**Jesus and
the Politics of His Day**

Jesus and
the Politics of His Day

EDITED BY
ERNST BAMMEL
*Reader in Early Christian and Jewish Studies,
University of Cambridge*

AND

C. F. D. MOULE
*Emeritus Lady Margaret's Professor of Divinity,
University of Cambridge*

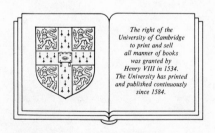

*The right of the
University of Cambridge
to print and sell
all manner of books
was granted by
Henry VIII in 1534.
The University has printed
and published continuously
since 1584.*

Cambridge University Press

Cambridge

London   New York   New Rochelle

Melbourne   Sydney

Published by the Press Syndicate of the University of Cambridge
The Pitt Building, Trumpington Street, Cambridge CB2 1RP
32 East 57th Street, New York, NY 10022, U.S.A.
296 Beaconsfield Parade, Middle Park, Melbourne 3206, Australia

© Cambridge University Press 1984

First published 1984

Printed in Great Britain at the University Press, Cambridge

Library of Congress catalogue card number: 77–95441

British Library Cataloguing in Publication Data
Jesus and the politics of His day.
   1. Jesus Christ   2. Christianity and
   politics
   I. Bammel, E.   II. Moule, C. F. D.
   232.9'01   BT590.P/

ISBN 0 521 22022 X

WV

Contents

Abbreviations

AnBibl	*Analecta Biblica*
ACO	*Acta Conciliorum Oecumenicorum*, ed. E. Schwartz (Strassburg, 1914 onwards)
AJT	*American Journal of Theology*
ARW	*Archiv für Religionswissenschaft*
Bb	*Biblica*
BFChTh	Beiträge zur Förderung christlicher Theologie
BJRL	*Bulletin of the John Rylands Library*
BibLeb	*Bibel und Leben*
BLit	*Bibel und Liturgie*
BZ	*Biblische Zeitschrift*
BZAW	Beihefte zur *Zeitschrift für die alttestamentliche Wissenchaft*
BZNW	Beihefte zur *Zeitschrift für die neutestamentliche Wissenschaft*
CBQ	*Catholic Biblical Quarterly*
CCL	Corpus Christianorum, Series Latina
CRAIBL	*Comptes rendus de l'Academie des Inscriptions et Belles-Lettres* (Paris, 1924)
CSEL	Corpus scriptorum ecclesiasticorum Latinorum
DJD	Discoveries in the Judaean Desert of Jordan
DLZ	*Deutsche Literaturzeitung*
EKK	*Evangelisch-katholischer Kommentar zum Neuen Testament*
EvK	*Evangelische Kommentare*
EvTh	*Evangelische Theologie*
ExpT	*Expository Times*
FRLANT	Forschungen zur Religion und Literatur des Alten und Neuen Testaments
GCS	Die griechischen christlichen Schriftsteller der ersten drei Jahrhunderte, hg. v. der Berliner Akademie der Wissenschaften
HAT	Handbuch zum Alten Testament
HThR	*Harvard Theological Review*
HUCA	*Hebrew Union College Annual*
IEJ	*Israel Exploration Journal*
IGRR	*Inscriptiones Graecae ad res Romanas pertinentes*, ed. R. Cagnat *et al.* (Paris, 1906–)
JBL	*Journal of Biblical Literature*
JBR	*Journal of Bible and Religion*
JJSt	*Journal of Jewish Studies*
JQR	*Jewish Quarterly Review*
JRS	*Journal of Roman Studies*
JSS	*Journal of Semitic Studies*
JThSt	*Journal of Theological Studies*
KuD	*Kerygma und Dogma*
MThZ	*Münchner Theologische Zeitschrift*

NAG	Nachrichten der Akademie der Wissenschaften in Göttingen, Philolo-gisch-historische Klasse
NGGG	Nachrichten der Göttinger Gelehrten Gesellschaft
NKZ	*Neue kirchliche Zeitschrift*
NovTest	*Novum Testamentum*
NovTestSup	*Novum Testament um Supplement*
NTSt	New Testament Studies
OrChr	*Oriens Christianus*
OGIS	*Orientis Graeci Inscriptiones selectae*, ed. Wilhelm Dittenberger (Leipzig, i, 1903; ii, 1905)
OLZ	*Orientalistische Literaturzeitung*
PG	J. Migne, *Patrologia graeca*
PL	J. Migne, *Patrologia latina*
PW	Pauly-Wissowa, *Real-Encyclopädie der classischen Altertumswissenschaft*
RArch	*Revue archéologique*
RB	*Revue biblique*
RdQ	*Revue de Qumran*
REJ	*Revue des études juives*
RGG	*Die Religion in Geschichte und Gegenwart* (3rd ed. Tübingen, 1957–65)
RHPhR	*Revue d'histoire et de philosophie religieuses*
RHR	*Revue de l'histoire des religions*
RIDA	*Revue internationale des droits de l'antiquité*
RQ	*Römische Quartalschrift*
RechSR	*Recherches de science religieuse*
SAH	Sitzungsberichte der Heidelberger Akademie der Wissenschaften, philosophisch-historische Klasse
StANT	Studien zum Alten und Neuen Testament
SB	*Sources bibliques*
S–B	H. L. Strack and P. Billerbeck, *Kommentar zum Neuen Testament aus Talmud und Midrasch* (München, 1922–8)
SBA	*Sitzungsberichte der Berliner Akademie*
SC	Sources chrétiennes
StEv	Studia Evangelica
SJTh	*Scottish Journal of Theology*
SNTS	Society for New Testament Studies
ST	*Studia Theologica*
TDNT	*Theological Dictionary of the New Testament* (ET Grand Rapids, 1967ff)
ThBl	*Theologische Blätter*
ThHK	Theologischer Hand-Kommentar zum Neuen Testament
ThLZ	*Theologische Literaturzeitung*
ThR	*Theologische Rundschau*
ThStKr	*Theologische Studien und Kritiken*
ThWNT	G. Kittel and G. Friedrich (eds.), *Theologisches Wörterbuch zum Neuen Testament*
ThZ	*Theologische Zeitschrift* (Basel)
TU	Texte und Untersuchungen zur Geschichte der altkirchlichen Literatur
VigChr	*Vigiliae Christianae*
ZAW	*Zeitschrift für die alttestamentliche Wissenschaft*
ZDPV	*Zeitschrift des deutschen Palästina-Vereins*

ZKTh	Zeitschrift für katholische Theologie
ZNW	Zeitschrift für die neutestamentliche Wissenschaft und die Kunde der älteren Kirche
ZRGG	Zeitschrift für Religions- und Geistesgeschichte
ZSTh	Zeitschrift für systematische Theologie
ZThK	Zeitschrift für Theologie und Kirche
ZWT	Zeitschrift für wissenschaftliche Theologie

Foreword

Many attempts have been made, particularly in recent years, to interpret the life of Jesus of Nazareth in terms of the Jewish nationalistic movements of his day. This collection of essays is aimed at throwing light on the events, and the motives behind them, of those significant days by a sober investigation of the evidence relating to Jesus's attitude to authority, both Jewish and Roman.

Owing to unfortunate delays, it is only now possible to publish these essays, some of which were completed about a decade ago. The authors must not be held responsible for not having brought their contributions up to date. To all of them the editors are greatly indebted, both for their willingness to undertake a task which, in some cases, involved considerable research, and for their patience in the face of delay. The editors wish to record their gratitude also to those who translated certain contributions, to those at the Cambridge University Press who have devoted skill and patience to the production of the book; and their special thanks to the Reverend G. M. Styler for much hard work in correcting the proofs and the Reverend Dr W. Horbury for assistance with the index.

E.B.
C.F.D.M.
1983

J. P. M. SWEET

The Zealots and Jesus

The theory that Jesus was mixed up with the movement or party of armed resistance to Rome commonly called the Zealots has never lacked proponents (cp. the following essay), but latterly it has achieved new force and publicity through a combination of factors: the excavation of the Zealot stronghold at Masada by Yigael Yadin, and the glorification of Zealot heroism;[1] current concern as to the authentic Christian role in resistance to oppressive regimes; and the work of the late S. G. F. Brandon. In his *Jesus and the Zealots* (Manchester, 1967), which built on his earlier book, *The Fall of Jerusalem and the Christian Church* (London, 1951), he claimed not that Jesus actually was a Zealot, a member of the party (if there was such a party in his time), but that Jesus and his disciples sympathised with the ideals and aims of the Zealot movement, and so did the earliest Christians.

Brandon's work was taken up as substantiating his own hunch by Colin Morris, formerly a Methodist minister in Zambia and adviser to President Kaunda, in a popular paper-back, *Unyoung, Uncoloured, Unpoor* (London, 1969). To quote the summary on the back,

> its theme is simply that the world is ruled by the Unyoung, Uncoloured and Unpoor and that only violent revolution will overthrow them in order to give the majority of the world's population their due place in the sun. Claiming that the Christian has both the right and the responsibility to take part in this struggle, Morris offers a re-interpretation of Jesus which challenges the traditional view that he was innocent of sedition against the Roman authorities.

Morris writes out of deep experience of the Third World and its dilemmas, and tries to work out what Jesus's attitude would be with passionate sincerity. There are other warnings from the Third World against a too easy acceptance of the non-violent Jesus. C. R. Hensman (a Sri Lankan, who has travelled widely in Asia and Africa as well as in the West) wrote a short life of Sun Yat-sen in 1971 in a series called 'Six Christians'. In justification of writing in such a series (the others were Martin Luther King, Simone Weil, Karl Barth, Teilhard de Chardin and George Bell) about one who to the church establishment of his time was a 'bad' Christian – a lifelong

---

[1] Martin Hengel had already demonstrated their deep roots in Jewish theological tradition and hope for the future, in *Die Zeloten* (Leiden, 1961; reprint with corrections and additions, 1976).

I

organiser of armed revolution, who fought against Western (including missionary) interests in East Asia and welcomed the Bolshevik revolution – he wrote this: 'To lead the poor and oppressed to rebel against their oppressors, and to join in the work of ridding the world of the violence, injustice and economic backwardness which causes impoverishment and oppression – these, one would suppose, are revolutionary tasks which Christians can ignore only by making their faith in Christ meaningless' (p. 12). Sun himself had remarked: 'I do not belong to the Christianity of the churches but to the Christianity of Jesus, who was a revolutionary.'

Finally one might mention from South America the admired and evocative figure (especially among students) of the Catholic priest Camilo Torres,[2] who joined the guerrillas in Colombia and was killed by Government forces in 1966. For him too 'the revolution' was not only permissible but obligatory for those Christians who see it as the only effective way to make love for all people a reality, and he painted a picture of Christ with a halo behind his head and a rifle behind his shoulder.

We are concerned here not directly with the Christian's duty in the present, but with the appeal to Jesus. Brandon, as we have said, claimed not that Jesus was a Zealot – the fact that one of the Twelve was known as Simon the Zealot distinguishes him from the rest of the band (*Zealots*, p. 355) – but that he and his followers were in fundamental sympathy with Zealot principles, the use of violence not excepted (p. 355, note 3). He claimed further that the New Testament documents, written in and for the Roman world, have done their best to cover this up and project a pacific image of Christ,[3] and that Josephus has similarly blackened the Zealots as mere brigands, in order to lay on them the blame, from the Jewish side, for the disastrous war against Rome.[4]

His theory starts from two sets of facts on which most would agree.

(1) Jesus was condemned by the Roman prefect of Judaea to the Roman form of execution for sedition, as 'King of the Jews', that is, as a nationalist leader who denied the kingship of Caesar. He was crucified between two brigands – one of the terms used for what today might be called 'freedom fighters'. One of his inner circle of disciples was Simon 'the Cananaean'

[2] See John Gerassi, *Revolutionary Priest – the complete writings and messages of Camilo Torres* (London, 1971).

[3] On *Tendenzkritik*, see C. F. D. Moule's essay, pp. 91–100.

[4] He drew extensively on the magisterial work of Hengel (see p. 1, note 1) to discredit Josephus's picture and establish their genuinely religious patriotism, but Hengel himself has been one of the firmest opponents of Brandon's thesis with respect to Jesus and the Christians – see review in *JSS* 14 (1969), 231–40; *War Jesus Revolutionär?* (Stuttgart, 1970) (ET *Was Jesus a Revolutionist?* (Philadelphia, 1971)); *Gewalt und Gewaltlösigkeit: zur 'politischen Theologie' in neutestamentlicher Zeit* (Stuttgart, 1971) (ET *Victory over Violence: Jesus and the Revolutionists* (Philadelphia, 1973)).

(Mark 3: 18), which the New English Bible renders as 'a member of the Zealot party',[5] and one at least of the disciples was armed when Jesus was arrested. Further, Jesus is represented in the gospels as condemning Sadducees, Pharisees, and Herodians but nowhere (explicitly) Zealots.

(2) This last point takes its significance from the second set of facts: that the Gospels were written for the Roman world, to commend Jesus as Son of God and Saviour, and therefore inevitably had an interest in demonstrating Jesus's innocence of the political charge on which he was executed. Further, the Roman world had a suspicion and hatred of the Jews which was exacerbated by the Jewish war; the Gospels therefore had an interest in dissociating Jesus and his followers from the Jewish cause (just as Josephus had an interest in blackening the Zealots).

If, then, there were any memories of Jesus having at any time condemned the Zealots, surely these memories would have been used by the evangelists, especially Mark who wrote in Rome at about the time of the Jewish War – so Brandon argued (see G. M. Styler's essay, pp. 104–5, on the use of *argumentum e silentio* in reverse). All this does not of itself give the lie to the Gospel picture. But it does show why, if the facts were really as Brandon and others suppose, the original picture was altered.

Brandon's picture can be briefly sketched as follows:

(1) Jesus was a patriotic Jew who believed passionately in God's exclusive sovereignty over Israel (the main tenet of the Zealot 'philosophy') and thought that he was commissioned to prepare Israel for its imminent enforcement. Though his attack was not directly against the Romans, it was against the Jewish hierarchy which collaborated with them: he was therefore understandably executed by the Romans on a charge of sedition. The earliest church was drawn from the same patriotic anti-Gentile, anti-collaborationist circles; it expected Jesus's imminent return as messiah, as leader of God's forces in the final battle against his, and Israel's, enemies.

(2) Through the work of Hellenistic Jews, pre-eminently Paul, Christianity became a mystery cult which welcomed Gentiles and presented Jesus to them as a divine saviour in entirely non-political terms. Paul was hounded by emissaries of the Jerusalem church as a traitor, and finally suppressed.

(3) In A.D. 66 the Jewish Christians centred on Jerusalem threw in their lot with the rebels, and were obliterated with them in A.D. 70. Thus by an accident of history the Pauline version of Christianity came out on top. The Acts of the Apostles legitimates it by painting Paul as a loyal Jew – in a purely religious sense of course – who worked in harmony with the

[5] Over-confidently – see note 8 on p. 5.

Jerusalem 'pillars'. The Gospels by the same token paint out all – or nearly all – the tell-tale evidence of Jesus's loyalty to his nation in its fight for freedom from heathen domination. He becomes the divine emissary of the unseen world, insulated from this world's political objectives and choices, his rejection by his own people and his acceptance by the Gentiles predetermined by God and advertised in the Jewish scriptures – for those who can read them aright.

Here then is a coherent interlocking picture of Christian origins, which has at first a certain attraction. There is very little concrete evidence for it, but that is only to be expected, because the post A.D. 70 church had every reason to suppress what did not perish in the ruins of Jerusalem. There is much that purports to contradict it, but that again is only to be expected since the church had every reason to depict a peaceful, non-political Jesus, and to dissociate him and itself from the hated Jews. There is a similar attraction in studies which show that the conventional picture of Richard III is the fabrication of Tudor historians with an obvious axe to grind, and piece together from little straws of evidence an astonishingly different portrait. As the bias of the sources is laid bare and pointers to a different state of affairs are amassed, the sympathies of the reader are engaged, especially if he has no specialist knowledge of the period.[6] If Brandon's picture is wrong, it can only be rebutted by a series of detailed methodological, historical and exegetical studies such as this book sets out to provide. Indeed the enquiry could well be carried further. There is here no detailed examination of Brandon's claims that the Jerusalem church was obliterated in A.D. 66 to 70 and that the tradition of its escape to Pella is pious legend – see E. Bammel, pp. 40–1. But this has been very thoroughly answered by M. Simon.[7] Again, the question of the Jerusalem church's relations with Paul and their respective understandings of Christianity is beyond this book's scope. Here Brandon would find more scholars to agree with him, but few would extend their agreement to support of his Zealot thesis. Arguments for Paul as an innovator provide no direct support for Brandon: on the other hand all the studies tell against him which bring out Paul's Jewishness and fundamental closeness to the Jerusalem church (cp. E. Bammel, pp. 41–2).

Since detailed professional study of each element in the argument is necessary, it is not the role of this general essay to investigate individual issues. It will simply set out what seem the essential points.

---

[6] See, for example, *Daughter of Time* by Josephine Tey (London, 1951). But this, unlike *Zealots*, was published as detective fiction.

[7] 'La Migration à Pella', *RechSR* 60 (1972), 37–54; cp. S. Sowers, 'The Circumstances and Recollection of the Pella Flight', *ThZ* 26 (1970), 305–20.

1 The historical background

Must Jesus, as a Galilaean, have shared the Zealot 'philosophy', as Brandon suggests? 'It is likely that many Galilaeans had taken part in the revolt of A.D. 6, and Jesus would have known some of the survivors and the families of those who had perished. To a Galilaean boy or youth these martyred patriots would surely have been heroes, and doubtless he would often have listened enthralled to tales of Zealots' exploits against the hated Romans' (*Zealots*, p. 65).

But (*a*) there were other models for a patriotic Jew than those provided by the Maccabees or the 'Fourth Philosophy' – Jeremiah, for example, with whom Jesus was connected by some, according to Matthew (16: 14); or the Hasidim, and the pattern of suffering fidelity presented in Daniel and the *Assumption of Moses*. (*b*) Many Jews *wanted* Roman rule, in preference to Herod's; others saw it as a divine imposition because of Israel's sins, and to be accepted humbly as such. (*c*) There is no firm evidence that there was as yet a 'Zealot party', as assumed by Brandon, and by the New English Bible at Mark 3: 18. The term 'Zealot' certainly had connotations of violence in defence of the Law, but not specifically of armed resistance to Rome and its collaborators.[8] (*d*) The expectancy of divine intervention was so vivid that there was danger to peace inherent in *any* popular movement, however peaceful its character and aims, particularly if miracles and prophetic utterance were involved – witness Josephus's accounts of rebel leaders, and the followings they attracted, and the reasons he gives for Herod's execution of John the Baptist: fear lest his great influence over the people might lead to a revolt (*AJ* xviii. 116–19).

The fact that Jesus was brought up in Galilee and that one of his chosen disciples was called 'the Zealot' (and the possibility that others may have been connected with the resistance movement) proves nothing as to his own attitude and aims.

2 The trial of Jesus

It follows from what has just been said that the fact of his execution by the Romans on a charge of sedition also proves nothing as to his own stance. In

[8] It is often assumed that what Josephus calls the 'fourth philosophy', stemming from Judas the Galilaean (*AJ* xviii. 23–5), is to be identified with those he calls 'Zealots'. But Josephus nowhere makes this identification. He uses the term 'Zealots' of a particular group only in his account of the War itself. See Morton Smith, 'Zealots and Sicarii', *HThR* 64 (1971), 1–19, and M. Borg, 'The Currency of the Term "Zealot"', *JThSt* n.s. 22 (1971), 504–12. The term has in fact a much wider currency. But its use for militant patriots has become general and does no harm provided that the wider sense is not forgotten.

the explosive atmosphere of the time the removal of someone who, however innocently, might become the focus of a popular uprising with its inevitable consequences, would be a natural and intelligible action; cp. the remark of Caiaphas in John 11: 50. Even if the Jewish non-involvement in his trial, for which Winter and others have argued, be accepted, even if the whole affair was merely Roman police action and the Christians later foisted the responsibility on to the Jewish leaders for apologetic reasons, there is still nothing to prove that the Roman verdict was justified – except in the pragmatic sense just mentioned, as seeking to curb popular unrest by removing one man, not for what he had said and done in itself so much as for the effect it might have on the people. The fact that Jesus alone was picked out and the Twelve went free is enough in itself to prove that the Romans did not see him as the leader of a seditious group.

In fact, however, the historical question about the responsibility for Jesus's death is still wide open. References to the continuing debate are given in the following essay and in the closing essays in this book. Few scholars would reject completely the Christian version, which can be traced back to one of Paul's earliest letters (1 Thess. 2: 15); it has even been argued that the Jews could themselves have carried out the crucifixion (see E. Bammel, pp. 431–45).[9] There is in any case very wide agreement that there was a religious issue between Jesus and his own people, which went far deeper than an attack on the collaborating priestly aristocracy; that he brought a theological challenge of the most fundamental kind, making claims for himself, whether directly or indirectly, which were either true or false, and if false demanded his condemnation and death.

As to the exact nature and significance of the triumphal entry, the cleansing of the Temple, the disciples' swords and the arrest of Jesus, the Barabbas episode and the trial or trials, there is hot dispute and no consensus is ever likely to be reached (see the closing essays in this book). Brandon's view remains a possibility, but in the eyes of the great majority of competent scholars the *probabilities* are heavily on the other side. This may seem too cavalier a treatment of such a crucial issue as the trial of Jesus, even for a general survey. But where every aspect of the question is enigmatic and controversial, it is perhaps enough to make the general point that even if the trial before the Sanhedrin was a Christian invention, even if, as H. Cohn has recently argued,[10] the Jews were involved only in trying to get Jesus off and failed through his non-cooperation, there is still no positive evidence that the Roman verdict was justified in the sense that Jesus

[9] See also E. Bammel, *The Trial of Jesus* (London, 1970), pp. 162–5. The view has been independently defended by Dr J. M. Ford, ' "Crucify him, Crucify him" and the Temple Scroll', *ExpT* 87 (1976), 275–8.

[10] *The Trial and Death of Jesus* (London 1972); cp. Bammel, pp. 49–51.

actually was a Zealot or para-Zealot. This can only be maintained by detaching him from all that we know of his past and (if we may so speak) his future.

3 The Jerusalem church

There is even less evidence that the first Christians were implicated in violent zealotry than that Jesus was. Josephus's accounts of rebel leaders end with the massacre of their followers, but there is no hint of Roman movement against any of the followers of Jesus. Acts records only attempted Jewish coercion on religious grounds, until the action of Agrippa I against James, son of Zebedee, and Peter recorded in Acts 12.[11]

Brandon might find more agreement with his estimate of Paul than of Jesus, but a very strong case can still be made, on the basis of Paul's own letters, for his fundamental unity with the 'pillar' apostles at Jerusalem. Even if it could be shown with high probability that the earliest Palestinian Christianity was far more Jewish than the Pauline version, and that it perished in the war of A.D. 66–70, there would still be not one shred of positive evidence that it was in any way aligned with the 'Fourth Philosophy'.

As for the Gospel of Mark, which Brandon held was written after A.D. 70 in Rome as an *apologia* to exculpate Jesus, and Christians, from their prima facie involvement with the Jewish national cause, there are strong arguments for dating it before the Jewish War and even stronger arguments for asserting its *theological*, not political, concern. The 'argument from silence' – that Jesus is recorded as condemning Herodians, Sadducees and Pharisees, but nowhere Zealots, and that if any such condemnation had been remembered surely Mark must have recorded it – is examined by G. M. Styler in a separate essay (pp. 101–9). He analyses the logic of the argument as Brandon employs it, and shows how each link requires individual testing if it is to carry conviction – and how, with equal logic, a different reconstruction is possible. Here it is enough to ask why, if the evangelists created so much else for apologetic purposes, they could not have created such a condemnation if it were really necessary to the argument. In actual fact, it was *not* necessary. Few non-Jews outside Palestine could have known anything about the Zealots (in Brandon's sense) in the sixties and seventies, before Josephus's works were published. It was the *Jews* who were known and hated, and Mark has done more than enough to distinguish Jesus and his followers from them.

The aftermath of Jesus's career, then, can no more bring evidence for his

---

[11] Cp. B. Reicke, below p. 147.

Zealot involvement than the background from which he emerged. The interlocking picture dissolves, on inspection, at either end. But what of the middle? The recorded teaching and behaviour of Jesus is the nub, to which we now turn.

4 Jesus's teaching

Brandon builds heavily on certain passages – for example, the tribute money question (Mark 12: 13–17 and parallels), 'I came not to bring peace but a sword' (Matt. 10: 34), and the 'arming' of the disciples (Luke 22: 35–38). These passages need detailed examination – see the essays by F. F. Bruce, M. Black and G. W. H. Lampe;[12] here it is enough to say that they can help Brandon's cause only if one shuts one's ears to the note of irony in Jesus's teaching. The far greater number of anti-violence sayings and actions are written off by Brandon as created later, especially by Matthew, in order to project the image of a pacific Christ, suitable for a religion for the Roman world. But many of these sayings, on the criteria of modern Gospel criticism, are most likely to be original; many reviewers have noted the arbitrariness of Brandon's critical method, accepting what fits his case and rejecting what does not, without reference to accepted procedures. For example, many of these sayings occur in the Q material. Admittedly Q has its sceptics, and the creativity of Matthew its champions. But even if all the sayings like 'if a man in authority makes you go one mile, go with him two . . . Love your enemies and pray for your persecutors' (Matt. 5: 41, 44), which in Jesus's time could not have been said without reference to the Romans, were the creation of Matthew, we are still left with Jesus's behaviour. His welcome for tax-gatherers and sinners, who to Zealots were even more abhorrent than the Romans, and what was worse, his eating with them, cannot be ironed out of the tradition. Brandon makes much of Simon the Cananaean among the Twelve, but nothing except one footnote of Levi or Matthew the tax-gatherer (*Zealots*, p. 201, note 4). It is *possible*, as Brandon hints, that the tax-gatherers whom Jesus attracted at once gave up their profession, whereas the revolutionaries did not, but again the probabilities are the other way. Jesus's attitude to and relations with 'sinners' are decisive evidence against any link between him and those whom Brandon calls the Zealots.

Brandon's theory, then, does provide a coherent picture of Christian origins, but it is a tissue of interlocking *possibilities* of varying weight, wholly lacking in positive evidence: many passages can be adduced which can be construed in support of the theory, if the theory is true, but none which is

---

[12] Pp. 249ff, 287ff and 335ff respectively.

actually evidence for its truth. The plea that the positive evidence has been destroyed, whether in the Jewish War or by the later church, is unanswerable, and warns us against regarding probabilities as certainties. But probability is still the guide of life.

Probability, however, is a guide which is only too often ignored by wishful thinking. The popularity of the Zealot or revolutionary interpretation of Jesus in the last decade witnesses to men's perennial propensity to look to him for support for their own ideals and aims. But it provokes the wry reflection that one can find support from Jesus for violent political action only by discounting those aspects of the traditional picture of him which give most reason for seeking his support.

E. BAMMEL

The revolution theory from Reimarus to Brandon

I

Milton, in his *Paradise Regained*, portrays his vision of Satan trying to lure Jesus to plot with the Parthians to deliver the ten tribes and to establish his realm 'from Egypt to Euphrates and beyond' and to set up a kingdom that 'Rome or Caesar not need fear'[1] and, then, improving on this by producing the yet more tempting prospect that Jesus should expel the monster Tiberius from the throne, 'a victor-people free from servile yoke' and aim 'at no less than all the world'.[2]

Just as according to the rules of the Greeks a satyr play follows the tragedy, so a burlesque of Milton's scene may perhaps be found in Schiller's *Die Räuber*, where Spiegelberg playfully suggests the idea of setting up as a descendant of Herod and calling forth all those who do not eat pork, pretending 'das Königreich wieder aufs Tapet zu bringen'.[3]

In this way the idea of political messianism, both in conjunction with Jesus and apart from him, attracted the imagination of the poets. On the plane of research, however, it was due to the work done by H. S. Reimarus that the problem came into focus. His essay on Jesus's and his disciples' goal is,[4] as has been maintained,[5] the first landmark of research on the life of Jesus.[6] It is startling that the question of a political involvement of Jesus already plays a role in this first analysis. Jesus was not just a teacher of

---

[1] III. 384f.   [2] IV. 100ff.   [3] I. 2.

[4] What became *geschichtsträchtig*, are the *Wolfenbüttelsche Fragmente* published by Lessing betweem 1774 and 1777, which represent an early stage of the work of Reimarus's lifetime, of the *Apologie oder Schutzschrift für die vernünftigen Verehrer Gottes*. This latter manuscript was not published in its entirety until 1972 (by G. Alexander (Wiesbaden, 1972), 2 vols.). There are three translations of the *Fragmente*: by C. Voysey (London, 1879), by R. S. Fraser (Philadelphia, 1970; London, 1971, ed. by C. H. Talbert), and by G. W. Buchanan (Leiden, 1970). For Reimarus's philosophy cp. H. Sieveking, 'H. S. Reimarus 1694–1768', *Zeitschr. d. Vereins f. hamburgische Geschichte* 38 (1939), 145ff.

[5] Albert Schweitzer, *Von Reimarus zu Wrede* (Tübingen, 1906), p. 13 (ET under the title *The Quest of the Historical Jesus* (London, 1910), p. 13); *Geschichte der Leben-Jesu-Forschung* (Tübingen, 1913), p. 13 (this second edition of the earlier work – considerably revised and augmented – has not appeared in English so far).

[6] The *Schutzschrift* soon became known abroad. Coleridge, for example, was made familiar with its views in Bristol; cp. E. Shaffer, '*Kubla Khan' and the Fall of Jerusalem* (Cambridge, 1975).

virtues; rather he was or became the herald of the 'kingdom'.[7] Jesus, Reimarus emphasises, must have been well aware of the political implications of a messianic pronouncement. In using this messianic terminology himself, he was conscious of awakening the Jews to the hope of a worldly messiah.[8] All the actions of Jesus agree with such an interpretation: his entry into Jerusalem, his 'interruption of order in the Temple',[9] his 'seditious speeches to the people against the high council'.[10] His suspicious and seditious actions were such that even more 'ungestüme Weiterungen' were to be expected.[11] A certain measure of force was not foreign to him – even the passage on the two swords is a highly suspect enigma.[12] It is due to certain misconceptions in strategy on his part and to the fact that he was only agreeable to the 'common rabble' that the Jerusalem action did not succeed and that he could be put to death. Indeed, he deserved his condemnation – 'nach allen Rechten und politischen Regeln'.[13] The presentation of Jesus's goal as suffering and death is a 'construction of his disciples'[14] who are portrayed in dark colours,[15] whereas the true facts give Jesus a place among the many messianic pretenders. It is to demonstrating the latter that the main interest of Reimarus is devoted. Still, from his reconstruction emerges the sketch of a Jesus whose activity is firmly rooted in the belligerent Jewish tradition. The difficulties of explaining, for example, the trial of Jesus on the basis of this do not concern him, so determined is he to demonstrate the rift between Jesus and his disciples.

Subsequent research had to deal with the question as it had been posed

---

[7] §4 (Talbert, *Fragmente*, pp. 66f).

[8] Reimarus's statements are not always consistent. In the *Fragmente* he affirms with vigour the nationalistic character of Jesus's message, whereas in the *Schutzschrift* – owing to the influence of Semler (cp. Alexander, *Apologie*, i, 31) – he admits and even praises such 'herrliche Lehren Jesu' (Alexander, *Apologie*, ii, 516, 173f, 176) as are not conditioned by Jewish particularism, while castigating Jesus's messianic claims at the same time (e.g. Alexander, *Apologie* ii, 156). This does not, however, mean that, as A. C. Lundsteen (*H. S. Reimarus und die Anfänge der Leben-Jesu-Forschung* (Copenhagen, 1939), pp. 46f, 146) assumes, in the opinion of Reimarus at a certain time there was a turning-point in Jesus's activity.

[9] §2 (Talbert, *Fragmente*, p. 137).

[10] §8 (Ibid., p. 148).

[11] Alexander *Apologie*, ii, 176.   [12] Ibid., 165.

[13] Ibid., 161. It is Reimarus's intention to show that Jesus's suffering cannot have had a vicarious character. As far as there is a bias in his work, it is to be found in this direction; he himself is not at all interested in revolution.

[14] T. Chubb had already attempted to bring out differences between Jesus and his disciples (cp. Lundsteen, *Reimarus*, pp. 132ff, 145); but his impressions lack any consistent idea.

[15] The *Schutzschrift* attributes a greater measure of blame to the disciples even during the lifetime of Jesus: they staged the scene of the entry into Jerusalem (Alexander, *Apologie*, ii, 159f).

by Reimarus. Two different solutions were offered. F. V. Reinhard[16] denied any connection on the side of Jesus with the idea of a Davidic messiah. He himself never accepted this appellation. His own design was nothing but spiritual. The other explanation, suggested by H. E. G. Paulus, centres the idea of political messianism in the person of Judas: he hoped to raise the crowds to intervene forcefully for the imprisoned Jesus.[17] A further step was taken by K. Hase,[18] who noticed two different periods in the ministry of Jesus, one in which he took up the messianic ideas of his environment without reserve, another in which he withdrew in order to go his own way. Without necessarily interpreting the messianology of Jesus's time politically himself, Hase nevertheless showed the direction in which the sting of a political interpretation could be removed.[19]

There the matter rested for most of the nineteenth century. The lives of Jesus and the detailed investigations of the problem – the books of T. Colani, G. Volkmar and W. Weiffenbach – take up one of these lines with certain qualifications; they set Jesus firmly against messianism, which they understand politically.[20] It is in this respect that the new school of eschatologists who followed the authors mentioned earlier, such as E. Issel, O. Schmoller, J. Weiss and A. Schweitzer, agree with their predecessors. Their own definition of and interest in eschatology as a supra-human

[16] *Versuch über den Plan, welchen der Stifter der christlichen Religion zum Besten der Menschheit entwarf* (Wittenberg, 1781).

[17] *Das Leben Jesu als Grundlage einer reinen Geschichte des Urchristentums* (Heidelberg, 1828).

[18] *Das Leben Jesu* (Leipzig, 1829).

[19] A more unequivocal echo of Reimarus's theory may possibly be found in a statement of Goethe. He writes in his *Maximen und Reflexionen*: 'Die christliche Religion ist eine intentionierte politische Revolution, die, verfehlt, nachher moralisch geworden ist' (Nr. 819 dated 3 February 1814; 'the Christian religion is an intended political revolution which, after failing, subsequently became an ethical one'). It is not absolutely clear whether the political dominance Goethe detects in Christianity refers to the time of Jesus or that of the apostles. If the former is the case, the statement has to be seen as the result of considerations sparked off by Reimarus. Assuming the latter, H. Petsch (cp. Hamburger Goethe-Ausgabe xii, Nr. 82, footnote) had tentatively thought of the communism of the early Christians. This phenomenon, however, would not merit the contrast between political and moral revolution which is stressed by Goethe. We will have to think of the life of Jesus and may possibly have to link Goethe's remark with the other reflection which was found in an unfinished form in his literary remains. According to this Jesus came to an end not dissimilar to that of Hamlet, and this end was all the more disastrous, since he let down those whom he had previously called (*Maximen*, Nr. 1305). The fact that the view of Jesus expressed in many statements of different periods of Goethe's life (cp. P. Meinhold, *Goethe und das Christentum* (Freiburg, 1958)) points to his appreciation of Jesus's *sittliche Hoheit* makes it likely that the two citations represent tentative reflections which he did not follow up.

[20] T. Colani, *Jésus Christ et les croyances messianiques de son temps* (Strassburg, 1864); G. Volkmar, *Jesus Nazarenus und die erste christliche Zeit* (Zürich, 1882); W. Weiffenbach, *Der Wiederkunftsgedanke Jesu* (Leipzig, 1873).

intervention led them so far as to view political messianism as a mere fringe feature even on the Jewish religious map,[21] and as something that hardly touched Jesus[22] and is of minimal concern for the examination of his message.

A. Rembe's *Christus der Mensch und Freiheitskämpfer* seems to be an exception.[23] He pictures Jesus as a world revolutionary, who comes out fervently against the wealthy class without, however, touching their wealth.[24] Jesus is the preacher of an ideal state beyond the clouds, who directs himself against the Temple and the Law as the institutions that keep the people in serfdom.[25] Tried for this reason, he proves to be the true fighter who, when defeated, triumphs over himself.[26] His disciples, incapable of understanding him, develop their own imagined ideas after his death. But it happens in the course of time that this 'geistige Sozialdemokratie'[27] is amalgamated with and swallowed up by the state. It is evident that the picture is an imprecise rehash of Reimarus's without any new impulse to critical investigation.

II

A new departure had already been made by W. Weitling in 1845.[28] Jesus, like Pythagoras, was striving for a radical revolution in the social conditions – so Weitling assumes.[29] Jesus was, however, fully aware both of the difficulty of expressing himself openly and of the shortness of time available to him. Owing to this we find statements of caution and even camouflage.[30] Nevertheless the main point is clear: it is a social revolution that he has in mind. Its aim is the abolition of property.[31] Luke 14: 33 is a pointer to the kernel of Jesus's message. The communalisation of work and of the means of production, and in consequence of leisure,[32] are required. Its success is forecast by Jesus in the statement of Luke 18: 29f.[33] The situation of the

---

[21] Schweitzer, *Geschichte*, pp. 232ff (*Quest*, pp. 237ff).

[22] Symptomatic is Schweitzer's discussion of Matt. 11: 12 (*Geschichte*, p. 404; *Quest*, pp. 355f): even this passage is taken to refer to those who try to wring the kingdom from God by penitence. Differently J. Weiss, *Die Predigt Jesu vom Reiche Gottes* (Göttingen, 2nd edn. 1900), who links the verse with the Zealot movement (p. 197).

[23] Leipzig, 1887.

[24] *Christus*, pp. 27ff.   [25] Ibid. p. 41.

[26] Ibid. p. 63   [27] Ibid. p. 75.

[28] *Das Evangelium eines armen Sünders* (Bern, 1845). A more extended edition appeared in 1846. It was this edition which was reprinted in Hamburg in 1971 (= *Philosophie der Neuzeit* 22).

[29] *Evangelium*, p. 25 (1845 edn.).

[30] Weitling assumes that Jesus like John was an Essene, and he toys with the idea that both men had been commissioned by the order to spread its principles in disguise.

[31] Weitling, *Evangelium*, p. 62.

[32] Ibid. p. 80.   [33] Ibid. p. 80.

early community reflects exactly what he had in mind: 'even those communists of our time, who take the most extreme position, could not go further than this body did'.[34] The principle is designed not only for Jesus's own fellowship but for the world at large – although Jesus is aware that allowances have to be made. In the end, however, faced with persecution from the side of the over-privileged, he himself retaliates in a like manner: 'dass Extrem gegen Extrem gesetzt werde'.[35] The 'revolutionary carpenter' advised his disciples to buy a sword and preached war.[36] Weitling does not go further in interpreting the last phase of the activity of Jesus;[37] but he emphasises that Jesus had worldly aims – John 18: 36 is only due to caution – and he draws the conclusion that similar actions may become necessary as long as the 'state of Christendom' has not yet materialised.[38]

Weitling sees a development in Jesus's teaching. In his first period he was still under the influence of national prejudices.[39] That means, the development of his preaching, the circumspect nature of its presentation and, eventually, blunt confrontation with the powers that be are due to Jesus's energetic and inquisitive mind and his concern for the poor.[40] All this is described in most engaging language, in a style reminiscent of that of the prophets and of the same dignity as that of Hebel and Büchner.[41, 42]

The social approach was in keeping with the feeling of the younger generation of the period. Thus Jesus in Wagner's sketch of 1843 is portrayed as saying, 'gemeinsam sei euch Hab und Gut',[43] while elements of political revolutionary activity are absent from his Jesus drama of 1848[44]

---

[34] Ibid. p. 64.   [35] Ibid. p. 122.   [36] Ibid. pp. 123f.

[37] He gives only a psychological interpretation of the betrayal of Judas (pp. 102–8).

[38] In this context he interprets λαμβάνειν (Luke 11: 10; John 16: 24) as a permission to take.

[39] *Evangelium*, p. 98.

[40] Weitling is genuinely inspired by the person of Jesus. His presentation is, however, partly conditioned by the fact that the bible is 'the book, which is to be found in every house and which is still accepted with confidence' (pp. 130f), and that apart from it there is no basis for agitation. Founding his communism on the teaching of Jesus is therefore partly a matter of pedagogical consideration.

[41] It seems that the view taken by J. A. Reichmuth (*Die Bibel in sozialistisch-kommunistischer Beleuchtung* (Bad Lauchstedt, 1921); cp. the summary given by J. Leipoldt, *Vom Jesusbilde der Gegenwart* (2nd edn., Leipzig, 1925, pp. 69f) is similar to that of Weitling.

[42] The political revolutionary explanation of Jesus's life can be understood as the secularised form of another one, according to which Jesus went up to Jerusalem in order to establish the messianic kingdom from the Temple, expecting divine intervention to assist him in this task. This view is not infrequent, e.g. R.v.d. Alm, *Die Urtheile heidnischer und jüdischer Schriftsteller* . . . (Leipzig, 1864), p. 148.

[43] *Das Liebesmahl der Apostel* in *Der junge Wagner. Dichtungen, Aufsätze, Entwürfe* 1832–49, ed. J. Kapp (Berlin, 1910), pp. 329ff.

[44] R. Wagner, *Jesus* (published Leipzig, 1887). He clings to the social ideal: 'Keiner sage von seinen Gütern, dass sie sein wären sondern es sei euch alles gemein' (p. 96).

although the author himself was soon to become a fighter on the barricades. Both Weitling and Wagner make Jesus dissociate himself from the nationalism of his environment: the one after having allowed for a quasi-Zealot initial phase, the other without such a concession,[45] the former disregarding the Barabbas problem (and, indeed, the trial itself), the latter stating *expressis verbis* that Jesus had no connection with the Barabbas rebellion.[46] A dichotomy thereby emerges which was to become typical for the following generations.

The interest changed after the failure of the 1848 revolution.[47] Professional scholars tended to become more cautious, whereas radicals did not feel any longer the same need to see themselves as the mouthpiece of history and to view the whole cultural heritage as leading up to and culminating in their own propositions.[48]

H. K. H. Delff's presentation is symptomatic.[49] He reduces the appeal to the Poor to a Galilaean feature, while in his view Jesus's activity in Jerusalem was by no means marked by a social stance.[50] He even views the Parable of the Great Feast as a portrait of Jesus's own activity: it is only in the last instance that he goes to the outcast.[51] He emphasises the need seen

[45] Wagner advances the startling theory that the aristocracy would have shown interest in a political messiah (*Jesus*, p. 25).

[46] In his view a 'matt ausgelaufene Meuterei' (Wagner, *Jesus*, p. 25; cp. 46).

[47] It was the combination of social interest with mediating tendencies which resulted in the proposition that a Christian has to be responsible but anti-revolutionary. This view became most influential in nineteenth-century conservative thinking. This was so especially on the continent, which had been shaken by the 1848 revolution and the experience of the Paris Commune of 1871. The formation of the Christian Anti-revolutionary Party in Holland in 1849 was a direct result of such consideration.

[48] A reaction to the situation is to be found in the important book of R. Todt, *Der radikale deutsche Socialismus und die christliche Gesellschaft* (Wittenberg, 1877). He declares that when basing our judgement on the N.T. we cannot deny 'Berechtigung dem Sozialismus nach seinem innersten Wesen' (p. 370). It is his intention to evoke understanding for socialism as it presents itself in his time and simultaneously to criticise it from the basis of the N.T. That means, factors implying a social motivation in the N.T. are admitted but taken as moderating factors in an issue that is already viewed as having come into existence independently of the Christian message. It is not that the N.T. is taken as a social challenge and manifesto. While he does not see it as taking the lead, it is certainly the author's opinion that revelation in history will have the last word – he takes up the ideas of Swabian speculation in order to demonstrate this. An escape in the opposite direction was made at the same time by E. von Hartmann, who attributes an asceticism hostile to work, family and all possessions to Jesus, and views him as a kind of precursor of his own philosophy of pessimism (*Briefe über die christliche Religion* (Stuttgart, 1870), p. 110 (the work appeared under the pseudonym F. A. Müller); *Die Selbstzersetzung des Christentums* (Leipzig, 1874), pp. 50f).

[49] *Jesus von Nazareth* (Leipzig, 1889).

[50] Ibid. pp. 318f.

[51] Ibid. pp. 337f.

by Jesus for new bottles or forms, so that the new force may not disperse itself in the 'formlose Revolutionäre',[52] into revolutionary anarchy; and he separates Jesus pointedly from the aims of his 'Zealot brother' James[53] and equally from every kind of zealotism.[54]

III

It was left to A. Kalthoff[55] to take up the general line of Weitling, whose writings, however, were unknown to him. The manner in which this was done shows characteristic differences. While Weitling takes the sources as they are handed down and explains diverging statements by reference to the arcane discipline and the caution with which Jesus had to proceed,[56] it is extreme scepticism vis-à-vis the traditions in the New Testament that guides Kalthoff's approach. Eventually he arrives at the conclusion that the Gospels were purely mythical in character and, combining this with the Tübingen idea of the origin of Christianity in the belief of the community rather than in the teaching of Jesus,[57] he goes so far as to deny that a particular event like the crucifixion of a certain Jesus, if its historicity is granted, or that the person of a 'founder'[58] could be of any constitutive importance.[59] Radicalising the view of the Tübingen school in this way[60] he advances a new perspective by giving Christianity its setting, even its origin, in the social situation of the empire. It is the product of certain converging factors in the ancient world. The revival of the social preaching of the prophets in the form of apocalypticism, the philosophy of the middle Stoa, the movement of the proletariat and, most important, the

---

[52] Ibid. p. 332.

[53] Ibid. p. 333. 'Zealot' seems to have a wider meaning in the context.

[54] Ibid. p. 340.

[55] An informative sketch of Kalthoff is supplied by F. Steudel in his preface to the posthumous edition of Kalthoff's *Zukunftsideale* (Jena, 1907), pp. v–xxxii. For criticism of Kalthoff's and Kautsky's views cp. A. Deissmann, *Licht vom Osten*, 2nd edn. (Tübingen, 1923), pp. 336, 403ff.

[56] Weitling, *Evangelium*, pp. 33ff, 43.

[57] F. C. Baur, *Kirchengeschichte der drei ersten Jahrhunderte* i, 3rd edn. (Leipzig, 1863), 40; cited by A. Kalthoff, *Entstehung des Christentums* (Leipzig, 1904), p. 24 (ET London, 1907, p. 29).

[58] The emphasis on the personality of Jesus is in his opinion nothing but an attempt at modernisation; nay, worse than this, it is 'die Angst vor dem kirchlichen Kommunismus, die in dieser Leben-Jesu-Theologie nachhinkt'; this theology fears for its 'privat-kapitalistische Weltanschauung, wenn es ihr nicht gelingt, in den Evangelien den kommunalen Christus durch den individuellen zu verdrängen' (*Entstehung*, p. 98 etc.; ET p. 123 etc.).

[59] Kalthoff, *Entstehung*, p. 108 (ET p. 139).

[60] For Baur's concept of Jesus, cp. W. G. Kümmel, *Das Neue Testament. Geschichte der Erforschung seiner Probleme* (2nd edn. Freiburg, 1970), pp. 174f; ET (London, 1973), pp. 141f.

emergence of semi-secret societies[61] brought about something that may be called the fulfilment of the times, the ripe fruit of which was produced in Christianity: all the currents of the time flowed together into this movement because each of them had already absorbed ideas of economic communism.[62]

This means that the Christian communities inherited a mentality and, already to some extent, a programme of radical social change. Revolutionary unrest was not something that invaded the communities from time to time and was combated especially by Paul, but was the very essence of these communities – the pointers to the contrary in the Pauline letters are viewed by Kalthoff as fabrications of a later period.[63] The community is seen as the incarnation, as the Christ–God;[64] the absolute unity of the members was already a revolutionary factor within the context of a totally different structure of the political world. The *agape* is constitutive for what is, speaking in economic terms, a community of consumption, the oblations and *primitiae* provide communal property.[65] An essential feature is the abandonment of private property in favour of communal ownership. Corresponding to this is the emphasis on work, that means on consumption and usufruct which is solely based on production. This is a step forward compared with the life of the thiasic congregations and a complete departure from the Roman concept of property (based on loot or power). What emerges with Christianity is a state within the state, an economic entity of co-operation within the agrocapitalistic society.[66] The thrift which is demanded in so many Christian regulations is only one side of a communist economic system.[67] The prohibition of interest, the emphasis on the fair price (without any gain) are other features. Indeed, we owe to the church 'the most comprehensive communist manifesto that was ever conceived'.[68]

Kalthoff's view is entirely conditioned by this analysis of the whole

---

[51] Which, indeed, caused the concern of the state and, at times, suppression (cp. Pliny, *Epist.* x. 33 and 34).

[62] For communistic tendencies in apocalypticism, cp. pp. 77f (ET pp. 98ff).

[63] Pp. 13ff; 111ff (ET pp. 16ff, 142). Cp. B. Kellermann, *Kritische Beiträge zur Entstehungsgeschichte des Christentums* (Berlin, 1906), pp. 45ff, who combines Kalthoff's ideas with those of Wrede. This particular view was anticipated in some ways already by the radical Dutch school and R. Steck (cp. R. Steck, 'Plinius im neuen Testament', *Jahrbücher für protestantische Theologie* 17 (1890), 545ff).

[64] Kalthoff, *Entstehung*, p. 110 (ET p. 141).

[65] Ibid. p. 125 (ET p. 162).

[66] Ibid. pp. 105f (ET pp. 135f).

[67] Ibid. p. 126 (ET p. 163). Communist ideas were emphasised especially by the church fathers of the post-Constantinian period, as E. Tröltsch (*Die Soziallehren der christlichen Kirchen*, Gesammelte Schriften i (Tübingen, 1912), 51) stated.

[68] Kalthoff, *Entstehung*, p. 140 (ET p. 181).

period. He takes it as a single entity and does not believe in crucial divergences, either for the better or for the worse. Therefore he does not believe in Jesus as the type of a revolutionary; this idea is just one form of an unhistorical, modernising individualisation,[69, 70] a tendency not in keeping with the necessity of placing everything in the developing *fluidum* of Christian culture.[71]

Having resisted the temptation to invoke Reimarus or Baur as patrons and to admit substantial change, he is compelled to regard the beginnings of Christianity as being on one plane and to shift the pieces of evidence so that they fit in. He therefore views the accounts of the passion as reflections of what happened in the time of the persecution under Trajan,[72] he sees Pliny under the mask of Pilate,[73] characterises Peter as the personification of the Roman community,[74] takes the Gospel reports as reflecting the struggle of the masses on the Italian estates[75] and transfers the Pauline letters to the second century. At the price of this new arrangement of the sources he is able to sketch the panorama he was interested in. The high-handed re-arrangement of evidence shows how much of an over-simplification it was to bring the Christian literature under the one vinculum of social tension. Nevertheless Kalthoff's venture has not only the suggestiveness of boldness; it is far superior in calibre and breadth to any other attempt at 'social' understanding of Early Christendom.[76]

IV

(*a*) Parallel to Kalthoff's, and yet distinctively different, is Kautsky's view.[77] His approach is tinged with scepticism towards the earliest Christian sources, he is doubtful whether it is possible to find out anything certain about Jesus's life and teaching[78] and is even not averse to the theory of

---

[69] Ibid. p. 98 (Christ is just the patron of the community; ET p. 126); p. 148 (ET p. 190); cp. *Das Christus-Problem* (Leipzig, 1903), pp. 38f.

[70] In fact most of the names of Christian literature are worthless (*Entstehung*, p. 92; ET p. 122). He draws attention to the anachronisms of the haggada (*Was wissen wir von Jesus* (Berlin, 1904), p. 39).

[71] Reflections in the style of R. Rothe are to be found on pp. 132ff of *Entstehung* (ET pp. 173ff).

[72] Kalthoff, *Was wissen wir von Jesus*, p. 38.

[73] Kalthoff, *Das Christus-Problem*, p. 43.

[74] Ibid. pp. 50ff.   [75] Ibid. pp. 57ff.

[76] Kalthoff's mythical theory was taken up (in a modified form) by P. Alfaric, *Origines Sociales du Christianisme* (Paris, 1959; GT Darmstadt, 1963).

[77] K. Kautsky, *Der Ursprung des Christentums* (Stuttgart, 1908). There are two English translations: New York, 1925 (repr. 1973) and New York, 1953 (by J. F. Mins). The page numbers refer to the former translation. The new German edition (Hannover 1968) contains an informative introduction supplied by K. Kupisch.

[78] Ibid. p. 25 (ET p. 43).

Jesus's unhistoricity.[79] In the main, however, he is inclined to accept the sources as not too far removed from what actually took place, and to attempt – with preference for Luke and with disapproval of the revisionist Matthew[80] – to draw a sketch of Jesus. Jesus's milieu is the rural proletariat;[81] the nearest parallel to the community which adopted his name is the Essenes, with the decisive difference, however, that the Christians were essentially a city organisation and therefore able to carry on as a secret society.[82] What is most characteristic of Jesus himself is his rebellious mentality,[83] which was directed against both the Jewish establishment and the Romans.[84]

The Poor are called by him because they are poor. The end, announced to them in the words of the Jewish kingdom expectation, demands violent action on their side. Luke 12:49 and 22:38ff are of heuristic value for Kautsky. Correspondingly he reconstructs a planned revolt after the successful assault against the Temple, the betrayal of which led to the downfall of Jesus.[85] His execution is very understandable if he was a rebel; otherwise it appears as a senseless act of wickedness.[86] It is only later tradition, tradition that arose after A.D. 70, that plays down these features and is partly successful in this attempt. The portrait of the suffering Christ replaces the tradition of the rebellious Jesus.

It is due to the organisation that he had himself already founded that his name survived and that the tradition was projected into the form of the resurrection myth. The belief in the coming Christ gave impetus to the communist organisation of the outcasts[87] and made it 'irresistible'.[88]

Kautsky had twice before[89] dealt with the origin of Christianity and had

[79] Ibid. p. 384; cp. pp. 17f, 22f (ET p. 364: 'whether he actually existed or was merely an ideal figure of men's visions . . .'; cp. pp. 35, 40).

[80] Ibid. p. 352 etc. (ET p. 335).

[81] He draws the conclusion that the partisans of the proletariat are much better equipped to comprehend the beginnings of Christianity than chairbound dons (p. viii; ET p. 12).

[82] Kautsky, Ursprung, p. 337 (ET p. 320).

[83] Ibid. p. 384 (ET p. 363): differently M. Robbe (Der Ursprung des Christentums (Berlin, 1967), p. 75) who emphasises the open, the embracing character of the Christian communities as contrasted with the Essenes.

[84] Kautsky, Ursprung, pp. 385ff (ET pp. 364ff).

[85] Ibid. pp. 387ff (ET pp. 365ff).

[86] Ibid. pp. 389 (ET p. 368).

[87] Ibid. p. 402 (ET pp. 379f). It has to be emphasised that, according to Kautsky (cp. p. 434; ET p. 409), the communist city organisation is singular and of decisive importance for the parting of ways with Judaism.

[88] Kautsky, Ursprung, p. 403 (ET pp. 380f). The class hatred of the early Christians was a feature that appealed to the non-Jews, while it brought the Christians into conflict with Judaism, which believed in united forces.

[89] 'Die Entstehung des Christentums' in Die neue Zeit 3 (1885), 481–99, 529–45; Die Vorläufer des neueren Sozialismus (Stuttgart, 1895), 40, 46ff.

stated emphatically that the person of Jesus was 'of comparatively small importance', was even 'bedeutungslos'.[90] The interest he took in the Jewish background in his third attempt is obvious. It seems that the scrutiny of this world had opened his eyes to the fact that the development was more complex than he had previously assumed. It was in this bewildering world of Judaism that he was able to allot a place to Jesus, as an exponent of the then dominant movement. He is neither placed at the cross-roads between the two cultures nor viewed as a *homo sui generis*. These are the limitations of Kautsky's sketch of Jesus. Early Christendom itself is seen entirely as a social movement.[91]

Kautsky holds that modern times are totally different from the days of the struggle of the peasant proletariat. He therefore refrains from taking Jesus as a direct example – that is the difference from Weitling. He sees Jesus himself, however, more clearly than Kalthoff was able to do in the situation of the Jewish struggle. The Zealot face of it is in his view a feature of the particular situation – he himself is not at all interested in this (or only negatively, in order to dispute the Christian portrait of Jesus). It only provides him with the means to give historical colour and logic to a life, the outcome of which appears almost ridiculous if viewed from the basis of the Christian sources as they stand.

The appearance of Kautsky's book was followed by a lively discussion. The anonymous 'A. D.' held against Kautsky that Jesus was only interested in and concerned for individuals, and that the radical tendencies are due to an *Umbiegung* in the early communities, which happened when the proletariat got control over them.[92] F. Mehring, on the other hand, stated his basic agreement with Kautsky while pointing to the influence of Paul, who – so he holds, citing a famous statement of Pfleiderer[93] – had succeeded in overcoming the tendencies hostile to any social order.[94] H. Windisch questioned the picture of militant Christian beginnings and admitted such tendencies only for the Apocalypse, explaining them as due to subsequent Judaisation (*nachträgliche Judaisierung*). If the early Christians had been revolutionaries, they would have joined the Zealot movement and have

---

[90] *Die neue Zeit* 3 (1885), 543. He mocks at the aim of his fellow socialist A. Dulk to recover early Christianity for his own belief (p. 545).

[91] Cp. the criticism raised against him by Tröltsch, *Soziallehren*, pp. 17f.

[92] 'Der sogenannte urchristliche Kommunismus', in *Die neue Zeit* 26 (1908), 482ff.

[93] O. Pfleiderer, *Die Entstehung des Christentums* (München, 1905, p. 186; ET London, 1906, p. 211): Paul rejected emphatically the communistic fanaticism related to the early Christian tendency to world-abrogation. This statement is found once and again in socialist writings, and was only recently used as a weapon against Paul by K. Farner (cp. note 394, pp. 61f). Kautsky himself wrote a very hostile review of Pfleiderer's book (*Die neue Zeit* 25 (1907), ii, 760).

[94] 'Der Ursprung des Christentums' in *Die neue Zeit* 27 (1909), i, 281ff.

perished with it.[95] He points especially to the fact that Psalm 2 and Amos were cited in Acts 4 and 15 in a way which is contrary to the original militant meaning of the passages. Kautsky refuted Windisch by drawing attention to comparable phenomena in Bohemian radicalism and communist sectarian movements, where militant beginnings are followed by an inclination to peacefulness. He fastens on the title ὁ χριστός: to call himself messiah would have been as absurd for a peace-loving martyr as if Tolstoi had described himself as a bomb-throwing terrorist. He interprets Windisch as having admitted three stages (Jesus peaceful, the first community rebellious, the later development peaceful again), and claims that in order to salvage Jesus from the presumption of a rebellious disposition Windisch is forced to assert Jesus's inability to exercise an influence on his rebellious disciples. He emphasises that the militant passages in the New Testament are 'Überreste einer tiefeingewurzelten Tradition.'[96]

(b) Soviet historiography, in its presentation of Early Christianity, is more dependent on F. Engels and his indebtedness to Bruno Bauer[97] than on any other radical Jesus researcher. Kautsky is rarely cited, and Kalthoff, although in the central historical issue more akin to Engels than Kautsky, is disregarded almost completely, while A. Drews was mocked by Lenin himself.

On the one hand, Soviet ideologists are attracted by what appears from their point of view as the parallel between early Christianity and the socialist movement, while on the other hand the contents of the bible are abhorrent to them. It is due to this hiatus that they felt drawn to the conclusion of the non-historicity of Jesus.[98] The diverging tenor of the early Christian statements on force and war are explained as products of different stages in the development of Christendom.[99] The radical ones are

---

[95] H. Windisch, *Der messianische Krieg und das Urchristentum* (Tübingen, 1909).

[96] K. J. Kautsky, 'Jesus' 'der Rebell', *Die neue Zeit* 28 (1910), i, 52. The opinion voiced by Hitler (Jesus is recommendable, while Paul was an 'instigator of the proletariat'; *Monologe*, ed. W. Jochmann (Hamburg, 1980), pp. 96f, 150, 412f; the last conversation recorded!) was in all likelihood started off by his reading of this controversy.

[97] It was Kautsky who drew Engels's attention to Bauer, who 'brachte fast das, was ich suchte' (*Fr. Engels Briefwechsel mit K. Kautsky*, ed. by B. Kautsky (Wien, 1955), p. 179). For a critique of Bauer, cp. E. Barnikol, *Bruno Bauer, Studien und Materialien* (Assen, 1972), pp. 238f. Cp. also J. Irmscher, 'Friedrich Engels und das Urchristentum', *Studii Clasice* 3 (1961), 99ff.

[98] B. Stasiewski, 'Ursprung und Entfaltung des Christentums in sowjetischer Sicht', *Saeculum* ii (1960), 169; *idem* in *Sowjetsystem und demokratische Gesellschaft* iii (Freiburg, 1969), 343ff. Robbe, *Ursprung*, p. 24, on the other hand, declares the question a matter of minor interest: even if he lived it was not he who became instrumental in starting Christianity but it was a general movement which gave rise to it.

[99] Stasiewski, *Saeculum*, ii (1960) 163; cp. 170.

considered to reflect the primitive state and it is for this reason that the Revelation of John is valued as the oldest and most significant Christian document.[100] The opinion that the early communities in their social unrest lacked awareness of their social position precludes these authors from appreciating early Christianity as anything that is substantially different from pre-Marxist communism of the beginning of the nineteenth century. Thus, even the radical or revolutionary tendencies found in early Christian sources do not dispose them favourably towards it.[101]

A shade of difference from this is found in S. I. Kovalev.[102] A considerable departure is, however, not noticeable before M. Machovec, who is the best informed among the eastern Marxist authors of this generation and whose sketch betrays sympathy and understanding for Jesus and equally for his message.[103] He starts with the presupposition that it would be surprising if Jesus had not developed a stand entirely of his own *vis-à-vis* the question of force,[104] and thereby avoids pinning down Jesus to one of the established positions in contemporary Judaism. It is the emphasis on activity[105] without the use of force[106] which is seen as characteristic of Jesus, while the eschatological prophetic element – a facet to which Machovec is able to give considerable value[107] is interpreted without being brought down to the level of social problems.[108] His portrayal of Jesus as utopian is, perhaps,

---

[100] A view – taken by F. Engels – is thus repeated (similarly Kautsky, *Ursprung*, p. 380; ET p. 360). Robbe, *Ursprung*, p. 181, deviates here from the dominant line by emphasising that the Apocalypse with its anti-state bias is not typical of Christian mentality.

[101] Typical is A. B. Ranowitsch, 'Das Urchristentum und seine historische Rolle' (in *Aufsätze zur Alten Geschichte* (Berlin, 1961) pp. 135ff). While paying tribute to the idea that Christianity, being a religion, was opium for the people (p. 135), and subsuming it under the vinculum of *Sklavenhaltergesellschaft* he characterises it as a new stage in the development of this society (p. 139) which made possible, for the first time in history, a world religion. Its origin is sketched without any reference to Jesus. Its earliest and foremost document is the Apocalypse with its hatred against a 'world of suppression' (p. 141). The mentality of revolutionary radicalism which conditioned certain features in the life of the communities (p. 145) remained alive, however, only in the side-branches of Christendom, while what became the official church developed a hierarchy of offices and encountered the world with the message of love instead of hatred. This olive-branch is a development of the second half of the second century (p. 158); it reflects the decrease of messianism and opens the door for an alliance with the world.

[102] Stasiewski, *Saeculum* ii (1960), 176f.

[103] *Jesus für Atheisten* (Stuttgart, 1972; ET under the title *A Marxist looks at Jesus*, London, 1976).

[104] Ibid. p. 128 (ET p. 106).

[105] Ibid. p. 133: love your neighbour is an iron demand without any compromise towards yourself (ET p. 110).

[106] Ibid. p. 131 (ET p. 108).

[107] He takes up ideas of M. Bloch (*Das Prinzip Hoffnung* i/ii (Berlin, 1955)).

[108] Cp. his criticism of Kautsky, pp. 287f (ET pp. 216f).

influenced by the religious heritage of Bohemia[109] but on the whole it is free from Hussite militancy and communist clichés. It is the first socialist approach that dispenses with the Marxist economic yardstick.[110]

(c) Marxism in the West had gone a different way in the meantime.[111] 'We cannot expect any recovery of the Jesus of history in those who are reconciled to the social order' is a statement[112] as typical of the consternation after the first world war as it is of the social tendency, and still worth contemplating. By taking a leap forward from this presupposition it is maintained that Jesus's call for inner repentance resulted of necessity in his struggle against the ruling classes – the reorganisation of society is his real aim[113] – while he withstood nationalist suggestions once and again.[114] The chasm between socialist and nationalist[115] interpretations of Jesus is opened thereby. The difference between these ways of 'environmental' understanding is, however, not exclusive: Jesus 'the social revolutionary' holds the Temple for three days[116] – the nationalist theory is made use of conveniently.

The early twentieth-century approach was taken up by A. Robertson.[117] He describes Christianity as a 'mass movement conditioned by a decaying slave society of antiquity'.[118] This is the normal socialist slogan. Robertson gives it a special slant by characterising the beginnings of Christianity as 'a revolutionary movement led first by John the Baptist and then by Jesus the Nazorean, and aimed at the overthrow of Roman and Herodian rule in Palestine and the establishment of an earthly kingdom of God'.[119] He thereby comes out for the historicity of Jesus;[120] he is most definite in this

---

[109] Cp. P. Roubiczek, *Warrior of God* (London, 1947).

[110] For the consequences, for the value attributed to Jesus as a monument, as a stimulus to social activity, cp. the summary in E. Grässer, 'Motive und Methoden der neueren Jesus-Literatur', *Verkündigung und Forschung* 18 (1973), 34–40.

[111] The rejection of Jesus had never been as thoroughgoing in the socialist parties of the West as in the Communist world of the East. Cp. the statements cited in H. Hartmann, *Die Stimme des Volkes* (München, 1920); G. Naumann, *Sozialismus und Religion* (Leipzig, 1921), pp. 78, 83; Leipoldt, *Jesusbild*, pp. 68f; W. Ilgenstein, *Die religiöse Gedankenwelt der Sozialdemokratie* (Berlin, 1914), p. 195. An element of propaganda cannot be ruled out in these lukewarm appraisals. An instructive defence against the materialistic view is to be found in H. Köhler, *Die sozialistische Irrlehre von der Entstehung des Christentums* (Leipzig, 1899).

[112] J. Lewis in *Christianity and Social Revolution* (London, 1935), p. 102.

[113] J. Macmurray, *Creative Society. A Study of the Relation of Christianity to Communism* (London, 1935), pp. 84f.

[114] The temptation story and John 6: 15 are interpreted along these lines.

[115] Cp. p. 87.

[116] Macmurray, *Society*, p. 88.

[117] *The Origins of Christianity* (London, 1953; GT Stuttgart, 1965).

[118] Ibid. p. 209 (GT p. 235).

[119] *Origins*, p. 93 (GT p. 104).   [120] Cp. n. 79, p. 20.

conclusion. While Kautsky had wavered, at least for a moment, in his approach to the question, Robertson even mocks at the myth school.[121] But it is symptomatic that his portrait of the Baptist is drawn more clearly than that of Jesus, and that he eventually reduces[122] the importance of both of them for the movement which they initiated or only represented.[123]

The 'primitive gospel', a document which purports to deal with Jesus, whereas in fact it was embellished with incidents which had been related of revolutionary leaders for generations back,[124] is a revolutionary manifesto for which it is characteristic that, while Pharisees and Sadducees are denounced, the Zealots are not. It was composed at the time of the Jewish war, in which the Christians took part.[125] It is to be mainly recovered from so-called Q-material which was deliberately suppressed by Mark.[126] Its mentality lived on in the Apocalypse.[127] Mark was written after 70 and tries to draw the sting of revolutionary messianism.[128] It does this by fusing the primitive gospel with Pauline theology: the old theory of Mark's Paulinism, rejected already by M. Werner,[129] is thus revived. Paul himself had established a different brand of Christianity, a religion that had little or nothing to do with Jesus, that represented middle-class sentiments in the Empire and was thus opposed to the revolutionary 'venom' spread by slaves and the like.[130] The history of the nascent church is seen as the confrontation and reconciliation, and eventually union between these tendencies: the Tübingen theory, projected on to the social level, is thus adopted.[131] A transformation from the material outlook to a spiritual one was the result for the primitive church.[132]

Compared with Kautsky the work displays a far better cognisance of the sources and a scrutiny of their respective value. Coinciding with Brandon –

[121] *Origins*, 76f. (GT pp. 8of, 85).

[122] Cp. Kautsky.

[123] '. . . round confused traditions of more than one leader the original gospel was written' (p. 209; GT p. 235).

[124] Robertson, *Origins*, p. 144 (GT p. 163).

[125] Ibid. pp. 140ff (GT pp. 158ff); the statements of Eusebius and Epiphanius to the contrary are rejected and positive evidence is found in Rev. 12: 7f; 14: 20; 17: 9f.

[126] Ibid. p. 150 (GT p. 170).

[127] Ibid. p. 156 (GT pp. 176f).

[128] Ibid. p. 149 (GT p. 169).

[129] *Der Einfluss paulinischer Theologie im Markusevangelium* (Giessen, 1923). It was revived at the same time in an even more radicalised form (Marcion is the author of Mark) by H. Raschke (*Die Werkstatt des Markusevangelisten* (Jena, 1924), pp. 31ff).

[130] 'Paul's attempts to inoculate the masses against revolutionary Messianism by spreading the cult of a purely mystical Christ . . .' (Robertson, *Origins*, p. 172; GT p. 190). 'He removed the kingdom of God from this world to the next. This was to cause trouble with the revolutionary Messianists' (p. 104; GT p. 116).

[131] Cp. the defence of F. C. Baur in Robertson, *Origins*, p. 102 (GT pp. 246f).

[132] Ibid. p. 80 (GT pp. 84f).

of whom he does not show knowledge – in the description of the guiding lines of the development, he differs in postulating that the bulk of tradition had come into existence before 70, in emphasising the social radicalism and in attributing a lion's share in the origin of the movement to the Baptist.

V

The mainstream of research on the life of Jesus continued to move in a different direction. This is not only true for the liberal lives which go on, more or less, in the tradition of Hase.[133] It is equally the case with what was then the modern theology, the eschatological approach. Thus Albert Schweitzer states that the 'apocalyptic movement in the time of Jesus is not connected with any historical event' and that there were no events 'calculated to give impulse to eschatological enthusiasm': 'Stille ringsum.'[134] It may be that the purely antiquarian approach of Schürer's *Geschichte des jüdischen Volkes* repelled any attempt to bridge the gap between the political world and the theological writings. It may be that the ingenious searching of nineteenth-century scholars for contemporary allusions in apocalyptic literature had been found to have reached a dead end.[135] In any case, it was owing to this turning away from the political scene that an interpretation of the message of Jesus continued to flourish which had dispensed beforehand with the possibility of any reference to contemporary events.

Even those who proclaimed a social messiah, a Jesus in fellowship with the Poor – a considerable number of writers did so[136] – did not really make use of the political circumstances as the foil to set off their portrait of Jesus. Exceptions, like M. Maurenbrecher,[137] who allowed for political side-issues, were torn to pieces by Schweitzer.[138] Indeed, even the social message itself was found incompatible with the principle of thoroughgoing

---

[133] Typical for the English scene is the portrait of Jesus by Seeley, of whom it is said that he did not discuss the relation of this *imperium in imperio* (Lewis, *Christianity* p. 77).

[134] *Von Reimarus zu Wrede*, pp. 366f; *Quest*, p. 368; cp. *Geschichte*, pp. 283f.

[135] It is typical that W. Bousset, who was in his period the outstanding authority on apocalypticism, felt drawn, for a time at least, to the solution of the unhistoricity of Jesus; cp. *The Modern Churchman* (1976), p. 106. For a one-sided discussion of Bousset's motifs, cp. F. Regner, '*Paulus und Jesus' im 19 Jahrhundert* (Göttingen, 1977).

[136] Leipoldt, *Jesusbild, passim.*

[137] *Von Nazareth nach Golgatha* (Berlin, 1909).

[138] *Geschichte*, pp. 575f (not in ET). An attempt was made by the philosopher W. Bröcker to insert the notion of a violent Jesus and of a riot caused by him in co-operation with his followers into the Schweitzerian scheme (W. Bröcker and H. Buhr, *Zur Theologie des Geistes* (Pfullingen, 1960), pp. 61f). The author himself leaves behind this feature in order to make room for a synthesis on another level, by a theology of the spirit.

eschatology in the interpretation of Jesus.[139] Mystical interpretations were not untypical for this period.[140]

It is significant that the Christian Socialist intelligentsia in Germany became increasingly aware of the difficulty of maintaining its position. Already in 1894 A. von Harnack tried to answer the question whether the gospel which proclaims a holy indifference *vis-à-vis* worldly problems can contribute towards the solution of the social question.[141] Friedrich Naumann, who had proclaimed '*Jesus der Volksmann*' in an earlier pamphlet,[142] stressed the incompatibility between Jesus's message and the necessities of capitalist society, and left the reader (as well as himself) with the dilemma.[143] The famous last page of the first part of Wellhausen's *Einleitung*, in which he pointed to certain features in the life of Jesus that are not acceptable to our own time, and where he went so far as to state: 'Wir können nicht zürück zu ihm, auch wenn wir wollten',[144] made a deep impression on this generation.

The position was clarified in the celebrated paper of W. Herrmann 'Die sittlichen Gedanken Jesu in ihrem Verhältnis zu der sittlichreligiösen Lebensbewegung der Gegenwart.'[145] While frankly admitting that there is nothing of the zealotism of a political or economic reformer in Jesus,[146] he declares that taking his way of life as a new law (as was done by Tolstoi) would be a betrayal of Jesus. He challenges us to ethical *Selbständigkeit* (self-reliance).[147] He does not defend Jesus by reference to his belief in eschatology, but he sees him as the source of *stete Unruhe* (continual

[139] Schweitzer, *Geschichte*, p. 574 n. 3.
[140] Cp. H. Weinel and A. G. Widgery, *Jesus in the Nineteenth Century and After* (Edinburgh, 1914), pp. 448f.
[141] *Die Verhandlungen des 5. Evangelisch-sozialen Kongresses* (Göttingen, 1894), p. 141. Cp. the statement of Tröltsch, who, pointing to the disinterest of the Christians in mundane affairs, holds that this is a revolutionary element but lacks any revolutionary intentions (*Willen zur Revolution*), *Soziallehren*, p. 50.
[142] *Jesus der Volksmann* (Göttingen, 1894).
[143] *Briefe über die Religion* (Berlin, 1903): the conflict, 'dass wir praktisch keine Christen im genauen Wortsinne des Evangeliums sein können, schätze ich ... für viel peinlicher als alle Konflikte der Lehre' (p. 58 in the edition of 1916). The gospel of the Poor is 'eine unserer Lebensnormen, aber nicht die einzige. Nicht unsere ganze Sittlichkeit wurzelt im Evangelium, sondern nur ein Teil derselben, allerdings ein äusserst wichtiger und leicht missachter Bestandteil' (p. 66). He confines himself to speaking of mere 'Stimmungen des Evangeliums' and maintains that they move 'nur wie ferne, weisse Sehnsuchtswolken über allem wirklichen Tun unserer Zeit' (p. 60). He drew the conclusion in his influential address to the Evangelisch-soziale Kongress in 1908, when stating that the New Testament contains neither a political nor a social doctrine, and for this reason cannot serve as the basis for social politics (*Verhandlungen* p. 39).
[144] *Einleitung in die drei ersten Evangelien* (Berlin, 1911), p. 104.
[145] *Verhandlungen* (Berlin 1903) pp. 9ff.
[146] Ibid. p. 19.
[147] Ibid. p. 29.

unrest)[148] and the promoter of ethical action which is conditioned by the conscience of the individual.[149, 150]

Only independent minds ventilated the political issue in this period. Wellhausen, rejecting an apocalyptic interpretation of Jesus, points to the political expectation, considers whether Jesus made use of this, recalls the violence at the cleansing and at the arrest, wonders whether other traces of this kind might have been obliterated, and concludes: '*bis zu einem gewissen Grade könnte* Reimarus Recht haben'.[151] In this way he testifies to the fact that every concept that takes the messianic terminology as constitutive and refrains from spiritualising it is under a certain obligation to admit quasi-Zealot ingredients in the Gospel accounts.

On the other hand, this is the period in which, challenged by the mythological theory of A. Drews,[152] scholars,[153] especially classicists,

[148] Ibid. p. 11.

[149] Ibid. p. 27. Cp. K. Weidel's statement: 'das Soziale liegt ihm überhaupt fern, er hat stets nur den einzelnen Menschen im Auge' (*Jesu Persönlichkeit* (Halle, 1908), p. 25; 3rd edn. 1921, p. 49). Cp. Naumann's confession that Jesus dealt with the *Einzelseele* (*Verhandlungen*, p. 41), while he himself ventured into the world of politics without the guidelines given by Jesus. For general information, cp. G. Kretschmer, *Der Evangelisch-soziale Kongress* (Stuttgart, 1972).

[150] The radical wing of the Christian socialists did not maintain this reserve and ended in an impasse. They used the Bible as a means of illustrating present-day problems without qualification; nevertheless, the form of the sermon proved inadequate for the purposes of socialist agitation (cp. W. Deresch, *Predigt und Agitation der religiösen Sozialisten* (Hamburg, 1971), pp. 69ff). Cp. A. Pfeiffer (ed.), *Religiöse Sozialisten* (=*Dokumente der Weltrevolution* 6) (Olten, 1976).

[151] *Einleitung*, 2nd edn. pp. 82ff.

[152] A. Drews, *Die Christusmythe I/II* (Jena, 1909–11); J. M. Robertson, *Jesus and Judas* (London, 1927); cp. Schweitzer, *Geschichte*, pp. 444ff. The myth theory was taken up by Raschke (*Werkstatt; Das Christusmysterium* (Bremen, 1954)) – his argument is far more original than that of his predecessors – and more recently defended by the same author in K. Deschner, *Jesusbilder in theologischer Sicht* (München, 1966), pp. 343ff. This approach was followed by G. A. Wells (*The Jesus of the Early Christians* (London, 1971), *Did Jesus exist?* (London, 1975)). He tries especially to give an explanation of the metamorphosis from mythology to history (*Early Christians*, p. 6). J. Kahl, *Das Elend des Christentums* (Hamburg, 1968; ET London 1971) comes very near to Wells's position. He mocks at Bultmann's emphasis on the 'that of Jesus's having come', finding it 'cryptic and meaningless, indistinguishable from a myth' (p. 70; ET p. 103), and comes out in favour of agnosticism about Jesus: 'we just do not know' (p. 81; ET p. 121). On the other hand, when he comes to charges against Christianity, he does not spare Jesus (p. 49; ET p. 73). The mythological interpretation did not meet with applause among Jewish students. It was, however, although with a characteristic deviation, taken up by J. b. Gorion, who identified Jesus with the Jesus ben Ananus mentioned by Josephus (*Jeshu b. Hanan* (Jerusalem, 1959)).

[153] K. Dunkmann, *Der historische Jesus, der mythologische Christus und Jesus der Christus* (Leipzig, 1911); E. Klostermann, *Die neuesten Angriffe auf die Geschichtlichkeit Jesu* (Tübingen, 1912); J. Weiss, *Jesus von Nazareth. Mythos oder Geschichte?* (Tübingen, 1910); A. Jeremias, *Hat Jesus Christus gelebt?* (Leipzig, 1911); H. Windisch, 'Der geschichtliche Jesus', *ThR* 13 (1910), 163ff and especially A. von Harnack, 'Hat Jesus gelebt?' in *Aus Wissenschaft und Leben* ii (Giessen, 1911), 167ff.

examined the non-Christian testimonia[154] to early Christendom with great sagacity.[155] Even the following generation benefited very much from this scrutiny, whereas this heritage and interest seems to have been lost to present-day theological researchers. The scrutiny of the national movements led to a better understanding of the time of Jesus and already cast certain doubts on the Schweitzer theory of a Jesus who was not troubled by political circumstances. Indeed, it is unlikely that he lived insulated from the political events of his time. This does not, however, mean that he joined with one of the forces of action.

This was especially the time of investigations into the social conditions of the ancient world and of nascent Christianity within them, and of at least one attempt to set early Christendom in the context of social radicalism. R. von Pöhlmann's magisterial *Geschichte der sozialen Frage*[156] pictures Jesus as a proletarian who addressed co-proletarians,[157] as someone whose message, although not without a different, a religious background,[158] became merely a class gospel (*Klassenevangelium*). It proclaimed the destruction of the existing economic system and of the social order. Pöhlmann holds that Jesus had completely lost contact with reality and that his views were fathered by *Zusammenbruchswahn.*[159] It is for this reason that no programme of social reform can be found in the Gospels. The expectation of the speedy

---

[154] Cp. K. Link, *De antiquissimis quae ad Jesum Nazarenum spectant testimoniis* (Giessen, 1913).

[155] The London papyrus of Claudius's letter to the Alexandrians, a source which came to light in 1923, was interpreted by one scholar at least as giving direct evidence for the subversive activities of Christian propagandists 'analogue, à ses yeux, au péril communiste dont beaucoup d'États se sentent menacés aujourd'hui' (S. Reinach, *CRAIBL*, p. 315, subsection of *RArch* 5th series, 33 (1931). The Reinach theory was supported by F. Cumont, 'La première allusion au Christianisme dans l'histoire', *RHR* 90 (1924), 108ff, and criticised by H.J. Bell, *HThR* 37 (1944), 189f. For an examination of the whole letter, cp. S. Lösch, *Epistula Claudiana* (Rottenburg, 1930). Of special importance is Tacitus *Ann.* xv. 44, the reference to the Neronian persecution. M. Joel considers it surprising that the Christians had not been mentioned before in Tacitus's account; he points to the fact that Tacitus's report of the years 29 to 32 is not any longer extant and is inclined to assume that this is due to the redactional activity of some Christians, and that it was in this report that Jesus was pictured as a revolutionary who had been executed by the Romans for this reason, and that the movement started by him had messianic revolutionary aspects as well (*Blicke in die Religionsgeschichte* ii (Breslau, 1883), 96ff). For a critical investigation, cp. K. Büchner, 'Tacitus über die Christen', *Aegyptus* 33 (1953), 181ff, and P. Corssen, 'Die Zeugnisse des Tacitus und Pseudo-Josephus über Christus', *ZNW* 15 (1914), 114ff.

[156] *Geschichte der sozialen Frage und des Sozialismus in der antiken Welt* i/ii (München, 1912; cited after the third edn. 1925).

[157] Ibid. ii. 467. Cp. the similarly sounding but substantially different statement of Naumann: Jesus put on a fight within the people and for the people ('im Volk und für das Volk').

[158] Pöhlmann, *Geschichte*, ii, 464, 473.

[159] Ibid. ii, 472.

establishment of an ideal world on earth is all the more ardent. The radical character of the phenomenon does not consist in individual revolutionary actions but in the total and fundamental denial of any reasonable and advanced form of social order. Pöhlmann points to the message of the prophets and states that Jesus's own lack of interest in prosperity was just possible in his own environment: Judaism had only been able to develop a *Halbkultur*.[160] He rejects, however, the possibility of secondary Essene (or Ebionite) influence: the communist tendencies are grounded in the basic ideas of Christianity (a *Wahlverwandtschaft* – an elective affinity – between Christian and pagan social romanticism is not thereby ruled out).[161] True, the communist organisation of the Jerusalem community was not imitated by those in the Greek world, but it served as a model and was considered as having been of crucial importance. Pöhlmann cites one church father after another – especially John Chrysostom, whose optimistic hope of 'establishing heaven on earth' does not lag behind the 'fantasies of [August] Bebel'[162] – as witnesses for the anti-capitalist sentiments. He describes Christianity as the greatest mass movement in world history;[163] he characterises it as the climax of social movements in antiquity and sees it as a mass illusion for which he has little taste. His oligarchic sentiments (not dissimilar from Macaulay's)[164] and his economic approach cause him to picture Christianity in a light not altogether different from Kautsky's portraits – however much he had poured scorn on the latter's *Halbbildung*.[165]

'Christian theology is the grandmother of Bolshevism' – this statement of Spengler (made after the first world war)[166] could be taken as echoing Pöhlmann's claims. Indeed, Spengler sees the same inclination towards egalitarianism and socialism at work in the Christian churches which Pöhlmann had marked down and which Nietzsche had previously stigmatised. He observes that all sectarian movements are in principle hostile to state and wealth,[167] and thereby illuminates an early stage of the development. He emphasises, however, that the church is a betrayal of religion, of the religion of Jesus especially; he paraphrases Mark 8: 36 to show a lack of interest on the part of Jesus in abolishing property and holds

---

[160] Ibid. ii, 470.   [161] Ibid. ii, 486.   [162] Ibid. ii, 488.

[163] Ibid. ii, 497. For a critique of the position of Pöhlmann, cp. the remarks of F. Oertel in the third edn. ii., 567–70.

[164] For a more recent form of a similar approach over against Christianity, cp. the works of A. Mohler and his publications in the periodical *Criticon*.

[165] Cp. the blow administered by him on Kautsky in 1894 in 'Extreme bürgerlicher und sozialistischer Geschichtschreibung' (reprinted in R. von Pöhlmann, *Aus Altertum und Gegenwart* (München, 1895), pp. 391–416 and, in an extended form, in the second edn. (1911), i, 346–84).

[166] O. Spengler, *Jahre der Entscheidung* (München, 1933; ET New York, 1934), p. 93 (ET p. 129).

[167] Ibid. p. 90 (ET p. 125).

that the 'communism' of the Jerusalem community is an indication of their scorn for the material world.[168]

The first world war, which altered the theological scene so decisively in a general way, brought about certain new accents in the portraits of Jesus. The 'militant Christ' was only a slogan[169] and of ephemeral importance. In contrast to this, the emphasis on the distance between Jesus and the issues of the day is a symptomatic feature of the post-war period. In America a number of studies appeared which took this line.[170] One of them, V. G. Simkhovitch's essay,[171] sharpens the issue by pointing out that Jesus's position was unique: it was non-resistance neither out of prudence nor owing to Hellenistic inclinations, and it was this attitude that brought about the 'great and fundamental cleavage' with the segments of Jewish society.[172] The 'heroic Jesus' – heroic rather in action than in suffering[173] – became the watchword that characterised the attempts of Chamberlain and of other German nationalists to conceive of a Jesus who was congenial to them.[174] Tinges of social colour in the characterisations of Jesus retreated into the background in this period apart from J. Leipoldt[175] and his pupil W. Grundmann[176] and a few Marxist sketches.[177] On the strictly scholarly level Jesus books appeared which started from the Schweitzerian position and included, in one way or the other, ideas of the new dialectic theology.[178]

[168] Spengler, *Der Untergang des Abendlands* ii (München, 1922), 60ff; (ET London, 1928, pp. 212ff; abr. ET London, 1959, pp. 280f).

[169] Like others of a later period: 'the greatest propagandist the world has ever known' (Lord Beaverbrook, *The Divine Propagandist*, London, 1962, p. 39); or 'the greatest revolutionary of all times' (F.C. zu Schaumburg-Lippe, *Dr. G. Ein Porträt des Propagandaministers* (Wiesbaden, 1964), p. 87; cp. p. 172).

[170] H. J. Cadbury, *The Peril of Modernizing Jesus* (London, 1937), p. 129.

[171] *Toward an Understanding of Jesus* (New York, 1921; 2nd edn. 1927).

[172] Ibid. p. 14.

[173] A. Rosenberg directs himself against the 'exhausted' theme of the suffering and proclaims the 'old–new' motto: Jesus the hero (*Der Mythus des 20. Jahrhunderts*, ed. München, 1936, pp. 604, 606, 616). Rosenberg holds that an old Phrygian legend about Chrestos, the saviour of the people in serfdom, which was given colour by the fate of Mithradates, was transplanted to Palestine, linked with the messiah myth and the person of Jesus. In this he is heavily dependent on W. Erbt, *Weltgeschichte auf rassischer Grundlage* (Frankfurt, 1925), pp. 134ff. Rosenberg does not take notice of the fact that the passage in question was omitted by the author in the second edition (Leipzig, 1934).

[174] H. S. Chamberlain, *Worte Christi* (München, 1901); A. Dinter, *Das Evangelium* (Leipzig, 1923); cp. M E. Winkel, *Der Sohn*, 2nd edn. (Berlin, 1938).

[175] *Jesusbild, passim.*

[176] *Jesus der Galiläer* (Weimar, 1940).

[177] See pp. 24f.

[178] R. Bultmann, *Jesus* (Tübingen, 1926; ET London, 1935); E. Hirsch, *Jesus Christus der Herr* (Göttingen, 1926); M. Dibelius, *Jesus* (Berlin, 1939; ET London, 1963); W. Groenbech, *Jesus der Menschensohn* (Stuttgart, 1941); E. Seeberg, *Christus, Wirklichkeit und Urbild* (Stuttgart, 1937).

A theological line was followed almost to the exclusion of any historical background and of the contemporary issues.[179] Eisler's *grosser Wurf* has to be viewed as a reaction against this.

VI

Robert Eisler's work[180] is a new departure of the greatest importance: it is based mainly on source material outside the Gospels and the revolutionary ambition and failure of Jesus is made the central issue of his book. True, the passages on Christian origins in the Slavonic version of Josephus had been initiated,[181] but nothing of a comparable penetration and so engaging an ingenuity had been presented to the learned world before.

These passages go back, in the opinion of Eisler, but for Christian mutilations, to the original Aramaic form of the Jewish War. They speak of a gathering of Jesus, of his 150 servants and of a great multitude on the Mount of Olives, of their insistence on Jesus's entering the city and defeating the Romans, of Jesus's consent,[182] the actual rising against God and Caesar,[183] the occupation of the Temple area, the denunciation by the Jewish leaders to Pilate, the latter's interference with the movement led by Jesus, the seizure of the Temple by Roman forces, Jesus's arrest and condemnation as sorcerer, robber, insurgent and would-be ruler/king.

The Gospel accounts are inserted into this scheme: those of the passion week and details from elsewhere, for example Luke 13: 1–9, which is viewed as reflecting on the failure of the revolt in the Temple and, therefore, as having been spoken on Jesus's last day before the arrest. Source criticism is not in the main line of Eisler's interest. He lists the differences between Matthew and Luke on the question of force,[184] but he disregards them immediately and proceeds to his selective use of sources. Eisler considers many passages as reliable pieces of evidence which are disputed by critical research, whereas he ignores some material, for example the controversy stories of Mark 11: 27 to 12: 34. Most striking is the absence of Judas and his

---

[179] Bultmann's radicalism and ahistoric position come out most bluntly in the report of an encounter at a meeting of the *Alte Marburger* given by H. Diem, *Ja oder Nein* (München, 1974), p. 267.

[180] Ἰησοῦς Βασιλεὺς οὐ βασιλεύσας, i/ii (Heidelberg, 1929f); *The Messiah Jesus and John the Baptist* (London, 1931). The English edition contains only certain sections of the German text. For a characterisation of Eisler, cp. G. Scholem, *Von Berlin nach Jerusalem* (Frankfurt, 1977) pp. 162ff.

[181] E.g. A. Berendts, *Die Zeugnisse vom Christentum im slavischen 'de bello Judaico' des Josephus* (Leipzig, 1906); J. Frey, *Der slavische Josephusbericht über die urchristliche Geschichte* (Dorpat, 1908).

[182] Eisler, Ἰησ. Βασ. ii, 298.

[183] Ibid. ii, 450f.

[184] Ibid. ii, 255f; *Messiah*, p. 364.

betrayal, a story that, like that of the denial of Peter, was so embarrassing to the Christians[185] that it cannot have been invented. The selective use of the Christian sources was justified, if the Slavonic Josephus could be taken as controlling evidence. In fact the account is of a mixed character.[186] Underlying the Christian redaction it contains a Jewish account, which is, however, based on the references to Jesus in Sanh. 43a and was extended into a form not dissimilar from the Jewish substratum of the Acts of Pilate and the Aramaic Toledoth Jeshu. Its evaluation is only possible if its *Sitz im Leben* in the Jewish–Christian controversy is recognised and the direct link with Josephus and the first centuries abandoned. It is a document like the elaboration on the basis of Josephus which is commonly cited under the name of Hegesippus; the one is Jewish, while the other is Christian. It should not be impossible to trace certain features worth considering for the student of Christian origins but the way to this is barred by the theory that the text represents the *Urform* of Josephus's *Jewish War*.[187]

The picture of Jesus that emerges out of Eisler's voluminous effort is the following: Jesus's approach is characterised by the attempt to pacify the world by a 'mere message' which is announced by the disciples sent out to perform the task.[188] Their lack of faith is a challenge to him to advance to radical action, the renunciation of everything dear to men's hearts, the return to the desert of the time of the pilgrimage: 'not revolt, but merely a breaking out'. This exodus is to happen via Jerusalem from where he will lead Israel back over the Jordan and erect the tent of the patriarchal period. At the same time he is aware of a fate of ignominy and death that he has to encounter.[189] The activists among his disciples, on the other hand, make sure of ambivalent orders given by the master[190] and, indeed, of the whole journey to Jerusalem, in order to gather together a large following, to give the entry into the Holy City the appearance of a messianic proclamation

---

[185] Cp. H. Merkel in *The Trial of Jesus. Festschrift C. F. D. Moule* (2nd edn. London, 1971), 66ff. Judas is not mentioned in one branch of the Jewish lives of Jesus.

[186] Points of criticism, different from those advanced above, were raised by H. Lewy in a famous review in *DLZ* 51 (1930), col. 481ff.; M. Goguel, *Jésus et le Messianisme politique* (Paris, 1930; reprinted from *Revue Historique* 162 (1929), 217–67); H. Windisch, 'Unser Wissen um Jesus', *Neue Jahrbücher f.Wiss.u. Jugendbildung* 7 (1931), 289–307; W. Stapel, *Der christliche Staatsmann* (Hamburg, 1932), pp. 45ff; W. Bienert, *Der älteste nichtchristliche Jesusbericht* (Halle, 1936) – his findings were summarised by H. W. Kars, 'Der älteste nichtchristliche Jesusbericht', *ThStKr* 109 (1937), 45ff; cp. J. W. Jack, *The Historic Christ* (London, 1933) and C. J. Cadoux, 'The Politics of Jesus', *Congregational Quarterly* 14 (1936), 58–67.

[187] For the evaluation of the Greek text see *Josephus-Studien. Festschrift O. Michel* (Göttingen, 1974), pp. 9ff.

[188] Eisler, Ἰησ. Βασ. ii, 689f; *Messiah*, p. 569.

[189] Ἰησ. Βασ. ii, 691; *Messiah*, p. 570. This element of Eisler's description is not really integrated into his picture.

[190] Luke 22: 36; cp. Eisler, Ἰησ. Βασ. ii, 268, 691; *Messiah*, p. 570.

and to stage the occupation of the Temple. Jesus is drawn into these events rather than having planned them himself.

For the first period of Jesus's activity the picture is not too dissimilar from the one given by Albert Schweitzer. The eschatological influence, maintained by Schweitzer, in the sending out of the disciples is, however, absent and it is due to this lack of motivation that the second period appears even less marked by Jesus's own personality. The combination of Rechabite motives with that of a role to be played on the stage of Jerusalem[191] is artificial and results in the minor figures dominating the scene. Eisler's picture is in fact the attempt to synthesise the account of the Slavonic Josephus with an enfeebled version of Schweitzer's view.

The concept of a new design conceived by the disciples after the death of the master, worked out by Reimarus, is adopted into the idea of a different goal entertained by them already during the lifetime of Jesus. If this picture is correct we do not understand why the attempt to execute this militant intention after the departure of the master was not repeated and repeated more vigorously. True, Eisler links almost every militancy in the subsequent generations with the following of Jesus[192] – even Bar Kochba is seen as a scion of Jesus's family[193] – but this is managed only by including persons who, in the opinion of Eisler, made use of the name of Jesus, and by leaning on the flimsiest evidence – the only piece of evidence worth considering, Ev. Petr. 26, does not receive a close examination.[194] It is, however, extremely unlikely that a person who already in his lifetime had become more and more a mere figure-head should have drawn so many under his vinculum after the disastrous failure of his own attempt. It is even more unlikely that parallel movements should have made common cause with them. It would be wrong to maintain that, in Eisler's view, Jesus was the 'arch-revolutionary'.[195] It is all the more surprising that Jesus's name should have served as a focussing point while the names of other persons (e.g. of the Baptist who, according to Eisler, had dominated the scene twice) had not received such recognition.

Eisler places nascent Christianity in the wider context of the social unrest of the time.[196] His sketch is, so to speak, the bold attempt to follow the line of Pöhlmann – to go even further than he did – and to give his findings a

---

[191] It is most significant that according to Eisler it was Peter who tried to dissuade Jesus from going to Jerusalem, whereas Jesus insisted on doing so ('Iησ. Βασ. ii, 276). Just the opposite would have been in line with the designs attributed to each of them respectively.

[192] 'Iησ. Βασ. ii, 691ff.

[193] Ibid. ii, 717; *Messiah*, p. 590: 'the clan of Jesus would in that case . . . have produced two kings anointed by the Lord.'

[194] Cp. p. 446.

[195] As Jack, *Christ*, p. 97, wishes to do.   [196] 'Iησ. Βασ. ii, 720ff (not in the ET).

deeper, a quasi-metaphysical meaning at the same time. The work, packed with information, is a warning against the dominance of the social side in Jewish and Christian messianism, while it admits this influx into the movement once it was on the way. Relevant as this knowledge is for the development and spread of Christianity, it does not, however, do more than contribute to knowledge of the circumstances of the life of Jesus, whereas his message, even in the description of Eisler, is barely conditioned by social demands. Eisler is torn between his interest in the oriental origin and the Jewish development of a political messianism – a theme he had intended to tackle in a special book[197] – and his findings on Jesus which hardly comply with this general line. Eisler may be right in mockingly alluding[198] to those who wish to give the impression that Jesus only made speeches and never proceeded to action.[199] It does not, however, follow that he performed such actions as have been attributed to him.

Eisler's theories caused an enormous stir.[200] Once the dust had settled, it emerged that his thesis on the origin of the Slavonic Josephus had met with little or no approbation,[201] while his reconstruction of the events of the life of Jesus was equally rejected. Neither Jewish nor Marxist historians felt challenged to give him substantial and massive support.[202] Only here[203] and

---

[197] *Messiah*, p. xi.   [198] Ἰησ. Βασ. ii, 461.

[199] It is a citation from G. B. Shaw that Eisler takes up in this (*Messiah*, p. x).

[200] While J. Warschauer, who had suggested a few years before Eisler that the cleansing was a 'carefully planned coup', that it was the intention of Jesus to force the advent of the kingdom – 'like those men of violence . . . with whom he sympathized' (*The Historical Life of Christ* (London, 1927), pp. 257ff) – passed almost unnoticed. He had, however, added that Jesus had considered the rendering of his life as a precondition for the coming of the kingdom.

[201] Cp. note 186, p. 33. Eisler answered Bienert, the most important of his critics, in his *Flavius Josephus-Studien* i (London, 1938). The problem was given a new twist by F. Scheidweiler, 'Sind die Interpolationen im altrussischen Josephus wertlos?', *ZNW* 43 (1950/1), 155ff, who selected a number of passages in the Slavonic Josephus, for the possible antiquity of which he gave reasons.

[202] S. Reinach (cp. *RArch* 5th series, 33 (1931), 215; 35 (1932), 130f) is the exception on the Jewish, J. Macmurray (see p. 24) on the Marxist side. E. Sahlin, while dissociating himself from much that Eisler has to say, describes his work as an 'einzigartige Leistung' which enables scholars to understand part of the activity of Jesus for the first time (*Schmollers Jahrbuch*, 55, ii (1931), 163ff). He himself tries to give a more balanced view, which is clearly influenced by Eisler, in 'Urchristentum und Staat', *Schmollers Jahrbuch* 55, ii (1931), 213ff.

[203] Eisler is given a sympathetic consideration by H. P. Kingdon, 'Had the Crucifixion a political Significance?', *Hibbert Journal* 35 (1936/7), 556ff. The author disagrees, however, with Eisler on the main issue: Jesus, in his opinion, gave himself up in order to open the eyes of his followers (565). Kingdon enlarged on this in a later essay. While emphasising that the Palestine of the time of Jesus was terrorised by 'Jewish Jingoes', admitting the inclinations of some of both his closer and his wider circle towards political messianism and stressing that the Barabbas uprising was 'in some way' connected with Jesus's entry into Jerusalem, he separates Jesus from the goal of that revolt: 'the supposed leader of the revolution gave himself up for

there[204] – not in every case from quarters Eisler himself was friendly disposed to[205] – were voices heard that took up part of his theory. Sound scholarly reasons were produced for its rejection.[206] The fact that Lietzmann suggested a substantially different solution of the problem of the trial of Jesus at the same time[207] – a solution which became widely accepted – did certainly play a role.[208] Another factor, however, came in as well. The

execution'. This was his design in order to bring them to understanding; 'he would save not only their lives, but their souls. He would give his life, a ransom for many' ('The Political circumstances of the Crucifixion', *The Student Movement* 43 (1941), 95). In this way he became a challenge to 'our complacement patriotisms and shallow pacifisms'. It is a drama presented almost in the Schweitzerian manner that the author sketches on these pages. J. Taubes (*Abendländische Eschatologie* (Zürich 1947)) is heavily dependent on Eisler. He alters the timing, however, of the Eislerian scheme and adds elements of Schweitzerian provenance: it was in the middle of his ministry that Jesus issued the call for a migration to the desert in order to establish a new kingdom. After having recognised his failure he decides in Caesarea to enter the course of suffering and death.

[204] Fr. Murawski, *Jesus der Nazoräer, der König der Juden* (Berlin, 1940). The same author gives an ornate picture of Early Christendom: Christianity kept aloof from the state because of its eschatological belief and it soon developed an attitude of hatred against this world (*Die politische Kirche und ihre biblischen ‹Urkunden›* (Berlin, 1938), pp. 86f). Essentially it was the religion of world revolution (p. 83), a revolution which it enacted by way of sabotaging the existing order (p. 89). The documents camouflage this: certain terms may have a religious meaning but also carry political overtones; the accounts of Pilate's belief in Jesus's innocence are another way of hiding what is the true kernel of Christianity (p. 54). This picture is not meant to recommend a radical form of Christianity. On the contrary, it is painting black on black, meant to be a warning against a political church which indulges in anarchistic dreams (p. 90). Eisler's theory is summarised with sympathy by F. Pzillas, 'Der Messiaskönig Jesus' in Deschner, *Jesusbilder*, pp. 181ff. (Deschner himself tends to adopt Eisler pp. 472f). In England it was *The Modern Churchman* that gave Eisler a favourable hearing throughout the years of the editorship of Major.

[205] For certain political connotations of Murawski's writings cp. J. S. Conway, *The Nazi Persecution of the Churches* (London, 1968), p. 406.

[206] Cp. note 186, p. 33. Still, theologians were not uninfluenced by Eisler. Goguel went so far as to state that there was a time when Jesus was about to be proclaimed king by his followers, i.e. to be put forward as the enemy of Rome, and that it was Mark who obliterated this feature because he did not want to cause damage to the spread of the gospel among the loyal subjects of Rome (*Jésus*, GT p. 243; ET pp. 376f). Windisch admitted that Eisler's combination of Mark 15: 7 with the cleansing is very debatable : Jesus gave expression to his messianic and kingly claim by causing an 'uprising' ('Unser Wissen', p. 306).

[207] *Der Prozess Jesu*, SBA 1931, pp. 313ff (repr. in *Kleine Schriften* II (Berlin, 1958), pp. 251ff). Lietzmann holds that the *Petruserzählung* is fundamental and therefore the arrest carried out by the Jews as well. They decided not to take the risk of a religious trial but to proceed along a more promising avenue by handing over Jesus to the Romans. The account of the Sanhedrin trial is therefore an addition to the original narration.

[208] J. Pickl composed a portrait of Jesus at about the same time which makes extensive use of Josephus, sets Jesus against the background of Jewish Zealotism and brings out a sharp contrast between these two worlds (*Messiaskönig Jesus* (München, 1935); 3rd edn. 1938). It is regrettable that his work, which displays a masterly knowledge

reluctance was partly due to the fact that the professionals,[209] accustomed to slow and steady progress in research, felt consternation at what appeared like the eruption of a volcano. Besides, the time was not ideal for thoroughgoing discussion. It had to happen that his theories were taken up by someone else and exposed to the scrutiny of the learned world once again. It was, perhaps, fortunate that this was undertaken by a scholar whose manner of arguing and presenting his case was so much at variance with Eisler's as S. G. F. Brandon.

Brandon stands on the shoulders of Eisler and he is not slow to admit this.[210] He refers to the Slavonic Josephus, so cherished by Eisler;[211] he cites the Hebrew Josippon and a number of other sources out of the wealth of material presented by Eisler. He is, however, less enthusiastic about these sources than Eisler is. His approach is not uncritical in detail,[212] although he has not really made himself familiar with the points of detailed criticism raised against Eisler. More than that, he is less dependent on this material than is Eisler. He found himself able to reconstruct to his own satisfaction a picture of nascent Christianity from such sources as belonged to the traditional armoury of scholars, a picture which more or less coincided with Eisler's impression. It is probably due to this that the dependence on Eisler is less marked in his later publications.[213] They appear, in part at least, like a regression from Eisler to the nationalistic interpretation and the treatment of sources favoured by the Franco-Jewish writer Rodrigues.[214]

of the Greek Josephus text, was never examined alongside Eisler's and used as a corrective to him. Eisler received some support. H. Braunert, 'Der römische Provinzialzensus und der Schätzungsbericht des Lukas-Evangeliums', *Historia* 6 (1957), 129ff, thinks that the date of the birth of Jesus given by Luke derives from a Judaeo-Christian group which was eager to make his birth coincide with the date given by Josephus for the beginning of the Zealot movement. It was in his opinion a Christian zealotic group which was responsible for this dating, a group which wanted to mark the date, which had a truly historical importance for the national struggle. He hints at the zealotic provenance of Judas and points to Farmer's findings as showing a close relation between Jewish nationalism and early Christianity, while leaving it open whether this merging took place during the ministry of Jesus or later.

[209] On the other hand the writer Max Brod shows himself greatly influenced by Eisler in his *The Messiah* (London/New York, 1931) (cp. G. Jasper, *Stimmen aus dem neureligiösen Judentum in seiner Stellung zum Christentum und zu Jesus* (Hamburg, 1958), pp. 109ff). The same is true for F. Andermann, *Das grosse Gesicht* (München, 1970).

[210] *The Fall of Jerusalem and the Christian Church* (London, 1951), pp. xf.

[211] Ibid. pp. 32, 114ff, 122f.

[212] Ibid. pp. 121f.

[213] Although – see *Jesus and the Zealots* (Manchester, 1967), pp. 367f – he is still inclined to link the Slavonic report on Jesus with Josephus and for this reason to consider it as a source of the highest importance.

[214] H. Rodrigues, *Histoire rationelle des premiers Chrétiens* (Paris, 1873). On Rodrigues, cp. D. Catchpole, *The Trial of Jesus . . . in Jewish Historiography* (Leiden, 1971), pp. 49f, 116.

Besides, Brandon confines himself to a few leading ideas, while Eisler fired a salvo of ideas at the reader, causing simultaneously stimulation and embarrassment. His presentation is at first cautiously worded in detail, but then his tentative conclusions are taken as a solid basis in the next section and the final summing up only too often lacks any features of caution.

The starting-point of Brandon's approach to the problems of early Christianity is a rigorous critique of the sources after the model of the Tübingen *Tendenzkritik* of the last century.[215] The Gospels, which are viewed as being almost completely products of the pens of single individuals,[216] are seen as having found their particular shape under the influence of certain apologetic tendencies of the respective evangelists. Mark, a Gospel which had often been taken as primitive, is characterised by Brandon as a sophisticated performance,[217] aimed at reversing the impression the Roman public had of Christendom. It carries through the idea of a pacific Christ, who taught love and was condemned by Pilate as a result of Jewish intrigues, whereas in reality the opposite had happened: he had been executed by the Romans on the charge of sedition after having come out openly against the payment of taxes, after an assault against the Temple and the preparation of armed resistance. His death gained him the sympathy of his fellow-countrymen, a sympathy which the Christians enjoyed likewise and which lasted beyond the death of Jesus's brother James[218] and enabled the Christians to join the ranks of the revolutionaries in their fight against Rome.

The picture of the events, coinciding with the one drawn by Eisler, does deviate in one particular point. Brandon emphasises that Jesus was not a member of a Zealot underground organisation: he stayed independent and his activity can only be described as para-Zealot in character. This, however, does not mean that he was less active than they were; on the

---

[215] Which kept him fascinated; see his 'Tübingen vindicated?', *Hibbert Journal* 49 (1951), 41ff. For the Tübingen principles cp. Kümmel, *Das Neue Testament*, pp. 156ff.

[216] This is done by Brandon in opposition to the then ruling school of *Formgeschichte* and was maintained by him in spite of the new *Redaktionsgeschichte*, a development he barely took stock of.

[217] The attribution to Mark of a tendency to belittle Jesus's disciples (*Fall*, 195ff; similarly and with much more acumen Raschke, *Werkstatt*, pp. 104ff; and cp. recently J. Schreiber, 'Die Christologie des Markusevangeliums', *ZThK* 58 (1961), 154ff, who actually maintains that Mark is directed against the early community) would be more credible if Mark had given indications pointing to others besides the disciples to be taken as exemplary figures.

[218] Brandon holds a very low opinion about the tradition according to which the Judaeo-Christians left Jerusalem for Pella at the beginning of the revolt. For his mistranslation of the decisive passage cp. W. Wink, 'Jesus and Revolution', *Union Seminary Quarterly Review* 25 (1969), 42.

contrary, he anticipated the Zealots in attacking the Temple,[219] while in directing himself against the Temple and the priestly oligarchy[220] he gave an indication that his emphasis did not completely[221] coincide with that of the Zealots, who were primarily anti-Roman in their outlook.[222] Eisler had linked Jesus more closely with the Zealot movement while on the other hand admitting that Jesus was likely to have been a man pushed forward by the masses and thus the victim of the situation.[223] This latter is emphatically denied by Brandon: Jesus was a 'dynamic leader', not a 'visionary who was swept away'.[224]

Another difference emerges in consequence of this. In attacking the Temple Jesus incurred the animosity of the high priests. Brandon has therefore no difficulty in assuming a Sanhedrin trial and, perhaps, a Jewish arrest,[225] while the cleansing, an action that had involved 'violence and pillage',[226] led of necessity to the condemnation by the Romans.

The evidence is found in certain data preserved in the gospels which could only be neutralised by the evangelists, not rejected: the Roman execution alongside two Zealots, the cleansing of the Temple; secondly in a few details which happened to survive because of the less circumspect procedure of Luke:[227] the tower of Siloam, the two swords, etc. These data and the assumed tendencies of the evangelists are used by Brandon as the focal points in between which every tradition at variance with these is eliminated.[228] Is it, however, likely that tradition which was not only

---

[219] Brandon, *Zealots*, p. 338.

[220] Ibid. pp. 342f.

[221] Although the difference should not be over-accentuated; thus Brandon thinks that a connection existed with the Barabbas insurrection which happened at the same time as the cleansing (p. 339). E. Stauffer, on the other hand, maintains that Mark 11: 17f are a stray piece of tradition which referred originally to Barabbas (*Jerusalem und Rom* (Bern, 1957), p. 146 n. 18).

[222] Brandon is not fully aware of the fact that the 'cleansing of the house of Israel' is equally an aim of the Zealots, a precondition for the coming of the messiah, at least as important in their view as the defeat of the Romans.

[223] 'Ιησ. Βασ. ii, 508ff; *Messiah*, pp. 500f.

[224] *Zealots*, p. 354.

[225] *The Trial of Jesus of Nazareth* (London, 1968), p. 149; cp. p. 130.

[226] *Zealots*, p. 338.

[227] Ibid. p. 324.

[228] Granted that Brandon is right in assuming this, why then did the evangelists not invent statements of Jesus giving an open warning against zealotism? Surely they would have been able to do so if they so wanted. The lack of such attacks against the Zealots does not mean what Brandon (*Zealots*, p. 201) makes it to mean, the tacit admission of the evangelists that Jesus had been associated with them in some ways, but rather that the whole question was of minor importance within the Christian communities or had been solved on the political level. The absence of any mention of the Zealots has its parallel in the almost complete silence about the priests and Sadducees. This shows that the Christians put down only such sayings as were still relevant in their own times and *vis-à-vis* their own adversaries.

authentic but grew without impediment until A.D. 70 left no more traces
than these? Is such a rigid carrying out of a single tendency really the
approach to be assumed for an evangelist? Can we even be sure that Mark
was written after A.D. 70?[229] Granted that Mark was stimulated by
apologetic tendencies to the extent assumed by Brandon, is he likely to have
met the reservations of the Roman administrators by his presentation?[230]
Does the treatment of the Temple really indicate a post-war origin?[231] Is the
description of the material that in the opinion of Brandon originated after
A.D. 70 always correct?[232]

Above all, what are in fact the changes in historical perspective which
were made after A.D. 70? There can be little doubt that these years left their
mark on the outlook of those who went through them.[233] Judaism provides
the most striking example of this. A thorough investigation of the
developments in this field, the listing of the changes that were made and the
working out of the criteria which became instrumental for the carrying out
of the alteration in the *Geschichtsbild* might indeed give criteria for the
singling out of corresponding features in Christian literature. This might
especially be promising for the analysis of the fragments of Judaeo-
Christian literature which have come down to us. Nothing has been done
along these lines.

The evidence of Judaeo-Christianity plays an important role in
Brandon's argumentation. Hegesippus's report about the migration of the
Jerusalem community to Pella before the encircling of the Holy City is

[229] Mark 13: 14f could be taken to reflect a situation before 70.

[230] The Romans, tolerant as they were, became very irritated about religious
propagandists, especially those with a magical touch. To keep clean at least the
metropolis was the sound principle of the administration. The *praefectus urbi* stepped
in once and again against the activities of magicians in the capital. We would
therefore expect a portrait of Jesus that is purged of features that are open to
magical interpretation. The opposite is the case. The Gospel describes Jesus as a
miracle worker and contains elements which might be taken as indicating magical
practices: 5: 1ff; 5: 28f; 9: 28 etc. Λεγιών in 5: 9 might have caused direct concern.
The case shows that the political tendency assumed by Brandon is not likely to have
played a role either.

[231] Both Mark 15: 38f and the Judaeo-Christian tradition (Ev. Naz. fr. 21) indicate that
the Temple lost its value after the death of Jesus. The problem of the delay of its
doom worries Matthew, who explains it by reference to the lack of faith on the side
of the Christians (21: 20–22). Would we not expect similar statements in Mark, if
the contents of the Gospel had been coloured by the experience of the Jewish war?

[232] The tendency to characterise the Judaeo-Christian gospels as products of a new
foundation (*Neubildung*) in the second century which had nothing to do with the
Jerusalem community is spreading and finds backing in the imprecise employment
of the term 'Judaeo-Christianity' as it is used by J. Daniélou (*Théologie du
Judéo-Christianisme* (Tournai, 1958)). The theory is, however, only supported by the
flimsiest evidence.

[233] Cp. H. Windisch, 'Der Untergang Jerusalems im Urteil der Christen und Juden',
Theologische Tijdschrift 48 (1914), 519–50.

completely rejected by him[234] and the Judaeo-Christians are made fellow-combatants in the uprising against Rome. If indeed his estimation of the fall of Jerusalem were substantiated, we would expect the crisis after the event to have shaken this branch of Christendom much more than other centres. Where, however, is the evidence? Brandon avoids this question by maintaining that the Jerusalem church had fallen into 'complete oblivion' and had been 'utterly destroyed by the Romans'.[235] He regards the Judaeo-Christian gospels, the anti-cultic tendency of which is so blunt and which is linked so closely with both the proclamation[236] and the death[237] of Jesus that there is no room for the theological concept of divine forbearance or the historical one of a development, as conditioned by the approach of the *Grosskirche*. It seems that the attitude of antagonism to the Temple, as we find it in the New Testament only in Acts 7: 48, was developed in these circles. True, this is not easily reconcilable with the Hegesippan report on James, who wore priestly dress and frequented the Temple so often in prayer that his knees grew hard like those of a camel.[238] This could point to a line more rigid than James's own attitude being taken up after his death by his community and, on the other hand, to the employment of embellishing colours by the annalists of the *Grosskirche*. Probably both forces were at work on their respective levels. There is not, however, evidence that the tendency of antagonism to the Temple had to be pushed through for the view that the priestly emphasis in the description of James is due to his officiating in the Temple,[239] let alone to his instigating the – *nota bene* Jewish – Levites against the high priests. On the contrary, the tradition, kept alive in Judaeo-Christianity, about the collapse of the lintel of the Temple after the death of Jesus[240] implies the ineffectiveness of the cult immediately after the departure of the Shekinah which is indicated by this event. No traces of a crisis caused by the year 70, nor vestiges of the employment of the Jewish catastrophe for apologetic purposes are noticeable in this literature. Without such evidence the Brandon theory, suggestive as it may be, is based on a *petitio principii*, is merely a *Luftgebäude* (castle in the air).

Brandon studies Mark in detail but he almost bypasses the large body of

---

[234] Brandon follows the direction given by Joel (*Blicke*, ii, 84f) and he is followed in this by G. Strecker, *Das Judenchristentum in den Pseudoklementinen* (Berlin, 1958), pp. 229ff and J. Munck, 'Jewish Christianity in Post-Apostolic Times', *NTSt* 6 (1959/60), 104. For criticism cp. S. Sowers, *ThZ* 26 (1970), 305ff.

[235] *Religion in Ancient History* (London, 1973), p. 281.

[236] Epiphanius, *Haer.* 30.16.22.

[237] Jerome, on Matt, 27.51.

[238] Eusebius, *H.E.* 2.23.6.

[239] Eisler, 'Ιησ. Βασ. ii, 584; *Messiah*, p. 542; Brandon, *Fall*, pp. 98f.

[240] It is to be understood in line with Ps. 24: 7, 9: God is leaving, therefore the lintel is collapsing.

Christian material we possess in the Corpus Paulinum. The outlook, with respect to the Romans, of the latter is basically the same as Mark's. But most of these letters were written before A.D. 70. The fact shows that a departure – if that is what it was – like that of Mark was possible without the impact of the Jewish war and already quite a number of years earlier. Quasi-Zealot antecedents are likely in the case of Paul.[241] Why then was he suspect to the Jerusalem community? Why did he embrace the para-Zealot belief of Christianity at all if he was moving politically in a different direction? Why, on the other hand, was a distinguishing position *vis-à-vis* zealotism like the one taken by the Christian Paul not already possible for Jesus? The differences between Jesus and Paul may be far less marked on the political level than in other questions.[242] True, Brandon gives his case support by reference to Acts 23: 16ff, in his opinion the attempt of Zealot members of the Jerusalem community to get rid of Paul by way of lynch law.[243] Quite apart, however, from the fact that Paul is reduced in size to the figure of an apostate, the points at issue between him and the Jerusalem authorities are such that they can hardly be subsumed under the rubric of political zealotism.

It is appropriate that scholars should look out for fixed points, in order to date the nascent Christian literature (a tendency which was particularly characteristic of nineteenth-century scholarship) and it is understandable that the Jewish war is taken as a touchstone. The argument based on the reference or otherwise to this event is, however, often overworked. The Christians, especially those who were at home in the Roman world, could interpret many events as signs of divine intervention, not only the destruction of Jerusalem but equally the anarchy after Nero's death, the eruption of Vesuvius – even a chain of such events might have been seen as significant. The absence of such references in writings scrutinised for them does not necessarily mean that these documents are of earlier date (*pace* J. A. T. Robinson);[244] it may very well mean that the authors were less concerned about the general scenery than we would want them to be. In the same way, an actual reference (if proven) does not necessarily imply that the event referred to had substantially changed the outlook of the writers; the reference may have been a casual one or of auxiliary importance (*pace* Brandon). True, the communities in Palestine had every reason to see God at work in the actions of Caligula, the expulsion of the Jews from Rome and, supremely, in the doom of Jerusalem. But they may have been readier to interpret the persecution the Christians themselves were undergoing as a

[241] Cp. *ZNW* 59 (1968), 108ff.
[242] Cp. W. R. Farmer, *The Modern Churchman* n.s. 11 (1967/8), 119.
[243] *Fall*, pp. 135, 151f.
[244] *Redating the New Testament* (London, 1976).

sign of the future[245] and they certainly did interpret the events mentioned above as consequential to the Cross – a view which substantially influenced the presentation of them.

Brandon's scheme, unlike Eisler's grand design, received little attention when it appeared in 1951. The political atmosphere had changed so much that the Zealot theory was hardly noticed or found worth mentioning.[246] His treatment of the New Testament sources was considered old-fashioned and the interest he took in the Judaeo-Christians militated against the then dominant ahistorical approach to the New Testament. It was the total change of scene rather than his own insistence in later publications that, in conjunction with the impact made by Jewish contributions,[247] led to a revival of the Eisler–Brandon theories in the late sixties.[248]

VII

The Jewish contribution to research in early Christendom was for a long time dominated by apologetic motifs. While their forefathers had maintained the rightness of the condemnation of Jesus, the sons – from the time of Mendelssohn onward – disclaimed involvement in the execution of Jesus.[249] This meant that the actual teaching of Jesus – not the christology of the Early Church – remained a kind of adiaphoron, which could be valued without prejudice. Indeed, already at the beginning of the nineteenth century it is stated that his thoughts are not at all at variance with Judaism.[250] At the same time it is, however, felt that there is something lacking in Jesus, something that is not only dear to the Jewish heart but

[245] Typical is the interpretation of the expulsion of the Jews from Rome, as we find it in I Thess. 2: 16; cp. *ZThK* 56 (1959), 294ff.

[246] C. F. D. Moule, *JThSt*, n.s. 3 (1952), 106–8 (review of Brandon, *Fall*). For a penetrating critique of Brandon's views cp. J. Jeremias, *Neutestamentliche Theologie* (Gütersloh, 1971), 219f (ET London, 1971, pp. 228f).

[247] It is typical that S. Sandmel, who confesses to be a sceptic with regard to the possibility of reconstructing the historical Jesus (*A Jewish Understanding of the New Testament* (Cincinnati, 1956), pp. 173ff), feels nevertheless drawn to Brandon's views and states his 'full agreement' with his thesis (*Saturday Review* (1969), p. 88).

[248] Although in the case of Brandon himself the findings are not meant to serve as a model for the present (Wink, *Union Seminary Quarterly Review* 25 (1969) 50 is mistaken in assuming this). On the contrary, it is rather an attempt to dissociate the church from certain features of its heritage. Nineham's various papers (*Explorations in Theology* (London, 1977); *The Use and Abuse of the Bible* (London, 1978)) may be viewed as a parallel phenomenon to that tendency – *mutatis mutandis* of course.

[249] Catchpole, *Trial, passim*.

[250] This tendency can go so far that S. Wise posed the question: 'because Christendom has renounced Jesus in fact, shall we continue to deny him now that we, his brother Jews, are free to face his life and teaching anew?' (cited by H. Danby, *The Jews and Christianity* (London, 1927), p. 111).

fundamental to the Jewish mind: the well-being of the Jewish nation as the *raison d'être* of the code of behaviour. This is noticed with disapproval already by J. Salvador[251] and sharply criticised by J. Jacobs: 'Jesus died . . . for that he cared naught for our national hopes.'[252]

The same sentiment is found in J. Klausner, the first Jew who ventured a life of Jesus[253] and who concludes with the statement: 'to adopt the teaching of Jesus is to remove oneself from the whole sphere of ordered national and human existence'.[254] But this is linked with another perspective, with a quasi-Zealot interpretation. 'During the earlier stage of his ministry it seemed as if he, too, were a political–spiritual messiah like the other messiahs of his age.'[255] Klausner accepts the idea of a Markan[256] watershed and comes out for the historicity of the announcement of the suffering of the messiah. This, he emphasises, does not mean the death of the messiah. Jesus had it in mind to announce himself publicly as messiah in Jerusalem and to cleanse the Temple in this context; he had foreseen hard times to come thereafter – times in which he might need armed protection and was to withdraw to Galilee[257] – but he believed in divine intervention. There is no reason to assume that he planned a revolt against the Romans and that the cleansing has to be seen as a political action.[258] The hostility of the Sadducees he aroused thereby could not have brought about his downfall, were it not that by giving an evasive answer on the question of the tribute money he forfeited the support of the nationalistic masses.[259] So the high-priestly party, infuriated because of Jesus's Temple action and somehow regarding him as a menace to the peace,[260] got hold of him in a surprise action which was made possible by the information supplied by Judas regarding his whereabouts. The tragedy of the event consists in the fact that Jesus, who had relinquished Zealot leanings and returned to a Pharisaic type of belief, had so much come to be at loggerheads with the Pharisees about questions of detail that he did not receive protection from

[251] *Jésus Christ et sa doctrine* i (Paris, 1838), 298ff, 385ff.
[252] *As Others saw Him* (London, 1895) p. 210. Cp. 'All Israel was pining to be freed from the Roman yoke, and he would have us pay tribute to Rome for aye. Did he feel himself in some way as not of our nation?' (p. 202; cp. p. 161).
[253] *Jesus of Nazareth*, Hebr. ed. Jerusalem, 1922; ET London, 1925; GT Berlin, 1930.
[254] ET *Jesus*, p. 397.
[255] Ibid. p. 206.
[256] Characteristic for his approach is the reliance on a high degree of credibility in the Christian sources, especially of Mark (cp. p. 294); in this he is an heir of the older type of Life-of-Jesus authors.
[257] So he interprets Luke 22: 36ff and Mark 14: 28.
[258] Klausner, *Jesus*, pp. 312f.
[259] Ibid. p. 318. The summary which I. Maybaum (*Trialogue between Jews, Christians and Muslims* (London, 1973), p. 85) gives of Klausner's portrait of Jesus is one-sided.
[260] Klausner, *Jesus*, pp. 336, 348.

their side and was, when it came to the point, at the mercy of the Sadducees who treated the case only as a matter of convenience.[261]

In giving this outline Klausner succeeds in bringing Jesus yet another step nearer to the paternal religion. For a time Jesus was the true mouthpiece of Judaism and it is only fatal deviation in his activity, his neglect of national life[262] and, at the same time, the features of 'exaggerated' Judaism[263] in his teaching, which separate him from Judaism proper.[264] 'He lacks the Prophet's political conception and the Prophet's spirit of national consolation in the political national sense.'[265]

This attempt at *Heimholung* – at Klausner's time emphatically opposed by orthodox Jews[266] – was taken up by Winter.[267] Unlike Klausner he made extensive use of, and certain detailed contributions to, source criticism. More important, his investigation appeared at a time when the Christian church was particularly prone to give fundamental reconsideration to its position *vis-à-vis* the Jews.[268] It was for these reasons that the book made history. Adopting that part of Lietzmann's theory on the trial that claims the unhistoricity of the report on the interrogation by the Sanhedrin and making himself a champion of it, he attempts to deny the existence of a formal Sanhedrin trial, while allowing for a preliminary investigation by the high priest and, perhaps, his collaboration in the arrest.[269] The involvement is minimal and affects only a few, while there was no discord between Jesus and the Pharisees.[270] The charge for the condemnation was

---

[261] Very similar, Jacobs, *As Others*, pp. 153ff.   [262] *Jesus*, pp. 371f.

[263] Ibid. p. 374: 'nothing is more dangerous to national Judaism than this exaggerated Judaism'.

[264] Ibid. p. 375: his teaching 'became, in a sense, non-Judaism'.   [265] Ibid. p. 414.

[266] Cp. A. F. Moore, 'A Jewish Life of Jesus,' *HThR* 16 (1923), 100ff; H. Kosmala, 'J. Klausners Jesus von Nazareth im liberalen und orthodoxen jüd. Urteil', *Saat auf Hoffnung* 68 (1931), 6ff.

[267] *The Trial of Jesus* (Berlin, 1961; 2nd enlarged edn. 1974).

[268] Cp. *Die evangelische Kirche in Deutschland und die Judenfrage* (ed. by Oekumenischer Rat der Kirchen (Genf, 1945)); A. Bea, *Die Kirchen und das jüdische Volk* (Freiburg, 1966). For a Jewish response cp. S. Zeitlin, 'The Ecumenical Council Vatican II and the Jews' in *Studies* ii (New York, 1974), 582ff.

[269] Winter, *Trial*, p. 48; 2nd edn., pp. 66f. S. b. Chorin, on the other hand, admits a Jewish trial and campaigns for its revision (*Juden und Christen* (Berlin, 1960), pp. 50ff).

[270] 'In the whole of the N.T. we are unable to find a single historically reliable instance of religious differences between Jesus and members of the Pharisaic guild, let alone evidence of a mortal conflict' (Winter, *Trial*, p. 133; 2nd edn., p. 186). This is much more marked in the second edition. Indeed, Winter gives arguments for a later date of the passages stating a hostility between Jesus and the Pharisees, which are very similar in kind to those presented at the same time by F. Weiss (in R. Meyer, *Tradition und Neuschöpfung im antiken Judentum*, Leipzig, 1965) and G. Baumbach (*Jesus von Nazareth im Lichte der jüdischen Gruppenbildung* (Berlin, 1971)). He stresses at the same time the connection of the Christians with the Jewish activists ('the sympathies of Jewish Christians were with those Jewish parties that opposed Rome

entirely a political one; it was the charge of rebellion.[271] The evangelists, especially Mark,[272] were at pains to convey the contrary impression[273] – it is in trying to unearth such a tendency that Winter stands nearest to Brandon – and they did so by inventing the story of a Sanhedrin trial. Winter is predominantly interested in demonstrating what was the Roman charge. He leaves it open how much was true in it. Indeed, he is even inclined, or rather not disinclined,[274] to deny the truth of the charge as far as Jesus is concerned[275] – the case was very different with those who surrounded him,[276] very likely so already in his lifetime.[277] This is not held against

and fought the Romans' (2nd edn., p. 180) or styles them as messianic troublemakers, a ferment owing to the activity of which the respective Jewish communities as a whole had to suffer (2nd edn., p. 182). He goes even so far as to claim that the adverse portrait of the Herodians in the Gospels is conditioned by the fact that Herod Agrippa II tried to dissuade the Jews from waging war against the Romans.

[271] Winter, *Trial*, p. 50; 2nd edn., pp. 68f; cp. 181, 189. It is obvious that these lines of argument are not consistent with each other. For criticism see Catchpole, *Trial*, pp. 72ff. Winter's argument runs as follows: the Romans were reluctant to interfere in religious matters but eager to stamp out political unrest – so they acted in the case of Jesus (pp. 15ff). On the other hand, the Sanhedrin had criminal jurisdiction, but there is no evidence that it made use of it in the case of Jesus. Therefore it was essentially a Roman matter. Winter finds additional evidence in Mark 14: 48b, 49, which verses he considers as a faint echo of a tradition according to which Jesus was arrested by the Romans as a precaution against insurrectionist activities (p. 50). Winter's theory is supported by O. Cullmann (*Der Staat im N.T.* (Tübingen, 1956) pp. 29f; ET London, 1957, pp. 66f), who claims priority (*Jesus and the Revolutionaries* (New York, 1970), p. 34). Cullmann is followed by E. Trocmé (*Jésus de Nazareth* (Neuenburg, 1971), p. 134), whereas F. Bovon (*Les derniers jours de Jésus* (Neuenburg 1974), p. 40) rejects a Zealot interpretation. Winter receives support in the thesis put forward by G. Braumann ('Dem Himmelreich wird Gewalt angetan' (Mt. 11.12), *ZNW* 52(1961), 104ff; 'Markus 15: 2–5 und Markus 14: 55–64', *ZNW* 52 (1961), 273ff), according to which Mark 14: 55ff is a doublet of Mark 15: 2ff, inserted in order to extend the guilt for the death of Jesus to the Jews (p. 277). A certain parallelism between the reports in the accounts of the Roman and the Jewish proceedings is obvious, but conditioned by the subject. More evidence is needed to justify the conclusion.

[272] Winter, *Trial*, p. 24.

[273] It is less the influence of the disaster of the year 70 than the apologetic needs of the urban communities that, in the opinion of Winter, caused the change.

[274] 'Only what his followers hoped . . . finds its expression in the gospels. What Jesus himself thought, . . . we simply do not know' ('The Trial of Jesus', *The Jewish Quarterly* 16 (1968), No. 2/3, p. 37).

[275] Winter, *Trial*, p. 50.

[276] 'We can say without hesitation that Jesus's followers cherished aspirations of Jewish national independence. We cannot say whether they were encouraged to such aspirations by Jesus himself' (*The Jewish Quarterly* 16 (1968), No. 2/3, p. 37); cp. n. 274. He seems to think of developments similar to those that happened in the environment of the Baptist: 'it was primarily the effect which his teaching exercised on certain sections of the populace that induced the authorities to take action against him' (Winter, *Trial*, 2nd edn., p. 189).

[277] Interesting is Winter's treatment of Sanh. 43a; he translates the accusation: 'led

him – Winter differs at this point from Klausner; on the contrary, Jesus becomes to him a symbol for the suffering of the Jewish nation, in his own time at the hands of the Romans, in other times at those of the Christians.[278, 279]

There seems to be a far cry from Eisler to Winter – indeed neither the former's name nor the source favoured by him plays a role in the latter's argument. Still, there are points of contact which are obliterated by the predominantly analytical procedure of Winter: the Zealot inclination among the disciples of Jesus, the more restrained attitude of Jesus himself, the Roman responsibility for trial and execution, the mitigating tendencies in the documents of the New Testament.

Owing to this, a blending of Winter's[280] and Eisler's approach could be achieved in the portrayal of J. Carmichael. It is Eisler's influence that is dominant, and thus we find a description of 'the violence that attended Jesus's movement, its anti-Roman political implications and, above all, perhaps its material failure'.[281] Jesus was reared in the environment of the Baptist, who himself had organised a group 'to oppose the authorities through physical secession from their territorial jurisdiction'.[282] He broke away[283] from John and attempted to establish the kingdom, not somewhere

Israel to revolt'. He assumes that, if it refers to Jesus's attitude to the Roman government, it derives – indirectly – from Luke 23: 2 and that, if it refers to the Torah, it was pure mystification. In any case, he denies any evidential value. It is necessary for him to disclaim the credibility of the passage, because it states that there was a Jewish trial and execution. He thereby deprives himself of the possibility of attributing revolutionary plans to Jesus and shifts the emphasis to Jesus's followers: 'there is reason for thinking that some expression of such aspirations occurred already in the life of Jesus' (*Trial*, p. 145; 2nd edn., p. 202). The Eislerian theory is re-established thereby in a weaker form.

[278] Conversely S. Asch pictures Jesus as having been crucified by Hermanus (*The Nazoraean* (ET London, 1939)).

[279] H.-W. Bartsch became an advocate of the views of Winter on the Trial (*Jesus. Prophet und Messias aus Galiläa* (Frankfurt, 1970); *Der Tod eines Revolutionärs* (Wuppertal, 1968)). He proceeds further, however, and expresses the opinion that the messianic demonstrations of entry and cleansing caused or necessitated Jesus's handing over to the Romans (pp. 43, 47, 53). He goes even so far as to state that the activities of his followers were such that the Sanhedrin saw no reason to enter into a collision course with Rome for the sake of so small a minority (p. 128).

[280] Dependent on Winter is P. E. Lapide, *Jesus in Israel* (Gladbeck, 1970), pp. 53f. Similar statements in Lapide's popular and diffuse book *Der Rabbi von Nazaret* (Trier, 1974). Like Winter in his second edition Lapide, in his later work, approaches the Zealot solution.

[281] J. Carmichael, *The Death of Jesus* (London, 1963; Penguin edn. 1966), p. 157.

[282] Ibid. p. 142. Similarly Andermann, who maintains that Jesus entered the underground organisation of John, who was a 'Tambour des Widerstands' although he remained aloof in the desert (*Gesicht*, p. 177).

[283] Here we notice a difference from Eisler. While the 'breaking out' is the final goal of Jesus according to the latter, it is the device of an initial phase according to Carmichael (cp. pp. 145f).

far away, but by storming Jerusalem.[284] He held the Temple in occupation
for a time – the so-called thieves at the Cross acted as subsidiary
commanders,[285] was probably supported by the younger men of the Temple
hierarchy[286] and exercised sovereignty there.[287] Carmichael, like so many
others, searches for a turning-point in the career of Jesus. He finds it
alluded to in Mark 13: 14 – a veiled reference to Pilate's defilement of the
sanctuary by setting up Roman standards in its precinct.[288] The
turning-point is thus neither an experience of the Schweitzer nor of the
Eisler type. It is an external event that sets in motion a man who, through
his connections with the Baptist and even more so after his break with him,
is anyhow ready for such an action. The idea of an earlier period,
substantially different, is quietly given up. Jesus is part of the mainstream
of Jewish life of his time. Messianic consciousness, usually admitted by
Jewish scholars, is denied.[289] The Sanhedrin trial does not interfere with
this, because Winter's thesis enables Carmichael to dispense with it
completely.[290] The man who acted as a Jew 'died as a Jew'[291] at the hands of
the Romans. The closer Jesus himself is linked with his fatherland, the
readier Carmichael is to allow for a quick transmission in Christianity. To
Jewish Christianity and the year 70 – the touchstones in Brandon's
criticism – no significant role is attributed.

H. Maccoby[292] goes even further than Eisler. While displaying an
extremely critical attitude vis-à-vis the Gospel reports, he bases his
understanding of Jesus on his own interpretation of contemporary history,
which is linked with certain facets of the Jesus tradition in such a way that
these are drawn in like metal shavings by a magnet. The period is viewed as
dominated by zealotism – to the exclusion of anything else and therefore
Jesus is made a para-Zealot figure as well: 'his preaching must have
contained denunciations of the Roman rape . . .'.[293] He was a preacher of
the 'ideological world-victory of Judaism'[294] and of the 'overthrow of
Roman power'.[295] Identifying himself with the task, he allows himself to be

---

[284] Carmichael, Death, p. 143. Jesus was assisted by 2,000 armed followers – so
Carmichael says, referring to what he calls ' a medieval copy of a lost version of a
work of Josephus' (p. 117).

[285] Ibid. p. 120.   [286] Ibid. p. 121.   [287] Ibid. p. 160.

[288] Ibid. pp. 167f. This is supported by general remarks on 'chronological dislocation'
in the Gospels (p. 159).

[289] Carmichael, Death, pp. 152ff.

[290] Cp. p. 158; although he admits that the cleansing made Jesus collide with the
Jewish authorities (p. 133).

[291] Carmichael, Death, p. 165.

[292] Revolution in Judaea. Jesus and the Jewish Resistance (London, 1973). Maccoby
developed his views in 'Is the Political Jesus dead?', Encounter 46 (1976), 80ff (Feb.
Nr.) Reply, Encounter 48 (1977), 88ff (April Nr.).

[293] Maccoby, Revolution, p. 130.   [294] Ibid. p. 173.   [295] Ibid. p. 157.

crowned a king, a scene which was transformed to that of the transfiguration,[296] to head for Jerusalem, to enter the city 'in an act of rebellion'[297] to occupy the Temple area and, perhaps, to appoint a new high priest.[298] Being an apocalypticist he did not, however, engage in battle against the Romans but expected salvation from a divine miracle, as had been announced in Zech. 9 – he waited for it in the agony of Gethsemane.[299] He was arrested by the Romans, kept in prison for 'some weeks or months'[300] and condemned as a revolutionary. His preaching was of the Pharisaic type;[301] nothing was outstanding in it;[302] he would have been forgotten in Judaism, were it not that Christianity had got hold of him by way of 'falsification of everything that Jesus stood for'.[303] The difference is such that, one would think, the assumption of the unhistoricity of Jesus would more easily explain the emergence of that 'sad masochistic Romanticism'[304] called Christianity and its fantastic Gospels than the author's portrayal of Jesus. There are many cracks in the picture and the speed with which the author proceeds from an unproven hypothesis to its use as a solid basis for the next idea is breathtaking. The influence of the Toledoth Jeshu is just noticeable,[305] an influence which had been much more in prominence in the Jesus portrait of H. J. Schonfield.[306]

A further stage is reached by H. Cohn.[307] Jesus himself is firmly placed within Judaism; no deviation is castigated. Nor is the onus put on the high priests; any treacherous inclination on their side is denied.[308] Even the cleansing had their support, at least tacitly.[309] It is Cohn's basic claim to have established the unanimity of the nation, which manifested itself in the utmost protection offered to Jesus.[310] The so-called Sanhedrin trial is, in

---

[296] Ibid. pp. 167ff.   [297] Ibid. p. 174.

[298] Ibid. p. 179.   [299] Ibid. pp. 193ff.

[300] Ibid. p. 217.   [301] Ibid. p. 129.

[302] Slightly different on Maccoby, *Revolution*, p. 191.

[303] Ibid. p. 191.   [304] Ibid. p. 135.

[305] Cp. n. 300 with the scheme of the Toledoth.

[306] *Jesus* (London, 1939). He accepts the Toledoth account of the arrest as historical (p. 254) and interprets it as referring to an action taken by the disciples: after having taken refuge they raised some of the Galilaean Zealots and made a demonstration in force. The authorities were forced to set Jesus free, but later on he was caught in the Temple etc.

[307] H. Cohn, *The Trial and Death of Jesus* (in Hebrew Tel-Aviv, 1968; ET London, 1972); cp. *Reflections on the Trial and Death of Jesus* (Jerusalem, 1967).

[308] *Trial*, p. 36; John 11:48 is cited in support of this.

[309] Ibid. p. 249.

[310] Jesus was arrested by the Romans. But the Jewish police force was present at the same spot and obtained permission to take Jesus into custody until the next morning. He was conducted into the high priest's palace and found the high priest already waiting for him: something had to be done quickly. What? 'To prevent the execution by the Romans of a Jew who happened to enjoy the affection and love of the people' (*Reflections*, pp. 23f). 'Witnesses had to be found to prove his innocence'

fact, nothing but the attempt of the leading men in Jewry to shield Jesus against the Romans and to achieve this by working out a scheme which could be staged on the following morning in front of the prefect. Thus, the Jews did for Jesus according to Cohn what they did for Barabbas according to the Gospels. The old idea of a show trial[311] is thereby given a new twist by Cohn.[312] When Jesus refused to play his part, they had no alternative but to

(p. 24). He himself had to be persuaded to promise that he would not in future engage in any treasonable activities (p. 24). The night meeting takes place in order to enable the Sanhedrin to intervene on Jesus's behalf. They satisfy themselves that the incriminating witnesses were false (p. 25). Jesus himself has to be persuaded not to plead guilty. In fact, Jesus remains silent for most of the time but when asked by the high priest he not only admits but even adds a prophecy of revenge – so the high priest 'gives up in despair' (p. 26). What Jesus said was not considered as blasphemy. Therefore it is only the high priest who rends his clothes and not the whole court. They deliver him to the Romans – it is likely that he is led unbound. When Jesus proves to be unwilling to collaborate with the leaders of the Sanhedrin, 'they could do nothing more' (p. 32). (N. Notowitsch, *Die Lücke im Leben Jesu* (Stuttgart, 1894), presents a picture of the Trial which is similar: the Jews do everything in their power to free Jesus, while only Pilate wants his execution. His sketch is based on sources which, he claims, he himself had discovered in Tibet.) The great advantage of this theory is that the author is able to combine (*a*) emphasis on the illegalities with (*b*) the suggestion that there was a meeting. But it is very difficult to follow his reason for positing a Jewish custody, if a Roman arrest and incrimination had taken place. The interpretation of the 'trial' is certainly engendered by the memory of what happened in Palestine during the time of the British mandate. But it needs more than a poet's imagination to interpret the report this way. And the whole participation of Jews in the trial before Pilate had to be interpreted out of existence. Cohn draws attention to the possibility of the Jews acting on two levels. Rightly so. It is most likely that understandings existed between the Jewish parties on the basis of which one of them carried out negotiations with the Romans, which were flanked by demonstrations or other actions engineered by other parties. The considerable success of the official speakers of Judaism had once and again before the outbreak of the Jewish revolt would be incomprehensible otherwise. It is likely that the trial of Jesus was influenced by dealings of this kind as well: several, if not all, of the Jewish parties (the fashionable view that the Pharisees had no share in the condemnation of Jesus (Winter, *Trial, passim*; Baumbach, *Jesus*, p. 91) has little to be said for it) had become involved, some of them had become very unfavourably disposed towards him, while at the same time the fate of Barabbas, who was very dear to one of these parties, hung in the balance. It is likely that this set of circumstances worked against Jesus.

[311] Cp. J. Blinzler, *Der Prozess Jesu* (Regensburg, 1969), p. 30.

[312] There is, of course, no room for the betrayal by Judas (*Trial*, pp. 79ff). The relative prominence given to Judas is very often a test case in modern literature. Those who admit a political issue in the life of Jesus tend to concentrate the problems around the figure of Judas (cp. G. Buchheit, *Judas Iskarioth* (Gütersloh, 1954); W. Jens, *Der Fall Judas* (Stuttgart, 1975), who gives the Zealot theory a sympathetic hearing (pp. 32ff), although the author himself is inclined to look in a different direction for the solution of the problem). It is in keeping with this that J. R. Harris views Judas as the foremost disciple (*The Twelve Apostles* (Cambridge, 1927), pp. 93f, while Shaw in the unpublished play *The Household of Joseph* goes so far as to picture Jesus as having been lured by Judas from his surroundings in Nazareth to the city of Jerusalem (W. S. Smith, *Shaw on Religion* (London, 1967), p. 15). This is not, however, the case

let fate have its way. The condemnation because of his pretension to be a king – something that 'smacks of treason'[313] – was the inevitable result.

On the basis of this thesis it is hardly comprehensible that a special fellowship of followers of Jesus came into existence, let alone that they diverged from the Jews and even less that they left Jerusalem for Pella and – this is the view taken by the contemporary Jews according to Cohn[314] – turned traitors. Cohn's theory shows that the attempt to confine Jesus within Judaism, if carried too far burdens the subsequent history with insoluble problems. It is, however, most symptomatic of how far Jewish scholarship – not only literary imagination[315] – can go in order to achieve the *Heimholung in das jüdische Volk*.

According to these views Jesus belongs, more or less, to the Pharisaic type. The question of his own[316] Zealot inclinations and those of his community[317] is left more open. The success reached by the incorporation of Jesus in Judaism is such that the particular question of affiliation to zealotism could be treated with a certain latitude. It may be, on the other hand, that the Zealot solution called for attempts to explore other connections as well. The latest attempt to portray Jesus as a thaumaturge[318] may be seen as such a case. Is it too bold to assume that after other solutions have been attempted the circle will be completed and Jewish scholarship will return to favouring a quasi-Zealot combination?[319, 320]

in Jewish tradition, where the 'traitor' does not figure in the majority and, possibly, the oldest forms of the texts. Eisler's reconstruction manifests an affinity with this strand of Jewish tradition. He is followed in this by Maccoby who, by ingenious interpretation, rules Judas and the treachery out of existence (*Revolution*, pp. 263ff). An interpretation of the betrayal, altogether different, is ventured by C. Roth, *Iscariot* (London, 1929). Cp. recently H. L. Goldschmidt and M. Limbeck, *Heilvoller Verrat? Judas im Neuen Testament* (Stuttgart, 1976).

[313] Cohn, *Reflections*, p. 177.
[314] Ibid. p. 262.
[315] Cp. A. A. Kabak, *The small path* (Jerusalem, 1938; in Hebrew).
[316] G. Vermes, *Jesus the Jew* (London, 1973), p. 50: 'Zealot or not. . . .'
[317] Cohn, *Reflections*, p. 249.
[318] Vermes, *Jesus*, pp. 58ff.
[319] A highly individual interpretation is given by H. Landau ('Jesus in jüdischer Sicht' in Deschner, *Jesusbilder*, pp. 397ff). It was Stephen, the Hellenist, who threatened the Jews with the destruction of the Temple to be performed by Jesus, who was – this is. Landau's suggestion – still alive at this time (J. O'Neil, *The Theology of Acts* 2nd edn. (London, 1970) holds an even more radical view in assuming that Stephen was not a Christian). This threat was found alarming, pressure was exercised on the Sanhedrin to get hold of Jesus, who was arrested without difficulty, whereas 'James and the others' escaped after an unsuccessful attempt to resist (p. 307). The trial itself is seen as entirely a Roman one (no proper reason is given), the Gospel reports – the earliest of which, Mark, was written a hundred years after the event (p. 310) – are stimulated by the desire to win Roman favour and to dissociate Jesus from the Jews; they are untrustworthy. The facts had been different. Jesus, an Essene and successor of the Teacher of Righteousness (p. 303) had enjoyed the veneration of the

The impulse given by the Zealot interpretation led on the non-Jewish side to reflections which manifested themselves in three different approaches. Pike's reconstruction – the title of the book[321] is a misnomer – follows most closely, both in details and outlook, the path of interpretation in terms of revolution; it is in fact a *florilegium* with a definite preference for Eisler and Brandon. The work, however, stops short of attributing a revolutionary intention to Jesus himself. The cleansing was meant to arouse the conscience of the nation and to bring about a situation which would enable God to intervene.[322] It was the divine action that Jesus was waiting for at Gethsemane, the non-arrival of which led him to prohibit his disciples from making use of the swords they had collected.[323] Deeply committed to the liberation of Israel, he wondered, however, whether the people were able to comprehend 'the kind of things he had been teaching his disciples and that were taught at Qumran'[324] or whether they had to be led through doom to the final liberation. Without having launched a revolt he became suspect because Barabbas had attacked the Antonia at the same time as he cleansed the Temple. He was arrested in a mopping-up operation after this event – the Barabbas incident may be based on fact[325] – and sent to the Cross by the Prefect who made use of his *imperium*.

The general view of the course of history is the Zealot one into which the New Testament data are inserted,[326] a procedure which results in a reluctance to accept all the consequences of the Zealot interpretation.[327] The development of Jesus's own action and, indeed, his reflection[328] is not thereby explained.

It is, on the other hand, a refinement of the theory of Reimarus that is to

whole population; they had pleaded for his release – the Barabbas account as it is found in the Gospels is due to a duplication (pp. 311ff). His memory was held in high regard even in the Talmud, the crucified one became the symbol of the state of the Jewish nation, and his name was passed over in silence until Israel's condition of deprivation came to an end (p. 308). Exploiting Lietzmann's theory on the Sanhedrin trial the author proceeds to theories of his own which are disconnected and confused.

[320] The only author who breaks out of this circle is H. J. Schonfield who maintains that Christianity as a religion will have to go, and equally Jewish nationalism will have to go, because they are both misinterpretations of the messianic idea (*The Politics of God* (London, 1970), p. 52). For his reconstruction of the historical events – he makes use of Brandon at this point – cp. his *The Pentecost Revolution* (London, 1974).

[321] *The Wilderness Revolt* by D. K. Pike and R. S. Kennedy based on ideas and notes of J. A. Pike (New York, 1972).

[322] Pike and Kennedy, *Wilderness Revolt*, p. 176.

[323] Ibid. p. 193.   [324] Ibid. p. 163.   [325] Ibid. p. 225.

[326] If there are difficulties, they are mastered by means of straightforward commonsense without applying critical tools.

[327] Pike and Kennedy, *Wilderness Revolt*, p. 193.

[328] The authors very often point to such 'reflections'. Is this a sign of a portrait of Jesus different from the one presented in the book?

be found in the writings of G. W. Buchanan,[329] according to whose view it was the ideology of and obsession with conquest that directed both Jewish and Christian theology. The concept of the kingdom in the New Testament is accordingly entirely nationalistic.[330] On the other hand, a concept of 'passive ethics' had emerged which involved the toleration of hardship and martyrdrom, the final goal of which was, however, the same as that of the first concept. By suffering and the performance of ascetic practices and thus the acquisition of treasures in heaven, God will be forced to step in himself and to bring about the fulfilment of the covenant–conquest pledges. Acquainted with both schemes Jesus, following the Baptist, adopted the former one. But the death of John 'may have required Jesus to rethink his whole program and to reconsider the role of the Messiah'[331] and, left without a divine command, to abandon the aim of military struggle in favour of meritorious suffering. It is again the idea of change which is developed here. It is presented in a way which combines Reimarus with the second phase of Schweitzer. This is done, however, in such a manner that Jesus suffers his death in keeping with this scheme – no indication of a new experience, as was assumed by Schweitzer, is included. There is therefore no room or need for reconsideration by the disciples after his death. The rapid formation and growth of the communities and equally their self-denying practice can be explained quite easily – this is the difference over against Reimarus. By retrojecting back the turning-point into the life of Jesus, Buchanan is also able to place militant[332] and 'pacifist' sayings of Jesus side by side – both are original in their respective periods; the rigid *Tendenz*-criticism of Brandon is avoided by this means. There is no doubt that an impressive picture is presented of forces which were for a long time dominant. It is achieved at the price of depriving both Jesus and nascent Christianity of anything that is outstanding and original. Both phenomena are only projections of concepts which had been in force already. Eisler's portrait of Jesus was already faded, Buchanan's lacks any significant features and makes it quite incomprehensible why early Christendom took a development so different from the Jewish sects which Buchanan emphasises as parallel phenomena.

Similar, although less one-sided, is J. Lehmann.[333] He more or less accepts Carmichael's thesis of political motives in the movement of Jesus and points to Zealot leanings of not less than six of Jesus's disciples.[334] He

---

[329] *The Consequences of the Covenant* (Leiden, 1970); H. S. Reimarus, *The Goal of Jesus and his Disciples* (Leiden, 1970; introduced by Buchanan), pp. 27–32.

[330] Buchanan, *Covenant*, pp. 69, 90.   [331] Ibid. p. 40.   [332] Ibid. pp. 38f.

[333] *Jesus-Report. Protokoll einer Verfälschung* (Düsseldorf, 1970; ET New York, 1971; London, 1972).

[334] Lehmann, *Jesus-Report*, pp. 126ff (ET pp. 104ff).

reprimands Carmichael, however, for having disregarded the new *Ansatzpunkt* and for having done so for convenience's sake:[335] this is Jesus's connection with Qumran. Jesus taught like the men of the desert community; little in his message was original.[336] He was neither a saviour nor a revolutionary[337] but just a rabbi. It was due to historical accidents that, at the end of his life, he, like the Essenes, engaged in a form of action which was interpreted as a political crime by the Romans.[338] Conversely, ecclesiastical filtering tried to obliterate any traces of both political involvement and Essene heritage.[339]

The Zealot theory is never far away from the Jewish mind when approaching Jesus. It is the approach which is the supreme achievement of making him equal to oneself.[340] It is so much the model that the social interpretation of Jesus is still almost entirely absent[341] from the Jewish enterprises.

Whereas this works in favour of giving Jesus a place in the Valhalla of the Jewish nation it has rather the opposite effect on the non-Jewish side. If the theory is carried through, and not only applied to one particular phase, it creates a portrayal of a Jesus engaged in particular questions, a portrayal which is bound to dissociate him from the great questions of mankind. This is especially noticeable in Lehmann,[342] who claims: 'the Christ whom the church preaches has nothing but the name in common with the historical

---

[335] Ibid. p. 31 (ET p. 28).
[336] Cp. Pike's view. The unguarded hovering between a Qumran and a Zealot approach is typical of a good part of the more popular literature. It would be justified if a closer link between Qumranites and Zealots could be established. This is indeed the theory of C. Roth, which, however, has not met with universal approval.
[337] Lehmann, *Jesus-Report*, pp. 139f (ET p. 113).
[338] Ibid. pp. 30, 120f, 140; cp. p. 188 (ET p. 27f, 98. 113; cp. p. 149).
[339] Ibid. p. 136 (ET p. 109f); J. Lehmann, *Die Jesus G.M.B.H.* (Düsseldorf, 1972), pp. 18f. For a critique of Lehmann, cp. E. Lohse, *EvK* 3 (1970), 652ff. The views taken by E. Bromme (*Allegorisierte Geschichte-gelebter Glaube* (Berlin, 1975)) form an imaginative climax. He persuades himself to his own satisfaction that the terminology used in the N.T. represents an allegorical presentation of military terms and, indeed, events; that 'beloved son' means an eminent and trustworthy emissary of the Essenes; that the fight against the demons means battles against human enemies; the healing of the centurion's servant the conquest of Capernaum; Jesus's teaching in synagogues means giving instruction to Essene communities; the transfiguration is Jesus's promotion to the position of independent commander; etc., etc.
[340] It enables the Jew thereby to shake off a certain cultural inferiority complex, which was apparent in former generations.
[341] Perhaps with the exception of a remark in F. Andermann: Jesus 'kam von der Basis der gesellschaftlichen Pyramide, und er brachte von unten her einen Radikalismus mit, vor dem es dem Johannes grauen musste' (*Das grosse Gesicht* (München, 1970), p. 177).
[342] The same is already true for F. Murawski.

Rabbi J(esus)';[343] he is only used 'as an excuse for an entirely different faith'.[344] This being so, the church lost the integrity which is necessary in order to approach the questions of life.

The effect, however, is almost the same on both sides. The Jew who incorporates Jesus into his own heritage does so at the cost of moving him away from Christianity, of widening the gap between Jewry and Christendom and of denouncing Paul and Christianity.[345] The non-Jew, who pictures Jesus as Zealot takes this as a sufficient reason for dispensing with a Christian heritage which is built on so strange a foundation. The Zealot interpretation serves as a means of and justification for dissociation from Christianity.

The socialist writers explain the origin of Christianity without admitting a constitutive influence of its 'founder', of the person of Jesus. Jewish historiography tends to explain early Christendom as a deviation from Jesus, who is interpreted solely within the Jewish context. Both views converge. They both benefit from the scheme of the Tübingen school from Baur to Bultmann and radicalise its findings.

On the other hand, Christian scholars of this generation find themselves under a certain pressure not to depart (too much) from what has become the *communis opinio* among Jews. An important change of climate is indicated by this. While the generation of Harnack felt – for scholarly as well as practical reasons – that the Greek line of development taken by the church's history, for all its shortcomings, was the right course, and while they had a deep distrust towards the attempts to enliven the oriental and Jewish roots of Christendom, the opposite is now the case: the climate is in favour of as little departure from the Jewish heritage as possible and – in certain questions at least – of a tacit agreement with what appears to be the Jewish position.

The effect is a stalemate. Scholars eager to fall in with the interests of their Jewish fellow-workers develop the Zealot theme with great gusto while they tend to remain silent about what is truly revolutionary in Jesus, his *animus* against the law, his lack of compliance with what was, on the basis of the law, the established order of the day, his relationship to God

---

[343] *Jesus-Report*, p. 187 (ET p. 149; not correct).
[344] Ibid. p. 192 (ET p. 153). H. Marsch (alias Berman Saklatvala), *The Rebel King* (New York, 1975) is, in spite of the title, not a Zealot portrait of Jesus, but rather an attempt to picture him as having parted company with the nationalistic expectation at the time of the temptation and as having remained disinclined to become a 'Rebel King'.
[345] It goes so far, in some cases, that it even affects the picture of the passion of Jesus; thus Landau claims: not those who rejected the preaching of Jesus but those who divinised him placed on his shoulders the cross, which he had to carry and fixed to which he was to die (*Jesusbilder*, p. 305).

and his regard for the individual. Men of genius from Nietzsche[346] to Werfel[347] and Camus[348] noticed this, while it plays a minor role in contemporary studies.[349] Jesus revolted against the Torah of his fathers, nay he wrestled with God, but it is not likely that he descended to ordinary revolutionary activity or allowed himself to be used by the mouthpieces of the different activisms of his day.

VIII

The scene of American intellectual church life in the first decades of this century was dominated by the eager zeal to present Jesus's message as a social gospel.[350, 351] It is typical for the American atmosphere that it was this

---

[346] He states: 'Dieser heilige Anarchist, der das niedere Volk . . . zum Widerspruch gegen die herrschende Ordnung aufrief – mit einer Sprache, falls den Evangelien zu trauen wäre, die auch heute noch nach Sibirien führen würde, war ein politischer Verbrecher, so weit eben politische Verbrecher in einer absurdunpolitischen Gemeinschaft möglich waren. Dies brachte ihn ans Kreuz' (*Werke*, ed. K. Schlechta (München 1955), ii. 1189). Cp. Nietzsche's penetrating characterisation of Jesus: 'die Leidenschaft gewordene Rechtschaffenheit' (*Der Antichrist*, p. 35).

[347] He makes Gamaliel say: 'Ich widerrufe meinen Willen über Jesus von Nazareth! Mag er ein heiliger Prophet gewesen sein, ich nenne ihn Feind. Der alte Widerspruch ist er, der Aufruhr in der Wolle des Lamms' (*Paulus unter den Juden* (Wien, 1927), p. 170). For the problem cp. E. Stauffer, 'Jesus und seine Bibel' in *Abraham unser Vater. Festschrift Otto Michel*, edd. O. Betz, M. Hengel and P. Schmidt (Leiden, 1963), pp. 440ff.

[348] 'Why hast thou forsaken me? This was a revolutionary cry (un cri séditieux), was not it?' (A. Camus, *La Chute* (Paris, 1956), p. 131; GT 118ff).

[349] Klaus Berger's *Die Gesetzesauslegung Jesu* I (Neukirchen, 1972), for all its merits, is a telling example of this state of affairs.

[350] S. Mathews, *The Social Teaching of Jesus* (New York, 1897); F. G. Peabody, *Jesus Christ and the Social Question* (New York, 1900; GT Giessen, 1903); W. Rauschenbusch, *Christianizing the Social Order* (New York, 1923); *Christianity and the Social Crisis* (New York, 1924). A different line is taken by F. D. Heuver, *The Teaching of Jesus concerning Wealth* (Chicago, 1903); cp. H. E. Lucock, *Jesus and the American Mind* (New York, 1930). For criticism cp. H. Frick, *Das Reich Gottes in amerikanischer und deutscher Theologie der Gegenwart* (Giessen, 1926).

[351] It is parallel to the Christian Social movement in Württemberg and Switzerland at the beginning of the century, which is marked by the names of Blumhardt and Ragaz. For an evaluation cp. U. von der Steinen, *Agitation für das Reich Gottes* (München, 1977) and M. J. Stähli, *Reich Gottes und Revolution* (Hamburg, 1980). Christian Socialism in Great Britain had developed along different lines. The movement started earlier – before the German lives of Jesus had become a force. There is little reflection on Jesus's own position. One gets the impression that the social tendencies emerged spontaneously and that the combination with the N.T. and, indeed, the O.T., is rather an afterthought (e.g. C. Kingsley interpreted Luke 4: 16 as referring to the Hall year in his famous sermon of 1851 and made this the starting point for his social propositions). The link is performed by the utilisation of certain N.T. features as mottoes (e.g. J. L. Davies, *Morality according to the Sacrament of the Lord's Supper* (London, 1867)), while very occasionally modern thoughts ('The work of Jesus Christ . . . is . . . shown to be secular work': S. Headlam, *The Service of*

aspect of politics that was discussed. The attempt to modernise Jesus in this way was carried out without much historical insight and with the help of arbitrarily selected citations from the works of German theologians. Something similar happened in the sixties when the view that Jesus was a revolutionary spread like a prairie fire over the five continents.

In the time in between a claim, substantially different but in other ways related, was made. The sentence 'Jesus was black' is recorded to have been expressed in 1924.[352] It is not clear what was meant by this: whether Jesus was actually black in his lifetime,[353] or the risen Lord gives his concern to the black, or whether the expression was intended to be symbolic. In any case, a special relation between Jesus and the black underdog is assumed. This is a line that was taken up many times. What may have been meant initially as a sentiment, an expression of consolation, became something different when it was linked with black aims. Whereas it had been the suffering Christ who had given comfort to the maltreated negro, it was now claimed that Jesus's violent death sanctifies violent struggles for justice.[354] Whereas God's compassion for the black man had been stressed, the emphasis is now shifted: 'black is holy'.[355] Whereas the simple life of Jesus had been taken as appealing to the black, it was now maintained that the Zealot-type activism called for similar actions.[356] Even where this

Humanity (London, 1882), p. 3) crop up. C. Noel is something of an exception. He describes Jesus as a revolutionary and his proclamation as directed towards a new world order, a kingdom of justice and comradeship, which he wishes men to build upon earth (*The Life of Jesus* (London, 1939), pp. 212, 486, 580). It is this 'collective hope' (p. 582) he finds significant. He therefore emphasises the political implications of the ministry and denies a pacifist interpretation (p. xviii, (2nd edn.) p. 487), while coming out even more sternly against a Zealot understanding (he is disinclined to follow Eisler (p. xix: Jesus would probably not have approved of the 'mad action' described in the Slavonic Josephus (p. 564)) and sets Jesus against the imperialism of the Zealots, pp. 274ff). The temptation of the kingdom is a temptation for Noel's internationalism as well; he avoids dissociating himself from Jesus by claiming that the Roman pretensions were based on external dominion and were therefore 'essentially inhuman' (p. 296). By interpreting the temptations as warding off particular expressions of political hope (cp. p. 284f) he finds himself able to maintain his concept of the kingdom, an idea Noel develops from the prophetic and Baptistic proclamation rather than from an interpretation of the dominical message. Much of Noel's concept looks like a secularised version of F. D. Maurice's *Kingdom of Christ* (London, i/ii 1937). For an evaluation of the whole movement cp. L. Brentano, *Die christlichsoziale Bewegung in England* (Leipzig, 1883) and, most recently, E. R. Norman, *Church and Society in England 1770–1970* (Oxford, 1976).

[352] Leipoldt, *Jesusbild*, p. 286.
[353] This is the opinion of A. B. Cleage, *The Black Messiah* (New York, 1968).
[354] B. Carr at the Lusaka Conference of 1974; cp. A. Hastings, 'Christianity and Revolution', *African Affairs* 74 (1975), 360.
[355] J. H. Cone, *Black Theology and Black Power* (New York, 1969), p. 69.
[356] Liberalism 'by any means necessary' as J. H. Cone puts it (*Black Theology*, p. 11).

reconstruction of the life of Jesus was not accepted it is argued that 'the Nazarene, although he was not a revolutionary Zealot, as risen Lord became involved in the black revolution'.[357, 358] A link is established in this way with the common belief of the black Christian. It is the returning Christ who plays a role in his life,[359] while the reference to the historic Jesus as an inspiration to revolution comes primarily from white counsellors.

The black man himself is inclined to single out certain elements in the Bible and to re-interpret them in the light of his own expectation. This can be done in a committed way and in a more detached manner which only makes use of the traditional material. Characteristic for the latter is the motto: 'seek ye first the political kingdom and all the rest will be added to you'.[360]

Basically it is lack of objective interest in Jesus and early Christianity that becomes manifest in this way. Even the sketch of the future as it is drawn in Christian and post-Christian religions developed by the coloured man tends to become a future without Christ in the majority of the sources.[361] It is, perhaps, symptomatic that the cypher 'Black Messiah' or

[357] J. H. Cone, 'Schwarze Theologie im Blick auf Revolution', *EvTh* 34 (1974), 13 (the whole issue, pp. 1–112 of *EvTh* entitled *Zur schwarzen Theologie*, was translated into English and appeared in *Union Seminary Quarterly Review* 31 (1975/6), iff).

[358] The same author maintains that Jesus is 'the complete opposite of the values of white culture' (*Black Theology of Liberation* (Philadelphia, 1970), p. 215), an analysis that would give him a position in between 'irrelevant for our times' and 'irrelevant for the time of the historical Jesus' (p. 214) and he maintains 'If Christ is not black then who is he?' (p. 217). He sees as the historical kernel of the N.T. reports the manifestation of Jesus as the Oppressed one whose earthly existence was bound up with the oppressed of the land (p. 202). In his recent *God of the Oppressed* (New York, 1975) Cone admits that a collaboration of Jesus with the Zealots cannot be defended on historical grounds (p. 274). He turns, however, the 'uncertainty' against those who advocate a different opinion and asks: 'How can we be sure that Jesus was not violent?' (p. 223). He sees those who disagree with him as 'the contemporary representatives of the scribes and lawyers' (p. 223), lists a whole series of 'establishment scholars' (p. 272f) and admits only one exception, Käsemann. For a sympathetic and searching consideration of Cone's principles cp. J. L. Segundo *Liberación de la teologia* (Buenos Aires, 1975; ET New York, 1976, esp. pp. 25ff). It must be added that in the opinion of Cone the term 'Black theology' does not comprehend the fullest meaning of the Divine revelation. It is, however, its necessary way of becoming concrete – like the liberation from Egypt, like the appearance of the man Jesus (*EvTh* 34 (1974), 88, 90).

[359] Cp. note 361. Also cp. Cone, *God of the Oppressed*, p. 119, who goes so far as to state that the emphasis on the humanity of Christ was the emphasis of black slaves.

[360] It is the nationalist version of the 'translation' given by S. Headlam: 'live as member of a righteous society, and individually you will benefit' (W. S. Smith, *The London Heretics 1870–1914* (London, 1967), p. 185). For the statement itself cp. H. J. Margull, *Aufbruch zur Zukunft* (Gütersloh, 1962), p. 70; M. Warren, *Problems and Promises in Africa today* (London, 1964), p. 40.

[361] This becomes obvious from the sources cited by Margull. The cases referred to on pp. 94 and 96 are rather the exception and represent movements of a period already bygone. The example of a revelation chain in which Christ represents a stage that is

'Black Christ' tends to be supplemented by 'Black theology'. If that feature should turn out to be of a lasting nature, it would indicate a departure that is far more crucial than the presentation of the portrait of a revolutionary Christ.

It is mainly through C. Morris[362] that the latter idea is suggested to the black man. The Winter–Cullmann theory, according to which Jesus was executed as a political criminal, is taken by Morris as probably matching the facts: Pilate may have been right in putting Jesus to death.[363] It results from this that Jesus was not non-violent.[364] And indeed Morris finds instances in the Gospels that support this view: Jesus's statement on the tribute money is 'fighting talk';[365] the entry had to be understood politically and the cleansing of the Temple, of that 'haunt of Roman collaborators', was meant to be a 'symbolic condemnation of any collaboration'.[366] He finds it significant that the Zealots are nowhere condemned in the New Testament, considers the pacific portrait of Jesus given by the evangelists as untrustworthy, nay, finds it hard to imagine that they themselves believed it[367] and states his agreement with Brandon.[368]

It may be that his sketch of Jesus is meant rather to awake the European Christians than to foster revolution in Africa. His advocacy of violence[369] may be taken this way.[370] It has to be emphasised that it is action Morris is interested in. His thinking revolves around what is said in the Parable of the Last Judgement.[371] He has harsh words to say on a theology of revolution which is all too often a way of avoiding action.[372] While Morris's manifesto had no immediate echo[373] in Africa, where it was written; while it was

superseded by the new prophet Hung is given on p. 103. For the tendency to view Jesus as a figure on the fringes or to proclaim the returning Christ as a political liberator, cp. E. Dammann, 'Das Christusverständnis in den nachchristlichen Kirchen und Sekten Afrikas' in E. Benz, *Messianische Kirchen, Sekten und Bewegungen im heutigen Afrika* (Leiden, 1965).

[362] *Unyoung, Uncoloured, Unpoor* (London, 1969).

[363] Ibid. p. 111.   [364] Ibid. p. 102.   [365] Ibid. p. 113.

[366] Ibid. pp. 116f.   [367] Ibid. p. 102.   [368] Ibid. p. 121.

[369] 'Violence may well not establish a Paradise but it can destroy an Inferno' (C. Morris, sermon in Great St Mary's, Cambridge, March 1970).

[370] There are features in Morris's activity which are open to question. It is his attempt to jump on the bandwagon and to be trendy. Action for social and political justice – in the tradition of old tendencies in the churches to reduce and to abolish outrageous injustice (cp. e.g. P. Marshall, *The Anti-Slave Movement and Bristol* (Bristol, 1968)) – tends to erode interest in personal salvation and to politicise the church (cp. R. E. Kendall, 'Political involvement for the Christian', *Epworth Review* 2 (1975), 64ff).

[371] *Include me out. Confessions of an Ecclesiastical Coward* (London, 1968 and, in a revised form, 1975), pp. 40, 113.

[372] *Include*, pp. 41, 46f. For C. Morris's basic attitude towards politics cp. L. Charlton, *Spark in the Stubble* (London, 1963), pp. 87f.

[373] The situation lends support to the view that the social structure of Africa contained

treated with reserve even by the sophisticated negroes of North America,[374] a parallel and far more radical battle cry had been promulgated already by A. B. Cleage. Jesus is seen as the inaugurator of a movement which became so widespread and well-established that the disciples could move freely without worries about money and other support. The Zealots functioned as the 'revolutionary underground part' of the same organisation.[375] Influences stemming from Brandon are obvious at this point; the matter is, however, expressed in overwhelmingly socialist terminology. This Jesus was 'in constant opposition to the established power structure',[376] he was 'engaged in a liberation struggle against the whole gentile world'.[377] It is the black man's task to let himself be called back to this, Jesus's original teaching.[378] It is in this activity that Jesus serves again as an example, not so much, or rather not at all, in his death.[379] Dark shadows fall on the church's attempts to give meaning to Calvary,[380] on the otherworldly conception of salvation,[381] which is stigmatised as individualistic and branded as counter-revolutionary,[382] on justification by faith,[383] against the 'old theology', which is Paul's and not Jesus's[384] – all this is nothing but a 'waste of the Holy Spirit'.[385]

Cleage names the 'Black experience' as basic for the developing of a new value system. The model for this experience is found in the history of Israel[386] rather than in the life of Jesus. The latter is mentioned occasionally but emphasis is given to the Old Testament, the history of which is linked, in a rather arbitrary way, with African tribal religion – so much so that the black people are singled out and proclaimed as 'God's chosen people'.[387]

so many balancing factors that an outburst was not inevitable (thus Hastings, *African Affairs* 74 (1975), 360f). How different the African situation still is becomes apparent from J. S. Pobee, *Towards an African Theology* (Abingdon, 1979).

[374] M. J. Jones, *Black Awareness* (Nashville, 1971), pp. 121f.
[375] A. B. Cleage, *Black Christian Nationalism* (New York, 1972).
[376] Ibid. p. 182; 'the Roman power structure including the temple in Jerusalem' (207f).
[377] Ibid. p. 45; cp. pp. 53, 174.
[378] Ibid. p. 175.   [379] Ibid. p. 188.
[380] Ibid. pp. 60f, 183. He compares it spitefully with 'the old Uncle Tom's ways' (p. 58 etc.).
[381] Ibid. pp. 183, 188, 201; cp. pp. 53, 73.
[382] Ibid. p. 58; cp. p. 217.   [383] Ibid. pp. 186, 190.
[384] Ibid. p. 136 and Y. b. Jochanan's attack against the 'dreamer' Paul, who turned to Rome (in Cleage, *Nationalism*, p. 291).
[385] Ibid. p. 256.
[386] Ibid. pp. 192, 202, 206f, 239 etc.; cp. Cone, *God of the Oppressed*, p. 137, and I. R. Washington, *The Politics of God* (2nd edn., Boston, 1970), p. 157.
[387] Cleage, *Nationalism*, p. 175; cp. p. 239. In a similar vein Washington, *Politics*, p. 156. Cleage holds that Judaism is essentially a black religion. He points to the Egyptian beginnings and lists a number of characteristic features which in his and his collaborators' opinion derive from African tribal religion. The conclusion that Jesus himself was black is obvious, and equally the deduction from it: 'historically both

Tendencies which are noticeable here and there are expressed much more openly and crudely by this author than in other publications. Whatever may be the outcome of the political movement started by Cleage, the tendencies he had given voice to are likely to come up again in this or another form.

A third focussing point of unrest was the explosive situation in South America. It was met by a church which was at first and at best only equipped with a Las Casas type of theology,[388] with compassion for the suppressed which is given expression in the act of protest. Even C. Torres is no exception to this. Certain scriptural passages – especially the Parable of the Last Judgement and Romans 13:8 – figure as mottoes in his pronouncements,[389] while what reflection there is on the situation has to be supplied from the Marxist intellectual armoury. The desire to enact an imitation of Christ[390] may have led him to force his violent death.

Apart from the situation which sparked off these manifestos it was the Christian–Marxist dialogue which influenced the state of discussion and led to theological penetration. This discourse, which started on a larger scale in the sixties, was opened by the Marxists'[391] confession that they were in agreement with and had even taken up *die Sache Jesu*.[392] Conciliation was voiced, appreciation of Jesus was expressed although it was admitted that Jesus was not a revolutionary 'like the Zealots, like Bar Kochba'.[393] It was in this dialogue that the appreciation of Jesus, described as the revolutionary *par excellence*, was turned against the church, against those who stamped out the fire which he had kindled.[394] It was in the same

religions belong to us' (*Nationalism*, p. 175). The author proceeds even further and declares that black people as such have 'the legitimate right to be Christian or Jewish if they wish' (p. 175). It is interesting that the terms 'Christian' and 'Jewish' are used interchangeably.

[388] Cp. C. Lange, 'Kolonialismus – das Zeugnis von Las Casas' (Diss. Berlin, 1972).

[389] C. Torres, *Revolution als Aufgabe des Christen* (Mainz, 1969), pp. 25f; *Vom Apostolate zum Partisanenkampf. Artikel und Proklamationen* (Hamburg, 1969), pp. 125f, 143. *C. Torres, Revolutionary Priest. Complete Writings*, ed. J. Gerassi (Pelican edition, London, 1973) pp. 270f. He also refers to Matt. 25 as a *movens* for his fight in his justification for the petition for laicisation; cp. H. Lüning, *C. Torres, Priester und Guerrillero* (Hamburg, 1969), p. 115.

[390] The statement his mother made after his death ('Would Christianity exist, if Jesus had died in his bed?'; Lüning, *Torres*, p. 158) is an indication of this.

[391] Some of them were neutralised and reprimanded in their own parties subsequently.

[392] Cp. E. Bloch's essay, *Im Christentum steckt die Revolte* (Zürich, 1971).

[393] R. Garaudy, *L'Alternative* (Paris, 1972), p. 124 (GT Wien 1973, p. 116, ET London, 1976, p. 96). Jesus is described as 'breaking tabus' (p. 118; GT p. 111, ET p. 91). 'He is not a revolutionary' (p. 124; GT p. 116; ET p. 96), but by being the man he is, he is just the person a revolutionary is able to agree with and even 'to believe in' (p. 126; GT p. 118; ET pp. 97f).

[394] The Reimarus scheme of a radical change after the death of Jesus is applied by K.

dialogue that Jesus was attacked as the man of 'total protest' whose attitude is more akin to the 'anarchism' of Baader, Meinhof and Mahler than to the principles of Marxist revolution.[395] On the other hand, it was in this discussion that Christian criticism in the manner of the prophets was invoked as the means of tracing the authentic Karl Marx, who had been neutralised by a satisfied Communist establishment[396] and even to bring about something like a permanent revolution.[397] Old patterns of reaction re-emerged in this way.

The reflection on the Christian side resulted in a 'theology of revolution',[398] a political theology,[399] political hermeneutics, a theology of

Farner in the following way: the church turned Jesus's protest into a kind of non-protest, an opiate. The theology of liberation might lead to a liberation of the theology. The theology of revolution might result in a revolution of the followers of Jesus: in a de-Christianisation in the direction of Jesus. He adds to this the important qualification: only forces of a general kind might be able to achieve this; 'the Christians are hardly able to accomplish it: they have been already far too long "just Christians"' ('Jesus als Brandstifter-Christus als Brandlöscher' in I. Fetscher (ed.), *Marxisten und die Sache Jesu* (München, 1974), pp. 62ff). Cp. K. Farner, *Theologie des Kommunismus?* (Frankfurt, 1969).

[395] L. Kofler, 'Jesus und die Ohnmacht', in Fetscher, *Marxisten*, p. 50. While Engels had compared early Christendom with the pre-Marxist communist societies of the early nineteenth century it is Kofler who sees Christ – he considered it as irrelevant whether he actually lived or not – in the line of those who proclaimed 'total protest' (p. 49), a line which culminates in anarchism: 'it is for this reason that Tolstoi could be a Christian and an Anarchist at the same time' (p. 49). The total *Ohnmacht* (helplessness) felt by 'Christ' led to resistance to the established order, to abstinence from it, to opting out entirely (*Verweigerung*). Thus Christ is the exponent of rebellion which is not at all identical with a revolution which is conscious of its aims. The use of the name 'Christ' as a motto in the modern political struggle is therefore an indication of the emotional, unreflected and non-rational character of the rebellion initially signalised by that name (p. 52). This is a caveat from the Marxist side which indicates the limits of their appreciation of early Christendom. The observation, although couched in sociological language, is not without certain grains of truth.

[396] A. T. van Leeuwen, *Revolution als Hoffnung* (Stuttgart, 1970), p. 213.

[397] R. Shaull in C. Oglesby and R. Shaull, *Containment and Change* (New York, 1967), p. 238. For a critique from the side of orthodox Marxism cp. I. Bauer and A. Liepert, *Die 'grosse Wende' des Roger Garaudy* (Frankfurt, 1971), pp. 59ff, 132f, and, not altogether different, C. Ordnung, *Christ und Revolution. Theologische Konzeptionen zwischen Desorientierung und Wegweisung* (Berlin, 1974), pp. 42ff.

[398] J. Comblin, *Théologie de la révolution* (Paris, 1970). The term had already been coined by M. Schröter in 1964 (cp. E. Feil and R. Weth, *Diskussion zur Theologie der Revolution* (München/Mainz, 1969), p. 291). Comblin's work was hailed by Garaudy; the idea of the nearness of God in Christ appeals to him and he goes so far as to describe Christianity as a 'religion of action' and indeed decision, and to justify 'militant action' from this basis (*De l'Anathème au Dialogue* (Paris, 1965), GT in R. Garaudy, J. B. Metz and K. Rahner, *Der Dialog* (Hamburg, 1966), p. 51 (ET, based on GT (London, 1967), p. 46)); Garaudy, *L'Alternative*, p. 118 (GT p. 111; ET p. 96).

[399] H. Peukert (ed.), *Diskussion zur politischen Theologie* (Mainz, 1969).

the world,[400] a theology of liberation,[401] in the search for a liberation of theology.[402] What is typical for these designs which began to flourish at about the same time is the attempt to give them a wider basis: in the exodus which is viewed as an act of legitimate disobedience,[403] in phenomena of church history from Joachim to Müntzer, in a covenant revelation, that means in progressive revelation,[404] in Jewish messianism, in Hegel's philosophy of history in the guise of E. Bloch,[405] in the heritage of natural theology,[406] while the reflection on Jesus plays only a minor role. It is typical for this approach that its leaders, Moltmann and Metz, are heavily indebted to the influence of Federal theology and Aristotelian Thomistic theology respectively.

Moltmann deals with the question of Jesus's own position at length,[407] follows Hengel[408] and is inclined to part with Brandon's Zealot theory,[409] while resurrecting a political theology for other reasons[410] and claiming that Christian theology postulates the 'Abbau politischer Herrschaftsverhältnisse',[411] the destruction of political power structures,

[400] J. B. Metz, *Zur Theologie der Welt* (Mainz/München, 1968; ET London, 1969). Metz describes Jesus as a 'revolutionary who comes, in action and suffering, into conflict with the establishment' (*Dialog*, pp. 126f) and attributes to early Christendom an expectation which is pugnacious (*kämpferisch*) and which aims at the transformation of this world; Christian hope is creative, it is to be described as 'productive eschatology'. On the other hand, he protests against the taking of political theology just as an 'ideological paraphrase of progressivism' (p. 129) and professes the Christian task to 'deritualize' the progressive ideology (p. 130). This theology is not unaware of the need for justification *vis-à-vis* Christ, without, however, being able to give concrete expression to this awareness. It is symptomatic that only such contributions to the Diskussion zur politischen Theologie which take up a critical position (H. Maier in Peukert, *Diskussion*, p. 8; W. Pannenberg, ibid., pp. 232ff) refer to dominical sayings as providing a norm.

[401] G. Gutierrez, *Theologia de la Liberacion* (Salamanca, 1972; ET London, 1974; GT München/Mainz, 1973).

[402] J. L. Segundo, *Liberación de la teologia* (Buenos Aires, 1975).

[403] Comblin, *Théologie*.

[404] J. Moltmann, *Theologie der Hoffnung* (München, 1964), pp. 85ff; ET London, 1967, pp. 95ff.

[405] Moltmann, *Theologie*, pp. 316f.

[406] Metz, *Theologie*; cp. G. Bauer, *Christliche Hoffnung und menschlicher Fortschritt. Die politische Theologie von J. B. Metz als theol. Begründung gesellschaftlicher Verantwortung* (Mainz, 1976).

[407] *Der gekreuzigte Gott* (München, 1972), pp. 119ff (ET London, 1974, pp. 137ff).

[408] *War Jesus Revolutionär?* (Stuttgart, 1970); 'Christus und die Macht' in E. Kellner, *Christliche Politik* (Wien, 1976), pp. 17ff. Cp., however, Moltmann's qualification, *Gott*, p. 135, note 59.

[409] Ibid. pp. 133ff (ET pp. 139ff).

[410] Ibid. pp. 293ff (ET pp. 317ff).

[411] Ibid. p. 304 (ET p. 328 does not give an adequate rendering). He goes so far as to say that the condemnation of Jesus in the name of the political authority of the day deprives such authorities of their credibility: 'Political rule can only be justified "from below" ' (p. 305; ET p. 328).

and leaving open the way in which this liberation is to be achieved.[412]

In South America itself a leap was felt to be necessary from a theology which appeared so traditional that its values could hardly be brought to life. North American influences, stemming from Niebuhr and his pupils[413] on the one hand and from Bonhöffer on the other, had given some preparation, when the revolutionary situation caused an eager appropriation of intellectual structures provided by Marxism and sophisticated theologies mainly of German provenance.[414]

Brandon's theory was picked up quickly in order to provide a biblical basis for activism. M. Dutheil became the protagonist of this approach in South America.[415] It is however significant that, partly under the influence of Cullmann, this approach soon faltered. G. Gutierrez, while denying the apolitical character of the message of Jesus most emphatically, and drawing out political connotations and dimensions to the maximum, comes to the conclusion that 'the Zealots were not mistaken in feeling that Jesus was simultaneously near and far away'[416] – a sentence which indicates the direction of his search and the extent to which he is intrigued by Eisler and Brandon.[417] On the one hand the measure of agreement is emphasised and Jesus's points of departure are characterised by the phrase 'even more revolutionary than the Zealots'[418]; on the other hand the non-violent aspects of this activity are stressed and a theology of revolution – revolution properly speaking – is treated with great reserve.[419] J. Miguez Bonino, while admitting that Jesus 'did not enroll himself with the Zealots' – 'for whatever reason' – 'contends that he left no doubts about whether he was on the side of the poor and oppressed or the power structures (religious and political)

---

[412] After having attempted to dissociate Christian eschatology from any philosophy of history, he falls prey to the danger of millenarianism which he himself had previously attacked (*Theologie*, pp. 210ff; ET London, 1967, pp. 230ff).

[413] Cp. A. P. Neely, 'Protestant Antecedents of the Latin American Theology of Liberation' (Diss. American University, Washington, 1977).

[414] For general information cp. F. Siebeneichler, 'Catolicismo popular – Pentecostismo', *Kirche: Religion in Lateinamerika* (Frankfurt, 1976); S. Wiedenhofer, *Politische Theologie* (Stuttgart, 1976); A. Blatezky, *Sprache des Glaubens in Lateinamerika* (Frankfurt, 1978); E. Dussel, *History and the Theology of Liberation* (New York, 1976); R. Gibellini, *Frontiers of Theology in Latin America* (London, 1980); M. Hofmann, *Identifikation mit dem Anderen* (Göttingen, 1978); L. Boff, 'Das Anliegen der Befreiungstheologie' in *Theologische Berichte* 8 (Zürich, 1979), 71ff. Morphologically not without parallels to the theology of German Christians, liberation theology may, however, last longer and develop differently because the external factors work rather in its favour than against it.

[415] 'El Cristo de la nación y el Cristo del Templo', in *La fe, fuerza historica* (Barcelona, 1971).

[416] *A Theology of Liberation*, ET (London, 1974), p. 231 (GT p. 223).

[417] Ibid., pp. 226f, 245 (GT pp. 216f).

[418] Ibid., p. 227 (GT p. 217).

[419] Ibid., p. 250 (GT p. 230).

of his time',[420] and he is able to deduce a justification of violence from Jesus's position.[421] J. Sobrino states: Jesus 'shared some of the basic views and outlooks of the Zealots',[422] but adds important qualifications.[423] The outcome of the consideration of this historical problem is – *mutatis mutandis* – not very different from the state of discussion in Europe, and adds some weight to the observation that the call for an indigenous theology has not made much headway so far: 'for the moment . . . the theology of liberation has not offered any improvement on the current slogans'.[424]

Symptomatic is the uneasiness about 'the lack of any sense of crisis about the meaning of Christ'[425] and the attempt to draw out certain features in the life of Jesus and to link them with other phenomena. So declares Fierro: Jesus's confrontation with the powers of his day is just as much a paradigmatic history as the Exodus story; it 'includes a theology of messianism'.[426]

The incorporation of the Exodus motif,[427] of the prophetic criticism,[428] of the messianic longing for a new order,[429] and the interest in John the Baptist,[430] provide the basis for the weaving of a 'mythistory' of a new kind[431] that becomes evocative for the man of today and enables him to proceed on what is called engagingly the 'long march'.[432] It is in this context that Marx is viewed as standing in the tradition of the Old Testament prophets.[433] Other representatives of liberation theology prefer to speak of messianic

---

[420] *Doing Theology in a Revolutionary Situation* (U.K. title *Revolutionary Theology Comes of Age*) (Philadelphia/London, 1975), pp. 122f.

[421] Ibid., pp. 117f; cp. pp. 125, 128.

[422] J. Sobrino, *Cristologia desde america latine* (Rio Hondo, 1976; ET *Theology at the Crossroads*, London, 1978), p. 212.

[423] Ibid. pp. 369f: an alternative to Zealotism.

[424] H. Assmann, *Practical Theology of Liberation* (London, 1975 (published in Mary Knoll under the title *Theology for a Nomad Church*) = *Teologia desde la praxis de la liberacion*, Salamanca, 1973), p. 76.

[425] Sobrino, *Cristologia*, p. 2.

[426] A. Fierro, *El evangelio beligerante* (Estella, 1974; ET *The Militant Gospel*, London, 1977), p. 160. Fierro writes in Spain, but is in close contact with South America.

[427] J. Severino Croatta, *Liberación y Libertad* (Buenos Aires, 1973).

[428] Miguez Bonino, 'Violence and Liberation' in *Christianity and Crisis* 32 (1972), 168ff. This was sharply criticised by K. Lehmann in 'Diskussion zur politischen Theologie', p. 193, and in K. Lehmann (ed.), *Theologie der Befreiung* (Einsiedeln, 1977).

[429] R. Shaull, 'Theology and the Transformation of Society' in *Theology Today* 25 (1968), 25.

[430] Not completely new: Ragaz had already pointed to this 'missing link' between O.T. and N.T. revolutionary prophetism (*Die Bibel. Eine Deutung* IV, 1948, p. 102).

[431] Fierro, *Militant Gospel*, p. 170.

[432] H. Gollwitzer in Feil and Weth, *Diskussion*, p. 43.

[433] Miguez Bonino, *Christians and Marxists* (Grand Rapids and London, 1976), pp. 68f.

presence[434] or messianic humanism.[435] The example of Jesus, directly or indirectly, is of varied importance.[436] It becomes, however, central again where suffering instead of revolutionary action is seen as the task of the day.

The tendencies are outflanked by the challenge to dispose of the *theologischer Mehrwert* of the theology of revolution.[437] This is directed against the attempt to distil any direct advice from the teachings of Jesus, against any rapid application of his teaching, and instead suggests taking the way of Jesus as a historical project which may function as a simile, working as a factor in the process of what is called 'socializing an entity'.[438] The bible and especially Jesus himself serve as a symbol[439] which evoke reflection on present-day tasks. It is true, the historical dimension is thus maintained. There is no hesitation in stating that Jesus is not completely identical with the political struggle of our days.[440] The identification with actual problems under the motto 'Christ the revolutionary' or even 'Christ among the Poor' is admitted to be short-sighted.[441] It is the combination of distance and practicability that is striking in this approach. What wins victory is serviceability for the strife: only such features in Jesus's way of life as make a contribution in one way or another speak to the revolutionary man.

The oscillation between eschatological[442] and historical[443] justification of

---

[434] P. Lehmann in Feil and Weith, *Diskussion*, p. 183. An exegetical basis for this is given by J. P. Miranda, *Being and the Messiah. The Message of St John* (Mary Knoll, 1977).

[435] R. Alves, *A Theology of Human Hope* (Washington, 1969), p. 98.

[436] Miguez concludes his *Revolutionary Theology Comes of Age* with the famous sentence with which Schweitzer brought to an end his *Quest* (p. 174).

[437] L. Ossa, *Die Revolution – das ist ein Buch und ein freier Mensch. Zur Inkulturation des Christentums in Lateinamerika* (Hamburg, 1973) p. 164.

[438] Ibid. p. 151. The realisation that the present time is not to be undervalued in relation to a post-revolutionary future (pp. 149f) serves as an example for the efficacy of the contemplation of Jesus's way.

[439] Ibid. p. 81.

[440] 'Ein gleichzeitiger, wenn auch politischer Christus praesens müsste stumm bleiben, da er nur die Gestalt der gegenwärtigen Ideale darstellt, die seine Vertreter in ihn projizieren' (Ossa, *Revolution*, p. 147).

[441] What is the nature of the difference? Is it the distance a revolutionary has to keep *vis-à-vis* his less perceptive followers? There is something in this comparison, although its value is restricted by the fact that it was not in a superficial way that Jesus intervened in the struggle of his time. Instead, he aimed at the greater *Steuerungskapazität* (capacity for self-determination) of men. Cp. J. G. Davies, *Christians, Politics and violent Revolution* (London, 1976), p. 101.

[442] Cp. p. 58. Cp. also H. McCabe: 'Every revolution which deals with structure less ultimate than this (death) is an image of, and a preparation for, the resurrection of the dead. The Cuban or Vietnamese revolution is a type of the resurrection in the sense that we speak of Old Testament events as types of Christ' (*Law, Love and Language* (London, 1968), pp. 133f).

[443] Thus R. F. Smith, 'Eine Theologie der Rebellion' (in Feil and Weth, *Diskussion*, pp. 159ff) claims that there is an affinity between Jewish–Christian and rebellious mentality. P. L. Lehmann sees Jesus as an offshoot of this heritage (Feil and Weth,

revolution is a feature which distracts from the main point, from the fact that the whole attention of these advocates of change is devoted to the present situation. Not only is it significant that this situation is given the one-sided description 'revolutionary';[444] it is more revealing that the criteria for reflection are taken from what appears to be the revolutionary process. This process becomes the καιρός, in which God is found, it is on the verge of becoming, so to speak, a source of revelation itself.[445]

This sentiment – prepared already by the lack of an objective foundation in the Bultmannian theology[446] – is a pervasive undercurrent, while secondary questions like the one on violence versus non-violence are openly discussed.[447] It was unavoidable in the logic of the process that the linkage with the past, even with the historical Jesus, proved to be too tenuous to last. Thus R. F. Smith turns against seeing as absolute an event of the past or of the future.[448]

L. Ossa tends to reduce the relevance of Jesus to those features in him which may serve as mirroring the political and social process.[449] J. H. Cone mocks at the emphasis on the humanity of Christ as the attitude of black slaves.[450] It is only a case of drawing the consequences of this, when the reference to 'historical texts' is rejected with contempt[451] and the relevance of the church is seen as entirely conditioned by its functioning in society.[452]

Diskussion, p. 176). Reliance on the Jewish heritage is a phenomenon parallel to the Jewish design to enlist Jesus in the Jewish pantheon.

[444] J. Moltmann, 'Gott in der Revolution' (in Feil and Weth, Diskussion, p. 82).

[445] Cp. A. Rich, 'Revolution als theologisches Problem' (Feil and Weth, Diskussion, p. 142).

[446] Admitted by Bultmann himself; cp. E. Busch, Karl Barths Lebenslauf (München 1975), p. 403; (ET London, 1976, p. 389).

[447] Cp. M. Hengel, Gewalt und Gewaltlosigkeit (Stuttgart, 1971, ET Philadelphia, 1973; London, 1975); Davies, Christians; A. Kee, A Reader in Political Theology (London, 1974), pp. 136ff; J. Ellul, Violence (London 1970); N.N., Violence in Southern Africa. A Christian Assessment (London, 1970).

[448] In Feil and Weth, Diskussion, p. 170.

[449] Die Revolution, pp. 142f.

[450] Black Theology, p. 119.

[451] W. D. Buckow, Das Elend der sozialistischen Opposition in der Kirche (München, 1969), p. 115.

[452] Buckow, Das Elend, pp. 99, 105f. Cleage is ready and eager to make use of the church as a basis for the building of 'Black counterinstitutions' (pp. 227f). He rejoices in the group experience, in the 'incarnation' accomplished in it (p. 254). He feels uneasy, however, about the term 'church' and would like to replace it by 'Black nation' (p. 134; cp. pp. 240, 246f). The church is, if anything, a cadre like the disciples, who were trained by Jesus to serve as cadres committed to the revolution (p. 221). The message of that institution would emerge from the Black experience, its task would be the liberation of the Black world rather than salvation, let alone an appeal to the individual (the animosity against the 'protestant heresy' of individualism is very strong; pp. 70f, 189, 251, 254 etc.).

Whether arising from contempt or not, from disregard or quiet moving away – the tendency indicates the extent of the inclination just to listen to the voice of the day, a tendency which may recall the saying: 'what shall it profit a man, if he shall gain the whole world, and lose his own soul?'[453]

[453] Brandon's theory has recently been taken up by G. Lüling. He sees the Passover meal of Jesus as the initiatory rite for a holy war and interprets especially the dipping of hands as a rite of swearing in of conspirators (*Verschwörungsritus*) ('Das Passahlamm und die altarabische "Mutter der Blutrache", die Hyäne, *ZRGG* 34 (1982), especially p. 141, 144–6). For a criticism of Brandon cp. J. Hadot, *Histoire des Origines du Christianisme, Jésus et les Zélotes. Etude critique des thèses de S. Brandon* (Brussels, 1977).

The date and character of Mark

I

'The Gospel of Mark' is our designation, but it is not Mark's: he sets out to relate what he calls 'the gospel of Jesus Christ, the Son of God', a gospel which begins with the ministry of John the Baptist. John's ministry marked the beginning of the fulfilment of those wide areas of Hebrew prophecy which looked forward to the consummation of Yahweh's saving work on earth. Jesus, introduced in the context of John's ministry, is the one through whom this saving work is accomplished. His designation as Son of God in the *prooemium* is not textually certain,[1] but no doubt of his identity is left by the heavenly voice which addresses him at his baptism, 'You are my beloved Son . . .' (Mark 1: 11), and acclaims him at the transfiguration, 'This is my beloved Son; listen to him' (Mark 9: 7). At the end of Mark's narrative, where we might expect to hear a similar affirmation, we do indeed hear it, but not from heaven: it is voiced at the cross by the most unlikely of the *dramatis personae* there. The Roman centurion, hearing Jesus's last shout and seeing the manner of his death, says, 'Truly this man was the Son of God!' (Mark 15: 39).

Otherwise Jesus is hailed as Son of God only by the demon-possessed, who might be presumed to have some contact with the wider knowledge available in the spirit-world (cp. Mark 5: 7).[2] The disciples do not speak to him in these terms, and Jesus makes no such claim himself – not, at least, until his appearance before the Sanhedrin. There, in answer to the high priest's question, 'Are you the Messiah, the Son of the Blessed?' he replies, 'I am'; but immediately recasts the words into those of his own choice: 'you will see the Son of man sitting at the right hand of Power, and coming with the clouds of heaven' (Mark 14: 61f).

In other words, says Mark, Jesus was indeed the Son of God, but he preferred to speak of himself as the Son of man – not by way of antithesis, but because the designation 'the Son of man' provided a more suitable

---

[1] In Mark 1: 1 'Son of God' is omitted after 'Jesus Christ' by ℵ * Θ 28 and a number of other witnesses. It is retained in NEB 'in view of its strong attestation (most of the ancient Greek MSS and all the Latin evidence) and as in keeping with the "Son of God" Christology of Mark' (R. V. G. Tasker, *The Greek New Testament* (Cambridge and Oxford, 1966), 413).

[2] Cp. Mark 1: 24 ('the Holy One of God'). The Matthaean addition of 'the Son of the living God' to Peter's confession (Matt. 16: 16) is absent from Mark 8: 29.

vehicle for what he wished to convey about his person and mission than 'Son of God' or even 'messiah' would provide.

II

The story of Jesus, as told in the Gospel of Mark, takes the *prima facie* form of a continuous narrative, falling into a few well-defined divisions:

- (*a*)   Introduction: the baptism and the temptation (1: 1–13)
- (*b*)   The Galilaean ministry (1: 14 to 9: 50)
- (*c*)   The road to Jerusalem (10: 1–52)
- (*d*)   The Jerusalem ministry (11: 1 to 13: 37)
- (*e*)   The passion narrative (14: 1 to 15: 47)
- (*f*)   The empty tomb (16: 1–8)

But the appearance of continuity could be due in large measure to the evangelist himself. The passion narrative, it is generally conceded, was handed down in Christian tradition as a self-contained unit: this is implied, for example, in Paul's remark that, on each occasion when the memorial bread and cup were taken, the story of 'the Lord's death' was recited (1 Cor. 11: 26). It should probably be added that Mark's general outline of Jesus's movements was also handed down in the tradition and indeed corresponded to historical fact, for he did teach in Galilee, he did meet his death in Jerusalem, and however frequently he journeyed from Galilee to Jerusalem, one such journey must have been the last, and that journey may well have taken in a Peraean ministry, as is implied in Mark 10: 1. Moreover, that the closing phase of his Galilaean ministry included the feeding of a multitude, followed not long afterwards by a crucial acknowledgement of his identity by Peter, is attested in the narrative of the Gospel of John, which represents a quite independent stream of transmission.[3]

While Mark's Gospel consists almost entirely of narrative, two bodies of discourse material are incorporated into the contexts of the Galilaean and Jerusalem ministries respectively: the parables of the kingdom in the former (4: 1–34) and the Olivet prophecy in the latter (13: 3–37). It is not unreasonable to expect that these discourses may illuminate the evangelist's understanding of the accompanying narrative.

When we come to the detailed material within the broad divisions of the narrative, such sequence as may be traced is probably topical and literary rather than chronological and continuous. The day is long since past when Mark's record could be regarded as so consecutive and watertight that a piece of non-Markan gospel tradition which could not be fitted into that record must be written off as unhistorical.[4]

[3] John 6: 1–14, 66–71.
[4] Cp. F. C. Burkitt's comments on the historicity of the narrative of the raising of

The death-blow was given to this assessment of Mark's narrative in 1919 by K. L. Schmidt, whose *Der Rahmen der Geschichte Jesu* (Berlin, 1919) presented his narrative as comprising independent *pericopae*, transmitted as separate units in primitive Christian tradition and arranged in their Markan order by the evangelist himself, who linked them together with short editorial summaries.[5] While Schmidt's thesis greatly influenced later interpreters of Mark like A. E. J. Rawlinson, it is but just to recall that many of his main emphases were anticipated by Allan Menzies, who in *The Earliest Gospel* (1902) expressed the view that what the tradition preserved consisted of detached incidents and sayings; the historical connections were forgotten. Some attempts to collect incidents and sayings together were probably made before Mark wrote his Gospel, but Mark, so far as we know, was the first 'to gather the narrative about Jesus together into a connected history'. To 'find the cord on which all these pearls were to be placed' and to 'fix their proper position on that cord' he 'must have been guided by one who knew the life of Jesus not only as a set of isolated stories but as a connected whole inspired by a growing purpose'.[6] In this last hypothesis Menzies differs from most of those who have more recently interpreted Mark in terms of form-criticism and redaction-criticism: at times, they allow, tradition may go back to eye-witness testimony but the idea that *redactional* material should have a historical basis is so far out of the question as hardly to be considered. Yet if an author, weaving independent units into a connected narrative, had some independent knowledge of the general course of events, there was no reason why he should not make use of that knowledge.[7]

C. H. Dodd in 1932 endeavoured to demonstrate that K. L. Schmidt's editorial summaries, when placed together, formed such a consecutive outline of the Gospel story as could be traced here and there in the New Testament epistles and in some of the speeches recorded in Acts.[8] His demonstration covered only the section from the beginning of the Galilaean ministry to the return of the Twelve from their mission (Mark 1: 14 to 6: 30), and was subjected to searching criticism in 1955 by D. E. Nineham.[9]

Lazarus in *The Gospel History and its Transmission* (3rd edn., Edinburgh, 1911), pp. 221ff. Cp. also J. A T. Robinson, below pp. 453–76.

[5] K. L. Schmidt, *Der Rahmen der Geschichte Jesu* (Berlin, 1919), pp. 18ff *et passim*.

[6] A. Menzies, *The Earliest Gospel* (London, 1902), pp. 27, 29.

[7] T. W. Manson goes farther: 'the title of the Marcan framework to be regarded as respectable historical material is as good as that of any detailed story in the Gospel' (*Studies in the Gospels and Epistles* (Manchester, 1962), p. 6).

[8] 'The Framework of the Gospel Narrative', *ExpT* 43 (1931–2), 396ff; reprinted in *New Testament Studies* (Manchester, 1953), pp. 1ff.

[9] 'The Order of Events in St Mark's Gospel – an Examination of Dr Dodd's Hypothesis', *Studies in the Gospels: Essays in Memory of R. H. Lightfoot*, ed. D. E. Nineham (Oxford, 1955), pp. 223ff.

Professor Nineham doubted if any *Sitz im Leben* could plausibly be posited to account for the preservation of a skeleton outline of the ministry. His criticism of Professor Dodd's thesis cannot be lightly ignored, but it would probably be less telling against the earlier thesis of Allan Menzies: individuals – and here we may think either of Mark himself or an older informant – do remember the general course of events which have taken place within their knowledge, even (or indeed especially) forty years before, although they may find it difficult to say when or where certain incidents took place or certain words were spoken. Historical or chronological curiosity, which is commonly denied to the early Christians, does not enter into such a situation.

III

We cannot pronounce on Mark's sources with anything like the confidence that characterises much source-criticism of Matthew and Luke, for one of the main sources of these two later evangelists has been preserved independently in Mark. Behind Mark we can trace, in addition to the continuous passion narrative, a collection of controversies and debates (2: 1 to 3: 6) and possibly a second such collection (12: 13–37),[10] a collection of parables (4: 1–34), and the Olivet discourse (13: 3–37), which in its present form may represent an elaboration of some *verba Christi* which first circulated in written form in A.D. 40, when Caligula's attempt to have his image erected in the Jerusalem Temple seemed to portend a re-enactment of Daniel's 'abomination of desolation'.[11]

Mark's record of the Galilaean ministry includes two parallel series of incidents (4: 35 to 6: 44 and 6: 45 to 8: 10) each of which begins with the stilling of a storm on the lake and ends with the feeding of a multitude. (The second series is missing from Luke's record.) Hilary of Poitiers suggested that the two feedings symbolise Jesus's communication of himself to the Jews and to the Gentiles respectively,[12] and numerical and other elements in the vocabulary of the two parallel feeding-narratives have been thought to confirm this suggestion.[13] More important in this regard is the fact that the

---

[10] B. S. Easton, noting that the collection of Mark 2: 1 to 3: 6 ends with an alliance between the Pharisees and Herodians while that of Mark 12: 13–37 begins with such an alliance, suggested that Mark received the two as one continuous collection which he divided (*Christ in the Gospels* (New York, 1930), p. 35). But the life-setting of the earlier collection is Galilaean while that of the latter is in Jerusalem.

[11] B. S. Easton points out that when the parallels to Mark 13 in Matt. 10: 16–23 are examined, some of the elements in the Matthaean version are earlier than some in the Markan version. 'The result is of course a problem of great perplexity' (*Christ*, p. 20).

[12] Hilary, *Comm. in Matthaeum*, Migne, *PL* ix. 999Cff, 1006Aff.

[13] Cp. A. Richardson, *The Miracle Stories of the Gospels* (London, 1941), pp. 94ff.

second feeding is preceded by a controversy between Jesus and the Pharisees regarding purificatory customs and other features of 'the tradition of the elders', leading up to a pronouncement in which Jesus effectively abrogated the Jewish food-laws and 'declared all foods clean' (7: 1–23). Since the food-laws constituted one of the principal barriers between Jews and Gentiles, it is probably more than a coincidence that Jesus's removal of this barrier is followed immediately by his healing of the Syrophoenician woman's daughter and then by a journey with the disciples through the Gentile territory north and east of the Lake, during which Jesus cures a deaf man in the Decapolis who has an impediment in his speech. But in the parallel sequence of 4: 35 to 6: 44 Jesus bestows blessing in the same Gentile regions: the Gerasene demoniac lives in Gentile territory (as may be gathered from the part played by the herd of swine in his neighbourhood), and he tells the story of his cure throughout the Decapolis (5: 1–20).

The possibility of Mark's dependence on Q, or on the sayings-collection behind Q, has been discussed by some scholars,[14] but it is practically impossible to reach any conclusion on this, since Q has no existence save in the non-Markan material common to Matthew and Luke. It is difficult to talk about Mark's dependence on a postulated document whose primary characteristic is its non-Markan content.

IV

In the twofold geographical setting of the Markan record – Galilee in 1: 14 to 9: 50 and Judaea from chapter 11 onwards, with chapter 10 providing the transition – theological significance has been discerned. For Mark, according to Ernst Lohmeyer and others, Galilee is the place of action and revelation, and Judaea (specifically Jerusalem) is the place of suffering and death; hence the disciples have to go back to Galilee for the revelation of their risen Lord (Mark 16: 7).[15] If there is any theological significance in these geographical data, it rests upon historical fact: Galilee was, after all, the main area of Jesus's public ministry, and Jerusalem was the place where he was crucified.

Lohmeyer's view that Jesus's instruction to the disciples to meet him in Galilee (Mark 14: 28; 16: 7) points to the expectation of his parousia there is elaborated by Willi Marxsen, who links this instruction with Mark 13: 14, where the setting up of the 'abomination of desolation' is the signal for those in Judaea to 'flee to the mountains'. This is identified with the oracle

---

[14] Cp. Easton, *Christ*, pp. 19f.
[15] E. Lohmeyer, *Galiläa und Jerusalem* (Göttingen, 1936), pp. 10ff; R. H. Lightfoot, *Locality and Doctrine in the Gospels* (London, 1938), pp. 59ff, 106ff.

mentioned by Eusebius (*H.E.* iii. 5. 3) in accordance with which the church of Jerusalem migrated to Pella before the siege of their home city began. As Marxsen interprets this, Mark thought of Pella as belonging to the general area of Galilee and, publishing his Gospel in Galilee, intended his readers to take the angel's words in 16: 7, 'there you will see him', as a promise that the glorious coming of the Son of man (13: 26) would be witnessed there.[16]

There may, in fact, be more of a deliberate contrast between Galilee and the wilderness than between Galilee and Judaea. The wilderness was the scene of John's ministry but for Jesus it was the scene of temptation, not ministry. For his ministry he turned his back on the wilderness (with its Zealot associations?) and proclaimed the good news of the kingdom of God in the populous and fertile region of Galilee.[17]

But so far as the theme of revelation is concerned, no revelatory moment in Galilee communicates so much of the truth of the Gospel as does Mark's account of what happened at the moment of Jesus's death.

V

The present arrangement of the gospel material is generally held to be the evangelist's own work. But Harald Riesenfeld has pointed out that this 'historically stylised' arrangement is crossed or overlaid by another, which he describes as 'theologically systematic', in which the two main divisions are:

(a)   The Son of man and Israel's call (1: 14 to 8: 26)

(b)   The Messiah as teacher and prophet (8: 27 to 13: 37)

The second of these falls into two subdivisions, the former of which (8: 27 to 10: 52), beginning with the Caesarea Philippi and transfiguration incidents, goes on to describe Jesus's training of the disciples, with the situation of the post-Easter and post-Pentecost church in

---

16 W. Marxsen, *Der Evangelist Markus* (Göttingen, 1959), pp. 73ff. The Lohmeyer–Marxsen line, according to which Mark 16: 7 points to the parousia and not (as Matthew understood) to a resurrection appearance of Christ in Galilee, is specially associated with the view (held also by some who do not follow that line) that Mark 16: 8 is the original and designed end of the Gospel. Despite all the evidence adduced to show that literary units could end with γάρ (cp., e.g., Lightfoot, *Locality*, pp. 1ff; P. W. van der Horst, 'Can a book end with γάρ? A note on Mark XVI. 8', *JThSt* n.s. 23 (1972), 172ff), I find it extremely difficult to believe that Mark intended to conclude his record at this point.

17 A different view is expressed by U. Mauser, who finds that in Mark, as in the Old Testament, the wilderness is 'the place of God's mighty acts, significant for all believers of all times and all places' (*Wilderness*, p. 14). According to him, it is Luke who treats the wilderness as 'a topographical symbol for the old epoch which is superseded by Jesus' (p. 148); cp. H. Conzelmann, *The Theology of St Luke* (ET London, 1960), p. 27.

mind, while the latter (11: 1 to 13: 37), beginning with Jesus's entry into Jerusalem, goes on to deal with his teaching in the capital.

Now this second, theological arrangement, giving expression to the evangelist's theological outlook, is self-evidently redactional; but if that is so, then the 'historically stylised' arrangement is probably traditional, part of what Mark 'received'.[18] And indeed a severely compressed form of the 'historically stylised' arrangement may be recognised in the summary of Peter's speech in the house of Cornelius in Acts 10: 37–40 (verse 41 is Lukan, but the preceding outline is mainly traditional). If the outline were amplified – if, for example, the statement that Jesus 'went about doing good and healing all that were oppressed by the devil' were illustrated by instances of his healing and exorcising activity – we should begin to have something not unlike the Markan record, 'beginning from Galilee after the baptism which John preached' and going on to the resurrection announcement.[19] Is it a mere coincidence with the second-century tradition of the Petrine authority behind Mark's Gospel that this outline should be ascribed to Peter?

VI

This second-century tradition is first attested by Papias,[20] and appears in another form towards the end of the century in the anti-Marcionite prologue to this Gospel.[21] Embellishments of it in Irenaeus and later writers probably have no factual basis independent of the testimony of Papias. On the authority of someone to whom he refers as 'the elder', Papias reports that:

> Mark had been Peter's interpreter and wrote down accurately all that he remembered, whether the sayings or the doings of the Lord, but not in order – for he had neither heard the Lord nor followed him, but followed Peter later on, as I said. Peter was accustomed to teach as occasion required,[22] but not as though he were making a compilation of the

---

[18] Riesenfeld, *Tradition* (Oxford, 1970), pp. 51f.

[19] Cp. C. H. Dodd, *Apostolic Preaching*, pp. 53ff.

[20] Quoted by Eusebius, *HE* iii 39. 15. It may be that only the first part of the quotation comes from 'the elder' and that the rest, from 'but not in order' onwards, is Papias's comment.

[21] Conveniently accessible in H. Greeven's revision of A. Huck, *Synopsis of the First Three Gospels* (Tübingen, 1981), p. ix; but note Greeven's reference *in loco* to J. Regul, *Die antimarcionitischen Evangelienprologe* (Freiburg, 1969).

[22] Gk. πρὸς τὰς χρείας. But χρεία had also the technical rhetorical sense of 'a concise and pointed account of something said or done, attributed to some particular person or in keeping with some person' (Theon, *Progymnasmata* 5), and this may be the meaning here. See R. O. P. Taylor, *The Groundwork of the Gospels* (Oxford, 1946), pp. 75ff; also M. Dibelius, *Die Formgeschichte des Evangeliums* (Tübingen, 3rd edn.

dominical oracles.[23] So Mark made no mistake in writing down certain things as he called them to mind; for he paid attention to one thing: to omit none of the things he had heard and to make no false statements in any of them.

Since Papias derived this information from a man of the generation preceding his own, it may go back to the end of the first century. It was composed for a purpose which must now be a matter of speculation – perhaps to explain why Mark deviates in content and sequence from Matthew, or even from the recently published gospel of John.

The first part of the anti-Marcionite prologue to Mark is missing; the surviving portion runs:

> ... (as) was asserted by Mark, who was called stump-fingered, because his fingers were short in proportion to his other bodily dimensions. He was Peter's interpreter, and after the departure of Peter himself he wrote down this Gospel in the parts of Italy.

Whatever the reason was for Mark's being called 'stump-fingered' (κολοβοδάκτυλος), the explanation given here is probably an unintelligent guess and could well be Papias's independent contribution. For the rest, all that the prologue adds to the elder's statement is that Mark wrote his Gospel in Italy.

What factual element underlies the statement that Mark was Peter's interpreter and *aide-de-camp* cannot be determined with certainty: it could be an inference from 1 Pet. 5: 13. Its historical value must be assessed on the basis of internal evidence.

C. H. Turner pointed out features in the Gospel of Mark which, he reckoned, justified the reader in calling it 'autobiographical' in contrast to Matthew and Luke. This Gospel 'records the experience of an eyewitness and companion'. In particular, Turner drew attention to the repeated occasions in Mark on which 'a sentence commences with the plural, for it is an experience which is being related, and passes into the singular, for the experience is that of discipleship to a Master'. That is to say, we begin with 'they' (the disciples) and pass over to 'he' (Jesus). If, then, 'they' is changed to 'we', the reader 'will receive a vivid impression of the testimony that lies behind the Gospel' – the testimony being that of Peter, whose spoken 'we' (reflected in Mark's written 'they') means 'my companions and I'.[24]

1959), pp. 150ff (where the χρεία is related to the 'paradigm'); W. R. Farmer, 'Notes on a Literary and Formcritical Analysis of Some of the Synoptic Material Peculiar to Luke', *NTSt* 8 (1961–2), 301ff; especially 307ff.

[23] Gk. οὐχ ὥσπερ σύνταξιν τῶν κυριακῶν ποιούμενος λογίων, as (according to Papias) Matthew did (*ap. H.E.* iii. 39. 16); cp. the title of Papias's work: λογίων κυριακῶν ἐξήγησις (*ap. H.E.* iii. 39. 1).

[24] C. H. Turner, 'The Gospel according to St Mark', in *A New Commentary on Holy*

T. W. Manson, following up this clue, drew up a 'tentative list of Petrine paragraphs', comprising those which exhibited 'Turner's mark' along with others which attached themselves naturally to these. These 'Petrine paragraphs', he found, fell naturally into two groups – one set against the Galilaean background, with Capernaum as the principal centre, and the other covering incidents on the last journey to Jerusalem, with events in Jerusalem during Holy Week up to Jesus's arrest and Peter's denial.[25]

How completely foreign this approach is to more recent studies of Mark may be seen if we compare it with D. E. Nineham's argument that, since by general consensus some of Mark's material 'bears all the signs of having been community tradition', it seems 'only logical' to go on and take the same view about the rest of his material; indeed, in his view all of it bears the same signs.[26] Professor Nineham does not rule out the possibility that some of the material might ultimately derive from Peter, but he thinks that the evidence rules out direct dependence on Peter. Probably we should recognise sections which bear the signs of community tradition and others which bear the signs of more positive Petrine influence, even if Professor Manson over-estimated the extent of the latter.

VII

T. W. Manson took seriously the statement in the anti-Marcionite prologue that Mark composed his Gospel in Italy after Peter's 'departure'. He thought, however, that later writers were wrong in thinking that Peter's 'departure' (*excessio*, probably reflecting Gk. ἔξοδος) meant his death. He suggested rather that Peter and Mark visited Rome between A.D. 55 and 60, that when Peter moved on elsewhere Mark stayed behind (he was still in Rome during Paul's period of house-arrest there, if this is the setting of Philem. 24 and Col. 4: 10) and, at the request of members of the Roman church, undertook to compile a written record of what Peter had told them, amplified by means of other material to which he had access.

If it be asked if there was any circumstance in the history of early Roman Christianity which would have brought Peter and Mark to Rome early in Nero's principate, one answer could be that the church was being reconstituted then after being dispersed by Claudius's edict expelling the Jewish community from Rome, and a visit from the prince of the apostles was just what was needed to establish it. Such a visit could explain Paul's language in Rom. 15: 20 about his reluctance to 'build on another man's

Scripture, ed. C. Gore etc. (London, 1928), *NT*, pp. 48f; cp. C. H. Turner, 'Marcan Usage', *JThSt* 25 (1923–4), 377ff; and especially 26 (1924–5), pp. 225ff.

[25] *Studies*, pp. 40ff.

[26] *The Gospel of St Mark* (Harmondsworth, 1963), pp. 26f.

foundation'. Professor Manson's suggestion – it was no more – involved a dating for Mark before A.D. 60, 'a few years earlier than is generally thought likely'.[27]

A commoner view is that it was composed in A.D. 64 or soon afterwards. This, of course, is in line with the traditional interpretation of Peter's 'departure' as meaning his death, and with the traditional dating of Peter's death to the persecution of the Roman Christians in the aftermath of the fire which devasted the imperial capital in July of A.D. 64. C. H. Turner makes Peter's death (A.D. 64–5) the *terminus a quo* for the writing of Mark, adding that 'it will naturally have been rather soon after the martyrdom that the need made itself insistently felt for a written record of his teaching'.[28]

But, quite apart from the tradition, this date is on various grounds probable for Mark's Gospel. Such a work, appearing on the morrow of a murderous outburst of hostility, 'had the character of a call to Christian loyalty and a challenge to a hostile world'.[29] The wildest travesties were in circulation about the origin and character of those people, 'loathed for their vices, whom the populace called Christians', as Tacitus puts it in his account of these events. He himself notes, with greater accuracy but no less unfriendliness, that 'Christ, from whom they got their name, had been executed by the procurator Pontius Pilate when Tiberius was emperor'; thus, he adds, 'the pernicious superstition was checked for the moment, but it broke out anew, not only throughout Judaea, where the trouble started, but throughout Rome itself, where all the horrible and shameful rites collect and find a following'.[30] But what did the Roman Christians themselves know of the origin of their faith? Were they able to answer current misrepresentations with a confident account of the real facts? Was it true that their Founder had been executed by sentence of a Roman magistrate? If so, was not the movement which he founded properly suspect in the eyes of the authorities?

Twelve years previously, or a little more, another Roman magistrate had given a ruling which worked for a time to the advantage of the Christian movement. When the leaders of the Jewish community in Corinth accused

[27] *Studies*, pp. 38ff. Cp. W. W. Harvey's note on Irenaeus, *Haer.* iii. i. 1. Perhaps this is the place to mention J. O'Callaghan's thesis that the Qumran Greek fragments 7Q5 and 7Q6.1, from two separate manuscripts independently dated on palaeographical grounds not later than A.D. 50, exhibit respectively the texts of Mark 6: 52f and Mark 4: 28 ('¿Papiros neotestamentarios en la cueva 7 de Qumran?', *Bb* 53 (1972), 91ff). The thesis has been conclusively refuted, on the basis of a study of the papyrus fragments themselves (as distinct from photographs), by P. Benoit, 'Notes sur les fragments grecs de la grotte 7 de Qumran', *RB* 79 (1972), 321ff.
[28] *New Commentary, NT*, pp. 44f.
[29] C. H. Dodd, *About the Gospels* (Cambridge, 1950), p. 2.
[30] Tacitus, *Annals* xv. 44.

Paul before Gallio, proconsul of Achaia, of propagating a religion not countenanced by imperial law, Gallio ruled in effect that what Paul was preaching was a variety of Judaism, and therefore entitled to the protection which imperial law extended to Judaism – provided, of course, that public order was not disturbed.[31] Had Gallio ruled *against* Paul, his ruling would have constituted a most unwelcome precedent for other magistrates. As it was, his refusal so to rule may have served as a negative precedent, thanks to which Paul in particular was able to discharge his apostolic ministry for several years more, until he found himself under house-arrest in Rome, still preaching the kingdom of God and telling the story of Jesus to his visitors, under the eyes of the imperial authorities. Even so, by this time it was no longer possible for Roman magistrates to regard Christianity as one among many varieties of Judaism, least of all in a city like Rome, where the Christian community was now predominantly Gentile. Unprotected by the law, the Christians of Rome provided convenient scapegoats when Nero found it advisable to divert suspicion of fire-raising from himself. Near-demoralised by the sudden attack, they sorely needed to be reassured of their identity. What was better calculated to restore their morale and their sense of identity than this little book which 'contained the Christian society's own account of the events out of which it arose, and of its martyred Founder'?[32]

The story is based on the main body of apostolic preaching: its intention is not biographical but kerygmatic and theological. It provided Christians not simply with an account of their historical antecedents but with an understanding of their identity over against Jews and pagans, especially in its revelation that the recent persecution in Rome was no strange or abnormal experience, but something all of a piece with the essence of their faith, which recognised in the suffering Son of man the ultimate manifestation of God.

Reference has already been made to W. Marxsen's view that Mark is a Galilaean Gospel, composed during the war of A.D. 66–70 to prepare the followers of Jesus for his impending parousia in Galilee. The generation between the death of Jesus and the parousia is filled by the proclamation of the gospel to the nations (Mark 13: 10) – Mark's interpretation of the 'testimony' spoken of in the *verbum Christi* of 13: 9.[33]

A date two or three years later than Marxsen's was proposed by S. G. F. Brandon, according to whom Mark's Gospel was written after the collapse of the Jewish revolt and the confirmation of its collapse in the triumph granted to Vespasian and his two sons in A.D. 71, in order to help the

---

[31] Acts 18: 12ff.   [32] Dodd, *About the Gospels*, p. 2.
[33] Marxsen, *Markus*, p. 119. He rightly links this proclamation with Rom. 11: 25.

Roman Christians to see where they now stood in relation to an event which, even for them, must have been traumatic.[34] Professor Brandon held that Jesus, though not a member of the Zealot party, sympathised with Zealot ideals and was consequently, and not surprisingly, executed by the Romans, and that the Jerusalem church, under the leadership of his brother James, shared the same sympathies. The Gentile churches, and pre-eminently the Roman church, would henceforth wish to be completely dissociated from Zealot ideas and policies.[35] The crushing of the Jewish revolt and the destruction of the Temple and city of Jerusalem not only meant the dispersion of the mother-church but indicated to Gentile Christians that the Jews were not God's peculiar people and that Jerusalem was not – or at least was no longer – the centre of his work on earth. The spectacle of the Temple furniture carried in the procession to the shrine of Jupiter Capitolinus (whence it was moved later to grace Vespasian's new Temple of Peace)[36] proclaimed that the once holy place had been deserted by the divine presence. If some of them were disposed to think it sacrilege that the purple curtains of the Temple were now hung in the imperial palace,[37] let them reflect that at the moment of Jesus's death the Temple veil was torn in two from top to bottom.[38] So Mark relates, arguing in effect from this act of God that, despite the Jewish origins of Christianity, the logic of the passion of the Christ detached Christianity from any essential dependence on these origins. Even if it had earlier been politic to deny that Jesus had ever spoken against the Temple,[39] now that the Temple lay in ruins it was apposite to recall how explicitly he had foretold that one stone of it would not be left standing on another (Mark 13: 2). When 'on that fateful day' the legionaries offered sacrifice to their standards within the sacred precincts and hailed Titus as *imperator*, then indeed the 'abomination of desolation' was seen 'standing where *he* ought not' – but Mark would not make the identification more explicit: 'let the reader understand', he says (Mark 13: 14).[40]

But, confidently as Professor Brandon presented his reconstruction, it

---

[34] 'The Date of the Markan Gospel', *NTSt* 7 (1960–1), 126ff; cp. his *Jesus and the Zealots* (Manchester, 1967), pp. 221ff.

[35] Hence, he suggests implausibly, Mark (followed by Matthew) distinguishes the second Simon among the Twelve as 'the Cananaean' (Mark 3: 18), knowing that the Aramaic word would be unintelligible to the Romans and less liable to suspicion than its Greek equivalent 'Zealot' (Brandon, *NTSt* 7 (1960–1), 140f; *Zealots*, pp. 243ff).

[36] Josephus, *BJ* vii. 148ff, 161.

[37] Josephus, *BJ* vii. 162.

[38] Mark 15: 38 (see pp. 87f below). In Jewish legend Titus sacrilegiously entered the Temple and slashed the curtain with his sword (TB *Giṭṭin* 56b).

[39] Mark 14: 57–9.

[40] Brandon, *NTSt* 7 (1960–1), 134.

can scarcely stand against the positive evidence that Mark's Gospel, and especially his version of the Olivet discourse, implies a life-setting earlier than the events of A.D. 70. Whatever Mark meant by the personal 'abomination of desolation', his standing 'where he ought not' was to be a signal to those in Judaea to 'flee to the mountains', and months before the Temple went up in flames the time for such flight was past.

An earlier form of the discourse may well have been circulated to meet the threatened crisis of A.D. 40, but it is its Markan form that is relevant for the dating of the Second Gospel. That its Markan form is *earlier* than A.D. 70 is indicated by those modifications of it in the gospel of Matthew which reflect the situation *after* that date. For example, the disciples' question which is answered by this discourse appears thus in Mark: 'Tell us, when will this be [viz. the destruction of the Temple, predicted by Jesus in 13:2], and what will be the sign when these things are all to be accomplished?' (13:4). 'These things' are the events of the end-time which, especially according to Daniel's visions, attend the desolation of the sanctuary, culminating in the establishment of 'everlasting righteousness' (cp. Dan. 8:11–14; 9:24–27; 11:31ff). In the Markan form of the question they apparently belong to the same temporal complex as the destruction of the Temple. But in Matthew the question is re-worded so that the destruction of the Temple is separated from the events of the end-time: 'Tell us, when will this be [the destruction of the Temple], and what will be the sign of your coming and of the close of the age?' (Matt. 24:3). For, when Matthew's Gospel was written, the destruction of the Temple had taken place, but the parousia and the 'close of the age' were still future. A distinction which was patent after A.D. 70 was not so obvious at an earlier stage, and it is such an earlier stage that is implied in Mark's wording. For Mark, the 'abomination of desolation' has not yet made his appearance, although he may well be expected imminently. The cryptic language seems to point to some intolerable encroachment of Caesar on the things that are God's.

VIII

An important milestone in the course of Markan study was the publication in 1901 of William Wrede's work on the messianic secret in the gospels. According to Wrede, Jesus's commanding silence when he is acknowledged to be the messiah (at Caesarea Philippi, Mark 8:30) or Son of God (Mark 3:12; cp. 1:25, 34) does not represent historical truth but is a device by which the gospel tradition (given literary form by Mark) endeavoured to reconcile the church's belief that Jesus was the messiah from the beginning of his career with the fact that this belief did not emerge until after the resurrection. Jesus was the messiah, so runs the 'traditional' and Markan explanation, but he kept his messiahship dark. Thus, when three of the disciples were granted a vision of his true glory on the mount of transfiguration and heard him acclaimed as the Father's dear Son, 'he charged them', says Mark, 'to tell no one what they had seen, until the Son of man should have risen from the dead' (Mark 9: 9). But this vision (according to Wrede), like Peter's confession at Caesarea Philippi, was originally related as a resurrection appearance and was artificially transposed back into the setting of the historical ministry.[41]

A realistic assessment of the 'messianic secret', however, will give it its most appropriate setting in the historical ministry. Jesus placed his own interpretation on the designation 'messiah' and, if that interpretation was conceded, he would not refuse the designation. But it was so regularly interpreted in a political and military sense that he preferred not to use it and discouraged its application to him by others. Even when Peter, at Caesarea Philippi, confessed him to be the messiah, he showed that his understanding of Jesus's messianic mission was far from adequate and had to be sharply rebuked for trying to dissuade his Master from thinking in terms of impending suffering.[42] During the ministry of Jesus its messianic character was not at all obvious.

The only parable of the kingdom of God which is peculiar to Mark, that of the seed growing secretly (4: 26–9), makes this point. When the seed has been sown, it does not matter that it is not seen: something is going on underground and will appear in due course. So, when once the kingdom of God has begun to work, it is a matter of small importance that its significance is not appreciated here and now: one day, within the lifetime of the present generation, it will have 'come with power'[43] and its effect will be manifest to all.

That the significance of the ministry was not generally appreciated is indicated further in the quotation of Isa. 6: 9f which in Mark 4: 11f introduces Jesus's interpretation to his disciples of the parable of the sower. We are frequently invited to penetrate behind the background of this 'hard saying' and discern in the underlying Aramaic a rather different meaning, related probably to a different context from that which Mark gives it. And if we are to determine *Jesus's* intention in speaking thus, this is probably the right procedure, and it is quite likely that he meant that, whereas the mystery of the kingdom, the divine purpose implicit in its proclamation, has been divulged to the Twelve and to other believers, it remains a riddle

[41] W. Wrede, *Das Messiasgeheimnis in den Evangelien* (Göttingen, 1901), pp. 34ff *et passim* (ET *The Messianic Secret* (Cambridge and London, 1972), pp. 35ff *et passim*).
[42] Mark 8: 32f (see p. 84 below).
[43] Mark 9: 1.

to those outside, who remain bereft of perception and understanding, and so do not repent and receive forgiveness.[44] But if we look for *Mark's* intention in recording the saying, we must examine his Greek text, not the underlying Aramaic, and view it in the context where he places it. We may then come to the conclusion that he is concerned, as was Paul, about the problem of Jewish unresponsiveness to the gospel, and sees in it the effect of that judicial 'hardening' of Israel which Paul also discerned, in fulfilment of prophetic words about unseeing eyes and unhearing ears.[45] To some an understanding of the 'mystery' was granted, but from others it was withheld, even when it was proclaimed in the graphic language of parable.

This is not the only respect in which Mark presents parallels to Paul without being dependent on him. If Paul lays it down that food-restrictions and the observance of special days are matters of religious indifference, on which each one must be 'fully convinced in his own mind' (Rom. 14: 2–6), Mark records the sovereign freedom with which Jesus disposed of the Sabbath law (Mark 2: 23 to 3: 5) and recognises in his pronouncement on the rules of levitical purity a declaration making 'all foods clean' (Mark 7: 14–19).[46]

IX

While Martin Kähler's description of Mark's Gospel as a 'passion narrative with an extended introduction'[47] is an exaggeration, it contains more than a little truth. The record of Jesus's ministry preceding his arrival at

---

[44] Cp. T. W. Manson, *The Teaching of Jesus* (2nd edn. Cambridge, 1935), pp. 75ff; J. Jeremias, *Neutestamentliche Theologie* i (Gütersloh, 1971), 133f, 243f (ET *New Testament Theology* i (London, 1971), 120f, 256).

[45] Cp. Rom. 11: 7ff.

[46] See p. 73 above. R. P. Martin, 'A Gospel in Search of a Life-setting', *EspT* 80 (1968–9), 361ff, argues that Mark's Gospel was published after Paul's death in order to provide a safeguard against two tendencies which Paul's kerygmatic theology had held in check – one which promoted a messiah who performed magical signs and another which promoted the figure of a heavenly redeemer detached from history. Mark's use of εὐαγγέλιον (1: 1, 14, 15; 8: 35; 10: 29; 13: 10; 14: 9) has Pauline affinities (cp. p. 79 n. 33 above). Martin's thesis is elaborated in his *Mark: Evangelist and Theologian* (Exeter, 1972). Two other theses can receive only the briefest mention here: that of E. Trocmé (*La formation de l'Évangile selon Marc* (Paris, 1963); ET *The Formation of the Gospel according to Mark* (London, 1975)), which holds that the original edition of Mark ended with chapter 13 and was written around A.D. 50 by someone of the outlook of Philip the evangelist, and that of T. J. Weeden (*Mark – Traditions in Conflict* (Philadelphia, 1971)), according to whom Mark opposes the θεῖος ἀνήρ christology of the disciples with the suffering messiahship of Jesus.

[47] *The So-Called Historical Jesus and the Historic, Biblical Christ*, ET (Philadelphia, 1964), p. 80. Kähler uses the expression in the plural, with reference to all the gospels, but makes Mark his chief example.

Jerusalem at the beginning of chapter 11 contains repeated adumbrations of the coming passion. The series of five controversies in Mark 2: 1 to 3: 6 includes a hint that one day the 'bridegroom' will be 'taken away' from his friends (2: 20) and ends with an account of a plot against Jesus's life by an unnatural combination of Pharisees and Herodians. The list of the Twelve in Mark 3: 16–19 ends with 'Judas Iscariot, who betrayed him'. The story of John the Baptist's execution, told as a 'flash-back' in Mark 6: 17–29, is ominous, for Herod Antipas, who has put John to death, thinks of Jesus as John *redivivus* when news of the mission of the Twelve reaches him. Later, the parallel between John and Jesus is made explicit: 'Elijah has come', says Jesus to the disciples after their descent from the mount of transfiguration, 'and they did to him whatever they pleased, as it is written of him' (Mark 9: 13) – that is, the recorded threats against the first Elijah's life which his enemies were unable to carry out (1 Kings 19: 2ff) have been fulfilled in the death of the second Elijah at the hands of *his* enemies. And as such things were 'written' concerning Elijah, so it is 'written of the Son of man, that he should suffer many things and be treated with comtempt' (Mark 9: 12). The last words, based in part on the fourth Isaianic Servant Song (probably) and in part on Psalm 118: 22 (certainly), belong to primitive tradition (for their transmission along a non-Markan line cp. Luke 17: 25).[48] They underlie the recurrent warnings of the impending passion which, according to Mark, Jesus impressed on his disciples from Caesarea Philippi onwards. Immediately after Peter's confession 'he began to teach them that the Son of man must suffer many things, and be rejected . . . and after three days rise again' (Mark 8: 31), but, for all the 'plainness' (παρρησία) with which he said so, Peter bluntly deprecated such language, expressing himself in terms which Jesus repudiated as a satanic, though well-meant, temptation to deviate from his appointed path (8: 32–4).[49] Later, in Galilee, he repeated the warning: 'The Son of man will be delivered into the hands of men, and they will kill him; and when he is killed, after three days he will rise' (9: 31). 'But', says Mark, 'they did not understand the saying, and they were afraid to ask him' (9: 22). Even on the road to Jerusalem they failed to understand him, when he foretold[50] his

---

[48] Cp. W. Michaelis, *TDNT* v, pp. 913ff (s.v. πάσχω).

[49] There is a striking similarity between Jesus's rebuke of Peter here ('Get behind me, Satan!') and his reply to the wilderness tempter in Matt. 4: 10; perhaps on both occasions he recognised the same temptation – to fulfil his mission otherwise than by suffering and death.

[50] That these predictions are not sheer *vaticinia ex eventu* is suggested by the fact that none of them speaks of crucifixion; indeed, apart from the reference to the disciples' taking up the cross in Mark 8: 34, crucifixion is not mentioned in this gospel before the passion narrative proper. Cp. R. H. Lightfoot, *The Gospel Message of St Mark* (Oxford, 1950), p. 36.

passion with unprecedented explicitness (10: 33f). Indeed, how little they appreciated what his words involved is emphasised by Mark in the following pericope, where the sons of Zebedee still imagine that their Master is about to establish a kingdom in which the chief places will attract such honour as is paid to dignitaries in the kingdoms of this world. They have yet to learn that their Master's closest associates must drink his cup and share his baptism, that in his fellowship the highest honour consists in rendering the lowliest service: 'For the Son of man also came not to be served but to serve, and to give his life as a ransom for many' (Mark 10: 35–45).

This theme of the suffering Son of man so pervades the central section of Mark's narrative that it must be recognised as crucial to his understanding of the ministry. The suffering of the Son of man is, moreover, something that is *written* concerning him: it is, in other words, foretold in Old Testament scripture. 'The Son of man goes as it is written of him', says Jesus at the Last Supper when indicating the presence of a traitor at the table (Mark 14: 21), and later the same evening he submits to his captors with the words: 'let the scriptures be fulfilled' (14: 49).

The Son of man in Mark is the 'one like a son of man' of Dan. 7: 13, who comes 'with the clouds of heaven' before the Ancient of Days to receive universal dominion from him when the beasts, which represent successive pagan world-empires, disappear from the scene. This is evident from the influence of Daniel's vision on those Markan passages where the Son of man is said to come with 'clouds' (Mark 13: 26; 14: 62). But it is difficult to see in Daniel's vision the source of the concept of the *suffering* Son of man. True, the 'one like a son of man' is interpreted in terms of the saints of the Most High, with whom the 'little horn' (i.e. Antiochus Epiphanes) 'made war ... and prevailed over them, until the Ancient of Days came, and judgement was given for the saints of the Most High, and the time came when the saints received the kingdom' (Dan. 7: 21f). But nowhere in the vision is the 'one like a son of man' described as suffering,[51] and while the modern exegete can see quite clearly that his suffering is implied, the earliest interpreters of Daniel appear to have distinguished him from the persecuted saints. He is associated but not identified with them: he is their champion and avenger, as he is the judge and executioner of their persecutors.[52]

If those interpreters of Mark are right who see behind the suffering Son of

---

[51] For the view that Daniel's 'one like a son of man' is exalted *after suffering*, see C. F. D. Moule, 'From Defendant to Judge – and Deliverer', *SNTS Bulletin* 3 (1952), 40ff; M. D. Hooker, *The Son of Man in Mark* (London, 1967), pp. 11ff.

[52] E.g. in the *Similitudes of Enoch* (1 Enoch 48: 4ff *et passim*); cp. Hooker, *Son of Man*, pp. 33ff.

man the suffering Servant of Yahweh in Isa. 52: 13 to 53: 12,[53] they may in some measure be bringing back to light the original intention of the book of Daniel to re-present the suffering Servant in the form of the suffering saints or *maskilim* of the persecution under Antiochus.[54] But whether that is so or not, the suffering of the Son of man in Mark demands a more explicit biblical background than Dan. 7: 13 can supply. The Son of man's giving his life as 'a ransom for many' (Mark 10: 45) is in line with the Isaianic Servant's giving his life as a reparation-offering ('*āshām*) and bearing the sin of many (Isa. 53: 10, 12).[55] 'How is it *written* of the Son of man, that he should suffer many things and be treated with contempt?' – how indeed, if the Son of man be not equated with the Servant of Yahweh?

Yet before his passion the Son of man is vested with exceptional authority: he 'has authority on earth to forgive sins' (Mark 2: 10) and claims to be 'lord even of the sabbath' – evidently as representative of man, for whom the Sabbath was made (Mark 2: 27f). His authority to forgive sins is quite unlike the judicial authority granted to Daniel's 'one like a son of man'[56] but is not unlike the Isaianic Servant's commission to 'justify the many' (Isa. 53: 11).

Jesus's own use of the designation 'the Son of man' – a designation almost without exception found on his lips alone – is not our object of study here. By Mark, the Son of man, whether exercising his present authority on earth, suffering betrayal, contempt and death, or 'coming in clouds with great power and glory' (13: 26), is identified with Jesus himself.

The Son of man and the kingdom of God are so closely associated that the one implies the other even if the other is not expressly mentioned. This is what might be expected in view of the plain statement in Dan. 7: 13f that the eternal kingdom is bestowed on the 'one like a son of man' – to which might be added the testimony of the fourth Servant Song that the Servant of Yahweh, after his suffering and death, is to be 'exalted and lifted up' and made 'very high' (Isa. 52: 13). As the Son of man exercises his authority in the ministry of Jesus, so the kingdom of God is at work in his ministry, as the parables of Mark 4: 1–34 declare. Yet, according to these parables, the kingdom's working is largely hidden at present, like the seed growing

---

[53] Cp. Manson, *Teaching*, pp. 227ff; V. Taylor, *Jesus and his Sacrifice* (London, 1937), pp. 39ff; W. Zimmerli and J. Jeremias, *The Servant of God*, ET (London, 1957), pp. 79ff; for a contrary opinion cp. M. D. Hooker, *Jesus and the Servant* (London, 1959).

[54] Cp. M. Black, 'Servant of the Lord and Son of Man', *SJTh* 6 (1953), pp. 1ff.

[55] Cp. C. K. Barrett, 'The Background of Mark 10: 45', *New Testament Essays . . . in Memory of T. W. Manson*, ed. A. J. B. Higgins (Manchester, 1959), pp. 1ff, for the view that a background to this saying should be sought rather in the Maccabaean martyrdoms than in Isa. 52: 13 to 53: 12.

[56] The judicial authority granted to the 'one like a son of man' implies authority to convict and condemn rather than to pardon and release.

secretly; it is unimpressive to outward appearance, like the minute mustard seed. But one day it will come visibly 'with power' (Mark 9: 1), just as the Son of man, after submitting to suffering and death, will be manifested in glory (8: 38; 14: 62).

X

The portrayal of Jesus as the Son of man, commissioned by God, exposed to suffering, destined to come in glory, is Mark's way of presenting him as Son of God. Whatever else he means by 'the Son of God', he means the one in whom God himself is fully revealed. Jesus is hailed by God, at the outset of his ministry, as his 'beloved Son' (Mark 1: 11). If we ask what kind of person God's 'beloved Son' is, Mark lets us see him in action and teaching, but he brings out the full significance of his character and mission by portraying him as the Son of man. So Jesus himself replies to the high priest's question, 'Are you the Messiah, *the Son of the Blessed?*' with the words: 'I am; and you will see *the Son of man . . .*' (Mark 14: 61f). And when the Son of man, betrayed and humiliated, has endured his final suffering, the truth about his person is proclaimed in the centurion's words: 'Truly this man was the Son of God!' (Mark 15: 39).[57]

It is not by chance that, immediately before recording the centurion's confession, Mark tells how, at the moment when Jesus breathed his last, 'the curtain of the temple was torn in two, from top to bottom' (15: 38). It is unlikely that this has anything to do with the display of the Temple furnishings in Vespasian's triumph, or with other portents in and around the sacred building which seemed in retrospect to foreshadow its destruction in A.D. 70. For Mark, this is the climax of his narrative. He may have in mind, like the writer to the Hebrews, the fact that Jesus by his death has opened up for his people a 'new and living way . . . through the curtain' into the presence of God (Heb. 10: 20); but still more he implies that in the death of Jesus God is revealed to men in the fullness of his grace. Once his presence was hidden from them behind the curtain which hung before the holy of holies, but now it is hidden no more. If in his works of creation we trace 'but the outskirts of his ways' (Job 26: 14), in the cross of Jesus he has bared his heart. The rending of the veil proclaims the same message as the centurion's confession. The centurion, paradoxically and unwittingly, divulges the messianic secret, which (as T. W. Manson said) 'is not

---

[57] The centurion's confession sums up Mark's message as Thomas's confession, 'My Lord and my God' (John 20: 28), sums up John's. Whatever the centurion might have meant by υἱὸς θεοῦ, Mark interprets the words as a confirmation of his own theme (hence 'the Son of God' in the 1962 and 1971 editions of RSV, as against 'a son of God' in the editions of 1946 and 1952).

concerned with the identity of the Messiah but with the nature of his task'.[58] When Jesus himself declared it 'plainly', his disciples misunderstood him. They took him to mean, perhaps, that the establishment of the kingdom would call for toil and tribulation, but that in the end the kingdom, with its power and glory, would be theirs. Their messianic expectations were in essence of the same order as those of most of their fellow-countrymen. Not until 'the Son of man was risen from the dead' did the truth begin to dawn on them, and even then it dawned gradually: the crucified Jesus is king – king in his crucifixion – and the way of the cross is the way of the kingdom. In emphasising this, Mark emphasises the heart of Jesus's mission and ministry. If his readers grasped this lesson, they would greet their own sufferings as a participation in those of the Son of man; let them confess him thus, and they would find him unashamed of them at his coming 'in the glory of his Father with the holy angels'.[59]

Additional Note

In December 1960 Morton Smith reported to the ninety-sixth meeting of the American Society of Biblical Literature and Exegesis a discovery which he made in 1958 in the monastery of Mar Saba, some twelve miles south-east of Jerusalem, while he was cataloguing the contents of its library. On the end-papers of a copy of Isaac Voss's edition of six Epistles of Ignatius, printed at Amsterdam in 1646, he found a manuscript copy of a Greek letter written in what was most probably an eighteenth-century hand. The copy is headed: 'From the letters of the most holy Clement, author of the Stromateis: To Theodore.' The actual text of the letter identifies neither the writer nor the person addressed. On stylistic grounds Professor Smith was disposed to accept the attribution to Clement of Alexandria (fl. c. A.D. 180); other scholars to whom he showed it varied in their assessment – thus A. D. Nock suggested a date of composition not later than the fourth century; J. Munck thought it might have been composed to support the claim of the church of Alexandria to have a special association with Mark.

The text of the letter was published by Professor Smith in Clement of Alexandria and a Secret Gospel of Mark (Harvard University Press, 1973). It refers to a longer edition of the Gospel of Mark, preserved at Alexandria, which included 'secret' acts and sayings of Jesus not found in the canonical Mark. Mark, according to the letter, came to Alexandria from Rome where

---

[58] 'Realized Eschatology and the Messianic Secret', Studies in the Gospels, ed. Nineham, p. 220.
[59] With the negative formulation of Mark 8: 38 cp. the positive counterpart in Luke 12: 8.

he had already published the shorter edition. At Alexandria he expanded this edition, adding the 'secret' material so as to provide 'a more spiritual gospel for the use of those who were being perfected'. Carpocrates, says the writer, further amplified Mark's expanded addition with some spurious material. This may be linked with Irenaeus's statement (*Adversus haereses* i. 25. 5) that in the Carpocratean writings it was claimed that Jesus gave esoteric teachings to his disciples and permitted them to transmit these to such of their adherents as were 'worthy'. According to samples of the expanded gospel quoted in the letter, it inserted after Mark 10: 34 the story of the raising of a rich young man from the tomb at Bethany – a story with resemblances to the Johannine narrative of the raising of Lazarus. James's and John's request to Jesus is next recorded (cp. Mark 10: 35–45). When, at the end of this incident, Jesus comes to Bethany (Mark 10: 46a), the rich young man's sister and mother are there with Salome, 'but Jesus did not receive them'. We recall that in several Gnostic Gospels Salome plays a larger and more colourful part than in the canonical writings.

A preliminary judgement is that here we have evidence of a Gnostic expansion of Mark, but further study must be devoted to the text, and to the rich apparatus of annotation with which Professor Smith has equipped it, before firmer conclusions are possible.

Some observations on *Tendenzkritik*

Tendenzkritik is a technique in historical research specially associated with
F. C. Baur and A. Schwegler and others of the Tübingen school, since it was
they who applied it to the reconstruction of the early history of the church.[1]
In principle, it is a matter of plain common sense, and was already in use
among secular historians before the Tübingenians adopted it. If it can be
established that a document was written with a clear propagandist
purpose, then it becomes probable (other things being equal) that its writer
bent the facts, or made a tendentious selection from among them,[2] to fit his
purpose; and it is therefore necessary to make allowance for such distortion,
in any attempt to get back to the truth about what actually happened.
Accordingly, a question of prime importance for the historian in
interpreting a document and estimating its worth is, What was this
document for? What did its author hope to achieve by it? A classic example
of *Tendenzkritik* is the estimate of Acts reached by New Testament scholars
over against Galatians. It is a familiar fact that, whereas the Epistle to the
Galatians shows Paul at one point taking issue with Peter, and reflects a
difference (if not a conflict) between the leaders of the Gentile and Jewish
missions respectively, the Acts presents a picture of basic harmony between
Paul and the leading figures in the Jerusalem church. Equally, it is well
known that, in certain details, Galatians and Acts are difficult, if not
impossible, to reconcile. *Ergo*, a strong case appears to emerge for treating
Acts – which, in any case, is later (perhaps much later) than Galatians – as
a tendentious re-telling of the story for the purpose of papering over cracks
which in fact existed between Paul and the Jerusalem leaders.

It is upon such assumptions, coupled with a particular chronology for the
writing of the New Testament and related documents, that the Tübinge-

---

[1] See, e.g., F.C. Baur's *Kritische Untersuchungen über die Kanonischen Evangelien*
(Tübingen, 1847), pp. 71–6. For a discussion, see P.C. Hodgson, *The Formation of
Historical Theology: a Study of Ferdinand Christian Baur* (New York, 1966), where it is
urged that it is incorrect to associate the method with Hegelianism. (See, e.g.,
p. 200.) For a convenient summary of Baur's *Tendenzkritik*, with excerpts (among
others illustrating other points) from Baur's *Paulus, der Apostel Jesu Christi* (Stuttgart,
1845) and his *Kritische Untersuchungen*, see W.G. Kümmel, *Das Neue Testament:
Geschichte der Erforschung seiner Probleme* (2nd edn. Freiburg/München, 1970), pp.
164ff (ET *The New Testament: the History of the Investigation of its Problems* (London,
1973), pp. 134ff). On Schwegler see ibid. pp. 177f (ET p. 145).
[2] See the note on 'the *argumentum e silentio*' by G. M. Styler, pp. 101–7 below.

nian version of the early years of Christianity rests. Subsequently to the days of Baur and his immediate successors, it has become habitual to question, indeed, the chronology of the Tübingen scholars (not least because of the massive criticism of it by J. B. Lightfoot and his colleagues),[3] but to endorse their assumption of tendentiousness in Acts, and, indeed, in the Gospels. Baur himself had already applied *Tendenzkritik* to the Gospels, bringing out Matthew as the earliest and most free from bias;[4] and *Redaktionsgeschichte*, so fashionable at the present time, has in some respects affinities with the method, although critical opinion today is not wont to set Matthew on any pedestal of objectivity above his fellows. Form-criticism too employs *Tendenzkritik* on a miniature scale, in its dealings with the small, independent units of tradition. One of the assumptions of form-criticism is that each unit had its own particular purpose in the life of the Christian church;[5] and when that purpose was an apologetic or propagandic one, then one must reckon with the possibility that the contents of the unit were shaped and modified so as to enhance its force: the size of a miracle or the effect of a polemical saying may be exaggerated; and so forth.

Now any man of integrity and common sense will agree that *Tendenzkritik* is not merely a legitimate but a necessary factor in the process of getting at the truth. It is on this principle (though not by that name) that the system of advocacy in a law court rests; and we use it every day, consciously or unconsciously, when estimating the truth of what we are told. Instinctively we make allowance for the fisherman's bias in his description of the size of his catch. But the principle ought not to be used uncritically. *Tendenzkritik* is a delicate tool, not a crowbar.

It involves two questions, which may subtly react on one another; and, when all is said and done, the answers to them have only a limited scope: and this needs to be recognised and accepted. One question concerns the author's aim and intention, and therefore the *a priori* likelihood of distortion; the other concerns the actually demonstrable extent of distortion in his tale. If it be established, in answer to the first question, that the author is indeed dominated by an apologetic or propagandic purpose, the presumption may be that he has distorted facts to gain his ends. If, in

---

[3] Especially through Lightfoot's edition of Ignatius.

[4] See Kümmel, *Neue Testament*, pp. 171f (ET pp. 138f), referring to *Kritische Untersuchungen*. But Baur is careful to qualify this judgement (*Kritische Untersuchungen*, pp. 620f). He believed that, in its present form, Matthew was not earlier than the second century.

[5] For some recent observations on this topic, see Morton Smith, 'Forms, Motives, and Omissions in Mark's Account of the Teaching of Jesus', in J. Reumann (ed.), *Understanding the Sacred Text* (in honour of Morton S. Enslin, Valley Forge, 1972), pp. 153ff.

answer to the second question, distortion can in fact be demonstrated, and demonstrated in the expected direction, then the existence of a dominant purpose is confirmed. A fisherman's story is *a priori* likely to be told to enhance his prowess; and if a palpable minnow comes out (not from the water, but from the story) as a sturgeon, then this intention is confirmed. But there are strict limits to the effectiveness of the method. If a definite aim is established, it still does not necessarily follow that there must be distortion. Conversely, if distortion is established, it may not invariably be due to bias, unless a whole series of distortions is detected, all pointing in the same direction. So there are many factors to be reckoned with, and it would not be wise to follow slavishly Baur's principle of requiring that the veracity of narrative material should be judged by a writer's tendency rather than by direct comparison with other sources (unless indeed the other sources are suspected of being themselves untrustworthy).[6] In this, Baur seems to have been over-reacting against D. F. Strauss's *divide et impera* methods.[7] There are many possibilities which must not be ignored. Suppose the man with whom we have to do happens to be not only a fisherman (and therefore, by definition, tempted to exaggerate) but also a modest and truthful man; in this case, he may successfully resist the temptation to elongate his minnow. And suppose he is as keen a naturalist as he is a fisherman, he will have an added reason for preferring accurate records about his catch to romances about his prowess. On the other hand, there might still be factors, not included in any of these circumstances, leading to mis-statements in his story. These are childish parables; but do but transfer them to the serious matter in hand, and it will be evident what damage can be done to scholarly judgement by the uncritical application of *Tendenzkritik* without sufficient regard for its limitations.

The thesis of Professor Brandon's *Jesus and the Zealots* (Manchester, 1967) depends on an estimate of Mark's Gospel as deliberately tendentious. Brandon believed that this Gospel was written, for use in Rome, immediately after the Flavian triumph of A.D. 71. This triumph, he believed, profoundly affected the Roman Christians: 'it brought, disturbingly, to their attention the fact that their faith stemmed from this Jewish people who had so fiercely revolted against Roman rule, and it faced them also with the serious possibility that they might be regarded by their pagan neighbours and the Roman authorities as being themselves infected with Jewish revolutionary ideas' (pp. 242f). The Gospel according to Mark reflects – so Brandon believed – the resulting embarrassment. For instance, Mark renders the disciple's name which, in Luke 6: 15 and Acts 1: 13, appears undisguisedly as Σίμων ὁ (καλούμενος) Ζηλωτής by the less

[6] *Kritische Untersuchungen*, 71ff.   [7] See Hodgson, *Historical Theology*, p. 198.

easily recognisable Aramaic form Σίμων ὁ Καναναῖος (Mark 3: 18). 'This masking of the fact', wrote Brandon, 'that one of the Twelve had been a Zealot indicates that the author of Mark was not concerned to present an accurate historical record of the career of Jesus, but that he was moved by a definite apologetical motive' (p. 245).

Such argumentation oversimplifies the matter. First, Brandon's estimate of the occasion and purpose of the writing of Mark's Gospel is by no means conclusive.[8] Starting from the assumption that Mark was written between A.D. 60 and 75 (rather than, as many – probably most – scholars would suggest, before A.D. 70), he proceeded to look for the date and occasion between these limits which seemed best to explain its contents, and lit on A.D. 71, for the reasons already indicated. But it is difficult to be sure that this is right. Is Mark's reference to the tearing in two of the veil of the Temple so obviously related to the sight of the Temple curtains (presumably intact) being carried in triumph? Were the Roman Christians oblivious, till then, of the fact that the Jews from whom their faith stemmed were openly rebellious against the Romans? The Epistle to the Romans and Acts 18: 2 (to mention no further evidence) suggests that there had for long been a large Jewish element among them, who must surely have been aware of what had been going on for so long. Again, if it was as vital as Brandon made out that Jesus should be shown as advocating the obedient payment of tribute to Caesar, why are his words in this connection as ambiguous as Brandon subsequently (pp. 345–9) makes them out to be? Brandon thinks that the original saying was a strongly pro-Zealot one, and meant that among the things *not* belonging to Caesar was Palestine, which must at all costs *not* be 'rendered' to him. But if one is going to extract this meaning from the saying at all, it is as easy to do so from the form of it which now appears in Mark; and it would surely be precarious indeed if the 'innocent' interpretation of the words could be so easily turned in a 'dangerous' direction by any hearer who was 'in the know'. Even if Brandon's answer was that the dialogue would have sounded very different in Palestine, and that Mark has de-fused it by the context in which he has set it, the argument still remains decidedly speculative.[9] Once again, if it was so important to establish that Christians were not disloyal to the emperor, why does Mark quote the seditious phrase, 'the Abomination of Desolation' at all – even if it is sufficiently oracular to be 'discreet' (p. 233)? If the presence among the Twelve of one who may (though the term does not actually prove it)[10] have

[8] See F. F. Bruce's essay, pp. 69–89 above.

[9] See F. F. Bruce's essay, pp. 249–263 below.

[10] See M. Hengel, *Die Zeloten* (Leiden, 1961), M. Borg, 'The Currency of the Term "Zealot" ', *JThSt* n.s. 22 (1971), 504ff, and M. Smith, 'Zealots and Sicarii: Their Origins and Relation', *HThR* 64 (1971), 1ff.

been a Zealot is so damaging to the Christian cause, why risk even an Aramic version of the term? If Mark 'is not concerned to present an accurate historical record', why does he trouble to preserve the offending term in any form? And why did he not, instead, call attention, in the list of the Twelve (as Brandon himself, for his own purposes, avoided doing), to the fact that they included also one who had been a collaborator – one of the tax collectors so hated by the Jews and so useful to the Romans? It suits Brandon's reading of the situation to regard as part of Mark's propaganda the whitewashing of Pilate. But it is generally agreed (and Brandon himself agrees) that, whatever Mark does to Pilate, Luke goes further in this direction. Yet Luke it is who is not embarrassed to call a Zealot a Zealot. Something seems to have gone wrong here in the interpretation of motives. If Brandon's *Sitz im Leben* for Mark were correct, Mark's Pilate ought to have been more like Luke's (or, rather, more like the Pilate of Luke's story of the trial: not the Pilate of Luke 13: 1). Conversely, if Brandon's reason for Mark's use of Καναναῖος were correct, then Luke ought also to have disguised the offensive Ζηλωτής. And if Brandon's answer were to be that, by the time Luke wrote, the word had lost its dangerous connotations (and, admittedly, Luke freely uses the word and its cognates in a non-revolutionary sense), this would need a good deal of evidence to establish it. Yet it is these unproved assumptions about the circumstances and purpose of Mark, and about his readers (or hearers), and about his readiness deliberately to misrepresent the facts, that provide the foundation on which rests Brandon's radical reconstruction of the story of Jesus. Whatever tendentiousness there may be in Mark, the evangelist does not appear to have the monopoly of it.[11] No doubt, the strength of Brandon's case is his construction of a total situation in which he can interpret Mark as he does. But so many of the links in his chain are weak that it cannot be accepted in its totality.

If one sets aside guesses as to what Mark is likely to have done, what more substantial evidence is there that Mark has misrepresented the facts? The whitewashing of Pilate has been mentioned; and even if Mark is surpassed in this direction by Luke, it might still be argued that the Pilate even of Mark is not the Pilate of Philo and Josephus (or, for that matter, of Luke 13: 1). But the issue is not as clear-cut as this.[12] In the first place, *Tendenzkritik* must, of course, be applied to Philo and Josephus, no less than to the Gospels, before it is assumed that they are right and the Gospels

---

[11] M. Hengel suggests that Brandon's method is 'a *reductio ad absurdum* of the older *Tendenzkritik*', in his review of *Jesus and the Zealots* in *JJSt* 14 (1961), 231ff (233, note 1).

[12] For a judicious estimate, with full bibliography, see E. Bammel in *RGG* 35, Spp. 383f; also W. Horbury, 'The Passion Narratives and Historical Criticism', *Theology* 75.620 (Feb. 1972), 58ff (65f).

wrong. But what a tangle of motives there is to be unravelled! Philo's account (*Legatio* 299–305), in any case, occurs in a passage purporting to be quoted from Agrippa's letter (see *Legatio* 276–93), and that is hardly likely to be unbiased. Moreover, the story in it is notoriously difficulty to reconcile with that in Josephus.[13] As for Josephus's references to Pilate,[14] it is as difficult to make allowance simultaneously for Josephus the Pharisaic Jew and Josephus the Roman collaborator as it is to give a simple account of the motives of the evangelists. And, when all is said and done, the non-Christian portraits of Pilate differ from the Christian mainly in no more than that they are explicit about his brutality (though Luke 13: 1 is explicit about this also, in another context). In the Christian accounts, it is only Luke and John who show him as having any serious concern to rescue Jesus. As for the evangelists' representation of Pilate as convinced that Jesus was not guilty, this is something that, in any case, has no parallel in Philo or Josephus, and must be judged independently; and even on this point Mark's emphasis is minimal. And even if the Barabbas story sounds implausible, it is a hasty verdict and an illegitimate use of the argument from silence[15] to declare it an apologetic fiction without more substantial evidence than that there is near silence elsewhere, and that, in general, the Gospels were probably tendentious.

At any rate, even if it were established that Mark has deliberately distorted the picture of Pilate, this would still not serve to eliminate the conflict between Jesus and the Jews as fictitious. On the contrary: it is difficult to avoid the conclusion that, before ever it came to the trial, Jesus's ministry had constituted a head-on collision with the Judaism of his day.[16] *Mutatis mutandis*, the account in the latter chapters of the Acts of Paul's position *vis-à-vis* Judaism and Rome respectively (see the summary in Acts 28: 17ff) presents a close parallel to what the Gospels, broadly speaking, suggest regarding the position of Jesus: in violent collision with many of the theological attitudes of Judaism, but politically and legally difficult to convict. And, details apart, this is perfectly plausible in both cases.

It is difficult to think where else to look in Mark for evidence of the sort of

---

[13] See E. M. Smallwood's note in her edition of the *Legatio* (Leiden, 1961), p. 291.
[14] *BJ* ii. 169–77, *AJ* xviii. 35; 55–9; 62; 64 – the *testimonium flavianum*, probably to be discounted; certainly not to be read in the Slavonic form, despite Brandon's attempt to revive Eisler's theory; 87–9; 177.
[15] See once again, G. M. Styler, pp. 101–7 below; and Horbury, *Theology* 75.620, (Feb. 1972), 66f.
[16] See H. Merkel's essay, 'The opposition between Jesus and Judaism', pp. 129–44 below; and his 'Jesus und die Pharisäer', *NTSt* 14 (1967–8), 194ff; and Horbury, *Theology* 75.620 (Feb. 1972), 64f; and D. Catchpole, 'The Problem of the Historicity of the Sanhedrin trial' in *The Trial of Jesus*, ed. E. Bammel (London, 1970), pp. 47ff (48ff).

tendentiousness postulated by Brandon. If we turn from Mark to other
New Testament writings, one instance of evident tendentiousness that
springs to mind is the devastating attack on the scribes and Pharisees in
Matthew 23. Even if it can be shown that some Pharisees were guilty of the
offences here described, it is clearly a selective and one-sided account when
judged by the ample evidence from Jewish sources about the character of
Pharisaism. It may, at least in this form, spring from a period subsequent to
the time of Jesus himself, and reflect the bitter antagonism that had sprung
up between church and synagogue in the latter decades of the first
century.[17] Much the same applies to the strictures on 'the Jews', as they are
generically called, in the Gospel according to St John. These, too, may well
reflect actual clashes with opponents of Christ or of Christians, and
epitomise the conflict between legalism generally and the Christian gospel.
Such phenomena undoubtedly point to tendencies in these writers; but it is
to be noted that the tendency is deduced not from any independent
evidence of the writer's purpose, but from the evidence of a number of
straws in the wind all blowing in the same direction: it is a matter of
tendencies detected (contrary to Baur's principle) by comparing each
relevant passage with some independent source, rather than of tendencies
deduced from knowledge (actual or alleged) of the writer's purpose. The
same seems to be true, notoriously, of the 'heightening' of Matthew's
christology, of which it is only one familiar example that when, in Mark,
Jesus appears to question his own goodness, Matthew seems deliberately to
alter the phrase:

Mark 10: 18 τί με λέγεις ἀγαθόν;

Matt. 19: 17 τί με ἐρωτᾳς περὶ τοῦ ἀγαθοῦ;

Similarly, Luke, as is well known, seems fairly consistently to reduce the
'eschatological tension' in comparison both with Mark and Matthew.[18]
(On a more trivial level and in parenthesis, it is possible that Luke is
displaying a measure of tendentiousness when he simply says (in the best
text of 8: 43) that the woman with the haemorrhage could not be cured by
anyone. Possibly they are right who think that it was the physician's
professional pride that forbade him to reproduce Mark's assertion (Mark
5: 26) that she had undergone treatment at much cost at the hands of many
doctors with no success. But that is a special and isolated instance of a
guessed *Tendenz*.)

But the main tendencies alluded to, and many besides, are detected by

---

[17] See, for a recent allusion to the question, A. F. J. Klijn, 'Jerome's quotations from a
Nazoraean Interpretation of Isaiah', *RechSR* 60 (1972), 241ff, suggesting (254) that
it is the author of Matthew who introduced the idea of hypocrisy.

[18] For a recent treatment of this theme, see J. Mánek, 'Geschichte und Gericht in der
Theologie des Lukas', *Kairos* 3–4 (1971), 243ff.

comparison with other documents, and by the frequency and consistency with which they occur, rather than deduced from generalisations about the writer's purpose. They still do not constitute examples of the successful application of the principle that events may be reconstructed by making allowance for distortion deducible from apologetic purposes. Nor, conversely, does a demonstrable mis-statement or distortion in itself constitute evidence for tendentiousness, but only (as has been said) if it is one of a series all pointing in the same direction.

These observations apply – if we now go back to the point from which we set out – to the Tübingenian estimate of the Acts. It was J. B. Lightfoot,[19] replying to the Tübingen scholars, who pointed out how little solid evidence there was for the alleged antagonism between the apostle to the Gentiles and the Jerusalem apostles, and how the assumption of the tendentiousness of Acts is thus called in question at the outset. The purpose of Acts might indeed have been to show that it was not the leaders on either side who were at variance but only the lesser men who were their adherents. But, if so, it might have been no more than the truth that it was showing. It may be added that if, contrary to Lightfoot's judgement, Galatians be assigned an early date, then certain other alleged discrepancies between Galatians and Acts also disappear. But this is not the place to pursue details of this prolonged controversy.[20] Perhaps it is, however, the place where a light-hearted aside may be permitted, calling attention to two passages in the Acts where the author seems deliberately to be giving an account of tendentiousness in others. In the story of Paul's arrest in Acts 21, the Roman commandant (whose name, it subsequently transpires, was Claudius Lysias) discovers only after the arrest – and that by chance and to his great surprise, when he is on the verge of having Paul beaten – that Paul is a Roman citizen. But the letter that Lysias is represented as writing to Felix when he sends Paul on to him in chapter 23 says (verse 27): 'This man was seized by the Jews and was on the point of being murdered when I intervened with the troops and removed him *because I discovered that he was a Roman citizen.*' The NEB is surely right in so translating the last clause: it would need the most improbable syntactical gymnastics to extort from μαθὼν ὅτι ʻΡωμαῖός ἐστιν any other tense-sequence; which means that Lysias is deftly represented by the narrator as claiming for himself more merit than the facts warranted: a surreptitious little bit of tendentiousness

---

[19] See, for instance, J. B. Lightfoot's famous dissertation on 'St Paul and the Three' in his commentary on Galatians (8th edn London, 1884), pp. 292ff; with interesting comments by C. K. Barrett in 'Joseph Barber Lightfoot', *The Durham University Journal* 64, 3 (n.s. 33.3) (June, 1972), 193ff.

[20] See F. F. Bruce, 'Galatian Problems. 4. The Date of the Epistle', *BJRL* 54.2 (Spring 1972), 250ff.

in one of the *dramatis personae*. Whether we are to believe that it was itself tendentiously introduced by Luke, who can say? It certainly looks like an example of the novelist's imaginative characterisation, which may or may not have been true to life, but is certainly plausible. The other passage is in Acts 25: 20, where Festus is represented as telling King Agrippa that he had asked Paul whether he would like to go to Jerusalem to be tried, *because Festus was at a loss* (ἀπορούμενος) over details of Jewish religion and over Paul's assertions about the aliveness of Jesus. But the narrative in 25: 9 had already made it clear that Festus's real reason for suggesting that Paul should go to Jerusalem was to win favour with the Jews, who wanted him sent to Jerusalem because they were plotting to assassinate Paul on the way (cp. verse 3).

Actually, when it comes to attempting to assess the motives of New Testament writers, there are not very many instances involving the narration of events when one may be quite sure of them. Nobody can doubt that in the little piece of narrative in Gal. 2: 3–5 Paul is struggling hard to establish a point which evidently had been and was being contested. We can no longer be certain whether Titus was or was not circumcised; but, whichever it was, Paul is evidently telling the story in order to make it plain that it in no way undermines the case for the freedom of the Gentiles. But it so happens that, whereas we are certain that he had this aim and held to it with passionate feeling, it is almost equally certain that he could hardly have distorted the facts, even if he had wished to, without being detected and ruining his cause. Here, then, is a case of known apologetic intention where the corollary of tendentiousness is resisted by the circumstances. There are few other passages of the New Testament involving the narration of events that can be decisively furnished with a purpose. If Brandon's arguments from contents are not conclusive, there is no support from tradition for the view that Mark's Gospel was written as apologetic to exculpate Christians from complicity in the Jewish revolt. Papias's hackneyed words state that Mark's aim was to record fully and accurately what Peter had said.[21] The newly-discovered fragment attributed to Clement of Alexandria contradicts the 'fully', saying rather that the Gospel represents only a selection of Peter's reminiscences, intended for the use of beginners.[22] But in both cases, the motive ascribed to the writer is simply to preserve traditions. Luke's Gospel (and, by implication, the Acts) claims for itself accurate investigation and declares the intention of instructing the reader (1: 3f). John's Gospel states for itself an evangelistic purpose (20: 31). The epistles (including those, such as the Epistle to the Hebrews, which may be more in the nature of treatises or homilies than of

---

[21] *Apud* Euseb. *H.E.* 3.39.15   [22] See F. F. Bruce, above pp. 88f.

normal letters) are clearly written with pastoral intentions. And the Apocalypse, too, is pastoral, aiming at fortifying those who are under stress and whose faith is in jeopardy. But in only a very few passages of the epistles and the Apocalypse is there narrative in which the course of history is at issue; and the method of *Tendenzkritik*, as originally applied by the Tübingen scholars, is therefore, to that extent, scarcely applicable here.

In sum, the technique of making allowance for distortions due to apologetic intentions, right and necessary though it is in principle, requires to be used with the utmost reserve because of the number and the complexity of the factors entering into each situation in actual life, and because of the large element of guesswork that therefore enters into the method. The instances where a New Testament writer's intentions (beyond the general intention to glorify Jesus Christ) can be ascertained with virtual certainty are rare; and even then it must not be assumed, without further evidence, that he has allowed his intentions to distort his representation of the facts. It is safer (*pace* Baur and Brandon) to stick to such direct evidence as may be available for testing his accuracy, and to deduce his tendency, if such there be, from the repeated and consistent occurrence of demonstrable distortion or selectiveness, rather than from speculations about his purpose.

Argumentum e silentio

The title of this note might perhaps be better in the plural: *argumenta e silentio*. It is not only that Dr Brandon draws attention to a number of instances of a surprising silence in the ancient sources, both Jewish and Christian. It must also be noticed that silence can be interpreted in more ways than one, and that different lines of interpretation rely for their force upon a different logic. It is with a brief glance at the different logical principles that we will begin.

First, there is the *direct* argument, which uses the silence of a witness to cast doubt upon an alleged, or otherwise attested, fact. It may be schematised like this:

(*a*)   X makes no mention of y;
(*b*)   X would surely have known y, if it were true;
(*c*)   he would surely have mentioned y;
therefore y is not true.[1]

This is the *argumentum e silentio* proper, and it is to this class that the chief arguments to be examined belong.

But secondly, there is also the *reverse* argument, which uses an alleged or agreed fact to cast doubt upon the integrity of a witness who is silent about it. In schematic form it runs like this:

(*a*)   X makes no mention of y;
(*b*)   and X must surely have known y;
(*c*)   and he ought surely to have mentioned it; therefore,
(*d*)   since y is a well-attested fact, or well-established inference, his silence is due to deliberate concealment.

Both the direct and the reverse argument are in principle sound. Whether in practice they will carry conviction will depend on the soundness of the individual links, (*a*), (*b*), (*c*) and (*d*). But if anyone employs both forms there is obviously a danger, if not exactly of circular reasoning, at least of an attempt to 'have it both ways', by using the same writer's silences positively at one time, that is, on the assumption of his general reliability, and negatively at another, that is, to impugn his reliability. Of course, both arguments may be in practice justified. But if so that will be because the individual links and the judgements of which these consist are

---

[1] Or 'probably not true' etc., according to the strength of the conviction with which (*a*), (*b*) and (*c*) are asserted.

sound. As far as logical form is concerned, it will often be possible for someone else, taking a different selection from the evidence as his starting-point, to employ the arguments from silence to reach the opposite conclusion.

Thus – to compress his long and careful reasoning into skeleton form – Dr Brandon holds (i) that the partial or complete silence of the earliest sources (Mark and Q) in respect of any open repudiation by Jesus of the Zealot outlook is to be interpreted *directly*, that is, as evidence that he did not repudiate it; (ii) that the small pieces of evidence which can be interpreted as indicating that Jesus in some measure shared that outlook should be handled in terms of what I have called the 'reverse argument', that is, they have been deliberately played down because of the writers' apologetic interests; and (iii) that any indisputable criticisms of the Zealot outlook should likewise be interpreted by the reverse argument, that is, ascribed to apologetic motives.

As far as formal validity goes, however, one could start from the opposite end: (i) the slimness of the evidence for the contention that Jesus accepted the Zealot outlook could be taken *positively*, and (ii) the silence of Mark (partial or complete) about his repudiation of it could be explained on the grounds that it was not necessary for him to emphasise it, or not part of his purpose.

Prima facie, either approach is legitimate. In other words, the mere silence of witnesses on a vital point is open to more than one interpretation. Dr Brandon is well aware that an *argumentum e silentio* will by itself prove very little, and he addresses himself very carefully to all the relevant considerations which must be assessed before a silence can be properly interpreted. No criticism of his basic logic is here intended; all that is claimed is that with equal logic a different reconstruction is possible.

Granted then that it is logically proper to employ arguments from silence in more ways than one, it will be seen that it is on the strength of what I have called the intermediate links that the validity of these arguments will depend. Each of these has to be established, and tested; any of them may be open to attack by an opponent. Thus – to pick up the letters used in the schematic version of the arguments given at the beginning of this note – it must be asked:

(*a*)   Is X's alleged silence established?

(*b*)   Might not X have been *ignorant* of y?

(*c*)   Might not X have omitted to mention y?

(*d*)   Is y sufficiently well established?[2]

A full examination of each of these intermediate links would range over

---

[2] (*d*) figures in the 'reverse' argument only.

the whole of Dr Brandon's case, in which he takes great pains in trying to establish each one; other essays in this collection examine individual points in detail. What is emphasised here is that arguments from silence cannot stand in isolation; they take their place and have their force in conjunction with the discussion, interpretation, and evaluation of every relevant piece of evidence and argument.

It will perhaps be of interest to proceed now to a brief summary of the main lines of investigation followed by Dr Brandon in which some use is made of the silence of witnesses. As will be seen, in some cases the silence is interpreted by the direct argument, in others by the 'reverse' argument.

(1) Josephus tells us much about revolutionary activities and the fate of bandits in the period before A.D. 66, but refrains from suggesting that the Zealot movement was clearly defined with an established and honourable place in the outlook and lives of the people. Philo and Agrippa, on whose evidence he purports to draw, are similarly reticent. Brandon uses the reverse argument here, and attributes the silence to motives of apologetic and prudence.

(2) Luke–Acts likewise contains a number of references to revolutionaries, often muddled but substantially authentic; but at several points where the politico-revolutionary background must almost certainly have been relevant to the experience of the Christian community (e.g. in connection with Agrippa I, with Cuspius Fadus, and Cumanus), Acts gives no hint of their impact on the Christian community, nor yet of the Christians' attitude towards them. Again, Dr Brandon applies the 'reverse' argument, and contends that the writer's apologetic motives have led him to conceal or to play down some embarrassing facts.

(3) The full importance of Peter and his missionary work is not adequately set out in our sources. Grounds for suspicion are found in numerous passages. For example, what was the 'other place' to which Peter went, according to Acts 12:17? Why does Mark say nothing of his restoration by the risen Christ? Why does Paul skate so lightly over what Peter did and taught? By the 'reverse' argument, Dr Brandon ascribes all such lacunae to embarrassment and deliberate concealment. Similarly we are told much less than we should like about James the Lord's brother. Indeed, if we had to reply on Acts alone we should not know that he *was* the Lord's brother. Our sources give us little or no direct and reliable evidence for the theological tenets of the Jerusalem Christians. What we can reconstruct by oblique inference suggests that all our extant writings, when they have not distorted these tenets, have concealed them.

(4) At the heart of Dr Brandon's thesis is his contention that, contrary to general Christian estimate and to a certain strand in the New Testament

itself, Jesus did not openly and definitely repudiate the outlook of zealotism; that, far from repudiating it, some of his actions and above all his execution by the Romans on the charge of sedition compel us to see him as, at least in some measure, in sympathy with it. With Dr Brandon's positive arguments we are not here concerned. What we here note is his use of the 'direct' argument from silence: viz. his claim that Mark, in contrast with passages in the later gospels, does not portray Jesus as openly repudiating the use of force and resistance to Rome. At most he does so by implication. The contrast with passages in the later gospels is significant, and highlights Mark's silence. So too, he claims, is the contrast between the strong criticism which the Jesus of Mark levels against the Jewish groups – against the Pharisees, the Sadducees, and the Herodians – and his silence concerning the Zealots.

(5) Similarly, Dr Brandon claims that the other early traditions of Jesus's teaching (i.e. what is generally denoted as Q) contain no evidence of the 'pacific' Christ. The main passages which explicitly portray him as 'pacific' are found only in the later gospels, and are independent additions to the tradition.[3]

(6) Finally, separate mention should be made of Mark's omission to supply a translation of the word 'Cananaean'. Dr Brandon uses the reverse argument here, and holds that, contrary to his usual practice, Mark gives no translation, because he does not want to draw attention to the fact that one of Jesus's disciples was a member of the Zealot party.

Out of these instances of the argument from silence it will be seen that items 1, 2, 3, and 6 employ the 'reverse' argument, and items 4 and 5 the direct argument. As has already been said, an answer to these arguments would have to cover as many points as Dr Brandon covers in his advocacy of them; and some of this is attempted in other essays. In particular it may be noticed that much will depend on what was listed as point (c) on page 101, viz. how strong is the expectation that the writer who is in fact silent *ought* to have spoken, and how strong is his alleged motive for concealment? But an attempt to answer the most direct use of the argument from silence is called for here, and it is to this that the final section of this note is devoted.

How complete, then, *is* the silence of the most important witnesses on the vital points? The three witnesses to be re-examined are Paul, Mark, and Q; and the vital points are those that define the traditional picture of Jesus as one who is essentially opposed to the use of violence for the sake of asserting one's rights. If that picture is basically veridical, then, whatever affection

---

[3] Cp. especially Matt. 5: 3, 5, 9; 26: 52–4; Luke 9: 52–6; 13: 1–3; 19: 38b, 42; 22: 51; 23: 34; John 18: 36–7.

Jesus doubtless had for Israel and its national heritage, it follows that he would ultimately be opposed to Zealot activism. To those brought up in the ordinary tradition it comes as a shock to find that this picture of Jesus is under suspicion of being a forgery, made for the purposes of political apologetic, or to underpin a non-historical religious myth. To many it will remain inconceivable – however the battle of scholarly argument turns out – that this picture of Jesus can be anything but a true picture of one who was uniquely creative, inconceivable that it could have been put together by accident and coincidence out of apologetic motives. Such judgements are of course 'subjective'. But perhaps 'intuitive' would be a better word to describe them. 'Subjective' has become a pejorative word, and is too often used to denote a judgement that is hasty or ill-considered. But the intuition which recognises in the traditional picture of Jesus something that is both unique and compelling is neither hasty nor ill-considered. At any rate, the widespread assurance that the character of Jesus is of priceless worth does at the least demand that Dr Brandon's assertions and arguments should be subjected to criticism as rigorous as he has applied to the New Testament.

The evidence of Paul ought not to be too quickly dismissed as irrelevant. It is true that the harvest of biographical information about Jesus from Paul's epistles is meagre. But the testimony to his essential *character* is steady and convincing.[4] Even on the traditional view it is *remarkable* how brightly the character of Jesus shines through in Paul's own ethical principles and teachings. It is certainly '*remarkable*', in view of the fact that Paul had not been a disciple of Jesus; but it is not *incredible*, given that Paul did receive the Christian tradition. What to the present writer *would* be incredible is that Paul, or his Hellenistic–Christian predecessors, should first have invented a soteriology out of the fact of the cross, and then have constructed this picture of Jesus to underpin that soteriology. If the soteriology alone could win converts, why bother to invent the picture? And if the picture is as old as the soteriology, where could it have originated, except in Jesus himself?

The evidence of Mark is twofold. First, there is the passage about the tribute-money.[5] Dr Brandon argues that the logion 'Render unto Caesar . . .' stood originally by itself and bore the meaning that no Israelite should concede to a pagan ruler the obedience due only to God, that is, it advocated *resistance*; and that Mark has reversed the original meaning by

---

[4] Cp. e.g., Rom. 12: 14–21; 13: 1; 15: 1f; 1 Cor. 2: 16; 9 (not asserting one's rights); together with 11: 1; 13; 2 Cor. 10: 1; Eph. 4: 2, 20f; Phil. 2: 1ff; Col. 3: 12–15. There is little to be gained by examining every passage in detail, although the *quantity* of the evidence is important to the argument. The argument has been vividly stated in the form: 'The picture of ἀγάπη painted by Paul in 1 Cor. 13 is *not* a self-portrait.'
[5] See pp. 241–63 below.

giving it its present setting. Against this, it must be argued that the concentration of attention on an actual imperial coin clearly guarantees a positive teaching that taxes *ought* to be paid, and by implication that Roman rule should not be resisted; and that this very concentration on the coin and its inscription will seem to many, as it does to the present writer, to be highly characteristic of Jesus himself, and his concrete approach to abstract questions. It is hard to believe in either the ingenuity or the perversity which Dr Brandon's suggestion ascribes to Mark.

Secondly there is the constant teaching of the divine necessity that the Son of man must suffer. It is possible, of course, along with Dr Brandon and many scholars, to *impugn* this evidence, to see it as a Pauline or post-Pauline construction, and to deny that Jesus, if he predicted his death, ever did so in these theological terms. But at least it is clear that *Mark* is not silent about Jesus's central convictions. And if there is an essential germ of truth[6] in this picture of Jesus's understanding of his vocation, then that confirms the traditional picture of his character.

The estimate we make, then, of Mark's silence will depend on a number of things: how complete we deem that silence to be, how far the exceptions to it can be explained away as motivated apologetically, and how far the situation in Jesus's own lifetime must have compelled him to speak openly if he wished to dissociate himself from revolutionary sympathies. Dr Brandon contrasts Jesus's silence here with his open denunciation of Pharisees, Sadducees, and Herodians. He is right in saying that the Jesus of Mark openly criticises the Pharisees; but his attitude to the Herodians is less plain,[7] and his attitude to the Sadducees emerges scarcely more frequently than his attitude to revolutionaries.

The kernel of any reply to Dr Brandon must be a defence of the traditional view that Jesus urged a religious dependence on God which treated human establishments, rights, and loyalties as secondary. Sometimes the details of what is implied are spelt out; but the context in which this is done is accidental, and the implications for any one range of human activity may be made plain only in one passage, and that may be one that occurs in only one gospel.

It is when we turn to examine the Q-material that Dr Brandon's case

---

[6] If the predictions of his death are retained, but radically rewritten, then of course a different inference will be indicated. But what happens on a *modest* rewriting of them? E.g., if Jesus predicted that he must die, in line with the fate of prophets before him, but without explicit reference to the details, or to the deeper theological meaning? Dr Brandon seems to me to be too quick in identifying loyalty to the prophetic ideas with a pro-Zealot outlook. Surely Jeremiah and Deutero-Isaiah might warrant a different estimate.

[7] As against *their* attitude to him. What is 'the leaven of Herod' (Mark 8: 15)? The answer is not obvious.

seems most vulnerable. True, it gives no explicit disavowal of the use of force in revolutionary situations. But the general injunctions of the spirit of love are so strongly expressed that the pacific implications are surely inescapable. 'Love your enemies; do good to those who hate you; bless those who curse you; pray for those who treat you spitefully. When a man hits you on the cheek, offer him the other cheek too; when a man takes your coat, let him have your shirt as well.'[8] Even Q, of course, is not immune from criticism and the suspicion that the genuine sayings of Jesus have been amplified in subsequent tradition. But in the passage quoted the present writer cannot doubt that we are hearing words that substantially represent the mind of Jesus, and that are incompatible with active zealotism. Q at least has broken silence.

[8] Luke 6: 27–9; cp. Matt. 5: 44 and 5: 39–40.

E. BAMMEL

The Poor and the Zealots

The economic conditions of Palestine were marked by a sharp rise in prosperity in the Hasmonaean period and a decline in the middle of the first century B.C., caused by the civil wars, the Roman intervention with its financial burden, and the remigration of such Jews as had been settled by the Hasmonaeans in territories which were separated again from the Jewish commonwealth by the Romans. The rule of Herod, the son of the financial ἐπίτροπος of the last Hasmonaean, meant a sophistication of the taxation system and, perhaps, an increase of the levy, but, by and large, a slow rise in prosperity. The many public edifices which were erected under Herod indicate the existence of certain financial resources and the new possibility of long-term commitments. The expansion of certain crafts and, indeed, the new establishment of others[1] must have been the consequence of this building wave. The economic situation was such that no special reason for discontent existed. The same is true for the Roman period. The new valuation of property,[2] a certain alteration in the fiscal system,[3] caused discontent, but there is no substantial evidence for an increase in the burden on the population.[4] Occasional sequestrations, like the appropriation of Temple-money for the improvement of the water supply of Jerusalem,[5] were for the benefit of the people, and major wars, such as would have demanded the use of the resources of Palestine, did not take place.[6] The pilgrimages, which were very important especially for Jerusalem,[7] are likely to have increased considerably in the times of the *Pax Augusta*. The conditions were different in the tetrarchy of Antipas, the wealth of which was minimal compared with that of the Roman province,[8]

<hr/>

[1] Cp. H. Kreissig, *Die sozialen Zusammenhänge des judäischen Krieges, Schriften zur Geschichte und Kultur der Antike* i (Berlin, 1970), 58.

[2] E. Stauffer, *Die Dauer des Census Augusti Festschrift E. Klostermann*, TU 77 (Berlin, 1961), pp. 9ff. Cp. A. Granovsky, *Land Taxation in Palestine* (Jerusalem, 1927).

[3] The details mentioned in Ket. 17:16 and B.B. 127b may reflect this.

[4] The corruption of the Roman administration (for Syria in the time of Tiberius see Tacitus, *Ann.* ii. 43) was probably more than matched by the decrease in costly donations to foreign countries, which was so very typical of the Herodian style of rule.

[5] *BJ* 2 §175ff.

[6] The removal of the threat of war by the agreement between the Romans and Parthians in 37 A.D. is of the greatest importance.

[7] J. Jeremias, *Jerusalem zur Zeit Jesu*, 3rd edn. (Göttingen, 1969), pp. 89–98 (ET London, 1969, pp. 77–84).

[8] H. Hoehner, *Herod Antipas* (Cambridge, 1972), pp. 65ff.

while Antipas nevertheless had to try to keep up the pattern of expenses set by his father.

The famine at the end of the forties, aggravated by the preceding Sabbath year,[9] and the uncertainty of communications, conditioned by the guerilla warfare of the *sicarii*,[10] are likely to have resulted in a certain economic decline. The completion of the Temple in A.D. 64 meant the redundancy of a great number of skilled workers and posed short-term economic problems. The only strike of which we know, however, is an action taken by the bakers of Temple bread and makers of incense.[11]

In fact the social condition of the Poor was not comparable with that of similar social strata in the surrounding countries.[12] The soil was not βασιλική χώρα but private property.[13] The peasants were not just λαοί, labourers without legal titles to land, but *personae*. The position had been different in Galilee, where the country had been divided between Hellenistic cities and royal estates in Seleucid times.[14] The conquest by the Hasmonaeans meant on the one side the dissolution of the city constitutions and on the other an improvement of the situation of the indigenous[15] rural population.[16]

True, a certain part of the land became the private property of the Herodians, and the majority of this was subsequently sold by the Romans.[17]

[9] Jeremias, *Jerusalem*, p. 159 (ET, p. 142), Whether these episodes had a more far-reaching effect on first-century Palestine than previous events still awaits investigation.

[10] This is stressed, perhaps even over-emphasised, by Josephus.

[11] According to Jeremias, *Jerusalem*, p. 27 (ET, p. 25), the only social movement at this time.

[12] The economic conditions resulting in comparative calmness, as they are presupposed in the Gospels, are much closer akin to those of the reformed period of the Roman *Kolonat* than to those of the Orient or of pre-Spartacus Rome. To conclude from this that the Gospels reflect Roman conditions rather than Palestinian ones, as was done by A. Kalthoff (*Die Entstehung des Christentums* (Leipzig, 1904), pp. 42f; ET pp. 54f), is wrongheaded.

[13] Kreissig, *Zusammenhänge*, pp. 26f; E. Bickermann, *Les Institutions des Seleucides* (Paris, 1938), p. 179. One-sided and not very clearly-developed views are expressed by H. G. Kippenberg, *Religion und Klassenbildung im antiken Judäa* (Göttingen, 1978), pp. 106ff. For the conditions after the Jewish war, cp. A. ben-David, *Talmudische Oekonomie* (Hildesheim, 1974), pp. 58ff.

[14] A. Alt, *Kleine Schriften* ii (München, 1953), pp. 408f.

[15] The opinion of W. Bauer (*Festgabe für Ad. Jülicher*, Tübingen, 1927, p. 21), that a judaisation of Galilee was impossible because of lack of settlers, is not supported by evidence. For the most recent discussion, cp. E. M. Meyers, 'The Cultural Setting of Galilee: The Case of Regionalism and Early Judaism' in *Aufstieg und Niedergang der römischen Welt* ii (Berlin, 1970), 686–702.

[16] The alliance between the Hasmonaeans and the penniless rural population which is stressed so much by W. W. Buehler, *The Pre-Herodean Civil War and Social Debate* (Basel, 1974), p. 67, may be partly due to this factor. This segment of the population was, however, much more prone to being attracted to messianic figures.

[17] Jos. *AJ* 18 §2.

But this happened under conditions which were more favourable for husbandmen and tenants than in the surrounding countries.[18] The number of smallholdings was comparatively large. This means that the percentage of those who were dependent either as tenants or as casual labourers was reduced in proportion. Slaves, at least Jewish slaves, were rare. Rural unrest was less motivated than in most countries of the Mediterranean world.

Nevertheless, Jewish literature is aware of the social differences as well as of the unnatural state of the Poor. The consciousness is kept alive by the memory of the Deuteronomic legislation, according to which the land was to be divided anew into equal allotments after fifty years, and is conditioned by the experience – spelled out chiefly in the Psalms[19] – that God is especially the God of the Poor. Thus those who were in a less destitute position than the corresponding classes in the neighbouring countries were able to give voice to their grievances in the knowledge of the divine assistance; and on the other side, whatever oppression existed in the Jewish commonwealth, it could not be carried to extremes, because even the oppressors were aware of the divine promises for the Poor. It is due to this almost unique conjunction of circumstances that something like a movement of the Poor could arise in Palestine, while the rest of the Orient remained silent and the Occident was shaken by uprisings of a purely economic nature.

The expression of their discontent is traceable only here and there,[20] testifying both to a subliterary status of the Poor and to the inseparable amalgam of social consciousness with other, religious, themes. The first document is derived from the end of the second century B.C., after the end of the Maccabaean wars and the emergence of a new and disappointing establishment. Incorporated in the Book of Sirach (13: 17ff), it is a piece on its own.[21] It states plainly that there is nothing in common between rich and poor, that there exists no κοινωνία between them (verse 15),[22] a

---

[18] A different view is taken by F. C. Grant, *The Economic Background of the Gospels* (Oxford, 1926), pp. 11f. Cp. A. Oppenheimer, *The 'Am Ha-aretz'. A Study in the social history of the Jewish people in the Hellenistic-Roman Period* (Leiden, 1977). There is no evidence for the assumption of H. G. Kippenberg and G. Theissen (*Soziologie der Jesusbewegung* (München 1977), p. 42 (ET London 1979, p. 41); it is an otherwise interesting sketch) that the sale resulted in an increase of social tension.

[19] Very characteristic is Ps. 145: 7–9: ἀδικούμενοι, πεινῶντες, πεπεδημένοι, κατερραγμένοι, τυφλοί, δίκαιοι, προσήλυτοι, ὀρφανός, χήρα.

[20] E.g. most strikingly in the Qumran pesher to Ps. 37.

[21] It is framed by a passage that gives casuistic advice (13: 9) at the beginning and comes out with a qualified support for wealth at the end (13: 24); a different view is taken by G. Wohlenberg, 'Jesus Sirach und die soziale Frage', *Neue kirchliche Zeitschrift* viii (1897), 342.

[22] (= חבורה); that means that *Volksgemeinschaft* does not exist any longer between them.

characterisation of class disruption that is highlighted by the fact that it starts off with the citation of the Stoic phrase: *homo homini amicus* (13: 15), and goes on to emphasise that, contrary to this, the poor man is like an ὄναγρος in the desert which is the prey of the lion[23] and even considered as a βδέλυγμα by the rich.[24] The passage, which disagrees with the whole outlook of Wisdom literature,[25] seems to have been taken from a manifesto of those who consider themselves as πτωχοί and at the same time as εὐσεβεῖς and ταπεινοί.

It is this intertwining of social and religious language that becomes typical for this literature. Characteristic are Enoch 109ff and Ps. Sol. with their equation of πτωχοί and ὅσιοι. The conviction that the Poor are the very tool of God finds its most thoroughgoing and forceful expression in the statement of *Ass. Mos.* 1: 12: the world was created because of the *plebs* (= *Amme ha-arez*).[26]

Formulations similar to those of the Book of Enoch occur in the Magnificat of Luke 1,[27] a passage that belongs to a set of stories on the birth of the Baptist,[28] the speaker of which is thought to have been originally Elizabeth the mother of John.[29] The social radicalism[30] of these verses is in

[23] So already Job 24: 5. The enemy of God is pictured as a lion in 1QHod. 5: 7–19; cp. Achikar 2: 57.

[24] Is this a phrase used by the rich who branded the poor as an element inimically disposed towards the present order?

[25] Cp. *ThWNT* vi 893f (ET vi, 894f).

[26] It is not necessary to smooth away the stern saying by suggesting a conjecture (as has been done by C. Clemen in his edition, *Die Himmelfahrt des Mose* (Bonn, 1904), p. 5). There is some truth in the famous statement of Nietzsche: 'In dieser Umkehrung der Werte (zu der es gehört, das Wort "arm" als synonym für "heilig" und "Freund" zu brauchen) liegt die Bedeutung des jüdischen Volks: mit ihm beginnt der Sklaven-Aufstand in der Moral' (*Jenseits von Gut and Böse*, Aphorismus 195).

[27] Luke 1: 53 is given by sy^cs in the form: he has filled the poor with his goodness and despised the rich, since they are empty (translated according to A. Merx, *Die vier kanonischen Evangelien nach ihrem ältesten bekannten Texte* (Berlin, 1897), p. 106. F. C. Burkitt, *Evangelion da-Mepharreshe* (Cambridge, 1904), ad. loc., regards the second half of the sentence as corrupt. The spiritualising reading is certainly secondary, but is possibly a parallel version that goes back to an early (cp. Rev. 3: 17), perhaps even pre-Christian period. The *Opus imperfectum in Matthaeum*, which derives from Italy, also reads: *pauperes impleuit bonis* (*PL* 56. 809).

[28] M. Dibelius, *Die urchristliche Ueberlieferung von Johannes dem Täufer* (Göttingen, 1911), pp. 67ff.

[29] The derivation of the Psalm of Mary from the Baptist tradition is made certain by the parallels Luke 1: 68ff and the prehistory and composition of Protoluke, independently of the reading 'Elisabeth' emphasised by A. van Harnack, 'Das Magnificat der Elisabet (Luk. 1, 46–55) nebst einigen Bemerkungen zu Luk. 1 und 2', *SBA* (1900), pp. 538ff; reprinted in *Studien zur Geschichte des Neuen Testaments und der alten Kirche* (Berlin, 1931), 62ff; cp. A. Meyer, *Das Rätsel des Jakobusbriefes*, (1930), p. 149, n. 3; H. Sahlin, *Der Messias und das Gottesvolk, Acta Seminarii Neotest. Upsaliensis* xii (1945), pp. 159ff; a different interpretation in L. Goppelt, *ThWNT* vi, 17 n. 43 (ET vi, 17 n. 43). On the possibility of an earlier origin, which would not

keeping with the tenor of what is, according to tradition, the general preaching of the Baptist,[31] whereas the special advice in Luke 3: 10–15 is so much of a piece with Luke's own social teaching that it can only be regarded as the evangelist's replacement of something that was more radical in character[32] and offensive to the ears of the Roman government.[33] The Baptist's attack against Antipas can be seen as a symbolic action in imitation of Phineas the Zealot. Confirmation for this is to be found in Josephus. His report, which states that a wider audience (ἄλλοι) became excited (ἤρθησαν)[34] and that it was possible to interpret the call βαπτισμῷ συνιέναι[35] as an undertaking that constitutes *nouarum rerum cupiditas* and might lead to ἀπόστασις and μεταβολή, makes sense only if the Baptist's preaching contained elements of the kind that is indicated in the Gospels.

The Zealot movement,[36] which – according to Josephus at least – arose in A.D. 6, immediately aimed at the consent and co-operation of the masses by focussing their resistance on the valuation of property (for the purpose of taxation) and the counting of the population. Social unrest, quite apart from the theological argumentation,[37] was bound to have been stirred up by this – Simon is said to have already destroyed the mansions of the wealthy.[38] The guerilla actions, carried out in the open countryside, depended equally on some kind of assistance given by the rural population. The social side of the activity is emphasised by the fact that one of the first actions carried out by the insurgents in Jerusalem in A.D. 66 consisted in setting fire to the archives where the deeds of loans were deposited, inciting thereby the

exclude handing down via and elaboration by Baptist circles, cp. Meyer, *Das Rätsel*, and P. Winter, 'Magnificat and Benedictus – Maccabaean Psalms?', *BJRL* 37 (1954), 328ff.

[30] For the reversal theology cp. D. L. Mealand, *Poverty and Expectation in the Gospels* (London, 1980), pp. 41ff. It must, however, be emphasised that the dominant forces in Judaism moved away from this position. Targ. Is. 53. 9 states that the wealthy will be an object of contempt, while nothing is said of the exaltation of the Poor. Syriac Baruch 70: 4 goes so far as to maintain that the preference given to the Poor will be a sign of the eschatological woes, which means a negative feature.

[31] His audience is the masses (Mark 1: 5; Matt. 11: 7), not the leaders (Mark 11: 27ff).

[32] Cp. *NTSt* 18 (1971/72), 105f. Kreissig's interpretation of the passage misses the point completely.

[33] For Luke's caution in this respect see W. H. C. Frend, *Martyrdom and Persecution in the Early Church* (Oxford, 1965), pp. 151ff.

[34] For this reading see W. Brandt, *Die jüdischen Baptismen*, BZAW 18 (1910), p. 145.

[35] Cp. E. Lohmeyer, *Das Urchristentum* i (Göttingen, 1932), 31f.

[36] For the problem of the priority of the *sicarii* and their relation to the Zealots see G. Baumbach, 'Zeloten und Sikarier', *ThLZ* 90 (1965), col. 727ff; *Die antirömischen Aufstandsgruppen* (in J. Maier and J. Schreiner, *Literatur und Religion des Frühjudentums* (Würzburg, 1973), pp. 273ff), and recently M. Hengel, *Josephus-Studien. Festschrift O. Michel* (Göttingen, 1974), pp. 175ff.

[37] Material in M. Hengel, *Die Zeloten* (Leiden, 1961), pp. 132ff.

[38] Josephus, *BJ*, 2 §57.

ἄποροι against the εὔποροι.[39] Their leader could be characterised as an οἰκεῖος δῆμιος.[40] Simon b. Giora, one of the leaders of the last phase of the rebellion, managed to gather a following by promising freedom to the slaves.[41]

It is evident that the currents of social unrest that existed in Israel were swallowed up by the Zealots. There is, however, no evidence that the terminology of the theology of the Poor played any role in their argument. On the contrary, the very fact that it was not before the end of the Bar-Kochba rebellion that a re-emergence of the πτωχός-consciousness, albeit with a significant change,[42] is noticeable among those who had been the activists, indicates that the ways of Zealots and the Poor had parted in the preceding period.

In the meantime the theology of the Poor was adopted by the Judaeo-Christians. This had already happened in Jerusalem in the first decades of the Christian church[43] and became a constituent factor in the outlook of that branch of Christendom. Such a phenomenon is intelligible only if there existed no other movement that seized upon the terminology of the Poor. It is reasonable to suppose that such elements among the Poor as did not agree with the activism of the Zealots found shelter, a new perspective and at the same time receptivity towards their own ideology in certain communities of nascent Christianity.

II

The problem of a possible influence on nascent Christianity consists of two questions: firstly, whether early Christianity emerged from those levels of society[44] and whether it in turn tried to influence them; and secondly,

---

[39] Ibid. 2 §427.   [40] Ibid. 2 §443.

[41] Ibid. 4 §508. Does Josephus apply a *topos*? For an interpretation of the passage cp. O. Michel, 'Studien zu Josephus. Simon bar Giora', *NTSt* 14 (1967/68), 402f; M. Hengel, *Gewalt und Gewaltlosigkeit* (Tübingen, 1971), pp. 30, 59f. (ET London, 1975, pp. 59f).

[42] It is מסכנותא = serfdom, not צניה = poverty, that is seen by Akiba as the state of Israel that indicates the impending salvation.

[43] Cp. *ThWNT* vi, 908, 911–13 (ET vi, 908, 912–14).

[44] Galilee had become notorious as the hotbed of nationalist unrest already at the beginning of Herod's reign, and continued to gain equal fame when the Romans took over (cp. E. Stauffer, *Jerusalem und Rom* (Bern, 1957), pp. 81f). The fact that some of the disciples of Jesus had names which commemorated the Maccabaean heroes shows that tendencies of this kind had taken root in the population. This does not, however, mean that everyone in Galilee was ready to support zealotism actively. The fact that Jesus started his preaching in synagogues, that is to say in essentially Pharisaic institutions, and that his argumentation is directed towards the Pharisees and against Pharisaic accusations shows that it was this world and climate that was his starting-point. The remark in Luke according to which

whether leaders of the church had special connections with political activists.

The indications given in the gospels on the first followers of Jesus point to the lower stratum[45] of independent or at least semi-independent professions,[46] without entirely excluding other spheres (Mark 2: 14; Luke 8: 3; John 18: 15).[47] The conclusion that they therefore represented the piety of the Anawins is mistaken.[48] Nor can the followers characterised by the term προσδεχόμενοι (Luke 2: 25, 38; Mark 15: 43) be brought into close association with this movement.

There is more evidence for some kind of a connection with the Zealots. Judas Iscariot was, according to the plausible suggestion of Wellhausen, a *sicarius*.[49] Simon is called Καναναῖος, a word that probably equals Zealot. Instead of Thaddaeus the name Judas Zelotes[50] is used in *abh* and some

---

προσδεχόμενοι were among the associates of Jesus's parents – a detail which is a more integral part of that tradition than the Magnificat – provides a further indication for a 'spiritual home' in a climate of peaceful expectation, although the knowledge of activist machinations can never have been far away from Jesus's sphere of action. There is no evidence for a Zealot provenance, let alone for more extravagant views such as the one according to which 'Mary seems to have trained several [of her sons] as pioneers of new revolutionary thought and action' (H. Johnson, *Christians and Communism* (London, 1956), p. 49). Nor is there any foothold for the view entertained by F. Andermann that Jesus's father met the end of a rebel (*Das grosse Gesicht* (München, 1970), p. 172).

[45] Cp. Acts 4: 13: ἀγράμματοι . . . καὶ ἰδιῶται.

[46] For the problem of the social level of the early Christian communities cp. A. Deissmann, *Das Urchristentum und die unteren Schichten* (Göttingen, 1908); M. Weber, *Grundriss der Sozial-Oekonomie* 3 (Tübingen, 1922), pp. 275ff; B. Grimm, 'Untersuchungen zur sozialen Stellung der frühen Christen in der römischen Gesellschaft' (Diss. München, 1975), pp. 36f and especially A. von Harnack, 'Das Urchristentum und die sozialen Fragen', *Preussische Jahrbücher* 131 (1908), 449f: 'the proletariate properly speaking has never exercised a dominant influence in the communities and those proletarians who joined the Christians were raised to a higher level thereby'.

[47] Luke points with a certain emphasis to people belonging to the higher strata of society in the environment of Jesus or on the fringes of Early Christendom; this is probably a secondary feature. There is no evidence that Jesus had been reared in a wealthy house as G. W. Buchanan, 'Jesus and the Upper Class', *NovTest* 7 (1964/65), 195ff, assumes.

[48] This is the line taken by W. Sattler in his influential contribution to the *Festgabe für A. Jülicher* (Tübingen, 1927), 'Die Anawim im Zeitalter Jesu Christi' (pp. 1ff). Similar ideas are found already in M. Friedländer, *Die religiösen Bewegungen innerhalb des Judentums im Zeitalter Jesu* (Berlin, 1905).

[49] *Das Evangelium Marci* (Berlin, 1903), p. 25; F. Schulthess, *ZNW* 21 (1922), 250ff. Different suggestions are made by H. Ingholl, *Studia Orientalia. J. Pedersen dedicata* (Copenhagen, 1953) and recently by B. Gärtner, *Die rätselhaften Termini Nazaräer und Iskarioth* (Uppsala, 1957), pp. 41ff; cp. D. Schirmer, 'Rechtsgeschichtliche Untersuchungen zum Johannes-Evangelium' (Diss. Erlangen, 1962), pp. 179ff, who adopts the theory of C. C. Torrey 'The Name "Iscariot"', *HThR* 36 (1943), 57ff.

[50] J. R. Harris, *The Twelve Apostles* (Cambridge, 1927), pp. 8of, goes so far as to identify him with Nathaniel.

other old Latin MSS. of Matt. 10: 3.[51] This evidence has to be taken together with the indications for Baptistic antecedents of some of the disciples[52] and the activist inclinations of two of them.[53] This is enough to show that the circle[54] was not a community far removed from the questions of the day.[55] But the fact that they had moved away from their former loyalties to Jesus and that Jesus acted as the undisputed authority among them is proof that nothing like a direct and immediate zealotic impregnation took place in the company of Jesus.

Two of the documents of nascent Christianity show a special interest in social questions. While Mark contains an ethical code (10: 1–31) with a short section on the dangers of wealth (verses 17–31),[56] Q is filled with remarks on the vicissitudes of the faithful. The special regulation for the disciples not to carry money etc. (Matt. 10: 9) may reflect this situation. The allusions to persecution and the appeal not to worry (Luke 12:22ff) are the dominant theme. There are, however, two sayings, the tenor of which is different and which demand special attention.

[51] This means that the last three names in the list of Matthew represent Zealot activists. Whether this reading originated by accident or goes back to an independent tradition must be left undecided.

[52] Cp. Dibelius, *Johannes der Täufer*, pp. 106ff.

[53] Mark 3: 17; Luke 9: 54; cp. A. Stumpff, *ThWNT* ii, 888 (ET ii, 886).

[54] It may be that the difference between the Baptist (and his circle) and Jesus was felt already at an early stage. A number of those who surrounded John and Jesus had been given additional names which characterised them. It is not unlikely that the solemn phrase of John 1:29 (ἴδε ὁ ἀμνός κτλ) is an extension of the simple appellation ἀμνός and that, in this form, it goes back to the Baptist. If that is the case, the name alludes to Jesus as to a man of peace in contradistinction to *inter alia* the 'sons of thunder'.

[55] R. Eisler, *Jesous Basileus* ii (Heidelberg, 1931), 69f, links Peter (and John) with the Barjonim who are mentioned in Gittin. Suppose that this combination were correct, it would rather point to an appellation coined with the intention of damning the Christians by giving the revolutionaries a 'Christian' name than to a linkage of Peter with revolutionary activists. It is, however, much more likely that *barjonim* is an opprobrious appellation by which the Zealots are sarcastically called 'Greeks' (thus L. Goldschmidt, *Der babylonische Talmud, ed. minor*, vi (Berlin, 1932), 364) – a characterisation which is very comprehensible from the background of Rabbinic theology. If this is true, the appellation ceases to have any connection with the Christians. In any case, the reference to the Barjonim derives from a *Sammelbericht* on the destruction of Jerusalem (Gitt. 55b–57a), the elements of which are of different provenance. The Syriac version of John 18: 10 makes Peter carry a sword habitually (cp. A. Merx, *Das Evangelium des Johannes* (Berlin, 1911), p. 428) – an interpretation which is not unnatural in the oriental environment and hardly sufficient an indication for listing him as a Zealot.

[56] The passage is largely parallel to 9: 33ff. 10: 13–16 equals 9: 36f, 42; 10: 17–28 is parallel to 9: 43–8; 10: 29–31 to 9: 49f; 10: 32–4 equals 9: 30–2 and 10: 35–45 is to be taken together with 9:33–5. This shows that ch. 10 is based on an earlier formation, which is introduced by the regulation on marital life (verses 1–12) and in which the section on offence is replaced by a paragraph on the specific danger of wealth.

III

Jesus's answer to the question of the disciples sent by the Baptist (Matt. 11:4ff; Luke 7:22ff) is given in the tradition of the Lukan text almost without variants.[57] Its sixth phrase should not be regarded as an addition by the evangelist;[58] Luke 7:18–23 is far too complicated to be laid in its entirety to the account of the writer[59] and it is verse 21 that strikes one as a redactor's insertion in which Luke made his own addition (πνευμάτων πονηρῶν).

It is made up of a formula based on expressions from Isaiah: 29:18f (κωφοί, τυφλοί, πτωχοί), 35:5f (τυφλοί, κωφοί χωλοί, μογιλάλοι), 61:1f (πτωχοί, συντετριμμένοι, αἰχμάλωτοι, τυφλοί), but it cannot be wholly explained from this source. Certain other lists are even closer. The substratum of the formula occurs in the form of a pattern in references to those excluded from the special community.[60] It is also handed down as a catalogue in connection with the inadequacy of idols[61] and in connection with the charitable actions demanded of man.[62] Finally it occurs as an eschatological doctrine, which proclaims the acceptance, healing, or preferential treatment in the messianic age of those indicated in its list.[63] In

---

[57] Omission of the fourth phrase by 998 b l, of the fifth phrase by 1574 033. The reversal of the fifth and sixth phrases by sys(c) 700 is the result of schematising application of the principle of crescendo. The Tatian tradition too gives the Lukan text almost without exception – the more remarkable since Tatian otherwise often follows Matthew.

[58] Thus E. von Dobschütz, 'Der heutige Stand der Leben-Jesu-Forschung', ZThK N.F.5 (1924): deriving from the 'pauperistisch gestimmten Lukas'. The same view in G. D. Kilpatrick, The Origins of the Gospel according to St. Matthew (Oxford, 1946), p. 125 (the latter apparently following F. C. Burkitt, Evangelion Da-Mepharreshe ii (Cambridge, 1904), 239).

[59] The passive form of the verb (cp. 4:18, 43) makes a Lukan origin unlikely.

[60] IQSa. 2:5f.   [61] Ep. Jer. 35–7.   [62] 5 Esr. (= 2 Esdr. 1–2) 2:18–20.

[63] Ginza R. 1:201 (sick, blind, lepers, cripples, those crawling on the ground (cp. E. Stauffer, 'Antike Jesustradition und Jesuspolemik im mittelalterlichen Orient', ZNW 46 (1955), 2, 17), deaf-mutes, the dead, preaching to the Jews). Parallel traditions: Ginza R. 2:1, 136; Johannesbuch 243 (twice). Paraphrases: (a) Johannesbuch 79f (blind, lame, dumb); (b) Slav. Jos. Bell. 1, 364ff (lame, blind, poor); (c) Sib. 8, 205ff (νεκροί, χωλοί, κωφοί, τυφλοί, οὐ λαλέοντες, κοινὸς βίος καὶ πλοῦτος; the position of νεκροί at the beginning is conditioned by the exclusively eschatological emphasis); Sib. 1, 351ff (νοσεροί, ἐπίμωμοι, τυφλοί, χωλοί, κωφοί, οὐ λαλέοντες, δαίμονες, νεκροί); Sib. 8, 279ff (οἰκτροί, νέκυας, νόσον) (d) Ps. Clem. Hom. 1, 6, 4 (κωφοί, τυφλοί, κύλλοι, χωλοί, πᾶσα νόσος, δαίμονες, λεπροί, νεκροί; cp. Sib. 1, 351ff); (e) Test. Adae (ed. E. Renan, Journal Asiatique (1853), ii, 444f), 3, 2f (blind, lepers, deaf, dumb, hunchbacks, those sick of the palsy, demons, possessed, the dead, the buried). Contrast with this the miracles of the Antichrist: Or. Sib. 3:66: νέκυας στήσει καὶ σήματα πολλὰ ποιήσει (cp. 2:167); the same in the Andreas-Commentary on Rev. 56:27 and the Elucidarium of Honorius (PL 172:1163); Ps. Hipp. 23, 106, 14: λεπροί, παράλυτοι, δαίμονες . . . νεκροί (the more striking since Ps. Hipp. – according to W. Bousset, Der

all these variations the formula points back to a pre-Christian period.[64] Noteworthy are (a) an original core: blind, lame, deaf (and dumb); (b) the introduction of the possessed or (respectively) δαίμονες not until the Judaeo-Christian tradition;[65] (c) the omission of the Poor outside Q, with the exception of 5 Esr. 2 (egens) and Slav. Jos. Bell. This allows one to conclude on the one hand that the formula already showed a certain tendency to vary in its Jewish setting, while on the other hand one may recognise tendentious elaborations as well as supplementary or decorative phrases.[66] The inclusion of the Poor must be regarded as one of the former.

In content this addition breaks the uniformity of the formula, which can otherwise be summarised under some such heading as πᾶσα νόσος. The difference is further emphasised by εὐαγγελίζονται;[67] as compared with

Antichrist (Göttingen, 1895), p. 25 (ET London, 1896, p. 41) – apart from this is from c. 22 dependent on Ephraem. The confutation of the raising of the dead must be a case of a more recent, possibly Christian, counter-form; in addition the other type: Ap. Eliae 33: 1ff.: lame, deaf, dumb, blind, lepers, sick, possessed, but no raisings from the dead (the same in Ap. Zeph. 125, and similar Ephraem Syr., Hom. de Antichristo 9; further material in Bousset, Antichrist, pp. 116f).

Compare with this the depictions of the Age of Salvation according to Lev. R. 18: 4 on ch. 15: 2 (S–B I, 594f): those with haemorrhages, lepers, lame, blind, dumb, deaf, cretins; Pesiq R. 7 (28a): lame, blind, dumb, deaf, those with haemorrhages, lepers; Midr. Song of Sol. 4: 7, 1: those with haemorrhages, lepers, lame, blind, dumb, deaf, cretins, simpletons, idiots, those with cleft palates.

[64] Ep. Jer. 'nicht später als 2 Jhdt. v. Chr'. (O. Eissfeldt, Einleitung in das Alte Testament (Tübingen, 1964), p. 737; ET Oxford, 1965, p. 595); 5 Esr. 2nd century A.D. (thus H. Weinel in Neutestamentliche Apokryphen, ed. E. Hennecke 2nd edn. (1924), p. 391; cp. on the other hand idem in HAT, pp. 332, 335); but 2: 20–23a (or b?) is morphologically a foreign body. Or. Sib. 3: 63ff first century B.C. (cp. Bousset, Antichrist, pp. 59f; ET pp. 95f); vaguer Rzach, PW IIA, 2131); in the same way Or. Sib. 8: 205ff is Jewish (cp. Rzach, PW IIA., 2144). Test. Adae, 3, 2ff has received Christian additions; for the Jewish basis cp. H. Weinel in Eucharisterion für H. Gunkel ii (Göttingen, 1923), 162. The rabbinic pronouncements on the period in the desert have no firm textual foundation and are therefore secondary historisations of what were originally purely eschatological statements. Thus they point unambiguously to an origin before the time of the floreat of those in whose names the tradition is handed down (Simon b. Jochai, Elieser b. Jose, both middle of the 2nd century A.D.).

[65] Ps. Clem. Hom. 1, 6, 4 (cp. note 58) and, in a shorter form Rec. v. 10. The formula in Pistis Sophia (ed. C. Schmidt, pp. 180f), which even starts the list with the δαιμόνια, seems to derive from this strand of the tradition. The summary in Jesus Messiah Sutra, logion 179 (P. Y. Saeki, The Nestorian Documents and Relics in China (Tokyo, 1951), pp. 142f) also includes the demons. The same is true for the beginning of Acta Pil. (ch. 1) and the letter of Pilate to Claudius.

[66] Interesting is the change of emphasis in Justin's presentation: the preaching to the Poor comes first (Dial. c. Tr. 12). This feature probably derives from a Gemeindetradition which reflects Judaeo-Christian influences (cp. TU 93 (1964), p. 61). Cp. notes 78 and 79, p. 120.

[67] Isa. 29: 19, 5 Esdras 2: 20 and Slav. Jos. 1, 364ff are to be understood in terms of a state of material prosperity. In Isa. 61: 1 (summarising title), this will be the case too despite the εὐαγγελίσασθαι.

the preceding verbs this indicates something quite different. The fact however that εὐαγγελίζονται is made formally parallel to ἀναβλέπουσιν κτλ. emphasises the effectiveness of the activity therein indicated: the Poor are put in possession of the message, they alone.[68] This emphasis is achieved by means of a new direction in content, made all the more striking when viewed against the formal reminiscence of Isaiah, the replacement of Isaiah's double event by a single happening.[69] The formula (Matt. 10: 8, 15: 30f; Mark 7: 37; on the other hand Matt. 10: 1 = Luke 9: 1 (cp. 10: 9)) thus reveals itself to be the expression of a conscious turning aside from the normal Jewish tradition[70] (nor can it be brought into connection in its *acumen* with the other formulae containing a phrase on the Poor).[71] Perhaps, however, this passage, which has its roots in the tradition of ideas about the Messianic Prince of Paradise,[72] also has an idiosyncratic position in Q, where Jesus is, apart from this, never designated as χριστός.[73]

In both parts the formula is not dominical.[74] It must have come into existence before the time of Q. That it should go back to Jewish circles is in itself possible, but the complete silence of the Jewish sources with regard to a phrase on the Poor, when they are so abundant apart from this, is against it. More likely it came into being within the Baptistic circles which had turned to the early Christian community, circles in which the political ingredient[75] had apparently quickly evaporated. Its later history – apart from the insertion of the δαίμονες or δαιμονιζόμενοι[76] – is marked by: (*a*) the disappearance of the gospel of the Poor in the early tradition of Matthew;[77] (*b*) the remodelling of the gospel of the Poor into a teaching

---

[68] Tanchuma B §7 and Lev. R. 18: 4 have their *acumen* in the fact that *even* the blind etc. are thought of as included in the Age of Salvation of the wandering in the desert, whereas in the formula of Luke 7 it is for the blind etc. *especially and preferentially* that salvation is claimed.

[69] In Isaiah a passage of time is envisaged between the proclamation and the event itself. Whether this was still the intention in the source of Luke 4: 17ff remains uncertain. Luke himself (cp. Acts 10: 38) conflates the two.

[70] With regard to which the breadth of this tradition – right up to the Qumranites and on the other side into the New Testament – is to be taken into account.

[71] 5 Esra 2 is just an imperative, it does not reflect on the objects of charitable activity. Slav. Jos. *Bell.* 1 is certainly post-Lukan – whether or not it is possible to attribute historical weight to the passage (as does F. Scheidweiler, 'Sind die Interpolationen im altrussischen Josephus wertlos?', *ZNW* 43 (1952), 168).

[72] Cp. R. Meyer, *Der Prophet aus Galiläa* (Leipzig, 1940), pp. 26f. The tradition is not otherwise taken up in Q, probably however in e.g. Mark 1: 13. The possibility of priestly tradition is considered by G. Friedrich, 'Beobachtungen zur messianischen Hohepriesterwartung in den Synoptikern', *ZThK* 53 (1956), 286.

[73] Cp. more recently E. Stauffer, 'Messias oder Menschensohn?', *NovTest* 1 (1956), 83.

[74] Cp. *ThWNT* vi, 907 (ET vi 908).

[75] It would have demanded the mention of the release of prisoners.

[76] Thus already Luke 7: 21.

[77] That it belonged to the original Matthaean text is made likely by: (*a*) the general

topic for the Jews in the Judaeo-Christian tradition;[78] (c) the cutting out of εὐαγγελίζονται in favour of πτωχοὶ εὐφραίνονται in a side stream, in particular of the Tatian tradition,[79] by means of which the last line loses its emphasis; and (d) certain abbreviating formulations.[80]

The Baptist's questioning of Jesus is historical.[81] The genuine core of what was handed down as Jesus's answer is to be found in Luke 7: 23/Matt. 11: 6[82] – perhaps it was spoken while Jesus was performing an act of healing.[83]

The first of the beatitudes[84] was given by Luke in a special form of its own, which relates directly to the audience (6: 19, more direct than in Matthew)[85] and secondly addresses them merely as πτωχοί.[86] The

improbability of post-Matthaean Lukan influence; (b) the witness of the Tatian tradition, which follows Luke here – because the texts of Matthew were not unanimous! (c) the substantial remodelling which Matthew has undertaken in the parallel passage 15: 30f; (d) if Matt. 11: 3 is a piece of its own with separate derivation in Q, it ended the sayings source in this and no other form; two forms at the time of Q are unlikely.   [78] Cp. Stauffer, *Jerusalem und Rom*, pp. 16f.

[79] Thus sy[c] and the MSS. B and C of sy[pal] in both synoptic passages (for the dependence of sy[pal] on the Tatian tradition cp. M. Black, 'The Palestinian Syriac Gospels and the Diatessaron', *OrChr* 36 (1941), 101, and C. Peters, 'Proben eines bedeutsamen arabischen Evangelientexts', *OrChr* 33 (1936), 195), and also the Persian Diatessaron (ed. G. Messina (*Biblica et Orientalia* 14 (1951)), 90ff. In content this means (a) a bridge to Isa. 29: 19 (just as sy[pal] and Arab. Diat. correct Luke 4: 18 according to the LXX) and (b) a compromise with regard to the division in the textual tradition of Matthew.

[80] Thus in Chrysostom's homily twice (blind, lame, deaf, poor; W. Till, *Mitteilungen d. Dt. Arch. Inst. Kairo* 16 (1958), p. 324. and in Sharastani (deaf, blind, palsy; Haarbrücker, *Ash-Sharastanis Religionspartheien und Philosophen–Schulen* i (Halle, 1850f), 260). On the other hand, elements of the formula are forged together with other notions, in order to give a full picture of Christ's activity (thus Ev. Nic. 1: . . . commanding the winds, walking on the lake and many other miracles).

[81] W. G. Kümmel (*Verheissung und Erfüllung* (2nd edn. Zürich, 1953), p. 103, ET London, 1957, p. 111) regards the narrative as an '*im wesentlichen alte, zuverlässige Ueberlieferung*'; (cp. also O. Cullmann, *Christologie des Neuen Testaments* (Tübingen, 1957), p. 162, ET London, 1959, p. 159; and Dibelius, *Johannes der Täufer*, pp. 33ff).

[82] Bultmann, *Tradition* (3rd edn. Göttingen, 1958), pp. 163f (ET Oxford, 1972, pp. 151f) regards verses 5f as original, but detaches the formula from the situation.

[83] Even if Luke 7: 21 is frame-narration, none the less there may be old tradition behind the detail; Luke here treats his source more carefully than does Matthew. F. Spitta, 'Die Sendung des Täufers zu Jesus' *ThStKr* 83 (1910), 534ff, regards verse 21 as older than verse 22.

[84] For the latest investigations see C. Michaelis, 'Die π-alliteration der Subjektsworte der ersten vier Seligpreisungen', *NovTest* 10 (1968), 148ff; H. Frankemölle, 'Die Makarismen', *BZ* n.s. 15 (1971), 52ff. C. Kähler, 'Studien zur Form-und Traditionsgeschichte der biblischen Makarismen' (Diss. Jena, 1974).

[85] At an earlier stage of the tradition those who are addressed as πτωχοί are the μαθηταί (cp. 6: 20a, 40), a state of affairs which, however, Luke (seduced by the cries of woe?) alters by means of the new addressees (cp. 6: 19; 7: 1; 6: 17 (levelling out formulation)). Adolf Schlatter, *Lukas* (Stuttgart, 1931), pp. 238f does not differentiate.

[86] The Matthaean form, which often appears in the textual tradition – already in sy[c]

pronouncement is elucidated by means of the following beatitudes, which address those who are oppressed or persecuted,[87] and therefore permit the conclusion that, in the first example as well, it is a case of outwardly visible suffering. The πτωχοί differ only in so far as their lack of impediment (for in the context πτωχοί is also a heading for the sick who are designated in 6: 17f) is a permanent condition, whereas the other addressees suffer the effects of particular situations in salvation history.[88] The saying is further illuminated by the symmetrically recurring cry of woe οὐαὶ ὑμῖν τοῖς πλουσίοις . . . (6: 24), which explains πτωχοί *e contrario* and excludes the possibility of an understanding according to Matt. 5: 3,[89] but also makes it clear that the βασιλεία is intended as a recompense (παράκλησις). This recompense takes place in the future – to this extent the saying can be understood eschatologically[90] but partly already in the present, since the addressees are already healed (6: 19).[91]

The saying, which is made up of eight parts, is not uniform. Items 4 and 7 (verses 22f and 26) are clearly amplifications,[92] whose removal makes the reference of items 2, 3, 6, and 7 (verses 21 and 25) to the situation of persecution uncertain, particularly since the pointer νῦν is also an addition.[93] None the less this does not entirely get rid of the difference between 1 (verse 20b) and 2 and 3 (verse 21), as the various ὅτι formulations that follow indicate. A separate provenance for 1 and 2+3 must therefore be regarded as possible. At least by this point 1 will already have had a social flavour. For the association of 1 with 2−3 is to be attributed also to the fact that the enemies of the Poor – the Rich – were the chief persecutors, with regard to which it is significant that the word πτωχός, clearly because it was traditional, was no longer adequate as an expression of the experience of persecution. A parallel to the amalgamation poor/persecuted may be seen in the formula μακάριοι οἱ πτωχοὶ καὶ οἱ διωκόμενοι ἕνεκεν δικαιοσύνης . . . (Pol. Phil 2: 3), which should most

---

(cp. H. von Soden *Die Schriften des Neuen Testaments in ihrer ältesten erreuchbaren Textgestalt* i (Leipzig, 1902) ad. loc.) – is a later assimilation. The earliest witness for the uncorrupt Lukan text is Tertullian (cp. A. von Harnack, *Marcion* 2nd edn. Leipzig, 1924), and, if H. von Soden is correct in his criticism of Harnack ('Der lateinische Paulustext bei Marcion und Tertullian', *Jülicher-Festschrift*, edd. H. von Soden and R. Bultmann, Tübingen, 1927, p. 239), even Marcion.

[87] The description in verse 22 is long-winded, because it aims at accuracy.

[88] Therefore νῦν or ἐν ἐκείνῃ τῇ ἡμέρᾳ is there added.

[89] Thus G. Bornkamm, *Jesus von Nazareth* (Stuttgart, 1956), p. 184, n. 21., ET p. 202, n. 21.

[90] Thus M. Dibelius, *Botschaft und Geschichte* i (Tübingen, 1953), 120.

[91] Although it seems as if the interpretation that is given to verse 20c in 24b intends to make the βασιλεία an exclusively future blessing.

[92] Which perhaps took place already at the time when the beatitudes and the cries of woe were combined.

[93] Cp. E. Klostermann, *Das Lukasevangelium* (Tübingen, 1929), p. 79.

likely be regarded as a separate formulation of Jewish or community theology origin, independent of Matthew and Luke.[94]

The indications that have emerged about the genesis of the Lukan passage show that the first beatitude does not derive from Luke himself (and cannot therefore be used for the evaluation of his own social tendencies without certain caveats). This does not yet, however, decide the question of the priority of either the Lukan or the Matthaean form. The hypothesis, occasionally ventilated, of a derivation from two independent sources finds support in the fact that the formula עניי־רוח = πτωχοὶ τῷ πνεύματι, the non-occurrence of which had been taken as the decisive argument for the more reliable wording of the Lukan beatitude, has been traced recently in a Qumran source (1 Q Mil 14.7). The assumption that different forms of makarisms of the Poor (with or without a promise) existed side by side – four formulae are known to us – and exercised their influence on different Christian manifestos is to be preferred to the attempt to trace them back to one form. The beatitudes were, in one form or another, a stock phrase at the time of Jesus and it is therefore unlikely that one of them belongs to those sayings which are typical of the dominical preaching.

On the other hand, the prominence given to the πτωχοί -formulae and their variety evince the flooding of the early communities with elements of the theology of the Poor and indeed the readiness of the Christians to expose themselves to such influences.

The growing influence of the Baptistic heritage in the early community is likely to have played its part in this development. It may have fostered and stimulated the emergence of the adulation of the Poor.[95]

IV

The view of the twelve disciples which became the standard one certainly militates against the hypothesis of Zealot influences on Jesus and his circle. John calls Judas Ἰσκαριώτης and at the same time κλέπτης. Both terms seem to describe the same thing. κλέπτης is an unfavourable expression for what is commonly called λῃστής[96] – a term applied to both Zealots and

---

[94] J. Weiss, Die Predigt Jesu vom Reiche Gottes (2nd edn. Göttingen, 1900), p. 181, conjectures that Polycarp used a 'vorkanonische Redaktion der Makarismen'. How far διωκόμενοι κτλ. goes back to Matthew himself, as is assumed by H. Köster (Synopt. Ueberlieferung bei den apostolischen Vätern, TU 65 (1957), 118), is not clear.

[95] The claim that Caiaphas took offence especially at Jesus's praising of the Poor and his promise of earthly redemption (Rec. I. 61) may reflect such developments in the early community.

[96] In Josephus the term λῃσταί points clearly to insurrection activity. Its meaning includes the notion of pretension to authority in certain cases (see R. MacMullen, The Roman Concept Robber–Pretender, RIDA 3rd Series 10 (1963), pp. 221f). In the political propaganda language of the empire it even describes the usurper.

sicarii. To this is added in John 12: 6 an interpretation which casts even more doubt on Judas's integrity.[98] The basis of the whole development in the blacklisting of Judas is the linking of the traitor with the Zealots and therefore, by inference, the separation of Jesus and his true followers from that movement.

It is in this context that an allusion in John 10: 8 gathers momentum: κλέπται καὶ λῃσταί are called 'those who came'.[98] This may refer to figures who came as contemporaries of Jesus and made saviour claims, to men who were of the Zealot type. The phrase had been used before in the parable of 10: 1, although only the first part of it was developed both in the course of the parable and in its subsequent interpretation (verse 10). The positive example is only expressed by one term. It is therefore likely that in a more primitive form the parable had contained only one negative term. As κλέπτης is the term which fits the contents of the parable it is to be assumed that this word belongs to the original narration,[99] while λῃστής came in in order to make a new point. It goes with the direct identification of the shepherd with Jesus as we find it in verses 11ff.[100] The καλὸς ποιμήν, a term capable of political interpretation in the ancient world, is reinterpreted in these verses. To give the negative term a political direction by the addition of καὶ λῃσταί would be a corresponding re-emphasis. It results from this that the λῃστής with its political associations is likely to have been brought in in order to emphasise the difference between Jesus's position in his church and that of pretenders among their followers.

The dominical kernel of the parable alludes to the religious leadership in

[97] The characterisation of the Judas as a money-grabber (John 12: 6) is thus to be taken as an artificial reinterpretation of the meaning of the attribute. The choice of the term κλέπτης (rather than λῃστής) may be partly due to the fact that the thief's work is often associated with night, while the very action which determined the portrait of Judas in the early church took place in 'the hour of darkness'.

[98] πρὸ ἐμοῦ is to be found only in part of the tradition. It is significant that the Syriac tradition, which is dotted with anti-Jewish statements does not seize upon this. On the other hand, it is equally characteristic that ℵ, a text which tends to compromise by omission, does not reproduce these words. Might it be that something like the reading of Nonnus (παρὸς ἐμοῦ) was the alternative before the scribe of ℵ and perhaps even the original reading? Cp. *As. Is.* 4: 6: I am God, before me there has been none. The second half of the saying was refashioned in Gnostic tradition. Basilides claims that all the prophets before the saviour spoke from the ruler of the firmament (*Hipp. Ref.* vii. 25: 5) and the Naassene Book of Baruch is even more specific: they had prophesied, because they had been enticed by the serpent. Failing to accomplish the same with Jesus, the serpent crucified him. It is in keeping with this tendency that Pistis Sophia, ch. 102 (257.25), gives the phrase 'keep away from robbery' (originally an extension of John 10: 8b?) an entirely metaphorical meaning.

[99] Merx, *Johannes* (Berlin, 1911), p. 250, holds the opposite view.

[100] According to J. Wellhausen, *Das Evangelium Johannis* (Berlin, 1908), p. 48, already in verse 7.

Israel, which will not be accepted by the door-keeper, that is, God. It is without direct political connotations. Its meaning could, however, be easily extended to refer to the new political self-styled leaders as well; and it certainly exposed Jesus and his followers to the animosity and even hatred of those who in their political direction pressed the nation into their own fold.[101]

Of crucial importance is the cleansing of the Temple.[102] It is this event that comes nearest to revolutionary activity and it is this narrative that contains the watchwords indicating Zealotism: ζῆλος and ληστής.

The story is preserved in two strands of tradition – surprisingly there is no record of it in Jewish or extracanonical sources. The narrative itself is supplemented by interpretative remarks. The Johannine report contains two sentences of this kind, each of them introduced by ἐμνήσθησαν.[103] Mark on the other hand contains a statement of Jesus, preceded by the description of an action (11: 16), which, however, is due to the redactor, as it is reproduced neither by Luke nor even by Matthew, to whose theology it would have been congenial. The statement itself is a combination of Old Testament passages in the manner of a Teacher of Righteousness exegesis – something that is in keeping neither with the Markan presentation nor with what we know of the dominical references to the Old Testament. It is therefore likely that the original form of the narrative lacked any interpretative statement, beyond, perhaps, a reference to the violated sanctity of the House – probably not in the form of a quotation.[104] An interpretation is, however, supplied by the story of the cursing of the fig-tree, which in its two parts frames the cleansing and which seems to form a unit with the latter already in pre-Markan tradition.[105] Jesus's action

---

[101] For recent investigations cp. O. Kiefer, *Die Hirtenrede* (Stuttgart, 1967) and A. Simonis, *Die Hirtenrede im Johannes-Evangelium* (Rom, 1967).

[102] For recent studies see G. Abramzik in *Festschrift M. Plaut* (Bremen, 1971), 69ff and E. Salin, 'Jesus und die Wechsler' in A. ben-David, *Jerusalem und Tyros* (Basel/Tübingen, 1969), pp. 49ff.

[103] The second of these refers both to the event itself and to the fragment of a controversy reproduced in John 2: 18–20. While it is the intention of verses 21ff to give a disarming interpretation of the preceding verse, this verse itself defies explanation; Jesus applies the technique of outmanoeuvring the challenge of his enemies by provoking them to do something – the actual suggestion to pull down the Temple was not out of place, as the building of the Herodian Temple was not undertaken without misgivings.

[104] The action thus opened itself to different explanations: the possibility that it was directing itself against the trade set up and monopolised by the house of Annas was one of them. Another, emphasised in Mark 11: 16, was that Jesus was expressing his opposition to the Herodian Temple. The ambiguity of his action to the outside world is a phenomenon that should not be disregarded.

[105] It is not connected with the entry pericope, as the lack of πάλιν in Mark 11: 15 shows (whereas in verse 27 it is present). The two locations given in 11: 1 are puzzling; but

deprives the fig-tree of its *raison d'être*. The cleansing interrupts the execution of the sacrificial system for one moment and thereby makes it invalid. The two actions correspond to each other:[106] the cursing of the fig-tree is the interpretation of the cleansing. It is a symbolic gesture that points to the end of the cultic approach to God. The re-interpretation offered in the two strands of the Gospel tradition portrays Jesus as a restorer of the original quality of the Temple, as someone who directs himself just against certain practices[107] and possibly is in favour of the more modest Zerubbabel Temple.[108] While the term ζῆλος, which was about to replace the older term *zedaka* at this time, is characteristic in the Fourth Gospel for the description of the attitude of Jesus,[109] it is in Mark that the anti-divine world is described by λῃστής. The former indicates a time in which the Christians were still able to use terms dear to the Jewish activists[110] and even to advocate their master's action by hinting at the example of the zealous Phineas,[111] whereas the latter marks a separation. The Johannine usage must be the earlier one, while the Markan, although a citation from Jeremiah, is probably employed here with the secondary intention of separating Jesus's action from the activities of the Zealots. Although this latter interpretation is a rewriting, it is not at this point at variance with the original meaning of the event: it is prophetic action that, by interrupting those procedures which precede the cultic performance (even the ἀγοράζοντες, the would-be worshippers, are turned away by Jesus, according to Mark 12: 15), symbolises the end of the cult, and it is not a political or revolutionary action. This interpretation agrees both with the Judaeo-Christian tradition on Jesus's attitude with respect to the Temple[112] and with the role attributed to the Temple saying in the Sanhedrin trial.[113]

they find their interpretation in the assumption that one of them was transferred when the units 11: 1ff and 11: 12ff were forged together.

[106] A different view is taken by W. R. Telford, *The Barren Temple and the Withered Tree* (Sheffield, 1980).

[107] Thus especially D. Chwolson, *Das letzte Passamahl Christi und der Tag seines Todes* (2nd edn. Leipzig, 1908), p. 127. Reinterpretations on the redactionary level are discussed by R. E. Dowda, 'The Cleansing of the Temple in the Synoptic Gospels' (Diss., Duke Univ., 1972).

[108] Mark 11: 16 could be taken as prohibiting the completion of the Herodian Temple.

[109] Deriving from Psalm 69: 10 – a psalm which came to be used christologically (cp. Mark 15: 36).

[110] Cp. Rev. 2: 9; 3: 9, where the term Ἰουδαῖος is still claimed by the Christian church, whereas it is abandoned in the Fourth Gospel.

[111] Later Christian tradition, however, makes him a descendant of Cain.

[112] Jesus is said to have come in order to abolish sacrifices. It is not until the compilation of the Apostolic Constitutions that the Jews accuse Jesus as destroyer of the Temple and taker away of sacrifices (verse 14).

[113] Both Matthew and Mark, although displaying significant differences in detail, agree in so far as they emphasise that the Temple accusation did not lead to the desired result. Had it been otherwise, a verdict would have been reached without

A third focussing point is to be found in the saying in Mark 11:23: the ὄρος must be a particular mountain; in all probability it is the Temple mount. Taken in this way the logion is a parallel to the form of Jesus's Temple saying which is expressed in Matt. 26:61: δύναμαι καταλῦσαι τὸν ναὸν τοῦ θεοῦ. What Jesus is said to have claimed for himself in the latter passage is promised to the very faithful disciple in the former. The two sayings are complementary. They display a similarly radical attitude vis-à-vis the Temple as is found in both the cleansing and cursing scenes.

Jesus equally kept aloof from *Schwärmertum*, from apocalypticism, the disposition which once and again amalgamated with national expectation and Zealotism. Statements like Luke 17:21 express unequivocally his reserve vis-à-vis apocalyptic speculation and expectation.[114] His departure from apocalypticism is the counter-proof, the proof for his parting from political expectation.

Matthew 26:52: πάντες ... οἱ λαβόντες μάχαιραν ἐν μαχαίρῃ ἀπολοῦνται, a proverbial saying which, possibly under the influence of Mark 8:34, came into existence in the early church, sums up fairly the position of Jesus.[115]

It is not inconsistent with this that a document, possibly going back to the first century, describes the hatred felt towards Jesus as caused by the fact that he had no zeal,[116] or was not a Zealot.[117] An echo of the impression of the time is found in a Jewish source of the Tannaitic period which claims that Jesus was put to death by Phineas, the robber.[118] ליסטאה, the Aramaic form of the Greek λῃστής, is obviously taken as an honorific title (like the Dutch '*geuzen*'), while Phineas, the hero of the Zealots, is referred to

[114] Even the synoptic apocalypse, a passage which is heavily overlaid by material of both Jewish and Early Christian provenance, directs its readers to phenomena which, contrary to apocalyptic time-tables, are viewed under the heading οὔπω τὸ τέλος (Mark 13:7); and is designed, it its redactional form at least (verse 10 is symptomatic; the addition of verses 32ff seems to express similar sentiments), to calm down rather than to whip up expectations.

ado. Temples were protected in the Roman empire and any violation was treated as an action against the public peace and punished most severely. Cp. D. Juel, *Messiah and Temple* (Missoula, 1977).

[115] It is doubtful whether more detailed advice was given in the community. The view that Matt. 5:41 refers to the Roman practice of forced labour and that the advice is implicitly pro-Roman and anti-Zealot (L. E. Keck, *A Future for the Historical Jesus* (London, 1972), p. 254) is too neat.

[116] Od. Sol. 28:10 – transl. J. H. Bernard (*Texts and Studies* 8.3 (1912), 110f); J. R. Harris, *An Early Christian Psalter* (Cambridge, 1910), p. 50.

[117] Thus translated by J. R. Harris, *The Twelve Apostles* (Cambridge, 1927), p. 34. For the negative meaning applied to ζῆλος in early Christian literature cp. Ps. Clem. *Hom.* 3.42, where the name Cain is interpreted by ζῆλος and every kind of Zealotism is blacklisted thereby.

[118] Sanh. 106b. The theories that Phineas is a mistake for Pilate and that *lista* derives from a Syriac *losta* = august are, of course, far-fetched.

as an indication of Zealot activity. The statement describes Jesus's death as due to or influenced by punitive action taken by Zealot elements.[119]

No definite tendency can be deduced in those passages on the Poor – they are by far the smaller proportion – that can be attributed to Jesus. The challenge given to the rich young man is not intended as a principle, nor is it meant to be an indication of the virtue of doing good to others;[120] it demands action, the action which Jesus's loving call[121] recognises as necessary. Jesus's love is directed to the individual; the words in which it is expressed are not meant to be understood as law. Occasionally the word πτωχός occurs in a *Beispielerzählung* (Luke 14: 13)[122] or is taken up in the words in which Jesus characterises a procedure which takes place before his eyes (Mark 12: 42). None the less, this happens surprisingly seldom. When Jesus describes the circle of men to whom especially he has turned his compassion he prefers other words. It is to the νήπιοι (Matt. 11: 25) that his glory is revealed; he himself calls the κοπιῶντες καὶ πεφορτισμένοι (Matt. 11: 28), he blesses the παιδία (Mark 10: 14), he portrays men in their special needs (Matt. 25: 25ff).

The κοπιῶντες are primarily those who suffer under the burden of the law. It is, however, true that the exercise of religion had become a privilege of those who had had some training in the law and of those who could afford to observe the law punctiliously. Those who suffer under the yoke of the law are therefore likely to belong to the lower strata of society.[123]

The only clearly defined pronouncement on the πτωχοί is Jesus's refusal (Mark 14: 7)[124] to allow himself to be tied down to a social principle or indeed to let his sympathies be regimented at all. Jesus does good himself (cp. Acts 10: 38 with Mark 14: 7), but he does not bind men to a law, nor

---

[119] It is to be mentioned too that John 16: 1f refers, according to Merx, *Johannes*, p. 400, to a persecution of the Christian community initiated by Zealots.

[120] Thus J. Jeremias, 'Die Salbungsgeschichte Mc 14 3–9', *ZNW* 35 (1936), 79.

[121] The oldest traceable form of the answer given by Jesus is near to the one handed down in the Ev. Hebr., in that the central section of Mark is lacking there. On the other hand, this pointing to the command of love is to be taken as a secondary transformation of the Markan ἠγάπησεν.

[122] Cp. Aboth 1: 5; Tos. Ber. 4: 8, where the Poor appear only as a supplement to the invited guests.

[123] There are, it is true, features in his teaching, which militate in favour of the Poor. The restriction of business life which was necessitated by a rigid observance of the Torah ceased to exist. Indeed, the blessing given to the transgression of the Sabbath law, as we find it in the D version of Luke 6: 5 at least, opened up a new avenue. The abolition of the hereditary law which bestowed titles exclusively on the male offspring, must have been brought about, if not by Jesus himself, very soon in Judaeo-Christianity (Shabb. 116a) and resulted in a better social condition both of widow and virgin. This does not, however, mean that social considerations played a role in Jesus's preaching.

[124] The story is 'wahrlich wert, im Evangelium zu stehen' – this is Wellhausen's judgement (*Marcus*, 2nd edn. p. 109).

does he emphasise the law; where he is, other legal principles with-draw.

All the same Jesus's way of life corresponds to that of the Poor. It is not just that his illustrations and sermons prefer to address the Poor and that it is chiefly the ὄχλος (John 7: 49) that attaches itself to him; he proceeds through the country as a man without possessions, dependent on help and protection from others (e.g. Mark 1: 31). He is put under pressure, persecuted (Luke 9: 58; 13: 33; 21: 37 etc.) and takes refuge (John 11: 54). He is conscious of his identity with the exploited and humiliated (Matt. 11: 28). Yet he does not make use of the slogan which indicated their position and their hopes. This is clearly because it had been excessively overlaid and distorted by glowing expectations.[125] Instead of this it is to the individuals in their various needs that Jesus speaks.

The most telling expression is given to this connection in Mark 8: 38/Luke 9: 26. This saying, the original wording of which seems to be 'whoever is ashamed of me and my (companions) . . .', refers to those individuals in his environment who are less respectable and less presentable, rather than to his disciples alone.[126] The verse expresses more than Jesus's concern for his group, it indicates his total identification with those whom he chooses to associate with.

Those who had to abandon their abode because of political or religious causes, or who from poverty had let themselves be led into actions of despair, will have experienced similar ways of life, although their backing in the population and the support given by their fraternities may have been more effective. Jesus's proclamation does not, however, coincide with the key-words of the activists' appeal. Πάτριος νόμος,[127] ἐλευθερία,[128] salvation of Israel[129] are absent from his language. His actions do not give a different impression; even the Cleansing of the Temple is rather a symbolic action than a political manifesto. Compared with the political movements of his day Jesus is what is expressed by Paul, albeit in a different context, in the one word παρεισελθών: he is the one whose words and deeds were different both from the preceding and from the surrounding world.

---

[125] The attempt of Sattler (Ad. Jülicher, pp. 1ff), which was taken up by W. Grundmann (Jesus, der Galiläer (Weimar, 1940)), to illustrate Jesus's self-consciousness from the background of the piety of the Anawim is thus hardly tenable.

[126] It is only the present context in Mark 9: 1 (if the verse is not meant as an introduction to the transfiguration story) which makes one think of the disciples.

[127] Josephus, AJ 14 §41.

[128] A. Reifenberg, Ancient Jewish Coins (Jerusalem, 1947), pp. 60–6 (חרות).

[129] Reifenberg, Coins, pp. 58, 60f, 63f (גאלה).

HELMUT MERKEL

The opposition between Jesus and Judaism

Jesus was a Jew. This indisputable fact[1] long ago led H. S. Reimarus, the founder of the study of the historical Jesus, to regard Jesus completely within the framework of Judaism, and to consider it evident 'that Jesus had not the slightest intention of doing away with the Jewish religion and putting another in its place'.[2] From this it became necessary to explain the New Testament accounts of conflicts between Jesus and the Pharisees as the product of exchanges between church and synagogue[3] – an early position which the form-critical approach has appeared to confirm.[4] But if Jesus lived in harmony with his contemporaries, then the reason for his violent end must have lain in his political activity. Accordingly, from Reimarus to R. Eisler down to S. G. F. Brandon Jesus has again and again been placed in the company of Zealot resistance fighters.[5]

Since the Enlightenment, too, the representation of Jesus as an Essene wisdom teacher has often been placed alongside representations of him as an orthodox Pharisee and a nationalistic resistance fighter.[6] Since the publication of the Qumran texts particularly, repeated attempts have been made to connect Jesus with the Essenes.[7]

---

[1] O. Michel, 'Jesus der Jude', in H. Ristow and K. Matthiae (eds.), *Der historische Jesus und der kerygmatische Christus* (2nd edn. Berlin, 1961), pp. 310ff.

[2] Quoted by A. Schweitzer, *The Quest of the Historical Jesus* (ET London, 1910), p. 17.

[3] Cp. G. Lindeskog, *Die Jesusfrage im neuzeitlichen Judentum* (Uppsala, 1938). More recent studies from this point of view include J. Isaac, *Jésus et Israel* (Paris, 1948), pp. 96ff; P. Winter, *The Trial of Jesus* (Berlin, 1961), pp. 111ff; S. Ben Chorin, *Bruder Jesus* (München, 1967), pp. 16f, 22, 74f; D. Flusser, *Jesus* (Reinbeck bei Hamburg, 1968), pp. 43ff, ET *Jesus* (New York, 1969), pp. 44–64. See also G. Jasper, *Stimmen aus dem neureligiösen Judentum* (Hamburg, 1958).

[4] R. Bultmann, *Geschichte der synoptischen Tradition* (6th edn. Göttingen, 1964), ET *The History of the Synoptic Tradition* (2nd edn. Oxford, 1968), p. 54. J. C. Weber, Jr., 'Jesus's Opponents in the Gospel of Mark', *JBR* 34 (1966), 214ff, entirely follows Bultmann's conclusions. A substantially different view is taken by H. F. Weiss, 'Der Pharisäismus im Lichte der Überlieferung des Neuen Testaments' in R. Meyer, *Tradition und Neuschöpfung im antiken Judentum* (Leipzig, 1965), pp. 89ff. Cp. also his article 'Φαρισαῖος' in *ThWNT* ix, 36ff.

[5] R. Eisler, ΙΗΣΟΥΣ ΒΑΣΙΛΕΥΣ ΟΥ ΒΑΣΙΛΕΥΣΑΣ ii (Heidelberg, 1930); S. G. F. Brandon, *Jesus and the Zealots: A Study in the Political Factor in Primitive Christianity* (Manchester, 1967). Further literature is cited in M. Hengel, *War Jesus Revolutionär?* (Tübingen, 1970) (ET *Was Jesus a Revolutionist?* (Philadelphia, 1971)).

[6] Cp. S. Wagner, *Die Essener in der wissenschaftlichen Diskussion vom Ausgang des 18. bis zum Beginn des 20. Jahrhunderts* (Berlin, 1960).

[7] Cp. especially A. Dupont-Sommer, *Les écrits esséniens découverts près de la mer Morte*

Over against all these stands an impressive list of scholars who have taken seriously the opposition of Jesus to his contemporaries which comes to light in various places in the Gospels. David Friedrich Strauss, the first radical critic of the Gospel tradition, recognised

> as the simple historical outline of the life of Jesus that he grew up in Nazareth, had himself baptized by John, gathered disciples, wandered around the Jewish countryside teaching, set himself in opposition to Pharisaism throughout and summoned men to the Messianic kingdom; that he was finally brought down by the hatred and jealousy of the Pharisaic party, and died on the cross.[8]

Since Strauss's time, the significance of the opposition between Jesus and the Pharisees has been often emphasised by both radical and conservative scholars.[9] Rudolf Bultmann lists the 'breaking of the Sabbath commandment, violation of the rules of purity, polemic against Jewish legalism, association with outcasts like tax-gatherers and prostitutes, sympathy for women and children' among the characteristics of Jesus's actions that can 'with some caution' be ascertained.[10] Most of the more recent critical portraits of Jesus also take account of the opposition between Jesus and the Pharisees,[11] though to be sure it has been a matter of debate whether Jesus attacked only Pharisaic casuistry or the Torah itself as well.[12] Recent study of the trial of Jesus has regarded this opposition as the decisive factor

---

(Paris, 1959), ET *The Essene Writings from Qumran* (Oxford, 1961), pp. 368–78. Further material may be found in H. Braun, *Qumran und das Neue Testament* ii (Tübingen, 1966), 54ff, 85ff.

[8] D. F. Strauss, *Das Leben Jesu* i (1st edn. Tübingen, 1835), 72.

[9] T. Keim, *Geschichte Jesu von Nazara* ii (Zürich, 1871), 337ff (ET *History of Jesus of Nazara* iv (London, 1879), 4–27); B. Weiss, *Das Leben Jesu* ii (2nd edn. Berlin, 1884), 99ff (ET *The Life of Jesus* ii (Edinburgh, 1883), 289–305); W. Beyschlag, *Das Leben Jesu* ii (Halle, 1886), 259ff; W. Bousset, *Jesus*, ET (London, 1906), pp. 59–70; P. Wernle, *Jesus* (3rd edn. Tübingen, 1917), pp. 107ff; M. Goguel, *La vie de Jésus* (Paris, 1932) (ET *The Life of Jesus* (London, 1933), pp. 343–6), GT (Zurich, 1934), p. 219f; W. Heitmüller, *Jesus* (Tübingen, 1913), pp. 97f.

[10] R. Bultmann, 'Das Verhältnis der urchristlichen Christusbotschaft zum historischen Jesus' (ET as 'The Primitive Christian Kerygma and the Historical Jesus', in C. E. Braaten and Roy A. Harrisville (eds.), *The Historical Jesus and the Kerygmatic Christ* (New York and Nashville, 1964), p. 22). The present translation differs slightly.

[11] G. Bornkamm, *Jesus von Nazareth* (5th edn. Stuttgart, 1960), pp. 88ff, ET *Jesus of Nazareth* (London, 1960), pp. 98–100; E. Stauffer, *Die Botschaft Jesu* (Bern, 1959), pp. 36ff; E. Haenchen, *Der Weg Jesu* (Berlin, 1966), *passim*; M. Hengel, *Nachfolge und Charisma* (Berlin, 1968), p. 63; H. Braun, *Jesus* (Stuttgart, 1969), pp. 72ff. Cp. my survey in *NTSt* 14 (1967–8), 194–208.

[12] An attack by Jesus on the Torah itself is disputed by J. Jeremias, *Neutestamentliche Theologie* i (Gütersloh, 1971), 198ff (ET *New Testament Theology* i (London, 1971), 204–8). For the contrary view see especially Stauffer, *Botschaft*; Haenchen, *Weg*; Hengel, *Nachfolge*, pp. 78f.

behind Jesus's indictment.[13] The supposed affinity of Jesus and the Zealots has also been recently questioned; it has indeed been proposed that there was an unbridgeable gulf between them.[14] The representation of Jesus as a Qumran Essene has not remained uncontested either.[15]

With such an abundance of opposing positions and views on the question, we might feel justified in giving up, especially since to many questions we feel able with a clear theological conscience to give a verdict of *non liquet* with an appeal to Kähler and Bultmann.[16] On the other hand, it has been shown that *faith* has an interest in the historical facts about Jesus,[17] although this subject will not concern us further here. But what can we say about the actual possibility of historical reconstruction?

I

It is today generally recognised that the Gospels are of a kerygmatic nature, so that an uncritical estimate of their value is out of the question.[18] The fundamental breakthrough to this recognition was made by form-criticism, although it had already operated in 'liberal' study around the turn of the century. Adolf Jülicher, for example, set out the problem strikingly in an evaluation of the achievements of Wrede, Wellhausen, and Harnack:

> The task will always be for us to distinguish within the Synoptic tradition what can probably be ascribed to the community, or perhaps what was composed by the community in venturing to correct older material, and what is more probably to be traced back to Jesus himself. Whenever

---

[13] So G. Lindeskog, 'Der Prozess Jesu im jüdisch-christlichen Religionsgespräch', in *Abraham unser Vater* (Festschrift O. Michel) (Leiden, 1963), pp. 325ff; D.R. Catchpole, 'The Problem of the Historicity of the Sanhedrin Trial', in E. Bammel (ed.), *The Trial of Jesus*, (2nd edn. London, 1971), pp. 47ff, and *idem, The Trial of Jesus* (Leiden, 1971), pp. 107ff.

[14] Hengel, *War Jesus Revolutionär?*; O. Cullmann, *Jesus und die Revolutionären seiner Zeit* (Tübingen, 1970) (ET *Jesus and the Revolutionaries* (New York, 1970)).

[15] Cp. the summary in Braun, *Qumran* ii, 54ff, 85ff.

[16] G. Strecker, 'Die historische und theologische Problematik der Jesusfrage', *EvTh* 29 (1969), 453ff.

[17] O. Michel, 'Der "historische Jesus" und das theologische Gewissheitsproblem', *EvTh* 15 (1955), 349ff; J. Jeremias, *Das Problem des historischen Jesus* (Stuttgart, 1960) ET *The Problem of the Historical Jesus* (Philadelphia, 1967); W.G. Kümmel, *Die Theologie des Neuen Testaments nach seinen Hauptzeugen* (Göttingen, 1969, pp. 22f); P. Stuhlmacher, 'Kritische Marginalien zur gegenwärtigen Frage nach Jesus', in *Fides et communicatio* (Festschr. M. Doerne), ed. D. Rössler *et al.* (Göttingen, 1970), pp. 341ff.

[18] This is the weakness of the comprehensive study of W. Beilner, *Christus und die Pharisäer* (Wien, 1959). The work of K. Berger, *Die Gesetzesauslegung Jesu* (Neukirchen, 1972), while rich in material, also raises doubts about method. What the author considers a 'comprehensive traditio-historical method' (Foreword), often operates like 'combinatorial magic'. Cp. also note 79, p. 140.

characteristic traits are striking in a disorganized mass of material, whenever words of peculiar stamp and character meet us, then this is . . . the surest proof of authenticity.[19]

Wilhelm Heitmüller, whose presentation of Jesus was debated by the Prussian chamber of deputies,[20] formulated five critical canons, of which the first was

> that in spite of legendary and mythological elements and in spite of the not inconsiderable overlaying attributable to the belief of the community that we have to clear away, we have material of historical value in the gospel tradition whenever there are elements in it which cannot be reconciled with the belief of the community to which the material as a whole belongs. What is not consonant with this belief cannot have grown out of it. These elements often show themselves to be at variance with the belief of the community through their omission or alteration by later writers.[21]

'We can have complete confidence [in the residuum of material satisfying this criterion]. We can extend this confidence to everything that stands in an organic relation to it.'[22] Further indicators of authenticity were the local colour of narratives, Aramaisms, and forms of traditional material suitable for memorisation. With these principles Heitmüller offered a way of making Jülicher's methodology more precise. Ernst von Dobschütz expressed himself similarly.[23]

This position changed with Bultmann. He wanted to abandon any presumption of reliability in dealing with the Gospel tradition,[24] believing that nothing more than the earliest stratum of the tradition could ever be discerned; to what extent Jesus was behind it could no longer be determined.[25] He also extended the criteria for authenticity: Jesus must

---

[19] A. Jülicher, *Neue Linien in der Kritik der evangelischen Überlieferung* (Tübingen, 1906), pp. 73f.

[20] *Jesus* (Tübingen, 1913). Cp. the Foreword, pp. iiiff.

[21] Ibid. pp. 34f.

[22] Ibid. p. 40.

[23] 'Der heutige Stand der Leben-Jesu-Forschung', in *ZThK* N.F. 5 (1924), 64ff. In order to prove that the Gospel 'did not originate in the ideas of the time or the aspirations of men', von Dobschütz emphasised two facts: (1) 'The gospel tradition made changes in words and narratives, a sign that it found some things offensive.' (2) 'In this process, some individual traits were preserved which could not have been made up since they are in direct contradiction with later attitudes . . .' (p. 65). He went on to refer to the local colour, Aramaisms, and Jewish concepts in the Gospels.

[24] A presumption still shared by Heitmüller, *Jesus*, and M. Dibelius, *Die Formgeschichte des Evangeliums* (4th edn. Tübingen, 1961) (ET *From Tradition to Gospel* (London, 1934), pp. 293f), and *Jesus* (3rd edn. Berlin, 1960, p. 19 (ET *Jesus* (Philadelphia, 1949), p. 22).

[25] R. Bultmann, *Jesus* (Berlin, 1926) (ET *Jesus and the word* (New York and London, 1934), pp. 12f).

stand out not only from the later community but also from Jewish moral teaching and piety.[26]

On this foundation rests the 'criterion of underivability' developed by Ernst Käsemann in his famous lecture.[27] Inasmuch as this formulation has been acknowledged in principle by scholars of widely differing opinions,[28] it can be considered an accepted result of the discussion of method to date.

The most weighty objection that can be raised – and which has been repeatedly raised[29] – against this criterion, was stated by Käsemann himself, viz., that 'we shall not, from this angle of vision, gain any clear view of the connecting link between Jesus, his Palestinian environment and his later community'.[30] To get a complete picture of the proclamation of Jesus, we could overcome this objection in part by following Heitmüller's method and regarding everything that was 'in organic relation' to the residuum of underivable material as authentic. However, for the question at issue here we have to discover first what this residuum of material is that unmistakably goes back to Jesus, and for this undertaking by itself the 'criterion of dissimilarity' (as Norman Perrin calls it) is suitable. Criteria of form,[31] however, can provide valuable checks: source-critical, form-critical, and redaction-critical analysis must obviously be combined with considerations of content.

This comprehensive method of investigation[32] may well overcome the

---

[26] R. Bultmann, *Geschichte der Synoptischen Tradition* (Göttingen, 1964), p. 222, ET *History of the Synoptic Tradition* (Oxford, 1972), p. 205.

[27] E. Käsemann, 'Das Problem des historischen Jesus', in *Exeget. Versuche* i (Göttingen, 1965) (ET 'The Problem of the Historical Jesus', in *Essays on New Testament Themes* (London, 1964), pp. 15–47): 'In only one case do we have more or less safe ground under our feet: when there are no grounds either for deriving a tradition from Judaism or for ascribing it to primitive Christianity, and especially when Jewish Christianity has mitigated or modified the received tradition, as having found it too bold for its taste' (p. 37).

[28] W. Grundmann, *Die Geschichte Jesu Christi* (2nd edn. Berlin, 1959), pp. 16f; H. Conzelmann, 'Jesus Christus', *RGG* iii, 623; Stauffer, *Botschaft*, pp. 10, 16; O. Cullmann, 'Unzeitgemässe Bemerkungen zum "historischen Jesus" der Bultmannschule', in Ristow and Matthiae, *Der historische Jesus*, pp. 266ff, esp. pp. 277f; E. Lohse, 'Die Frage nach dem historischen Jesus in der gegenwärtigen neutestamentlichen Forschung', *ThLZ* 87 (1962), 168; E. Bammel, 'Erwägungen zur Eschatologie Jesu', in StEv iii, 3ff, esp. p. 19; C. Burchard, 'Jesus', in *Der kleine Pauly* ii (Stuttgart, 1967), 1346; N. Perrin, *Rediscovering the Teaching of Jesus* (London, 1967), pp. 38f; H. G. Klemm, 'Das Wort von der Selbstbestattung der Toten', *NTSt* 16 (1969/70), 6off, esp. 74; Jeremias, *Theologie* i 2 (ET p. 2); Hengel, *Nachfolge*, p. 96.

[29] Cullmann, 'Unzeitgemässe Bemerkungen'; P. Stuhlmacher, 'Kritische Marginalien'; Jeremias, *Theologie* i, 2.

[30] Käsemann, 'Das Problem' (ET p. 37).

[31] Jeremias, *Theologie*, pp. 19ff (ET i, 3–37).

[32] M. Lehmann, *Synoptische Quellenanalyse und die Frage nach dem historischen Jesus* (Berlin, 1970), also proposes a 'co-operation of criteria'. For similar proposals, see P. Stuhlmacher, 'Thesen zur Methodologie gegenwärtiger Exegese', *ZNW* 63 (1972),

sceptical attitude (which seemed at first to be required by form-criticism) that it is impossible to get back behind the post-Easter community. We appeal here to the fundamental remarks of H. Schürmann, who has shown that it is not the post-Easter community but the pre-Easter circle of disciples that is the earliest recoverable social entity.[33] We may resolutely give up all *a priori* guarantees for the trustworthiness of the tradition as a whole.[34] Everything depends on the examination of individual traditions.

II

The Gospel tradition has preserved several instances in which Jesus placed himself in direct opposition to Jewish religious practice.

(*a*) First of all there is the saying in Matt. 8: 22 par. in which Jesus invites the violation of something that is a religious duty in all cultures. Matthew and Luke have blunted the edge of the saying by altering its context, and the further history of its exegesis shows that this saying remained offensive.[35] There can, then, be no doubt of its authenticity.[36]

(*b*) It has long been recognised that Jesus's attitude to women was unusual.[37] The extraordinarily low estate of women in Judaism[38] and the generally reserved and critical estimate of them in early Christianity[39] guarantee, at least in principle, that those traditions in which the 'religious equality of women'[40] can be read do go back to Jesus.

(*c*) Jesus's rejection of fasting, in its original form in Mark 2: 18f, must have been astonishing and, for a religious teacher, disqualifying.[41] The fact

---

18ff, esp. 22; and D. G. A. Calvert, 'An Examination of the Criteria for Distinguishing the Authentic Words of Jesus', *NTSt* 18 (1971–2), 209ff, esp. 219.

[33] H. Schürmann, 'Die vorösterlichen Anfänge der Logientradition', in Ristow and Matthiae, *Der historische Jesus*, pp. 342ff.

[34] Against H. Riesenfeld, *The Gospel Tradition and its Beginnings* (Oxford, 1957), and B. Gerhardsson, *Memory and Manuscript* (Lund, 1961). The references to the rabbinic transmission of tradition may perhaps serve as a counterweight to radical scepticism, but they do not bear examination in individual cases. Cp. the criticism of W. D. Davies, *The Setting of the Sermon on the Mount* (Cambridge, 1964), pp. 464ff, and Hengel, *Nachfolge*, pp. 58ff.

[35] Cp. also Klemm, 'Dass Wort'.

[36] So also Hengel, *Nachfolge*, p. 16.

[37] Cp. A. Oepke, 'γυνή', in *TDNT* i, 784f; Stauffer, *Botschaft*, pp. 68ff; Braun, *Jesus*, p. 102f; Hengel, 'Maria Magdalena und die Frauen als Zeugen', in *Abraham unser Vater*, pp. 243ff.

[38] Cp. esp. S–B iii, 611f; iv, 1226f; and J. Jeremias, *Jerusalem zur Zeit Jesu* (3rd edn. Göttingen, 1962), pp. 395ff (ET *Jerusalem in the Time of Jesus* (London, 1969), pp. 359–76).

[39] 1 Cor. 11: 7f; 14: 34ff; 1 Tim. 2: 11f; Luke 14: 26; Rev. 14: 1ff.

[40] Hengel, 'Maria Magdalena', p. 243.

[41] For this see my argument in 'Markus 7.15 – das Jesuswort über die innere Verunreinigung', *ZRGG* 20 (1968), 360–3; and J. Roloff, *Das Kerygma und der irdische Jesus* (Göttingen, 1970), pp. 223ff.

alone that this pericope in its Markan form actually constitutes a justi-fication for the practice of fasting in the church (ἐλεύσονται δὲ ἡμέραι . . . τότε νηστεύσουσιν),[42] shows that verse 19a, which is critical of fasting, cannot be derived from the thinking of the early church, which (as Matt. 6: 16ff and Did. 8.1 clearly show) placed a high value on Christian fasting.[43] The form-critical objection to the authenticity of Mark 2: 18f holds that Jesus is here defending not his own but his disciples' conduct, and that by this device the community is appealing to Jesus to justify its own conduct.[44] This line of argument is spelled out twice by Bultmann;[45] none the less it should now be given up, since it is quite natural that Jesus should have been called to account for shortcomings in the conduct of his followers.[46]

Jesus's critical position toward the Sabbath and ritual purity will be treated in detail below, since in these cases it is a question not only of characteristically Jewish custom but of the Law itself.

III

Jesus's attitude to the outcasts of society must have given rise to very serious conflicts.

(a) Tax-gatherers were among the most hated classes of people in ancient Judaism.[47] Their profession belonged to that class of occupations which 'were not only despised, nay hated, by the people; they were *de jure* and officially deprived of rights and ostracized'.[48] The special favour of Jesus for the tax-gatherers,[49] evidenced in all strata of the tradition, has to be understood as an outrageous provocation from the Jewish point of view. On the other hand, the question was no longer a problem for the later church, whose references to tax-gatherers, although widely distributed, are few in

---

[42] Dibelius, *Formegeschichte*, pp. 62f (ET pp. 65f).

[43] Roloff, *Kerygma*, p. 226, continues to defend the authenticity of the rule of fasting in Matt. 6: 16ff. None the less, the picture of Jesus as a reformer of the religious institutions of Judaism seems to fit the Matthaean christology rather than the historical Jesus.

[44] Bultmann, *Synoptischen Tradition*, p. 17 (ET p. 16).

[45] Ibid. p. 48.

[46] So especially, E. Stauffer, 'Neue Wege der Jesus Forschung', in *Gottes ist der Orient* (Festschrift O. Eissfeldt) (Berlin, 1959), pp. 167ff. Cp. the earlier essay of C. H. Dodd, 'Jesus as Teacher and Prophet', in G. K. A. Bell and A. Deissmann (eds.), *Mysterium Christi* (London, 1930), pp. 53–66; Roloff, *Kerygma*, p. 55; and D. Daube, 'Responsibilities of Master and Disciples in the Gospels', *NTSt* 19 (1972–3), 1ff.

[47] Cp. S–B i, pp. 378f.

[48] Jeremias, *Jerusalem*, p. 346 (ET p. 311).

[49] Mark 2: 15–17 (pre-Markan; see R. Pesch, 'Das Zöllnergastmahl', in *Mélanges Bibliques en hommage au R. P. Béda Rigaux* (Gembloux, 1970), pp. 63ff); Matt. 11: 18f par. (Q); Luke 18: 9–14; 19: 2–10 (L-material); Matt. 21: 31f (M-material).

number.[50] This fact admits of the conclusion that the texts which describe Jesus's association with tax-gatherers correspond to neither Jewish nor Christian thinking, and so reflect Jesus's own attitude. It must have been scandalous to all Jesus's contemporaries that he received into his company the 'notoriously sinful Israelites who have separated themselves from the true Israel'.[51] The reproach taken up by Jesus that he was a 'glutton and a drinker, a friend of tax-gatherers and sinners' (Matt. 11: 18f par.) is the best possible illustration of this attitude of Jesus and its rejection.[52] It is not merely a moral disqualification that is expressed here, but the accusation according to religious law that Jesus was a 'disobedient son', who, according to Deut. 21: 20f, was punishable by stoning.[53]

(b) The mixed race of the Samaritans was just as hated and scorned in the time of Jesus as the tax-gatherers.[54] When Jesus, in the undoubtedly authentic[55] parable of the 'good Samaritan' (Luke 10: 30ff), let the deed of human kindness be performed ideally by none other than a Samaritan, it must have been taken as an insulting affront by any patriotic Jew. H. G. Klemm has rightly pointed out that in Luke 10: 30–5, just as in the parables

[50] In the synoptics, the mention of tax-gatherers is almost always taken over in traditional material. R. Pesch, 'Levi-Matthäus', ZNW 59 (1968), 40ff, tries to show a redactional origin for Mark 2: 13f. Two facts tell against this thesis: (1) the discontinuity between verses 14 and 15 (noticed as early as J. Wellhausen, Das Evangelium Marci (2nd edn. Berlin, 1909), p. 17, which would have been avoidable if verse 14 was editorial; and (2) the absence of the name Levi from Mark's list of apostles in 3: 16ff. Matt. 5: 46 has been regarded since A. Harnack, Sprüche and Reden Jesu (Leipzig, 1907), pp. 46f (ET (London, 1908), p. 62), as the more original form of the saying paralleled in Luke 6: 32f. Matt. 18: 17 seems to have its origin in pre-Matthaean tradition (see R. Hummel, Die Auseinandersetzung zwischen Kirche und Judentum im Matthäusevangelium (2nd edn. München, 1966), p. 23. Matt. 21: 32 may be redactional (so Bornkamm, 'End-Expectation and Church in Matthew', in G. Bornkamm, G. Barth and J. Held, Überlieferung und Auslegung im Matthäusevangelium (Neukirchen, 1960), pp. 22ff, ET Tradition and Interpretation in Matthew (London, 1963), pp. 27f; G. Strecker, Der Weg der Gerechtigkeit (2nd edn. Göttingen, 1966), p. 153; Hummel, Auseinandersetzung; U. Luz, 'Die Jünger im Matthäusevangelium', ZNW 62 (1971), 154), or indeed the whole parable: see my argument in 'Das Gleichnis von den "ungleichen Söhnen" Mt XXI. 28–32', NTSt 20 (1972–3), 254ff. The Johannine tradition ignores all encounters between Jesus and tax-gatherers.

[51] O. Michel, ThWNT viii, 103 (ET TDNT viii, 104).

[52] On the authenticity of Matt. 11: 18f, see E. Schweizer, 'Der Menschensohn', in Neotestamentica (1963), 72f; C. Colpe, ThWNT viii, 434, ET TDNT viii, 431; and J. Jeremias, Die Gleichnisse Jesu (7th edn. Göttingen, 1965), pp. 16of (ET The Parables of Jesus (London, 1963), pp. 161f).

[53] Stauffer, 'Neue Wege', p. 175; Jeremias, Theologie, i, 265f (ET 261f). Brandon touches on this complex of issues only in a subordinate clause (Zealots, p. 201), without considering its far-reaching implications.

[54] S–B i, 538ff; Jeremias, Jerusalem, pp. 387ff (ET pp. 352ff).

[55] Jeremias, Gleichnisse, pp. 202ff (ET pp. 202ff); Perrin, Teaching, pp. 122ff; H. G. Klemm, 'Das Gleichnis vom Barmherzigen Samariter' (Diss. Erlangen-Nürnberg, 1967).

in Matt. 18: 23ff, 25: 32ff, and Luke 15: 11ff, a 'reversal of perspectives, a victory of human kindness over inflexible principles and hardened attitudes' is accomplished.[56] Jesus's lack of prejudice, evident in this parable, is reflected also in the story of the 'grateful Samaritan' (Luke 17: 11ff) and in the conflict between his disciples and the inhabitants of a Samaritan village (Luke 9: 52ff).[57] Only the saying in Matt. 10: 5f shares the prejudice of the time against the Samaritans. Joachim Jeremias has to be sure demonstrated the great antiquity of this text,[58] but the evidence of Aramaic idioms proves only that the saying was handed down by the earliest, Aramaic-speaking church. Since Matt. 10: 5f fits into the Jewish and Jewish–Christian horizon and at the same time contradicts authentic tradition about Jesus, the conclusion that it is of secondary origin is attractive.[59]

(c) If our assignment of Matt. 10: 5f to the Jewish–Christian church is correct, then one of the most difficult texts for the problem of 'Jesus and the Gentiles' is removed from the discussion. No planned limitation of the Christian mission can be seen in the earliest sources; the historical Jesus could not have imposed it on himself or his disciples.[60] To be sure, we may not follow F. Spitta[61] and make Jesus the first missionary to the Gentiles, but the texts make it clear that Jesus displayed a fundamental openness to Gentiles which corresponded to his attitude to 'tax-gatherers and sinners' and Samaritans. As illustrations there are several specific individual cases (Mark 7: 24ff par., Matt. 8: 5ff par.), whose original history is in any event not easy to reconstruct, as well as the sayings in Luke 10: 23, 11: 29ff, 13: 28f,[62] in which Jesus sets up the Gentiles as contrasting examples over

[56] Klemm, *Gleichnis*, p. 421.

[57] The authenticity of Luke 17: 11ff was doubted already by P. Wernle, *Die synoptische Frage* (Freiburg, 1899), p. 94, and thoroughly disputed by R. Pesch, *Jesu ureigene Taten?* (Freiburg–Basel–Wien, 1970), pp. 35ff. Cp., however, the reply to this criticism by M. Hengel, *Gewalt und Gewaltlosigkeit* (Tübingen, 1971), p. 65. Roloff, *Kerygma*, considers the narrative to be independent tradition but the mention of the Samaritan secondary. On Luke 9: 52ff, cp. Hengel, *Nachfolge*, p. 67. Both texts are organically related to the residuum of underivable material.

[58] J. Jeremias, *Jesu Verheissung für die Völker* (2nd edn. Stuttgart, 1959), pp. 16f (ET *Jesus' Promise to the Nations* (London, 1958), pp. 19f).

[59] So too E. Käsemann, 'The Beginnings of Christian Theology', in *New Testament Questions of Today* (ET (London, 1969), p. 87); F. Hahn, *Das Verständnis der Mission im Neuen Testament*, (2nd edn. Neukirchen-Vluyn, 1965), p. 87; Haenchen, *Weg*, p. 228; M. Hengel, 'Die Ursprünge der Christlichen Mission', *NTSt* 18 (1971/72), 36. The argument of H. Kasting, *Die Anfänge der urchristlichen Mission* (München, 1969), pp. 110ff, that Matt. 10: 5 and 15: 24 are compositions of the evangelist, is not convincing, since Aramaisms do not occur in redactional material.

[60] Against Jeremias, *Verheissung*.

[61] F. Spitta, *Jesus und die Heidenmission* (Giessen, 1909).

[62] Jeremias, *Verheissung*, p. 48 (ET p. 85), favours the Matthaean form of this saying, but W. Trilling, *Das wahre Israel* (3rd edn. München, 1964), pp. 88f, has shown that

against the failure of Israel. Finally, this openness of Jesus even with regard to non-Jews, is connected with the fact that Jesus detached religion from national soil.[63] By this 'un-limitation' he made the essential preparation for the Gentile mission.[64] This fact, that Jesus burst through traditional ways of thinking in his position toward tax-gatherers, Samaritans, and Gentiles, goes unappreciated by Brandon. Every representation of Jesus as a religious conformist runs aground on it.

IV

It was a binding axiom for all Jews that the Torah was the final dispensation of the purpose of God, although differences might appear in the interpretation of this divine precept.[65] It is widely assumed that Jesus shared this contemporary view,[66] but several texts have to be adduced in which a conflict of Jesus with the Torah can be denied only by a forced exegesis.

(a) The saying of Matt. 8: 21f par. discussed above not only represents a disregard for part of the 'core of Jewish piety' but can be 'taken as an attack on the reverence toward parents enjoined in the Fifth Commandment'.[67] The same goes for the narratives of the calling of the disciples in Mark 1: 16ff, which, as Rudolf Pesch has shown, rest on 'recognizable historical foundations'.[68] 'In Mark 1: 20, the unconditional willingness to follow Jesus is at stake. In this case the call of Jesus requires a break with the Fifth Commandment.'[69]

(b) Strict observance of the Sabbath was required by the Torah,[70] and special *halakhot* for its more exact observance were developed in Qumran as well as Pharisaic circles.[71] Now there is widespread agreement among

Luke is the earlier. Against Jeremias's wide-ranging conclusions from the Lukan 'inaugural sermon', cp. Haenchen, *Weg*, p. 272, n.2.

[63] A. Harnack, *Mission und Ausbreitung des Christentums* i (4th edn. Leipzig, 1924), 39 (ET *The Mission and Expansion of Christianity in the First Three Centuries* (2nd edn. London, 1908), p. 36).

[64] Cp. Hengel, *NTSt* 18 (1971–2), 36.

[65] S. W. Gutbrod, *ThWNT* iv, 1054–9; H. Braun, *Spätjüdisch häretischer und frühchristlicher Radikalismus* i (Tübingen, 1957), 2ff, 15ff, 48ff, 90ff.

[66] See the literature cited in note 3, p. 129, and Jeremias, *Theologie* i, 204–8.

[67] Hengel, *Nachfolge*, p. 29.

[68] Pesch, 'Berufung und Sendung, Nachfolge und Mission', *ZKTh* 91 (1969), 1ff (quotation p. 18).

[69] Stauffer, *Botschaft*, p. 29.

[70] For this and what follows, see W. Rordorf, *Der Sonntag* (Zürich, 1962); (ET *Sunday* (London, 1968)).

[71] Qumran: CD X.14–XI.18; cp. Braun, *Radikalismus* i, 69f; E. Lohse, *Umwelt des Neuen Testaments* (Göttingen, 1971), pp. 73f, 128f; S. T. Kimbrough, Jr., 'The Concept of Sabbath at Qumran', *RdQ* 5 (1966), 483ff. For rabbinic material see S–B i, 615ff.

scholars that the controversies over the Sabbath reported in both the Synoptic and Johannine traditions reflect the attitude of Jesus.[72] It is not merely a matter of an attack on the Pharisaic Sabbath *halakha*, as Jeremias maintains,[73] since the sayings in Mark 2: 27 and 3: 4 plainly qualify the absolutely unquestionable commandment to keep the Sabbath holy, whose violation is made punishable in the Torah by death.

Even the oldest Gospel did not tolerate the saying in Mark 2: 27 in its unconditional form, in which the welfare of man is placed above the norm fixed by the Torah, but blunted it by a christological argument: not man, but the 'Son of man', is lord of the Sabbath.[74] Finally, Matthew omits Mark 2: 27 and lets the conflict over the Torah fade away.[75] In the same way, Matthew recasts the second controversy over the Sabbath in Mark 3: 1ff. 'The Sabbath commandment remains in force in principle. The Torah is the common ground of the debate. Only its interpretation and practical application are at issue.'[76] From all this, the underivability of Jesus's criticism of the Sabbath can be concluded.

(c) The subject of cultic purity and impurity is also among the most important elements of the Torah; in Qumran and among the Pharisees it underwent various halakhic treatments.[77] The saying in Mark 7: 15, οὐδέν ἐστιν ἔξωθεν τοῦ ἀνθρώπου εἰσπορευόμενον εἰς αὐτὸν ὃ δύναται κοινῶσαι αὐτόν, offers a radical criticism of this whole concept. I have

---

[72] Cp. E. Lohse, 'Jesu Worte über den Sabbat', in *Judentum-Urchristentum-Kirche*, Festschr. J. Jeremias (2nd edn. Berlin, 1964), pp. 79–89; and Rordorf, *Der Sonntag*, pp. 55ff (ET pp. 61–5).

[73] Jeremias, *Theologie* i, 201 (ET p. 209).

[74] Cp. Käsemann, 'Das Problem', 38f; Braun, *Radikalismus* i, p. 70 n. 1; Rordorf, *Der Sonntag*, pp. 63ff. The analysis of Roloff, *Kerygme*, overlooks the connection between Mark 2: 25f and 28 demonstrated by Bammel, 'Erwägungen' and also pointed out by H. Hübner, *Das Gesetz in der synoptischen Tradition* (Witten, 1973), p. 120.

[75] By the introduction of ἐπείνασαν, Matthew emphasises the correspondence to the example of David (Matt. 12: 1), he adds a second proof-text which, in contrast to Mark 2: 27, actually satisfies the rabbinic demands (see D. Daube, *The New Testament and Rabbinic Judaism* (London, 1956), p. 71), and he calls the disciples innocent (12: 7). The omission of Mark 2: 27 by Matthew and Luke seems to have been differently motivated: what seemed to Jewish Christians too critical of the Torah could have seemed to Gentile Christians too partial to the institution of the Sabbath. The conjecture of Wernle, *Synoptische Frage*, p. 55, that the omission could reflect an earlier text of Mark is thus unnecessary, and more than unnecessary since Luke's takeover in 6: 5 of the Markan transitional formula καὶ ἔλεγεν αὐτοῖς betrays his knowledge of Mark 2: 27. This tells against the hypothesis of Hübner, *Gesetz*, pp. 117ff, who supposes that Matthew and Luke were influenced by a Q form of the controversy. But even if he were correct, it would remain unexplained why Matthew and Luke should simultaneously desert Mark in favour of Q.

[76] Hummel, *Auseinandersetzung*, p. 45.

[77] Lev. 11f; 15; Num. 5: 1ff; 19; Deut. 14: 3ff; 23: 9ff; etc. For the rabbinic material see S–B i, 695ff; for Qumran material see Braun, *Radikalismus* i, 29, 34f, 54, 58, 104ff. On the whole question see W. Paschen, *Rein und Unrein* (München, 1970).

elsewhere presented a detailed survey of the many softenings and re-interpretations that this saying of Jesus has suffered in the last 200 years.[78] Unbiased exegesis, however, can only maintain that 'the man who denies that impurity from external authority can penetrate into man's essential being is striking at the presuppositions and the plain verbal sense of the Torah, and at the authority of Moses himself'.[79] Again in this case the state of the secondary additions and later omissions offers the most probative check on the authenticity of the saying. Mark himself blurs Jesus's opposition to the Torah by connecting 7: 15 with the controversies over hand-washing and the validity of the *halakha* (7: 1ff). He also limits the saying, which applies to all the commandments about purity, to the food laws (7: 19c), and he diverts attention from the deeper opposition by means of the peremptory, 'parenetically sonorous but theologically inoffensive catalogue of vices'.[80] The transformation of the whole debate by Matthew, a

[78] *ZRGG* 20 (1968), 341–50.

[79] Käsemann, *Exeget. Versuche* i (1965), 39; so Bornkamm, *Jesus*, p. 90, ET p. 98; Braun, *Qumran* ii, 72; Stauffer, 'Neue Wege', in *Gottes ist der Orient*, p. 171; Haenchen, *Weg*, pp. 256f; Perrin, *Teaching*, pp. 146f; S. Kawashima, 'Jesus und die jüdischen Speisevorschriften' (Diss. Erlangen-Nürnberg, 1969); Hübner, *Gesetz*, pp. 142ff. Against this, it represents a step backwards when Paschen, *Rein*, understands the whole saying on the basis of verse 15b. Verse 15a should be taken at least as seriously! This must also be said against Jeremias, *Theologie* i, 202 (ET pp. 209f).

The attempt of Paschen and Hübner to trace an earlier form of the tradition behind the saying of Jesus in Mark 7: 15 cannot be discussed here. My own reconstruction is treated critically by W. G. Kümmel, 'Äussere und innere Reinheit bei Jesus', in *Das Wort und die Wörter* (Festschrift G. Friedrich) (Stuttgart, 1973), pp. 35–46. The difference of views is determined by a difference in the degree to which the 'criterion of dissimilarity' is accepted. Happily, Kümmel's recognition of the force of Jesus's criticism of the Torah is not impaired.

Berger, *Gesetzesauslegung*, pp. 463ff, goes too far in softening the criticism of the Torah in saying 'The notion of purity is not abolished, but only transferred to the realm of the spiritual' (p. 464), in order to be able to illustrate 'the great proximity of this maxim to Hellenistic Judaism' with a comparison with Philo, *de Spec. Leg.*, iii, 208f. I have previously shown (ZRGG 20 (1968) see note 41, p. 135) that the spiritualised notion of purity was well known, but Berger is still at fault in his contention that the annulment of the letter of the Torah went along with this internalising in Hellenistic Judaism. Philo, Berger's authority, expresses himself definitely to the contrary: 'There are some who, regarding laws in their literal sense in the light of symbols of matters belonging to the intellect, are overpunctilious about the latter, while treating the former with easy-going neglect. Such men I for my part should blame for handling the matter in too easy and off-hand a manner: they ought to have given careful attention to both aims, to a more full and exact investigation of what is not seen and in what is seen to be stewards without reproach. . . . These men are taught by the sacred word to have thought for good repute, and to let nothing go that is part of the customs fixed by divinely empowered men greater than those of our time.' (*de Migr. Abr.* 89f, transl. by F. H. Colson in Loeb Library, *Philo*, iv, p. 183).

[80] Stauffer, 'Neue Wege', in *Gottes ist der Orient*, p. 172.

masterpiece of his scribal method,[81] keeps the conflict over the Torah out of sight, and implies by the concluding formula τὸ δὲ ἀνίπτοις χερσὶν φαγεῖν οὐ κοινοῖ τὸν ἄνθρωπον that only the problem of hand-washing had been discussed. 'In fact, the debate in Matthew ends with Jesus formulating a particular *halakha* concerning hand-washing which contradicts the Pharisaic one.'[82] Here too the tradition has preserved the attitude of Jesus only with qualifications, and so testifies to the individuality of Jesus.

(*d*) Finally, the saying in Mark 10:9, which denies the possibility of divorce, is in explicit contradiction to the Torah (Deut. 24:1ff).[83] Already in the oldest tradition it was thought necessary to underpin the unconditional saying of Jesus with a proof-text (Mark 10:6-8),[84] and it is supplemented with casuistic stipulations (verses 11f)[85] in which the possibility of divorce is

---

[81] The earlier thesis of von Dobschütz that Matthew was a converted rabbi ('Matthäus als Rabbi und Katechet', *ZNW* 27 (1928), 338ff) has been more recently seconded by Hummel, *Auseinandersetzung*, and (cautiously) by Weiss, 'Der Pharisäismus' in Meyer, *Tradition*, p. 127, and still awaits refutation. The latest advocate of a Gentile Christian origin for Matthew, R. Walker (*Die Heilsgeschichte im ersten Evangelium* (Göttingen, 1967)), has done more harm than good to this thesis. It will not do to assert of all the Jewish elements in Matthew that they are 'completely antiquated' or have only 'illustrative value' or are 'purely homiletical examples', etc. Certainly Walker's magic formula 'that traditional material is one thing, the *literary use* made of it by the author of the Gospel is another' (p. 128) comes to grief in the controversies between Jesus and the Pharisees: in these Mark is clearly the source, and the rabbinic elements are to be credited to Matthew. The case is similar to the μηδὲ σαββάτῳ of Matt. 24:20, which Walker asserts is 'an anachronism which has remained in the text as an irrelevancy' (p. 134); a glance at the synopsis contradicts this. The judgement of the rabbinic scholar D. Daube still applies: 'Matthew's is a Rabbinic Gospel' (*Rabbinic Judaism*, p. 60). For the Jewish Christian provenance of Matthew, see also H. Stegemann, ' "Die des Uria." Zur Bedeutung der Frauennamen in der Genealogie von Mt 1.1-17', in *Tradition und Glaube*, Festgabe für K. G. Kuhn, ed. G. Jeremias *et al.* (Göttingen, 1971), pp. 246-76, esp. pp. 274f; E. Lohse, *Entstehung des Neuen Testaments* (Stuttgart–Berlin–Köln–Mainz, 1972), pp. 88f; W. G. Kümmel, *Einleitung in das Neue Testament* (14th edn. Heidelberg, 1965), ET 1966, pp. 80ff; A. Wikenhauser and J. Schmid, *Einleitung in das Neue Testament* (6th edn. Freiburg–Basel–Wien, 1973), pp. 243ff.

[82] Hummel, *Auseinandersetzung*, p. 46.

[83] Wellhausen long ago recognised the criticism of the Torah in this saying (*Marci*, p. 79), and he is followed by Bornkamm, *Jesus*, pp. 90f (ET pp. 98f); Stauffer, 'Neue Wege', in *Gottes ist der Orient*, p. 175; Braun, *Radikalismus*, p. 110; Jeremias, *Theologie*, i, 200 (ET 207); Haenchen, *Weg*, p. 341. For the authenticity of Mark 10:9 see also B. Schaller, 'Die Sprüche über Ehescheidung und Wiederheirat in der synoptischen Überlieferung', in *Der Ruf Jesu und die Antwort der Gemeinde*, Festschrift J. Jeremias (Göttingen, 1970), pp. 226ff.

[84] On this see Haenchen, *Weg*, pp. 339ff.

[85] Since the discussion of E. Bammel, 'Markus 10:11f. und das jüdische Eherecht', *ZNW* 61 (1970), 95ff, this verse can no longer be considered a late, Hellenistic addition (against Schaller, 'Die Sprüche', in *Der Ruf Jesu*, p. 229, n. 7). For the question of authenticity, which Bammel explicitly leaves open (p. 101), the contradiction with Jesus's absolute prohibition of divorce in 10:9 is still the deciding factor.

again presupposed. Matthew tacitly restores the authority of Moses by putting the exception for adultery on the lips of Jesus as part of his concluding pronouncement (Matt. 19: 9, cp. 5: 32). In the Matthaean form of the debate, Jesus is again presented as a Pharisaic scribal authority[86] who defends the view of the school of Shammai in what was at the time a much-debated subject,[87] but who upholds the Torah according to its original intention.

It emerges clearly from the foregoing texts we have briefly examined that for Jesus the Torah formed 'no longer the focus and ultimate standard. . . . Jesus – unlike the whole body of his Jewish contemporaries – stood not *under*, but *above* the Torah received by Moses at Sinai.'[88] This is the deepest reason why there could be no understanding between Jesus and a Jew of Qumran or Pharisaic practice. The attack of Jesus on the Torah confronts us finally with the unprecedented claim of Jesus to authority, a fact which is being increasingly recognised by scholars.[89]

V

Since the Zealots stood near to the Pharisees doctrinally,[90] they too must have been shocked by Jesus's criticism of the Torah, as well as by his association with those who collaborated with the occupation government and by his openness towards the Gentiles.[91] If only by reason of the fundamental difference in their ways of thinking which appears here, any alliance between Jesus and the Zealots is quite improbable. Three texts, however, have to be pointed out which imply Jesus's unequivocal renunciation of the Zealot ideology.

(a) The discussion of tribute-money (Mark 12: 13ff),[92] whose authenticity cannot be doubted,[93] presupposes the problem raised by Judas of Galilee in forming the resistance movement: tribute to the pagan ruler was idolatry.[94] In his answer to the artful question, 'Jesus neither allowed himself to be lured into conferring divine status on the existing power

---

[86] Cp. Hummel, *Auseinandersetzung*, p. 344.

[87] So already von Dobschütz, *ZNW* 27 (1928), p. 344.

[88] Hengel, *Nachfolge*, p. 78.

[89] Ibid. pp. 76f; Jeremias, *Theologie*, i, 239ff, ET pp. 250ff. Cp. also H. von Campenhausen, *Die Entstehung der christlichen Bibel* (Tübingen, 1968), pp. 10f, ET *The Formation of the Christian Bible* (London, 1972), p. 13.

[90] M. Hengel, *Die Zeloten* (Leiden, 1961), pp. 89ff; cp. *War Jesus Revolutionär?*, pp. 30f (ET pp. 11f).

[91] Hengel, *Die Zeloten*, pp. 190ff.

[92] For this see Stauffer, *Die Botschaft Jesu*, pp. 95ff; Bornkamm, *Jesus*, p. 110 (ET pp. 121ff).

[93] So even Bultmann, *Tradition*, p. 25 (ET p. 26).

[94] Hengel, *Die Zeloten*, pp. 143ff.

structure, nor concurred with the revolutionaries who wanted to change the existing order and compel the coming of the Kingdom of God by the use of force.'[95] Brandon's attempt to discover beneath the Markan form of the discussion of the tribute-money an anti-Roman statement of Jesus which was recast for apologetic reasons, lacks any support.[96]

(b) The Parable of the Patient Husbandman (Mark 4: 26ff) is best explained on the hypothesis that Jesus is here placing himself in opposition to Zealot activism.[97] Just as the husbandman cannot advance the moment of the harvest, αὐτομάτη ἡ γῆ καρποφορεῖ, so neither can anyone force the Kingdom of God to come. Faith should wait for everything from God. Indeed, Jesus reinterprets the conception of the coming of the Kingdom of God still further: it is no longer merely in the future, but in his work has already broken in! This is expressed not only in a number of parables[98] but also in a saying from the sayings-source in Luke 11: 20 par.: εἰ δὲ ἐν δακτύλῳ θεοῦ ἐγὼ ἐκβάλλω τὰ δαιμόνια, ἄρα ἔφθασεν ἐφ' ὑμᾶς ἡ βασιλεία τοῦ θεοῦ.[99] Here again it becomes clear that the proclamation of Jesus cannot be separated from his person. Brandon overlooks this range of issues.

(c) The crucial difference between Jesus and the Zealots, however, becomes clear in the matter of the attitude to one's fellow-men. Whereas the Zealots believed that it was necessary in the service of God's cause to root out rigorously all law-breakers,[100] Jesus demanded unconditional love of one's neighbour and even one's enemy (Matt. 5: 43ff par.). In dealing with

---

[95] Lohse, Umwelt, p. 59.

[96] Brandon (Zealots, pp. 346–9) adduces two arguments, which cannot however be sustained by the texts in question: (1) Jesus would not have been recognised as messiah if he had not refused to pay the tribute. Against this one must at least say with O. Cullmann, Die Christologie des Neuen Testaments (3rd edn. Tübingen, 1963), p. 126, ET The Christology of the New Testament (2nd edn. London, 1963), p. 126, that 'Jesus showed extreme reserve toward the title Messiah. He actually considered the specific ideas connected with the title as satanic temptations.' (2) Jesus is accused by the Jews in Luke 23: 2 of forbidding payment of tribute to Caesar. But the discussion by G. Schneider in this volume, pp. 403–14, removes the force of this reference. On this problem, cp. also the contributions of F. F. Bruce, pp. 249–63, and of G. M. Styler, pp. 105–7.

[97] For Zealot activism, see Hengel, Die Zeloten, pp. 127ff. For the parable, see Jeremias, Gleichnisse, pp. 151f (ET pp. 151f), and Bammel, StEv iii, 11.

[98] C. H. Dodd, The Parables of the Kingdom (London, 1935).

[99] In favour of authenticity are W. G. Kümmel, Verheissung und Erfüllung (Zürich, 1956), pp. 98ff (ET Promise and Fulfilment (London, 1961), pp. 105–7); J. Becker, Johannes der Täufer und Jesus von Nazareth (Neukirchen-Vluyn, 1972), pp. 82f; H. W. Kuhn, Enderwartung und gegenwärtiges Heil (Göttingen, 1966), pp. 190ff; Perrin, Teaching, pp. 63ff; Bammel, 'Erwägungen', StEv iii, 13. Against it is Haenchen, Weg, p. 148, but the considerations in this direction do not seem probative. The problem of the relation of present and future eschatology cannot of course be discussed here.

[100] Hengel, Die Zeloten, p. 230.

this passage, the tendentiousness of Brandon's judgement once again interferes:

> Matthew, moved by the dangers which threatened the church in Alexandria during these difficult years, not only presented Jesus to his fellow-Christians as the Messiah who rejected armed violence to promote his cause, but he represents him as commanding his followers to show themselves similarly pacific in their conduct.[101]

In this Brandon of course neglects the fact that the commandment to love one's enemy is to be found already in Q (see Luke 6: 27f, 32ff)! In fact, since parallels to this unconditional requirement are lacking in both Qumran and rabbinic literature,[102] and since the primitive church took up other themes (cp. Rom. 12: 19; John 13: 34f; 1 John 3: 23; Rev. 6: 10), we may well apply the criterion of underivability: this 'Magna Charta of *agape*'[103] can only go back to Jesus himself.

If conduct toward one's fellow-men is to be so totally determined by love that not only are vindictive acts and thoughts to be eschewed but even intercession for one's enemy is required, then there can be no justification for Zealot acts of violence against a fellow-man. All ideals, however great or sacred they may be, must be subordinated to love for one's neighbour. With this precept Jesus placed himself outside all parties and groups of his time. Once we become aware of how often Jesus burst through the bounds of conventional thought and behaviour, we must regard a conflict between him and the representatives of the traditional order as unavoidable. In fact, the proclamation of Jesus 'cannot be set within the Judaism of the time without supposing that it made a fundamental breach in the framework of Judaism'.[104] This historical situation is suitably reflected theologically in Rom. 10: 3 and John 1: 18. Paul and John have preserved here a significant feature of the proclamation of Jesus, even though the outlines of the earthly Jesus may not otherwise show up clearly in their writings.[105]

---

[101] *Zealots*, p. 210.
[102] So Jeremias, *Theologie*, p. 207 (ET p. 213); Braun, *Jesus*, p. 124.
[103] Hengel, *War Jesus Revolutionär?* p. 20 (ET p. 27).
[104] Hengel, *Nachfolge*, p. 79.
[105] The article was translated by Dr J. F. Coakley. Some aspects of the more recent discussion are dealt with in my article 'Jesus im Widerstreit' in *Glaube und Gesellschaft* (Festschrift W. F. Kash), (Bayreuth, 1981), pp. 207–17.

Judaeo-Christianity and the Jewish establishment, A.D. 33–66

During the middle third of the first Christian century, that is, between the crucifixion of Jesus, c. A.D. 33, and the outbreak of the first Jewish war, A.D. 66, the centre of Christianity acknowledged by all was constituted by the Jewish Christians in Palestine (Matt. 24: 16 with par.; Acts 15: 2; 1 Thess. 2: 14; Rom. 15: 26f; Acts 21: 18). Our understanding of the political attitude adopted by the church in the days of the apostles – including the question whether the disciples of Jesus had connections with Jewish zealotism – must depend on what can be observed about the relations of the Jewish Christians in Palestine with the Jewish authorities of the period. Because the country was controlled by the Romans, the Jewish establishment represented by the high priest and the Sanhedrin was supposed to maintain good relations with the Roman establishment represented by the prefect in Caesarea and the governor in Antioch, and indirectly with the *princeps* and senate of the empire. For the same reason the positive or negative relations between the Jewish Christians of the Holy Land and the Jewish rulers and leaders were of importance for the political attitude of the entire church during the apostolic period, A.D. 33–66.

I

The story of the passion told by the evangelists implies that Jesus was accused of two different crimes before the Sanhedrin and the prefect: (*a*) of false teaching and (*b*) of rebellion. Since the forensic context was in each case a different one, there had to be this double charge. (*a*) Before the Jewish Sanhedrin, the high priest referred to Jewish legislation and accused Jesus of religious false teaching, here called blasphemy (Matt. 26: 65 with par.).[1] (*b*) Before the Roman prefect, the high priest referred to Roman interests, and presented Jesus as a political troublemaker (Luke 23:2) who claimed to be the King of the Jews (Matt. 27: 37 with par.). Thus the Nazarene was 'reckoned with transgressors' (Luke 22: 37), sacrificed by the

---

[1] J. C. O'Neill, 'The Charge of Blasphemy at Jesus' Trial before the Sanhedrin' in E. Bammel (ed.), *The Trial of Jesus, Cambridge Studies in Honour of C. F. D. Moule* (London, 1970), pp. 72–7.

populace instead of a revolutionary assassin (Mark 15: 7), and crucified together with two bandits (Matt. 27: 38 with par.).

After the death of Jesus, c. A.D. 33, until the exodus of the Jewish church shortly before the outbreak of the first Jewish war, A.D. 66 (Eusebius, *H.E.* iii. 5.3), the Palestinian Christians were repeatedly molested by the Jewish establishment or by the mob. Several prophecies were also quoted in order to show that Jesus had already foreseen this analogy between himself and the believers (for instance, Matt. 10: 17–25; 24: 9–22 with par.). But the historical evidence available implies that his disciples were in fact only accused of false teaching or blasphemy (*a*), and there is no trace of their having been accused of rebellion (*b*). This is certainly an important circumstance with regard to the question whether the Palestinian Christians had connections with the so-called Zealots, those Jewish nationalists who, during the period in question, fought desperately against Greek influence and Roman sovereignty.

II

Disciples of Jesus were in fact merely accused of (*a*) false teaching or even blasphemy in connection with different persecutions ascribed to the apostolic period, but never of (*b*) rebellion.

In three cases the charge was blasphemy, which had to be punished by stoning (Lev. 24: 16): (1) at the trial of Stephen, A.D. 36 (Acts 6: 14; the blasphemy was his statement that Jesus is superior to Moses and the Temple); (2) at the arrest of Paul, A.D. 58 (Acts 21: 28; 24: 6; Paul was alleged to have polluted the Temple); and (3) of James the brother of Jesus, A.D. 62 (according to Josephus, *AJ* xx. 200, he was accused of transgression of the Law; according to Hegesippus in Eus. *HE* ii. 23.4, it was the scribes who stoned James because his confession of Jesus as the messiah irritated them).

In connection with two other persecutions of Christians in Palestine during the apostolic period, the charge was false teaching (below, 1 and 2); in two further cases there is no hint of any denunciation or incrimination (below, 3 and 4).

(1) The arrest of Peter and John in the Temple, c. A.D. 34, was said to have been arranged by the captain of the Temple together with other priests, and by the Sadducees (Acts 4: 1). They were embarrassed by the great success the apostles experienced among the people, who had seen them heal a lame man and heard them preach the gospel of resurrection which the Sadducees rejected as false teaching (4: 2). For the moment, however, the Sanhedrin was not able to find them guilty of any crime (4: 14–16).

(2) Some time afterwards, c. A.D. 35 – according to a parallel tradition

also used by Luke, and presented by him in similar terms – the high priest arrested the apostles since he was jealous of the enormous interest Peter aroused among the people because of the signs he did (Acts 5: 17), but also since he was afraid of being accused of having caused the death of Jesus (5: 28). This time, it was reported, the Pharisaic Rabbi Gamaliel I declared before the Sanhedrin that if there were any reason for it God himself would destroy the community as he dissolved the infamous movements of Theudas and Judas the Galilaean, the pioneer of zealotism (Jos. *AJ* xviii. 23; *BJ* vii. 253); but otherwise he would protect the Christians against every human attack (Acts 5: 36–9). Luke wanted to make clear that Gamaliel and the Sanhedrin left the question open whether the apostolic community led by Peter was comparable to the rebellious movements led by Theudas and Judas, or quite different from them. The subsequent development of the Nazarene movement was supposed to be the criterion, for if Christianity did involve anarchy, it would certainly be destroyed by God like the insurrections of Theudas and Judas. Every reader of Acts knew that the church was flourishing, and the famous Pharisaic scholar had therefore given Christianity a double testimony confirmed by historical facts: the gospel was not comparable to any propaganda of the Jewish revolutionaries, but inspired by God.[2]

(3) Judaea became a kingdom again for the years 41–4 under Agrippa I, the grandson of Herod I. It was this snobbish Herod who, around A.D. 42, gave orders to kill James the son of Zebedee, and later to arrest Peter (Acts 12: 2–4). The execution of James was said to have pleased the Jews, and Luke saw here the reason why the persecution was continued by the arrest of Peter (12: 3). This explanation is quite in harmony with the pro-Jewish and pro-Pharisaic policy that Agrippa I began to practise as soon as Claudius had made him king of Judaea (Jos. *AJ* xix. 293–302, 327, 330–4). During the years 37–40, when Caligula had favoured Hellenism in the empire, Christianity had rapidly been spread over the whole of Palestine and even to Phoenicia, Cyprus and Syria, reaching Hellenistic areas of great importance (Acts 8: 4 to 11: 30). As was evident at the persecution of Stephen in the year 36 (Acts 6: 1, 9), the success of the Gospel among the Hellenists irritated orthodox Jews. Though he favoured Hellenism abroad, Agrippa I arranged the persecution of James and Peter around the year 42 in order to confirm that he was the great protector of Judaism in Palestine. It was for the same political reason that he neglected the interests of the Hellenistic centres, Caesarea and Samaria, the population of which rejoiced when he died in the year 44 (Jos. *AJ* xix. 356–9).[3]

---

[2] B. Reicke, *Glaube und Leben der Urgemeinde* (Zürich, 1957), pp. 55–114.
[3] Seeing that James, the son of Zebedee, was reported to have been killed 'by the

(4) Though the famine around A.D. 46 and the apostolic council of the year 49 reduced the Judaistic opposition to Hellenism and thus also to Christianity (Acts 11:28–30; 15:19–29; Gal. 2:9f), the years 50 to 52 brought about violent quarrels between legalistic Jews and their neighbours in Rome, Alexandria, and Palestine. Indirectly the Christians had to suffer from this *Kulturkampf*. By an edict of A.D. 50, Claudius expelled the Jews from Rome because of constant rioting among them in connection with the messiah (Suetonius, *Divus Claudius* xxv. 4 speaks of a man called Chrestus), and for this reason Aquila and Priscilla came to Corinth (Acts 18:2). Between the Greeks and Jews of Alexandria there had been violent struggles in A.D. 38, and they began again *c.* A.D. 50, when both groups had to send delegates to Rome. Claudius, in the year 52, and under the influence of Agrippa II, decided the issue in favour of the Jews (*Acta Alexandrinorum* IV A, ii. 16f; IV C, ii. 21–4, ed. H. Musurillo: *The Acts of the Pagan Martyrs* (Oxford, 1954); *Acta Alexandrinorum* (Lipsiae, 1961)). At the same time, a real war took place in Palestine. First the Jews were irritated by the soldiers of the Roman procurator Cumanus, then they went to war against the Samaritans, well knowing that Cumanus protected the population of the Hellenistic *poleis*, Caesarea and Sebaste. Their attacks were especially carried on by demagogic anarchists under the leadership of a famous Zealot, Eleasar Dinaei, but also supported by aristocratic patriots under the leadership of the former High Priest Jonathan. Like the Alexandrian struggle, this Palestinian war led to a trial before the Emperor in A.D. 52, and since Agrippa II was successful in his defence of the Jews, Cumanus and the Samaritans were condemned (Jos. *BJ* ii. 223–46; *AJ* xv. 105–36). The same revival of Judaism was the background of the Jewish abuse of Christians in Judaea, of which Paul complained in a letter written in A.D. 52 (1 Thess. 2:14–16). Paul did not refer to any details and Luke avoided the story with regard to Agrippa II, but in different ways Jewish Christians of Palestine must be understood to have become the victims of the reinforced Jewish patriotism and zealotism, which triumphed in the trials of A.D. 52.

Thus the historical evidence available shows that the double charge preferred against Jesus, implying (*a*) false teaching and (*b*) rebellion, was extended to Jewish Christians in Palestine only with regard to (*a*) religious heresy, but never with regard to (*b*) social or political rebellion. Some

sword' (Acts 12:2), S. G. F. Brandon has concluded that Agrippa I was also concerned about the seditious aspect of Christianity: *The Trial of Jesus* (London, 1968), p. 48. But in connection with this persecution, *c.* A.D. 42, the king's concern was expressly said to be to please the Jews (12:3), and his general ambition to strengthen Pharisaism was emphasised by Josephus. There was no reason for any Jewish opposition to Rome under the glorious King Agrippa, and there is no reason to believe that James and his fellow Christians had ever appeared to be a danger to the empire.

persecutions took place without any legal trial, and no accusation is referred to. Generally the Christians were exposed to Jewish zeal for the law. The trials of the years 34 to 36 were led by two high priests belonging to the family of Annas, and the charge implied preaching the gospel of resurrection (Acts 4: 1f; 5: 17, 28) or criticism of Moses and the Temple (6: 11–14; 7: 1; 9: 1); in *c.* A.D. 42 the persecution was organised by Herod's grandson Agrippa I simply in order to please the Jews (12: 1); in *c.* A.D. 52 the Zealot movement involved the Christians in the general terror (1 Thess. 2: 14); in A.D. 58 Paul was nearly lynched by the mob because of their zeal for the Temple (Acts 21: 28, 24: 6), and made the Sadducees furious because of his belief in the resurrection (23: 6); eventually, the trial of the year 62 was caused by another high priest of the Annas family who accused James the Lord's brother of transgressing the Jewish law (Jos. *AJ* xx. 200). In all these contexts the Christians are represented as the victims of the Jewish establishment which fostered patriotism and zealotism.

III

The history of the church during the years 33–66 is only known from Luke in Acts and Paul in his letters, and it must be admitted that both authors might have left out details which they found embarrassing. Luke and Paul adopted an optimistic attitude to the Roman establishment (Acts 25: 11; Rom. 13: 4), and in Rome it was especially important for them to give the gospel a good reputation in official circles (Acts 28: 30f; Phil. 1: 13; 4: 22). Is it not possible that some of the Jewish Christians shared the antagonism of the Jewish Zealots against Rome, although Luke and Paul did not describe any movement of that kind?

Here one has to observe the difference between the first and last half of the apostolic era, that is, between (1) the period 33 to 54 when Tiberius, Caligula and Claudius governed the empire and Peter was the leader of the Jewish believers (Gal. 2: 7), and (2) the period 54 to 66 when Nero was emperor, when Jewish zealotism became more and more predominant in Palestine, and James, the Lord's brother, was the leader of the Judaean churches (Acts 21: 18).[4]

(1) There is not the slightest hint of any connection between Jewish insurgents and Christian believers during the years 33 to 54. On the contrary, the Christians were repeatedly the victims of Jewish patriotism and zealotism during this period. An *argumentum e silentio* is here inevitable, for the only alternative is the illogical conclusion that members of the churches led by Peter were Zealots because the sources do not mention it.

[4] B. Reicke, *Neutestamentliche Zeitgeschichte*, 3rd edn. (Berlin, 1982), pp. 191ff, 238ff (ET *The New Testament Era* (London, 1968), pp. 188–224, 237–51).

(2) But indications of a certain Christian zeal for the law are in fact given by Luke in Acts and Paul in his letters with regard to the years 54 to 66. This was the period when the notorious Hellenism of Nero caused a reaction of Judaism which became more and more violent, and then led to the first Jewish war, A.D. 66–70. If the Zealot troubles had already imposed severe difficulties upon the Christians of Judaea around A.D. 52 (1 Thess. 2: 14), they grew into a veritable terror after Nero's enthronement in A.D. 54. This terror compelled Jewish Christians to combine their belief with a zeal for the law, but it cannot be proved that they ever took part in revolution and violence.

Josephus was seventeen years old when Nero became emperor in A.D. 54, so his description of the reaction in Palestine was based on personal recollections. He had been an eager student of law under the guidance of Pharisees, Sadducees, and Essenes, but then suddenly left Jerusalem, and spent the years 54 to 56 with a baptist community in the desert (Jos. *Vita* 9–12). Bearing in mind his remarkable opportunism, one understands that Josephus seized the opportunity to avoid the political terror which broke out in the first years of Nero's pronouncedly Hellenistic government. In his works on the Jewish war, he gave dramatic reports of the violent resistance characteristic of this period (Jos. *BJ* ii. 254–65; *AJ* xv. 160–72). Just after Nero's enthronement bandits of a new kind came up in Jerusalem, the assassins called *sicarii*, because they carried a curved dagger (*sica*) under their clothes. With this Parthian weapon they secretly killed people supposed to collaborate with the Romans. Throughout the country they set fire to the houses of those who refused to support the resistance. Josephus said that everybody expected death any moment as one might in time of war (*BJ* ii. 256).[5]

Under the pressure of this political terror, Judaean Christians began to ask themselves whether it would not be advisable to accept the Jewish zeal for the law, and so be able to avoid the mortal danger. This led to a development of Judaism within Christianity during the years 54 to 61; and the spread of the zeal for the law can be followed in Paul's opposition to it.

Although the apostolic council of A.D. 49 had guaranteed equal rights to Jewish and Greek believers, supporters of James, the Lord's brother, made Peter and Barnabas uncertain some years later, and they withdrew from

---

[5] M. Smith, 'Zealots and Sicarii. Their Origins and Relation', *HThR*, 64 (1971), 1–19, wants to find three stages in the development of zealotism: (1) several representatives of 'zeal' in the sense of resistance to direct Roman government (p. 18); (2) the rise of the *sicarii* A.D. 54 (pp. 13, 18); (3) the organisation of the Zealots, A.D. 67 (p. 19). The impetus given by the *sicarii* was in any case important for the further development of the resistance movement.

intercommunion with the uncircumcised. Paul was obliged to criticise Peter for this when he met him in Antioch after his second journey, A.D. 54 (Gal. 2: 11–14). He had earlier been a Jewish Zealot who fought violently against the Christians to defend the traditions of the fathers (1: 14), and knew the destructive effects of any zeal for the law (2: 18f). Having left Antioch for his third journey, Paul was shocked to see the same exclusive Zealot movement dominating the Christians of Galatia (4: 17). Then he was confronted with the Judaistic movement at Ephesus in 55 (Acts 18: 25), and finally at Corinth in 56 (1 Cor. 1: 12). Writing from the capital of Greece in 58, Paul warned the Roman Christians against unlawful behaviour and zealotism (Rom. 13: 1, 13). He came back to Jerusalem a few months later, and there found thousands of Christians who had become Zealots for the law (Acts 21: 20). To avoid troubles, the friends of James, the Lord's brother, advised him to demonstrate a certain solidarity with Moses in the Temple (21: 23f). It did not help, for the mob accused Paul of sacrilege, and only the Roman garrison saved him from being stoned (21: 27–32). Just as Paul had earlier been a zealous enemy of the Christians, so he was now exposed to severe Jewish fanaticism. Luke indicated this analogy in a speech ascribed to Paul (Acts 22: 3). Paul himself referred to it while he was still in captivity after the Zealot riot in Jerusalem, and in very sharp language warned the Philippians against the influence of Judaistic materialism (Phil. 3: 2, 6, 19). In the capital of the empire the danger of zealotism was especially great, as was later confirmed by Clement of Rome when he found zeal to have been the reason for the persecution of several Christians as well as for the catastrophe of Israel (1 Clem. 5: 1 to 6: 4).

It is thus evident from Luke's narrative in Acts and from Paul's opposition in his letters that a certain zeal for the law was developed by Jewish Christians during the years 54 to 61. But it can only be said of this limited period. The zeal was caused by a desire to avoid the dangers of the Jewish reaction against the pro-Hellenistic emperor Nero. For this very reason the documents seem to give a reliable picture when they do not indicate the slightest Christian participation in the Jewish activities whether these activities were led by patriots or Zealots. On the contrary, Christians who did not join the extreme nationalists in Judaea were probably exposed to pressure or persecution, as emphasised by Josephus with regard to his countrymen in general (Jos. BJ ii. 264f; AJ xx. 192). Paul experienced this in Jerusalem and Caesarea, A.D. 58 to 60 (Acts 21: 28; 23: 12; 25: 3). James, the Lord's brother, although the leading authority of those Christians who recommended concentration on Mosaic traditions (Gal. 2: 12; Acts 21: 18, 20), was made the victim of Jewish nationalism in A.D. 62. He was accused of transgression of the law and stoned by the High Priest Ananus, then leader of the aristocratic patriots who, during the years

62 to 66, competed in rebellion with the demagogic Zealots (Jos. *AJ* xx. 185–214).

The trial of James, the Lord's brother, implies that he no longer represented that zeal for the law characteristic of his supporters in the years 54 and 58 – at least not so definitely that it satisfied the Jewish establishment. It is probable that James as well as Peter, although both represented pronounced Jewish-Christian points of view in A.D. 54 (Gal. 2: 12), were driven to change their policy around A.D. 60, and desist from Jewish nationalism. At any rate the Epistles which carry their names reject inclinations to isolation and zealotism (James 4: 2; 1 Pet. 3: 13). It must also be observed that many Christians left Jerusalem and Palestine during the years before the war began in 66 (Eus. *H.E.* iii. 5: 3). While there may have been some contacts between Jewish Zealots and Christians in the period 54 to 60, this possibility is reduced to a minimum in the subsequent years.

A.D. 70 in Christian reflection

The capture of Jerusalem by Titus and the burning of the Temple seem, so far as we can judge from the literature of the succeeding century and a half, to have made a surprisingly small impact upon the Christian communities. It was only a comparatively short time after the rejection of the messiah and the persecution of his followers by the leaders of Judaism when the spiritual and civil centre of Judaism was spectacularly destroyed, and the Temple laid in ruins.[1] We might expect Christian apologists to have exploited to the fullest extent the extraordinary opportunity offered to them by that shattering event to vindicate the church's claim to be the true Israel, the rightful heir to the promises and blessings of the covenant, and to declare God's judgement upon the 'stiff-necked and uncircumcised in hearts and ears' (Acts 7:51) who had so stubbornly opposed that claim. No special prophetic insight would have been required for any Christian to see in that disaster the decisive revelation of God's condemnation of the enemies of Jesus and his reversal of their verdict. We might also expect the year 70 to mark a turning-point in the relationship between Jewish Christianity and Judaism and so too, perhaps, between Jewish and Gentile Christians.

Yet in fact the literature of the Christian movement contains relatively few allusions to the fall of Jerusalem. The New Testament passages which may allude to it are somewhat enigmatic. Some are fairly certainly *vaticinia post eventum*, but most, and perhaps even all, could just be interpreted without total implausibility as genuine prophecies of a catastrophe which the troubled history of Judaea in the three or four decades preceding the outbreak of war would make it easy to foresee. The earliest Christian writing in which the destruction of the Temple is plainly and directly referred to in an historical statement, as distinct from a prophetic prediction or a parabolic saying, is the Epistle of Barnabas (16:4). It is therefore most precarious to argue from the silence of any book of the New

[1] K. W. Clark, 'Worship in the Jerusalem Temple after A.D. 70', *NTSt* 6 (1959/60), 269ff, argues for the continuance of the cultus on the Temple mount between the year 70 and the Second Revolt, at least to the extent to which it is widely believed to have been maintained during the Babylonian Exile. There is certainly no evidence that the ruins, or site, of the Temple were officially closed to worshippers, like the temple at Leontopolis. In any case, Clark is right in his insistence that the decisive catastrophe was not the destruction of the Temple by Titus but Hadrian's establishment of the cult of Jupiter on its site. Had there been a Josephus to narrate the events of 135 we might appreciate this fact more easily.

Testament about the fall of Jerusalem that it must have been written before 70.[2] It is equally misleading to suggest that no author writing after that date could speak of the Temple cultus in the present tense and fail to mention that in fact it had ceased to exist. The author to the Hebrews does this; but so does the author to Diognetus (1–3). J. Moffatt,[3] speaking of the need to place a work of literature in its contemporary intellectual, social and political setting in order to understand it properly, points out that 'as the early Christian literature was not national . . . such synchronisms yield less for the New Testament than for almost any other group of ancient writings'. 'As a matter of fact', he continues, 'the catastrophe is practically ignored in the extant Christian literature of the first century. Beyond slight traces in the synoptic, especially the Lucan, version of the eschatological predictions made by Jesus, and a possible echo in one of the sources underlying the Apocalypse, no vibrations of the crisis can be felt.'

If the idea that the fall of Jerusalem was an epoch-making event (in the strict sense of that term – a decisive turning-point in history) is strikingly absent from the early Christian literature, it is scarcely more prominent in contemporary Jewish writings. A. B. Davidson, discussing the theory that the Epistle to the Hebrews was addressed to Jewish Christians whose faith had been shaken by the destruction of the Temple, asserts bluntly that 'such a despair ought to have seized all Hebrews alike, whether Christians or not; but there is no historical evidence of such a thing'.[4] M. Simon contends that the evidence shows that the crisis of 70 had little effect on Diaspora Judaism in general; the Jews of Rome, Carthage, and even Alexandria and Antioch, remained indifferent to an event which changed nothing in their own situation.[5] Others have gone further. According to E. Deutsch,[6]

> The Priesthood, the Sacrifices, the Temple, as they all went down at one sudden blow, seemed scarcely to leave a gap in the religious life of the nation. The Pharisees had long ago undermined these things, or rather transplanted them into the people's homes and heart. Every man in Israel,

---

[2] The most that the advocates of an early dating for some or all of the books of the New Testament, of whom the most persuasive is J. A. T. Robinson, *Redating the New Testament* (London, 1976), can hope to demonstrate is that no passage in the New Testament absolutely *necessitates* a later date than the fall of Jerusalem. They cannot show that any particular book which fails to mention that event, even when to allude to it might seem to us to be particularly relevant and apposite, *must* have been written before it happened.

[3] *Introduction to the Literature of the New Testament* (3rd edn. Edinburgh, 1918), p. 3, partly cited by Robinson, *Redating*, p. 13.

[4] *Hebrews* (Edinburgh, 1882), p. 21.

[5] *Verus Israel* (Paris, 1948), p. 54.

[6] 'Notes of a Lecture on the Talmud', in *Literary Remains of Emmanuel Deutsch* (London, 1874), p. 139.

they said, is a priest, every man's house a temple, every man's table an altar, every man's prayer his sacrifice. Long before the Temple fell, it had been virtually superseded by hundreds of synagogues, schools, and colleges, where laymen read and expounded the Law and the Prophets.

This is one-sided rhetoric. Rabbinic Judaism itself was more varied in its reactions, and besides the Pharisaic tradition idealised by Deutsch there existed also apocalyptic hopes of a rebuilding of Jerusalem and the downfall of the empire of the Flavians (cp. 2 Esdras 11: 1 to 12: 3), Josephus's presentation of the tragedy as the outcome of, and divine penalty for, folly and wickedness, the insistence of 2 Baruch (7: 1; 80: 1–3) that it was a signal instance of divine judgement on Israel, and of Book 4 of the Sibylline Oracles (115–27) that it was part of God's universal judgement, directed primarily against the devotees of temples, altars and animal sacrifices (27–30) and recently manifested in the homeland of the Romans themselves in the eruption of Vesuvius in the year 79. It seems clear, nevertheless, that the early Jewish reaction to the event of 70 scarcely suggests that it was seen as the totally catastrophic end of an age. On the contrary, mainstream Judaism appears to have accommodated itself remarkably easily to the cessation (if such it really was) of the Temple and the cultus.

It is, however, only with Christian attitudes that we are now concerned. Here the evidence shows that by the time Christians had begun fully to develop an apology against Judaism which made use of the themes of the supersession of the Temple and the sacrifices, the vindication of the Christian argument from prophecy, and the punishment of the Jewish people for the crime of the crucifixion, the second Jewish war had been fought, and the memory of the fall of Bether was fresher than that of the sack of Jerusalem by Titus. The event which evidently made an especially strong impression on Christian apologists was the exclusion of the Jews from the heart of their own land. This took place, declared Eusebius, primarily by the will of God, as the prophets had prophesied, and secondarily by the prohibitions enacted by the Roman government (*Chron.* A.D. 135). 'The whole nation', said Aristo of Pella, 'was prohibited entirely from setting foot upon the country round Jerusalem by the decrees and ordinances of a law of Hadrian which forbade them even from afar to gaze on the soil inherited from their fathers' (Eusebius, *H. E.* 4.6.3). 'So', adds Eusebius, 'when the city was thus emptied of the nation of the Jews and its old inhabitants utterly destroyed, and when it was peopled by an alien race, the Roman city which then arose changed its name, and was called Aelia in honour of him who was ruling, Aelius Hadrianus' (4.6.4). Justin was greatly impressed by this exclusion of the Jews from their own land on pain of death. To him it fulfilled such prophecies as Isa. 1: 7, 2: 15, 64: 10–12, and Jer. 50: 3; it meant also that circumcision, the former sign of the covenant which some Jewish Christians in Justin's time still maintained, had become a kind of brand of Cain, marking out Jews as wandering exiles.[7] The events of the year 70 thus tended to be remembered in association with, and to some extent only as a prelude to, the even more final and crushing judgement of God executed in 135 against the opponents of the church's claim to be the authentic Israel; and by the latter date the church's main preoccupation lay no longer with the establishment of its position over against Judaism, but elsewhere.

The outcome of the first Jewish war made relatively little difference to the church's understanding of itself and its mission, and had no decisive effect on the situation even of Jewish Christians. It had become clear by that time that the future of the Christian mission lay with the Gentile churches, a conclusion which had much more to do with the progress of the Pauline and other missions to the Gentiles than with the fate of Jerusalem and the Temple. By the sixties the growing-points of the church lay far from Judaea, and the notion entertained by Origen (*Hom.* IX. *10 in Jos.*) and by Sulpicius Serverus (*Chron.* 2.30.7) that the aim of the Romans in 70 was to destroy both Judaism and Christianity at one blow is quite anachronistic. Jewish Christianity, as well as Gentile, had by this time established its own identity. It is true that the romantic imagination of Hegesippus, or perhaps the romantically nostalgic traditions of Palestinian Christianity in the second century, pictured an extremely close link between the church of Jerusalem under James and the Temple and its cultus. Hegesippus describes James as a priestly figure, constantly offering intercessory prayer for the Jewish nation (Eus. *H.E.* 2.23. 4–7). After the war, of course, no such relationship was possible; but it is unlikely that it ever existed in the manner portrayed by Hegesippus, whose idea of James belongs to the exaggerated tradition, developed in the second and third centuries, according to which the leadership of James in the church of Jerusalem was imagined to have involved something like a transference of the high-priesthood.

During the war and in the ensuing three or four decades, it is true, the separation of the Jewish Christians from Judaism became complete. According to Eusebius (*H.E.* 3.5.3) and Epiphanius (*Haer.* 29.7, 30.2, *Mens.* 15.2–5), perhaps using Hegesippus as their common source, they left Jerusalem for Pella before the siege. Some at least returned to Jerusalem after 70 and maintained a Jewish Christian succession of bishops there during the period between the two wars (Eus. *H.E.* 4.5.1–4), continuing to observe the Law. There is no evidence, however, that this church was at all interested in the question of the restoration of the Temple. No Christian echoed the Jewish prayer, 'May it be speedily rebuilt in our days' (*Tamid*

---

[7] Cp. Justin, *Dial.* 16, 17. 1–4, 22, *1 Apol.* 47.

7.3 (33b), *Ta'anith* 4.8 (26b), *Baba Metzi'a* 28b). The messianic and apocalyptic expectations of the period of 2 Esdras, the Apocalypse of Baruch, the war in Trajan's reign, and the revolt of Bar Kochba were not shared by Christians; it is possible, indeed, that such warnings as Mark 13: 5–6 and its parallels may reflect their reaction against them. When the Second Revolt came these Jewish Christians became the object of fierce persecution by the nationalists (Justin, *1 Apol.* 31). In the meantime, during the inter-war period, the Christians came to be excluded from the synagogue (cp. John 9: 22) and cursed in the words of the twelfth of the *Eighteen Benedictions* (cp. Justin, *Dial.* 16). But this state of affairs was by no means new or unprecedented. It represented only an intensification of a mutual separation and hostility between Jews and Jewish Christians in Palestine which had caused the latter to suffer violent persecution as early as the writing of 1 Thess. 2: 14, and which is reflected in the traditions recorded in Acts. The war, the flight to Pella, and the fall of Jerusalem may have sharpened this separation and hatred and accelerated its development, but they neither created it, nor, in all probability, greatly affected its growth, which the links of the Jewish Christians with Gentiles made inevitable.

The main principles of the Christian position had been established against Judaism well before the first Jewish war and the destruction of the Temple. The fall of Jerusalem might indeed be expected to have raised in a most dramatic manner fundamental questions about the identity of God's elect people, and about the divine vindication of the claims which Christians made for Jesus. Yet in fact it could do no more than confirm what Christians in the churches of the Gentile world already believed. For them, as indeed for Jewish Christians as well, the decisive event which vindicated Jesus as the Christ, the Lord, the Son of God, was not the destruction of his enemies but his resurrection from the dead and his exaltation to God's right hand. The teaching of Paul had vindicated the claim of the church to be the authentic Israel. The seed of Abraham was the community of those who, like Abraham, were justified by faith; the covenant of faith was therefore both older and newer than the covenant made at Sinai. Christ had been shown by Paul to be 'the end of the Law' (Rom. 10: 4) in more than one sense of the word 'end'. By implication, at least, the Pauline gospel meant that the sacrificial cultus had been superseded; and well before the year 70 the foundations had already been laid for the theological structure that was to be built by the authors of the Fourth Gospel and the Epistle to the Hebrews in relating, in their different ways, the work of Christ and his priesthood 'after the order of Melchizedek' to the priesthood and the sacrifices of the Old Covenant. From the letter to the Galatians Christians had learned that they were children of the

Jerusalem which is 'above', the community which, because it enjoys the freedom of the Spirit, stands over against its antithesis, the earthly Jerusalem which is in servitude to the Law (Gal. 4: 25–6, cp. Phil. 3: 20). The foundations, once again, had been laid for the later development of the theme of the 'heavenly Jerusalem' in Hebrews (12: 22), the 'new' or 'holy' Jerusalem which, according to the Revelation of John (3: 12; 20: 9; 21: 2), is to descend from heaven and in which the presence of God will not be focussed or localised in any temple, and for the reinterpretation by the Fourth Evangelist of the idea of a holy place, established by God for worship, in terms of a community which worships in the Spirit and truth (John 4: 21–3). Paul had already taught that the holy temple of God, indwelt by the Spirit, is the congregation of Christian people, the temple of the living God in which his presence assures the fulfilment of the covenant promise, 'I will be their God and they shall be my people' (1 Cor. 3: 16–17; 2 Cor. 6: 16); and Paul had also shown that in a secondary sense each individual believer is the temple of the indwelling Holy Spirit (1 Cor. 6: 19). In this area of Christian theology, too, the foundations of later developments, such as the teaching of Eph. 2: 21 and 1 Pet. 2: 5, and, through a combination of the themes of the 'temple of the Spirit' and the 'body of Christ', of John 2: 21, had been firmly laid in the years before the Jewish war.

A strong tradition, indeed, derived the idea of the destruction of the Jerusalem Temple, and its replacement by a spiritual or heavenly temple 'not made with hands', from Jesus himself (Mark 14: 58; Matt. 26: 61). Although the evangelists assert that it was false witnesses who accused Jesus of having spoken in this sense, the charge is repeated by mockers at the Cross (Mark 15: 29; Matt. 27: 40), and Luke, who omits this in his Gospel, introduces the same theme in his account of the trial of Stephen: false witnesses allege that they have heard Stephen say that this Jesus the Nazarene will destroy the Temple (Acts 6: 14). Long before 70, therefore, the church as a whole, despite differences between, and within, the Gentile and Jewish Christian communities on christology and the place of the Law, had taken up its position on the central issues of the vindication of the messiahship of Jesus, the church's claim to be Israel in the true Abrahamic succession, the appropriation of the scriptures as testimonies to Jesus and the church, the cessation of the sacrifices and the reinterpretation of the significance of cultus and priesthood, and the replacement of the earthly Jerusalem and the material Temple by a heavenly city and a spiritual sanctuary, In some respect these conclusions were themselves based on attitudes current in Diaspora Judaism, where Law and synagogue, rather than Temple and sacrifice, formed the heart and focus of devotion, and where, in circles influenced by Alexandria, cultus, priesthood and Temple had been reinterpreted along the lines of Philonic 'spritualisation'. Even those Christians who, like Papias, Justin and Irenaeus, interpreted the Apocalypse and its prophecies of the millennium literalistically, and located the reign of Christ and the saints in Jerusalem (e.g. Justin, *Dial.* 81), did not imagine a restoration of the Temple and its system.

Answers had also been worked out early in the history of the church to the problem posed by the rejection of Jesus and the gospel by the leaders of Judaism and most of their followers. In the Epistle to the Romans Paul argued that the hardening and blinding of the Jews were included within God's purpose for the salvation of the world. It was a temporary divine dispensation to enable the Gentiles to hear and accept the gospel and so to stimulate the Jews, in their turn, to claim their rightful place within the true Israel of the church. A more pessimistic mood informs Paul's violent attack on the Jews in 1 Thess. 2: 14–16 – so different from the thought of Romans 9 to 11 as to suggest to some commentators the possibility that the passage is an interpolation. In a fury of indignation at the way in which his mission has been obstructed, Paul charges the Jews collectively with the murder of the Lord Jesus and the prophets (cp. Acts 2: 23, 7: 52), and with persecuting himself. They are displeasing to God and hostile to all men, preventing Paul from preaching salvation to the Gentiles, and thus 'filling up the full measure of their sins always'. Now, says Paul, God's wrath has come upon them 'utterly' or 'for good and all', in anticipation of the final Judgement. Assuming that this denunciation is authentic, we can easily appreciate how little there was left for Christians to say when disaster actually overtook the Temple and the priesthood. In this mood, at any rate, Paul was ready to believe that the eschatological wrath of God had already come upon Judaism because, and in the very fact that, it had slain Christ and the prophets who had proclaimed him before the event, and was now persecuting and hindering the missionaries who were preaching him after the event. According to Romans 9 to 11, Judaism was soon to become merged with the Gentile church by conversion and thus lose the separate identity which God was allowing it to retain only for the time during which the Gentiles were being gathered in. Alternatively, according to 1 Thess. 2: 16, Judaism was already subject to irrevocable condemnation. In either case the destruction of the Temple would evoke little surprise. It would seem a natural outworking of a situation which had long been established and to which the events of 70 made no essential difference.

In the later books of the New Testament and in the literature of the following century or so we find a development and consolidation of attitudes towards Judaism which had already been formed in the time of Paul. Thus the conviction that Christians are Israel, possessors of a new and better covenant mediated by Jesus, reaches fuller expression in such passages as Eph. 2: 19ff; Heb. 2: 16; 7: 22; 8: 6–13; 1 Clem. 31.2, and in varying forms it is implicit in the main thrust of the argument of Luke–Acts, Matthew, and, indeed, most of the New Testament and early post-canonical writings. Paul's argument concerning the covenants of the Law and the Spirit (Gal. 4: 21–31) is transformed by the author of Barnabas (13, 14), admittedly an extremist, into a virtual denial that the Israel of the Old Testament ever received God's covenant at all; the Jews never were the authentic Israel. At the same time the belief that the blindness of Judaism is temporary and providential gives way to the alternative conviction that the Jews have irrevocably rejected the gospel and have themselves been rejected by God. Luke firmly believes that the gospel was the fulfilment of the true tradition of Israel, as the speeches of Stephen and of Paul in his own defence (Acts 7: 2–53; 22: 1–21; 23: 6; 24: 10–21; 26: 2–23) plainly declare; but although, right to the very end of Luke's narrative, there are some Jews who understand that this is so and who become converted (Acts 28: 24), the eyes of official Judaism remain closed, its ears are dulled, its mind has become gross: it has fulfilled the prophecy of Isa. 6: 8–10, and within the true Israel which now embraces both Jews and Gentiles the future clearly lies with the Gentile element (Acts 28: 26–8). [Matthew presupposes a situation in which the church stands over against the renewed and consolidated Pharisaic Judaism of the period after 70; the separation of church from synagogue is complete, the church has its own organisation and ordinances (Matt. 18: 15ff; 23: 7–12), and Pharisaism is a powerful and bitter enemy. For the Fourth Evangelist 'the Jews' collectively are of the devil (John 8: 44). The seer of the Apocalypse even denies them the honourable name of Jews; they are Satan's synagogue (Rev. 2: 9).

Just as these attitudes towards Judaism had their roots in the decades preceding the Jewish revolt, so, too, the loyal, and sometimes even enthusiastic, attitude to the Roman empire of Christian writers of the period after 70 followed earlier precedent. Except for the Revelation of John, this attitude is remarkably consistent, and it is probably right to interpret that book's denunciation of Rome and its prophecies of Rome's destruction as directed against the demonic aspect of Rome's sovereignty, that is, the imperial cult and the consequent persecution of Christians in the name of a false king, lord and saviour (in fact, an anti-Christ), rather than against the empire itself from the standpoint of Jewish, or Christian–Jewish, nationalism. There was always an inevitable ambivalence in the Christian attitude to the empire. The duty of loyal citizenship, on the one hand, was matched on the other by the duty of passive resistance and martyrdom if the state demanded the worship which Christians believed to be due to God alone. Apologists such as Tertullian found no inconsistency in extolling the virtues of the Christians as loyal citizens who prayed constantly for the welfare of the emperor, and at the same time threatening those who persecuted Christians in the emperor's name with God's judgement and hell fire. There need have been no more inconsistency in the co-existence within the church during the sub-apostolic age of the apocalyptist's visions of the beast with the exhortations of 1 Peter to honour the emperor and fear God as parallel and related aspects of Christian duty. Luke's picture of the imperial authorities as the friends of Jesus and the church, at least when they were not intimidated by the Jews, and his careful explanations that it was only through ignorance or misunderstanding that Christian leaders could be associated with, or confused with, Jewish revolutionaries like Judas of Galilee, Theudas, or the 'Egyptian' (Acts 5: 36, 37; 21: 38), are fully in line with Clement's emphatic assertion of devotion to the empire (1 Clem. 60–61) and his remarkable choice of the Roman army as a model for ecclesiastical discipline (37). This is an attitude which leads on to the claim of Melito of Sardis that it was by divine dispensation that Christianity and the empire of Augustus originated at the same time; that the empire can assure its own prosperity by protecting Christianity ; and that it was only the wicked emperors, Nero and Domitian, who persecuted the church and then only because they had been misled by malignant persons (Eus. *H.E.* 4.26.7–11). All this, except conceivably 1 Peter, belongs to the period after 70; but the sentiments are not new, for they merely echo and enlarge upon the almost equally forceful words of Paul in Rom. 13: 1–7, inculcating the Christian duty of obedience to the emperor as a minister of God.

55 –
60 AD

To the period after 70 there very probably belong some, at least, of those 'prophetic' passages in the Gospels which may allude to the fate of Jerusalem. In the Markan tradition, followed by Matthew and Luke (Mark 13: 2, Matt. 24: 2; Luke 21: 6), the context of the apocalyptic discourse of Jesus is furnished by his prophecy of the total destruction of the Temple. It is possible to regard this as an actual prophecy, and to connect it with the obscure and ambiguous evidence that Jesus expected the Temple 'made with hands' to be superseded. In any case, it resembles and echoes the prophecies of Micah, Jeremiah and Ezekiel that God's imminent judgement on Israel would involve the overthrow of the Temple (Mic. 3: 12 cited at Jer. 26: 18; Jer. 7: 14–15; Ezek. 24: 21). Yet the doom of the Temple is pictured in terms of such extreme devastation ('Not one stone will be left upon another, all will be thrown down') as to suggest that a catastrophic fulfilment of the prediction may be alluded to (not necessarily, of course, with precise literal accuracy: the Temple was burned rather than demolished), and that it either originated or was sharpened after the event which it predicts.

The enigmatic prophecy of the 'abomination of desolation' (Mark 13: 14;

Matt. 24: 15) may also refer to the events of 70. In its Markan form this is a vague and imprecise application to a coming catastrophe in Judaea of a traditional apocalyptic symbol derived from the heathen altar, and probably also the statue, erected in the Temple by Antiochus Epiphanes (Dan. 9: 27; 11: 31; 12: 11; 1 Macc. 1: 54; cp. 2 Macc. 6: 2). It has to be borne in mind that early Christian eschatology tended to be cast in the mould of the Maccabaean crisis and therefore to follow a pattern laid down in the book of Daniel. This typological convention makes it extremely difficult to assign such material as that contained in 2 Thess. 2: 3–12 or in the 'synoptic apocalypse' to particular historical situations.

The implication of this passage is that the Temple (Mark speaks of the 'abomination' standing where it (properly, he) ought not, and Matthew explains this phrase as meaning 'in the holy place') will suffer some horrible heathen profanation. Among many interpretations which have been offered we find: the emperor Gaius's attempt to introduce his statue into the Temple in 39 to 40; the expected appearance of antichrist (cp. 2 Thess. 2: 3–4); the desecration of the Temple by the internecine strife among the Jewish factions during the Roman siege (but Daniel's 'abomination' must denote heathen idolatry); the entry of the Roman forces; or, as some late patristic commentators supposed, the introduction into the Temple precincts of a statue of Titus.[8] Luke reinterprets this saying. He substitutes 'the desolation' of Jerusalem for the allusion to the 'abomination of desolation', and explains that this will be brought about by besieging armies (Luke 21: 20). It is likely that Mark and Matthew as well as Luke may be thinking of an invasion of the Temple by Roman forces, and that they are associating this with some specific act of desecration. Possibly this was the famous occasion when the troops of Titus brought their standards to the Temple, set them opposite its eastern gate, and offered sacrifices to them.[9]

It must, however, again be remembered that the language of this passage, even in its Lukan form, is quite imprecise. The symbol of the 'abomination of desolation' was an apocalyptic commonplace, part of the Danielic typology of Antiochus Epiphanes and his violation of the Temple. Even Luke's picture of a besieged city, though true enough as a description of what befell Jerusalem in the war with Rome, is an echo of many passages of the Old Testament. This is equally true of the similar prophecy of a siege

---

[8] See G. R. Beasley-Murray, *A Commentary on Mark Thirteen* (London, 1957), pp. 54–72.

[9] Jos. *BJ* 6.316; cp. 1QpHab. 6.3–5: '(The Kittim) sacrifice to their standards and worship their weapons of war'; Tert. *Apol.* 16: 'The whole military religion of the Romans consists in venerating the standards, swearing by the standards, setting the standards before all the gods'.

and destruction of the city in Jesus's lamentation over Jerusalem (Luke 19: 43–4) with its echo of Isa. 29: 3–4.[10] The prophecy may be only a general warning that, as in the days of Jeremiah whose theme was the association of false religion with the Temple, the rejection of prophetic warnings of judgement by the leaders of the nation, and impending divine punishment, God's judgement is again approaching and will again be executed by heathen enemies.

Yet a saying may have a specific application to a particular historical situation even though it may be expressed in general terms and in conventional typological forms. We still have to ask why the evangelists gave prominence to this passage, and the most probable answer seems to be that it is really a 'prophecy' after the event, whether in its Lukan form only or in the Markan/Matthaean as well. If this is so, it indicates the beginning of Christian reflection on the significance of the disaster of 70. The proper response of Christians in Judaea was to flee from the city without delay; the use of the second person, 'pray (ye)', in Mark 13: 18/Matt. 24: 20 indicates that the whole warning is to be understood as being directly addressed to Jesus's followers. It is, again, a warning which echoes the traditional Maccabaean pattern: Christians are to act like the loyal devotees of the Law in the time of Antiochus, when Mattathias and his sons fled to the mountains, leaving all their possessions in the city (1 Macc. 2: 28). The question is whether this passage may possibly be referred to by Eusebius when, probably following Hegesippus, he records that the Jerusalem church received an oracle by revelation, as a result of which they moved out of the city to Pella before the outbreak of the war (*H.E.* 3.5.3). The destruction of Jerusalem was evidently seen, according to this tradition, as an act of divine vengeance for the violence done to Christ and his apostles, executed after God's holy people, the Christians, had been evacuated from the city like Lot from Sodom. We need not now consider the vexed question whether the command to flee, given in the 'Synoptic apocalypse', may have been suggested after the event by the actual flight of the Christians to Pella, or whether (as seems much less probable) it may have been itself the origin of the entire Pella tradition. Nor is it important that the command, literalistically interpreted, would have been impossible to carry out; flight would no longer be possible from Jerusalem (though perhaps still feasible from the rest of 'Judaea') once the city had been encircled by armies and the 'abomination' had arrived. What is relevant here is the fact that if it is indeed *post eventum* this passage contains the beginnings of Christian theological reflection on the fall of Jerusalem.

---

[10] See C. H. Dodd, 'The Fall of Jerusalem and the "Abomination of Desolation"', *JRS* 37 (1947), 47–54.

The event of 70 is God's judgement. These are the 'days of retribution' (cp. Luke 21: 22) which fulfil the Deuteronomic prophecy of God's wrath upon apostate Israel (Deut. 32: 35), and which, according to Luke's picture of Jerusalem 'trodden down by the Gentiles until the times of the Gentiles are fulfilled', also bring the fulfilment of the prophecy of Zech. 12: 3. In other passages peculiar to his Gospel Luke develops the theme of God's judgement on Israel, provoked by the rejection of the appeal and challenge of Jesus: in the warning to the daughters of Jerusalem (Luke 23: 27–31); and, more subtly, at the end of the Passion story: 'The crowd who had assembled for the spectacle, when they saw what had happened, went home beating their breasts' (23: 48). Taken together with Luke's insistence on the responsibility of the Jews for Jesus's death after Pilate's threefold verdict of acquittal, these words imply that already, at the time of the crucifixion, the people of Jerusalem were expecting that divine retribution would be exacted from them. Later tradition makes this explicit. According to a 'Western' manuscript tradition,[11] the crowds cry, 'Woe to us for the things that have been done today on account of our sins; for the desolation of Jerusalem has drawn near'. This seems to be derived from the tradition in the Gospel of Peter (25) which enlarges on the guilt and terror of the Jewish leaders. After the begging of the body of Jesus, 'the Jews and the elders and the priests, knowing what great evil they had done themselves, began to lament and to say, "Woe for our sins; the judgement and the end of Jerusalem has drawn near" '.

In the parable of the wicked tenants (Mark 12: 1–9; Matt. 21: 33–41; Luke 20: 9–16), the threat of destruction is possibly, but by no means certainly, an allusion to the fall of Jerusalem. Matthew (21: 43) strengthens the threat by adding, 'Therefore I tell you that the kingdom of God shall be taken from you and given to a nation producing the fruits of it'. God's special relationship to Israel, with its promises, blessings and obligations (for this is apparently what is meant in this context by the phrase 'the kingdom of God', not as usually in Matthew, 'the kingdom of heaven'), is to be transferred to the Christian church. This need not, however, contain a veiled allusion to the destruction of Jerusalem; it could equally well refer to the supersession of Pharisaic Judaism by Christianity.

The 'Q' tradition includes a warning that the rejection of Jesus, the climax of the long history of Israel's persecution of the prophets, must bring a divine judgement on Jerusalem (Matt. 23: 37–9; Luke 13: 34–5). It is quite possible, but again by no means certain, that this passage, which, in the warning 'your house is left to you (desolate)', echoes Jer. 22: 5, reflects the actual destruction of the Temple and the city. If, however, it is only a

---

[11] g¹, sysᵃᶜˑ, Tatian; cp. J. M. Creed, *The Gospel according to Saint Luke* (London, 1930) p. 288.

general and imprecise threat of judgement against the leaders of Judaism, it seems probable that it has been developed and made more specific in the Lukan lament of Jesus over Jerusalem (Luke 19: 41–4), with its explicit references to the siege and total destruction of the city. Admittedly, this is a conventional picture, employing familiar Old Testament imagery; but this is not inconsistent with its use by the evangelist or his source as an allusion to the events of 70: an allusion need not take the form of a literal description. The inference is that Jerusalem was blind to 'the things belonging to peace'. It did not recognise the time of God's visitation; and it was for this reason, so Christians reflected, that the city perished.

Luke is not alone among the evangelists in linking the divine condemnation of Jerusalem directly with the rejection and crucifixion of the Christ. Matthew similarly implies this in his story of the washing of Pilate's hands and the cry of 'all the people' (that is, Israel), 'his blood be on us and on our children' (Matt. 27: 25). In this dramatic scene Matthew makes the people themselves endorse the warning recorded in the 'Q' tradition that 'all righteous blood' (Matt. 23: 35f), or 'the blood of all the prophets' (Luke 11: 50f) will be paid for by 'this generation'.

A further important contribution to Christian reflection on the fall of Jerusalem is probably to be found in Matthew's peculiar insertion into his parable of the marriage feast: 'but the king was infuriated and sent his troops and destroyed those murderers and burnt down their city' (Matt. 22: 7). A case against the interpretation of this passage as a *post eventum* allusion to the Jewish war has been argued, notably by K. H. Rengstorf.[12] He maintains that the theme of an insult to a king or his representatives, provoking a punitive expedition and the destruction of the offenders' city by fire, is a traditional commonplace. The story recalls that of the book of Judith, and the episode of David and the Ammonites (2 Sam. 10: 1 to 11: 1), and its pattern recurs in the Old Testament, the Assyrian annals, and Josephus. It is, in fact, a *topos*, used as such in rabbinic parables. Rengstorf claims that it would be strange to see Vespasian's forces as armies sent by God (despite the fact that Josephus finds no difficulty in believing that they destroyed Jerusalem because God had condemned it – *BJ* 4.323,6.250), and he maintains that Matthew's parable is not historically focussed; it was not the destruction of the city itself but the ruin of the Temple and the cessation of the cultus that was the real disaster of 70. He does not, however, answer the difficult question why Matthew should have introduced this awkward digression into a story of the rejection of God's messengers by those whom he had originally invited, and of the bringing in of others to take their place

---

[12] 'Die Stadt der Mörder (Mt. 22: 7)', in W. Eltester, *Judentum, Urchristentum, Kirche* (Festschrift für J. Jeremias), *ZNW* Beiheft 26 (1960), 106–29.

at his feast – a story which, like its parallel in Luke 14: 16–24, would run smoothly and intelligibly but for this obtrusive verse about the king's revenge. It will not do to reply that Matthew seems in any case to have conflated two stories (that of the replacement of the invited guests, and that of the man without a wedding garment) into a single parable, and that he may in fact have also combined these two with a third: a tale of the insulting behaviour of a king's intended guests and of the way in which he avenged his messengers. For the question remains why Matthew should have chosen to confuse his parable by interrupting its sequence with another story, inartistically and awkwardly inserted in what is virtually a parenthesis. The obvious explanation would seem to be that Matthew sees in this parable, probably to be assigned to the 'Q' material, an opportunity to develop the theme of the parable of the wicked tenants (21: 41ff) and to drive home its point by an actual allusion to the fall of Jerusalem. He uses a conventional *topos* in order to do this; but the historical event itself of the revolt and its suppression could almost be said to follow a conventional recurrent pattern.[13]

Matthew, then, like Luke, sets the rejection of the Christ within the long history of Israel's persecution of the prophets, of which it is the final culmination. It means that God has abandoned non-Christian Judaism, and the destruction of Jerusalem and the Temple is the concrete evidence that this is so. Because the leaders of Judaism failed to believe in Jesus, the Romans had come and removed the Temple and the nation – as the Fourth Evangelist, with his typical irony, makes Caiaphas say they would do if the Sanhedrin were to let Jesus go and all men were to believe in him (John 11: 48).

Christian apologists naturally pursued this interpretation of the fall of Jerusalem as God's punishment of the Jews for the crucifixion; but, apart from these rather scanty allusions in the Gospels, it occurs neither so early nor so often as we might expect. Where it is found it often stands alongside other apologetic arguments, such as the claim that the destruction of the Temple vindicated the argument from prophecy for the messiahship of Jesus, that the Old Testament cultus was intended only as a temporary dispensation, that the cessation of the priesthood and sacrifices implies the supersession of the Law. Barnabas asserts that one purpose of the incarnation was that the full number of the sins of those who persecuted and slew the prophets might be summed up (5.11). This implies, like the parable of the wicked tenants, that Christ's death set the seal on the long

---

[13] See further L. H. Gaston, *No Stone on Another, NovTestSup* xxiii (Leiden, 1970); W. Trilling, *Das Wahre Israel*, StANT to (München, 1964); S. Pedersen, 'Zum Problem der vaticinia ex eventu', *ST* 19 (1965), 167–88; W. Grundmann, *Das Evangelium nach Matthäus*, ThHK (Berlin, 1968).

catalogue of Israel's ill-treatment of God's envoys, but it does not explicitly say that it brought about the events of 70. Earlier in this epistle the fate of the Jews is held up as a warning to Christians. Even after so many signs and wonders had been done among them, the people were abandoned by God. Christians, in their turn, must take heed not to be found to be the 'many called but few chosen' (4.14). Here the desolation of Jerusalem is seen as punishment or as a sign of reprobation, but it is not directly connected with the rejection of Christ.

Justin, too, argues that the scriptures attest the justice of God's punishment of the Jews by defeat and exile (*Dial.* 110); the fact that they had been banned from Judaea under Hadrian's legislation, and circumcision had become a sign which debarred them from entering their own land, was a measure of their rejection by God (*1 Apol.* 47, *Dial.* 16). Justin is chiefly concerned to develop the argument from prophecy. The fate of the Jews was part of the purpose of God disclosed by the Old Testament prophets; it confirms the Christian interpretation of the messianic prophecies. Justin does, however, at one point assert a direct connection between the downfall of the Jews and the death of Christ: 'It is right and just that these things have happened to you. For you killed the Righteous One and his prophets before him' (*Dial.* 16; cp. Acts 3: 14–15; 7: 52). In the Gospel of Peter this theme is developed: the destruction of Jerusalem was retribution for Christ's death. It is just possible that the same thought appears in the Preaching of Peter. An extract from this work, cited by Clement (*Strom.* 6.15.128), says that in the prophets we find the parousia (that is, the incarnation) of the messiah, his death, his cross, the punishments inflicted on him by the Jews, his resurrection and ascension, πρὸ τοῦ Ἱεροσόλυμα κτισθῆναι, καθὼς ἐγέγραπτο ταῦτα πάντα, ἃ ἔδει αὐτὸν παθεῖν καὶ μετ' αὐτὸν ἃ ἔσται. Von Dobschütz (TU xi, pp. 24–5) proposed to read κριθῆναι for κτισθῆναι, understanding this to refer to the 'judgement' of Jerusalem in 70, to which he believed μετ' αὐτὸν ἃ ἔσται to be an allusion. For a similar use of κριθῆναι he compared Isa. 66: 16 and 1 Clem. 11.1, and for the idea itself he compared the Gospel of Peter 25, already mentioned above: ἤγγισεν ἡ κρίσις καὶ τὸ τέλος Ἱερουσαλήμ. Others have conjectured ληφθῆναι, ἀλωθῆναι, or καθαιρεθῆναι for κτισθῆναι. Von Dobschütz may be right; on the other hand it is possible to repunctuate the passage so that it only means that some messianic prophecies are so old that they antedate the foundation of Jerusalem: πρὸ τοῦ Ἱεροσόλυμα κτισθῆναι καθὼς ἐγέγραπτο. ταῦτα πάντα, ἃ ἔδει αὐτὸν παθεῖν . . ., ταῦτα οὖν ἐπιγνόντες ἐπιστεύσαμεν.

Origen quotes Josephus as saying that the events of 70 came as retribution for the death of James the Just 'who was a brother of Jesus who was called Christ, since the Jews killed him who was a very righteous man'

(*C. Cels* 1.47, cp. *Comm. in Matt.* 10.17). Eusebius also reproduces these alleged words of Josephus, probably from Origen since he cites them in exactly the same form (*H.E.* 2.23.20). It seems likely that Hegesippus took this view, for his account of the martyrdom of James, excerpted by Eusebius (*H.E.* 2.23.4–18), ends: 'He has become a true witness both to Jews and Greeks that Jesus is the Christ. And immediately Vespasian attacked them.' Indeed, it is quite probable that Origen, and Eusebius following him, confused Hegesippus with Josephus. Alternatively, the passage was a Christian interpolation in Josephus *AJ* 20.200. Origen himself, however, is sure that the idea that the fall of Jerusalem was a punishment for the death of James is wrong: 'He ought to have said that the plot against Jesus was the reason why these catastrophes came upon the people, because they had killed the Christ who had been prophesied.' This theme recurs in Origen's writings. The Jews and their city, he says, were destroyed by the wrath of God which was consequent on their treatment of Jesus (*C. Cels.* 4.73), and their fall marks God's purpose of saving the Gentiles (*C. Cels.* 6.80 citing Rom. 11: 11–12, 25–6). Celsus himself was sufficiently familiar with Christian ideas to know of their belief that because the Jews had punished Jesus and given him gall (χολήν) to drink, they had drawn down on themselves God's fury (χόλον) (*C. Cels.* 4.22).

Origen's theory that the events of 70 were God's vengeance for Christ's death had been anticipated by Tertullian, who repeats Justin's contention that it was as a just punishment that the Jews had been prohibited from entering Jerusalem and circumcision had become a sign of their contumacy (*Jud.* 3.6). The doom prophesied by Amos (8: 9–10) has been fulfilled in the captivity and dispersion which overtook the Jews after Christ's passion (*Jud.* 10.15); these things have happened as a punishment for his death (*Marc.* 3.23).

Hippolytus developed this argument more fully. Because of their treatment of Christ the Jews are condemned to perpetual slavery (fulfilling Ps. 69: 25ff) and the loss of the Temple. It was not on account of idolatry (the golden calf), nor murder (of the prophets), nor Israel's fornication that the Temple was destroyed, but because of the slaying of the Son of the Benefactor (*Euergetes*). All this had been foretold by the Psalmist (*Dem. adv. Jud.* 6–7). Hippolytus (if this treatise is genuine) may have Jewish apologiae for the destruction of Jerusalem in mind. One of these explanations was that, whereas the first Temple had been destroyed because of idolatry, fornication and murder, the second Temple's ruin was caused by groundless hatred, which is as bad as those three cardinal sins (*Yoma* 9b). Another was that the fall of the Temple was a punishment for eight shortcomings on the part of Israel: the sabbath was desecrated, the reading of the *shema*ʿ neglected, the education of children neglected, the inhabitants of Jerusalem showed no respect to one another, small and great were made equal, they did not rebuke one another, scholars were despised, and men of faith ceased to be (*Shabbath* 119b). More generally, it was said that a judgement of God had been executed by the enemies of Jerusalem (*2 Bar.* 3.5), or, more optimistically, that exile was meant to afford opportunity for proselytising, and that God would surely rescue his people (*Pesachim* 87b). Josephus maintained that the destruction was caused by seditious tyrants among the Jews (*BJ* 1.11), and that it was not, in any case, a unique disaster; other nations, Athenians, Spartans, Egyptians and others, have suffered likewise (*C. Apion* 2.11). Answers on these lines were needed to counter the obvious arguments of pagan polemics: that the fate of the Jews demonstrated that the one God whom they worshipped was too weak and powerless to be able to prevent human beings, the Romans, from taking himself and his nation captive (Minucius Felix *Octavius* 10), or Apion's contention that the servile condition of Israel shows that God had abandoned them (Jos. *C. Apion.* 2.11). Such arguments had, in fact, appeared long before the Jewish revolt (e.g. in Cicero *Pro Flacco* 28).

The view that the fall of Jerusalem avenged Christ's death became a commonplace of later Christian apologetic. It is repeated frequently by Eusebius (*H.E.* 1.1.2, 2.6.8, 3.6.28), who believed not only that the Temple was destroyed as a punishment for the 'murderous killing of the Lord' but that Constantine's church, set up opposite its site, was in some sense a replacement of it, a 'new Jerusalem' (*V.Const.* 3.33). It recurs in Hilary: as a penalty for laying impious hands on the Lord and Saviour the Jews are scattered, captives, without Temple, priest or king. They were banned from Judaea, prophecy was silenced, sacrifices ceased, the Temple was made desolate (*Comm. in Ps.* 58.7). Jerome (*Comm. in Ezek.* 36: 16ff), Sulpicius Severus (*Chron.* 2.30), and Augustine (*Civ. Dei* 18.46) are among the later authors who repeat this standard argument.

In earlier apologetic much emphasis had been laid on the importance of the fall of Jerusalem as a confirmation of the argument from prophecy. It is treated in this way by Justin (*1 Apol.* 47). The Blessing of Jacob (Gen. 49: 8–12) showed that after the coming of the Christ there would be neither prophet nor king among the Jews; and 'after the appearance of Jesus our Christ in your race there has been no prophet anywhere, nor now exists, and, further, you have ceased to be under your own kings, and, in addition, your land had been laid waste' (*Dial.* 52). According to Tertullian, the fulfilment of the prophecies, especially Isa. 1: 3ff, in the destruction of Jerusalem proves that the Christ has actually come (*Jud.* 13.24ff). So, too, there is now no conceivable alternative to the Christian exegesis of Mic. 5: 1–3. This prophecy must refer to Jesus, for no leader of Israel can now or henceforth originate in Bethlehem; it is forbidden territory to all Jews, who can only 'behold the land from far off' (Isa. 33: 17f). Nor can the Jews expect a future messiah, for with the abolition of the Temple there is now no horn of oil with which he could be anointed (*Jud.* 13.2–3). Cyprian's *Testimonia* included proofs from Isa. 1: 7ff that the Jews would lose Jerusalem in accordance with the words of Jesus at Matt. 23: 37f, and from 2 Sam. 7: 4–5, 12–14, 16, with Matt. 24: 2 and Mark 14: 58, that the old Temple was to cease and be replaced by a new Temple which is Christ himself (*Test.* 1.6, 1.15). Eusebius ascribes the banning of Jerusalem to the Jews primarily to the command of God, proclaimed beforehand by the prophets, and only secondarily to the Roman legislation (*Chron.* A.D. 135). It was because the prophecies indicated that the Temple had been predestined to lie in ruins till the end of time (cp. Eus. *D.E.* 8.2.24f) that Julian's project for its rebuilding aroused so much excitement.

Christian apologists could also derive some telling arguments from the cessation of the sacrifices. Tertullian merely noted the fact that Vespasian's conquest put an end to the cultus (*Jud.* 8.17), but Justin had already used it as part of his demonstration that the sacrifices had been intended to be temporary: to typify Christ and to cease at his advent. Thus it is no longer possible to sacrifice the Passover lamb, a type of Christ, because Jerusalem is in the hands of the Jews' enemies (*Dial.* 40). According to the *Clementine Recognitions* (1.64), the destruction of the Temple, the setting up of the abomination of desolation, and the preaching of the gospel to the Gentiles, have come about because of the failure of the Jews to recognise that the time when sacrifices were to be offered had been completed. Barnabas goes further. The sacrifices were annulled by God so that in the new law of Christ there might be an offering not made by men (2.6). It was a heathenish mistake of the Jews to set their hopes on the Temple building instead of on God who made them to be his true house. They consecrated God in the Temple, almost like Gentiles; and so, 'because they went to war, it was destroyed by their enemies'. 'Now', says Barnabas, 'the very servants of their enemies shall build it up.' He means, of course, not that the material Temple is to be rebuilt but that the Gentile church is to replace it. He goes on to explain that the 'delivering up' of the city, the Temple and the people of Israel was shown forth in prophecy (he cites Enoch 89.56, 66), and that the community of believers is now being built up as God's real Temple (16.1).

In his argument against Trypho Justin pointed out that since the cultus had ceased it had become impossible to keep the entire Law (*Dial.* 46). Some apologists went on to argue that the Law is binding in every part (cp. Gal. 5: 3). Therefore, the impossibility of observing some of its precepts demonstrates that the whole Law has been abrogated. The *Apostolic Constitutions* (6.25) even maintain that because the Jews can no longer observe the cultic Law they have incurred the curse pronounced by Deut. 27: 26, and the Christians have inherited the Deuteronomic blessings since, through the gospel, they are in fact adherents of the Law and the Prophets. Chrysostom argued along similar lines (*Jud.* 4.6). The conclusion of all these arguments, however, had been summed up briefly, long before this time, by Tertullian (*Apol.* 21): the Jews are scattered wanderers, excluded from their own land of Judaea; this shows how they erred and forsook their calling, and how Judaism has been, therefore, superseded by Christianity.[14]

[14] [The late Professor Lampe was asked by the editors to do a study of early Christian reflection on A.D. 70. It scarcely needs to be said that the sentiments he reports are not to be taken as they stand as a record of a present-day Christian's views. – Ed.]

The trial of Jesus in the *Acta Pilati*

It is probable that an official record of the trial of Jesus before Pilate was made at the time and preserved. The authentic *acta* of the Christian martyrs are among the evidence which suggests that this would have been done, and they may indicate in a general fashion the form which it would have taken. We do not know, however, whether the prefect of Judaea would have sent a copy of the record to Rome, but that he should have reported the trial and execution of Jesus to Tiberius seems inherently probable, especially in view of the fact that it was the general belief in antiquity not only that Pilate would have done this but that his *acta* must be extant in the archives of the imperial government.

Several Christian writers mention the 'acts of Pilate', and Justin gives the impression of referring to an actual document, the contents of which he knows himself and which the emperor and his associates, to whom his *Apology* is nominally addressed, can be invited to consult. In the course of developing an argument from prophecy Justin enumerates those details of Christ's passion which fulfilled prophetic passages in the Old Testament. These include the piercing of the hands and feet of Jesus and the distribution of his garments, as foretold in Psalm 22, and also the setting of Jesus on the judgement seat (*bema*), as part of the mockery, with the cry 'Judge for us.' This last incident is based on a possible interpretation of John 19: 13 which takes the verb transitively and supposes that the mockers made Jesus sit on the judgement seat during the trial before Pilate. This is seen by Justin as a fulfilment of Isa. 58: 2. To confirm his argument from these incidents Justin adds, 'And that these things took place you can learn from the *acta* of the things done under Pontius Pilate' (*1 Apol.* 35). It is, however, highly unlikely that Justin had in fact either seen or obtained actual information about such a document. The inclusion in the mockery of Jesus of this act of setting him on the seat of judgement appears also in the Gospel of Peter (3), and it is conceivable that this was Justin's source. If not, then both Justin and the Gospel of Peter (which gives it in the form: 'They put on him a purple robe, and made him sit upon the seat of judgement, saying, "Give righteous judgement, thou king of Israel" ') must presumably derive it from a current exegetical tradition of the Johannine text. It seems probable that Justin believed that the incidents in the passion which were narrated in the canonical Gospels and embroidered in church tradition must also have been recorded in Pilate's official *acta*, and that he could therefore make a good propaganda point in the confidence that his imperial readers could plausibly be asked to verify from official sources the facts that were familiar to Christians from their own literature.

The idea that Pilate reported to Tiberius is developed by Tertullian. He maintains that Tiberius recommended to the senate that Christ should be admitted among the gods of Rome, on the strength of a report from Palestine which disclosed the truth of his divinity, and that, although the senate refused, Tiberius did not alter his opinion; consequently, he threatened to punish those who brought accusations against Christians (*Apol.* 5). Tertullian also asserted, more specifically, that the eclipse at the crucifixion was recorded in the Roman archives, and that the facts concerning Christ's death and resurrection were reported to Tiberius by Pilate who was already 'pro sua conscientia Christianus' (*Apol.* 21).

It is not at all probable that either Justin or Tertullian had in mind the extant Christian book known as the *Acta Pilati* or, with the addition of an awkwardly attached 'Part II' on the Descent into Hades and Christ's activity there (mainly contained in Latin MSS and absent from the oriental versions of the *Acta*), as the *Evangelium Nicodemi*. This almost certainly belongs to a much later date, and it is worth notice that neither the setting of Jesus on the judgement seat nor the piercing of his hands and feet is mentioned in it. It is quite possible, however, that the composition of the *Acta Pilati* may have been suggested by Tertullian's idea that Pilate must have reported not only Jesus's death but also the resurrection, that he would have done this from the standpoint of a Christian believer, and that, as Tertullian implies, the central theme of his report would have been the divinity of Jesus. The claim that Jesus is the Son of God, vindicated by the fully attested fact of his resurrection, is the main point which the *Acta Pilati* are designed to establish.

Nor need we necessarily suppose that when Epiphanius mentions 'acts of Pilate' he is actually referring to this book. He tells us that the Quartodecimans based their claim to accuracy in the dating of the passion on the authority of 'acts of Pilate' which mentioned the fact that it took place on 25 March (*Haer.* 50.1). The *Acta Pilati* do in fact begin with an elaborate date: the fifteenth year of Tiberius, the nineteenth year of Herod of Galilee, the 25th of March, the consulship of Rufus and Rubellio, the fourth year of the two hundred and second Olympiad, the high-priesthood of Caiaphas. These dates, however, were traditional. Tertullian gives the same year and the same consuls, and specifies the 25th of March. Similar dating is given by Clement (*Strom.* 1.21.146), Hippolytus (*Dan.* 4.23), and Lactantius (*Inst.* 4.10.18, *Mort. Persec.* 2), and after the time of Epiphanius it reappears in Augustine (*Civ. Dei* 18.54). The date may well have been arrived at, not through an independent tradition but by reflection on a combination of Luke 3: 1 ('the fifteenth year of Tiberius') with Luke 4: 19 ('the acceptable year of the Lord') which Clement explicitly states that he takes to mean a single year which included the events from Christ's baptism to his death. The day of the month may have been a guess, or possibly the result of an early attempt to combine that particular year with other New Testament data: that the crucifixion took place on a Friday which was either the eve or the day of the Passover. It is possible that Epiphanius is alluding to the date given in our *Acta Pilati*, but it is more likely that the Quartodecimans had followed an early and widespread tradition and, assuming that Pilate's official record must have been preserved, supposed that this traditional date, like the rest of the Christian narratives of the passion and resurrection, must have been derived from it.

The assumption that *acta* of Pilate would naturally be extant was not confined to believers. It was pressed into the service of pagan propaganda, according to the well-known account given by Eusebius (*H.E.* 9.5.1, 9.7.1), by Maximin Daia in the last stage of the final great persecution. 'Memoirs of Pilate' were forged, Eusebius tells us, containing every kind of blasphemy against Christ, and sent round for public exhibition and to be learned by children in the schools. This is notable as the only attempt by a hostile emperor, apart from Julian, to reinforce persecution of the church by the dissemination of officially produced anti-Christian propaganda. So obvious a step had been strangely neglected by the pagan state in spite of the great volume of Christian apologetic which was in circulation at all times and the effective use of the acts of the martyrs to recruit sympathy and support. It may have done some damage, even at this very late date, for Maximin's 'Memoirs of Pilate' were evidently not allowed to survive after the persecution ceased. We have, therefore, practically no evidence about what they contained. One clue, however, may be found in the account of the martyrdom of Lucian of Antioch which Rufinus adds to his version of Eusebius's history at 9.6. Rufinus speaks of Christ not deceiving by his death us for whom he rose on the third day – not like the falsely composed *Acts of Pilate*. This observation, together with Eusebius's description of these *Acts* as full of blasphemy against Christ, may lead us to infer that Maximin's object was to discredit the Christian claims concerning Christ's divinity and the truth of the resurrection. From at least as early as the time of Tertullian Christian apologists had tried to cite Pilate as a witness to these two claims. It is very probable that Maximin sought to turn their own weapon against the Christians by producing, as the actual record which they had always believed to exist, acts of Pilate which denied these cardinal points in the Christian argument. There is no evidence whatever that these 'memoirs' sought to embarrass the Christian movement by presenting Jesus as a nationalist agitator or any kind of political revolutionary; the argument in the fourth century, and, indeed, at all times when 'acts of Pilate' were appealed to, moved in quite a different area from that, and was concerned with the religious question whether Jesus was divine. If this was the purpose of Maximin's publication, it is tempting to think that the Christian *Acts of Pilate* may have been composed as a counter-blast to it. It is, however, unlikely that the work as we have it is earlier than the fifth century, although it is just possible that it may be a re-working of a somewhat earlier composition. Its argument, too, though concentrated on the themes of Christ's divinity and resurrection, is developed in a way which suggests that it is directed against Jewish rather than pagan opposition.

The *Acts* proper, excluding the appended 'Descent into Hades', are preserved in their earlier form (Recension A) in Greek and in Latin, Coptic, Syriac and Armenian versions. A late re-working (Recension B) adds further legendary material, including stories which became very popular in the Middle Ages, such as those relating to Judas's wife and her cock and to Dysmas, the penitent thief. The wide currency which was achieved by the former led T. Mommsen[1] to suggest that the work, though subsequently re-worked, perhaps many times, must have been of early origin; but it is more probable that the number of versions and manuscripts reflects its popularity rather than antiquity. A prologue prefixed in some manuscripts asserts that the *Acts*, or rather, according to the wording of the title, the 'Memorials of our Lord Jesus Christ done in the time of Pontius Pilate', were compiled by Ananias, or Aeneas, a *protector* of praetorian rank and a *iuris peritus*, in the seventeenth year of Theodosius II, and that they were translated from memorials written in Hebrew and deposited with Pilate. The *Acts* draw most of their material from the canonical Gospels, using them eclectically for the most part, but naturally depending mainly on the Fourth Gospel for the interrogation of Jesus by Pilate and taking the narrative of crucifixion from Luke. The non-canonical material, which predominates in the opening chapter and in the long section which deals with the resurrection, and is interspersed through the rest of the work alongside matter derived from the Gospels, is often very awkwardly harmonised with the latter and sometimes involves inconsistencies.

This author's picture of the trial of Jesus represents an extreme development of tendencies that were already present in the Fourth Gospel. There is only one trial: that before Pilate. The Jewish trial or trials have altogether vanished from the story and Pilate is the sole judge of Jesus. He is

---

[1] 'Die Pilatus-Akten', *ZNW* 3 (1902), 198–205.

actually the judge, trying the case from beginning to end, and his task is in no way concerned with confirming or rejecting the findings of another court. Jesus is a free agent when he is summoned to appear, and it is implied that there was no arrest, though later the author's familiarity with the New Testament leads him into an inconsistency on this point: Pilate sentences Jesus to be crucified in the garden where he had been arrested. The effect is to eliminate the Jewish leaders from any role but that of prosecutors. Jesus is a defendant in a trial which is purely Roman throughout; Herod plays no part. Yet the charges are religious. Kingship appears only as one aspect of divine Sonship, though the *Acts* follow the Gospels in making Pilate sentence Jesus because his nation has 'convicted him as a king'. The real issue is Christ's blasphemous claim to divinity, to which other charges are secondary: profanation of the Sabbath, seeking to destroy the Temple, being a sorcerer, being 'born of fornication', fleeing with Mary and Joseph to Egypt 'because they had no confidence among the people', and being the cause of the slaughter of the children at Bethlehem. These are issues familiar in the history of Christian–Jewish controversy over a period of centuries. Celsus makes his Jewish objector traverse most of this ground: that Jesus was born of adultery, that he fled to Egypt and became a magician there, that the massacre at Bethlehem was discreditable to him, that Christians regard him as Son of God because he healed the lame and the blind but he really did these things by sorcery (Origen, *C. Cels.* 1.28, 32, 38; 2.48–53). They recur constantly in rabbinic and Christian literature; and the concluding sections of the *Acts* deal with objections like those of Celsus's Jew when he is made to complain that there were no witnesses to the resurrection, which ought to have been publicly manifested, except one woman and some of Jesus's own friends (*C. Cels.* 2.70).

These are the topics of later polemics between Christians and Jews which the *Acts* incongruously make the subjects of an enquiry conducted by a Roman governor in the reign of Tiberius. The Sanhedrin does not come into the picture at all as a judicial body until Joseph of Arimathaea and other followers of Jesus are persecuted by the Jews after the burial of Jesus – in scenes which owe a good deal to reminiscences of the early chapters of the Acts of the Apostles. The Jewish authorities play no role in the earlier part of the story except as accusers, solely responsible for bringing about the death of Jesus. In the later part, after the burial, it is even suggested that the crucifixion was carried out by the Jews (cp. John 19: 16); Joseph, defending his action in burying the body of Jesus, tells the Jews: 'You did not repent when you had crucified him, but you also pierced him with a spear' (12.1), though this is inconsistent with the narrative of the crucifixion itself (cp. John 19: 23, 32, 34) which is mainly a condensed version of Luke's account and speaks of 'the soldiers' and the centurion, who is named as Longinus.

Not that the blame is thrown indiscriminately upon the Jewish people; among them are many supporters of Jesus and witnesses for the defence, and the first part of the book ends with a Christian apologist's dream of the ideal outcome of the controversy between church and synagogue: the recognition of the truth by the Jewish leaders and the singing of a psalm of praise by all the people.

In these *Acts* Pilate is more than a sympathetic judge. He is virtually a Christian. He is 'circumcised in heart' (12.1). The author does, indeed, make him go through the motions of paganism; he uses the conventional language of polytheism, calling Helios to witness that he finds no fault in Jesus (3.1) and, in answer to the accusation of the Jews that Jesus casts out devils by Beelzebub, declaring that 'this is not to cast out devils by an unclean spirit, but by the god Asclepios' (1.1). Even so, it is interesting that the gods named by Pilate, the Sun and the Healer, are the two who were least offensive to post-Constantinian Christians and lent themselves most readily to assimilation to Christ; there is no question of Asclepios being himself regarded as a demon. Pilate is also made to swear a pagan oath, and to ask the Jewish sympathisers with Jesus to take it also, which they refuse to do because they are absolutely forbidden to swear; but it is not the regular pagan formula, 'by the *genius* (τύχη) of Caesar' (cp. *M. Polyc.* 9.2, *M. Scillit.* 3 and 5), but the modified form κατὰ τῆς σωτηρίας καίσαρος which came to be generally acceptable to Christians (cp. *A.Jo.* 10, *Cod. Theod.* 2.9.3). Apart from these artificial touches of partial verisimilitude Pilate looks very much like an official of the Christian empire. He is virtually a believer, asking in all seriousness, 'How can I, a governor, examine a king?' (1.2), echoing the words of John 10: 32–3: 'For a good work do they desire to put him to death?' (2.6), speaking as an advocate for the defence rather than a judge (8), and making a speech to the Jews on the lines of Stephen's apology in Acts 7, reminding the Jews of the days of the Exodus, the manna, quails and water from the rock, and accusing them of being always a seditious and rebellious nation which has angered God by its idolatry from the time of the golden calf onwards (9.2). Of course, in the end, when the Jews say that Caesar alone is their king, and not Jesus, and recount the story of the visit of the magi, Herod's attempt to slay Jesus, and his massacre of the children, Pilate's opposition collapses suddenly and implausibly, and he condemns Jesus to death because his nation has convicted him of being a king. Having represented Pilate as virtually conspiring with the followers of Jesus to outwit the prosecution, the author has given himself an impossible task to explain at all convincingly how it came about that Jesus was after all crucified. He has to do what he can with two lines of explanation. One is the threat, taken from the Fourth Gospel, 'You are not a friend of Caesar if you let this man go; for he called himself the Son of God and king' (9.1). The other is that Jesus told Pilate that he was predestined to condemn him. It had been 'given him'; and to Pilate's question, 'How has it been given?', the answer is, 'Moses and the prophets foretold my death and rising again' (4.3). In any case, although Pilate has to condemn Jesus, the story of the crucifixion is passed over in a brief summary of Luke's narrative and the author hurries on, after first describing the distress of Pilate and his wife at what has been done, to the much longer section of the book which deals with the resurrection and ascension.

The *Acts* begin with the Jewish leaders, for whom Annas and Caiaphas are the chief spokesmen, coming to Pilate and presenting their charges: that Jesus, the son of Joseph and Mary, claims to be Son of God and king, defiles the sabbath, and destroys the Law. He heals on the Sabbath, and exorcises by sorcery. Pilate, however, ascribes his exorcisms to the power of Asclepios, and resists the demand that Jesus be brought to trial by asking how he, as a governor, can judge a king. Pilate then sends a *cursor* to bring Jesus without violence, and on meeting Jesus this messenger removes his turban and spreads it for Jesus to walk upon, afterwards explaining to Pilate that he is following the example of those who greeted Jesus as 'he that comes in the name of the Lord' at the entry. Pilate asks the Jews for a translation of the Hebrew words which were used on that occasion, and on hearing their meaning he asks how the messenger can have offended in repeating in Greek what the crowd had then said in Hebrew. Jesus is accordingly summoned to the court in royal dignity, and the Roman standards, or rather the images on the standards, miraculously bow in reverence as he comes in. This episode, one of the few wholly non-canonical episodes in the earlier chapters, is drawn out at some length. It serves to introduce the central theme of Christ's divinity. Conceivably it may have been suggested by a reminiscence of the story of Pilate introducing Roman standards into Jerusalem (Jos. *AJ* 18.55ff), perhaps combined with Pliny's account of Pompey's visit to Posidonius: 'forem percuti de more a lictore vetuit, et fasces litterarum ianuae summisit is cui se oriens occidensque summiserat' (*NH* 7.30.112). Our author is not concerned with historical accuracy here, nor with the fact that, even though the relation of military to civil authority in the provinces is not always clear, there would have been no standards, as opposed to the *fasces*, in Pilate's court. That this is so was made clear by Mommsen[2] who pointed out, in reply to von Dobschütz's attempt in the same volume (pp. 89–114) to claim that the *Acts* reflect authentic Roman judicial procedure, that on many other points as well, such as the relation of the *bema* to the *praetorium*, the function of the *velum*, the credibility of a dialogue between witnesses and judge, and many matters of procedure, the author shows himself ignorant or confused. The story is a fantasy, but it provides a popular–dramatic prologue to the trial proper.

The incident of Pilate's wife's dream follows. Here it serves to introduce the question of sorcery, for the Jews ascribe the dream to Jesus's magic. They also bring in the other charges relating to his illegitimate birth, the destruction of the Bethlehem children, and the flight to Egypt. The first accusation is repudiated by twelve friendly Jews who, denying that they are themselves Greek-born proselytes who have turned Christian, affirm that they are true Jews and that they were present at the espousals of Joseph and Mary. Pilate then enters into an implausible consultation with these witnesses, asking why the prosecution want to kill Jesus. The reply is 'Jealousy, because he heals on the sabbath', which elicits Pilate's protest that they should wish to kill Jesus 'for a good work.' He goes out of the *praetorium* and acquits Jesus, calling Helios to witness. The narrative then follows the Fourth Gospel fairly closely, the Jews pointing out, in answer to Pilate's 'Take and judge him according to your law', that it is not lawful for them to put any man to death; but this prohibition is taken to refer to the Sixth Commandment, for Pilate replies: 'Has God forbidden you to kill and allowed me?' The dialogue concerning Jesus's kingdom and truth proceeds as in the Johannine story, with some additions, after which Pilate again acquits Jesus. The Jews' response is to introduce at this point the charge of claiming to be able to destroy the Temple and build it in three days. The *Acts* thus bring one of the charges laid against Jesus at the trial before the Sanhedrin, according to the synoptists, into this Roman case; they also suppose that it was Solomon's Temple which took forty-six years to build. Pilate then declares himself guiltless of the innocent blood and the Jews cry, 'His blood be on us and on our children.' This is an episode which the *Acts* are anxious to emphasise strongly, for they repeat it later at the hand-washing.

Pilate does not pursue the theme of the Temple. He narrows down the charges to healing and profaning the Sabbath, and again acquits Jesus; but now the main charge from the synoptists' Sanhedrin trial is introduced: blasphemy. Although this is a religious charge its introduction in Pilate's court is made slightly less implausible by the way in which the Jewish leaders lead up to it: 'If a man blasphemes against Caesar, is he worthy of death?'; 'If a man be worthy of death if he blasphemes against Caesar, this man has blasphemed against God.' Pilate again tries to hand the case over to the Jews, but they insist that Jesus must be crucified, because he called himself the Son of God and king.

The *Acts* supply an obvious deficiency in the New Testament narratives of the trial: the absence of any defence or witnesses to testify for Jesus. Nicodemus takes the part of Jesus's advocate, arguing, with an echo of Gamaliel, that 'if the signs which he does are of God they will stand, but if they are of men they will come to nothing', and a procession of witnesses speak of the miracles: the paralytic, the man born blind (both of these being composite characters from the Johannine and the synoptic traditions), one who was made straight, a leper, the woman with the issue (named as Bernice or Veronica), and a multitude who testify to the exorcisms. If the devils were subject to Jesus, asks Pilate, 'why were your teachers not also subject to him?' The incident of Barabbas follows here, after which Pilate makes his speech rebuking the Jews for their age-old provocation of God by idolatry and disloyalty, a speech which is, strangely, followed immediately by the threats of the Jews concerning another king besides Caesar, and the sudden collapse of Pilate's resistance. There is the washing of the hands, the repeated cry, 'His blood be on us . . .', and the sentence to scourging and crucifixion. There is no mocking before the crucifixion. The crowning with thorns takes place at the execution, which otherwise follows the Lukan narrative closely.

After the burial of Jesus the story develops into a complex series of testimonies to the resurrection. Joseph of Arimathaea is imprisoned by the Jews and miraculously released in the manner of Peter and the apostles in Acts 5 and 12. Then the guards from the tomb report to the Jewish leaders the descent of the angel, the rolling away of the stone, and the words of the angel to the women. A priest and a teacher arrive from Galilee and tell of Jesus and his disciples sitting on a mountain and the commission to 'go into all the world' being given to them (from the longer ending of Mark). These messengers also testify to having seen the ascension. The Jewish leaders institute a search for Jesus, modelled on the search for Elijah in 2 Kings 2: 17, which results in the discovery of Joseph, who in due course testifies to having received a visit from the risen Christ; not a ghost, as Joseph knows, for he applied the test of reciting the commandments, which would cause a ghost to flee. Subsequently, at a meeting of the teachers, priests and levites, a rabbi, Levi, speaks of Jesus's Godfearing parents and tells the story of the Presentation in the Temple. Lastly, when the witnesses of the ascension have again been sent for from Galilee the Jewish leaders are given a detailed account of the way in which Jesus was taken up.

These naive and somewhat jejune stories were evidently thought by this author to be highly important for his main purpose, which was to confirm the truth of the resurrection and ascension by producing public evidence for those events, which had been actually communicated to the Jewish leaders who had brought about the death of Jesus. The narrative of the trial is more interesting: not because it has any historical value or throws any light on the problems presented by the canonical accounts, but for the way in which it transposes the New Testament material into a framework constructed out of the Christian–Jewish theological controversies of a much later age, and enlists the advocacy of Pilate as a Christian apologist.

W. HORBURY

Christ as brigand in ancient anti-Christian polemic

The ancient world described Christ in language also readily associated with criticism of government. Christian apologists used words such as 'prophet', 'teacher' or 'wonder-worker' to present Christ as a divinely-authenticated philosophical guide.[1] Domitian's expulsion of philosophers and astrologers from Rome is simply one instance of a general recognition that such teachers might be significant politically. Their followers' terms of praise had well-worn pejorative counterparts suggesting deception and subversion. The very words which offered the apologists common ground with paganism could therefore facilitate their opponents' depreciation of Christ's teaching.[2] Justin's *teacher* and doer of *mighty works*, Tertullian's *illuminator and guide of humanity*, is Lucian's *crucified sophist* and Celsus's *charlatan* and *leader of sedition*.[3]

This polemic claims attention here in so far as it links Jesus with Jewish nationalism or, in its own terms, with the sedition considered characteristic of Jewry.[4] Robert Eisler took early *antichristiana* of this kind to confirm his own derivation of Christianity from a messianic independence movement.[5] This chapter is devoted to one such pagan criticism singled out by Eisler.[6]

---

[1] For apologetic based on Christ's predictions see Justin, *1 Apol.* i. 12, *Dial.* xxxv, li (ed. J. C. T. Otto (Jena, 1843) i, 162: ii, 118, 164), with the title *prophet* at Origen, *Contra Celsum* ii. 13f (cp. *In Jo.* xiii. 54, on 4: 44) GCS, Origenes 1, pp. 143f; 4, p. 285, and Eusebius, *D.E.* ix. 11, *PG* xxii, 689; for *teacher* Justin *1 Apol.* i. 12f, xxxii, pp. 162, 164, 204, Otto, *Justin* ii. 5, and *Apollonius* xxxvi–xli in H. Musurillo, *The Acts of the Christian Martyrs* (Oxford, 1972), pp. 42, 100, Arnobius, *Adversus Nationes* i, 63, ii. 11 (CSEL 4, pp. 44, 55f), Lactantius, *Div. Inst.* iv. 24f (CSEL 19, pp. 371–7); with *wonder-worker* (in a defence of the cursing of the fig-tree), Chrysostom, *Hom. in Matth.* 67: 1, on 21: 18 (*PG* 58.633). For apologetic on the miracles, G. W. H. Lampe and M. F. Wiles in C. F. D. Moule (ed.), *Miracles* (London, 1965), pp. 205–34.

[2] For polemic against philosophers, magicians and prophets see R. MacMullen, *Enemies of the Roman Order* (Cambridge, Mass., 1967), pp. 46–162.

[3] Justin, n. 1 above and *1 Apol.* xxx, p. 200 Otto; Tertullian, *Apol.* xxi. 7 (CCL 1, p. 123); Lucian, *Per.* xiii (Loeb Classical Library v, p. 14); Origen, *C. Cels.* i. 71, etc., viii. 14, (R. Bader, *Der ΑΛΗΘΗΣ ΛΟΓΟΣ des Kelsos* (Stuttgart–Berlin, 1940), pp. 62, 197).

[4] 'Non cessat gens illa habens seditiones, et homicidia, et latrocinia', Origen, *Comm. in Matth.* 121, on 27: 16f (GCS 38, p. 256); cp. J. Juster, *Les Juifs dans l'Empire Romain* (Paris, 1914), i, 147, n. 1⁹ and 220, n. 8: ii, 182, n. 2.

[5] R. Eisler, ΙΗΣΟΥΣ ΒΑΣΙΛΕΥΣ ΟΥ ΒΑΣΙΛΕΥΣΑΣ (Heidelberg, 1929–30), i, xiii–xxxv (ET *The Messiah Jesus and John the Baptist* (London, 1931), pp. 3–21).

[6] Eisler, ΙΗΣΟΥΣ i, xxvf, ET 10f; further references in section III below.

Cited in Lactantius, *DI* v. 3, 4, it attaches to Christ's ministry the heavily-loaded term of *brigandage*. Some remarks on the historical context of this charge (I) may serve to introduce an examination of the text (II), followed by an estimate of its significance (III).

I

Assertions about *Christ* such as this occur in polemic which is anti-*Christian*, concerned primarily not with history but with the contemporary church. The Christian *secta*, like others, might be expected to imitate its founder; 'they worship their crucified sophist and conform their lives to his precepts' (Lucian, *Per.* xiii; see p. 183, n. 3). Two facts of Christ's life freely admitted by Christians proved especially useful to their opponents: his crucifixion and his gathering of disciples. Sources ranging from a rabbinic text of the tannaitic period to Celsus, an oracle ascribed to Apollo and the anti-Christian *Acts of Pilate* view the cross as a just punishment.[7] The consequent labelling of the crucified as a criminal – κακὸν ποιῶν, βιοθανής, κακοῦργος, *noxius* – was easily transferable to his followers; 'they worship what they deserve' (Minucius Felix, *Oct.* ix. 4).[8] Again, on the call of the disciples, Tertullian and Christians in general stress that 'a vast multitude' turned to Christ, while rabbinic sources see him as, *inter alia*, the leader-astray of whole communities, and for Celsus he is the initiator of *stasis*.[9] The contemporary force of these historical claims appears when we find the church likewise designated *factio*, and the judicial estimate of St Cyprian's episcopal work related as 'You have gathered to yourself many other vicious men in a conspiracy'.[10] Such early non-Christian interpretations of Christ's ministry were offered in a period when persecution was commonplace.[11] It is a paradigm of the close relationship which could

---

[7] Sanh. 43a; Origen, *C. Cels.* ii. 5, p. 63 Bader, *Kelsos*; Porphyry in Augustine, *Civ. Dei* xix. 23 (ed. B. Dombart and A. Kalb (Leipzig, 1929), ii, 393); Rufinus's version of Eusebius, *H.E.* ix. 6 (GCS 9.1, pp. 813, 815).

[8] For the epithets see John 18: 30, *Martyrium Cononis* iv. 6 (p. 188 Musurillo, *Martyrs*), *Acta SS. Tarachi, Probi et Andronici* in T. Ruinart, *Acta primorum martyrum sincera et selecta* (2nd edn. Amsterdam, 1713), p. 442, and Minucius Felix, *Octavius* xxix. 2 (ed. J. P. Waltzing (Leipzig, 1912), p. 50); for the passage cited in the text see Waltzing, *Octavius*, p. 12.

[9] Tertullian, *Apol.* xxi. 18; (CCL 1, p. 126); for a 'multitude' of disciples see already Luke 6: 17 (contrast Matthew 4: 25, Mark 3: 7). The multitude fed with loaves and fishes are disciples at Origen, *C. Cels.* ii. 46, iii. 10 (GCS pp. 168, 210). For Jesus as leader-astray of communities see Sanh. 43a; the offence is described in M. Sanh. vii. 10, Deut. 13: 13–18, EVV. 12–17. Celsus is cited at n. 3, p. 183 above.

[10] Tertullian, *Apol.* xxxix. 1 (CCL 1, p. 150); Minucius Felix, *Octavius* viii. 3, p. 10 Waltzing; *Acta . . . Cypriani* iv. 1, p. 172 Musurillo, *Martyrs*.

[11] The chief evidence for this view is summarised in K. Aland, 'The Relation between

obtain between assertions about Christ and attacks on the church that the fabricated *Acts of Pilate* were circulated to support the persecution under Maximin Daia.[12]

The claim that Christ practised brigandage, a further hostile interpretation of the gathering of disciples, should therefore be considered in relation to anti-Christian charges. It specifies Christ's offence unusually. The general term 'evil-doer' was commonly particularised with words like those already noted applicable to dubious teaching and wonder-working (see p. 184, n. 8).[13] Here Christ is identified as a violent criminal. That remains damaging to the church, however brigandage is understood; but, as Eisler did not fail to note and as recent study has amply documented,[14] the charge of brigandage may of course in ancient usage amount to that of sedition.

The innuendo of sedition readily adhered, as noted above, to anti-philosophical and anti-Christian charges of deception and magic. It already figures alongside deception and magic in the Gospels as an express allegation (pp. 403–14 in this volume).

Brigandage, however, although it may overlap with sedition in usage, remains distinct. *Stasis* in this sense and *seditio* commonly retain some reference to faction, *lesteia* and *latrocinium* to robber-like activity. Thus in polemic *stasis* may be used of the church's emergence from Jewry (Celsus, see n. 3, p. 183), seen as the revolt and secession of a new party, while *latrocinium* typically denotes brigand-like political violence (so in Cicero of the Catilinarian conspiracy),[15] misgovernment (St Leo the Great had many precedents in pagan political satire when he applied it to a church synod),[16] or misappropriation (as in critiques of territorial gains in Roman or Jewish origins).[17] It accords with this usage when jurists treat pretenders as brigands (n. 14, above). Josephus touches this range of meaning, but

Church and State in Early Times: a Reinterpretation', *JThSt*, n.s. 19 (1968), 115–27 (120–2).

[12] Eusebius, *H.E.* i. 9, i. 11, ix. 5 (GCS 9.1, pp. 72, 80, 810).

[13] W. Bauer, *Das Leben Jesu im Zeitalter der neutestamentlichen Apokryphen* (repr. Darmstadt, 1967), pp. 484f.

[14] R. MacMullen, 'The Roman Concept of Robber-Pretender', *RIDA* 3rd series, 10 (1963), 221–6; M. Hengel in O. Betz, K. Haacker and M. Hengel (eds.), *Josephus-Studien* (Göttingen, 1974), pp. 176f, n. 7.

[15] Cicero, *Pro Murena* 39 (84) 'hoc Catilinae nefarium latrocinium', cited among other passages by I. Opelt, *Die lateinischen Schimpfwörter und verwandte sprachliche Erscheinungen* (Heidelberg, 1965), p. 132.

[16] Leo, *Ep.* xcv. 2 (*ACO* 2. 4, p. 51); parallels in MacMullen, *RIDA* 3rd series 10 (n. 14 above) and Opelt, *Schimpfwörter*, pp. 132f, 168f. Recently 'MP likens leadership to thugs', part headline in *The Times* of 13 March 1976, p. 1.

[17] For Rome parallels to Augustine, *De Civ. D.* iv. 4 (i, p. 150 Dombart-Kalb) are collected by MacMullen, *Enemies*, p. 350, n. 30; for Jewry see Ber. R. i. 2 (ed. A. A. Halevy (Tel-Aviv, 1956), p. 2) discussed with parallels in W. Bacher, 'The Supposed Inscription upon "Joshua the Robber"', *JQR* 3 (1891), 354–7.

remains close to the literal sense of the word, when he calls rebel-bands *lestai*.[18]

With this distinction in mind it can be understood that up to the time of our citation brigandage is not prominent in anti-Christian charges of sedition.[19] The necessary points of comparison were not well marked. Unlike Josephus's rebels or the factions of the late Roman republic, Christians were not notorious for resort to arms, being indeed well-known for the numbers of women and children in their churches.[20] Unlike emperors, imperially-summoned synods at a later date, or pretenders to power, the third-century church did not exercise what was recognisably established government or tyranny. Unlike Rome or Jewry, it had no territorial claims. It looked to hostile observers like a people scattered everywhere, comparable with the Jews in atheistic and anti-social exclusiveness,[21] or like a network of secret societies,[22] or like a quarrelsome religio-philosophical party.[23] Words like *genus, stasis, factio, conspiratio* suited these points of view better than *latrocinium*.

An instance in which Christians were accused as brigands shows the unusual circumstances in which the charge might become plausible. A body of Syrian Christians, according to Hippolytus, followed their bishop into the desert in expectation of Christ's coming and were in danger of being massacred by the governor as brigands and arousing general persecution.[24] It can be inferred that enthusiastic groups, especially where Christianity had penetrated the countryside,[25] might despite discouragement from within the church[26] sometimes lay themselves open to the charge of brigandage by looking like robber-bands. The failure of brigandage to

---

[18] For the importance of the literal sense in Josephus see M. Smith, 'Zealots and Sicarii, Their Origins and Relations', *HThR* 64 (1971), 1–19 (14); S.J.D. Cohen, *Josephus in Galilee und Rome* (Leiden, 1979), pp. 211–14.

[19] Its absence from Celsus (see pp. 189f below) and Minucius Felix is especially striking. For polemic on Christians as public enemies see A. Harnack, *Der Vorwurf des Atheismus in den drei ersten Jahrhunderten* (TU 28.4, Leipzig, 1905), pp. 8–15 and *Die Mission und Ausbreitung des Christentums in den ersten drei Jahrhunderten* (4th edn. Leipzig, 1924) i, 281–9: ET *The Expansion of Christianity in the First Three Centuries* (London, 1908) i, 266–78.

[20] Lucian, *Per.* xii, Loeb Classical Library v, p. 12; Minucius Felix, *Octavius* viii. 4, p. 11 Waltzing.; Origen, *C. Cels.* iii. 55f (GCS pp. 250f).

[21] Harnack, *Mission* i, 281f (ET i, 266–8).

[22] Celsus in Origen, *C. Cels.* i. 1, viii. 17, pp. 39, 198 Bader; Minucius Felix, *Octavius* ix. 1f, pp. 11f Waltzing.

[23] Celsus, n. 3, p. 183 above.

[24] Hippolytus, *In Dan.* iv. 18 (GCS 1, pp. 230–2).

[25] The extent of rural Christianity at the end of the third century is estimated by Harnack, *Mission* ii, 948f (ET ii, 327).

[26] Hippolytus, *In Dan.* iv. 18; Eusebius, *H.E.* v. 16, 18 (episcopal attempts to restrain Montanism), vii. 24 (Dionysius of Alexandria rebuts chiliasm in Arsinoe) (GCS 9.1, pp. 459–68, 472–8, 684–90).

bulk large in anti-Christian polemic nevertheless indicates that such cases will have been exceptional.

Brigandage is however mentioned when Christians complain, and their opponents stress, that Christ and members of his church have been put to death in a way appropriate to robbers (see, with other examples,[27] Origen, *C. Cels.* ii. 44, p. 190, n. 51 below). The tone of the complaints (p.186, n. 26) confirms that the point at issue is the moral disgrace implied in such a death and emphasised in the polemic on the cross discussed above. The innuendo of sedition may be present, but is unexpressed.

To assert Christ's brigandage would certainly have contributed to the general impression that Christians were seditious. J. A. Fabricius compared our passage with Suetonius on the Roman Jewish riots *impulsore Chresto*, understood as a reference to Christians.[28] However Suetonius is to be interpreted, the comparison identifies the damaging aspersion of threat to public order cast by this polemic. Our passage might even recall, although the likelihood has not seemed great, an instance of Christians being charged with brigandage. Yet in view of its failure to correspond to any frequently-attested form of the anti-Christian charge of sedition, its value to the polemist seems likely to have lain principally in its moral denigration (p. 184, n. 8). We may then compare the eagerly-pressed claim of the anti-Montanist writer Apollonius that Alexander the Montanist martyr had once been convicted not for his faith but as a brigand (*lestes*).[29]

It is relevant here that the universally-encountered brigand[30] held a sure place in popular imagination. Robbers are the villains of the Midrash and the New Testament Apocrypha as well as of pagan romance.[31] Their resemblances to established government are a standing joke[32] and their rivalry with it may win sympathy from those who feel oppressed,[33] but they remain the archetypal evil-doers. When Clement of Alexandria tells of a Christian youth who defects to become a brigand-chief, his bishop is made

[27] Eusebius, *H.E.* vi. 41 (martyrdom of Nemesion) (GCS 9.1, p. 608); Lactantius, *DI* v. 20, 6 (SC 204, p. 242).

[28] J. A. Fabricius, *Salutaris Lux Evangelii* (Hamburg, 1731), p. 158n.

[29] Eusebius, *H.E.* v. 18 (GCS 9.1, pp. 474–6).

[30] To the rich material in MacMullen, *Enemies*, pp. 255–68 add the adoption of *lestes* as a loan-word in Hebrew, Aramaic and Syriac: S. P. Brock, 'Greek Words in the Syriac Gospels', *Le Muséon* 80 (1967), 389–426 (406).

[31] S. Krauss, *Griechen und Römer* (Monumenta Talmudica V. i, repr. Darmstadt, 1972), pp. 161–3, nos. 383–90; R. Söder, *Die apokryphen Apostelgeschichten und die romanhafte Literatur der Antike* (Stuttgart, 1932), pp. 168f.

[32] Eisler, ΙΗΣΟΥΣ, i, xxv (ET 10) and n. 17 above; cp. Stith Thompson, *Motif-Index of Folk-Literature* (revised edn. Copenhagen, 1955–8), v, 418 U11.2: 'He who steals much called king; he who steals little called robber.'

[33] On Palestine before the First Revolt see Josephus, *BJ* ii. 253 with A. Schlatter, *Die Theologie des Judentums nach dem Bericht des Josefus* (Gütersloh, 1932), p. 171.

to say that the young man is 'wicked, abandoned, and more than all, a robber'.[34] For the wicked man and shedder of blood *par excellence* of Ezek. 18: 10, where the Greek versions render *pariṣ* with words for evil-doer in general (LXX has *loimos*, applied to St Paul at Acts 24: 5), St Jerome keeps the specific *latro*.[35] In *Cena Cypriani*, when the biblical characters attend a fancy-dress party, it is Cain who comes attired as a brigand.[36]

II

An anti-Christian work by a writer who later helped to implement the Diocletianic persecution affirmed, according to Lactantius, 'that Christ, driven out by the Jews, gathered a band of nine hundred men and committed acts of brigandage': 'Christum . . . a Iudaeis fugatum collecta nongentorum hominum manu latrocinia fecisse.'[37]

The writer, not named by Lactantius here, is probably to be identified with Sossianus Hierocles, governor of Bithynia in 303 and prefect of Egypt in 307.[38] He led the persecution in both provinces. His work addressed to the Christians appears like that of Celsus to have attacked the New Testament both by criticism and – as our passage indicates – by counter-assertion. Eusebius wrote a reply in which he claimed that, apart from its comparison of Christ with Apollonius of Tyana, the book was entirely derivative.[39] Internal evidence at any rate suggests that the passage cited by Lactantius here did not originate with Hierocles.

It consists of three articulated statements: Christ was expelled by the Jews, he gathered his band, he committed acts of brigandage.[40] To be 'driven out by the Jews' implies withdrawal by Jesus some time before the

---

[34] Clement of Alexandria, *Quis Dives Salvetur*, xlii. 9 cited in Eusebius, *H.E.* iii. 23 (GCS 17, p. 189).

[35] Jerome, *In Ezechielem* vi, on 18: 10 (CCL 75, p. 242).

[36] A. Harnack, *Drei wenig beachtete cyprianische Schriften und die 'Acta Pauli'* (TU 19.3b, Leipzig, 1899), pp. 5 (dating the work *c.* 300–600), 12 (text). For Cain as brigand cp. Josephus, *AJ* i. 61, 66.

[37] Lactantius, *DI* v. 3, 4; P. Monat, *Lactance: Institutions Divines, Livre V*, 2 vols., SC 204–5 (Paris, 1973) i, 140f: ii, 44, 50.

[38] A. H. M. Jones, J. R. Martindale and J. Morris, *The Prosopography of the Later Roman Empire* (Cambridge, 1971), p. 432, summarise evidence for the identification further discussed by Monat, *Lactance*, ii, 44 and T. D. Barnes, 'Porphyry *Against the Christians*: Date and the Attribution of Fragments', *JThSt* n.s. 24 (1973), 424–42 (437f, 441). J. Geffcken, *Zwei griechische Apologeten* (Leipzig and Berlin, 1907), p. 291 n., not discussed by the foregoing, doubts the identification because Eusebius (see following note) says that Hierocles admits Christ's miracles and calls him a man of God; but polemic is not always consistent, and admission of the miracles is regularly allied as in Celsus with grave moral charges.

[39] Eusebius, *C. Hieroclem* ı (*PG* xxii. 797).

[40] Eisler, ΙΗΣΟΥΣ, i, xxv: ET 10 obscures the order of events by a mistranslation.

end of the ministry as a result of opposition from the nation as a whole. Such collective opposition at an early stage is envisaged at John 5: 16, 18 (cp. the opposition from more limited circles at Mark 2:6 and parallels). Withdrawal, at a later stage in the Johannine tradition as we have it, but before the end of the ministry, is described at John 11: 54.[41] Retrojection of collective opposition is as natural to the narrator as it is useful to the polemist. Hostile accounts from that of the Jew of Celsus onwards link it with the withdrawal.[42] The closest parallel to our statement is in Toledoth Jeshu where Jesus flees from Israel, represented by the Wise, near the beginning of his ministry, and gathers a band of evil disciples.[43] This first statement in Lactantius is then one instance of a development of traditions which received a different treatment in the Gospels as we now have them.

The gathering of nine hundred stands in contrast with the minimising of the disciples' numbers in Celsus (i. 62, 65; ii. 46; iii. 10; pp. 58, 76, 86 Bader). It may perhaps have arisen from the early emphasis on large numbers (p. 184, n. 9). This emphasis reappears in Christian sources up to Hierocles's time, Origen replying to Celsus that there were not merely ten disciples, nor only a hundred, nor only a thousand[44] and Eusebius envisaging many apostles in addition to the twelve and the seventy.[45] In Jewish tradition large numbers are assumed in one of the charges against Jesus formulated in the tannaitic period (n. 9, p. 184). Samuel Krauss compared with our passage the number 310 or 320, or general references to large numbers, found in descriptions of the disciples in Toledoth Jeshu.[46] Here again the statement in Lactantius is a not unparalleled instance of development of tradition attested in the New Testament.

Acts of brigandage, the theme of the third statement, are not clearly asserted of Christ in earlier polemic as now preserved (cp. p. 186, n. 19).[47] It has however been claimed, in line with Eusebius's judgement of the work in general, that Hierocles simply took over the charge from Celsus.[48] The

---

[41] E. Bammel, 'Ex illa itaque die consilium fecerunt . . .', in E. Bammel (ed.), *The Trial of Jesus* (London, 1970), pp. 11–40 (35, 38).

[42] Bammel, in *Trial*, pp. 30–2.

[43] P. 191 below and the texts printed in S. Krauss, *Das Leben Jesu nach jüdischen Quellen* (Berlin, 1902), pp. 40f, 68f.

[44] Origen, *C. Cels.* ii. 46; cp. iii. 10 (GCS pp. 168, 210).

[45] Eusebius, *H.E.* i, 12 (GCS 9.1, p. 82).

[46] Krauss, *Leben Jesu*, p. 173.   [47] Bauer, *Leben Jesu*, p. 468.

[48] G. Loesche, 'Haben die späteren neuplatonischen Polemiker gegen das Christenthum das Werk des Celsus benutzt?', *ZWT* 27 (1883), 257–302 (284) finds the germ of the idea in *C. Cels.* ii. 12, viii. 14; Geffcken, *Apologeten*, 291 also pointed to ii. 12; Bauer, *Leben Jesu*, p. 468 saw it as impossible to identify the source, but referred in a footnote to *C. Cels* i. 30, ii. 12 and 44, iii. 59. Among the passages cited by these scholars, i. 30 (GCS i, p. 81) is Origen's own statement that Christ's persuasiveness was not that of a tyrant, a robber, or a rich man; the others, all from Celsus or his source, are summarised in the three following notes.

Alethes Logos in fact appears to preserve Celsus's own view of Christian origins,[49] together with the independent view of his Jewish source[50] – both close to our passage in different ways – as well as incidental remarks from both Celsus and the Jew likening Christ or Christians to robbers.[51] None of the passages concerned, however, can be said to offer an exact parallel.

That most closely related to our citations is likely to be i. 62, where the Jew of Celsus claims that the disciples were ten or eleven infamous men who got their living by disgraceful and importunate beggary. It belongs to the same class of narrative polemic and, like the two statements of Hierocles already considered, finds a parallel in inner-Jewish tradition.[52] Yet it seems improbable that Hierocles has himself adapted the text in Celsus. That would have meant not only changing beggary to robbery, but also contradicting the argument on numbers to which Celsus clung (p. 189 above). It is more likely that Hierocles reproduces an existing variant of the Jew of Celsus's story.

This third statement, based on an existing narrative as it thus appears to be, nevertheless lacks the degree of contact with New Testament traditions noted in the two preceding clauses. It makes both Christ and the disciples men of habitual robber-like violence. The New Testament shows the disciples as (to begin with) multitudinous (p. 184, n. 9 above, and Monat, *Lactance* ii, 50), ready to use arms for defence at Christ's arrest (Luke 22: 35–8, 49; John 18: 10), expecting an earthly kingdom and opposed at least in Peter's case to Christ's will to endure (Mark 8: 32, pp. 393–4 in this volume).[53] For Christ himself, however, we can only compare his suffering a robber's death, as is underlined by the Barabbas story (Monat, ii, 50) and the crucifixion between two robbers or malefactors 'in the same condemnation', Luke 23: 40 (Eisler and Bauer, p. 188, n. 40 and p. 189, n. 47). The narrative of the two swords, Luke 22: 25–38 (pp. 335–51 in this volume), linked with our statement by Eisler, ii, 270: ET p. 370, needs

---

[49] The faction-ridden church (iii. 10, 12; viii. 49, pp. 86, 205 Bader) began from Christ's *stasis* against Jewry (iii. 1, 5; viii. 14, pp. 85, 197 Bader, cp. p. 184 above); the few early Christians (iii. 10, presumably including the disciples, see next note) must then by inference be regarded as seditious, but this is not made explicit.

[50] The disciples numbered ten or eleven (i. 62, 65; ii. 46, pp. 58, 76 Bader) and lived by begging (i. 62).

[51] Christians being self-confessed sinners are the sort of people a robber would call, Celsus in iii. 59, p. 97 Bader, perhaps dependent on ii. 12, 44, pp. 65f, 76 Bader, where the Jew claims that Jesus did not keep his followers' loyalty even as well as a *lestarchos* might have, and that anyone as shameless as the Christians could assert that a punished robber and murderer was a god, because he foretold his sufferings to his *syllestai*. For the moral burden of this polemic see p. 187 above.

[52] J. J. Huldricus, *Historia Jeschuae Nazareni* (Leiden, 1705), pp. 51–3.

[53] C. H. Dodd, *Historical Tradition in the Fourth Gospel* (Cambridge, 1963), pp. 77–80.

drastic exegesis (two swords for each disciple, Eisler, ii, 268: ET p. 369) before it gains close resemblance. Christians continue to admit the disciples' sinfulness (Barn. 8: 9) and the shame of the cross, and polemists fasten as seen already on these points (p. 184, n. 8). In the fifth-century *Altercatio Simonis et Theophili*,[54] as E. Bammel notes,[55] the Jewish debater is depicted as drawing an implicit comparison between Christ and Absalom the parricide. Yet apart from our citation surviving polemic does not attach the charge of brigandage to Christ or the disciples in the ante-Nicene period.

For passages of more marked similarity we must turn, as Eisler and M. Lods both observed, to later Jewish material.[56] Huldrich's text of Toledoth Jeshu (p. 190, n. 52) makes the ministry begin when Jesus kills his father. Israel refuses to associate with him, 'vain and wanton men', 'violent men' (*pariṣim*), and finally a brigand chief (*r'osh beryonim=archilestes*) join him, and he flees with 'his men' to the desert.[57] In other text-forms, as Eisler noted, Jesus's numerous followers (n. 46 above) use force against the Jews, attempts to rescue him during the ministry developing into a war after his death.[58] The standard designation of the disciples in these texts is *pariṣim*, which in biblical Hebrew, as in Jer. 7: 11 (LXX σπήλαιον λῃστῶν, cited at Mark 11: 17 and parallels), may denote robber, but also comes to mean (cp. the Greek versions of Ezek. 18: 10, p. 188 above) any violent transgressor. The same word is applied to 'Jesus and his companions' who encourage Gaius Caesar to impose emperor-worship on the Jews in a story related to Toledoth Jeshu found in two texts of Josippon (see pp. 197–209 in this volume).[59] Dan. 11: 14, where the word is used for 'The men of violence', is regularly applied to Christians by Jewish writers from Saadia (tenth century) onwards.[60] Thus used it was no doubt often taken, as by Jefet b. Ali (tenth century),[61] of breach of religious law; but its wider

---

54 B. Blumenkranz, *Les auteurs chrétiens latins du moyen âge sur les juifs et le judaisme* (Paris, 1963), pp. 27–31, no. 13.

55 E. Bammel, 'Christus Parricida', *VigChr* 26 (1972), 259–62.

56 Eisler, ΙΗΣΟΥΣ ii, 253, n. 3 (ET pp. 363 n. 2, 370 n. 1); M. Lods, 'Étude sur les sources juives de la polémique de Celse contre les chrétiens', *RHPhR* 21 (1941), 1–33 (18f).

57 Huldricus, *Historia*, pp. 35f.

58 Eisler, ΙΗΣΟΥΣ ii, 516–18, citing Krauss, *Leben Jesu*, pp. 42, 45, 47, 76f, 82, 120f; further texts in W. Horbury, 'A Critical Examination of the Toledoth Jeshu' (Diss., Cambridge, 1970), pp. 188, 192, 195, 242–4, 246f, 291, 295.

59 Eisler, ΙΗΣΟΥΣ i, 498; I. Lévi, 'Jésus, Caligula et Claude dans une interpolation du Yosiphon', *REJ* 91 (1931), 135–54 (139).

60 The list in Judah Rosenthal, *Studies and Texts in Jewish History, Literature and Religion* (2 vols., Jerusalem, 1967) i, 204 includes among others Maimonides, Rashi, Ibn Ezra and Abravenel.

61 D. S. Margoliouth, *A Commentary on the Book of Daniel by Jephet ibn Ali the Karaite* (Oxford, 1889), pp. 61f.

application is illustrated by Josippon's use of it for Josephus's *lestai*.[62] *Latrocinia* in the sense of highway robberies are not specified of Christ in these sources; but the disciples use violence during the ministry, although, at this stage of the narrative, as opposed to that dealing with events after the crucifixion, the theme is subordinate to the ruling emphases on miracle and false teaching. These thematically-related passages may be held to strengthen the likelihood that the source of Hierocles's third statement is Jewish.

The three statements may now be considered as a unity. They look like a fragment of a longer story. A comparable fragment-like series, relating events from the conception to the first self-predication of Jesus, occurs among the passages ascribed by Celsus to the Jew (ii. 28, p. 53 Bader) and is fully paralleled in inner-Jewish sources.[63] Similarly the statements in Hierocles are only paralleled with the same interconnection in inner-Jewish sources. Recalling other patristic evidence for Jewish accounts of Christ[64] we may propose an ultimately Jewish source for this citation. The narrative could then have reached Hierocles directly from a Jew or through a pagan, and it could have arisen at any time up to shortly before the date of his book.

Its potential in the hands of a polemist was obviously considerable. The Jews, to whose writings Christians constantly appealed, could be shown to have lost no time in rejecting Christ's claims. The numerous disciples vaunted by the Christians were engaged in nothing else than brigandage. As already noted, the charge of sedition was thus reinforced; and, most importantly, both Christ and his followers were branded with the mark of the most cordially detested class of violent evil-doers (section I above).

In the context of the present enquiry the historical value of the story especially concerns us. The first two items in the narrative may be considered as hostile interpretations of traditions which also entered the Gospels (notably John 11: 54, Luke 6: 17, see p. 189 above). Brigandage, the third item, whether taken as robbery or insurrection, by contrast necessarily implies habitual acts of violence on the part of Jesus. It thereby conflicts with the range of New Testament traditions on his character. The Pauline epistles already presuppose a portrait of the earthly Christ with which this implication would be wholly inconsistent. Appeals to the self-abnegation and gentleness of Christ such as those of Rom. 15: 3, 1 Cor. 10: 33 to 11: 1, 2 Cor. 10: 1, even if they allude to the condescension of the nativity as well as to the ministry, would have been stultified, as C. K.

---

[62] G. D. Cohen, *The Book of Tradition by Abraham Ibn Daud* (London, 1969), p. xxxix.

[63] Lods, *RHPhR* 21 (1941), 31f.

[64] E.g. H. L. Strack, *Jesus, die Häretiker und die Christen nach den ältesten jüdischen Angaben* (Leipzig, 1910), pp. 8*–11*, 14*; B. Blumenkranz, *Die Judenpredigt Augustins* (repr. Paris, 1973), pp. 87f.

Barrett points out, had it been known that the life of Jesus differed in character from what the Gospels now depict.[65]

This discord with the range of New Testament evidence, then, makes it probable that we have here later invention, perhaps in a development, out of contact with Christian tradition, of the tale of beggary cited by the Jew of Celsus (i. 62). The crime of the crucified has been made to fit his punishment.[66]

III

For Eisler[67] Hierocles stood pre-eminent among ancient non-Christian witnesses to Christ, Josephus of course excepted. Eisler linked our passage with the charge of magic in Celsus and Lucian, and with Celsus's phrase *leader of sedition* (p. 183, n. 3 and p. 190, n. 49), as typifying the pagan estimate of Jesus. He valued our passage especially, however, because he took it as a clear exposition of the Roman view of Jesus as a rebel, and the best commentary on Pilate's *titulus*.

Eisler took *latrocinia* here in the legal sense of high treason. He pointed out that for the jurists (p. 185, n. 14) a pretender is *latronum dux*, his adherents *latrones*. Elsewhere in his book he gathered modern instances of the same nomenclature, including contemporary newspaper reports of the Nicaraguan independence movement.[68] He thrice suggested in passing that the passage illuminated other aspects of the ministry. Thus he thinks, as noted already (p. 183 above), that armed disciples would have been called *sicarii* by Josephus, just as Hierocles terms them robbers. Indeed, Christ's several hundred followers begging their way must have been called *latrones*, their importunity being comparable with that of mediaeval 'sturdy beggars'.[69] Lastly, he sees general agreement between our citation and the report in Slavonic Josephus that a hundred and fifty helpers and a multitude of the people joined Jesus on the Mount of Olives.[70] In this instance Eisler's mistranslation (p. 188, n. 40), that Jesus 'was *defeated* by the Jews *when he had been* committing robberies', may by wrongly referring our passage to the arrest have caused him to see a greater resemblance between

---

[65] C. K. Barrett, *A Commentary on the Second Epistle to the Corinthians* (London, 1973), p. 246, on 10: 1. For Paul's concern with the character of the earthly Jesus see G. N. Stanton, *Jesus of Nazareth in New Testament Preaching*, SNTS Monographs 27 (Cambridge, 1974), pp. 99–110. Cp G. M. Styler, above p. 105.

[66] P. 187 and p. 190, n. 51, and Bammel in *Trial*, p. 165.

[67] Eisler, ΙΗΣΟΥΣ, i, xxvi: his words on the importance of this passage are omitted in ET p. 11.

[68] Ibid. i, 194, n. 3 (this section omitted in ET).

[69] Eisler, ΙΗΣΟΥΣ, ii, 253f, n. 3 (ET p. 363 (lacking the mediaeval analogy)).

[70] Ibid. ii, 440, n. 51, omitted in ET p. 457.

the two texts than really obtains. His rendering does not, however, seriously affect the argument for his main contention, that the passage rightly expounds Jesus's offence under Roman law. While Jews saw Christ as a leader-astray, for pagans, Eisler claimed (over-estimating the distinctiveness of their polemic), he was a magician, an instigator of rebellion, and a leader of robber bands. This pagan interpretation, especially as exemplified in our passage, closely approximated in Eisler's view to a true estimate of Jesus's ministry.

Eisler's keen eye for whatever might support his theory rightly discerned that this passage deserves attention. It is his merit to have shown that, so far from being a wholly isolated absurdity,[71] it has links with the common anti-Christian charge of sedition and with the sketch of the disciples as men of violence in Toledoth Jeshu. Our present study of the passage in the same context of pagan and Jewish polemic has suggested that it is older than Hierocles, forming in all probability a fragment of an originally Jewish narrative of Christ's life taken up, like the stories of the Jew of Celsus, by a pagan polemist. Yet is has also seemed probable, in contrast with Eisler's view, that as polemic the passage aims more directly at moral denigration than the charge of sedition, and that as historical assertion it rests in its most important detail, *latrocinia fecisse*, on hostile invention. Its significance for the historian lies rather in its interconnected but fragmentary character, suggesting the existence of a fuller story and confirming that narrative polemic on Jesus, comparable with that current in later Jewish–Christian debate, must be reckoned with in any account of contacts between Jews, pagans and Christians in the ante-Nicene period.

The New Testament evidence on the questions raised by our passage is examined elsewhere in this volume. Within the limits of the present study we may note one final consideration arising from the material under review. Early anti-Christian polemic as preserved to us in respect of the life of Jesus concentrates to a marked degree on teaching and wonder-working. So already where the New Testament records corroborative evidence for the charge 'king of the Jews' it refers to what an opponent would have called charlatanry or deception rather than brigandage, γοητεία or ἀπάτη rather than ληστεία.[72] Luke 23: 2, 5, 14 speak of *teaching* such as might raise

[71] So for example P. de Labriolle, *La Réaction païenne* (Paris, 1942), p. 310.

[72] For the distinction see Josephus, *BJ* ii. 254–64, where the *sicarii*, 'another kind of λησταί' (254), differ from 'another body of villains, with purer hands but more impious intentions' (258) who pretend to inspiration but are πλάνοι . . . ἄνθρωποι καὶ ἀπατεῶνες (259); 261–3 deal with the Egyptian false prophet (γόης, 261); and finally γόητες and ληστρικοί band together (264). (This passage is misleadingly said to equate the two, in E. Schürer, *History of the Jewish People in the Time of Jesus Christ*, as revised by G. Vermes and F. Millar (2 vols. to date, Edinburgh 1973–9) i, 462, n. 29; but they are justly distinguished with reference to *BJ* vi. 286, ibid. ii, 605f

sedition,[73] in John 11:47f *miracles* are specified; in John 19:7 the accusers bidden to support their charge, point to *teaching* in breach of the Torah. These are simply negative views of the activities identified in Luke 24:19 as prophetic *deed and word*. Despite the innuendo of subversion in polemic on these points (p. 183, n. 2) and the recurrent charge of sedition (p. 184 and nn. 9 and 10), polemical accounts of Christs's life continue to depict him as a false prophet rather than a bandit. W. Bauer's collection of material shows that, even allowing for possible loss, our passage is exceptional.[74]

There are instances, as we have seen, where polemical narratives of Christ seem to depend ultimately on traditions incorporated into the New Testament rather than the New Testament writings themselves. It is the more striking that pagan and Jew, no less than Christian, appear to have proceeded from data on the life of Christ in which practices definable as the sorcery and deceit of a false prophet predominated over activity which could be straightforwardly identified as insurrection.

(by C. T. R. Hayward).) The men of violence are likewise linked but contrasted with teachers and wonder-workers at the parallel *AJ.* xx. 167 (the distinction is overlooked by Eisler, ΙΗΣΟΥΣ i, 512f (ET (abbreviated) p. 110)): τὰ μὲν οὖν τῶν λῃστῶν ἔργα defiled the city, οἱ δὲ γόητες καὶ ἀπατεῶνες persuaded the people. On γόης as the pejorative equivalent of προφήτης (n. 3 above) see E. Fascher, *ΠΡΟΦΗΤΗΣ* (Giessen, 1927), pp. 207f; for γοητεία as primarily referring to self-proclamation, ἀπάτη to its effect E. Bammel in Betz–Haacker–Hengel (eds.), *Josephus-Studien*, p. 13 and n. 34.

[73] That this language was probably taken by the evangelist to signify a political charge, but may in fact preserve a trace of an accusation under Jewish law, is suggested by Dodd, *Historical Tradition*, p. 117 n. 1, p. 217 n. 2.

[74] Bauer, *Leben Jesu*, p. 468.

E. BAMMEL

Jesus as a political agent in a version of the Josippon

The restoration of Augustus meant a return to the ancestral religion in its different forms.[1] Non-compliance with this, *impietas*/ἀσέβεια, tended to be equated with *odium humani generis*, to be viewed as κοινὴ νόσος.[2] Whereas this was an accusation the Jews just managed to ward off, the charge haunted the Christians all the more. Without the privileged position of a *religio licita*, without an established claim of being an ancestral religion and of presenting time-honoured truths, they were almost defenceless against the pressure of the *Zeitgeist* and open to politico-juridical suspicion.

The situation was made even more difficult by the fact that there existed an inclination on the side of the Jews to direct the rising anti-Semitism in the Roman administration[3] against those who had split off from the main body of Judaism. Paul already encountered this tendency in Corinth (Acts 18: 12). Josephus positions his description of Jesus ominously close to that of certain detestable Jewish charlatans and describes his followers as men who proceeded from bad to worse.[4] Still, it took some time for the pagan observers to make themselves familiar with Christianity.

Suetonius knows from hearsay that the Jews of Rome, instigated by a certain Chrestus (*impulsore Chresto*), were causing continual disturbances (*assidue tumultuantes*) and had to be expelled from the metropolis in the time of Claudius.[5] There is nothing in this report that indicates Christian ambitions directed against the government, if indeed it is true that Christians had played an active role in the clashes referred to by the Roman historian. Still, the incident shows that strife within an ethnic group could

---

[1] For the sentiment of the time cp. J. Leipoldt, *Der soziale Gedanke in der altchristlichen Kirche* (Leipzig, 1952), pp. 9ff, 203. This became constitutive for the following centuries. Symmachus, the spokesman for the *mos majorum* in fourth-century Rome, gives expression to the same thing when he says: 'we pray for peace to the ancestral gods; for they all . . . mean the same' (*Relatio* iii. 10; O. Seeck = Monumenta Germaniae Historica. Auctores Antiquissimi 6 (Berlin, 1883).

[2] The term is used in Claudius's letter to the Alexandrians and interpreted by S. Lösch, *Epistula Claudiana* (Rottenburg, 1930).

[3] Cp. W. H. C. Frend, *Martyrdom and Persecution in the Early Church* (Oxford, 1965), pp. 154f, 158f and especially 164f. This point is over-emphasised by P. Styger, *Juden und Christen im alten Rom* (Berlin, 1934).

[4] Cp. *Josephus-Studien. Festschrift O. Michel* (Göttingen, 1974), pp. 15ff.

[5] Claudius 25.

be taken as sufficient reason for enacting administrative measures summarily.

While the Christians themselves are not referred to directly by Suetonius, it is different with his contemporary Tacitus.[6] He agrees fully with those who found the Christians propelled by *odium generis humani*,[7] while indicating some reserve *vis-à-vis* the accusation raised against them of having set fire to the city of Rome. That means that although he disclaims any actual political crimes,[8] he recognises an evil disposition[9] in the mentality of the Christians and he views them as potentially dangerous.[10] The reaction of the administration should be guided by the *utilitas publica*[11] rather than by any other considerations. It must, however, be added that the Christians are viewed as being as contemptible as every form of Eastern and especially Jewish[12] cult, and that their objectionableness is even deduced from the Judaean origin and outlandish character of their movement.

Celsus sees exactly the same impulse in Judaism. The Jews decamped from Egypt like slaves running away from their master. Instigated by the γοητεία of Moses[13] they broke with the religion which they had there, yet everything of any value in Jewish religion is derived from the Egyptians. The principle underlying this criticism is clearly regard for the traditional religion as venerable in its various manifestations and worthy of protection

---

[6] *Ann.* xv. 44. The short reference had been taken to be the only surviving part of a large section in the *Annales* in which Tacitus describes Christ as a revolutionary, and which was mutilated by a Christian scribe for that reason (M. Joel, *Blicke in die Religionsgeschichte zu Anfang des zweiten christlichen Jahrhunderts* (Breslau, 1883) ii, 96f). For criticism cp. C. F. Arnold, *Die neronische Christenverfolgung* (Leipzig, 1888), pp. 28ff. G. A. Müller, *Pontius Pilatus* (Stuttgart, 1888), pp. 28ff.

[7] For an interpretation of the phrase, cp. H. Fuchs, 'Tacitus über die Christen', *VigChr* 4 (1950), 84ff; H. Hommel, 'Tacitus über die Christen', *Theologia Viatorum* 3 (1951), 19ff; J. B. Bauer, 'Tacitus und die ersten Christen', *Gymnasium* 64 (1957), 561f.

[8] The matter would be different, if R.v.d. Alm's interpretation 'wegen ganz neuer Vorkommnisse Strafe verdienten (novissima exempla meritos)' could be substantiated (*Die Urtheile heidnischer und jüdischer Schriftsteller der ersten vier Jahrhunderte über Jesus und die ersten Christen*, Leipzig, 1864, p. 14). This is, however, hardly the case.

[9] Tacitus characterises the religion as a 'malum', taking up thereby an established terminology (νόσος, νόσημα, λοιμός, *pestis*), which had been used once and again against Judaism already; cp. Lösch, *Epistula*, pp. 14, 23ff.

[10] Cp. R. Freudenberger, *Das Verhalten der römischen Behörden gegen die Christen im 2. Jahrhundert* (München, 1967), pp. 180ff.

[11] Freudenberger, *Verhalten*, pp. 184ff. It is in keeping with this that Pliny desists from taking the initiative against the Christians and that he only proceeds to action if Christians have been denounced by other citizens, while taking into consideration the general situation in his province.

[12] Tacitus, *Hist.* v. 5.1: *adversus omnes alios, hostile odium*.

[13] Origen, *C. Cels.* v. 41.

by state and society.[14] The Jews deserted this ancestral religion, they are νεώτεροι[15] and, even worse, they attempt to make others abandon their own religion and adopt Judaism.

Seen in this way, Christianity is a potential danger to an intensified degree. Derived from Judaism by a similar revolutionary process,[16] it turned itself against it; it is the product of an *infinita revolutio*. And indeed, the principle that governed Jewish as well as Christian history is still effective. Jesus is called στάσεως ἀρχηγέτης[17] – perhaps in a playful allusion to Acts 15: 31[18] – but his disciples are worse than he was. And the fact that the Christians split among themselves is the supreme example of their character[19] and serves as a demonstration for the 'Gesetz, nach dem sie angetreten.'

Admittedly the Christians say that their God is the God of Moses. If one looks closer, however, it is by no means apparent whose law is taken as valid, that of Moses or that of Jesus. Celsus points to the difference between the precepts of the two.[20] The discussion is not an academic one, if one recalls that Judaism was a *religio licita*, whereas Christianity was not, if it could not identify itself as Judaism. Therefore the reproach of ἀθεότης, of *sacrilegium*, which, because of its constitutional position, one could raise against Judaism only in a modified way, falls on Christianity with undiminished weight. The man who venerates no ancestral gods has no gods, he is godless, he regards nothing as holy.[21] Therefore Christianity lacks all respectability.

[14] Thus the teaching which Celsus sets against Christianity is not his own invention but rather the sum of what was universally recognised, the wisdom of all people. He calls it κοινὸς νόμος (i. 1) and ἀρχαῖος λόγος (i. 14) or, emphatically taking up a term which is often used by Plato, ἀληθὴς λόγος.

[15] *C. Cels.* iii. 5.

[16] For the details of Celsus's view on the revolutionary character of both Judaism and Christianity cp. A. Wifstrand, *Die wahre Lehre des Kelsos* (Lund, 1942), pp. 13ff.

[17] viii. 14; cp. iii. 7, 13, 14. In ii. 44 he speaks of the possibility that someone who is a λῃστής or ἀνδροφόνος may claim with similar impudence that he is a god. This makes it likely that στάσεως ἀρχηγέτης is not used in its literal meaning. The equation Jesus = λῃστής was taken up and given a different slant by a polemicist whose work is attacked by Lactantius (*Mort. Pers.* v. 2.12f). He is very often but not universally (cp. the reservations made by J. Geffcken, *Zwei griechische Apologeten* (Leipzig, 1907), p. 291) identified with Hierocles.

[18] The meaning, however, is different. In Acts the intention is to emphasise the position of Jesus, whereas Celsus, while stating that the στάσις of the Christians had its starting point in Jesus, directs his displeasure and horror wholly against those who had followed him.

[19] *C. Cels.* ii. 12. A similar term is used in the Acts of the Alexandrian anti-Semitic martyrs: Appian calls the emperor λήσταρχος (*Acta Appiani* iv. 8; W. A. Musurillo, *The Acts of the Pagan Martyrs* (Oxford, 1954), p. 67).

[20] vii. 18. Is Acts 24: 14 where the claim is made that the Christians serve the πάτρῳος θεός to be taken as an answer against like accusations?

[21] Eph. 2: 12 is, perhaps, the first Christian answer to this reproach. Cp. A. v.

And indeed, Jesus appeared on the scene yesterday or the day before yesterday.[22] This only confirms that there is no ancient tradition in Christianity. The dominical saying that one cannot serve two masters is a φωνὴ στάσεως[23] and this impression is given weight by individual features such as the rejection of the oath. The claim that Jesus and the Christians came from the lowest levels of society and direct themselves to these levels belongs to this context. The welcome given to sinners shows that the Christians have no law and no discipline and justifies the inference that they themselves are κακοῦργοι.[24] His disciples are heaped with all imaginable scorn – they are characterised as members of despicable professions, as stupid and without any integrity – but revolutionary behaviour in the strict sense of the word is not ascribed to them. Their behaviour towards their master was worse than what is common in a society of robbers, who would not have deserted their λῃστάρχης, as Jesus's disciples did.[25] Their activity resulted in a number of factions. It is rather the disposition of the Christians than any specific action that makes their religion a source of danger to society.[26]

Στασιάζειν πρὸς τὸ κοινόν is the key phrase of Celsus's characterisation of the Christians.[27] He thereby combines two different points raised against them: (a) their turning away from the λοιποὶ ἄνθρωποι[28] and (b) their inclination to res novae.[29] If they had had their roots in one of the time-honoured and accepted religions, they would not have been attracted to a secluded form of life. If they had felt their responsibility for the common

Harnack, *Der Vorwurf des Atheismus in den drei ersten Jahrhunderten*, TU 28 (1905); Tertullian *Ad Nat.* 1.10 (*divortium ab institutis majorum*); Lactantius, *Mort. Pers.* 34 (*relinquere sectam parentum*).

[22] ii. 4; vi. 10.

[23] iv. 23. The term στάσις plays already a role in the philosophy of Plato (cp. G. M. A. Grube, *Plato's Thought* (London, 1935), pp. 129–49) and of Platonism (cp. J. Dillon, *The Middle Platonists* (London, 1977), pp. 368f). The meaning is however different.

[24] iii. 44ff.

[25] *C. Cels.* ii. 12; ii. 59.

[26] Cp. W. Nestle, 'Die Haupteinwände des antiken Denkens gegen das Christentum', *ARW* 37 (1941/2), 70, 90f, 97; 'Zur altchristlichen Apologetik im N.T.', *ZRGG* 4(1952), 120f.

[27] v. 25. Sedition is, of course, a theme that was very much in the mind of the Alexandrians. Josephus defends his own nation (that means those residing in Egypt) against the accusation of *seditio* (*C. Apion* ii. 68). Agrippa II praises the Egyptian Jews for not having let themselves be enticed by the ἀποστάσεως κέντρον of Alexandria (*BJ* ii. 385). He thereby accuses the Greeks of Alexandria of inclination to στάσις.

[28] viii. 8; cp. Libanius, *Oratio* 30. This put the Christian apologists in a difficult position. Some of them – Aristides, Diognetus, Bardesanes (*Patrologia Syriaca*, ed. F. Nau, ii (Paris, 1907), 607; 550–3) – still boasted the newness of the Christian religion, whereas others – Justin, Theophilus, Tatian – shied away from this and emphasised the antiquity of Christianity.

[29] The Christians are called νεώτεροι by Libanius, *Oratio* 30.

welfare, they would not be tempted to look ahead to a complete change of things. The phrase is thus rather the Platonic philosopher's general conclusion and an admonitory exclamation than a reference to events initiated or performed by the Christian community.

Even the charge that the Christians are opposed to all civil authority – a commonplace in the polemical literature[30] – points to *inertia*, reluctance or refusal to carry out public duties,[31] rather than to specific actions[32] directed against the government or its representatives. Celsus's position over against Christianity is reasoned and based on a scheme which is more fully developed than that of Tacitus.

The polemicist magnifies tendencies, he warns against potential dangers. What he fastens on are dispositions rather than actions. It is moral stigmatisation that is intended by Celsus's calumnious picture of Christian principles. It is an appeal to reconsider their position rather than a direct accusation that is in his mind. This does not rule out the possibility that the argument could have practical consequences in a time of high tension. Indeed, this was the reason why Origen felt it necessary to refute him in the time of the persecutor Decius.

Jewish tradition presents a variant of this scheme. The connection between Judaism and Christianity is crystallised in the person of Jesus. He is described as a prophet who became a pseudo-prophet,[33] or as a teacher who taught strange teachings.[34] These characterisations, however, come to be replaced by another: he was the pupil of a rabbi. Since he was only this he was unable to teach any teaching: anyone who teaches a teaching in the presence of his master is worthy of death.[35] And it was more than doubtful whether he was in a position to utter prophetic pronouncements. Any deviation from the traditional teaching was nothing but disobedience towards those who taught him. It is for this reason that the narratives about his behaviour *vis-à-vis* his teachers stress rather the impudence, the lack of

---

[30] *C. Cels.* viii. 55, 65, 67; Ps. Lucian, *Philopatris* 25.26; cp. below pp. 371f.

[31] For an interpretation of *inertia*, an accusation mentioned by Suetonius in his account on T. Flav. Clemens (*Dom.* 15.1), cp. W. Pöhlmann, 'Die heidnische, jüdische und christliche Opposition gegen Domitian' (Diss. Erlangen, 1967), 38ff.

[32] The στάσις of the Christians consists in his view in their refusal to take part in the *munera* and the ὠφέλεια they gain therby for themselves (iii. 14). Tertullian, on the other hand, emphasises that the Christians do not take part in the revolutionary activities of the day: 'numquam Albiani, nec Nigrini vel Cassiani inveniri potuerunt Christiani' (*Ad Scap.* 2).

[33] The identification with Bileam serves this purpose.

[34] Although not entitled to do so.

[35] The teaching of a teaching in the presence of a master, as it is supposed to have happened in the case of Jesus (Strassburg version, ch. 2; S. Krauss, *Das Leben Jesu nach jüdischen Quellen* (Berlin, 1902), p. 39; Vienna version, ch. 4; Krauss, p. 68) is *eo ipso* not only an act of irreverence but of insurrection against the tradition which was ordained by God.

respect on the side of Jesus than the teaching of abominable statements. It seemed inadvisable to reproduce Jesus's teachings and it was more serviceable to point to the underlying defects of Jesus's character and – this is the supreme Jewish argument – to a background and surroundings which explain everything in him.

The only allusion to his teaching is the claim that he intended to abrogate the Law,[36] and the conclusion is spelled out that he rebelled against the great God,[37] against the great God of heaven.[38] The Jewish polemicists occasionally give expression to this by using an opprobrious name for Jesus like רשע . The most far-reaching of these terms is בן סורר [39] = son of revolution, which is interpreted in the context by reference to his promulgating a new Torah; that means that it is used as a way of pin-pointing Jesus's departure from the document of the covenant. The other term which is capable of political interpretation is פרוץ . It is, however, significant that the term is normally used when the strife between Jews and Christians[40] is pictured. This fight is a standing feature in the accounts of the events after the crucifixion and in some versions is said to have taken place already during the lifetime of Jesus.[41] While פריצים is the normal term in these descriptions, a term used to denote the breach between Judaism and the new movement, it is not frequently employed in relation to the fellowship of Jesus. אנשיו is the standard expression in the Huldreich version of the Toledoth,[42] while פריצים is used only once when the disciples are listed. Most surprisingly, however, it is not Jesus who is the

[36] The Aramaic text published by Ginzberg only implies that 'Jesus the wicked' had intended to make vain the Torah and the Law and the Commandments (Schechter Memorial volume ii, 328 Ms Ib l.10), while it enlarges on the reaction which all Israel rose to engage in. The Huldreich text (J.J. Huldreich, ספר תולדות ישוע הנוצרי Historia Jeschuae Nazareni (Leiden, 1705), p. 43) states bluntly that Jesus commanded (אמר) that the Law be abolished (לבטל את התורה).

[37] Ginzberg text 2a, line 24.

[38] Ginzberg text 2b, line 6.

[39] J. D. Eisenstein, Ozar Midrashim (New York, 1915), pp. 215a, line 28f.

[40] The Huldreich version adopts on the whole the same style (pp. 59, 96f, 125f), while in a few places (100, 122) פריצים refers to relatives of Jesus.

[41] Wagenseil (Tela ignea, Altorf, 1681), p. 16; Vienna text (Krauss, p. 76); Yemenite text (Krauss, p. 120). Obviously motifs of the post-Easter stories had been inserted into the Jesus story on a secondary level. The claim of Hierocles – see p. 199 – is neither a närrischer Einfall (G. Lösche, 'Haben die späteren neuplatonischen Polemiker gegen das Christenthum das Werk des Celsus benutzt?', ZWT 27 (1883), 284; cp. Geffcken, Apologeten p. 291: 'das Histörchen von Christus dem Räuber') nor his ureigene Erfindung (H. Kellner, Hellenismus und Christenthum (Köln, 1866), p. 222) but deduced from stories of this kind. These Toledoth passages were referred to recently by H. J. Schonfield (Jesus, London, 1939; 2nd edn. 1948, p. 254), taken as historical evidence that points to a revolutionary activity of the disciples of Jesus carried out with the intention to set free the already imprisoned Jesus.

[42] The Josippon interpolation uses the phrase רעיו .

'head of the insurgents' (רוש הפריצים) but John the Baptist.[43] Another text, the addition to Josippon, gives the impression that the פריצים had come into existence almost independently from Jesus; it uses the formula 'the פריצים and Jesus' and lists the latter only once as a פרוץ together with two other פריצים who are executed at the same time. It emerges that פריצים in the majority of cases depicts the turning away from Judaism by establishing new laws etc. It is equally capable of indicating a violent clash which happened in consequence of this. The term, as it is mainly used, carries a meaning not very different from משומדים.

The reluctance to apply the term to Jesus is all the more significant as the Wagenseil version starts by characterising Jesus's putative father as a warrior (גבור מלחמה) and as someone who engaged in robberies and licentiousness.[44]

The case of Jesus is treated as a domestic affair in the Jewish references. The offence he gave and the verdict passed on him are described in Jewish terminology, and equally the authority that had to deal with him is taken to be the normal Jewish court. This is almost an ubiquitous feature in Jewish sources. But there are also subsidiary factors worth mentioning. Ulla explains the long time gap between the verdict and the execution of Jesus,[45] a time which made it possible to call for mitigating circumstances by reference to Jesus's connections with the government (מלכות) implying that these connections made it desirable for the court to proceed with the utmost care and to allow for as many interventions as possible. The general picture is the same: it was entirely a Jewish matter, but the case is justified vis-à-vis the non-Jewish world. The remark may be taken as the defence against assertions to the contrary, claims which are likely to have circulated already at the beginning of the Constantinian era.

On the other hand, in one branch of the Jewish lives of Jesus, mainly in the Aramaic tradition, a direct involvement of the Romans is claimed. A confrontation between the rabbis on the one side and Jesus and John on the other takes place before Caesar. As the result is not in Jesus's favour the Jews are permitted to take Jesus and John and to proceed with them according to their law. That means, the checking of the evidence takes place before the judgement is passed. The emperor, as a neutral witness, is viewed as involved in the fact-finding process, but the judgement and execution are still in the hands of the Jews.[46] Tiberius (and Pilate) are peripheral persons.

---

[43] Huldreich, p. 36.   [44] גזל וחמס (Wagenseil p. 3).

[45] Sanh. 43a. Cp. p. 360 n. 52.

[46] The texts were edited by L. Ginzberg, Ginze Schechter i (New York, 1928), 324ff and corrected by W. Horbury, Festschrift C. F. D. Moule (2nd edn. London, 1971), pp. 116ff. The report of Agobard, based on a type of Toledoth not dissimilar to this,

The matter is different in a story which is found in two manuscripts of the Josippon,[47] although it is not of a piece with that chronicle.[48] An encounter between Jesus and Caesar dominates the central section of the story. It is, however, not the accused or already condemned Jesus who is met by the emperor and given a chance to redeem himself, but a Jesus who is a commanding figure and eager to establish an influence on his counterpart. Pretending to be a messenger of God[49] he hails Caesar – his name is Gaius – as God on earth (אלהי׳ בארץ) and advises him to erect altars to himself as to a god. The story goes on with the account of the likeness of the emperor being sent to Jerusalem and the resistance of the Jews against giving it a place in the holy city. Herod sends an embassy to Rome – the names of the rabbis who act as emissaries are given – but without any success. Gaius decides to destroy the country of the Jews and he is supported by 'the impudent ones (פריצים) and Jesus and many of our nation'.[50] The Jews hold a fast and implore God's intervention. Gaius is killed as a result of this – cut to pieces which are eaten by the dogs – and Claudius, who had intervened on behalf of the Jews already during his predecessor's rule,

speaks actually of Tiberius's verdict (*Tiberii judicio in carcerem retrursum*), but it is not clear whether this includes the condemnation to death because of magical activity which is mentioned subsequently. It may be that the summary of Agobard is not correct in every respect (cp. S. Krauss, *Das Leben Jesu nach jüdischen Quellen* (Berlin, 1902), p. 6).

[47] A critical edition of the passage was presented by I. Lévi, 'Jésus, Caligula et Claude', *REJ* 91 (1931), 1ff. A new edition was undertaken by A. A. Neuman, 'A Note on John the Baptist and Jesus in Josippon', *HUCA* 23 2 (1950–1), 137ff; the interpretation the author offers is wide of the mark. The text was studied by R. Eisler, *Jesous Basileus* (Heidelberg 1930/1), *passim* (Eisler's thesis is summarised by S. G. F. Brandon, *The Fall of Jerusalem* (2nd edn. London, 1957), pp. 121f), and by W. Horbury, 'A Critical Examination of the Toledoth Jeshu' (unpublished thesis, Cambridge, 1971), 134ff. The story is not as unique as was assumed by Eisler. The Huldreich version of the Toledoth contains the narrative about the attempt of the inhabitants of Ai, i.e. the Christians, to put up a statue of Jesus and Mirjam in a way which offended the Jews and especially the son of king Herod, and tells how the king objected to it and issued a warning to the Christians, that these Christians approached the emperor and asked for his support and that they had to submit to the Jews and burn the statue because they had been denied the help they had craved (Zürich, 1705, p. 122). The similarity is obvious. Different, however, are two points. The event is supposed to have taken place in the period of the early community. The effigy is that of Jesus and his mother, which means the initial connection with the Roman sphere is lacking. Both destruction and replacement are features of a secondary development. The story is a kind of appendix to the Huldreich text. It must have remained in circulation and arrived eventually in a distorted and developed form in the milieu where the Huldreich version happened to be compiled.

[48] The Josippon account displays on the whole an anti-Herodian tendency (cp. Eisler, *Basileus* i, 480f), while it is different here: Herod is pictured as a stern defender of Judaism.

[49] מלאך אלהי׳.   [50] Ed. Lévi, p. 140, 1.11f.

rehabilitates the members of the Jewish embassy who had been sent away in disgrace by Gaius. He gave the Perizim into their hands, took three of them who had fled, killed them and gave their corpses to the dogs in order to exclude the possibility that their wandering followers should steal them at night.[51]

The backbone of the story is the incident at the time of Caligula known from Philo and Josephus. It is narrated in a way which includes Jesus and makes him the dominant figure behind the external pattern of historical events. Consequently it is upon his own and his companions' downfall that the interest is focussed.

Caligula's *Cäsarenwahnsinn* is explained (and in some ways excused) by the claim that he acted at the instigation of Jesus. It is said of the latter that he had advised Gaius against Herod and that he was responsible for the emperor's decision to destroy the holy land. Jesus appears as a political activist whose whole ambition is geared to actions detrimental to the Jewish nation. His sly machinations to this end are dominant, while his intention to alter the interpretation of the law[52] is only an incidental feature without any consequences in the story.[53]

The picture that emerges of his activity is the following: utmost submissiveness to the emperor, ruler-worship in its most outrageous form is not Caligula's own invention but almost forced upon him from outside, by Jesus. Equally the abhorrent suggestion to erect altars for him, for example in Jerusalem. It is probably the view of the narrator that Jesus made his (false) claim and put the idea into the head of Caligula in order to provoke the Jews who had no choice but to resist. Caligula's decision 'to destroy the holy land' is a reaction of stupidity possibly again instigated by Jesus. The emperor's death by an act of God brings Jesus's machinations to a quick end. He is, it seems, executed in the capital. The activity takes place in Rome but it is geared to Palestine, where those live whom he persecutes with his hatred.

This account is framed by another in which the 'impudent ones' play the main role. They are made to appear before the court of the judges of the Jews. They appeal to the Roman overlords – the account speaks of Edom while the main section refers directly to Rome – and claim that they are tried because they had revolted against 'their law' and adopted Caesar's

---

[51] The execution is understood as having taken place in Rome. Thus, the motif known from the *Mart. Petri* ('Romam venio iterum crucifigi'; Lipsius-Bonnet, *Acta Apost. Apocr.* i. 1ff) appears here in a very different form.

[52] Plural formulation in the text.

[53] He acts together with a whole band of followers in the capital as well as in Palestine. This is the basic difference from the Petersburg text published by A. Harkavy (*Hebräische Bibliographie* xv (Berlin, 1875), p. 15).

law. They did so successfully. The Romans gave them protection when they swore by the life of Caesar. At the end we are informed that Joshua and his companions – the members of the Jewish embassy – had returned to Jerusalem and brought the rest of the Perizim before the Sanhedrin. Judas Iskariot enquires on the orders of the king which verdict is appropriate for those who had advised the emperor against him. He actually hangs them on the tree. In consequence of this others are stoned. But the action is carried out only with partial success. It is not possible to wipe out the Perizim because they act in secrecy. The rest continue to exist and even convert many to follow them in secret.

Beginning and end are not entirely of a piece: the protecting Romans have disappeared, while the motif that the Christians hold on by means of acting secretly is introduced. The basic story of the ups and downs of the Christian community is, however, the same. The link with the middle section consists mainly in the introductory remark according to which 'Jesus and his companions' went to see the emperor. In the story Jesus appears almost single-handed. No reference is made to the Jewish threat and the Roman protection. This suffices to show that the framework and central portion are entities which did not belong together originally.

The framework is constructed out of elements each of which is paralleled in the Hebrew Toledoth.[54] The central part of the story is interlarded with features mainly reminiscent of the Aramaic part of the Toledoth. The names of the Jewish messengers, Jesus's claim of divine sonship, the intention attributed to him to alter the interpretation of the law, the fast of the Jews for three days, the motif of the hindrance of childbirth, the fear of the improper use of the corpses of the executed ones – all this is paralleled in the Toledoth, although the individual elements are sometimes given a slant different from the one they have in these texts.[55] On the other hand, Caligula's name appears surprisingly at the end of the Aramaic Toledoth text published by Ginzberg[56] and this very name seems to figure slightly disguised in the Hebrew text of Strassburg,[57] which stands somewhat apart from the rest of the Hebrew part and displays Aramaic features. This shows

[54] It is this branch which takes an interest in the Christian community and its relation to Judaism.

[55] E.g. Jesus is a messenger of God in order to proclaim Gaius god on earth.

[56] Page 2b, line 3: טברינוס קיסר וקליגוס הגמון according to W. Horbury, 'The Trial of Jesus in Jewish Tradition' in *The Trial of Jesus*, Festschrift C. F. D. Moule, London, 1970, p. 120. Caligula appears here, together with Pilate, as an official of Tiberius. In this way two traditions are combined.

[57] The Strassburg MS mentions, besides יהודא אסכריוט טא , a second person who became instrumental in the tracing and catching of Jesus: גיסא (Krauss, *Leben Jesu*, p. 44). The term signifies a composite person: elements of Judas, who very often is given the by name גינאה , seem to be mixed with גיוס (the names are often rendered with Aramaic endings in this text; cp. כיפא, Krauss, p. 49).

that a cross-fertilisation must have taken place, a fact which makes it impossible to dismiss the two texts as fanciful products of an ingenious mind of a time as late as the renaissance period.[58] The varying provenance, extent and degree of the influence give an indication of different strata.

If one concentrates on the central piece the temptation has arisen to think of a replacement of Apion by Jesus[59] carried out by a scribe with whimsical inclinations. Certainly the influence, direct or indirect, of the accounts by Philo and Josephus of the Jewish embassies sent to Rome is noticeable, although – this must be emphasised – the main point that someone else had instigated Gaius to send his statue to Jerusalem is absent from both Philo and Josephus. But there is more to be said. Already Irenaeus expresses the opinion that Jesus was crucified when he was in his forties and he dates this event *expressis verbis* as having taken place under Claudius; he refers for this to the view taken by the elders of Asia.[60] Two fragments, one from Milan and another from Padua, even give A.D. 46 as the date of the crucifixion. Above all Pilate's letter to Claudius points in the same direction. Is there a connection? In all the sources apart from Victorinus of Pettau which favour the view that Jesus died at an advanced age, that view is linked with the synchronism of Luke 3: 2;[61] that means, it occurs in an already mutilated form. It is likely originally to have existed independently and to have been more widespread. The references we possess point to the East as the region of origin,[62] from which it spread to the West. It cannot be ruled out that, somewhere on this route, this view of the dates of Jesus was picked up by a Jewish controversialist.[63]

Claudius was famed as an upholder of good old Roman tradition, and likewise he was recommended by Josephus as one keen to give due honour to the Jews. To link such a person with the execution of Jesus was certainly a construction which was inviting for a Jew. It was equally inviting to view Jesus's activity as having taken place in collaboration with Caligula who

---

[58] Thus Neuman, *HUCA* 23 2 (1950/1), 148f.

[59] Thus Levi p. 150.

[60] *Haer.* 2.22.5f. For a treatment of the question cp. E. von Dobschütz, *Das Kerygma Petri* (Leipzig, 1894), pp. 136f; W. Bauer, *Das Leben Jesu im Zeitalter der neutestamentlichen Apokryphen* (Tübingen, 1909), pp. 292ff; A. Strobel, *Ursprung und Geschichte des frühchristlichen Osterkalenders* (Berlin, 1977), pp. 281ff.

[61] Bauer, *Leben Jesu*, p. 295.

[62] For Irenaeus cp. n. 60. Victorinus depends on Alexander of Jerusalem. Justin, who may have shared the view (*Dial.* 88; cp. Bauer, *Leben Jesu*, p. 293), was himself a native of Palestine.

[63] The view taken in the Josippon passage corresponds especially to that of the 'very old' (Bauer 293) interpolation in the Daniel commentary of Hippolytus (iv. 23.3), according to which Jesus died in the first year of Claudius. The Christian claim of an *aetas perfecta* – an idea which influenced Justin and Irenaeus – may have been partly brought about by the Jewish accusation that people like Bileam (an alias for Jesus) will not see the half of their days.

belongs to the category of evil princes, as even eulogistic historiography was very ready to admit. Jesus's association with him meant justification of the condemnation pronounced by his successor. Still, the association is described in such a way that the main guilt is on the side of Jesus rather than the emperor.

The Christians are called פריצים and this appellation is applied once to Jesus as well, and to the two who are executed together with him. Still, their rebellious mind is presupposed rather than made explicit. Their rejection of the Torah did not lead to anarchism but, on the contrary, to an eager embracing of the law of Caesar. No attempt is made to picture Jesus and his followers as a conspiracy after the model of Catiline. The desertion of the ancestral law led of necessity to utmost submissiveness vis-à-vis the emperor. Still he was seen through by Claudius whose function it was to represent the true Roman tradition. By this means the story reconciles two motifs: Jesus on the side of the government and Jesus acting against the government. The one is his pretence, the other expresses the real state of affairs. He did indeed, as the Aramaic Toledoth put it, act 'against God and king'.[64]

The story is in fact the Jewish reply to the Christian claim that it was only the bad Caesars who turned against Christianity, and that they only did so because they had been exposed to the influence of wicked advisers.[65]

The dramatis personae utilised in the story are different from those in the talmudic accounts; they direct the reader's mind to the world outside Judaism. So do certain details. One is led to suspect that it may have played a role in the Jewish–Christian controversy. The features are not without parallels. The Aramaic Toledoth, which are extant in an abbreviated form redacted for home consumption, derive from a probably Greek *Vorlage*, which has striking similarities with the anti-Christian Acts of Pilate which circulated in the time of Maxentius.[66] These Acts were likely to have been influenced by the Jewish accounts. The Christian Acts of Pilate reflect the judicial machinery of the time around A.D. 300.[67] They are to be seen as an answer to the Acts of the time of Maxentius and they do indeed refute details of the Jewish accounts. The *Acta Silvestri*[68] and similar accounts direct themselves to the same task. The parallels show that the Jewish picture of the life of Jesus had been an issue in the ancient world for quite a time.

---

[64] Ginzberg, fo. 1b line 26. The same phrase is used in the Slavonic Josephus (cp. Eisler *Basileus* ii, 454).

[65] Melito according to Eusebius, *H.E.* 4.26.7–11.

[66] Eusebius, *H.E.* 1.11.9.

[67] E. v. Dobschütz, 'Der Prozess Jesu nach den Acta Pilati', *ZNW* 3 (1902), 89ff. Cp. above, pp. 173ff.

[68] Cp. W. Levison, *Aus rheinischer und fränkischer Frühzeit* (Düsseldorf, 1948).

The assumption that the central section of the narrative, in its original form at least, found its shape in this period and atmosphere gives it a *Sitz im Leben* which is more plausible than any other hypothesis. Certain individual features may lend a measure of support to this suggestion. Fourth-century Roman historiography was well aware that Caligula belonged to the number of evil princes.[69] The contorniates, the medallions issued in order to spread propaganda for the Roman tradition and against Christianity,[70] give special attention to scenes connected with the circus and were possibly distributed amongst the audience at the beginning of a show.[71] A narrative that enlarges on Caligula's end in the circus must have been greeted with interest in this world. The command of the emperor to worship his statue, while otherwise protecting the Jewish religion ('your feasts and your Sabbaths – keep them'),[72] presupposes a state of affairs in which the Jews enjoyed guaranteed religious freedom. Such a guarantee was given in the form of an exemption from emperor worship in the otherwise notorious decree of Diocletian.[73] The consequences of this licence are noticeable in the politics and legislation of the following generations.

Taken this way the little story is not without interest. It shows how Judaism liked to explain Christian origins to the non-Jewish world, when it was completely at liberty to do so. Branded as Jesus is, he is portrayed as the evil genius of an emperor, as, so to speak, a negative Josephus.[74] His and his followers' revolt against the Torah is presupposed but no attempt is made to shift this to a political level and to denounce the Christians as revolutionaries in the strict sense of the word.

[69] The portrait of Caligula in the epitome to *Origo Gentis Romanae* is entirely negative (*Epit.* 3.4; 5 and 7): cp. J. Schlumberger, *Die Epitome de Caesaribus* (München, 1974). The same is true of the sketch in the Historia Augusta; cp. J. Straub, *Heidnische Geschichtsapologetik in der christlichen Spätantike* (Bonn, 1963), p. 131, n. 7.

[70] A. Alföldi, *Die Kontorniat-Medaillons* i (Berlin, 1976). Cp. J. Wytzes, *Der letzte Kampf des Heidentums in Rom* (Leiden, 1976).

[71] Cp. J. M. C. Toynbee, *JRS* (1945), 115ff (review of A. Alföldi, *Die Kontorniaten* (Budapest, 1943)).

[72] The provision is a stock feature in those Toledoth which deal with the early church as well. It is there that the advice to give freedom to the Jews to exercise their own worship is put into the mouth of Peter, indicating a different situation, in which the voice of the church rather than that of the political authorities became to be of crucial importance.

[73] For the exemption of the Jews cp. J. Juster, *Les Juifs en Empire Romain* i (Paris, 1914), 247 n. 1.

[74] D. Daube, *Josephus* (München, 1978).

E. BAMMEL

The Feeding of the Multitude

I

The Feeding of the Multitude is represented in no less than five different places within the tradition of the canonical Gospels, as well as in a variety of forms in that of apocryphal sources.[1] This is a surprising state of affairs in Gospel tradition and, especially as two versions are to be found in one and the same Gospel, it hints at a bifurcation of the traditions concerning the Feeding already at a pre-literary stage.

It is this fact that makes it *a priori* unlikely that a simple solution can be advanced, or that a reduction of the reports to one or two versions would be possible in this case.[2] Mark 8 cannot simply be styled as a doublet of Mark 6,[3] nor can Matthew 14 and Luke 9 just be considered as reformulations of Mark 6, let alone John 6 be viewed as an offshoot of the Markan account. The differences are too marked to allow acquiescence in the kind of solution which has proved advisable in many other cases.

The Markan account is part of a pre-Markan composition, as the parallel in chapter 8 shows. The Feeding is followed there by the journey over the lake (verses 13–21), the Pharisaic demand for a sign from heaven (verses 11f) and, finally, a healing story (verses 22–6). All these elements are present in chapters 6 and 7 as well. Lake stories are reproduced in 6: 45–52 (56), the Pharisees appear in 7: 1ff, a healing is narrated in 7: 31–7.[4] The scheme is the same, with the single exception that the items in 8: 11–21 are interchanged. The scheme is preserved in its integrity in the second composition, whereas different material came to be included in the first one.[5] The existence of the parallel formations shows that the Feeding story

---

[1] A collection of this material is to be found in E. Stauffer, 'Antike Jesustradition und Jesuspolemik im mittelalterlichen Orient', *ZNW* 46 (1955), 1ff.

[2] A different view is taken by I. Buse, 'The Gospel accounts of the Feeding of the Multitudes', *ExpT* 4 (1962/63), 167ff.

[3] Nor is it possible to take the tradition about two feedings as original because it is analogous to the Elijah story (thus W. Erbt, *Das Markusevangelium* (Leipzig, 1911), p. 32).

[4] The similarity between the two healing stories – and this is especially true for the first part – is striking.

[5] It is likely that 7: 1ff just indicates the heading of the pre-Markan composition whereas the actual point of controversy was changed when the formation came to be included in the Gospel. For the latest investigation of the Markan version cp. R. M. Fowler, *Loaves and Fishes* (Chicago, 1978).

cannot be viewed in isolation but receives its interpretation in part from its context.[6]

The Markan account is introduced by a section which speaks (a) of a gathering or return of the ἀπόστολοι to Jesus; (b) of his suggestion that they should withdraw and rest for a time away from the crowds; and (c) the claim that the crowds counteracted this by assembling in the place of the multiplication of the loaves. This is too much for the purposes of an introduction. Furthermore it does not hold together. The reason given for the withdrawal into solitude (in verse 31b) is all the more strange in that the disciples are supposed to have come back from a period of public activity. Verse 33 defeats the purpose of verse 31 and is a most artificial bridge between the introduction and the feeding story. This means that what we find here is not just a filler, designed to link two pericopes, but rather a conglomeration of different material which was combined not entirely successfully. A redactional level is indicated by the term ἀπόστολος which is foreign to the body of the gospel[7] and the use of which is intended to establish a link with 6: 7, where however the term δώδεκα is used. Something similar is the case with verse 31b β (οὐδὲ φαγεῖν εὐκαίρουν). It is an attempt to establish a bridge to the following pericope and thereby points to a similarly late level.[8] The matter is different in 31a β (δεῦτε . . . τόπον). It is a piece of advice given to others,[9] which is interpreted in verse 32 as referring to a joint undertaking. It is this remark which seems to be the *membrum archaeum* of the tradition.[10]

Who were the original recipients of the advice? It seems that the redactional addition of ἀπόστολοι has distorted the original context. The advice appears to be given to men who do not normally stay with Jesus. The

---

[6] This was noted in a general way by M. Goguel, *La vie de Jésus* (Paris, 1932; GT Zürich, 1934, p. 230; ET London, 1933, p. 359).

[7] Even in 3: 14 the term seems to be secondary. It is not unimportant to see that Matthew uses a less stylised formulation at this point than Luke, for whom the identification of μαθηταί and ἀπόστολοι is characteristic (cp. 6: 13; 17: 5; 22: 14). The redactional touches seem to have been added to the Markan gospel in more than one stage. It is not at all impossible that 6: 30 was formulated with knowledge of Luke.

[8] Almost the same formulation is given in 3: 20, in a passage which shows the marks of redactional activity as well. W. Erbt, on the other hand, maintains that the whole of verse 31 is redactional (*Markusevangelium*, p. 29).

[9] The meaning of δεῦτε became weakened in Hellenistic Greek. Is it the remainder of a fuller formulation (δεῦτε ἄγετε)?

[10] The consideration that the vision of Ezek. 34 played a considerable role in the shaping of the Feeding scene and the fact that ἀναπαύεσθαι is already used in that chapter (verse 14) gives support to the view that ἀναπαύεσθαι belongs to the original stock in verse 31 as well. Of course not in the present form (ὀλίγον!), but perhaps in a wording analogous to that of Matt. 11: 29 (εὑρήσετε ἀνάπαυσιν).

counsel has to be given to them *expressis verbis*: their following is not the normal way of life of those who are accustomed to accompany their master. It is therefore likely to be advice given to a group of men who are not identical with the Twelve.

A narrower identification of this body is given in the reading of sy[sin], according to which[11] the disciples (*sic!*) had come and told Jesus what 'he' had done and taught. This is in all probability John the Baptist, and thereby the disciples are defined as his followers. The reading is, however, so close to Matt. 14: 12 that it is difficult to consider it as genuine within the Markan context.[12] The state of the Markan passage is such that it must be assumed that the original opening, which gave details about the arrival and the intentions of the men addressed by Jesus, was detached. Jesus's answer is likely to have contained a redirection of some kind of those who are spoken to. The original account is likely to have continued[13] with a remark that Jesus himself follows in the same direction subsequently.[14] The supposed original wording was worked over in order to obliterate any notion of flight.[15]

One of the characteristic features of the Markan report on the Feeding is 34a: ἐσπλαγχνίσθη κτλ.[16] It is a surprising statement in the light of verses 30b, 31b, and even 33; but it is very likely if taken together with the reconstructed beginning of the scene; the puzzled few on the one side, the helpless crowds on the other. The citation from Ezek. 34, which is not likely to have been added at a later stage,[17] underlines this motif.

This is especially true for the Matthaean and Lukan parallels to the Markan account. They contain a number of agreements over against Mark:

[11] The heritage of the reading is still noticeable in D; and A. Merx (*Die vier kanonischen Evangelien nach ihrem ältesten bekannten Texte* (Berlin, 1897), pp. 242f; *Matthaeus* (Berlin, 1902), p. 233) comes out in favour of the genuineness of the reading.

[12] This does not rule out the possibility that it was inserted in the knowledge of oral tradition, as indeed Syriac Christianity knew more of the Baptist than was taken up by the authors of the New Testament (cp. *NTSt* 18 (1971/72), 119ff).

[13] Such a procedure in stages is typical of Z (John 7: 3ff; 11: 3ff).

[14] As is the case in chapter 6: 45ff.

[15] The redactor rather gave the impression of a success story: verses 30, 31b, taken together with 7b, 13 lead one to expect a crowd which is eager and devoted to Jesus. Of seminal importance is an observation of Wellhausen: the original sequence ('der ursprüngliche Pragmatismus'), according to which Herod had caused the flight of Jesus across the lake, had been destroyed by Mark (*Einleitung in die drei ersten Evangelien* (2nd edn. (Berlin, 1911), p. 48). The opposite view is taken by E. Meyer, *Ursprung und Anfänge des Christentums* i (Stuttgart, 1921), 137. Cp. Mark 9: 33, where the reference to Capernaum is at variance with 9: 30 and results in the obliteration of the impression of a flight of Jesus.

[16] E. Hirsch, *Frühgeschichte des Evangeliums* i (2nd edn. Tübingen, 1951), 76, however, considers it as addition of Mark II.

[17] E. Schwartz, *Aporien im vierten Evangelium* iv, NGGG (1908), 498.

Matt. 14: 13 ἀνεχώρησεν/Luke 9: 10 ὑπεχώρησεν,[18] οἱ ὄχλοι[19] instead of Markan πολλοί (Matt. 14: 13, 15, 19; Luke 9: 11, 12, 16). A reference to the boat voyage (Mark 6: 32) is lacking in both Gospels.[20] On the other hand they both emphasise Jesus's healing activity, while they omit the contents of Mark 6: 34b.[21] The reference to the five loaves and two fishes (Matt. 14: 17b, Luke 9: 13) comes from the disciples of their own accord and is introduced by οὐκ ἔχομεν/εἰσὶν ἡμῖν. Both Gospels speak of τὸ περισσεῦον (-σαν) at the end of the account and both reports too place ὡσεί in front of the calculation of those present at the occasion (Matt. 14: 21, Luke 9: 14). The agreements over against Mark are such that the influence of a second source apart from Mark must be taken for granted.[22] It is very likely that certain features which occur only in one of the two accounts derive also from this same source.[23] This result is all the more important as the influx of a second source is already noticeable in the first half of Matthew's account of the beheading of the Baptist,[24] a narration the end of which too is completely at variance with Mark[25] and which – different again from Mark – runs directly into the beginning of the story of the Feeding of the Multitude.

It is reasonable to take these features as deriving from one entity, which

---

[18] The evangelist himself added a geographical location which is somewhat at variance with the verb.

[19] Matthew presents the plural formulations, while Luke gives the singular twice, probably for stylistic reasons. Cp. J. Schmid, *Matthäus und Lukas* (Freiburg, 1930), p. 117 – Ὄχλος is a Q word, as appears from Luke 3: 7; 7: 24; 9: 11f, 16.

[20] In Matthew 14: 13 according to the reading of Γ sy^sc, which is to be preferred here.

[21] Is this a post-Markan addition?

[22] Similarly H. Helmbold, *Vorsynoptische Evangelien* (Stuttgart, 1953), pp. 33ff.

[23] ἀποδεξάμενος (Luke 9: 11), βασιλεία as the object of teaching (11), the subsequent description of the location as ἔρημος τόπος (12; is verse 10b not any longer in its original state?), the absence of the 200 denarii, the change from ὄχλος to λαός (13), the addition of αὐτούς to εὐλόγησεν (16), the number of those present in verse 14 already – these details have to be taken into consideration.

[24] It is a passage where the correspondence between Mark and Matthew is less marked than in most pericopes (see G. Styler in C. F. D. Moule, *The Birth of the New Testament* (London, 1962), p. 229; W. Bussmann, *Synoptische Studien* i (Halle, 1925), 81f). This is especially the case in verses 3 to 5 and verse 12, whereas the intervening verses show a Markan influence (especially verse 9 λυπηθείς; cp. Mark 6: 26). It is reasonable to suppose that the Matthaean account is a contamination of a special source with the Markan description. The Markan report itself poses a problem. Its style does not agree with that of the first half of the Gospel (see L. Wohleb, 'Beobachtungen zum Erzählungsstil des Markusevangeliums', *RQ* 36 (1928), 192; cp. M. Zerwick, *Untersuchungen zum Markusstil* (Rome, 1937), p. 22). The pericope belongs to the redactional level of the Gospel.

[25] Wellhausen's criticism of Matt. 14: 12, that he accommodated Mark to his own design and turned the sequence of pericopes into chronological order (*Das Evangelium Matthaei* (Berlin, 1904), p. 75; similarly Fr. Spitta, *Die synoptische Grundschrift* (Leipzig, 1912), p. 217), would have to be subscribed to, were it not that Matthew already produces different information in 14: 3ff.

was – with difficulty – pressed into the Markan framework. What is characteristic of this sequence is the direct link between the two stories: the disciples of John recount the execution of their master to Jesus and it is in consequence of this that Jesus ἀνεχώρησεν. The report can only mean that by taking this action the disciples recognise Jesus as the successor of John, that they adopt him as their own master. Jesus's reaction is characterised as well: ἀναχώρησις is a term that describes the refuge one takes from fiscal or some other form of oppression.[26] It thereby establishes a bridge between Herod's punitive measure against John and the course of action taken by Jesus, a decision which may be seen as comprehensible on the assumption that the action taken by Herod is not necessarily limited to John but may be extended to other persons as well. It is in keeping with this that Antipas's action against the Baptist is described as being undertaken after deliberation (Matt. 14: 5) and not as the unfortunate result of a weak moment. It is the kind of action that is likely to lead to consequential measures. The fact that the crowds are not excluded from knowledge of Jesus's abode fits in with this scheme: it is important that Jesus is secure from Antipas, whereas the masses are not, as is the case in Mark, taken as something to keep aloof from.

The Johannine account[27] agrees more closely with the synoptic parallel than any other pericope of the Gospel.[28] Apart from introducing a few subsidiary motifs[29] which result in a disproportionate presentation,[30] it contains three distinct features over against the synoptic reports: (a) the ὄρος; (b) the mention of the impending Passover; (c) the sentiments of the people and Jesus's own reaction thereto, which is spelled out in verses 14f. The motif of the mountain is of central importance in Ezek. 34 (verses 6, 13f, 26) and inserted here – although at variance with verses 16ff – in order to establish a link with that *locus classicus* of Jewish eschatology. It is in the

[26] Cp. E. Bickermann, 'Utilitas Crucis', *RHR* 112 (1935), 214f.

[27] John 21: 1ff is to be seen as based on the story of the Feeding; it is a side-product of the tradition (J. Wellhausen, *Das Evangelium Johannis* (Berlin, 1908), p. 97). Cp. however R. T. Fortna, *The Gospel of Signs* (Cambridge, 1970), pp. 87ff.

[28] The dialogue with the disciples (verses 5bff) brings out something that is typically Johannine: the sovereignty of Jesus in every situation (cp. 11: 42). The means by which this is highlighted, the test of the disciples, is a motif that may have been developed out of the idea alluded to in Mark 6: 37. The παιδάριον that possesses the five loaves and two fishes is introduced because of the sacrificial overtones: only a child can serve such bread as is fit to be used for bread of life. The two hundred *denarii*, known from Mark, are said to be inadequate, a feature that is inserted in order to heighten the miracle. The gathering together of the multitude takes place at the command of Jesus and already symbolises the gathering in of the nations.

[29] The names of two disciples, the παιδάριον and the eucharistic phrases εὐχαριστήσας and ἵνα κτλ.

[30] 'Der reale Hintergrund der Geschichte ging verloren' (S. Mendner, 'Zum Problem "Johannes und die Synoptiker"', *NTSt* 4 (1957/58), 287).

same chapter that the Davidic ἄρχων is announced: καὶ ἔσται αὐτῶν ποιμήν (23f). This salvation came to be expected at Passover in Late Judaism.[31] Verse 4 is to be viewed in this context. Far from being a tiresome chronological notice introduced by the redactor,[32] it is an essential indication, the function of which is to heighten the tension. It serves the same purpose as the mention of the miracles wrought by Jesus that we find in Q, but the Johannine detail is an even more telling pivot, its meaning is an even more precise[33] indication of what is expected to happen. The most important feature is verses 14f. The remark is so extraordinary that it is considered by most scholars out of keeping with the preceding story. Different explanations are given. The verses are seen either as a redactional addition[34] or as a text that had originally followed verse 2a[35] or – interestingly – as the only remaining fragment of a different story which had been replaced by the multiplication of the loaves.[36] The answer is, however, not as easy as that. Verse 15a (Ἰησοῦς οὖν γνοὺς κτλ.) bears unmistakably the marks of Johannine theology;[37] by its interpretation it gives a new direction to the context and thereby suggests that the rest of the verse belongs to an earlier level. Verse 15c ἀνεχώρησεν or rather φεύγει[38] πάλιν is at variance with the beginning of the chapter, where nothing had been said about a movement of this kind by Jesus. On the other hand it contains an admission that is hardly reconcilable with the bold claim the redactor made in verse 6, and thereby evinces an earlier layer of the tradition. So it is an indication of an introductory notice not entirely consistent with the one which now opens the chapter. The evidence shows that verses 14f belong in part at least to a pre-redactional level of the pericope.

This view could be reconciled with the theory according to which the Feeding story is an addition on the redactional level.[39] Is it, however, a foregone conclusion that verses 14f are unrelated to the story? Verse 14 starts with a reference to one particular σημεῖον which is at variance with the plurality of signs mentioned at the beginning. The pointing out of a

[31] Cp. A. Strobel, *Untersuchungen zum eschatologischen Verzögerungsproblem* (Leiden, 1961).

[32] Wellhausen, *Johannes*, p. 28; W. Wilkens, *Die Entstehungsgeschichte des vierten Evangeliums* (Zürich, 1958), p. 29.

[33] It may be for this reason that the headings are omitted (or rather shifted to the background). Another reason is possible as well: the prophet (verse 14) is expected to perform one qualifying miracle.

[34] R. Bultmann, *Das Evangelium des Johannes* (Göttingen, 1941), pp. 157f (ET p. 213f).

[35] Mendner, *NTSt* 4 (1957/58), 296.

[36] Schwartz, NGGG iv (1908), 501.

[37] Cp. 2:25; 6:6; 11:42; 13:11.

[38] ℵ* lat sy^c – Ἀνεχώρησεν may be due to synoptic influence. The acceptance of the reading may have been facilitated by the parallel, chapter 11:54.

[39] The theory of J. Dräseke that John 6:1–29 is a later interpolation ('Das Johannes evangelium bei Celsus', *NKZ* 9 (1898), 139ff) did not meet with applause in his time.

difference between a miraculous border region of the activity of Jesus and the σημεῖον that calls for action – it is typical for the Z source[40] – demands the description of a special sign in the preceding verses. Does the Feeding story meet this demand? It is most certainly not an ordinary miracle in the eyes of the person who wrote down the account of John 6. It is a miracle that is wrought in the presence of the multitude and the divine origin of which was thereby guaranteed as had been the case in the time of Moses.[41] The efficacy of the miracle is vouchsafed by the existence of the 'remainder'. It can indeed be called a miracle in the highest sense, much more so than the cures mentioned in verse 2. It is hardly possible to think of another story that might have fulfilled this demand more effectively.[42]

The appreciation of the crowds is defined as an evaluation of Jesus's personal status and as a declaration of the role they wished him to play for them. The former – whether ὁ ἐρχόμενος κτλ. belongs to the source or not – is an allusion to Deut. 18: 15; the latter is based on the interpretation of Num. 27: 17, which is found in Ezek. 34.[43] It agrees with the emphasis on the mountain and the Passover period and points to an understanding of the scene by the people in the light of the desert imagery, which resulted in the attempt to nominate[44] Jesus as messianic king. This triangle of motifs is all the more important as it is not underlined by the redactor: he is much more interested in the subsidiary motifs of the narrative.

We encounter a picture of the Feeding according to which the event was such that the imagery of Israel in the desert impressed itself on those present, and did so to such a degree that people felt bound to see in Jesus the antitype of those events.

The description of Jesus's reaction to this endeavour has been characterised as due to revisionary activities, as an attempt to bring out the concept of the pacific Christ 'at this place'.[45] Φεύγει is, however, hardly congruent with the portrait of Christ which is presented by the evangelist: when referring to Jesus's withdrawals he uses terms like ἐξῆλθεν with or without ἐκ τῆς χειρὸς αὐτῶν (8: 59; 10: 39), indicating thereby the sovereignty of Jesus.[46]

---

[40] *Miracles*, ed. by C. F. D. Moule (London, 1965), pp. 195ff.   [41] *Miracles*, p. 192.

[42] Mendner's statement: 'one cannot see how such an action alone could have resulted in the proclamation as king' (*NTSt* 4 (1957–8), 296) is more rash than considered.

[43] Motifs deriving from this tradition can be found in a number of places in the synoptic Gospels apart from the feeding stories, e.g. in Matt. 8: 34; 10:·6; 18: 12; Mark 14: 27.

[44] καὶ ἀναδεικνύναι, the reading of א * (q), recommends itself. It is more Semitic in character than the reading starting with ἵνα and it agrees with the role the multitude is expected to play in the eschatological events.

[45] S. G. F. Brandon, *Jesus and the Zealots* (Manchester, 1967), p. 353.

[46] It might be possible to argue that this motif belongs to a pre-Johannine *Urform* of the story.

The story of the Feeding has a firm place in the apocryphal[47] and even in the Jewish[48] tradition. The occasion for the reference to it is normally a summary of the life of Jesus.[49] It is certainly seen as one of the distinctive features, although less frequently mentioned than the walking on the water. Both features are, however, introduced as elaborations of the scheme of Matthew 11. It may be due to this that in the Syriac Acts of John we have a combination where the healings of Matthew 14/Luke 9 are interpreted as performed vis-à-vis sick, lepers, lame and blind, and this is followed immediately by the orders given by Jesus for the Feeding.[50] The miracle is mentioned in Or. Sib. 1.356ff as the climax[51] of Jesus's messianic deeds, and the form in which it is enacted is not based on the Gospel reports.[52] It is the cardinal event, belief in which is decisive for salvation and condemnation in the great scene of Sur. 5 of the Koran.[53] The Feeding is described as the banquet table sent down from heaven, as a miracle that proves that Allah is the best guardian and confounds those unwilling to believe. This again is a form which is not directly dependent on the Gospel reports.[54]

A very particular view is taken in the encomium in praise of the Baptist, which is attributed to John Chrysostom.[55] This text, which is probably of Judaeo-Christian origin,[56] describes the Feeding as a love-feast, arranged by Jesus, for his 'friend and kinsman' John.[57]

[47] The representation of the scene in Christian art, especially in the paintings of the catacombs, where it figures prominently (cp. A. Grabar, Christian Iconography (Princeton, 1968), pl. 6; J. Stevenson, The Catacombs (London, 1978), p. 93) demands an investigation of its own.

[48] E.g. the standard form of the Toledoth (J. C. Wagenseil, Tela Ignea Satanae (Altorf, 1683), div. II v. 57). The Huldreich version of the Toledoth contains a scene with Jesus and two of his disciples in the desert (Sepher Toledoth Jeschua ha-Notzri (1705), p. 54). It is based, directly or indirectly, on the Johannine report, where two disciples, Philip and Andrew, are singled out. Origen, Contra Celsum i. 68, a passage cited from the pamphlet of the Ἰουδαῖος, is the oldest piece of evidence for a Jewish tradition on the Feeding.

[49] E.g. Act. Thom. 47; Acta Pauli 79 (Hennecke ET ii. 382). Differently in Epist. Apost. 5, where a summary of the miracles (especially the walking on the water) is followed by a more detailed account on the Feeding and its explanation as a symbol of the five elements of Christian belief.

[50] Cp. R. H. Connolly, 'The Original Language of the Syriac Acts of John', JThSt 8 (1907), 572.

[51] Therefore it follows after the walking on the water. Similarly VI. 15f. Cp. M. Monteiro, As David and the Sybils Say (Edinburgh, 1905), p. 56.

[52] Two points where it is different: only one fish is served (the same in VIII. 275) and the remainder is described as destined εἰς παρθένον ἁγνήν.

[53] 5.112–15 – For the interpretation cp. E. Stauffer, 'Antike Jesustradition', ZNW 46 (1955), 20ff.

[54] Islamic tradition has it that 1,300 persons were healed on the occasion (E. M. Wherry, A comprehensive Commentary on the Quran (London, 1896), ad Sure 5.112–14).

[55] Ed. W. D. Till, Mitteilungen d. Dt. Arch. Inst. Abteilung Kairo 16, 2 (1958), 322ff.

[56] Cp. NTSt 18 (1971–2), 127f.

[57] Till, Mitteilungen, p. 323.

II

While clearly pointing to the same event and coinciding in quite a number of details, the four branches of the tradition diverge in other respects. So it appears; but there are several details where a closer connection seems to exist.

Mark mentions that the multitude sat down ἐν χλωρῷ χόρτῳ. The remark agrees with the Passover reference in John 6:4 and militates against the theory[58] that the first part of the verse is not a constitutive part of the Johannine account.

John points to the ὄρος as the place of Jesus's activity. The word does not occur in the direct synoptic parallels. If its meaning is טורא = open, hilly area,[59] it is the same as expressed by the Markan ἔρημος τόπος.[60] Ὄρος itself is, however, prominent in Matt. 15: 29, where it seems to be the kernel and starting point of the First Evangelist's elaboration on the narration of the Feeding of the Four Thousand. No indication of a direct dependence either way is noticeable.

Matthew and Luke mention the miracles wrought by Jesus, a reference which seems to derive from Q. This feature is outstanding within Q. While narrating the one inaugural miracle of Jesus (Luke 7: 1ff) and referring to the multitude of δυνάμεις performed by him (Luke 10: 13, 23; 7: 21, if the verse derives from Q), Q refrains from outlining Jesus's healing activity. The exception must have been conditioned by the form of the tradition as it became known to the compiler of Q. Matthew has the feature in his own explanation in 15: 30. John is not without it, but it is presented in the account of what immediately preceded the event – very similarly to Matt. 15: 29f. This is probably a more developed, a standardised[61] form of the same feature. Mark, however, has the puzzling remark on the sheep without a shepherd (6: 34). Surely, it was the opinion of the evangelist that Jesus did not leave the multitude in this state – ἐσπλαγχνίσθη must have been taken by him as a sufficient indication of what in his view Jesus was about to do. Q/John on the one side and Mark on the other side seem to reproduce parts of what had originally been a whole.

[58] W. Wilkens, *Entstehungsgeschichte*, pp. 25ff. The festival references of the Fourth Gospel normally occur in connection with Jerusalem. This is not the case here. It is, however, likely that the second part (ἡ ἑορτὴ τῶν Ἰουδαίων) came in through the redactor.

[59] E. Klostermann, *Das Matthäusevangelium* (Tübingen, 1927), p. 135; A. Merx, *Markus und Lukas* (Berlin, 1905), p. 62.

[60] The parallels Matt. 18: 12 and Luke 15: 4 show clearly that ὄρος, which is used in the former, and ἔρημος, which is used in the latter, have the same meaning.

[61] Very suggestive is B. H. Streeter's explanation (*The Four Gospels* (London, 1924), pp. 413f).

The ὄρος-motif is reminiscent not only of the Sinai tradition but also of
1 Kings 22: 17[62] and above all of Ezek.34 where the word occurs no less
than five times. 'Sheep without shepherd' figure in both these passages.
While the first (1 Kings 22: 17) is a prophecy of doom, the second (Ezek.
34: 5, 8, 12) is a prophecy of divine favour. It is in keeping with this that
miracles are alluded to in Ezek. 34. Λιμός will be absent (verse 29) – the
central event of the New Testament story could be taken as foreshadowed
by this. Besides, God is seen as the one who will sustain the
συντετριμμένον (verse 16) and the ἐκλεῖπον (verse 16; cp. 21) and will be
on the side of the ἀσθενής (verse 20). The miracles could be seen as a
dramatic enacting of this promise. This is a sufficient indication of the
influence of the concept of Ezek. 34 on the presentation of the Feeding story
in different branches of its tradition. What appeared to be different at first
sight turns out to be interrelated if viewed in the light of Ezek. 34. This
underlying unity is even more important than the convergence of individual
features in the reports. The 'Ezekiel 34 tradition' must have developed in
different ways – probably inadvertently. It was taken as self-evident
that elements of the tradition mentioned here and there were not isolated
fragments but parts of a continuous whole, the knowledge of which could be
taken for granted. These points of allusion came to be handed down in
tradition as individual items at a time when their context was not any
longer known.

What is absent from Ezek. 34 is the reference to Passover. This element,
which is already closely linked with the Sinai tradition, had become an
integral part of late Jewish eschatology: 'the second will be like the first' and
therefore take place at the same time.[63] It was the Sinai tradition that was
enriched by claims of miraculous events: a full restoration of health is
supposed to have happened while Israel was standing round the mount of
Sinai[64] – later tradition extended these miraculous features to the whole
desert period.[65] The desert tradition, which had exercised its influence
already on Ezek. 34, in a later form enriched the response to this chapter
which is found in the narrative of the Feeding.

Those features which reflect theological ornamentation are less likely to
represent original tradition. This may be the case for the remarks on the
healing activity of Jesus,[66] while ὄρος should be taken as a stylisation of

---

[62] Cp. W. A. Meeks, *The Prophet-King* (Leiden, 1967), p. 97.

[63] A. Strobel, *ZNW* 49 (1958), pp. 164ff, 183ff.

[64] Lev. r. ad 15: 2 (Simon b. Jochai); Mek. Ex. 20: 18 (Eliezer b. Hyrkanos); Pes. 106b
(Jehuda b. Simon; cp. W. Bacher, *Die Agada d. pal. Amoräer* III (Strassburg, 1899),
pp. 207f); Numb. r. ch. 7 (Joshua b. Levi); Shabb. 88b (Joshua b. Levi; only an
allusion on the motif).

[65] Lev. r. ad 15: 2 (18.3) (Eliezer the Galilaean).

[66] Although the fact that Q, apart from the standard inaugural miracle expected from

ἔϱημος τόπος. It is different with χλωϱὸς χόϱτος. The mention takes place without theological elaboration and is therefore likely to be a *Restüberliefe-rung* which happened to survive and which supports the Passover remark in John 6: 4. The puzzling notice on the seating order κατὰ ἕκατον κτλ. in the same verse of Mark receives momentum in this context. The figure fifty is constitutive, all the more so as it is the only one mentioned in Luke (or Q?[67]). While the relation 1→10→100→1000 seems to be normal, and indeed the Roman army is based on this progression,[68] it is different in Jewish tradition. This is clear from the regulations set out in Exod. 18: 25, Deut. 1: 15 and 1 Sam. 8: 12 (cp. Isa 3: 3). It is true for the order of the Qumran community as well[69] and the idealised picture of the past as it is found in PsPhilo.[70] It occurs again in Chag. 14a and, interestingly, in 1 Clem. 37: 3. Fifty is the constitutive figure which recurs together with various multiples and, as an appendix, the smaller figure ten.[71] That means, this detail emphasises the 'true' Jewish character of the event and underlines the exodus motif in its presentation.[72]

On the other side, the eucharistic overtones were brought out by the early church in its interpretation. This happened both in the synoptic[73] and in the Johannine[74] tradition. It is all the more important to notice that the above-mentioned features, although capable of a eucharistic interpreta-tion, were not used in this way. A kernel of the tradition is discernible, in which an event is described as having taken place in the desert, in

the man of God (Luke 7: 1ff), refers to Jesus's δυνάμεις only in general terms (Luke 7: 22 – if the remark derives from Q; 10: 13), while it refrains from sketching Jesus's working of miracles, should make one cautious in assuming this.

[67] If Luke did not make up πεντήκοντα out of antiquarian interest.

[68] Even the army of insurrectionaries led by Josephus was formed in this way, as ῥωμαιϰώτεϱος στϱατιά (*BJ* 2 §578). The order of the Tartar army is well known (H. Dörrie, *Drei Texte zur Geschichte der Ungarn und Mongolen*, NAG (1956), p. 176).

[69] 1 QS 4: 2; 6: 11. Cp. Enoch 69: 3 (leader of 100, 50 and 10).

[70] 27: 3–5, 15.

[71] The reading of sy[sin] is דמאא מאא וחמשין = 150. The figure occurs in Slavon. Josephus in the account of the disciples of Jesus (ii. 9.3). Fifty is the standard figure in the Iranian educational societies (G. Widengren, *Feudalismus im alten Iran* (Köln, 1969), pp. 85, 92); 150 occurs as well (Widengren, *Feudalismus*, pp. 89, 99).

[72] For the latest attempts to give a meaning to the description see the theories of H. W. Montefiore ('Revolt in the Desert?', *NTSt* 8 (1961/62), p. 137) and D. Derrett ('Leek-bedes and methodology', *BZ* n.s.19 (1975), 101ff). Merx's opinion (*Markus und Lukas*, p. 60) that the phrase points to 50 companies of 100 and indicates the overall figure does not take into account Mark 6: 44 which would be unnecessary if he were right.

[73] G. H. Boobyer, 'The Eucharistic Interpretation of the Loaves in St. Mark's Gospel', *JThSt* n.s.3 (1952), 161ff; B. v. Iersel, 'Die wunderbare Speisung und das Abendmahl in der synoptischen Tradition', *NovTest* 7 (1964/65), 167ff; G. Schille, 'Zur Frage urchristlicher Kultätiologie', *Jahrbuch für Liturgik und Hymnologie* 10 (1965), 35ff.

[74] C. H. Dodd, *Historical Tradition in the Fourth Gospel* (Cambridge, 1963), pp. 188ff.

springtime, an occasion for which the crowds gathered together and on which they felt fed miraculously.

Such an event was of necessity understood messianically. The gathering of crowds in the desert as a starting point for messianic ventures is well-known from contemporary history.[75] That is what is described in John 6: 16f. There is nothing in this remark that appears unlikely from a general point of view. This outcome is, however, mentioned only in this Gospel. It is an integral part of the report,[76] while, on the other hand, the motif expressed in these verses is not in the forefront of the evangelist's presentation.

The reaction of the people is, on the whole, in this Gospel not a feature that sets events in motion. It is either a reaction of belief or of unbelief without, however, causing Jesus to let himself be influenced by this in words or actions. The occasions where other people act at the forefront of the stage are very rare,[77] and these indications appear to belong to one particular source.[78] The messianic-political perspective is almost completely absent from the Gospel. It only occurs in the form of an allusion in chapter 10 and in a more general way in 18: 33ff. The terminology is not typically Johannine either.[79]

The substance of the verses is not redactional[80] but rather pre-Johannine. It has no direct parallel in the synoptic accounts, although the sequel, Jesus's withdrawal over the lake, is expressed equally clearly in both Mark 6: 45 and 8: 10 (cp. Matt. 16: 5), while the traces of the Q report disappear at this point. There are, however, several traces which point to something more specific. The enigmatic statement in Mark 8: 15 belongs to a pericope which is in part an appendix[81] to and development of the Feeding story. While the surrounding verses deal with the possibility of a continuation of the miraculous Feeding,[82] this verse directs itself against an understanding of the event which must have been alluring for the disciples. If it is not to the

---

[75] Cp. p. 230.

[76] The attempt to link it solely with verses 1 to 3 and to take the narrative of the Feeding as a later ingredient is a desperate one.

[77] Cp. C. H. Dodd, 'The Prophecy of Caiaphas', *Neotestamentica et Patristica*, Festschrift Cullmann (Leiden, 1962), pp. 134ff.   [78] Cp. p. 232.

[79] Βασιλεύς is used in a different way in 1: 49. Γινώσκειν is used with a personal object (it is Jesus apart from 2: 24) apart from here. Ἔρχεσθαι normally has a heightened meaning and is not used elsewhere in an everyday context. Ἀναχωρεῖν and ἀναδεικνύαι are *hapax legomena* in the Fourth Gospel. The only Johannine phrase is found at the end of verse 14: ὁ ἐρχόμενος κτλ., conspicuously similar to 4: 42 (and 1: 29). The terminological relationship to 10: 12 is surprisingly close (ἔρχεσθαι, ἁρπάζειν, φεύγειν). It seems that the passage, which is secondary in the context (cp. Wellhausen, *Johannes*, p. 49), is based on 6: 14f.

[80] Thus Bultmann, *Johannes*, pp. 157f. (ET Oxford 1971, p. 213).

[81] J. Wellhausen, *Das Evangelium Marci* 2nd edn. (Berlin, 1909), p. 61.

[82] Similar to John 6: 26: there it is described as a reaction of the people, here of the disciples.

expectation of further acts of a similar kind that the verse refers, it must be to a reaction which is presented from a negative point of view in the fragment of a parallel[83] tradition in 8: 11: while the Pharisees are not (yet) convinced by the miracle and demand the sign from heaven as convincing proof, the disciples are. What is in common between the reference to the Pharisees and the one to the disciples is the question of messiahship that had arisen in consequence of the multiplication of the loaves. Additional evidence had been demanded by one side, whereas the other must have hailed the event enthusiastically. The answer returned by Jesus describes the whole attitude as ζύμη, as something that is normally viewed as negative by Jewish eyes,[84] as a speculation that is typical for the Pharisees and Herod.[85] That means, Jesus turns against messianism according to this tradition as well.[86] John 6: 14f concentrates this understanding of Jesus on the crowds, whereas Mark 8: 14ff thinks of the disciples. It is in keeping with and in consequence of this that Mark brings to the fore the problem of messiahship in what is virtually the next pericope, in 8: 27–33. The passage, in its present form, is his own creation; but the significant sequence of themes must be viewed as rooted in tradition.

Besides, the pericope hints at a detail which is lacking in the other strands. The Pharisees ἐξῆλθον. This is not a redactional feature 'noch viel ungeschickter'[87] than so many others, but the remainder of a tradition according to which the Pharisees went out in order to inspect the situation. It is a feature parallel to the one mentioned in 3: 22, 7: 1 and John 1: 19, 24. which is given a redirection by Mark by the insertion of πειράζοντες, a label typical for his treatment of the Pharisees.[88]

This tradition is independent of the Johannine report, but converges with it on a different plane: the question of questions, the one as to the messianic status of Jesus, is supposed to have been raised in consequence of the Feeding; not only by the crowds but by the disciples and by critical observers as well.

What follows the Feeding in Mark is as enigmatic as the introduction. Jesus brings the scene to an end by forcing (ἠνάγκασεν) the disciples[89] to

---

[83] Cp. the introductions in verses 10 and 13. The disciples are still on the way (only Matthew alters this).

[84] B. T. D. Smith, *The Parables of the Synoptic Gospels* (Cambridge, 1937), p. 122.

[85] The messianic interests of the Pharisees are well-known. Inclinations to messianic claims in the house of Herod are equally demonstrable (cp. R. Eisler, 'Ιησοῦς βασιλεύς 1 (Heidelberg, 1930),348, nn. 3–7).

[86] Does Luke 9: 11 (ἐλάλει κτλ.) reflect something similar? Is the link with the healings an unfortunate Lukan arrangement? The phrase itself (ἐλάλει περί) is rather pre-Lukan than Lukan.

[87] Wellhausen, *Evangelium Marci*, p. 60.   [88] Cp. 10: 2; 12: 15.

[89] The Georgian *Martyrdom of Eustathius of Mzketha* (D. M. Lang, *Lives and Legends of the*

embark in a boat and by despatching (ἀποταξάμενος) the crowds. The verb used for the dismissal of the crowds would have been more appropriate for the commissioning of the disciples, whereas ἀναγκάζειν is a term most unusual for Jesus's dealings with the Twelve. Besides, two reasons are given for the sending away of the disciples, one of which is identical with what is said in Mark 8: 9. The difficulties are such that the verses are considered as a mixture of tradition and redaction.[90] It is hardly possible to take 6: 46b (ἀπῆλθεν κτλ.) as the starting-point which called for the additions.[91] On the contrary, the motif of the prayer on a hill is well-known; the short remark is possibly patchwork, whereas the two unusual verbs are to be seen as the poles of the old tradition. The present context in which they function is as pale as it is unsatisfactory.[92] The 'forcing'[93] is only justified if it was preceded by something else that either culminated in the forcing or was answered by this action. As ἀποταξάμενος αὐτοῖς probably referred to the disciples in the substratum of the verses, it is likely that ἀναγκάζειν described the action that was answered by Jesus by the dispatching of the disciples. So it must have been an action of the masses, by which they (plural) forced the disciples to fall in with their intentions. Something must have preceded verse 45 and something else was omitted in verse 45 itself.

III

The problem the interpreter is faced with at the end of the story appears, although with different emphasis, at the beginning as well: while the Johannine report seemed to say more at the end it remains silent at the beginning.

The matter is, however, different, if the view is accepted that chapter 6 follows chapter 4[94] and if allowance is made for the possibility that even

---

Georgian Saints (London, 1956), p. 107) obliterates the difference: Jesus and his disciples walk together on the lake. Harnack held that the report is based on some form of the Diatessaron.

[90] R. Bultmann, *Geschichte der Synoptischen Tradition* 3rd edn. (Göttingen, 1955), p. 231 (ET (Oxford, 1972), p. 216); cp. W. Bussmann, *Synoptische Studien* iii (Halle, 1931), p. 83.

[91] This seems to be the line taken by E. Lohmeyer, *Das Evangelium des Markus* (Göttingen, 1937), pp. 131f.

[92] Προάγειν is a variation of προέρχεσθαι (verse 31), ἀπολύειν coincides with chapter 8: 9.

[93] P. Wendling, *Die Entstehung des Marcus-Evangeliums* (Tübingen, 1908), p. 83 lists a number of remarks of interpreters and persuades himself to assert: 'ἠνάγκασεν ist . . . aus der Psyche . . . des Redaktors zu verstehen'.

[94] J. Wellhausen, *Erweiterungen und Änderungen im Vierten Evangelium* (Berlin, 1907), pp. 15ff. Cp. J. Jeremias, *DLZ* 64 (1943), col. 416 (review of Bultmann, *Johannesevangelium*).

verses 5 to 42 of chapter 4 were moved from a place later in the Gospel by the redactor.[95] The passages 4: 1ff, 43ff are full of historical detail. They describe Jesus's removal because of the Pharisees and point to his contact with a βασιλικός. It is implied that this happened after the arrest of the Baptist.[96] The statement in its general outline is similar to that of Mark and Q: a striking change of the whereabouts of Jesus caused by influences from outside. The persons mentioned in the different sources are very similar: the Pharisees and the βασιλικός in the passage of the Fourth Gospel, Herod and, as it seems,[97] the Pharisees in the synoptic accounts. The designation of the actual force that was instrumental in making Jesus move is different in the two strands of tradition. The stray notice of Luke 13: 31 points to a laudable[98] attitude on the side of τινες Φαρισαῖοι. It had been found puzzling that the officer with Roman rank of the Q account appears as a βασιλικός in John. The riddle finds its natural explanation if the source John made use of intended to point to a contrast between the βασιλικός who put his hope in Jesus and the βασιλεύς himself who had done the opposite. The closeness of the story, which already in Q had been given a most crucial although different significance, to the notice of the Baptist's 'decrease' makes this likely, quite apart from the fact that the inclination to draw attention to positive exceptions to the rule in the segments of society that surrounded Jesus is noticeable quite often in the Gospel literature. That means, the actual text of John contains a faint echo of an earlier, more precise statement according to which the Feeding scene happened in consequence of the death of the Baptist.

IV

The later the Gospel traditions are, the more they lose interest in the Baptist or concentrate their interest in special points of a theological or hagiographic nature. The most valuable sources are found in Q and Z.[99] It emerges from these that the contact between Jesus and John continued beyond the one day of the baptism of the former in the presence[100] of the latter. Indeed, Jesus himself carried on with the rite administered by the

---

[95] Wellhausen, *Evangelium Johannis*, p. 20.
[96] This is brought out by part of the Western text of ch. 3: 36. The Arabic Tatian and the Codex Fuldensis, on the other hand, place the remark on the Baptist in the wording of Luke 3: 20 after John 4: 3.
[97] Cp. p. 228.
[98] The description of the Pharisees as emissaries of Herod (W. Grundmann, *Lukasevangelium* (Berlin, 1969), p. 288) is based on a one-sided interpretation of verse 32.
[99] Cp. *NTSt* 18 (1971/72), 122ff.
[100] So the reading of D of Luke 3: 7.

Baptist:[101] he set up an order of close followers, similar to that of those who surrounded John and partly consisting of his former disciples, he gave them rules, in part coinciding with and in part differing from the rules of John, and above all he proclaimed a message that could be summarised in the same words as are found in tradition as characterising John's preaching (cp. Matt. 3: 2 with 4: 17). The Baptist himself must have exercised a lasting influence on this neophyte of his.[102] After John's execution it came to pass that people viewed Jesus in the light of the figure of the Baptist, and even considered him as the reincarnation of John;[103] indeed Jesus himself more than once compared his own mission with that of the Baptist. If the community of the Baptist wanted to continue, it had to look for a new representative. It must have been the obvious course for part of John's followers at least to turn to Jesus, since he had established himself already and had succeeded in exercising an influence that rivalled[104] that of the Baptist.[105] The indication given by Q is in tune with this: it only supports what would otherwise have been deduced from circumstantial evidence.

Josephus, in his sketch of the Baptist, gives a reason for Herod Antipas's action against John that differs at first sight from the one stigmatised in the New Testament. According to his report the excitement of the masses and Herod's fear that something of a revolutionary character[106] might arise from this were responsible. Both reasons coincide if John's criticism of the leading representative of the Jewish nation was meant to be an initial stage in the cleansing of the house of Israel, an action that had to precede the final events.[107] The excitement of the masses must have been eschatological joy in anticipation, such as is alluded to in the New Testament as well.[108] It is evident from this that Antipas, once he had taken action, became entangled in the movements stirred up and influenced by the Baptist[109] – Mark 6: 14–16 gives pictorial expression to this. Close surveillance of Jesus and of his circle must have been imperative; even more so, as Jesus had taken Galilee as the centre of his ministry, while John, after having left Peraea (chased out by Antipas?), had stayed in Samaria and had entered Antipas's

[101] John 4: 1f.   [102] Cp. Luke 7: 18ff.

[103] Mark 6: 16; cp. C. H. Kraeling, 'Was Jesus accused of Necromancy?', *JBL* 59 (1940), 146ff; E. Stauffer, *Jesus. Gestalt und Geschichte* (Bern, 1957), p. 150.

[104] Cp. Merx, *Johannes*, p. 65.

[105] John 4: 1f.

[106] *AJ* 18§118: νεώτερον ... γενέσθαι. Cp. Philostratus, *Vita Apollonii* 8.7.13: νεώτερα πράττειν – the accusation against Antipas.

[107] Cp. *HThR* 51 (1958), 101ff.

[108] John 5: 35; cp. the ingenious transposition of πρὸς ὥραν suggested by E. Schwartz (*Aporien* iv, 522).

[109] The information we have of Baptistic communities comes solely from the diaspora. This shows that the Baptistic movement, in so far as its members did not join the Christian church, had been stamped out successfully in Palestine.

territory only in a last provocative bid. And indeed, it was from this time that Jesus, to all appearances, avoided the country of Herod.[110] Bethsaida (Mark 6: 45; 8: 22),[111] the region of Tyre (7: 24), the Decapolis (7: 31), Caesarea Philippi (8: 27), the region on the other side of the Jordan (10: 1) are mentioned as his abode, while only a speedy journey through Galilee is related (9: 30ff). This change is indicative and points to Jesus having felt himself to be in a state of danger after the beheading of his baptiser.[112] Mark 6: 30ff notes this change, while Matt. 14: 13 produces the reason as well since ἀκούσας in the phrase ἀκούσας . . . ἀνεχώρησεν . . . εἰς ἔρημον τόπον not only gives the date but also the motive:[113] he flees from the impending persecution of his sovereign.[114] What was meant to be an escape,

[110] It was J. G. Herder who was the first and for a long time the only scholar to have had a feeling for the crucial nature of the execution of the Baptist in Jesus's public life. He states in his *Vom Erlöser der Menschen. Nach unsern drei ersten Evangelien* (Riga, 1976): 'Fortan war für Jesum in Galiläa keine bleibende Sicherheit mehr; Herodes stellte ihm nach dem Leben' (*Werke*, ed. B. Suphan, xix (Berlin, 1880), 179). Cp. J. Wellhausen, *Einleitung in die drei ersten Evangelien*, (2nd edn. Berlin, 1911), p. 40. Valuable remarks are found in M. Maurenbrecher's *Jesus von Nazareth* (Berlin, 1909), pp. 230f. Most important are Merx's observations on Mark 6: 55: ἀπέδραμον (sy) indicates a text different from the present one. The original text had referred to the disciples' flight, not to the healing scene (*Markus*, pp. 64f). F. Spitta goes further and takes it that the command to silence followed closely the question of Herod about the character of Jesus in the synoptic *Grundschrift*; he draws the conclusion that the command was essentially a measure of precaution *vis-à-vis* the inquiring action of Antipas (*Grundschrift*, pp. 214ff). Spitta is right in positing a historical situation for Jesus's reaction. The direct link with the Herod passage is, however, a questionable hypothesis, while the Feeding provides a setting which explains Jesus's answer and allows for a meaning which exceeds by far the ephemeral one suggested by the link with the Herodian scene.

[111] Is the Gennesaret scene (6: 53) a variant of 5: 21, 25ff?

[112] A different scheme is proposed by Maurenbrecher: Jesus did not start his activity before the execution of the Baptist. What did he do in consequence of the event? 'er stürzte sich in die Nähe des Fürsten, der den Gottesgesandten hatte ermorden lassen': there was the place where he had to proclaim the arrival of the kingdom (*Jesus*, p. 220).

[113] A. Plummer, *Matthew* (London, 1909), p. 46.

[114] *Contra* A. Schweitzer, *Leben-Jesu-Forschung*, pp. 574f (cp. ET pp. 350f). The reason given in the earlier part of Mark (e.g. 1: 44f) for Jesus's staying outside the inhabited area does not apply here. It is the merit of Spitta and still more of M. Goguel to have realised the importance of Antipas for the development of Jesus's activity. The latter suggests that Luke 9: 9 originally contained a statement about Antipas's intention to kill Jesus (*La vie de Jésus*, GT p. 226; ET p. 354) and that it even gave the reason; he assumes that it was the commissioning of the Twelve that alarmed Antipas and that, owing to the warning given by some Pharisees, Jesus was able to escape the net spread for him (p. 228; ET p. 357). The masses are aware of this and rush to the desert, because they know that Jesus will not be able to return to their abode (pp. 233, 235; ET pp. 365, 367). The hostility of Antipas will have increased Jesus's popularity and kindled the expectation of his coming forth like a new Maccabee in battle with an Antiochus (p. 236; ET p. 367). The demanded sign – it had been asked for not by the Pharisees but by the followers of Jesus – was meant as the signal for the messianic uprising, while Jesus's own command of secrecy is

a matter of life and death, turned out to be at this stage at least a triumph beyond all imagining: the fugitive is followed by an innumerable multitude. The multiplicity of sources[115] reflects the singularity of the event.

The crowds had been roused into a state of agitation by the activity of John. The circumstances of his death must have increased the impetus he had given to them – as indeed evidence shows that the nature of the figure he presented remained as a subject of discussion for a long time.[116] The precursor's violent end could be viewed on the apocalyptic plane as the necessary step before the ushering in of the final events. It is clear that people looked for guidance in this situation and that it was possible for a determined person to establish himself and to further his cause.

On the other hand, the complexities of the interactions of the Jewish parties made a 'coming and going' necessary. The spreading of news, the channelling of information, the exploiting of the situation for particular purposes were part of the game. The Pharisees were in a crucial position: while they had connections with the Herodian house,[117] they were able to exercise influence on the masses as well, and above all they had had contact with both John and Jesus. The stray notice of Luke 13: 31 according to which τινες Φαρισαῖοι warned Jesus against the intentions of Herod Antipas – a detail which is unlikely to have been invented – fits this situation, whereas the claim that the Pharisees and the Herodians[118] took council in order to destroy Jesus (Mark 3: 6)[119] is likely to reflect the result of the realignment that developed after the execution of John.[120]

This was the situation in which the gathering took place. We have to differentiate between the movements of a group of people who are redirected by Jesus into the desert, Jesus's own withdrawal, and the

conditioned by the persecution of Antipas (pp. 247ff; ET pp. 381ff). Goguel is basically correct in his estimate of Antipas's position with respect to Jesus. He greatly overestimates, however, the significance of this feature by making it the explanation for the attitude of the masses and by reducing the Feeding to something of minor importance.

[115] G. Schille is even of the opinion that the reference to 500 brethren in 1 Cor. 15 is based on this event (*Das Judenchristentum im Markusevangelium* (Berlin, 1970), p. 48).

[116] Jos. *AJ* 18 §116; Mark 11: 30ff.

[117] They had already succeeded in establishing reasonable relations with Herod the Great and were to be on very good terms with Agrippa. It is *a priori* likely that they also had working arrangements with Antipas.

[118] The opinion that 'Herodians' is a cover name for Zealots (Y. Yadin, *The Temple Scroll* i (Jerusalem, 1978), Appendix II, pp. 111ff hardly recommends itself.

[119] The verse is the climax of a set of controversy stories which is independent of the sequence of events sketched out in the Gospel. A different historical occasion is assumed by Stauffer, *Jesus*, p. 71 (ET pp. 75f).

[120] While the importance of the Baptist for the movements of Jesus is passed over by most researchers, it was R. Reitzenstein who went so far as to maintain that Jesus was condemned in Jerusalem as a disciple of John (*Das mandäische Buch des Herrn der Grösse und die Evangelienüberlieferung* (Heidelberg, 1919), pp. 68f; cp. pp. 70f.

surprise event of a mass gathering out of the towns (of Galilee). It is this coming together of different groups and the interaction of tendencies which did not wholly coincide that is the significant feature of the day.

Those who had been redirected by Jesus do not come into the open at the event. They had probably mingled with the crowds and become their mouthpiece in the way that is described in John 6: 14f. The masses themselves are viewed by Jesus as men in the state of a flock without a shepherd. The remark is often taken as a reflection of the state of despair the masses were in. This does not, however, mean that they themselves were filled only by such thoughts. The fact that large crowds coming from different places all went in one direction suggests the existence of hopes, expectations and even demands which, although vacillating, may have been expressed pointedly. Even if elements of despair were not absent from their minds, the main direction is different: it is the call for a shepherd, based on the apocalyptic idea that the death of the Baptist must have its meaning in the process of ushering in the world to come. The speeding up of the events that seemed to be indicated by John's martyr death meant that the person who was to follow him could have an even greater task than the one with which he had been entrusted – if not the final eschatological commission. To all appearances the experiences of the day lent support to this view and raised expectations to the highest degree. The distribution of food and the blessing[121] administered by Jesus showed him performing a priestly function like the one every Jewish father of a family performs at Passover[122] and which is, in one way or the other, a prefiguration of the eschatological meal. This became the starting-point for the bold suggestion: ἀληθῶς ὁ προφήτης.[123]

It is in keeping with Jewish tradition that the truth about a man of God is brought out not by himself but by others. Samuel knew that God had selected Saul.[124] The presence of the multitude was already important on the occasion of the promulgation of the Torah and rose in prominence in late Jewish tradition. The progression prophet–king is equally based on the Saul story: he proves to be of royal stature by being able to prophesy with the prophets. Similarly the first claims about Jesus are made by persons

---

[121] There is no blessing on the grass. This militates against the theory of J. H. A. Hart ('A Plea for the Recognition of the Fourth Gospel as an historical Authority', *The Expositor* (1906), 377; (1907), 48ff), who, taking 2 Macc. 5: 27 as a parallel, thinks that χορτός was actually used as food.

[122] Philo, *De Decal.* §159 (. . . ἱερωσύνην τοῦ νόμου χαρισαμένου τῷ ἔθνει παντὶ κατὰ μίαν ἡμέραν ἐξαίρετον ἀνὰ ἔτος εἰς αὐτουργίαν θυσιῶν).

[123] Is the actual text a conflation of two readings? Does the text of D (οὗτός ἐστιν ὁ προφήτης) represent one of them?

[124] Motifs on 1 Sam. 8ff are noticeable especially in the Johannine presentation: the παιδάριον (cp. 1 Sam. 9: 7f), who happens to possess what is needed.

from his environment. John designates him as the lamb that carries the sin of the world and Nathaniel hails him as the king of Israel – a designation which is supplanted by a different one from Jesus himself. True, the influence of 1 Sam. 9f is noticeable in the story; but the motifs are applied in such a way that they cannot be taken just as a literary scheme.

What this amounts to is a threefold office: priest, prophet and king,[125] and thereby the consummation of offices. It is this ideal of perfection, indicated by the accumulation of offices, that plays an important role in late Judaism.[126] Moses is already seen in this function,[127] the high priests of the Hasmonaean period invest themselves with this dignity.[128] The concept took root in Christian tradition as well.[129] It clearly lies behind the narrative, but it is not brought out demonstratively and therefore not likely to be a theological embellishment. While the appreciations given to Jesus are normally confined to one title,[130] it is here that much more is maintained. This is said on the basis of an act he himself had performed. Such an appreciation should – one would think – have met with the approval of Jesus. What happens is, however, the opposite. Jesus withdraws.

The narrator phrases it in such a way that Jesus's prophetic quality is brought out once again: he knew beforehand what they were preparing to do. That means, the point at issue was in his view the kingly role attributed to him. It cannot have been different on the historical plane, as a prophetic quality was never disclaimed by Jesus.[131]

The messianic king is to 'redeem' Israel. This function of the messiah is dominant in all branches of Jewish eschatology. It was this form of expectation that flared up in these very years and led to scenes not dissimilar to the events surrounding the Feeding. Theudas persuaded a large multitude to follow him to the Jordan with their possessions.[132] Several 'deceivers' who appeared in the time of Felix lured people to migrate to the desert.[133] Jonathan was to lead the Jews of Cyrene into the wilderness.[134] The migration to the desert was in these cases the starting-point for further actions. It is an open question, whether John

---

[125] John 6: 11 (εὐχαριστήσας) indicates the priestly element.

[126] Cp. *ThLZ* 79 (1954), col. 351ff. For the three offices in the tradition on the Teacher of Righteousness see P. Schulz, *Der Autoritätsanspruch des Lehrers d. Gerechtigkeit in Qumran* (Meisenheim, 1974), esp. pp. 214f.

[127] Philo, *Vit. Mosis* 2. 6; his prophetical status is subsumed under that of the νομοθέτης.

[128] Jos. *AJ* 13 §299; *BJ* 1 §68.

[129] Cp. I. A. Dorner, *Entwicklungsgeschichte der Lehre von der Person Christi* i, 2nd edn. (Stuttgart, 1845), 261ff.

[130] The exceptions are Acts 2: 36; 3: 14; 5: 31; Heb. 3: 1.

[131] Cp. R. Meyer, *Der Prophet aus Galiläa* (Leipzig, 1940), *passim*.

[132] Jos. *AJ* 20 §97f.   [133] *AJ* 20 §167.   [134] Jos. *BJ* 7 §438.

himself had announced the coming of the Lord or of a messenger, but it is clear that his activism was the point he had in common with the messianic pretenders. It was only too natural for the crowds who had been greatly influenced by the Baptist to view Jesus in this light and, possibly, to test him, since he was reluctant to reveal himself[135] to those who surrounded him, while, on the other hand, it is equally possible that the proof a person has given of his prophetic status raises the expectation of a forthcoming political role.[136] Luke 24: 19, 21 is typical of this view; it is, so to speak, an expanded form of what is concentrated in the hopes said to have been expressed on a single day in John 6: 14f.

It is equally clear that the problem of messiahship must have posed itself to the self-consciousness of Jesus. Knowing about his commission he must have wondered which of the forms indicated in his bible God required him to take upon himself. The hints to be found in the oldest tradition about Jesus give the impression that this pondering was not the contemplation of one hour alone, but a question that accompanied his whole ministry and, perhaps, found its answer and expression only in the period when he approached passion and death.

The opinion other people had of him cannot have been without relevance for Jesus. Not so much what the sages thought, but the view taken by simple individuals and also that of the crowds in general mattered to him. This was in keeping with the Jewish tradition.[137] The messianic proposition put forward to him by the crowd, by a multitude that could be viewed as representing the nation, presented him with an inviting prospect. Besides, John had already attributed to him a role which lent itself to messianic interpretation.[138] Jesus's reaction may be understood as a refusal[139] or as the expression of his decision to remain in the waiting position of a *Messias incognitus*.[140] The suggestion made by the crowds was already the second invitation – an even more demanding one and not uncommon in this milieu.[141]

Jesus, however, decides not to take up this challenge.[142, 143] Whatever may

---

[135] Cp. E. Stauffer, 'Agnostos Christos' in *The Background of the New Testament and its Eschatology* (*Dodd-Festschrift*) (Cambridge, 1956), pp. 287ff.

[136] For examples in Late Judaism cp. *AJ* 20 §97f 169ff.

[137] Cp. *Miracles*, ed. by Moule, p. 192.

[138] Luke 7: 19; Matt. 11: 3. This interpretation is actually supplied in Matt. 11: 2.

[139] Cp. *ThWNT* vi, 907, note 212 (ET p. 908). A different line was taken by E. Renan, who put forward the interesting idea that Jesus met the Baptist after having preached independently before and that John exercised an unfortunate influence on Jesus (*Vie de Jésus* (9th edn. Paris, 1864), p. 76; GT Berlin, 1889, p. 92).

[140] Cp. John 2: 23ff.

[141] For the motif cp. Matt. 21: 32; Luke 7: 33ff.

[142] The analogy to the Saul story breaks down here (a different view is taken by D. Daube, *N.T. and Rabbinic Judaism* (London, 1956), p. 19). While Saul οὐχ εὑρίσκετο

have been the case at the beginning of his ministry,[144] the outcome here shows Jesus and the people miles apart.[145] His retreat from messianology and the introduction of the concept of transfiguration and suffering – both together – are the characteristic ideas of the following period.

John adds to the scene the significant notice: 'from that time many of his disciples . . . walked no more with him' (6: 66).[146] The same is presupposed in Mark 8: 34. In both cases the close circle of the disciples is referred to. The crowds have disappeared from the scene already, but the ventilation of what had happened continues. The division among the disciples underlines two facts: that the course Jesus had taken was not something that could have been expected and, secondly, that the decision he had made was seen as irrevocable.[147] Is it to be assumed that some of those disciples who had been closely attached to the Baptist went away?

The Gospel tradition is united in the suggestion of a turning-point during the ministry of Jesus[148] – even the Jewish accounts of the life of Jesus contain an echo of this.[149] It seems that this happened on the day of the Feeding and

(1 Sam. 10: 21), before he is traced and made king, Jesus's flight from kingship is final and decisive and the terminology is different. The early church felt uneasy about the flight as the alleviating reading shows. It would have been possible to cover up the matter by repeating the language of 1 Sam. 10: 21f. This was not done. Reimarus eliminates the importance of John 6: 14 by pointing to the Entry and stating: 'In der abgelegenen Wüste . . . war es nicht die Zeit . . . sondern dieser solenne Actus sich für einen König ausrufen zu lassen, war der Hauptstadt Jerusalem vorbehalten' (*Schutzschrift* ii, 159).

[143] The end of the story is so strange that Wagner, obviously in all innocence, decides to alter it: having mercy on the multitude that detains him, Jesus delays his departure and teaches the crowds about the kingdom etc. The story is made the main teaching occasion in his ministry (*Jesus* (Leipzig, 1887), pp. 7f; is the sketch on pp. 5f to be taken as an alternative?).

[144] Do we have to allow for an activity more in line with the popular eschatology? Differences in the attitude of Jesus *vis-à-vis* the messianic question have been ventilated here and there. Goguel is right in positing a development (*Jésus*, note 623; ET p. 366 n. 2), not however in his estimate that Jesus moved towards an awareness of his future messianic role (GT pp. 234f, 248; ET pp. 366, 383).

[145] The opinion that verse 14 shows the power of attraction Jesus had over the Zealots (O. Cullmann, *Jesus und die Revolutionären* (2nd edn. Tübingen, 1970) p. 22; ET New York, 1970, p. 8) is already one-sided. The conclusion that it shows partial agreement with the Zealots (G. Gutierrez, *A Theology of Liberation* (New York, 1973), p. 227) is certainly a more than forced interpretation. H. G. Wood in his penetrating note 'Interpreting this Time', *NTSt* 2 (1955/56), 265) sees in Mark 6: 45 an indication for Jesus's decision to break off the public ministry. This is not, however, the primary point. The fading away of mass support is conditioned by the negation of messianism.

[146] Verses 60 and 66 are parallel formulations. The latter represents early tradition (cp. F. Spitta, *Das Johannes-Evangelium als Quelle der Geschichte Jesu* (Göttingen, 1910, pp. 160ff), whereas the former came in by way of analogy.

[147] This is completely disregarded by Reimarus (cp. note 142).

[148] F. C. Burkitt, *Jesus Christ* (London, 1932), p. 66.

[149] Cp. *NTSt* 13 (1966/67), 325ff. Certain modern Jewish writers recognise a difference

in connection with it.[150] Mark, who differentiates so emphatically between those outside and those inside, was almost forced to move an event of this calibre of significance to a pericope dealing exclusively with the disciples. His scheme, which has become so important since the emergence of critical scholarship, obliterates reason and place for the change, although it retains indications of the older tradition.[151] It is not Caesarea Philippi that points to the location of the turning, it is not so much the *Leidensgeheimnis* itself that is the new departure; the Feeding of the Multitude must be viewed as the occasion where the break with the popular messianism and, indeed, the baptistic eschatology took place.[152] What is called the *Leidensgeheimnis* is only the other side of what was enacted by Jesus when his way parted from those whom he had fed.

V

The theme of the feeding of a multitude occurs in another passage of the Gospels as well, in the temptation story. It has been taken as surprising that a tradition according to which Jesus did refuse to perform such a miracle was handed down side by side with an account of an actual multiplication of loaves.[153] It is, however, not so easy to drive a wedge between the two traditions. In Mark 8: 14ff Jesus does not submit to performing a repetition of the miracle, while in John 6: 14f he avoids letting himself be lured into certain consequences. The matter is even more intriguing, if it is true that Q itself contained not only the temptation story but an account of the Feeding as well.

between the attitude of Jesus and that of the crowds and try to interpret this by assuming a divergence of intention and action that came into the open during the passion week. The feeling expressed in these sentiments is right. The occasion, however, at which the rift appears to have come to the surface is a different one: it is the Feeding.

[150] W. R. Farmer, whose concern it was to set Jesus against the background of both Jewish nationalism and apocalypticism, argued that the fact that Jesus allowed himself to be arrested indicated his final break with Zealotism (*Maccabees, Zealots, and Josephus* (New York, 1956), p. 198). This was, however, rather the consequence of the break which happened after the Feeding. Farmer argues that Jesus never detached himself from Jewish nationalism (p. 191). The evidence to be found in Jesus's attitude in the trial (cp. p. 421), however, leads one to qualify this statement. Illuminating remarks about the suggestiveness of the 'Zealot option' for Jesus are found in J. H. Yoder, *The Politics of Jesus* (Grand Rapids, 1972) and in A. Nolan, *Jesus before Christianity* (London, 1976), pp. 91ff.

[151] Cp. p. 238f.

[152] Did Mark (or someone before him) move the χριστός response from the meal to the Caesarea Philippi scene?

[153] R. Meyer, *Prophet*, p. 156f. For the spectrum of interpretations of the passage see P. Keller, *Die Versuchung Jesu nach dem Bericht der Synoptiker* (Münster, 1918) and E. Fascher, *Jesus und der Satan* (Halle, 1949).

Early Christian tradition understands the temptation as Jesus's successful effort 'to overcome the Adversary by means of deception';[154] he gives ambiguous answers, so as to prevent the Devil from getting a clear idea of his identity.[155] The story is thus lowered to the level of a farce, in which one side attempts to trap the other.[156] It is clear that this cannot be the original meaning. The matter was very much more serious.

What is at stake is implied by the protasis εἰ υἱὸς εἶ τοῦ θεοῦ (4: 3), repeated in Matt. 4: 6. Couched in the Son of God terminology which is conditioned by the juxtaposition with the baptism story[157] the phrase poses the messianic question. The messiah in his capacity as prophet like Moses is expected to perform the latter's miraculous works.[158] As an old tradition[159] which is embodied in Pes. R. 36 puts it: a miracle[160] that qualifies the messiah[161] will take place at the moment when he announces the glad tidings. It is with the third[162] suggestion that the possession of the

---

[154] W. Bauer, *Das Leben Jesu im Zeitalter der neutestamentlichen Apokryphen* (Tübingen, 1909), p. 147.

[155] The Jewish interpretation of the temptation as a victory won by Satan can be understood from this background.

[156] There is no need to think of a Hellenistic ingredient.

[157] Bultmann, *Tradition*, pp. 272f (ET pp. 254f), who, following Schlatter, directs himself against a messianic interpretation, is unaware of the fact that the problem of a magical miracle is of importance only in the context of the question of messiahship. It is not the temptation of engaging in the activity of a magus who usurped divine power (thus S. Eitrem, *Die Versuchung Christi* (Oslo, 1924), p. 18) that is described here, but the tempting suggestion made by the Devil pretending to be an agent of God.

[158] The theme of the prefiguration of Jesus giving up his life that Gerhardsson (cp. n. 164, p. 235) pp. 61, 83 discovers in the account on the second temptation is less obvious.

[159] Cp. M. Friedmann, *Pesiqtha rabbathi* (Wien, 1880), pp. 1ff.

[160] The miracle itself (cp. on this O. Michel, 'The light of the Messiah', *Donum Gentilicium*, Festschrift D. Daube (Oxford, 1978), p. 49) is different from the one suggested in Matt. 4: 6; but this is of secondary importance.

[161] Cp. *Miracles*, ed. by Moule, pp. 188f; cp. 4 Esd. 14: 50. The problem of the qualifying miracle does indeed play a role in the Jesus tradition. Q reproduces one miracle after Jesus's speech on the plain (Luke 7: 1ff); it is performed in public, under the surveillance of the representatives of the synagogue; it is recounted as the one qualifying miracle. Mark emphasises that Jesus's first miracle was performed in a synagogue (1: 23) and that one of the following healings was to be checked by the priestly authorities. Pap. Egerton 2 1.40ff presupposes that such a miracle was accepted as evidence by the persons concerned and that it led to subsequent questions. The Jew of Celsus, on the other hand, claims that Jesus, when challenged to perform a miracle in the Temple (so as to exclude the employment of magic) was unable to comply with the request (*c. Cels.* 1. 62). Justin states that Jesus's qualifying action consisted in his entry into Jerusalem (*Dial.* 88); cp. A. von Harnack, *Judentum und Judenchristentum in Justins Dialog mit Trypho* (Leipzig, 1913); p. 77.

[162] The Matthaean sequence seems to be original; cp. A. von Harnack, *Sprüche und Reden Jesu* (Leipzig, 1907), p. 34; ET p. 44).

lands shown to him,[163] in other words full power over the earth,[164] is offered to Jesus. While the first two suggested actions[165] are only of a preliminary nature – they are meant to be indications of the character of the person presented to the nation – it is in the third one that the final goal of the messianic venture is expressed. One may wonder whether Matt. 4: 9b (ἐὰν πεσὼν προσκυνήσῃς μοι) reflects a theological development of the narrative by which is interpreted in advance what is expressed in Jesus's answer in verse 10.[166] Jewish tradition has it that, after the destruction of the peoples, the messiah will be placed by God on a high mountain,[167] that he will step on the peak of Mount Zion,[168] in order to proclaim glad tidings to Israel. The presupposition εἰ υἱὸς κτλ. is not any longer necessary, because the proposition made to Jesus takes his messiahship for granted.[169] It is in this context that an unambiguous[170] answer of Jesus is reproduced: ὕπαγε, σατανᾶ. The one who was up to this moment a devil in disguise[171] – in the guise of a Zealot rabbi – is exposed thereby.[172] The bestowing of worldly power gives evidence for the diabolic character of the one who claims to possess this power. Even if 'Macht an sich' – to cite Burckhardt's famous phrase – is not considered as evil, the opinion is certainly held that power with messianic overtones is of a diabolic nature.[173] That means, the rebuff which is addressed to Peter in Mark 8: 33 and, in a less direct form, to the Baptist[174] in Matt. 3: 15[175] is put into the mouth of a superhuman figure in

---

[163] Cp. D. Daube, *Studies in Biblical Law* (Cambridge, 1947), pp. 24ff.

[164] It is not so much the temptation of wealth (B. Gerhardsson, *The Testing of God's Son* (Lund, 1966), pp. 64ff) that is meant in the story.

[165] Simkhovitch surprisingly interprets the ἄγγελοι (Luke 4: 10) as referring to the battle against Rome, whereas the βασιλεῖαι signify in his opinion the Hellenistic–Roman civilisation as an alluring possibility.

[166] H. P. Kingdon, on the other hand, sees in verse 9b the main point and interprets it as a symbol for the Herodian policy of feathering one's nest with the branches of Roman imperialism ('Had the Crucifixion a Political Significance?', *The Hibbert Journal* 35 (1936–7), 561).

[167] 4 Esd. 13: 6f.

[168] Pirqe Mashiah; cp. S–B iii. 10; 4 Esd. 14.35f.

[169] This is obliterated in the Lukan version, where the tempter appears as an agent of God, who gives (a share of) his commission to other persons.

[170] The two preceding answers can be understood within the framework of Jewish controversy, as answers which do not deny the messianic supposition.

[171] The term διάβολος had appeared so far only in the narrative part of the pericope. It may be assumed that an earlier form of the temptation story had only contained the term ὁ πειράζων.

[172] In Mark it is Peter who acts as seducer (Satan). He is addressed by the same ὕπαγε; the addition of ὀπίσω μου does not alter the meaning, it 'fügt dem ὕπαγε . . . nichts hinzu' (Wellhausen, *Evangelium Marci*, p. 66; cp. E. Klostermann, *Das Markusevangelium* (Tübingen, 1926) ad loc.).

[173] This is not seen by Noel (see p. 57). A deeper understanding of the pericope is given by S. Liberty, *The Political Relations of Christ's Ministry* (Oxford, 1916), pp. 43ff.

[174] There is a parallelism between Matt. 3: 15 (τότε ἀφίησιν αὐτόν) and 4: 11 (τότε

the temptation story. The reluctance to let Jesus express this fellowship with men (Matt. 3: 15), the refusal to let him go the way of suffering (Mark 8: 33) and, above all, the alluring suggestion of a messianic career are seen as the crucial points where a confrontation with inimical forces takes place.

The traditions about the occasion,[176] the length,[177] the opponents[178] and the character[179] of Jesus's temptation vary; indeed, different Jewish ideas about both the testing and tempting of the man of God were already available. Q, the earliest account of the ministry of Jesus, presents a

ἀφίησιν αὐτὸν ὁ διάβολος). This supports the view that 3: 14, 15 derive from Q and that there is a connection between the seducing questions of Satan and the tempting suggestion of John. It may be that just πᾶσα δικαιοσύνη is a product of the evangelist, while the beginning and the end of the sentence are pre-Matthaean. The standard translation of the line is dependent on ἄφες at the beginning of the sentence which is, however, more a *Füllsel* than a constitutive element. The proposed interpretation is compatible with a rite of baptism in which the 'baptiser' is merely the witness (thus in Jewish baptism) or in this case the one who admits to baptism (cp. Luke 3: 7 v. l.).

175 Mark's presentation is quite different. Jesus wages a running battle with the demons. He encounters them in the majority of his healings. Moreover, in Mark 8: 33, Satan addresses him again in the person of Peter. The answer that Jesus gives brings us on to the level of Q: the Son of God who thinks τὰ τοῦ θεοῦ and is therefore transfigured before he goes to Jerusalem! In Q the opinion of others that Jesus acts in the name of Beelzebub is all that remains of this.

176 The Judaeo-Christian tradition has it that Jesus in his baptism had already been purified by fire (cp. *TU* 93 (1966), pp. 53ff).

177 Luke views the temptation as occupying the whole period of forty days, whereas Matthew puts it at the end of this period, when Jesus was hungry. Mark emphasises that Jesus was with the wild beasts. This means not a fight against them, such as had been performed by so many giants right up to Siegfried the dragon-slayer, but rather community with the animals, i.e. the restoration of Paradise. After sending out his Son it pleased God to place him in the setting and conditions of the first man. This happens in the wilderness where he is alone, in surroundings untouched by human culture or decadence or sin. The desert is the place of salvation. When Jesus leaves this setting, he is immediately in a situation of conflict with Pharisees etc. The emphasis which is thus brought to light allows one to conclude that verse 13a is not original, but rather an insertion intended to bring the story into close connection with Matthew and Luke. Therefore the story as told by Mark has a quite different significance: it relates how God confirms the baptismal proclamation in a further action, whereas in Q this proclamation is tested. The continuing significance of the scene corresponds to the testing, while in Mark the testing proper begins with 1: 23 and ends with the transfiguration.

178 Cp. p. 235 nn. 171 and 172.

179 In Q the temptation is the necessary correlative to the Baptism. Therefore it is the test of Jesus's claim to be Son of God. It would after all have been possible for Jesus to have used the status bestowed on him for private purposes, to have regarded this status as an ἁρπαγμός. It is in keeping with this fundamental importance of the temptation that Jesus is attacked by Satan himself – after all an angelic figure! – who is forced to admit defeat by retreating. Satan knows exactly who Jesus is and his only chance is to seduce him to something that is in line with Jewish expectation. In Mark Jesus is harassed by the demons, who gradually recognise him while they are never able to lure him. Each of these designs indicates a more developed, a more 'mythical' christology than what we find in John 6.

heightened picture. It is a telescoped sketch of events – a form not unfamiliar to the student of Jewish literature – rather than just a poetical figment.[180] This enabled the author to bring out most forcefully what was the true temptation in the life of Jesus: the messianic claim. Q agrees in this with what seemed to be the kernel of the Feeding scene. It is in keeping with the thoroughly stylised character of the pericope that Satan withdraws (ἀφίησιν) at the end of the scene,[181] while the accounts of the Feeding agree in indicating that Jesus withdraws. The two remarks are complementary and underline the crucial nature of what happened. Thus, Q does in fact lend support to the view that the events surrounding the Feeding mark the decisive turn in the ministry of Jesus.[182]

VI

The messianic question must have posed itself to Jesus. Almost all of the charismatic figures of this century harboured inclinations in this direction,[183] very often with a Zealot bias. Jesus himself was a scion of the house of David, of that house with which messianic expectations were closely linked. As soon as he had entered the arena, the consideration whether the authority which he radiated had anything to do with his descent and whether he was put under an obligation by it must have impressed itself on the audience and on Jesus likewise. It is indicated in many details of the Gospel reports that the question was presented to Jesus in its different facets. His closer following was no exception to this.[184] It is especially the Lukan work that indicates the closeness of the disciples to an expectation which included the λύτρωσις of Israel – up to the cross and even beyond[185] – and takes pains to dissociate Jesus from such suggestions.

---

[180] Thus E. Meyer, *Ursprung und Anfänge des Christentums* i (Stuttgart, 1921), 94. If he were right, it would reflect the experience of the community behind Q.

[181] Luke qualifies this with ἄχρι καιροῦ. In 22: 3 he reappears and takes possession of Judas, who thereupon seeks an εὐκαιρία (verse 6) to take steps against Jesus; and indeed in 22: 53 the ὥρα . . . τοῦ σκότους has arrived. This is the first new intervention of Satan according to the scheme of this Gospel, i.e. the ministry itself is untouched by his skirmishes. It is the acceptable year *par excellence*.

[182] The proposed interpretation is in its main point in agreement with the brilliant exposition given by O. Pfleiderer, 'Die evangelische Erzählung von der Versuchung Jesu in der Wüste', *ZWT* 13 (1870), 201ff.

[183] Cp. H. Gressmann, *Der Messias* (Göttingen, 1929); J. Klausner, *The Messianic Idea in Israel* (New York, 1955). Onias is the exception.

[184] Peter's confession reflects the terminology of messianism. It is, however, in this context the stock phrase a puzzled disciple clings to rather than the attempt to push Jesus forward. Traces of entreaties among the disciples may possibly be found in Luke 9: 54.

[185] The theme of the λύτρωσις is given prominence at the beginning (1: 68; 2: 38) and at the end (24: 21) of the Gospel. The correction is only slightly indicated in the first

The almost complete lack of χριστός-statements in the other Gospels and of their refusal to take them as the consummation of witness to Jesus where they occur underlines this. Whereas in the Feeding stories the meal is the occasion at which the break between Jesus and the popular eschatology takes place, it is in Luke 24 that the meal gives illumination to the disciples assembled in Emmaus.

Jesus withdraws.[186] Still, the event must have made its impression on those who took part. The masses follow Jesus[187] – different branches of the tradition converge in assuming this.[188] Indeed, the Feeding could be taken as the beginning of the revival of the wondrous events of the desert time, as part of a sequence of actions which would culminate in 'salvation'. The entry to Jerusalem show that such hopes were latent even at this stage and could be kindled at any time.

It is against this background of the flaring up of old expectations that Jesus's statements have to be viewed. Not only had the enthusiasm of the multitude been dashed, not only was the crafty machination of the few brought to naught, but equally the perseverance of those who had taken a close interest in Jesus[189] was to be disappointed. It is in consequence of this that Peter's confession is given a cool, if not directly hostile,[190] reception,

place, while it is made the central point of the last teaching of Jesus: neither is the liberation the task of Jesus nor Israel his object, but the suffering and the entering into his glory. The suffering might have been taken as a prelude to the liberation – and indeed it is taken so by the malefactor who is pictured sympathetically – but this is excluded as well: there will be not a ἡμέρα τῆς ἐλεύσεως (23: 42 in D), Jesus is not to return ἐν τῇ βασιλείᾳ σου, in a state of royalty, but to be moved to the παράδεισος, a place which does not figure in the terminology of messianism. The confrontation with messianic aspiration is also emphasised in the main body of the Gospel.

186 It may be that the D addition ἐξεγερθείς (translated brilliantly by Hirsch, *Frühgeschichte* i, 77: 'er raffte sich auf') to ἠνάγκασεν is original. It points to movement and tension on the side of Jesus. The mention of the prayer in the following verse is in keeping with this. Goguel draws attention to the fact that the prayer which follows Jesus's withdrawal is one of three recounted in Mark and he assumes (*Jésus*, GT 240f; ET 373f) that it is equal in importance to the prayers at the beginning and at the end of his ministry.

187 Mark 6: 54f is a puzzle. It is not only the case that a *Sammelbericht* which starts with 55b is linked with something else (cp. Wellhausen, *Evangelium Marci*, ad loc.). Verses 54, 55a are not of a piece. Matthew who shortens the whole pericope, presents a longer text at this place, possibly an attempt at reconstructing one which had been lost by mutilation. The readings ἀπέδραμον (referring to the disciples) and περιέδραμον (referring to the masses) seem to represent the beginning and end of the line lost by mutilation.

188 Mark 6: 55 περιέδραμον = they rushed round the lake: John 6: 24ff.

189 We have to think especially of the Baptistic movement. Does the Chrysostom text (see note 55, p. 218), while leading in the right direction, single out only one side of what happened?

190 E. Wendling maintains that verse 33a, b followed verse 29 in Urmarkus (*Entstehung*), p. 116; slightly deviating from his *Ur-Marcus* (Tübingen, 1905), p. 29.

and that it is replaced by the proclamation of the Son of man's suffering – a point which is so crucial that even the ὄχλος is informed about it. The evangelist emphasises that – contrary to his normal procedure of speaking in symbols (parables) – it happened plainly;[191] that means that Jesus dissociated himself from messianism unmistakably and publicly.[192]

Messianic aspirations were dangerous at this time – the fate of so many pretenders gives ample evidence of this. One would expect Jesus to be safer after having disclaimed such ambitions. The denial of messianism was, however, equally dangerous. The messianic idea was deeply rooted in Jewish history and the expectation had reached boiling point in contemporary Judaism.[193] Whatever differences existed about the time and the person, no one was prepared to come out openly against messianism in principle.[194] The turning away[195] of someone who had been reared in the atmosphere of messianic expectation kindled by the Baptist's proclamation, and who perhaps at one time had wondered whether such a future might be his own vocation – this renunciation could be taken as a backsliding; it was bound to provoke those who were disappointed to hold Jesus's descent and former statements against him and to assemble such ammunition as could be found.

No wonder that critical observers[196] felt obliged to gather direct

Mark 8: 36 was the end and climax of the story and followed verse 33 immediately (p. 114).

[191] Mark 8: 31.

[192] E. Meyer (*Ursprung* p. 117) assumes that Peter's confession was followed in the original text by his urging Jesus to play the role of the messiah in line with the standard Jewish eschatology, and that it was this challenge that forced Jesus to reprimand him. It is possible that something of this kind happened (cp., however, note 184, p. 237) although traces of such an event are not any longer noticeable.

[193] According to R. Leszynsky (*Die Sadduzäer* (Berlin, 1912), pp. 99, 103) even in the Sadducaic party.

[194] Josephus's own position is a telling example; cp. W. Weber, *Josephus und Vespasian* (Berlin, 1921), pp. 250ff.

[195] Hebbel, who wrote sketches for a drama '*Christus*' in the year of his death (1863), made the difference between the Baptist and Jesus the basis of the development of the play. John is the deceiver, Jesus the deceived. Innocently he becomes a tool in the hands of the Baptist, who makes use for his own purposes of Jesus's power to work wonders and the messianic appearance which he has given without himself being aware of it. When John comes to his end he confides to Jesus his machinations and urges him to proceed likewise: pious fraud after the example of Moses ('*es ist das grösste Opfer, was du zu bringen hast, dass du dich zum frommen Betrug entschliessest, wie Moses*'). It is this event which opens Jesus's eyes. Gradually he is able to leave behind the Baptistic influence, to free himself even from the thought of an earthly kingdom and to proclaim a heavenly one (F. Hebbel, *Sämtliche Werke*, Erste Abteilung v (Berlin, 1904), 316ff). It is not clear from the fragments what aims the poet had visualised for the Baptist.

[196] The view taken by M. Goguel (*Jésus*, note 630; ET p. 372 n. 1) that the sign had been demanded by followers in the original tradition can hardly be maintained; even less

information. The mention of a questioning by the Pharisees, of attempts[197] to expose his position with complete clarity, had its place in these circumstances. Its outcome must have been unsatisfactory from the Pharisaic point of view. One might have thought that the Pharisees, who had stayed aloof from political intrigues in recent generations,[198] who seemed to have made it a principle to keep away from the realm of political action,[199] and who waited for a messiah sent by God, would have been pleased with a move which would have recommended Jesus to them, had it not been the case that he denied messianism altogether. This fact, however, made it imperative for them to fall in with what the ruling powers in Jerusalem had already indicated by their preliminary action.[200] Apart from τινες they turned against Jesus.

Jesus's withdrawal was by no means a move which would dispel the suspicion[201] felt against him by the Herodian administration: who could be sure that his retreat was a final one, that he was not preparing for another period of action? The fact that Jesus had to remain outside the territory of Antipas shows that vigilance continued. The situation which was to become decisive in the Trial emerges on the scene.

A series of actions taken by friends and sympathisers was aimed at removing Jesus either physically[202] or mentally[203] from a course of confrontation. A period which is marked by division,[204] fear[205] and yet determination[206] among his disciples was to follow. Jesus himself must have wondered what course to take. Eventually he made his decision, which, almost two hundred years ago, received its most apt characterisation from Herder: 'Meuchelmörderisch wollte Jesus nicht umkommen; er ging frei nach Jerusalem vors Angesicht der Obrigkeit und seiner Hauptfeinde. Wenn es das Leben galt, so wollte er dort sterben.'[207]

the opinion that the sign was meant to be the signal for a messianic uprising (GT p. 240; ET p. 372).

[197] Mark 7: 1; 8: 11–13; 9: 14.

[198] J. Wellhausen, *Die Pharisäer und die Sadducäer* (Greifswald, 1874), p. 101.

[199] A. Schlatter, *Die Theologie des Judentums nach dem Bericht des Josefus* (Gütersloh, 1932), p. 212; he seems however, to put too much trust in claims made by Josephus for apologetic reasons.

[200] Mark 3:22 is to be interpreted as a statement which has judicial relevance: a solemn warning is issued, which was to be followed by even sterner action.

[201] It is one-sided to characterise Jesus's movements as conditioned by his 'innere, ihn fast verzehrende Unruhe, zum Ziele zu gelangen' (K. Weidel, *Jesu Persönlichkeit*, 3rd edn. Halle, 1921, p. 96).

[202] Luke 13: 31   [203] Mark 8: 32.

[204] Mark 8: 15: John 6: 66. Goguel's description that Mark – over against the facts – wants to depict the situation of a gradual awareness of the character of Jesus by his disciples (*Jésus*, GT p. 237; ET pp. 369f) cannot be maintained.

[205] Mark 10: 32.   [206] John 11: 16.

[207] *Erlöser*, cited from *Werke*, ed. by Suphan, xix, 179.

The coin of 'Render unto Caesar . . .' (A note on some aspects of Mark 12: 13–17; Matt. 22: 15–22; Luke 20: 20–26)[1]

The provocative question ἔξεστιν κῆνσον Καίσαρι δοῦναι (Mark 12: 14: D and some other authorities read for κῆνσον, epexegetically, ἐπικεφάλαιον – we have to do with a poll-tax, not with indirect taxation) introduces what, maybe, was the first instance of the use of a coin, imaginatively, as a 'visual aid', in teaching. It added vividness, and a sense of drama, to the tale. Jesus calls for the appropriate coin φέρετέ μοι δηνάριον ἵνα ἴδω (Mark 12: 15; Matt. 22: 19 varies this – ἐπιδείξατέ μοι τὸ νόμισμα τοῦ κήνσου.) It is immediately forthcoming. No one doubts that it is indeed 'the money of the tribute'. The δηνάριον is the kind of coin in which the tribute is calculated and in which, by implication, it is to be paid.[2] We may note in passing that perhaps Jesus did not have such a coin about him. This is not stated. But it was perhaps so, for whatever reason. It would have been artistically desirable for the dénouement that the coin should have been provided by the Pharisees and Herodians who have posed the original question and no doubt they are the 'they' of οἱ δὲ ἤνεγκαν (Mark 12: 16; Matt. 22: 19 οἱ δὲ προσήνεγκαν αὐτῷ δηνάριον). But there is no reason to suppose as some have supposed that Jesus had no such coin about him because such a coin was itself an idolatrous object at which in the spirit of the strictest of the those strict sectarians mentioned by Hippolytus,[3] or of the famous Nahum

---

[1] This note is intended to supplement the treatment of the incident as a whole by Professor F. F. Bruce in this volume under the title 'Render to Caesar' (see pp. 249–63). Some of the evidence assembled for this note has accordingly been suppressed, to avoid overlap, but it has not been found convenient to avoid all overlaps.

[2] This is compatible with the provisions of the Palmyra inscription (*IGRR*, III, 1056, *OGIS* 629) of which use is made by Professor Bruce (p. 258). Cp. the comment, on the Gospel story, of Leo Kadman the distinguished numismatist of Israel: 'These questions and answers were only possible when Jesus could assume that the silver pieces found in the purse of the man in the street were Roman or Roman imperial coins, with the image and legend of the emperor', *Congresso Internazionale di Numismatica* (Rome, 1961), ii, *Atti* ii (Rome, 1965), 70.

[3] Hippolytus, *Refutatio omnium haeresium* ix. 26, ed. P. Wendland (Leipzig, 1916). They would not even carry coins, equating them with images.

or Menahem the son of Shimai,[4] Jesus might have been reluctant even to look. On the contrary he declared himself quite ready to look at it – φέρετέ μοι δηνάριον ἵνα ἴδω – calling for it for this very purpose. The coin was produced – for all to see. No question was made by any involved in this encounter of the idolatrous or blasphemous character or implication of the type and legend to be seen on the coin. The point of the story was not there.[5] The question which followed was a straightforward question: τίνος ἡ εἰκὼν αὕτη καὶ ἡ ἐπιγραφή;[6] the answer, certainly dramatic, perhaps reluctant, is equally straightforward – in one word Καίσαρος. All our three witnesses are in agreement. The coin which was called for, and was forthcoming, was in the correct tribute currency. It was a δηνάριον, a *denarius*. The point of calling for the coin, and of the subsequent question, was that the issuing authority was Caesar's. It was Caesar's money.[7] Both portrait and legend, εἰκών and ἐπιγραφή, testified precisely to this.

Perhaps the preliminaries were somewhat mystifying. But they introduced the ruling of Jesus (Mark 12: 17) on the original question,[8] with telling effect. It caused great surprise (Mark 12: 22, Luke 20: 26b). It was unanswerable (Luke 20: 26a).

But the concern of this note is not with the climax of the whole encounter but with the coin. Can we suggest with any confidence to what series of Roman imperial *denarii* the *denarius* which was shown to Jesus, and exhibited for all to scrutinise, belonged? There is a standard 'identification' which is probably quite right.[9] It should however be remembered that no such 'identification', however probable, can ever be proved to be right, nor will it add anything to our understanding of the Gospel narrative. What the

[4] On Nahum and the rabbinic evidences for him, see, conveniently, the discussion by Herbert Loewe in his book *Render unto Caesar* (Cambridge, 1940), pp. 88ff. Nahum earned the high title of 'a man of the holy of holies' 'because all his life long he never gazed upon a coin', 'because on coins there were human devices and devices of living creatures'.

[5] Cp. 'the images of princes printed or stamped in their coins, which when Christ did see in a Roman coin, we read not that he reprehended it'. Homily *Against Idolatry* (the two books of Homilies appointed to be read in churches, Oxford, 1859).

[6] For a similar question, in a very different context, Arrian, *Disc. Epict.* iv. v. 17. τίνος ἔχει τὸν χαρακτῆρα τοῦτο τὸ τετράσσαρον; for εἰκών as in the Gospels here cp. Herodianus (historicus) 1.9.7 καὶ νομίσματα ἐκόμισαν ἐκτετυπωμένα τὴν ἐκείνου εἰκόνα.

[7] 'Caesar's money' or 'coin' was probably a popular phrase, almost equivalent to 'legal tender', cp. τὸ τοῦ καίσαρος νόμισμα in Arrian, *Disc. Epict.* iii.

[8] A very interesting conjecture about the form of Jesus's *responsum* is made in J. Duncan M. Derrett, *Law in the New Testament* (London, 1970), p. 335.

[9] The standard identification (see next paragraph) is very widely accepted. It is not usual to trace it back beyond the first edition (1864) of F. W. Madden, *History of Jewish Coinage and of Money in the Old and New Testament* (London, 1864, reprinted New York, 1967), p. 247, although the 'identification' is older than Madden.

coin had to contribute as a 'visual aid' is all recorded there. Our question springs only from natural curiosity.[10]

If as is probable the *denarius* was a *denarius* of Tiberius himself,[11] the reigning Caesar whose tribute and tribute money is under discussion, there is remarkably little choice and a highly probable 'identification'. The imperial mints of Tiberius are listed in the great catalogue of Mattingly.[12] All his *denarii* are attributed to the mint of Lugdunum in Gaul. There are only two series: (*a*) a series dated to A.D. 15/16 (TR POT XVII) which was not continued,[13] and (*b*) the series of the standard 'identification'.[14] It bears no dates, but the titles of the emperor are continued on the *reverse* with PONTIF MAXIM, and as Tiberius became Pontifex maximus on 10 March A.D. 15[15] we have a *terminus a quo* for the series which was issued in quite extraordinary numbers[16] at intervals throughout the rest of his reign. The legends (*obverse* TI CAESAR DIVI AVG F AVGVSTVS and *reverse* PONTIF MAXIM) remain constant, the types (*obverse* head of Tiberius laureate, and *reverse* seated lady, perhaps Livia as PAX[17]) also remain constant, save for minor, though doubtless significant, variations in the presentation of the seated lady who persists as the *reverse* type. Annotated examples may be studied in Mattingly, *Coins of the Roman Empire*, plates 22 and 23. The series belongs with a long series of *aurei*[18] also of Tiberius from the same mint, and both were issued in continuation as it were of a series of *aurei* and *denarii* issued late in the reign of Augustus which shared the same fundamental reverse type.[19] This 'type is of special significance', writes Dr Michael Grant, 'because, when the *princeps* [Augustus] died soon afterwards, his successor Tiberius – changing only

---

[10] Cp. Derrett, *Law* p. 329, and the beginning of note 2, ibid. p. 338.

[11] The provisions made by Germanicus in the Palmyra inscription (cp. F. F. Bruce, below p. 258) make it probable that there was a notable increase in the availability of Roman imperial coins in Syria in the early years of Tiberius's reign.

[12] Harold Mattingly, *Coins of the Roman Empire in the British Museum*, i (London, 1923), 120ff.

[13] Mattingly, *Coins* i, p. 121, numbers 7–11.

[14] Mattingly, *Coins*, i, pp. 125ff, numbers 34–8, 42–5, 48–60. M. Grant in R. A. G. Carson and C. H. V. Sutherland, *Essays in Roman Coinage presented to Harold Mattingly* (Oxford, 1956), p. 112, suggests they were minted 'at more than the single mint of Lugdunum'.

[15] Evidence, conveniently, V. Ehrenberg and A. H. M. Jones, *Documents illustrating the reigns of Augustus and Tiberius* (Oxford, 1949), p. 47.

[16] The extraordinary numbers of this series found in modern times had already attracted the attention of Joseph Eckhel, see his *Doctrina Numorum Veterum*, Vol. vi (Vienna, 1796), p. 188.

[17] For this identification of the lady, Mattingly, *Coins*, i, 124, and pp. cxvii, and cxxxi; M. Grant, *Roman Anniversary Issues* (Cambridge, 1950), p. 39; C. H. V. Sutherland, *Coinage in Roman Imperial Currency* (London, 1951), p. 84, note 8.

[18] Mattingly, *Coins*, i, pp. 124ff, numbers 30–3, 39–41, 46, 47.

[19] Mattingly, *Coins*, i, p. 91, number 544 (*aureus*) and numbers 545f (*denarii*).

the obverse – continued to use the same reverse type, and scarcely any other, throughout the twenty-three years of his reign'. It is interesting to read in continuation 'this type was issued in many millions of examples (including, perhaps, the "Tribute Penny" of the New Testament) over a period of nearly a quarter of a century. This is a duration more characteristic of our modern coinage than of the incessantly changing coin-types of the Roman Empire. . . .'[20] In another place Dr Grant classifies this *denarius* among coins intended for empire-wide circulation.[21] The proposal to see here τὸ νόμισμα τοῦ κήνσου, and δηνάριον of our narrative, was first made long ago,[22] and has been generally accepted by New Testament scholars, and is very probable indeed. More than that – note Dr Grant's wise word 'perhaps'[23] in the above quotation – can hardly be said. Any *denarius* of Augustus, or a *denarius* of Tiberius in the dated series to which reference has been made above, might also be a candidate for the distinction of this 'identification'. The conditions are plain. The coin must be one which it is natural to call a *denarius*.[24] It must bear the εἰκών and ἐπιγραφή of Caesar. Augustus and Tiberius are the only two Caesars who can be considered, for obvious chronological reasons. The great numbers in which the *denarius* of the standard identification were issued tell powerfully in its favour. It is statistically the most probable suggestion.

Is it consistent with the monetary situation in Roman 'Palestine'[25] in the period of the ministry of Jesus? The answer is yes. But the question demands some scrutiny because hitherto early imperial *denarii* (i.e. those of

---

[20] M. Grant, *Roman Imperial Money* (London, 1954), pp. 133f.

[21] In Carson and Sutherland, *Essays*, p. 112.

[22] Cp. note 9, p. 242.

[23] He is, understandably, a little less cautious elsewhere. See his *Roman History from Coins* (Cambridge, 1958), pp. 83f, where he mentions very numerous finds of this *denarius* of Tiberius in southern India, and says 'This is the so-called "Tribute Penny" of the Bible. It is identified with the "penny" that was brought to Jesus. . . . No other *denarius* of Tiberius circulated nearly so extensively.'

[24] This tells against the suggestion to bring into consideration the coins of Philip the Tetrarch, e.g. in E. Klostermann, *Das Markus-evangelium* (Tübingen, 1950), on Mark 12:16. Philip issued no silver coins.

[25] For this much-studied subject reference may be made to the following: E. Schürer, *Geschichte des Jüdischen Volkes im Zeitalter Jesu Christi* (Hildersheim, 1964, reproducing Leipzig edition of 1907, ii, 71ff); L. C. West, *Gold and silver standards in the Roman Empire*, Numismatic Notes and Monographs, Number 94 (New York, 1941), pp. 47f; F. M. Heichelheim, *An Economic Survey of Ancient Rome*, iv, (Baltimore, 1938), 212f; A. N. Sherwin-White, *Roman Society and Roman Law in the New Testament* (Oxford, 1963), p. 124. None of these relate the literary to the numismatic evidence. Such studies are only beginning. For that see the paper of Dr C. H. V. Sutherland at the International Numismatic Convention at Jerusalem, 1963 to which reference is made below, and the sadly incomplete paper entitled 'The monetary development of Palestine in the light of coin hoards' by the late Leo Kadman who died at the beginning of that convention, printed in the *Proceedings*, pp. 311ff. Cp. information derived from Dr Ya'akov Meshorer cited below.

Augustus and of Tiberius) have been rather few in authentic finds in Palestine. J. Spencer Kennard, Jr, made much of this in *Render to God, A study of the Tribute passage*, and was able to quote only four specimens of the *denarius* of the standard 'identification' which were known to have been found in Palestine. He does not seem to doubt that a *denarius* was indeed shown to Jesus, or that it was likely to have been a specimen of the standard 'identification'. But he denies that it was the money of the tribute.[26] He sees the *denarius* as a rare novelty in the context of the Gospels. He argues that the tribute would have been paid in other silver currency, not minted far away at Lugdunum in Gaul. The cogency of arguments so based is however very questionable, since there has been no systematic recording of the detail and locality of finds until quite recent decades. Kennard's book was published in 1950 and the right comment even then would probably have been 'wait and see'. In an important paper entitled 'The pattern of monetary development in Phoenicia and Palestine during the early Empire' read at the International Numismatic Convention in Jerusalem in December 1963, Dr C. H. V. Sutherland notes: 'It is for the period down to A.D. 70 that literary evidence is most generous in giving a complementary impression of monetary economy in the area, and especially in Palestine.'[27] He refers to the evidence afforded by the New Testament and pronounces the picture 'a normal Greco-Roman one of the time'. He says later: 'There is little, until now, in the nature of hoard-evidence to amplify the sketch afforded by mint-analysis and literary evidence for the early Julio-Claudian period, though this will assuredly come in due course.'[28] The right comment on our question in 1963 was still therefore 'wait and see'. Then there is the *Isfiya* Hoard of about 4,500 ancient silver coins discovered in 1960 near Isfiya on Mt Carmel. This was all too briefly described by Leo Kadman who found in it 3,400 Tyrian shekels, about 1,000 half-shekels, and '160 Roman denarii of Augustus'.[29] Here is hoard evidence beginning to corroborate the picture afforded by the literary evidence of the New Testament and Josephus, certainly adding to the scanty evidence of earlier authenticated finds, that the Roman *denarius* played its part in the monetary system of Palestine in the time of the Gospels. Kadman did not publish a detailed list of the 160 *denarii* of Augustus, and there was here no news of more *denarii* of

---

[26] 'The *denarius* represented the coinage of the West; it was not the coin of tribute', Kennard, *Render to God*, p. 51.

[27] *Proceedings of the International Numismatic Convention, Jerusalem 1963* (Tel Aviv–Jerusalem, 1967), p. 91.

[28] Ibid. p. 93.

[29] In passing, as it were, in his very interesting paper 'Temple dues and currency in ancient Palestine in the light of recently-discovered coin-hoards', pp. 69ff of *Atti*, ii, (Rome, 1965). Another version of this paper is in *Israel Numismatic Bulletin* 1 (Jerusalem, 1962), 9–11.

1 and 2 are *denarii* of Augustus, 3 and 4 are *denarii* of Tiberius. Any of such coins, but most probably such a coin as 4, may therefore have been τὸ νόμισμα τοῦ κήνσου. 5 is a billion *tetradrachm* of Alexandria. It is perhaps the best candidate, other than a *denarius*, for the 'identification'. It was roughly equivalent in value to a *denarius*; but there is the problem of the monetary isolation of Egypt (see further H. St J. Hart, 'The Crown of Thorns in John 19, 2–5', *JThSt* n.s. 3 (1952), 66f. 6 is a 'shekel', 7 a '½-shekel', both of the mint of Tyre. According to Mishnah, *Bekhoroth*, viii. 7, it was in Tyrian currency that the Jewish 'shekel-dues' were paid. The Temple tax is discussed in this volume by W. Horbury (see pp. 265–86).

Nos. 2–4 by courtesy of the British Museum.

Nos. 1 and 5–7 by courtesy of the Fitzwilliam Museum, Cambridge.

Detail

1. Augustus. Lugdunum. *Denarius*. Undated but '*c.* 2 B.C.–A.D. 11'. Cp. Mattingly, *Coins*, i, no. 538. Obverse: Head, laureate. CAESAR AVGVSTVS DIVI F PATER PATRIAE. Reverse: Gaius and Lucius: between them two shields and two spears. In field, *lituus* and *simpulum*; below these X. C L CAESARES AVGVSTI F COS DESIG PRINC IVVENT.

2. Augustus. Lugdunum. *Denarius*. Undated, *c.* A.D. 11–13. Mattingly, *Coins*, i, no. 546. Obverse: Head, laureate. CAESAR AVGVSTVS DIVI F PATER PATRIAE. Reverse: Seated female figure. PONTIF MAXIM.

3. Tiberius. Lugdunum. *Denarius*. A.D. 15–16. Mattingly, *Coins*, i, no. 8. Obverse: Head, laureate. TI CAESAR DIVI AVG F AVGVSTVS. Reverse: The emperor in quadriga. IMP VII TR POT XVII.

4. Tiberius. Lugdunum. *Denarius*. Undated. Mattingly, *Coins*, i, no. 60. Obverse: Head, laureate. TI CAESAR DIVI AVG F AVGVSTVS. Reverse: Seated female figure. PONTIF MAXIM.

5. Augustus. Alexandria. Billon tetradrachm. Cp. J. G. Milne, *Catalogue of the Alexandrian Coins in the Ashmolean Museum* (Oxford, 1933), nos. 38ff. Obverse: Head of Tiberius, laureate. Τιβεριος Καισαρ Cεβαστος. Date, L Z (= 6 = A.D. 20). Reverse: Head of Augustus, radiate. Θεος Cεβαστος.

6. Tyre. Shekel. *Sylloge Nummorum Graecorum*, iv (London, 1971), no. 6089. Obverse: Head of Herakles/Melkart. Reverse: Eagle on prow. Τυρου Ιερας Και Ασυλου. Date, ZM (= 80–79 B.C.).

7. Tyre. Half-shekel. *Sylloge*, iv, no. 6093. Types and legend as on 6. Date = 10/9 B.C.

Tiberius.[30] So, mindful of Dr Sutherland's prophecy, cited above, I wrote to my very learned friend Dr Ya'akov Meshorer, of the Israel Museum in Jerusalem. From his reply, dated 1 April 1971, I am grateful to quote, with his kind permission, as follows:

> You rightly assumed these Tiberius denars are quite rare in this part of the world, though I occasionally spot one in the market. Excavations and published material is not much more encouraging. The only good example of a find including such coins is the famous hoard of Mount Carmel, discovered in 1960. It was never properly published although most of it was registered by Mr L. Rachmany of the Israel Antiquities department.
>
> The hoard was discussed briefly in a paper published by Kadman in the *Israel Numismatic Journal*, 1 (1962), pp. 9–11. This hoard includes 3,400 Tyrian shekels, and 1,000 half-shekels dated from 40 B.C. to 53 A.D., and also 160 Roman denars. Although Kadman wrote that all the denars are of Augustus, I can say for sure that at least 30 of them are of the Tiberius type you are interested in. Some of these coins are in the possession of the Israel Antiquities Department, some are apparently in the collections of the 'Coins and Medals Co.', Jerusalem, and the rest were sold on the open market.

and later in the letter: 'Father A. Spijkerman of the Franciscan Biblical School in Jerusalem, four years ago bought such a denarius in Jericho, which had been found there.'

In the light of this evidence we may conclude, with Kennard and many others, that the standard 'identification' is in all probability right. We may go further, against Kennard in 1950, and with many others before and since, and accept the implication – it is quite unexceptionable – of the Gospel narrative – that the Roman imperial *denarius*, of whatever contemporary variety, was indeed τὸ νόμισμα τοῦ κήνσου (Matt. 22: 19). It remains highly probable that the coin shown to Jesus was one of the huge second series of *denarii* of Tiberius according to the standard 'identification'. To determine between this and his earlier series, or some earlier *denarius* of Caesar Augustus himself, also bearing the εἰκών and ἐπιγραφή of Caesar, is not now in our power, nor is it probable that it ever will be.[31]

---

[30] In the Rome version Kadman had already noted one *denarius* of Tiberius among the 160 *denarii*.

[31] See also the plate and its annotations.

Render to Caesar

I

In the context of Jesus's ministry in the outer court of the Temple during his last week in Jerusalem Mark (followed by the two other synoptic evangelists) records this incident:

> They send to him some of the Pharisees and the Herodians to catch him in a statement. They come and say to him, 'Teacher, we know that you are true and court no one's favour: you do not regard anyone's status,[1] but teach the way of God truly. Is it permissible to give tribute to Caesar or not? Shall we give it, or shall we not give it?' Knowing that they were acting a part he said to them: 'Why do you try (to catch) me (like this)? Bring me a *denarius*; let me see it.' They brought him one; and he says to them, 'Whose image is this? Whose name is inscribed (on the coin)?' 'Caesar's', said they. So Jesus said 'Give Caesar's property back to Caesar; give God what belongs to God.' They were lost in amazement at him.[2]

While the point of the incident is preserved in all three synoptic records, it is generalised in later stages of the tradition. Thus, in Papyrus Egerton 2, it appears in the form:

> They came to him and tested him with a question: 'Master[3] Jesus, we know that you have come from God, for the things which you do bear witness beyond all the prophets. Tell us therefore: Is it permissible to render to kings the things that belong to their rule? Shall we render these things to them or not?' Jesus, knowing their mind, was angry and said to them: 'Why do you call me "Master" with your mouth without listening to what I say? Well did Isaiah prophesy of you when he said,[4] "This people know me with their lips, but their heart is far from me. In vain do they worship me, [teaching] commandments [of men]." '[5]

---

[1] Literally: 'you do not care for (meddle with) any one, for you do not look at the face of men' (cp. 1 Sam. 16: 7, 'man looks on the face [MT 'eyes'], but Yahweh looks on the heart'). In general βλέπειν πρόσωπον is, like θαυμάζειν πρόσωπον (Jude 16), synonymous with λαμβάνειν πρόσωπον, 'to be partial', 'to show favouritism'.

[2] Mark 12: 13–17; cp. Matt. 22: 15–22; Luke 20: 20–6.

[3] Gk διδάσκαλε. With the sentence introduced by this word cp. John 3: 2.

[4] Isa. 29: 13 (cp. its quotation in Mark 7: 6f).

[5] Fragment 2 recto, *Fragments of an Unknown Gospel and Other Early Christian Papyri*, ed. H. I. Bell and T. C. Skeat (London, 1935), pp. 10–13.

More succinctly, in the Gospel of Thomas, Logion 100 runs thus:

> They showed Jesus a piece of gold and said to him, 'Caesar's people are asking taxes from us.' Said he to them: 'Give Caesar what is Caesar's, give God what is God's,[6] and give me what is mine.'[7]

These last two passages are of interest for the development of the tradition under divergent influences; they throw no light on the significance of the pericope in its earliest form, but reflect a situation in which the original urgency of the question has been forgotten.

The pericope in Mark can be categorised as an apophthegm or paradigm in the conventional terminology of form-criticism. It was related for the sake of the punch-line – the epigrammatic saying of Jesus which forms its climax. The saying cannot have circulated on its own: it is intelligible only as part of the pericope.[8]

The editorial hand is seen only in the introduction to the pericope: the mention of Pharisees and Herodians together is striking. An alliance between the Pharisees and Herodians, with the aim of destroying Jesus, has been mentioned earlier, in Mark 3: 6, in a Galilaean setting, at the end of a series of five controversial incidents. The suggestion that, in the material as Mark received it, the controversies of 12: 13ff followed continuously on the five of 2: 1 to 3: 6 is not convincing:[9] those of 2: 1 to 3: 6 have a different form from those of 12: 13ff, and the incident with which we are concerned presupposes a Judaean setting. It was in Judaea, not Galilee, that the tribute question was one of practical moment, with the risk of an impolitic answer being construed as seditious. The presence of Herodians here is not surprising if Herod Antipas was temporarily resident in Jerusalem (cp. Luke 23: 7).

The Pharisees may have taken up a variety of attitudes towards the Roman administration of Judaea, ranging from Sadduq, the Pharisee who joined with Judas of Gamala in leading the revolt of A.D. 6,[10] to Yoḥanan ben Zakkai, who counselled submission to Rome at the time of the greater

---

[6] 'God' is not found elsewhere in the Gospel of Thomas; here the God of the Old Testament, the demiurge, is probably intended, so that we have an ascending order of dignity: Caesar, God, Jesus. He whom Jesus reveals is 'the Father', not 'God'; to embrace the saving knowledge imparted by Jesus as revealer of the Father is to give Jesus his due.

[7] *The Gospel according to Thomas* (Coptic text with English translation), ed. A. Guillaumont, H.-Ch. Puech, G. Quispel, W. Till and Yassah 'Abd al Masih (Leiden and London, 1959), p. 51.

[8] Cp. R. Bultmann, *Die Geschichte der synoptischen Tradition* (5th edn. Göttingen, 1961), p. 25 (ET *The History of the Synoptic Tradition* (Oxford, 1963), p. 26): 'There is no reason, in my view,' he adds, 'for supposing that this is a community product.'

[9] Cp. B. S. Easton, *Christ in the Gospels* (New York, 1930), pp. 35f.

[10] Josephus, *AJ* xviii. 4.

revolt sixty years later and acknowledged Vespasian in advance as world-ruler and Temple-destroyer.[11] The majority of them probably looked on the Roman dominion as a necessary evil, like Ḥanina the deputy high priest (prefect of the priests) who is credited with the admonition: 'Pray for the peace of the empire (mal^ekūṭ), since if it were not for fear of it men would devour each other alive'.[12]

As for the Herodians, they were not a religious group but a party that promoted the interests of the Herod dynasty and probably hoped for the re-integration of Herod's kingdom under one of his descendants. Although this would mean the end of government by imperial procurators, they must have been pro-Roman in their policy: only as allies or vassals of Rome could the Herods exercise any authority in Palestine.[13]

It was as representatives of two groups, then, that were not in principle hostile to the occupying power, that the deputation from the Pharisees and Herodians approached Jesus. The implication of the narrative is that, if he had denied the propriety of paying tribute to Caesar, they would have denounced him to the provincial government. This is Luke's explicit account of their motive: they hoped, he says, that Jesus's answer would enable them 'to deliver him up to the authority and jurisdiction of the governor'.[14] But their plan was thwarted. On the other hand, men who shared the Zealot outlook would have welcomed him as a sympathiser and ally had he returned a negative answer and would certainly not have denounced him to the authorities. The best that they could hope for, if they were already opposed to him, would be that an affirmative answer to the question 'Shall we give?' would lose him the sympathy of all who chafed under the Gentile yoke. But a question like this from men of Zealot outlook would more probably have been designed simply to find out where Jesus stood on this (to them) all-important issue. As it is, the question came from men whose motives, as Jesus read them, were more than suspect.

II

Judaea first became tributary to Rome when Pompey occupied it in 63 B.C.: 'he laid the region and Jerusalem under tribute', says Josephus.[15] For a time

[11] TB *Giṭṭin*, 56b; cp. TB *Yoma*, 39b.

[12] *Pirqe 'Aḇoṯ* 3: 2. The designation of Hanina as s^egan hakkōh^anim implies that he flourished before the fall of the Temple: 'probably the last to hold this office' (H. L. Strack, *Introduction to the Talmud and Midrash*, ET (New York, 1959), p. 109).

[13] Cp. W. Otto, in *PW* Suppl. ii, cols. 200ff (s.v. 'Herodianoi'); H. H. Rowley, 'The Herodians in the Gospels', *JThSt* 41 (1940), 14ff. The Herodians disappear completely from Luke's narrative: in Luke 20: 19ff it is spies from the scribes and chief priests who ask the question about the tribute money.

[14] Luke 20: 20.   [15] *BJ* i. 154; cp. *AJ* xiv. 74.

it seems to have formed part of one taxation unit along with Syria,[16] and may well have suffered the disadvantages of tax-farming by *publicani*, as so many other provinces did under the republic. Julius Caesar granted the Judaeans certain concessions in respect of tribute, showing special consideration for the circumstances of the sabbatical year, in which the fields were allowed to lie fallow.[17] Caesar's concessions were confirmed by the Roman Senate after his assassination.[18]

With the Parthian conquest and brief restoration of the Hasmonaean dynasty in Judaea (40–37 B.C.), tribute was withheld from Rome; and when Herod made effective the kingship over the Jews which the Senate had conferred on him, and reigned as ally of the Roman people (*rex socius*) from 37 to 4 B.C., Judaea was no longer tributary to Rome. Herod naturally knew that handsome gifts to the Roman rulers would not be unappreciated, and he kept this practice up to the end of his life, for in his will he bequeathed 1,000 talents of silver (10,000,000 Attic drachmae) to Augustus and half as much to the Empress Livia and other members of the imperial family.[19] He had other sources of revenue to defray his costly establishment and building enterprises than what his kingdom could supply, but it appears that the annual revenue which he drew from his kingdom was around 1,000 talents.[20]

No doubt his subjects felt his taxation burdensome enough, although there were other features of his reign more burdensome than this. On one occasion at least (*c.* 20 B.C.) he remitted one-third of their taxes;[21] five years earlier he had realised his own gold and silver plate to buy grain from Egypt for them during a famine.[22] Nevertheless, the first request they made of Archelaus after Herod's death was for a reduction in their annual taxation.[23]

When his kingdom was divided between three of his sons by Augustus after his death, Judaea (with Samaria) was allotted to Archelaus. Augustus, we are told, remitted one-fourth of the Samaritans' tribute (presumably their tribute to Archelaus, not to Rome) because they had not

---

[16] Cp. Cicero, *Prov. Cons.* 10.   [17] Josephus, *AJ* xiv. 202, 205f.
[18] Josephus, *AJ* xiv. 219ff.
[19] Josephus, *AJ* xvii, 146, 190. On the talent in Josephus cp. F. Hultsch, 'Das hebräische Talent bei Josephos', *Klio* 2 (1902), 70ff.
[20] This is computed by adding together the revenues of the territories into which his kingdom was divided after his death – especially Archelaus's ethnarchy, 400 (*BJ* ii. 97) or 600 talents (*AJ* xvii. 320); Antipas's tetrarchy, 200 talents, and Philip's tetrarchy, 100 talents (*AJ* xvii. 319). From a kingdom practically equal in extent to Herod's, Agrippa I later drew a revenue of 1,200 talents (*AJ* xix. 352). See W. Otto in *PW* Suppl. ii, cols. 87ff (s.v. 'Herodes'); A. Schalit, *König Herodes* (Berlin, 1969), pp. 262ff.
[21] Josephus, *AJ* xv. 365.   [22] Josephus, *AJ* xv. 305–9.
[23] Josephus, *AJ* xvii. 204.

engaged in revolts such as had disturbed the peace of Galilee and Judaea after Herod's death.[24]

According to Josephus, the annual revenue derived by Archelaus from his ethnarchy was 400 talents (so in the *Jewish War*)[25] or 600 talents (so in the *Antiquities*).[26] The figure given in the *Antiquities* may be a correction of that given in the earlier work, or conceivably the two figures come from two different sources, and represent two variant ways of calculating a talent. In either case, his subjects felt that the burden of providing this revenue was too heavy. When they greeted his appearance at his father's funeral with an appeal to have their annual payments reduced, he listened patiently enough, so anxious was he to command popular good will, and promised to consider their plea on his return from Rome, for which he was about to leave in order to secure the succession. But while he was in Rome a delegation of Judaeans arrived to seek an audience of Augustus and begged that their land might be relieved of Herodian rule altogether.[27] Their hopes that the accession of Archelaus might bring an alleviation of the high level of taxation and other exactions demanded by Herod did not run very high: Archelaus had already, in a matter of weeks, shown himself to be a true son of his oppressive father. What they desired, therefore, was to have their land attached to the province of Syria and to be ruled by the imperial legate posted there – their idea no doubt was that, subject to his overriding authority, they might enjoy more internal home rule than they had done under Herod.

Archelaus nevertheless was confirmed in his position as ethnarch of Judaea (including Samaria), but his subjects' forebodings were amply realised, and in less than ten years Augustus deposed him, because his rule was so intolerably oppressive, and banished him to Gaul (A.D. 6).[28] Now those Judaeans who had asked for direct Roman rule were at last granted their request. Judaea received the status of a Roman province of the third rank, to be governed by a prefect appointed by Augustus from the equestrian order. Such a province was liable to pay tribute to the Roman state, and so a census was held under the supervision of the legate of Syria, P. Sulpicius Quirinius, to assess the annual amount which the new province could reasonably be expected to raise.[29] Under the principate the tribute consisted mainly of a tax on landed property (*tributum agri* or *tributum soli*), calculated on the estimated annual yield in crops and cattle, together with a tax on personal property of other kinds (*tributum capitis*).[30] We do not

---

[24] Josephus, *AJ* xvii. 319.   [25] *BJ* ii. 97.

[26] *AJ* xvii. 320.

[27] *BJ* ii. 8off; *AJ* xvii. 300ff. There may be an allusion to this delegation in Luke 19: 14.

[28] *BJ* ii. 111; *AJ* xvii. 342ff.   [29] *AJ* xvii. 355, xviii. 1ff.

[30] Cp. *Digest* L, xv. 4. 2; 8. 7. Josephus probably transfers the situation of his day into

know the amount of tribute fixed by Quirinius's assessment; there is no reason to suppose that it was excessive by Roman standards, and it may have done little more than defray the expense of maintaining the military and civil administration of the province.[31] Eleven years later, indeed, we find the provincials of both Syria and Judaea petitioning for a reduction of tribute because the scale of payment was so burdensome.[32]

There were, of course, many kinds of indirect taxation (customs dues and so forth) superimposed on the direct taxation in the form of tribute. But for the Jews of Judaea the burden of financial outlay was exceptionally heavy. In addition to the Roman tribute and other secular dues, they were obliged by religious law to pay for the maintenance of the Jerusalem Temple and its large staff of priests, Levites and other Temple servants. The tithe which they had to pay regularly for this purpose (over and above the annual half-shekel poll-tax) was originally designed as an inclusive ten per cent income tax to be paid by subjects of a theocracy.[33] The Deuteronomic 'second tithe' was originally an alternative to this but had now to be paid in addition to it, every third year.[34] But when the imperial tribute was superimposed on the theocratic dues, the burden was well nigh intolerable: only an approximate estimate is possible in the absence of anything like precise data, but the total taxation could have approached something like forty per cent of the provincial income.[35]

III

Yet it was not because of the sheer weight of taxation that the question of tribute to Caesar was such a burning one in Jesus's day. The Herodian tribute had already been payable over and above the religious dues, and it may have been as high as the Roman tribute which replaced it. But at the time of Quirinius's census in A.D. 6 a new doctrine began to be taught in Judaea, so distinctive that those who held it could be classed as a separate school of religious thought.[36]

According to this new doctrine, the payment of tribute to the Romans

an earlier period when he represents David as exacting these two forms of tribute from Edom (*AJ* vii. 109).

[31] According to *BJ* ii. 405, arrears of tribute amounting to 40 talents were paid, at the instance of Agrippa II, in the summer of A.D. 66; but it is not clear what period this amount covered.

[32] Tacitus, *Ann.* ii. 42. 6.

[33] Num. 18: 21ff.

[34] Deut. 14: 22ff; cp. Mishnah *Ma'aśer Sheni*.

[35] Cp. F. C. Grant, *The Economic Background of the Gospels* (Oxford, 1926), p. 105.

[36] Josephus calls it an innovation and revolution (ἡ τῶν πατρίων καίνισις καὶ μεταβολή, *AJ* xviii. 9). Cp. M. Hengel, *Die Zeloten* (Leiden, 1961), pp. 132ff *et passim*.

was incompatible with Israel's theocratic ideals. This must have been because the Romans were pagans: no *religious* objection seems to have been voiced against the payment of taxes to Jewish rulers, mortal men though they might be[37] – not even to the Herods, who were undeniably Jews by religious law. The author of this new doctrine was Judas of Gamala in Gaulanitis (otherwise Judas the Galilaean),[38] designated by Josephus as the founder of the 'fourth philosophy' among the Jews[39] (the first three being the Pharisaic, Sadducean and Essene orders). Josephus represents the Jewish religious parties as 'philosophies', by analogy with the philosophical schools among the Greeks, and for the same reason he refers to Judas as a 'sophist'.[40] But Judas was indeed a religious teacher and the founder of a new school of thought in so far as his insistence on the sinfulness of paying tribute to a Gentile ruler appears to have had no precedent in Israel. On the contrary, when Israel and Judah in earlier days became tributary to foreign rulers, the general attitude of their religious leaders, and especially the prophets, was that this was Yahweh's judgement on his people for their unfaithfulness, and must be endured until he lifted it; until then, the withholding of tribute from the foreign ruler was an act of rebellion against Yahweh. This was pre-eminently true of Zedekiah's withholding tribute from Nebuchadrezzar, although Zedekiah compounded his offence by committing perjury too, since he had sworn in Yahweh's name to be Nebuchadrezzar's loyal vassal. For his double offence he was denounced by the prophet Ezekiel.[41] Jeremiah, for his part, had warned Zedekiah from the beginning of his reign that Nebuchadrezzar was Yahweh's servant, to whom Yahweh had given his imperial sovereignty, and that Judah's security lay in submitting to the Babylonian yoke.[42] Even after Zedekiah's rebellion, when in desperation during the siege of Jerusalem he sent for Jeremiah to ask his advice, the prophet assured him that he might yet salvage something from the wreck if even at this late date he would capitulate voluntarily.[43]

After the Babylonian exile, when Judaea became a minor province of the Persian Empire, no one seems to have suggested that there was anything wrong in paying tribute to the Great King.[44] Nehemiah, as governor (*peḥāh*) of Judaea under Artaxerxes I, refused to draw the governor's allowance

---

[37] When Josephus represents Judas as castigating the Jews for tolerating 'mortal masters' after God (*BJ* ii. 118), this is a piece of rhetoric.

[38] He is called the Galilaean in *BJ* ii. 118, 433, and *AJ* xviii. 23, xx. 102 (cp. Acts 5: 37); in *AJ* xviii. 4 he is described as 'a Gaulanite from the city of Gamala'.

[39] *AJ* xviii. 9, 23.   [40] *BJ* ii. 118.

[41] Ezek. 21: 25ff.   [42] Jer. 27: 4ff.

[43] Jer. 38: 17ff.

[44] If Haggai and Zechariah think of the fall of Persian power, it will be accomplished by the act of God (Hag. 2: 20ff; Zech. 4: 7).

because of the impoverished economy of the province.[45] His predecessors (and, we may be sure, his successors) were not so considerate, but no one questioned their right to the allowance, whether they were Jews or Gentiles.[46] His near-contemporary Malachi makes a passing allusion to the practice of giving nothing but the best to the (Persian) governor (*peḥāh*), with the implication that it was perfectly natural and proper.[47]

The Persian system was taken over by Alexander and his successors, and was accepted from 331 B.C.[48] until 'the yoke of the Gentiles was removed from Israel'[49] in the days of Simon the Hasmonaean (142 B.C.). The decades of Jewish independence under the Hasmonaeans made the imposition of the Roman yoke in 63 B.C. the more irksome; yet there were pious people in Israel, like the Qumran community and the authors of the 'psalms of Solomon', who showed themselves true sons of the prophets by recognising in the Roman conquest (with the ensuing exaction of tribute) a divine judgement on the Hasmonaeans.[50] No voice, so far as we know, was raised at that early stage of the occupation to protest against the impiety of Israel's being required to pay tribute to Rome. Whether or not the resistance leader Hezekiah, executed by Herod in his capacity as military prefect of Galilee in 47 B.C.,[51] was the father of Judas of Gamala (and there is no evidence that he was),[52] he is not credited with this attitude.

The first occasion when it was propounded, so far as our evidence goes, was at the time of the Quirinius census when Judas of Gamala, together with Ṣadduq the Pharisee, raised the standard of revolt.[53] Of this Ṣadduq we hear no more, but he may be linked with the Galilaean 'Sadducee' – meaning perhaps 'follower of (this) Ṣadduq' – who, according to the Mishnah, found fault with the Pharisees for including the name of the (Gentile) ruler (for dating purposes) on their divorce certificates along with the name of Moses (as author of the law of divorce).[54]

---

[45] Neh. 5: 14ff.

[46] In addition to Zerubbabel and Nehemiah, the names of two other Jewish governors of Judaea under the Persians are recorded on jar-handles found in 1960 at Ramat Rahel, accoring to Y. Aharoni, 'Excavations at Ramat Rahel', *The Biblical Archaeologist* 24 (1961), 98ff, esp. 111f.

[47] Mal. 1: 8.

[48] Cp. Josephus's account of members of the Tobiad family who secured the contract for tax collecting in Coelesyria under the Ptolemies and Seleucids (*AJ* xii. 160ff).

[49] 1 Macc. 13: 41.

[50] Cp. 1QpHab ix. 2ff; Ps. Sol. 17: 5ff.

[51] Josephus, *BJ* i. 204; *AJ* xiv. 159 (he calls Hezekiah an ἀρχιληστής).

[52] Judas, who raided the royal arsenal in Sepphoris after Herod's death in 4 B.C., was a son of the ἀρχιληστής Hezekiah (*BJ* ii. 56; *AJ* xvii. 271f), but Josephus does not identify him with the leader of the revolt of nine years later.

[53] *AJ* xviii. 4.

[54] Mishnah, *Yadayim* 4: 8. The 'Sadducee' is otherwise called 'a Galilaean heretic'. The Pharisees point for a precedent to Exod. 5: 2, where the name of a pagan ruler

The revolt was put down, but the 'fourth philosophy' was not extinguished: to it, indeed, Josephus traces the insurgent policy which involved the Jewish state in the disaster of A.D. 70.[55] Although he does not explicitly call Judas of Gamala the founder of the Zealot party, it is difficult to avoid the conclusion that this is precisely what he was, and that the new doctrine that it was impious to pay tribute to Caesar was the distinguishing feature of the Zealot outlook.

New the doctrine might be; it could not fail to be popular. Many Judaeans would in any case resent the payment of tribute to Rome on patriotic and economic grounds, and they would not readily reject the idea that it was contrary to the law of their God. Even if they went on paying it reluctantly, they could not but admire their fellow-countrymen who had the courage of their Zealot convictions and endured savage reprisals for refusing to acknowledge Caesar's sovereignty or his right to tax them. If we accept Mark's dating of the question about the tribute money during Holy Week, then around that very time there had been an outbreak of insurgency involving bloodshed, in which Barabbas played a prominent part.[56] Popular sympathies were engaged on the subject, and it was on no purely academic point of legal interpretation that Jesus was invited to give a ruling.

IV

The disproportionately lengthy preamble to the question was scarcely framed with the simple purpose of flattering Jesus: his questioners probably knew that he was not susceptible to such an approach. It indicates in general that they knew that they would get an impartial answer from him, because he did not adapt his answer to his hearers' preferences. It made no difference, they implied, who asked the question: the answer would be a straight one, truly expounding 'the way of God'. Such a topical question, posed in a public place, would immediately attract an eager crowd of listeners, and the unsolicited testimonial given to Jesus in the preamble was probably intended as much for their ears as for his, with the idea of putting him publicly on the spot.

'Is it permissible', they asked (meaning 'permissible' in terms of the law of Israel's God), 'to give tribute to Caesar or not?' The word rendered 'tribute' is κῆνσος, a loanword from Latin *census* ('assessment', 'tax');[57] it occurs as a loanword in rabbinical literature also, and could perhaps have

---

(Pharaoh) not merely accompanies but precedes the name of Yahweh himself.

[55] *AJ* xviii. 6ff.   [56] Mark 15: 7.

[57] So also Matt. 22: 17; Luke substitutes φόρος (20: 22).

been used by Jesus's questioners if they spoke to him in Aramaic, or even in Hebrew.

Jesus's reply, 'Bring me a *denarius*; let me see it',[58] suggests that the Roman tribute was to be paid in Roman money. That this was indeed so is indicated on a Greek inscription from Palmyra (dated A.D. 136/7)[59] which lays down that various dues are to be paid in *denarii* (εἰς δηνάριον) and cites as evidence a rescript of Germanicus Caesar (who exercised a *maius imperium* in the eastern provinces from A.D. 17 to 19) to Statilius (perhaps financial procurator of Syria), directing that all state taxes (τέλη) are to be collected in *asses* (εἰς ἀσσάριον),[60] i.e. in Roman coinage (the *as* being then one-sixteenth of a *denarius* in value).

The verb translated 'render' is ἀποδίδωμι, the natural verb to use in such a context. It is used of Jesus's handing back the scroll in the Nazareth synagogue to its lawful custodian (Luke 4: 20). It is specially used of paying various kinds of dues – of returning a deposit to its owner (Lev. 6: 4, LXX), of refunding an advance, as in the parable of the good Samaritan (Luke 10: 35), of restoring goods wrongfully taken, as in the Zacchaeus incident (Luke 19: 8), of repaying debts to a creditor, as in the parables of the unforgiving servant (Matt. 18: 34) and the two debtors (Luke 7: 42), of paying a fine or damages, as in Matt. 5: 26 par. Luke 12: 59, or (as here) of paying taxes (cp. Rom. 13: 7). In these instances it is implied that the person to whom payment or repayment is made is the rightful owner or recipient of whatever is paid or repaid; the action amounts to giving back to someone property to which he is entitled. Caesar, it is implied, is entitled to demand tribute; to pay him tribute is to give back to him what is in any case his. And the tribute money has just been acknowledged to be his. Mark does not explicitly say '*Therefore* render to Caesar . . .', as do Matthew[61] and Luke,[62] but the 'therefore' is as clearly implied in Mark's asyndeton as it is expressed by Matthew and Luke.

It could be said, of course, that the Judaeans' use of Caesar's coins did not necessarily imply their recognition of Caesar's sovereignty or his right to demand taxes from them. As Professor Derrett points out, Jews in Judaea and elsewhere used Tyrian coinage at this time to pay their Temple dues, but this would not be taken to mean that they acknowledged Tyrian sovereignty (how could they, since Tyre itself was subject to Rome?) or that

---

[58] So Luke 20: 24; Matthew has τὸ νόμισμα τοῦ κήνσου, 'the coin for the tribute', but adds: 'And they brought him a *denarius*' (22: 19).

[59] W. Dittenberger, *OGIS* 629, lines 153–6.

[60] We might understand εἰς ἀσσάριον in the sense of Lat. *ad assem* ('to the last *as*'), but the analogy of εἰς δηνάριον two lines above is probably determinant. In any case, Roman coinage is indicated.

[61] ἀπόδοτε οὖν (Matt. 22: 21).

[62] τοίνυν ἀπόδοτε (Luke 20: 25).

the Tyrians ought to have their tetradrachms and didrachms given back to them as though they belonged to Tyre because they had been minted there.[63] But the Tyrian coins bore no human ruler's name or image, and in any case the use of Tyrian coins for the payment of the Temple tax was not a political issue.[64] We must recognise the *ad hoc* and *ad hominem* character of Jesus's reply: the *denarius*, he argued, belonged to the man whose name and likeness were so plainly stamped on it – let him have it back!

His reply may well have carried an implication beyond this. So offensive, because of the breach of the Second Commandment involved,[65] was a human image on a coin in the sight of some strictly orthodox Jews that the exceptional holiness of a third-century rabbi, Nahum ben Simai, is illustrated by the fact that never in his life did he allow his eyes to look at the portrait on a coin.[66] Hippolytus, to the same effect, says of some Essenes whose practice of self-discipline went beyond the normal rules of their order that they would not even touch such a coin, since they held it unlawful not only to make, but even to carry or look at images of any kind.[67] There may, then, be the further *ad hominem* implication in Jesus's answer that such a coin as was produced for his inspection was fit only for Gentiles to handle, so that the best thing a pious Jew could do with it was to turn it over to them at once.

We must go farther and enquire what Jesus meant by adding 'render to God what belongs to God'. One interesting suggestion made in recent years is that of Professor Brandon (from whom I differ with reluctance), according to whom these words were the real gravamen of his reply, since they effectively nullified the superficial meaning of the words immediately preceding them.[68] Among the things that belonged to God was the land of Israel,[69] and therefore no part of its produce should be handed over to a pagan ruler. Had Jesus meant this, his meaning was expressed so cryptically that it might well have been missed. True, the Zealots would have agreed that the things belonging to God comprised both the land of

---

[63] J. D. M. Derrett, *Law in the New Testament* (London, 1970), p. 321. Derrett's chapter, 'Render to Caesar . . .', pp. 313ff, provides a specially full and valuable bibliography.

[64] The acceptability of the Tyrian tetradrachm for paying the Temple tax was due not to its being imageless – it bore on one side the likeness of Melkart (!) in the traditional form of Herakles, and an eagle the other side – but to its consistently high level of silver purity. Cp. A. Ben-David, *Jerusalem und Tyros* (Tübingen, 1969), pp. 6ff.

[65] Cp. also Lev. 19: 4, 'do not turn (your face) to idols'.

[66] TJ *'Abodah Zarah* 3: 1; cp. TB *Pesaḥim*, 104a, where he is called Menaham.

[67] Hippolytus, *Refutatio omnuim Haeresium* ix. 26.

[68] S. G. F. Brandon, *Jesus and the Zealots* (Manchester, 1967), pp. 345ff; cp. his *The Trial of Jesus of Nazareth* (London, 1968), pp. 66ff.

[69] Cp. Lev. 25: 23, 'the land is mine'.

Israel and the sovereignty over it which was acknowledged by the paying of tribute. But the words would not have been understood thus unless the hearers knew independently that this was the speaker's view. Certainly such a subtle way of giving a Zealot response would have provided no opportunity of denouncing Jesus to the Roman administration. It would probably be just as inopportunely subtle to say in criticism of this interpretation that even if the things belonging to God included the land of Israel, this would exclude the payment of the *tributum agri* (*soli*) but not of the *tributum capitis*. It is much more to the point to observe that the particularity of Jesus's question about the *denarius*, bearing the imperial inscription, leads straight to the conclusion that it is self-evidently Caesar's: whatever else belongs to God, a coin which by its very form and appearance contravenes his law cannot be regarded as his.

More important still: Jesus's attitude in such a matter is much more likely to have followed the tradition of the prophets than the much more recent precedent of the 'fourth philosophy'. It was not for nothing that, according to Matthew, some of Jesus's contemporaries said he was Jeremiah.[70] Jesus's counsel of non-resistance to Rome was on all fours with Jeremiah's counsel of submission to Babylon, and equally liable to be denounced as treasonable. Yet in the last days of the Judaean monarchy the country had no more devoted patriot than Jeremiah, and in A.D. 30 no one more earnestly than Jesus prayed for the peace of Jerusalem and endeavoured to make the city see that its welfare lay in quietness and not in armed rebellion.[71] The kingdom of God which he proclaimed would indeed supersede the current world-empire, but the triumph of the kingdom of God would be inherited by the 'little flock', not by the men of violence.[72]

According to Professor Derrett, Jesus meant that by giving Caesar what was Caesar's they would be giving God what was God's – in other words, 'Obey the commands of the king [emperor] and obey (thereby) the commandments of God', or 'Obey the commands of Caesar provided that the commandments of God are not broken in your doing so'.[73] This ruling he regards as based on Eccles. 8: 2, 'Keep the king's command', to which Jesus appealed in default of anything so explicit in the Torah.[74] The words

---

[70] Matt. 16: 14.   [71] Cp. Luke 19: 41ff.
[72] Luke 12: 32; 16: 16 (cp. Matt. 11: 12).   [73] Derrett, *Law*, pp. 335f.
[74] Ibid., pp. 323f; cp. I. Abrahams, 'Give unto Caesar', in *Studies in Pharisaism and the Gospels*, series 1 (Cambridge, 1917), pp. 62ff, and H. Loewe, *Render unto Caesar: Religion and Political Loyalty in Palestine* (Cambridge, 1940), pp. 21, 115f, both of whom mention the reference to Eccles. 8: 2 in *Tanḥuma* (*Noaḥ*, §10, exposition of Gen. 8: 16), where the paying of taxes is explicitly stated to be one way of keeping the king's command. Loewe also mentioned Prov. 24: 21, where fearing Yahweh and the king is coupled with the injunction not to meddle with those who are given to change (MT; LXX is different); any connection with our present pericope, more

of Eccles. 8: 2 are literally rendered 'Watch the king's mouth', which Professor Derrett relates to Jesus looking at the emperor's face on the coin – and also, allusively, to the unusual expression in Mark 12: 14, 'you do not look at (into) the face of men'. This account of the matter is interesting, but of doubtful cogency.

Even less convincing is the view that 'what belongs to God' here is the Temple tax, as though Jesus meant, 'You must pay your tribute to Caesar, and you must also pay your annual half-shekel to God.'[75] There is a pericope in the First Gospel which deals with the payment of the Temple tax,[76] but the introduction of this subject would be less appropriate here. Jesus placed a very low value on money or, as he commonly called it, 'mammon'; in saying that Caesar was welcome to the money which belonged to him in any case, he was (by his own standards) paying no excessive honour to Caesar.[77] In this context no great honour would have been ascribed to God by a ruling that God should have the money which was due to him, or to the maintenance of his Temple. 'What belongs to God' is much more likely to mean the dedication of one's whole life: the seeking of his kingdom and righteousness. Obedience to God's will is not compromised by letting Caesar have the money which bears his name.

If among the bystanders there were Zealots or Zealot sympathisers, 'Jesus' answer must have seemed a deplorable compromise';[78] nothing less than a categorical denial that Caesar had any right to tribute from the people of God would have been acceptable to them. By their standards giving to Israel's God what belonged to him demanded the withholding from Caesar of the produce of his land or the property of his people.

As for Jesus's questioners, they derived little advantage from their attempt to impale him on the horns of a dilemma. He had in so many words acquiesced in the payment of tribute to Rome, and given them no occasion to report him to the governor. Perhaps they hoped that he would forfeit the

---

particularly with οὐ μέλει σοι περὶ οὐδένος (Mark 12: 14), is a very remote possibility.

[75] Cp. Grant, *Economic Background*, pp. 100, 102, where such a view is envisaged – although Dr Grant's own interpretation is that 'the lawfulness of earthly tribute becomes a petty question of politics, best settled by acquiescence, since that frees the minds and energies of men for their true task as sons of God and members of His Kingdom' (p. 135).

[76] Matt. 17: 24–7. Cp. W. Horbury, below, pp. 265–86.

[77] Cp. E. Salin, 'Jesus und die Wechsler' (appendix to A. Ben-David, *Jerusalem und Tyros*), p. 53: 'You belong to God; therefore give yourselves to the God to whom you belong. Money is mammon, and the Roman emperor is the representative of mammon on earth. Away then with money, away with mammon; throw the money to Caesar, whose likeness it bears.' See also R. Eisler, *The Messiah Jesus and John the Baptist* (London, 1931), pp. 330ff.

[78] O. Cullmann, *Jesus und die Revolutionären seiner Zeit* (Tübingen, 1970), p. 64 (ET *Jesus and the Revolutionaries* (New York, 1970), p. 45.

good will of those around who cherished sentiments of national independence, but by bringing the explosive political issue down to such a matter-of-fact level he defused it (for the time being, at any rate). When it was considered in this light – the handing back to a Gentile ruler of coins which bore his name and image, coins which for that very reason no truly pious Jew ought to possess – it could not continue to be treated as a matter of the highest religious principle. Letting Caesar have his own coins could in no way limit the true liberty of any Israelite, or of the community of Israel as a whole. 'What belongs to God' is much more important than what belongs to Caesar; see to it that God is not deprived of *his* due, whether by giving it to Caesar or to any other person or cause. Jesus not only avoided the dilemma but turned it to emphasise the central theme of his ministry. If, however, untimely hopes of a declaration of independence had been raised by his entry into Jerusalem a day or two before, the answer about the tribute money must have discouraged them. Jesus did not command the same popular enthusiasm in Jerusalem by the end of Holy Week as he did at its outset, and his words on this occasion may help to explain that.

V

What, now, are we to make of the charge brought against Jesus before Pilate, according to Luke's narrative, of 'forbidding . . . to give tribute to Caesar'?[79] That Luke did not believe there was any substance in this charge is plain from the fact that he has previously incorporated the incident of the tribute-money and reproduced the Markan form of Jesus's reply practically word for word. Luke is the only evangelist to formulate explicitly the charge brought against Jesus by his accusers, but all the others imply that it included a claim on Jesus's part to be king of the Jews. Luke spells it out in detail: 'We found this man perverting our nation, and forbidding us to give tribute to Caesar, and saying that he himself is Christ a king.' Possibly Luke, having some knowledge of judicial practice, puts into words what Mark implies, without any other source to draw upon; possibly he had access to an independent account of the trial in which the charge was formulated in these threefold terms. Either way, his representation is consistent with Roman *cognitio* procedure, and is 'technically correct'.[80] But when Jesus's accusers informed Pilate that he claimed to be a king, they intended Pilate to understand 'king' in the ordinary political sense of resistance-leader, which inevitably involved a repudiation of Caesar's

[79] Luke 23: 2. Cp. H. P. Kingdon, *Messiahship and the Crucifixion*, StEv iii = TU 88 (Berlin, 1964), pp. 77ff; and G. Schneider, below, pp. 403–14.

[80] A. N. Sherwin-White, *Roman Society and Roman Law in the New Testament* (Oxford, 1963), pp. 25, 32.

authority and a refusal to countenance the payment of tribute to him. Luke's words, 'forbidding . . . to give tribute to Caesar', add nothing to what can be inferred from the other gospels, and cannot be used as an argument suggesting that, despite the plain implication of Mark's tribute-money incident, Jesus did nevertheless deprecate the paying of tribute to Caesar.

Like many other Gospel *pericopae*, that about the tribute money has more than one life-setting. Its life-setting during the ministry – more particularly during the later Jerusalem ministry – of the historical Jesus is plain enough. But it was not remembered and recorded simply as an interesting incident in the life of Jesus: it was recorded as a precedent for the guidance of his followers. Thus when Paul directs his Christian readers to render rulers their dues – 'taxes to whom taxes are due, revenue to whom revenue is due'[81] – he may not be quoting, or even recalling, Jesus's words but he certainly reproduces their intention, albeit in a less inflammable atmosphere. A time was soon to come, however, when Caesar demanded from the followers of Jesus things which they believed were due to God alone, and they discerned the logic of their Master's teaching clearly enough to say 'No' to Caesar.

[81] Rom. 13: 7; cp. 1 Pet. 2: 13ff. See C. D. Morrison, *The Powers that Be* (London, 1960).

The Temple tax

The early church could learn the Lord's teaching on taxation from Matt. 17: 24–7, Mark 12: 13–17 and parallels, and a passage of the Unknown Gospel (Pap. Egerton 2, Fragment 2, recto).[1] Matt. 17: 24–7, viewed with the narratives of the tribute-money, was often also referred to Roman taxation,[2] although the half-shekel was sometimes recognised as a Jewish levy.[3] The story continues to figure in discussion of Jesus's attitude to tax

---

[1] It is unnecessary to follow Hornschuh in conjecturing that *Epistula Apostolorum* 5 presupposes an independent variant of the story in Matt. 17 (M. Hornschuh, *Studien zur Epistula Apostolorum* (*Patristische Texte und Studien*, Bd. 5, Berlin, 1965), p. 11).

[2] Harold Smith, *Ante-Nicene Exegesis of the Gospels* iii (London, 1927), 211–13 (quoting St Clement of Alexandria, *Paed.* II. i 14. 1, Origen on Ezekiel, *Hom.* xii 2, on St Matthew, *Tom.* xiii 10, on Romans, *Lib.* IX, 30). In an unpublished typescript 'And to God the things that are God's,' kindly made available by Prof. M. Black, T. W. Manson also cites St Irenaeus, *Haer.* v. 24. The levy is understood as Roman tribute by St Jerome ad loc. (CCL 77, pp. 154–6), St Ambrose, *In Hexaemeron* v. vi (CSEL 32, p. 151) and *In Luc.* iv. 73–5, on Luke 5: 4 (CCL 14, pp. 133f), and St Augustine, *Enarr. In Psalmos* cxviii. 31, cxxxvii. 16, on Pss. 119: 161, 138: 8 (CCL 40, pp. 1770, 1988f). This interpretation became standard in the west, as shown by the portrayal in Masaccio's *Tributo* (1426). The passage was therefore quoted to establish clerical tax-immunity on the one hand ('liberi sunt filii', verse 26), and the liability to taxation of churchmen and all subjects, on the other ('da eis pro me et te', verse 27). See, for the former point, p. 286, n. 103, below, and Beryl Smalley, 'John Baconthorpe's Postill on St. Matthew', *Mediaeval and Renaissance Studies* 4 (1958), 91–145 (126–32); for a mediating position when dominion is pagan, Aquinas, *Summa Theologiae* IIa IIae x. 10; and for the latter point, Herbert von Einem, *Masaccios 'Zinsgroschen'* (Cologne and Opladen, 1967), pp. 14–17, to whose mediaeval references (Amarcius, York Anonymous, Aquinas, Antoninus of Florence) may be added Marsilius of Padua, *Defensor Pacis* II. iv. 9–11 (ed. C. W. Previté-Orton (Cambridge, 1928), pp. 134–9), the sermon 'Of Servants and Lords' in F. D. Matthew, ed., *The English Works of Wyclif Hitherto Unprinted* (London, 1880), p. 230, and the Homilies 'of Obedience' (1547), Part II, and 'against Wilful Rebellion' (1571), Parts II and V, in [John Griffiths, ed.] *The Two Books of Homilies* (Oxford, 1859), pp. 115, 568, 585.

[3] Melito, *Peri Pascha* 86 (ed. S. G. Hall, Oxford 1979, pp. 48f); Hilary of Poitiers, *Commentarius in Evangelium Matthaei*, XVII. 10 (*P L* 9. 1017f); Apollinarius ad loc., in J. Reuss, *Matthäus-Kommentäre aus der griechischen Kirche*, TU 61 (Berlin, 1957), pp. 27f; Cyril of Alexandria ad loc. in Reuss, *Matthäus-Kommentäre*, p. 222 and on John 4: 22 in P. E. Pusey, *Sancti Patris Nostri Cyrilli Archiepiscopi Alexandrini in D. Joannis Evangelium* i (Oxford, 1872), pp. 281–3 (ii. v). Chrysostom, *Hom. in Matth.* LVIII, identifies the didrachma as the redemption of the first-born (Num. 3: 46f), but sees (ibid. LXX) its payment by Jesus as a relevant precedent in the question of the tribute-money (*PG* 58 566f, 655). For later followers of both Chrysostom and Jerome see the clear analysis of Maldonatus, *Commentarii in Quatuor Evangelistas*, ad loc., ed. J. Martin (2nd edn. Mainz, 1853), i, 237f.

and government.[4] It is examined here with this question in mind. We consider the distinctive features of the passage, the light thrown by criticism on its evidential value, and its setting in Jewish history and the life of Jesus. On this basis an attempt is made to understand its primary meaning and historical significance.

I

Matthew 17: 24–7, a paragraph peculiar to this Gospel, stands out from the other taxation-narratives in both content and form. It begins with a question from tax-collectors rather than disputants, on the Temple half-shekel rather than the tribute-money. St Peter, who replies, is then met and taught by the Lord indoors, and commanded to pay for himself and his master with a stater to be found in a fish's mouth. The dominical teaching – payment is not obligatory, but advisable in practice to avoid offence – resembles apostolic injunctions on secular tax,[5] and is more explicit than the reply on the tribute-money.[6]

Formally, the section combines characteristics of a disputation (*Streitgespräch*)[7] with those of a miracle-story; yet the Lord does not meet the questioners, and the miracle itself is not recounted. The language has Matthaean characteristics,[8] and is striking within this Gospel as 'reasonably stylish' Greek.[9] Semitic equivalents have however been suggested for some words and phrases.[10] Verse 25 has been seen to resemble

[4] H. Loewe, '*Render unto Caesar*' (Cambridge, 1940), pp. 66–71; S. G. F. Brandon, *Jesus and the Zealots* (Manchester, 1967), pp. 49, 332n. On these see p. 284 below.

[5] Rom. 13: 5, 1 Pet. 2: 13–15, compared with the Matthaean passage in C. F. D. Moule, *The Birth of the New Testament* (3rd edn. London, 1981), p. 192.

[6] For the suggestion that τὰ τοῦ θεοῦ means the Temple tax, see J. D. Michaelis, *Commentaries on the Law of Moses* (ET by Alexander Smith, London, 1814), iii. 18f (Book IV. i, Art. 173); E. Stauffer, (*Christ and the Caesars* (ET London, 1955), pp. 133f.

[7] Especially typical of this form is the antithetical question in verse 25: see M. Albertz, *Die synoptischen Streitgespräche* (Berlin, 1921), p. 68. For an interlocutor's contribution to the argument here and in two Synoptic dialogues, see C. H. Dodd, *Historical Tradition in the Fourth Gospel* (Cambridge, 1963), p. 318.

[8] G. D. Kilpatrick, *The Origins of the Gospel according to St Matthew* (Oxford, 1946), p. 41.

[9] Moule, *Birth*, pp. 278: idem, *An Idiom-Book of New Testament Greek* (2nd ed. Cambridge, 1963), pp. 172f.

[10] τὸν ἀναβάντα (intransitive for passive) and another example of a personal pronoun used reflexively (as in ἀντὶ ἐμοῦ καὶ σοῦ, cp. F. Blass, A. Debrunner and R. W. Funk, *A Greek Grammar of the New Testament and Other Early Christian Literature* (Cambridge and Chicago, 1961), §283(2)) are cited as Aramaisms by J. Wellhausen, *Einleitung in die drei ersten Evangelien* (2nd edn. Berlin, 1911), pp. 18f, 26; also auxiliary λαβών by M. Black, *An Aramaic Approach to the Gospels and Acts* (3rd edn. Oxford, 1967), p. 125. Post-biblical Hebrew equivalents for προέφθασεν, τί σοι δοκεῖ, οἱ βασιλεῖς τῆς, τέλη, κῆνσον, ἐλευθεροί and στατῆρα are given by A.

Pap. Egerton 2 in speaking of rulers and taxes only in general;[11] but this resemblance is not more than formal.

On the age of the passage three views are held: that in its entirety it corresponds to an incident in the life of Jesus;[12] that, on the contrary, it has no basis in the life of Jesus, but was formed by the early church;[13] and that it is composite, a dominical saying or dialogue having been glossed in the church.[14] It is here taken as probable that both teaching and payment should be assigned to Jesus's ministry, since the two cohere with one another (I.(5) below) and are comprehensible within the settings of contemporary Judaism and the life of Jesus. First, however, it is necessary to review the chief arguments for dating. They are arranged below under seven headings, according to the points on which they depend.

(1) Style

That the passage contains 'features [especially participial constructions] which are linguistically the opposite of Semitic' has been thought to turn the balance of probability against the evangelist's having taken it from a source.[15] A similar conclusion has been drawn from its Matthaean impress.[16] If, then, this section of the Gospel depends on oral transmission, whereas other traditions of the ministry were available to the evangelist in

---

Schlatter, *Der Evangelist Matthäus* (Stuttgart, 1929), pp. 538–43, for τὸν ἀναβάντα πρῶτον by H. Strack and P. Billerbeck, *Das Evangelium nach Matthäus erläutert aus Talmud und Midrasch* (München, 1922), p. 773. That ἐλευθεροί corresponds to פטורים 'not liable to tax', as in Shek. i 6–7, is suggested by A. Wünsche, *Neue Beiträge zur Erläuterung der Evangelien aus Talmud und Midrasch* (Göttingen, 1878), p. 207. 'Στατήρ is one of the earliest Greek words to penetrate the Semitic languages' (first dated example 402 B.C.): S. P. Brock, 'Greek Words in the Syriac Gospels', *Le Muséon* 80 (1967), 389–426 (418).

[11] C. H. Dodd, *New Testament Studies* (Manchester, 1953), pp. 38f.

[12] Loewe, '*Render Unto Caesar*', pp. 66–71: J. D. M. Derrett, 'Peter's Penny: Fresh Light on Matthew xvii 24–7', *NovTest* 6 (1963), 1–15, revised and enlarged as *idem Law in the New Testament* (London, 1970), pp. 247–65.

[13] Fully elaborated hypotheses in R. Eisler, *Orpheus – The Fisher* (London, 1921), pp. 91–106 (99, n. 2); E. Hirsch, *Frühgeschichte des Evangeliums* ii (Tübingen, 1941), 326f; D. Flusser, 'Matthew XVII, 24–7 and the Dead Sea Sect', *Tarbiz* 31 (1961–2), 150–6. On these see pp. 272f, 276 below).

[14] A. Loisy, *Les Evangiles Synoptiques* ii (Ceffonds, 1908), pp. 63–6; C. G. Montefiore, *The Synoptic Gospels* (2nd edn. London, 1927), ii, 243–5: Kilpatrick, *Origins*, pp. 41f; H. W. Montefiore, 'Jesus and the Temple Tax,' *NTS* 10 (1964–5), 60–71; H. van der Loos, *The Miracles of Jesus* NovTestSup 8 (Leiden, 1965), pp. 680–7; R. Banks, 'Jesus and Custom', *ExpT* 84 (1973), 265–9 (266).

[15] Moule, *Birth*, pp. 217f.

[16] G. Strecker, *Der Weg der Gerechtigkeit* (FRLANT 82, Göttingen, 1962), pp. 200f; M. D. Goulder, *Midrash and Lection in Matthew* (London, 1974), pp. 396f (arguing from content as well as style).

writing, it might be suggested – although to the writer's knowledge this has not been argued explicitly – that the oral source is the less likely to have preserved pre-Easter tradition. The possible fidelity of Semitic oral transmission might be adduced against such a suggestion; but in any case, earlier steps in the argument would be open to question. On the most striking example of un-Semitic subordination, verse 25 καὶ ἐλθόντα κτλ, it may at least be asked if the elegant participle is not a secondary stylistic correction of the crude and Semitic ὅτε εἰσῆλθεν found in the Koine text (evidence in E. Nestle, K. and B. Aland, *Novum Testamentum Graece* (26th ed. Stuttgart, 1979), p. 48). Similarly, for verse 26 εἰπόντος δέ there is a 'strong v.l.' (Blass–Debrunner–Funk, §423) λέγει αὐτῷ (Nestle-Aland, loc. cit.). The number of words and phrases which can easily be rendered into a Semitic language must also be taken into account. Lastly, out of Kilpatrick's seven examples of Matthaean diction in the passage,[17] two only (προσῆλθον, τί σοι δοκεῖ) satisfy W. L. Knox's criteria of significance: one (ἀνοίξας) is a borderline case.[18] Their presence betrays the evangelist's hand, but by no means excludes the possibility of his having had a written source.[19]

(2) Position in the Gospel

The paragraph is linked with its context by the theme of precedence among the disciples. In 16: 13–20 Peter receives the power of the keys; in 17: 1–8 Peter, James and John are singled out to witness the transfiguration; in 17: 14–20 none of the disciples can heal the demoniac boy; in 17: 24–7 Peter alone shares the Lord's stater; immediately afterwards in 18: 1 the disciples ask who is greatest in the kingdom of heaven; and in 18: 18f all the disciples receive the power entrusted to Peter in 16: 19.[20]

There are indications in the Gospel that the evangelist stood at a certain

[17] Kilpatrick, *Origins*, p. 41.
[18] In a critique of Kilpatrick's collection of Matthaean expressions from Matt. 1: 18–25 and 2, W. L. Knox suggests that, for an expression to be regarded as typically Matthaean, it should be used in Matthew about twice as often as in Mark or Luke, and that where a word occurs less than ten times there should be a clear majority of five in Matthew, except perhaps where a word is peculiar to him and the other evangelists use a different word. See W. L. Knox, *The Sources of the Synoptic Gospels* (ed. H. Chadwick) ii (Cambridge, 1957), 123–5.
[19] For the conclusion (reached apparently without consideration of textual variants) that, despite Matthaean characterstics, the wording of the paragraph cannot be ascribed to the evangelist in its entirety see A. Fuchs, *Sprachliche Untersuchungen zu Matthäus und Lukas* (An Bibl. 49, Rome, 1971), p. 132. Cp. in general the conclusion in Knox, *Sources*, ii, 125, and his rebuttal of a stylistic objection to the search for sources (in this case in Mark) ibid. i (Cambridge, 1953), 1.
[20] Origen, *In Matth*. xiii. 14, on 18: 1 (GCS 40, pp. 213–16); A. M. Farrer, *St Matthew and St Mark* (2nd edn. Westminster, 1966), p. 118n.

remove from the milieu of his traditional material.[21] He is, however, unlikely to have placed the passage solely from thematic considerations, for it is internally limited to Galilee. As Knox points out, it has to occur where Peter can conveniently be sent to catch a fish.[22] Moreover – although any influence of this point upon the story might perhaps have been felt more strongly at an earlier stage than that of the evangelist himself – it seems likely that the Temple tax was collected in communities before being forwarded by them in bulk to Jerusalem.[23] Collectors would thus be met at a man's place of residence. According to tradition utilised in Matt. 4: 13 (cp. 9: 1 with the Markan parallel), but attested also in Mark and, probably independently, in the third and fourth Gospels, during the Galilaean ministry Jesus resided at Capernaum.[24]

The story would thus tend to locate itself by the sea of Galilee and at Capernaum where both Jesus and Peter lived for a time. If a form of Mark with a reference to Capernaum like that in our Mark 9: 33 already lay before the evangelist, it could in view of such possibilities have affected the placing of the passage at least as strongly as thematic considerations. Equally, the degree of prominence which the story enjoys in its position immediately before an important discourse may be fortuitous.

Care is therefore needed in arguing from the position of the passage to its date. If, for instance, the evangelist's wish to emphasise teaching relevant to a contemporary problem could be said to have gained this prominence for the passage, an origin for the story near to the time of the Gospel's composition might be made to some extent more probable; but the other considerations involved make it hazardous to infer that the placing of the passage results from such a wish. Again, it has been noted that the evangelist does not juxtapose the stories of the Temple tax and the tribute money, whereas some ante-Nicene Fathers (see n. 2 on p. 265) gave these scenes the same reference. This interpretation, as T. W. Manson points out, could most easily arise after 70, when the Temple tax became the Roman *fiscus iudaicus*.[25] May the fact that such an interpretation has not

[21] C. F. D. Moule, 'St Matthew's Gospel: Some Neglected Features', in F. L. Cross (ed.), *Studia Evangelica* ii (= TU 87, Berlin, 1964), 91–9.

[22] Knox, *Sources* ii, 101.

[23] Shek. ii. 1 'If the people of a town sent their Shekels [to the Temple] and they were stolen or lost . . .'; cp. Maimonides, *Mishneh Torah* III. vii. 2, par. 4 (edn. Amsterdam, 1702–3, Vol. I, f. 285b foot (ET in S. Gandz and H. Klein, *The Code of Maimonides, Book Three: The Book of Seasons* (New Haven, 1961), p. 414)). The importance of this point for the location of the story is emphasised by Schlatter, *Matthäus*, pp. 538, 542f.

[24] Dodd, *Historical Tradition*, pp. 235f.

[25] Manson, *loc. cit.* in n. 2, p. 265. The fact that Origen, who knows that the Jews still pay the didrachma to Rome (*Ep. ad Africanum* 14 (*PG* 11. 81)), takes the Gospel passage to deal with Roman taxation, may bear out this observation.

affected the evangelist's placing of the story indicate that he is working before 70?[26]

Two considerations seem to speak against this possibility. The tribute debate is placed by all synoptists in Jerusalem, whereas the Temple tax incident, as noted already, is internally limited to Galilee. Literary reasons would therefore forbid juxtaposition. Secondly, the exegesis of Melito and his followers (see n. 3, p. 265) shows that the interpretation in question, although widespread (see n. 2, p. 265), was not universal either early or later in the patristic period. That the evangelist should have been unaffected by it is conceivable either before or after the Jewish War.

(3) Literary analysis

Bultmann, who classifies the story as a 'legend', notes that verses 25f have a primitive ring.[27] C. G. Montefiore therefore allows for the possibility that this old logion – perhaps, as Bultmann suggests, originally bearing a different meaning – was used in the composition of a story which arose only after Jesus's death, even though it may be true that Jesus paid the tax.[28] More definite suggestions are made by G. D. Kilpatrick.[29] He sees the old core, verses 25f, as combined secondarily with a Petrine dialogue; thirdly, to meet the post-70 situation, verse 27 was introduced; lastly, the evangelist attached the story to its present setting by using Mark 9: 33. H. W. Montefiore likewise treats verse 27 as an accretion, but sees the earliest form of the story as a question to Jesus about the tax, with a reply as in verses 25f, and in conclusion a command to pay. This earliest form represents an incident in the life of Jesus.[30]

It is worth noting that the morphological distinction between the logion and its context need not imply a post-Easter origin for the latter. If the story preserves a genuine reminiscence, the saying will have been preserved by the hearer, he will have recounted it, and other tradents will have described both saying and scene. After transmission the characteristic distinction between a saying and its setting would be observable, irrespective of the setting's historical value. Secondly, as H. W. Montefiore points out, the command in verse 27 fits the situation before 70, and the period before Jesus's death, as well as (or better than) the post-war period. It will be suggested below that the allusion to miracle is not necessarily secondary.

[26] The question is raised with caution in Moule, *Birth*, p. 174 n. 1.
[27] R. Bultmann, *Geschichte der synoptischen Tradition* (6th edn. Göttingen, 1964), pp. 34f (ET *The History of the Synoptic Tradition* (Oxford, 1963), pp. 34f).
[28] C. G. Montefiore, *Synoptic Gospels* ii, 243–5.
[29] Kilpatrick, *Origins* pp. 41f.
[30] H. W. Montefiore, *NTS* 10 (1964/65) 64–8.

These analyses do not therefore permit any conclusion on the age of the story.

(4) The Temple tax

With occasional exceptions,[31] exegetes agree that the interest governing the transmission (some add, the origin)[32] of the story was the question of Christian Jews' liability to the Temple tax or its successor, the *fiscus iudaicus*. The relevance of the passage to relations with Rome in general is also stressed.[33] These observations would be consistent with an origin of the story at any time up to the composition of the Gospel itself.

Wellhausen, however, argued that the story could not be later than 70.[34] Verses 25f draw an implied analogy between the 'kings of the earth' and the divine king of Israel. They must thus refer to a tax being levied in God's name (the Temple tax was paid 'to God')[35] on his own people – who, by analogy with earthly practice, should be exempt. The saying cannot therefore (Wellhausen concluded) apply to the *fiscus iudaicus*.

This view has been challenged as introducing 'an unsuitable scientific precision into a midrashic pericope'.[36] It is true that some early interpreters (see n. 2, p. 265) applied the verses to taxation of any kind. Still – to anticipate the exegesis of the saying – such an application makes them comparatively clumsy. Instead of the parallel between earthly and heavenly kings being implied from the first, the analogy now only becomes clear as such when the word 'sons' is reached. That word will still keep the undesirable associations of its literal meaning 'sons of a Gentile King', and its metaphorical application to Israel will be harsh and sudden. It seems better to retain Wellhausen's explanation, whereby the verses are consistently metaphorical from the beginning, and plainly recall the

[31] Loewe, '*Render unto Caesar*', takes seriously the possibility – since espoused by A. N. Sherwin-White, *Roman Society and Roman Law in the New Testament* (Oxford, 1963), p. 126 – that a Roman tax is in question. John Lightfoot, *In Evangelium Sancti Matthaei Horae Hebraicae et Talmudicae* (Cambridge, 1658), p. 211, ad loc., hesitates to decide between tribute and Temple tax: the tendency of later study emerges from comparison of verse 24 AV 'tribute (*money*)' with RV 'half-shekel'.

[32] Eisler, Hirsch, Flusser (see n. 13, p. 267).

[33] Eisler, *Orpheus*, esp. pp. 95–100; W. D. Davies, *The Setting of the Sermon on the Mount* (Cambridge, 1964), pp. 389–91; R. Walker, *Die Heilsgeschichte im ersten Evangelium* (FRLANT 91, Göttingen, 1967), pp. 101–3, 134.

[34] J. Wellhausen, *Das Evangelium Matthaei* (2nd edn. Berlin, 1914), pp. 85f.

[35] Josephus, *AJ* XVIII. ix. 1 (312), τῷ θεῷ (cp. *BJ* vi. 335); Mekilta, *Yithro, Bahodesh*, i, on Exod. 19: 1 (cp. p. 280 below), לשמים .

[36] Davies, *Sermon*, p. 391, criticising E. Klostermann, who reproduces Wellhausen's view. B. W. Bacon, *Studies in Matthew* (London, n.d.), pp. 228f, to which Davies refers, does not meet Wellhausen's point. Kilpatrick, *Origins*, does not discuss Wellhausen's argument.

common midrashic comparison of God with a 'King of flesh and blood'.[37]

It is argued, again, that verses 25f can only refer to the *fiscus iudaicus*, and were probably composed in Rome under Domitian, since the Jewish half-shekel was neither paid to 'the kings of the earth' nor due from 'strangers' rather than sons, whereas the Caesars were 'kings of the earth' and their taxes were due from conquered 'strangers' rather than legally immune Roman citizens. The 'sons' on this interpretation are Christian Roman citizens, who are acknowledged in this composition to be free according to law but are urged for the sake of peace with the government to pay like their Christian Jewish brethren and indeed on behalf of the paupers and the clergy (Matt. 10: 8–10) among them.[38] This attractive theory also seems less than convincing because, like the Ambrosian exegesis on which it builds (n. 2, p. 265), it fails to recognise the metaphorical character of the saying.

Three other datings of the passage proceed from the treatment of the tax. It has been urged that the problem of liability would arise only for Christians who no longer felt themselves to be within the Jewish community. It would have been unlikely to impinge on a church such as that of the early chapters of Acts, and is still less conceivable in the life of Jesus. This point is seen as confirming suspicions of late origin.[39] Yet considerations apparently neglected here are the fact that the tax was disputed in pre-Christian Judaism (see section II below), and the likelihood that this comparatively light exaction,[40] which was not reduced for the poor,[41] would raise practical problems of payment only or especially in 'poor' communities such as those of Jesus's disciples and the early Jerusalem church.[42] Lohmeyer's conclusion,[43] that the passage represents a late compromise reached after an initial struggle with Judaism, seems to depend rather on an overall view of primitive church history than on anything in the story itself. Lastly, Flusser, who starts from the position

---

[37] For the comparison with rabbinic parable see Dodd, *Historical Tradition*, p. 381n. (with a different view of the 'moral'); Flusser, *Tarbiz* 31 (1961/62), 151f.

[38] Eisler, *Orpheus*, esp. pp. 94–7.

[39] C. H. Dodd, *History and the Gospel* (London, 1938), pp. 90f: a similar view in D. F. Strauss, *Das Leben Jesu für das deutsche Volk bearbeitet* (Leipzig, 1864), pp. 487f (ET *A New Life of Jesus* ii (London, 1865), 239).

[40] For first-century Egyptian Jews the *fiscus iudaicus* which replaced the half-shekel has been estimated as, despite an apparent surcharge, not in itself financially burdensome. See V. Tcherikover, *The Jews in Egypt in the Hellenistic–Roman Age in the Light of the Papyri* (2nd edn. Jerusalem, 1963), pp. XII (English summary), p. 94 (Hebrew); V. Tcherikover and A. Fuks (eds.), *Corpus Papyrorum Judaicarum* (Cambridge, Mass., 1957) i, 81f.

[41] Exod. 30: 15: a charitable man might pay on behalf of the poor, Shek. i. 7.

[42] So J. Kreyenbühl, 'Der Apostel Paulus und die Urgemeinde', *ZNW* 7 (1907), 180.

[43] E. Lohmeyer, *Lord of the Temple* (ET, Edinburgh, 1961, of *Kultus und Evangelium* (Göttingen, 1942)), p. 56.

that the story is a church creation, finds its origin in the Qumran community, which had reservations (see p. 279 below) on the payment of the tax. The church transferred the teaching to Jesus and added the miracle.[44] This conjecture depends on the initial assumption, which has no sufficient grounds in the story itself.

(5) The provenance of the stater

Widely disparate arguments are brought to bear on the dating of verse 27 and of the passage as a whole in the light of that verse.

(a) Critical considerations prompt the suggestion that, since the story here touches a common motif of folklore, a current legend may have been reapplied.[45] Still within this sphere it is conjectured that verse 27 was meant as a humorous hint to raise the money by selling the fish,[46] or even making a wealthy convert,[47] or that its present form is secondary and results from misunderstanding of an original injunction of this kind.[48]

Historical considerations such as those noted in the previous section may be allied with these literary–critical suggestions in an argument that the verse is a later appendix.[49]

(b) A different range of arguments from philosophy and theology can be adduced to show that if, as is probable, the text means to imply a miracle, the implication is baseless. A prominent consideration of this sort is the claim that such a miracle would lack moral justification.[50] Hence, once again, the verse would be in large part deprived of evidential value, although of course it could still be maintained that payment was made in an ordinary way (so, for instance, H. W. Montefiore, see n. 14, p. 267). On the other hand, the moral point is used by Johannes Weiss (n. 50, p. 273) to

---

[44] Flusser, *Tarbiz* 31 (1961/62), 150–6.

[45] Rich material from folklore is gathered by Eisler, *Orpheus*, pp. 100–5; for Jewish traditions see R. Meyer, 'Der Ring des Polykrates, Mt 17, 27 und die rabbinische Überlieferung', *OLZ* 40 (1937), 664–70; cp. Dodd, *Historical Tradition*, p. 225n., for further examples from Hans Andersen and modern Cyprus.

[46] H. E. G. Paulus and other eighteenth-century exegetes reviewed by C. T. Kuinoel, *Evangelium Matthaei* (2nd edn. Leipzig, 1816), pp. 505–9, ad loc.; similarly G. M. Lee, 'Studies in Texts: Matthew 17. 24–7', *Theology* 68 (1965), 380f, and Goulder, *Midrash*, pp. 396f. For criticism of such renderings see F. Field, *Notes on the Translation of the New Testament* (*Otium Norvicense, Pars Tertia*, revised) (Cambridge, 1899), pp. 13f.

[47] Eisler, *Orpheus*, pp. 93f, taking up allegorical patristic interpretation of the fish.

[48] van der Loos, *Miracles*, p. 687; J. Jeremias, *Neutestamentliche Theologie* i (Gütersloh, 1971), p. 91 (ET *New Testament Theology* i (London, 1971), 87).

[49] Different datings in Kilpatrick, *Origins*, p. 41; H. W. Montefiore, *NTSt* 10 (1964/65) 66.

[50] Strauss, *Leben Jesu*, pp. 486–9 = *New Life*, ii, 237–41; J. Weiss, *Die Schriften des Neuen Testaments* (2nd edn. Göttingen, 1907), i, p. 348; van der Loos, *Miracles*, pp. 686f.

clinch the conclusion that the whole paragraph is legendary. This range of argument is often combined with the critical considerations noted under (a).

Literary-critical considerations, examined so far as may be in isolation from philosophico-theological ones, seem not to support as unambiguously as is often assumed the conclusion that the verse is secondary to its context. It has long been recognised that reports of miracles commonly begin to circulate within the lifetime of the person to whom they are attributed, and do not simply by their presence mark as late or otherwise discredit the narratives in which they occur.[51] Further, two small but perhaps significant differences between the Gospel narrative and its folkloric parallels have been noted. E. Hirsch pointed out that whereas in folklore the precious object is found in the fish's belly, St Peter's fish has the stater in its mouth.[52] Similarly J. D. M. Derrett notes that, by contrast with the parallels, there is no question in the Gospel of the recovery of lost property.[53] These differences may be taken to reduce the likelihood that current folklore has been reapplied *tout court*. Lastly, the conjectures that the verse represents misunderstanding of commonplace advice on how to raise the money, or is a later appendix to verses 24–6, must be weighed against the observation that the method of payment described in verse 27 is peculiarly appropriate to the teaching of verses 24–6. By using a lost coin rather than drawing on the common money box (John 12: 6, 13: 29) Jesus meets the demand without acknowledging it as a legitimate charge.[54] Verse 27 thus coheres with what precedes it.

---

[51] A. Harnack, *Das Wesen des Christentums* (Leipzig, 1900), p. 17; ET *What is Christianity?* (London, 1901), p. 26; Knox, *Sources*, i, xi.

[52] Hirsch, *Frühgeschichte*, ii, 327. Note, however, among numerous parallels concerning the fish's belly, two where the precious object is found in the mouth Eisler, *Orpheus*, p. 101. That Hirsch's point is not nullified is however suggested by the fact that St Hilary of Poitiers (see n. 3, p. 265), Maldonatus ad loc. (ed. Martin, i, 238), and Strauss, *Leben Jesu*, p. 488 = *New Life* ii, pp. 240 of all note the strangeness of the coin in the mouth; while precisely this detail is assimilated to the majority of the parallels by a classicising paraphrast: 'huius pandantur scissi penetralia ventris;/illic inventum duplex dissolve tributum', Juvencus, *Libri Evangeliorum* iii. 394f. (CSEL 24, p. 95).

[53] Derrett, *Law*, p. 259n. (not in *NovTest* 6).

[54] Maldonatus ad loc. i, 239 Martin; Derrett, *NovTest* 6, 11f = *Law* p. 258; D. Daube, 'Responsibilities of Master and Disciples in the Gospels', *NTSt* 19 (1972), 1–15 (13–15). In view of Luke 8: 3, John 12: 6, 13: 29 it seems better to conclude that Jesus deliberately refrained from using the common purse (one possibility entertained by Jerome, ad loc., taken up by Hervaeus Natalis, *De Paupertate Christi et Apostolorum* (ed. J. G. Sikes in *Archives d'histoire doctrinale et littéraire du moyen age* ix (1938), 209–97 (280)) than that he had not enough to pay (the first possibility considered by Jerome, ad loc., taken up by Aquinas, *Summa Theologiae* III. xl. 3 and Wellhausen, *Matthaei*, ad loc.), perhaps because the main body of disciples was absent (Maldonatus, ad loc. i, 239 Martin; cp. Derrett, *NovTest* 6 (1963), 6, 11 =

Philosophical and theological criticism can be considered here only in so far as it is directly linked with exegesis. First, it should be noted that the *datum* of verse 27 for the theologian is not necessarily a miracle of power. 'Here I am at a loss which first to admire, the Saviour's prescience or his might' (St Jerome ad loc. (see n. 2, p. 265)). No doubt many from the first have thus understood creative power as well as foreknowledge to be in evidence here; but the implication intended may simply be foreknowledge, as probably in Mark 11:2–5, 14:12–16 and parallels, Luke 5:1–11.[55] Secondly, this is not the only synoptic miracle-story which has been thought to lack moral justification.[56] The criticisms made in this case, as stated representatively by Johannes Weiss – that the miracle satisfies no need of mankind, attains no religious goal, and appears selfish[57] – perhaps do less than justice to the moral connotations of verse 27 *lest we cause them to stumble* and the theological point, noted already, of this particular mode of payment.[58]

The likelihood of elaboration must be taken especially seriously when we verge as closely as is the case here on a motif of folklore. A scrutiny of criticisms nevertheless makes evaluation of verse 27 appear less simple than the abundance of parallels might suggest. For our present purpose it is not necessary, even if it were possible,[59] fully to reconstruct an incident in the Galilaean ministry such that verse 27 came into being. These observations may however support two conclusions bearing on historical assessment of this text. First, negatively, verse 27 provides no firm basis for dating the whole paragraph late or questioning its evidential value. Secondly, and positively, the difference between verse 27 and its legendary parallels, the coherence of the verse with its context and the moral and theological significance of payment in this particular way indicate that, despite the

---

Law, pp. 253, 257). Origen and Chrysostom (notes 2 and 3 on p. 265) emphasise that the Lord did not pay from his own resources.

[55] Hugo Grotius, *Annotationes in Novum Testamentum* i (Amsterdam, 1641), 310; Schlatter, *Matthäus*, p. 542.

[56] C. F. D. Moule (ed.), *Miracles* (London, 1965), p. 243, places the Synoptic miracles of the swine and the fig-tree in this category.

[57] Weiss, *Schriften*, i, p. 348.

[58] The force of such criticisms was less felt in patristic exegesis, which fastened on the symbolic character of the deed, setting it beside the feeding miracles (*Epistula Apostolorum* 5) as an act of divine mercy done on our behalf and foreshadowing redemption (Origen and Jerome, n. 2, p. 265; Acts of Thomas 143, adduced in different versions by F. C. Burkitt, *Evangelion Da-Mepharreshe* ii. (Cambridge, 1904), 274; St Hilary of Poitiers, n. 3, p. 265).

[59] Our ignorance of many circumstances is underlined by the variety of reasons propounded for the means of payment and its extension to Peter as well as Jesus. See the lists in St Thomas Aquinas, *Catena Aurea*, ad loc. (ed. J. Nicolai (Avignon, 1851), ii, 378) and M. Pole (Poole), *Synopsis Criticorum aliorumque Sacrae Scripturae Interpretum*, ad loc. (ed. J. Leusden (Utrecht, 1686), iv, col. 448).

strong *prima facie* case for suspecting the narrative, it is more likely to have originated in an incident than in pious imagination alone. The teaching of verses 24–6 would then have been followed, as H. W. Montefiore suggests, by payment of the tax, probably from lost property rather than the common fund.

(6) The Petrine interest

This story, like some other parts of the material peculiar to St Matthew, is strongly Petrine in interest. St Peter is sole recipient (and therefore sole transmitter) of the Lord's commands.[60] E. Hirsch founds his theory of origin on this trait.[61] He explains the story as basically a Petrine vision, analogous to that of Acts 10, received when St Peter as halakic authority was faced by the half-shekel problem. In course of time the vision was recounted as an event in the life of Jesus. This ingenious conjecture could claim consideration only if the story were in fact inexplicable as such an event.

(7) Doctrine presupposed

A pre-Easter setting for verses 24–6 has been urged on the ground that these verses, if taken as a church creation, would presuppose teaching which is atypical of primitive Christianity. This teaching would comprise an estimate of non-Christian Jews as foreigners and a claim that Christians are the true heirs of the Temple.[62] It is not clear, however, that either this estimate or the associated claim would have been unthinkable in the primitive church. That the Jews may become aliens is suggested by the warnings of Matt. 8: 11f = Luke 13: 28f, Mark 12: 9 and parallels. Outside the synoptic Gospels the theme recurs in a wide range of sources: notably Acts 3: 22f, among Pauline texts (but contrast Rom. 11: 28f) Gal. 4: 30, Phil. 3: 2f, 1 Thess. 2: 15f, in the Johannine writings John 8: 44 (cp. Rev. 2: 9, 3: 9). The repeated later query *adversus Iudaeos* 'whether this [Christian] people or the former people is the heir' (Barn. 13: 1) expects an answer already given in primitive Christianity. Again, the Temple is used constantly by Christians according to Luke–Acts (Luke 24: 53, Acts 2: 46, etc.), but no exclusive Christian claim to it is recorded, although such a claim has been conjectured.[63] The second-century accounts of St James the

---

[60] Wellhausen, *Matthaei*, p. 86. For the plural readings in verse 25 see Nestle–Aland, ad loc. and (for their secondary character) A. Merx, *Das Evangelium Matthaeus* (Berlin, 1902), p. 260.
[61] Hirsch, *Frühgeschichte*, ii, 326f.
[62] H. W. Montefiore, *NTSt*, 10 (1964/65), 67.
[63] A. A. T. Ehrhardt, *The Acts of the Apostles* (Manchester, 1969), pp. 16–19.

Lord's brother entering the Holy Place, and St John the Apostle wearing the high-priestly πέταλον (a privilege also later ascribed to James)[64] show that later thought could view the first Christians as presiding over the Jewish cult. It seems hazardous to exclude the possibility that defence of Christian access to the Temple might have taken the form of a claim to be the only legitimate worshippers there. Verses 24–6 cannot therefore be dated with any confidence on these doctrinal grounds.

This survey of criticism has led largely but not entirely to negative conclusions. A date before or after 70 cannot be argued from the position of the story, nor a date before Jesus's death from doctrine implied in verses 24–6. On the other hand, origin late in the pre-70 period, or after 70, cannot be deduced from the treatment of the Temple tax or the provenance of the stater. Verse 27 coheres with what precedes it: the ancient ring of the dominical logion does not mean that its context is only likely to have been provided after the resurrection: and the style of the whole passage does not preclude the possibility of its having been taken from a source. Lastly, the logion of verses 25f only retains consistent force if applied to tax levied in the name of God, an application only possible before 70.

The central saying therefore suggests a pre-70 date, and nothing else in the story rules this out. The passage can reasonably be considered as a whole. With these points in mind we turn to its setting in Jewish history. What was thought and practised as regards the half-shekel tax in the time of Jesus?

II

It has long been suspected that the annual half-shekel Temple tax did not arise until late in the post-exilic period.[65] Exodus 30: 13f was understood by the Pharisees as instituting an annual due, whereby all Israel shared responsibility for the cult (Shek. iv. 1). Payment of this due came to be ranked among the Positive Commandments of the Torah.[66] The Pentateuchal text, however, ordains only ransom-money on the occasions when

---

[64] Hegesippus and Polycrates of Ephesus *ap*. Eusebius, *H.E.* ii. 23, iii. 31, v. 24 (GCS 9.1, pp. 166, 264, 490): St Epiphanius, *Panarion* xxix 4 (GCS 25, p. 324).

[65] Michaelis, *Commentaries*, iii, 1–19 (Book IV i. Arts. 172–3); J. L. Saalschütz, *Das Mosaische Recht* (2nd edn. Berlin, 1853), pp. 291–3; A. Edersheim, *The Temple* (London, n.d.), pp. 72–4.

[66] No. 171 in the enumeration of Maimonides, *Sepher ha-Miṣwoth* ii (ed. Warsaw, 1883), 34: ET in C. B. Chavel, *The Book of Divine Commandments* i (London, 1940), 295. On the cult as the responsibility of all Israel see I. Abrahams, *Studies in Pharisaism and the Gospels, First Series* (Cambridge, 1917), pp. 88f.

the people are numbered. In the other relevant biblical passages[67] a yearly offering is only specified at Neh. 10: 32 (where the tax is new and the amount is one-third of a shekel)[68] and 2 Chron. 24: 5 (where no amount is named, and the account is composite). On one occasion some Elephantine Jews offered two shekels a head 'to the god *yhw*', but it is not clear if this was a regular custom.[69] Three inter-testamental sources which deal with Temple offerings fail to mention the half-shekel: Tobit 1: 6–8, the Letter of Aristeas, and Jubilees.[70] On the other hand, whatever contributions may have been levied earlier,[71] it appears that royal subsidies to the Temple sacrifices continued up to Maccabaean times.[72] This evidence has been taken to suggest that an annual half-shekel due only became regular in the Hasmonaean period,[73] perhaps at the time of the Pharisaic–Boethusian controversy over the provision of the *Tamid* in the reign of Salome Alexandra, or even later.[74]

[67] Exod. 38: 25f, 2 Kings 12: 4–16 (Hebrew 5–17), 2 Chron. 24: 4–14, Neh. 10: 32f. Cp. J. Liver, 'The Ransom of Half Shekel' [*sic*], in M. Haran (ed.), *Yehezkel Kaufmann Jubilee Volume* (Jerusalem, 1960), Hebrew section pp. 54–67: *idem*, 'The Half-Shekel Offering in Biblical and Post-Biblical Literature', *HThR* 56 (1963), 173–98.

[68] For rabbinic exegesis of this verse, not uniformly referring it to the Temple tax, see Strack–Billerbeck, *Matthäus*, p. 761 and Liver, *Kaufmann Volume*, p. 62n. = *HThR*, 56 (1963), 184n. Manasseh ben Israel, reconciling it with Exod. 30: 13, cites the opinions that Nehemiah's tax was new and distinct from the Pentateuchal one (Ibn Ezra): or, alternatively, that it was the same as the Pentateuchal tax, the shekel having increased in value (Nachmanides). See E. H. Lindo, *The Conciliator of R. Manasseh ben Israel* i (London, 1842), 198.

[69] For the papyrus listing male and female contributors (with two who made an offering to other deities) see A. [E.] Cowley, *Aramaic Papyri of the Fifth Century B.C.* (Oxford, 1923), pp. 65–76 (No. 22). For the dating in 419 B.C. (Cowley, *Papyri*, p. 66) 400 is preferred by E. G. Kraeling, *The Brooklyn Museum Aramaic Papyri* (New Haven, 1953), p. 62. Neh. 10: 32f is compared at Kraeling, *Papyri*, p. 100.

[70] E. Bickerman, 'Héliodore au Temple de Jérusalem', *Annuaire de l'Institut de Philologie et d'Histoire Orientales et Slaves* 7 (1939–44), 13f, reprinted in E. Bickermann, *Studies in Jewish and Christian History* ii (Leiden, 1980), 159–91 (167f). The significance of this silence is questioned by V. Tcherikover, *Hellenistic Civilization and the Jews* (ET Philadelphia, 1959), pp. 155, 464f (notes 6 and 12), on the ground that no relevant source deals with the Temple income. But Tobit and Jubilees, at least, treat the Israelite's responsibility for offerings, and might therefore have been expected to mention the half-shekel.

[71] Nehemiah's levy is regarded as temporary, that of 1 Chron. 24 as corresponding to the offering of Exod. 25: 1f rather than the half-shekel of the ransom (so also Michaelis and Saalschütz (see n. 65, p. 277)) in Liver, *Kaufmann Volume*, pp. 58–62; *HThR*, 56, 178–85.

[72] Ezra 6: 9, 7: 21–3; Josephus, *AJ* xii. 140 (Antiochus III); 2 Macc. 3: 3 (his son, Seleucus IV Philopator); for the idea cp. 1 Macc. 10: 39 (offer of Demetrius I Soter), 2 Macc. 9: 16 (Antiochus Epiphanes's deathbed vow).

[73] Bickerman, 'Héliodore', p. 14.

[74] Liver, *Kaufmann Volume*, pp. 66f: *HThR* 56 (1963), 189f. For a modern re-statement of the tradition that 2 Kings 12: 4 (Hebrew 5) implies an existing half-shekel levy see C. Albeck, *Einführung in die Mischna* (GT Berlin, 1971), pp. 7f.

If the annual tax was, as seems probable, of comparatively recent origin, it might be expected still to be controversial in the first century A.D.; 4Q159 (Ordinances)[75] points in this direction. A fragmentary halakic commentary on verses from the Torah, it treats the half-shekel (col. ii, lines 6ff) with emphasis: 'as for the half-[shekel, the offering to the Lord] which they gave, each man as a ransom for his soul: only one [time] shall he give it all his days'.[76] This is best understood as polemical. With the Pharisees it assumes that Exod. 30:13 institutes a regular offering. Against the Pharisees, however, this offering is seen as due only once in a man's lifetime,[77] not once a year. This exegesis probably reflects one possible legal interpretation of the period before the triumph of the Pharisaic view; while its sectarian retention shows the continuance of opposition to an annual half-shekel levy.[78]

Rabbinic sources further illuminate this opposition.[79] Rabban Johanan

[75] First edited and linked with Matt. 17:24–7 by J. M. Allegro, 'An Unpublished Fragment of Essene Halakhah (4Q Ordinances)', *JSS* 6 (1961), 71–3: republished in J. M. Allegro and A. A. Anderson, *Qumran Cave 4: I (4Q158–4Q186)*, Discoveries in the Judaean Desert of Jordan, v (Oxford, 1968), pp. 6–9 and Plate II: corrections in J. Strugnell, 'Notes en marge du volume V des "Discoveries in the Judaean Desert of Jordan" ', *RdQ* 7 (1970), 163–276 (165, nn. 3–5, and 175–9).

[76] This rendering follows the restoration and interpretation of J. Liver, 'The Half-Shekel in the Scrolls of the Judaean Desert Sect,' *Tarbiz* 31 (1961–2), 18–22 and *HThR* 56 (1963) 190–5. From his recognition of a parallel to Exod. 38:25f in Col. ii, lines 8–9 it follows that the lacunae at the end of the lines may be more extensive than allowed for in Allegro's edition, and hence that the reference to valuation money at the beginning of line 6 need not be taken to identify it with the half-shekel, but may form the end of a separate lost clause. The main point of interest in the present connection – the half-shekel payment only once in a lifetime – is, however, equally clear if Allegro's text is followed. This remains true after the corrections of Col. II, lines 6f in Strugnell, 177.

[77] Liver, *Tarbiz* 31 (1961–2), 21 and *HThR* 56 (1963), 191.

[78] A non-Qumranic origin for the law of the fragment, with the reservation that the influence of the Qumran sect's view of the Temple may be discernible in the particular instance of the half-shekel, is suggested by F. D. Weinert, 'A Note on 4Q159 and a New Theory of Essene Origins', *RdQ* 9 (1977), 223–30. Even if the interpretation of Exod. 30:13 in the fragment should turn out to be distinctively Qumranic, Shek. i. 4 (cited in the following paragraph) shows that the meaning of the verse was disputed beyond the bounds of the Qumran sect.

[79] The statement of R. Samuel (Babylon, first half of third century) cited in this connection from Ket. 106a, T. J. Shek. iv. 2 by M. Beer, 'The Sects and the Half-Sheqel', *Tarbiz* 31 (1961/62), 298f, is of doubtful historical relevance. It includes among those paid from the half-shekel the disciples of the Wise (Pharisaic sages) who taught the priests how to perform their duties. If this was so, another motive for non-Pharisaic opposition to the tax is clear. The statement may be trustworthy: cp. J. Jeremias, *Jerusalem zur Zeit Jesu* (3rd edn. Göttingen, 1962), pp. 130f (ET *Jerusalem in the Time of Jesus* (London, 1969), p. 115). On the other hand, it may simply be an inference from the principle that all ancillary Temple expenditure should be public (derived from the half-shekel) rather than private. As time goes on more such expenses are specified: with Shek. iv 1, T. Shek. ii 6 compare the longer list in Ket. 106a, T. J. Shek. iv. 2, 48a (10b in the edition in the Romm/Wilna

b. Zaccai concerned himself with the tax. In a frequently cited passage (Shek. i 4) he fiercely denied the priests' claim to immunity. His haggadah expounded the moral significance of the half-shekel, its ten component gerahs standing for the ten transgressed commandments.[80] These sayings illustrate the Pharisaic advocacy of the tax.[81] The attitude against which the Pharisees contended is illuminated by a third saying in his name, lamenting the outcome of the Jewish War with reference to Song of Solomon 1: 8: 'You would not serve God, now you are made to serve the lowest of the Gentiles, the Arabs: you would not pay to God the beka a head, now you pay fifteen shekels under your enemies' rule: you would not repair the roads and open places for the pilgrims, now you repair the posts and stations for those who go to the kings' cities.'[82] In this tripartite statement the second and third members substantiate the opening accusation 'You would not serve God.' The first supporting example is the non-payment of the Temple tax, termed the 'beka a head' in accordance with Exod. 38: 26.[83] The second example is the non-fulfilment of a duty closely associated with the payment of the tax at Shek. i. 1; the language is identical with that of the Mishnah. Thus in the speaker's eyes a chief offence of Israel has been unwillingness to pay the due which the Pharisees advocated.

The half-shekel also figures in a Mishnaic discussion of the effect of the wording of vows upon their validity, Ned. ii. 4. Here R. Judah is said to rule: 'If the vow was of undefined heave-offering, in Judaea the vow is binding, but in Galilee it is not binding.' An explanation is immediately added: '– for the men of Galilee do not recognise (or, distinguish: 'eynam makkirin) the heave-offering of the chamber' (lifted up from the half-shekels, Shek. iii. 1–4). A second ruling follows: 'If the vow is of undefined devoted things, in Judaea it is not binding, but in Galilee it is binding.' The explanation is: '– for the men of Galilee do not recognise the devoted things of the priests'.

Talmud Babli). That Pharisaic sages settled Temple procedure is itself doubted by J. Neusner, *The Rabbinic Traditions about the Pharisees before 70* (Leiden, 1971) iii, 228, 288.

[80] T. J. Shek. ii 3, 46d (6a in the edition in the Romm/Wilna Talmud Babli); W. Bacher, *Die Agada der Tannaiten* i (2nd edn. Strassburg, 1903), 32.

[81] The haggadic interpretation of Exod. 30: 13, whereby God shows Moses the fiery likeness of a coin, has obvious didactic value, and may be mentioned as further suggesting the kind of teaching which the Pharisees may have given. See Targum Ps. Jonathan and Rashi ad loc., B. Mandelbaum, *Pesikta de Rav Kahana* i (New York 1962), 34, and L. Ginzberg, *The Legends of the Jews* iii (Philadelphia, 1911), 146f.

[82] Mekilta, *Yithro, Bahodesh* i, on Exod. 19: 1; H. S. Horovitz and I. A. Rabin, *Mechilta d'Rabbi Ismael* (repr. Jerusalem, 1960), pp. 203f. For parallels see J. Neusner, *A Life of Yohanan ben Zakkai* (2nd edn. Leiden, 1970), pp. 185–7, and for an annotated text and translation S. Krauss, *Griechen und Römer* (Monumenta Talmudica V. i, repr. Darmstadt, 1972), pp. 158f, no. 372.

[83] Rendered 'einen halben Schekel' in the translation of Johanan's saying by Bacher, *Tannaiten* i, 42.

The two rulings are both given in the parallel at Tos. Ned. i. 6, where the second is credited to Eleazar b. Zadok, but the explanatory comments only occur in the Mishnah. It has been conjectured that the first comment may reflect first-century Galilaean reluctance to pay the half-shekel annually.[84] The suggestion is made tentatively, because the debate reflected in the Mishnah probably belongs to the end of the second century. This consideration is underlined by the Tosefta, for it is not impossible that its version preserves an earlier form, to which the stylised explanations of the Mishnah have been added. In any case, the object of the first explanatory comment is to show that, in a vow made in Galilee, undefined 'heave-offering' is likely to mean the priest's portion (Num. 18:8) rather than the offering from the Temple tax; and the vow is therefore invalid, since it does not mention an offering intended directly for God. Devoted things can likewise be set apart either for the Temple ('unto the Lord', Lev. 27:28) or the priest (Num. 18:14, cp. Lev. 27:21); but in this case, according to the second comment, the Galilaean is likely to mean things devoted to the Lord, and so his vow will be valid. The implication is not that Galilaeans are unwilling to pay the half-shekel, but that, unlike Judaeans, they do not have 'the heave-offering of the chamber' in mind as *the* heave-offering. The outlook envisaged as Judaean may perhaps be illustrated from Shek. iii. 3, where the household of Rabban Gamaliel are said to have cast their coins at the officer's feet in order to ensure that they were included in the heave-offering from the half-shekels, and not left over in the surplus. Ned. ii. 4 therefore hardly constitutes evidence that the Galilaeans formed a further group who were reluctant to pay an annual half-shekel in the first century; but it does show that the offering heaved up from the Temple tax was thought to have attained such a degree of significance for Judaeans, near the Temple, that it was considered 'the heave-offering' *par excellence*.

This Mishnaic comment coheres with evidence that the redemptive significance of the half-shekel, given its identification with the ransom-money of Exod. 30:13, was recognised both in Palestine and the Diaspora; the finding of a ransom may well have provided, as Philo suggests, a chief motive encouraging payment.[85] The sayings in Johanan b. Zaccai's name show, however, that despite this motive, and despite Pharisaic advocacy, Palestinian Jews at least were not paying the tax in a manner beyond

---

[84] S. Freyne, *Galilee from Alexander the Great to Hadrian* (Wilmington and Notre Dame, 1980), pp. 277–81.

[85] 'R. Eleazar said: While the Temple stood, a man paid his shekel and made atonement for himself', Bab. B. 9a: αἱ δ'εἰσφοραὶ λύτρα προσονομάζονται, Philo, *De Spec. Leg.* 1. 77 (L. Cohn and P. Wendland, *Philonis Alexandrini Opera quae supersunt* v (Berlin 1906), 20).

reproach.[86] This testimony agrees with the fact that the Mishnah provides for distraint and payment in arrear (Shek. i. 3, vi. 5). It is consistent, also, with other Palestinian evidence for the non-payment of sacred dues such as tithes, and for the evasion of civil taxes.[87]

The tax, then, probably of comparatively recent origin as a regular institution, was strongly advocated by the Pharisees. Its universal incidence would entitle all Israel to the benefits of the cult. Its redemptive significance was felt, but there was, at any rate in Palestine, less widespread willingness to pay than is often suggested.[88] The priests claimed exemption, the Qumran sect did not agree that the tax should be annual, and there were many who, for whatever reason, in practice did not pay.

III

It is this pre-70 background which the survey of criticism suggested as relevant. The tax-collectors' questions and the Lord's response can now be viewed within this setting and with reference to Jesus's life and teaching.

'Does your master pay the half-shekel?' is an understandable question, if it was known that Jesus and the disciples were supported by charity. The collectors might simply wonder if Jesus's tax was paid by a patron (Shek. i. 7). On the other hand they might suspect that Jesus would refuse to pay on some such principle as that of the Qumran community. Objections on principle, as seen already, were attacked by the Pharisees. It is then also possible that the collectors' question was linked with the Pharisaic testing on Jesus. Perhaps, in view of the searching character of the response, this is the most likely explanation. The collectors may have known that Jesus had the reputation of attacking Torah,[89] or they may have been instructed to discover his attitude on a halakic point which the Pharisees stressed.

Jesus teaches that the levy is wrong in principle, and he only pays in a manner not admitting liability. Two formal aspects of the teaching give a measure of confirmation to the view that it is dominical. The first is the primitive ring of verses 25f, where the antithetical question formally corresponds to synoptic sayings widely accepted as authentic.[90] Secondly, in Aramaic this question is likely to have had a degree of alliteration, a

---

[86] Philo (as cited in the previous note) says that the tax was paid προθυμότατα. Allowance should be made, however, for idealisation (he is emphasising the perpetuity of the Temple income) and also, perhaps, for particular devotion to the Temple in the Diaspora.

[87] Jeremias, *Jerusalem*, pp. 120–4, 141f; ET pp. 105–8, 125f.

[88] E.g. L. Finkelstein, *The Pharisees* (3rd impression, Philadelphia, 1946), i. 281; Derrett, *NovTest* 6 (1923), 2 = *Law*, p. 248.

[89] So St Cyril of Alexandria (above, n. 3, p. 265).

[90] See p. 270 above, and n. 7, p. 266.

feature characteristic of Jesus's sayings.[91] More generally, as noted already, its location in the Jewish thought-world is suggested by its resemblance to the common rabbinic comparison of God and king. A detail bearing this out is the fact noted by Schlatter that the phrase 'kings of the earth' was current in midrashic literature in a form differing from the biblical one.[92] Its usage here is thus consonant not only with direct dependence on the Bible, but also with an indirect dependence through living tradition.

In content the saying, as already noted, is most easily comprehensible if applied to this particular tax. Even earthly kings exempt their 'sons'[93] from toll and tribute. It is best to take the 'sons' as Israel in general, rather than Jesus and his followers in particular, since the unadorned description of other Jews as foreigners which the latter would imply does not occur elsewhere in Jesus's teaching. In other sayings it is Israel's election which is taken for granted (notably Mark 7: 27: cp. Matt. 10: 5f, 15: 24), while rejection is threatened rather than assumed (Matt. 8: 11f = Luke 13: 28f: Mark 12: 9 and parallels).

The Jews, then, are God's sons, and (it is argued) an interpretation which pictures their divine king as exacting something like a tribute from them does not rise to a true theology. Jesus's teaching is thus implicitly but radically critical of the Pharisaic view. The overturning of the money-changers' tables in the cleansing of the Temple would be consistent with this saying, even though the principal motives of the cleansing were probably different.[94]

Retroversion of the last words of the instruction to pay (ἐκεῖνον κ.τ.λ.) gives notably succinct Aramaic with a striking assonance.[95] As seen already, payment from lost property does not contradict the teaching. The principle on which it is made is complementary to that assumed in Mark 9: 42 par. Matt. 18: 6, Luke 17: 2: there others are not to offend the 'little ones', here the disciples are not to cause outsiders to stumble. Jesus and his followers might do so in this case either by appearing to controvert the Torah itself (the Pharisaic interpretation being assumed as correct) or by seeming to oppose the Temple. Jesus criticised Pharisaic interpretations,

---

[91] A frequent initial *Mem* would be probable, if something on the following lines may be conjectured: מאי דעתך שמעון מלכי ארעא מן מן נסבין אינון מכסא ומסא   For alliteration cp. Black, *Aramaic Approach*, pp. 160–85: Jeremias, *Theologie*, i, 371; ET pp. 27–9.

[92] Schlatter, *Matthäus*, p. 540, citing Mekilta, *Yithro, Amalek* i, on Exod. 18: 1,   מלכי האדמה (Horowitz and Rabin, *Mechilta* p. 188).

[93] I.e. their own people as opposed to subject aliens: so Wellhausen, *Matthaei*, pp. 85f; Stauffer, *Caesars*, p. 130; NEB. For tribute as a sign of servitude see Tertullian, *Apology* xiii. 6. If 'sons' is understood as 'family' or 'household' (so Derrett, *NovTest* 6 (1963), 7–9 = *Law*, pp. 254f) the interpretation offered in the text can still stand.

[94] Cp. Jeremias, *Theologie* i, pp. 144f, 200f; ET pp. 145, 207.

[95] סב והב חלפי וחלפך ? ; cp. Peshitta and Old Syriac ad loc.

and even the Torah itself (notably Mark 10: 5), while he venerated the Temple as the house of God (Mark 11: 17 and parallels, Matt. 23: 21).[96] He did not however scruple to announce its doom, and this announcement figured in the charges against him.[97] The care not to cause stumbling is therefore perhaps more likely to concern respect for the Temple.[98]

The whole passage, then, can be understood within the life of Jesus and contemporary Judaism. We consider, in conclusion, its bearing on Jesus's attitude to tax and government.

IV

Jesus's teaching here defines no doctrine on taxation levied by 'the kings of the earth', even though it has constantly been applied to secular taxes. Some modern historians, however, find in verses 25f a criticism of the Roman census, and therefore teaching comparable with Zealot belief.

Herbert Loewe[99] notes, after C. G. Montefiore, that Jesus respected the Temple. The passage, he thinks, may therefore be condemning the census rather than the half-shekel. Comparing rabbinic sayings on the tax-immunity which in principle belongs to the pious, he includes the passage in the evidence for Jesus's teaching on taxation. He draws the conclusion that Jesus's attitude here is doubtful but, on the whole, indicates that payment should be made.

D. Flusser,[100] who takes the passage as a church creation (above p. 273), accepts that it deals with the Temple tax. He thinks, however, that the saying which likens the Temple tax to the census is negative in its attitude to the latter: it means that the 'sons' (Israel) ought not to be obliged to pay it. This is comparable with the Zealot belief. Flusser sees here one more indication that the saying is not dominical: for (he argues) on the census Jesus's attitude was one of greater compromise (Mark 12: 17). The church took over this material, with its zealot-like implications, from Qumran.

S. G. F. Brandon,[101] without discussing the passage at any length or expressing an opinion on its origin, sees it as significant in connection with other evidence – such as that of the tribute-money pericope – that the payment of tribute continued to be resented in the years following Judas of Galilee's rising. He notes with approval E. Klostermann's interpretation,

[96] For a recent discussion see Jeremias, *Theologie* i, 1971; ET pp. 203–11.
[97] Mark 14: 58, 15: 29 and parallels: John 2: 19. Cp. Dodd, *Historical Tradition*, pp. 89–91: D. R. Catchpole, *The Trial of Jesus* (Leiden, 1971), pp. 126–32.
[98] A completely different explanation in Derrett, *NovTest* 6 (1963), 9–11 = *Law*, pp. 255–8.
[99] Loewe, *Render unto Caesar*, pp. 66–71.
[100] Flusser, *Tarbiz* 31 (1961–62) especially pp. 153f.
[101] Brandon, *Zealots*, pp. 49, 332n.

rejected here, that Jesus and the disciples are in principle immune from tax.

The factor common to all these views is the interpretation of verses 24–6 as criticism of the census. How justified is this interpretation?

The saying as a whole urges, as Flusser acknowledges, that God's people should not be taxed in the name of their divine king. Two points speak against the opinion that the census also is criticised. First, it is not mentioned by itself, but as one of two representative taxes, τέλη ἢ κῆνσον. Secondly, and more fundamentally, to find a criticism of the census here means neglecting the metaphorical character of the saying (cp. p. 271 above). This is not teaching about *portoria* or poll-tax, but an argument that, as the 'sons' of the kings of the earth are protected from these impositions, so Israel should be free from taxation in the name of their God. To substitute 'Israel' for 'sons', without also understanding God for the kings and the half-shekel for the secular taxes, is illicit.

To summarise: the passage originally refers to a particular problem in the interpretation of Jewish law. Does the Torah justify an annual collection of the half-shekel? The Pharisees advocated this regular levy, which entitled all alike to benefit from the sacrifices they subsidised. Jesus, on the other hand, was closer to those who attacked the innovation of annual payment, although his criticism was far more profound than that expressed in the variant *halakoth* of the priests and Qumran. He paid the tax so as not to cause offence, but in a way which did not admit liability. His teaching, couched in metaphorical form akin to that of the Midrash, sets this halakic problem in the light of the doctrine of election. He made no incidental criticism of Roman taxation. In what he said and did far-reaching principles are expressed: God does not treat his people like a subject race, offence is not to be given without cause. Yet the immediate context of both teaching and deed is provided by Jesus's relation with other interpreters of Torah.

As the early comments and the Diatessaric addition in verse 26[102] attest, the saying was soon transferred from Israel to Christ and his church. Equally, the half-shekel was sometimes, though by no means always (nn. 2 and 3, p. 265), removed from its context of Jewish law, and seen as exemplifying secular tribute. Clearly such an interpretation could support a negative attitude to civil power, Christians being considered in principle tax-free. St Jerome's deduction of this view from the passage formed the

---

[102] Christ commands St Peter: 'Thou too give, therefore, as one of them who are strangers.' Cp. Burkitt, *Evangelion* ii, 274; W. Bauer, *Das Leben Jesus im Zeitalter der neutestamentlichen Apokryphen* (1909, repr. Darmstadt, 1967), pp. 390f.

foundation of a later argument for clerical tax-immunity *iure divino*.[103] Michaelis tells of the Matthaean text being used by a Pietist to justify evasion of the Prussian excise.[104] If any first-century Christian may have wished to base similar arguments on the dominical saying,[105] he was authoritatively discouraged from doing so (Rom. 13: 5–7, 1 Pet. 2: 13–15).[106] The Lord's command in verse 27, seen within this new context as an order to pay tribute, was strongly emphasised. Its citation in the Middle Ages to defend Caesar's right to tax church and people (n. 2, p. 265) simply continues one well-marked ante-Nicene interpretation. Jesus's payment became for the early Christian an interpretative parallel to his answer on the tribute-money,[107] and the prime example of the rendering of dues enjoined in apostolic teaching.[108]

[103] St Jerome *ad versum* 25 (see n. 2, p. 265 above): for the canonists' argument, see n. 2, p. 265; Cornelius à Lapide *ad versum* 26 (*Commentaria in Scripturam Sacram*, ed. A. Crampon, xv (Paris 1877), 396) and J. Bingham, *Antiquities of the Christian Church* V, iii, 1 (ed. London, 1843, ii, 25–7).

[104] Michaelis, *Commentaries* ET iii, 14.

[105] This is assumed by Morton Smith, *Clement of Alexandria and a Secret Gospel of Mark* (Cambridge, Mass., 1971), 189, 249.

[106] Cp. E. von Dobschütz, *Die urchristlichen Gemeinden* (Leipzig, 1902), p. 97: ET *Christian Life in the Primitive Church* (London, 1904), pp. 130f.

[107] So St Clement of Alexandria and Origen (see n. 2, p. 265 above).

[108] Origen cites the passage to illustrate Rom. 13 (see n. 2, p. 265 above), and St Ambrose on Luke 5: 4 (see n. 2, p. 265 above) calls it 'magnum . . . et spiritale documentum, quo Christiani viri sublimioribus potestatibus docentur debere esse subiecti' (Rom. 13: 1).

'Not peace but a sword': Matt 10: 34ff; Luke 12: 51ff[1]

Quoted out of context – as they often are – these verses seem more appropriate to the Qur'an than to the Gospels; they sound like a cry of Muhammad proclaiming a Jihad or holy war, rather than a genuine utterance of the Prince of Peace.

Their context in the Gospels, however, is important if we are to seek to understand their original meaning. They are found in the 'double tradition', the source Q – which seems to have weathered continuous criticism – and appear in a variant form in Luke: 'do you suppose I came to establish peace on earth? No, indeed, I have come to bring *division*' (NEB) (διαμερισμόν for μάχαιραν, 'sword'). In both Matthew and Luke this saying is followed by an adaptation of Mic. 7: 6,[2] so that, for the common source of both evangelists, the conflict of division, which Christ here declares he had come to bring, was not one within nations, or even within a single nation, but *within families* – a situation all too familiar in Christian missionary history. Although omitted by Matthew, Luke 12: 49 contains a similar kind of saying ('I came to cast fire upon the earth . . .') which, there is good reason to think, comes from the same source (Q) and which certainly occurs in the same logia-group (Luke 12: 49–53), so that any interpretation of Matt. 10: 34 par. would then require to take some account of its twin-saying at Luke 12: 49.

There is ample and conclusive evidence in this sayings-complex in the Gospels that Matthew and Luke (and earlier the 'author' of Q) are 'editing' a traditional saying cast originally in poetic form[3] and composed originally in Aramaic. We should translate Luke 12: 49 (with the NEB): 'I have come to set fire to the earth, and how I wish it were already kindled!'[4] Matthew

---

[1] Another version of this article appeared in *ExpT* 81 (1969–70), 115ff, and the present article is printed by kind permission of the former editor of that journal, Dr C. L. Mitton.

[2] 'I have come to set a man against his father, a daughter against her mother, a son's wife against her mother-in-law; and a man will find his enemies under his own roof' (NEB).

[3] Cp. C. F. Burney, *The Poetry of our Lord* (Oxford, 1925), p. 90.

[4] For this use of exclamatory τί see my *Aramaic Approach to the Gospels and Acts* (3rd edn. Oxford, 1967), p. 123.

and Luke reproduce (and edit) alternative versions of an original Aramaic sayings-source.[5]

In an unpublished note, T. W. Manson has further suggested that Matt. 10: 36 is possibly a case where ἄνθρωπος should have been read as (ὁ) υἱός (τοῦ) ἀνθρώπου: the term οἰκιακός, 'member of his house', recalls Matt. 10: 25b, where it refers to 'members of the household of Beelzebul'. Luke 12: 52 could well be a paraphrase or 'targum' of this saying. This possibility widens the conflict to a 'division' between the kingdom of God and the kingdom of Satan.[6]

The parallel in Luke, 'division' – possibly a deliberate softening of the harsher expression in Matthew – makes it seem reasonable to assume that 'sword' is to be interpreted in this context in a figurative rather than in any literal sense. 'There are . . . sayings where Jesus spoke of the sword quite figuratively. This is true of Matthew 10: 34, where he says: "I am come not to bring peace, but the sword." Here the allusion is to the persecution to which every disciple will be exposed.'[7]

The assumption that there is a reference to persecution is frequently made, and, no doubt, it is chiefly in situations of persecuted minorities that such divisions are found. It is important to emphasise, however, that, so far as the evangelists are concerned, it is the division of loyalties within a 'family' which the 'sword' here signifies. The 'Micah' theme has become a commonplace of Jewish life, history and literature; and the gospel verses are simply a Christian extension of the same theme. Thus at Jubilees 23: 16, 19: 'and in that generation the sons will convict their fathers and their elders of sin and unrighteousness. . . . And they will strive with one another, the young with the old, and the old with the young'; *Mishnah, Soṭah*, 9, 15: 'with the footprints of the Messiah presumption shall increase. . . . Children shall shame the elders and the elders shall rise up before the children, "for the son dishonoureth", etc. (Micah 7: 6). The face of this generation is as the face of a dog, and the son will not be put to shame by his father.' (Danby, 306). The division 'three against two and two against three' is explained as the division of old and young, the 'generation gap';[8] the household consists of the father and mother on the one side (2), and the son, his wife and daughter, on the other (3). T. W. Manson comments: 'The

[5] Matt. 10: 34 ἦλθον//Luke 12: 51 παρεγενόμην; cp. Jud. 6: 5; 9: 37; 19: 10; 2 Kings 10: 16, LXX παρεγένοντο; Aq. ἦλθον. Heb. ויבאו ; Targ. ואתו. Foı βαλεῖν = δοῦναι, Jer. 37 (44): 18: LXX δίδως; Aq. ἔδωκας; Symm. ἐβάλετε: Heb. נתתם ; Targ. יהבתון . It is possible that חרבא (if this was the original) may have been misread as חרתא in Luke. I owe these observations to the note of Manson, mentioned above.
[6] See further below, p. 289.
[7] Oscar Cullmann, *The State in the New Testament* (London, 1957), p. 32.
[8] Cp. Mark 2: 21ff; 3: 31–5; Luke 9: 59–62; 14: 26.

picture here drawn by Jesus of the results of His work is in startling contrast to the kind of expectation shown in the rôle assigned to Elijah in Malachi 4: 5f. Here again Jesus reverses current expectations about the coming of the Kingdom.'[9]

Many will no doubt be satisfied with such an explanation of the 'sword'. We cannot be absolutely certain, however, that these words were originally spoken by Christ with sole reference to the division of loyalties which allegiance to him would bring within the family. It could conceivably have had a wider reference. If the suggestion of Manson is accepted and verse 36 is translated 'and the enemies of the Son of Man ([τοῦ υἱοῦ] τοῦ ἀνθρώπου) shall be those of his own household', the split Christ prophesied would be not just within families but within Israel itself. The conflict is then between the Son of man (or the kingdom of God) and Satan (the kingdom of Beelzebul). Luke 12: 51–2

> dwells further on the point made in verse 49. The manifestation of the Kingdom means war to the bitter end against evil; and evil is so firmly entrenched in human life and human relations that much suffering and heartbreak are inevitable before it can be cast out . . . The coming of Jesus brings tension: it brings to sharpest issue the struggle between the kingdom of God and the forces of evil. It compels man to take sides; and members of the same family may be in opposite camps.[10]

Moreover, one does not get rid entirely of the difficulty of Matthew's harsh term 'sword' by describing it as purely figurative, for while 'division' may imply 'conflict' but not necessarily 'violence', the 'sword' has all its associations with violent conflict and with the use of the armed hand.

It is on the strength of sayings like this that Jesus of Nazareth has, not infrequently, been cast in the role of political revolutionary. One of the earliest liberals, H. S. Reimarus, represented him as secretly working and preparing for a national uprising. Twice Jesus believed it to be near at hand, first when he sent out his disciples on the mission to Israel (Matt. 10: 23); the second and last occasion was after the triumphal entry, the violent challenge to authority in the Temple cleansing, and the great incendiary harangue at Matthew 23. But Jerusalem and the Jews did not respond by rising in rebellion, as they had failed to do when the disciples were sent out to rouse them.[11]

The 'political' theory of Jesus's messiahship has never been completely disproved or abandoned,[12] and, indeed, has been attracting interest again

[9] *The Sayings of Jesus* (London, 1949), p. 121.
[10] Manson, *Sayings*, pp. 120f.
[11] See further, A. Schweitzer, *Von Reimarus zu Wrede* (Tübingen, 1906), p. 19 (ET *The Quest of the Historical Jesus* (London, 1954), pp. 19f).
[12] The 1930s saw a number of these 'political' interpretations of the life of Jesus in this

in recent discussion. Thus, following the theory of Robert Eisler and Joseph Klausner that Jesus was a Galilaean Zealot, Professor S. G. F. Brandon of Manchester has reviewed the evidence again, in particular in the light of our fuller knowledge of first-century zealotism furnished by the Qumran discoveries.[13]

Jesus and his movement were, in fact, Dr Brandon argues, politically involved (Simon, one of the twelve, is called a 'Zealot', Luke 6: 15; Acts 1: 13); Jesus was crucified on charges of *lèse-majesté*. All this the Roman Gospel of Mark seeks to suppress, and Mark's apologetical interpretation of Jesus is further modified by the other evangelists into the traditional portrait of the 'pacific Christ', the Prince of Peace.

Matthew 10: 34 is cited on the frontispiece of Dr Brandon's book and referred to more than once in support of his theory: 'Verses 35f (Luke 11: 52f) appear to be an attenuated explanation of the original Messianic pronouncement.'[14] This secondary explanation of the original 'uncomfortable saying' was inspired by the primitive community's experience of what discipleship of Jesus meant in human relationships. The original pronouncement of Jesus, however, is to be understood as clearly indicative of a zealotic attitude and mission. (Cp. the statement on p. 20, 'his recorded sayings and actions signify variously both pacifism and violence'; a further reference to Matt. 10: 34 follows.)[15]

'Sword' is thus taken in the sense of violence to be applied for political ends and refers to political zealotism. This understanding of the text is further supported by Dr Brandon in his interpretation of the episode recorded at Luke 22: 35–8, which is understood as a 'record of Jesus arming his disciples, or rather his checking on their armament'.[16]

To see the possibility of a Zealot uprising behind the passion story is surely, however, to read too much into such scraps of evidence; and, in any case, as Cullmann has argued, the bearing of weapons for defensive purposes (in a land where violent attack might be expected in any situation) is all that the evidence at Luke 22: 35 need imply. Self-defence is quite different from embracing zealotism:[17]

country: Conrad Noel, *Jesus the Heretic* (London, 1939), *The Life of Jesus* (2nd edn. London, 1939); John Lewis, *Christianity and the Social Revolution*, ed. J. Lewis, K. Polanyi and Donald K. Kitchin (London, 1935); and in more recent years, Hewlett Johnson, *The Origins of Christianity* (London, 1953). Cp. also the discerning study of H. G. Wood, 'Interpreting This Time', *NTSt* 2 (1955/56), 262ff. Cp. E. Bammel above, pp. 11–68, esp. n. 351, p. 56f.

[13] *Jesus and the Zealots* (Manchester, 1967).   [14] P. 320, n. 2.

[15] For a recent clarification of Professor Brandon's views, see his note on ' "Jesus and the Zealots": A Correction', *NTSt* 17, 4 (1971), 453. Is this note completely consistent with earlier views?

[16] P. 340, note 7. Cp. also G. W. H. Lampe below, pp. 335–51.

[17] Cullmann, *State*, pp. 32f.

It is for their defense that they are to be equipped with a sword at this time. If we regard the saying as genuine (and I hold it impossible to assail its authenticity), then we must in consequence take this command seriously. Even so I do not believe we may draw the conclusion that Jesus really embraced Zealotism here, even for a moment ... He reckons with eventualities in which, for the sake of the proclamation of the Gospel, defensive sword-bearing may become a necessity for the disciples.

The passage, it seems to me, is not to be taken entirely literally as Cullmann is inclined to do. The selling up of the outer garment (the ἱμάτιον), a garment which was necessary for life,[18] and the purchasing of a sword, is vivid language to underline the extreme gravity and danger of the moment.

What has hitherto been unnoted (so far as I know) is that the word-play in τελεσθῆναι (is fulfilled) and τὸ περὶ ἐμοῦ[19] τέλος ἔχει (what concerns me has an *end*) is even more striking in Aramaic, since a very common word for 'sword' is *sayefa* (see Tj Exod. 17: 30, 2 Kings 3: 21); there is every reason why this word should have been employed in the original *logion*.[20] The Aramaic equivalents of τελεσθῆναι and τέλος are s u f (e.g., Dan. 4: 30, LXX τελεσθήσεται) and s o f a (Dan. 7: 28): τὸ γεγραμμένον δεῖ τελεσθῆναι (l e m i s o f) ἐν ἐμοί . . . τὸ περὶ ἐμοῦ τέλος (s o f a) ἔχει.

It has been argued that this genuine, apocalyptic word suggests that the message of Jesus did in fact include references to the messianic war; here Jesus is in direct contact with his Jewish apocalyptic milieu. The 'little apocalypse' is further evidence for this, even if the role played by Christian disciples seems there a purely passive one. By this word Jesus is, symbolically at least, predicting the coming final armed conflict.[21] (See further, below, p. 292f.)

Such evidence, however, could also lead to the suspicion of a 'non-dominical' zealotic origin and inspiration for our saying, in particular if it was in fact an isolated saying which the evangelists have given a 'comfortable' context: 'On the whole, there is much to be said for the suggestion that some astray Zealot phrases have somehow intruded their way into the Gospel record.'[22]

---

[18] Cp. Manson, *Sayings*, p. 51.
[19] What Aramaic lies behind τό περὶ ἐμοῦ? Has 'i l l a αἰτία (cp. Dan. 6: 5, 6) been omitted before 'a l a i περὶ ἐμοῦ, the original reading ἡ αἰτία περὶ ἐμοῦ (better κατ' ἐμοῦ) ('i l l a 'a l a i) τέλος ἔχει?
[20] The reason why, in the Greek of Luke, not ξίφος (i.e. סיפא) but μάχαιρα is used will then be simply that, since the paronomasia could not be preserved in Greek, the most natural word for sword was chosen.
[21] Cp. H. Braun, *Qumran und das Neue Testament* (Tübingen, 1966), p. 93.
[22] F. W. Beare, *The Earliest Records of Jesus* (Oxford, 1962), p. 229.

A different approach to the problem but one leading to a similar result is found in the work of modern German interpreters. R. Bultmann, for instance, removes the difficulty altogether by explaining the words as a community saying:

> We are also faced with difficulties in considering Lk 12: 51–53; Mt 10: 34–36. The prophecy in Lk 12: 52f. par. is the well-known prediction of the troubles of the end from Mic. 7: 6, which is also the source behind Mk 13: 12. Cp. E. En. 100.2; Sanh. f. 97a: 'In that age, when the son of David comes . . . the daughter will rise against her mother and the daughter-in-law against her mother-in-law'. That this prophecy now appears in Mt 10: 35 in the form ἦλθον γὰρ διχάσαι κ.τ.λ. is obviously a secondary transposition. *The Church, putting Jesus in God's place as the ruler of history, has made him proclaim that he will bring the time of terror*, and had obviously experiened the fulfilment of the prophecy in its own life. But then it is clear, that the previous saying Mt 10: 34 = Lk 12: 51 has the same meaning: in the experience of the Church can be seen the fulfilment of that eschatological prophecy, and in it all the Church knows, to its comfort in suffering, that Jesus himself has both willed it and brought it to pass. There is express defence against doubting his person and work in μὴ νομίσητε (or the questioning δοκεῖτε), which also introduces the saying in Mt 5: 17 which comes from the debates of the Church.[23] (Italics mine.)

A fresh approach to the problem which seeks to take seriously the 'zealotic' phrases (and the reality behind them) is to be found in an article entitled 'Jesu heiliger Krieg' (Jesus's holy war) by Professor Otto Betz.[24] Betz argues in this study that concepts and language coming from the Hebrew tradition of 'holy war' may be traced in the teaching of Jesus; the dark saying, for instance, about the 'storming' of the kingdom of God (Matt. 11: 12, Luke 16: 16). It was not, however, against the Roman enemy but against the embattled forces of Belial, the strong one (cp. Matt. 12: 29), that this spiritual warfare was being waged. Within this universe of discourse Matt. 10: 34 is to be understood. It is a threat (*Drohwort*) against an adulterous generation, against the godless who have no peace but will fall by the sword that will be divinely drawn in the final war when the Last Judgement breaks in on a godless world; and the no-man's-land between righteous and godless will be found even within the close fellowship of the family itself (p. 129).

---

[23] *Die Geschichte der synoptischen Tradition* (5th edn. Göttingen, 1961), p. 166. ET *The History of the Synoptic Tradition* by John Marsh (2nd edn. Oxford, 1968), pp. 154–5. For another 'solution' of the problem, see Foerster in *ThWNT* ii, 412, and cp. Stephen Neill's comment: 'this takes seriously neither what Jesus says nor the tremendous significance of what he means' (*The Interpretation of the New Testament, 1861–1961* (Oxford, 1964), p. 334).

[24] *NovTest* 2 (1958), 116f.

Micah 7:6 is adapted by the original author of this passage to give expression to this last terrible thought, but Dr Betz claims that the verse in Q also falls within the traditions of the Qumran sect. In one of the *Testimonia*[25] it is said of Levi that he will no longer know either father or mother, children or brothers, since he holds God's word and covenant in greater honour. Zeal for God may even turn his hand against the very life of members of his own family. Betz argues that behind this Qumran 'zealotry' lies Exod. 32:27–9 and Deut. 13:7–12, when all the Levites assembled to receive the command of Moses to take the sword and destroy the idolatrous worshippers of the golden calf: 'Thus saith the Lord God of Israel, Put every man his sword by his side . . . and slay every man his brother, and every man his companion, and every man his neighbour' (Exod. 32:27). So also Jesus, Betz argues, as 'the Holy One of God' (John 6:69; Mark 1:24), brings just such a sword of judgement. In the Apocalypse of John, which one could describe as a kind of 'War Scroll' of Christianity, the sword is the sign of Christ triumphant. He carries a sharp, two-edged sword which proceeds out of his mouth (Rev. 1:16; 2:12, 16; 19:15, 21). It serves for judgement on the godless, the heathen (19:15–21) or the unrepentant members of the church (2:16); but as the sword of his mouth it is a spiritual sword, the sword of his Word.

Whether Jesus himself shared in the Qumran expectation of the holy war of the last days (the Armageddon of the Apocalypse) which would herald the end and the last judgement, it is impossible to say. C. H. Dodd once noted, in a discussion of Matt. 10:34, that Jesus did expect a general upheaval to follow the crisis of his death.[26] If we can take Matt. 26:52–3 as authentic dominical utterances, then they not only make it abundantly clear that Jesus dissociated Himself absolutely from political zealotry,[27] but at the same time (verse 53)[28] would seem to imply belief in the possibility of the intervention in the destiny of the world of 'legions of angels', a heavenly warrior host, exactly as in the apocalyptic war of the Sons of Light with the Sons of Darkness. If Jesus did in fact share this item in the Zealot creed, then the sword he foretold in our text was the sword of the Lord of Hosts, or rather of his triumphant messiah. While not a political Zealot, Jesus could perhaps be claimed as an apocalyptic Zealot, proclaiming a final impending war against Belial and all his followers in heaven and on earth, even in the same family. The sword would then be an image of this terrible

[25] J. M. Allegro, 'Further Messianic References in Qumran Literature', *JBL* 75 (1956), 182f.

[26] *The Parables of the Kingdom* (rev. edn. London, 1961), p. 50.

[27] 'Put up your sword. All who take the sword die by the sword' (NEB).

[28] 'Do you suppose that I cannot appeal to my Father, who would at once send to my aid more than twelve legions of angels?' (NEB). The 'twelve' seems to be symbolic of the army of the heavenly Israel.

prelude to the last judgement, the manifestation of the wrath of God by the armies of heaven.

The 'uncomfortable words' would then follow appropriately on 12: 49 in Luke, a saying whose authenticity not even Bultmann challenges,[29] and which I have suggested earlier is a twin-saying to Matt. 10: 34.

The figure of 'fire' at Luke 12: 49 is almost certainly to be interpreted as a symbol of the divine judgement. The only satisfactory meaning the words can have in their Lukan context, where the 'fire' is parallel to and to some extent explained by the 'baptism' of Christ's death (verse 50), is that Christ anticipated that this divine judgement would be precipitated ('kindled') by his death. 'The "fire" probably signifies the fire of judgement, to be kindled as a result of the completion of his mission through death.'[30] It may well be that Christ is here represented (or interpreting his own mission) as a messianic fulfilment of the prophecy of John the Baptist (Matt. 3: 11 par. 'I baptize you with water . . . he will baptize you (with the Holy Spirit and) with fire').[31] Recent exegesis of the verse goes on to interpret Christ's death as the first instance of this impending divine judgement,[32] an anticipatory exercise of the divine *jus gladii*, but διὰ τὴν δικαίωσιν ἡμῶν. It is certainly clear that, within the whole context of verses 49–53 (and contrary perhaps to current expectations of a messianic reign of peace), Christ's baptism of fire, the penal judgement to which he willingly submitted, would be the beginning of a greater conflagration, possibly Armageddon and the final judgement itself.

To this vivid biblical symbolism of 'fire' for the wrath of God in judgement is added in Matt. 10: 34 the symbolism of the sword. The final judgement of God on the earth will be by fire and sword. The later New Testament understanding of the latter as the sword of the Spirit could be a spiritualisation of the original apocalyptic imagery, but not one that necessarily distorts or obscures its original meaning; it simply underlines the nature of the realities against which this 'holy war' was conducted, the cosmic powers of evil which the New Testament firmly believed to be at work in the universe as well as in the world of men.

[29] *Geschichte*, p. 165 (ET p. 154).

[30] G. W. H. Lampe, *Peake's Commentary* (rev. edn. London, 1962), ad loc.

[31] Cp. Manson, *Sayings*, pp. 120f.

[32] See E. Earle Ellis, *The Gospel of Luke* (London, 1966), pp. 181ff and G. Delling, βάπτισμα, βαπτισθῆναι, *NovTest* 2 (1958), 92ff (109).

W. GRUNDMANN

The decision of the Supreme Court to put Jesus to death (John 11: 47–57) in its context: tradition and redaction in the Gospel of John

I

Mark, the evangelist followed by Matthew and Luke, introduces the passion event with Jesus's entry into Jerusalem, which is preceded by the healing of a blind man as Jesus leaves Jericho (Mark 10: 46–52 par.; Matt. 20: 29–34; Luke 18: 35–43). Immediately afterwards come the cleansing of the Temple, the question about authority and the parable of the wicked husbandmen.[1] At the end there stands in all three synoptics the intention to seize Jesus, which, however, his opponents are prevented from doing because of fear of the people (Mark 12: 12). After the associated debates and the apocalyptic discourse, the decision is made in the high court to take Jesus 'by stealth' in order to put him to death. But in order to avoid a riot this is not to take place in the presence of the festival crowd.[2] 'By stealth' means therefore: secretly, without the people observing it. Fear of the people who are attached to Jesus is once again apparent. The decision of the council is fixed by Mark with a time-note: two days before the feast. The reason for the decision is made plain: the cleansing of the Temple and the parable of the wicked husbandmen which had been interpreted by the Sanhedrin members as an unmistakable attack on themselves. The Temple hierarchy, who played a leading role in the Sanhedrin, applied themselves to Jesus's arrest and destruction. While the Pharisees, or as the case may be, the scribes among their membership, often appear in the Gospels as Jesus's opponents, now they recede into the background. The Temple hierarchy leading the Sanhedrin brings about Jesus's death,[3] in that they are the persons who hand him over to the Romans.

---

[1] The fig-tree pericope (Mark 11: 12–14, 20–5; Matt. 21: 18–22) is absent from Luke, who instead offers the parable of the fig-tree elsewhere (Luke 13: 6–9).

[2] In Mark 11: 10f, 19f, 27; 14: 1 there can be seen traces of a time-scheme which spread the event over several days. Cp. W. Grundmann, *Das Evangelium nach Markus* (6th edn. Berlin, 1971), pp. 245–7; cp. J. Jeremias, *Die Abendmahlsworte Jesu* (3rd edn. Göttingen, 1960), pp. 65–7 (ET *The Eucharistic Words of Jesus* (London, 1966), pp. 71–3).

[3] Cp. G. Baumbach, 'Jesus und die Pharisäer', in *BLit* 41 (1968), 112–31, esp. 114f.

This synoptic scheme does not appear in the Fourth Gospel. Since it is difficult to accept that John knows any of the synoptic Gospels, the difference between him and the synoptics is not a question of literary criticism but rather one of tradition. Is the connection between the Temple cleansing, the question about authority and the parable of the wicked husbandmen one which was received by Mark or first constructed by him?[4] Only in the former case would one have to take account of some acquaintance with this tradition on the part of the fourth evangelist, and consequently of a deliberate transformation being undertaken by him. Since he draws the Temple cleansing back to the beginning of his Gospel with the question about authority still connected to it,[5] the key element in the Markan scheme is not available as the ultimate reason for the passion in his account. He is therefore bound to give an account of the cause of Jesus's death which diverges from the synoptics. In the Fourth Gospel this is found closely connected with the raising of Lazarus; that event is followed by the decision of the Supreme Council to put Jesus to death; joined to that is the account of the anointing in Bethany, that is, the anointing of the messianic king as he nears his death; the extension to Lazarus (12: 10f) of the plan already formed by the high priests to put Jesus to death is attached to this and shows the significance of the Lazarus event. The entry into Jerusalem, which is depicted as the reception of a king and which also contains the Lazarus reference (12: 17f)[6] triggers off the request of the Greeks. This constitutes for Jesus the signal that 'the hour is come in which the Son of man will be glorified' (cp. 2: 4; 7: 30; also 7: 6–8; 12: 23; see also 7: 39; 11: 4; 13: 1, 31; 17: 1f). The passages which speak of the hour that is future and yet is now, Jesus's glorification of the Father and his own glorification by the

---

[4] This question has been raised recently with reference to the shorter form of passion narrative, by E. Linnemann, *Studien zur Passionsgeschichte* (Göttingen, 1970); the same applies all the more to her own presuppositions. It is scarcely possible to affirm a connection between the 'triumphal' entry and the parable of the wicked husbandmen in the narrative sequence which came down to Mark in oral tradition.

[5] H. Schürmann, 'Der Bericht vom Anfang', in *Traditionsgeschichtliche Untersuchungen zu den synoptischen Evangelien* (Düsseldorf, 1968), pp. 69–80 suggests that there was a tradition concerned with the beginning of the story of Jesus. If this meets with approval then it becomes clear that in John not only the report of the end but also that of the beginning has been given a new form. On his theological viewpoint cp. W. Grundmann, Verkündigung und Geschichte in dem Bericht vom Eingang der Geschichte Jesu im Johannesevangelium', in H. Ristow and K. Matthiae, *Der historische Jesus und der kerygmatische Christus* (Berlin, 1960), pp. 289–308. By means of 1: 29; 2: 1, 4 and the position of the cleansing of the Temple and its interpretation, 2: 13–22 and 3: 14f, the Gospel of John is planned from the beginning with an eye to the crucifixion and resurrection. Cp. also J. A. T. Robinson below, pp. 455–60.

[6] Cp. M. Dibelius, *An die Thessalonicher I, II* (3rd edn. Tübingen, 1937) on 1 Thess. 4: 17; E. Peterson, *ThWNT* i, 380 (ET *TDNT* i (1964) 380f), and also 'Die Einholung des Kyrios', in *ZSTh* 7 (1929–30), 682ff.

Father, the role of Lazarus whom Jesus loves[7] – all these show clearly not only that tradition is available but also that this tradition is deliberately moulded and worked over redactionally. The redactional work of the Fourth Evangelist, however, bears an explicit theological stamp.[8] The pattern of it brings to light the interpretation of the passion event: Jesus is the giver of life; in the carrying out of the sign of giving life to Lazarus is to be found the prime cause of his own death. The giving of life by the life-giver brings death to him. That is made plain by the bringing together in the same context of the raising of Lazarus and the decision of the Sanhedrin to kill Jesus (11: 45–7). At the same time the high priest's prophetic statement makes clear that the death of the life-giver means the gift of life to mankind. In this way the fourth evangelist interprets the saying of the high priest (11: 51f), and in this way the thought is carried through in the narrative sequence from the anointing in Bethany to the request of the Greeks. The passage which tells of the redemption by Christ's passion, is set by the fourth evangelist in the context of one central theological idea and so betrays consciously undertaken redactional activity; in it the pericope about the resolution by the Sanhedrin plays the part of an essential connecting link. That his giving of life should bring death to the life-giver, and that this death is his gift of life to mankind is declared in the pericope which encloses the total event of the decision to put him to death. It has therefore a fundamental significance as theology mediated through redaction, though, at the same time, elements of tradition can still be clearly discerned in it. It must therefore be investigated in terms both of its theological redaction and of its historical contents as formed by tradition.

II

Two things are noticeable. Firstly, by contrast with the synoptic tradition, the Pharisees are involved in the decisive resolution. Secondly, this decision to put Jesus to death is not as in Mark 14: 1 fixed two days before the Passover, but quite a while earlier, some time between the Feast of Dedication in December (John 10: 22) and the Passover in April (11: 55).

The significance which the Pharisees have here is to be found in the development which occurred between the time of Jesus and the period after

---

[7] The striking emphasis on the love and friendship of Jesus for Lazarus and the extended reference suggest the thought that for the Fourth Evangelist Lazarus is the disciple whom Jesus loved (11: 3, 5, 11, 36; 13: 23; 18: 15; 19: 26; 20: 2; 21: 7, 20).

[8] On the question of tradition and redaction, cp. R. Bultmann, *Das Evangelium des Johannes* (Göttingen, 1941), p. 301, footnote 4 (ET *The Gospel of John* (Oxford, 1971), p. 395, footnote 4); E. Hirsch, *Studien zum vierten Evangelium* (Tübingen, 1936), pp. 87–94.

the Jewish war.[9] Whereas before the war they had been one group among others, they became after it the leading group which promptly determined the reorganisation of Israel and eliminated other forces. This development is reflected in the Gospel tradition; these people who become the decisive opponents of early Christianity and inflict a curse upon it[10] are made the essential enemies of Jesus too, and the dispute between Jesus and his opponents concentrates on them. Other associated Jewish groups like Zealots and Essenes do not appear, although Jesus may well have been involved in debate with them as well. All this is particularly plain in Matthew. It is all the more noteworthy that the synoptics' passion narrative speaks about the Sanhedrin and its grouping but says nothing about the Pharisees; this is therefore clear evidence of knowledge of the situation at the time of Jesus.[11] In the Gospel of John, however, the Pharisees appear more as an official body than as a party (John 1:24; 9:13–16; 11:46f).[12] Since in John the opponents of Jesus are 'the Jews',[13] account must be taken of the possibility that the passages which give to the Pharisees a directly official character and which regard them, along with the high priests, as the Sanhedrin (7:32, 45; 11:47; 18:3), belong to the tradition which has flowed into this Gospel.[14]

The decision to put Jesus to death is fixed some time before his entry into

---

[9] On the Pharisee question, cp. R. Meyer, *Tradition und Neuschöpfung im antiken Judentum* (Berlin, 1965); H. F. Weiss, *Der Pharisäismus im Lichte der Überlieferung des Neuen Testaments* (Berlin, 1965); R. Meyer–H. F. Weiss, *ThWNT* ix, 11–51 (ET *TDNT* ix (1974), 11–49).

[10] Cp. the twelfth petition of the Eighteen Benedictions prayer. S–B iv, pp. 212f.

[11] This limited judgement on the role of the Pharisees does not impinge on the problem of the controversial passage Mark 14:53, 55–65. This must be treated in its own right and by a comparison with other traditions. On this, cp. the discussion in P. Winter, *On the Trial of Jesus* (Berlin, 1961) and J. Blinzler, *Der Prozess Jesu* (3rd edn. Regensburg, 1960) (ET of 2nd edn, *The Trial of Jesus* (Cork, 1959).

[12] There are however passages where the sense is of a group or party, cp. 3:1; 9:40; according to 12:42 they are the powerful opponents of Jesus of whom even the Jewish ἄρχοντες are afraid.

[13] On this, cp. W. Bauer, *Das Johannesevangelium* (3rd edn. Tübingen, 1933), excursus on 1:19; W. Gutbrod, *ThWNT* iii, 378–81, 387f (ET *TDNT* iii (1965), 377–9, 385f); E. Grässer, 'Die antijüdische Polemik im Johannesevangelium', *NTSt* 11 (1964–5), 74–90.

[14] E. Bammel, 'Ex illa itaque die consilium fecerunt . . .', in *The Trial of Jesus: Cambridge Studies in honour of C. F. D. Moule*, ed. E. Bammel (London, 1970), p. 21 concludes that the formulation 'the high priests and the Pharisees' does not appear to be a Johannine figure of speech; he regards it as typical of the period from Agrippa to the war rather than of the preceding one. It is necessary, however, also to reckon with the possibility that it was fashioned after the Jewish war. In connection with the Pharisees there would then be within that developing situation an historicising tendency, just as in Matthew's formulation 'the Pharisees and Sadducees' (Matt. 3:7; 16:1, 6, 11f). On this cp. R. Hummel, *Die Auseinandersetzung zwischen Kirche und Judentum im Matthäusevangelium* (München, 1963), pp. 18–20. Cp. further in the text.

Jerusalem; it is publicised openly, and it issues in a demand to inform on Jesus. On the basis of this decision and with the assistance of Judas Jesus is arrested, examined and handed over to Pilate for trial (18:1 to 19:16). This account diverges from that of the synoptics. In common with Luke, John has no Jewish sentence of death (Luke 22: 66–71; John 18: 12–14, 19–24, 28), while Mark and Matthew give a report of proceedings against Jesus before the Sanhedrin which culminates in the declaration that he deserved death (Mark 14: 53, 55–65; Matt. 26: 57, 59–68); this is followed by his being handed over to Pilate (Mark 15: 1; Matt. 27: 1f). Over against this John has an explicit interrogation of Jesus based on a Sabbath healing in Jerusalem and the defence of this action by reference to his working together with the Father (John 5: 2f, 5–18). Jesus's apologia[15] is an extended discourse in which he answers the charges brought against him and also goes over to the offensive (5: 19–47). To this there is attached a discussion (7: 15–24).[16] While this discussion refutes the accusation of Sabbath-breaking (7: 21–4), the apologia deals with his relationship to the Father, which is the reason why the Jews want to assassinate him (cp. 5: 18). The whole event occurs at the Feast of Tabernacles, that is, a considerable time before the final Passover. The ensuing discussion about and with Jesus, which lasts right through to the end of the festival, is followed by a session of the high priests and Pharisees (7: 45, as also 11: 47) in which members of the Temple police report on the abortive attempt at an arrest of Jesus for which they had been commissioned.[17] This attempt had also been initiated by the chief priests and Pharisees (7: 32), just as the ultimate arrest is authorised by them (18: 3). In the events of the passion there is no completion of the debate with the Jews: that has already been finished. Rather, the climax is reached in the confrontation between Jesus

---

[15] As we have before us in John 5: 19–47 the literary form of the apologia, so in 13: 1 to 16: 33 we have that of the symposium.

[16] The original sequence may possibly have run as follows: 4: 43–54; 6: 1 to 7:13 (with 7: 12–13 forming the introduction to what follows); 5: 2–47; 7: 15–24. On this, cp. W. Strathmann, *Das Evangelium nach Johannes* (6th edn. Göttingen, 1951); W. Grundmann, *Zeugnis und Gestalt des Johannesevangeliums* (Berlin and Stuttgart, 1961), pp. 9–12.

[17] The sequence does exhibit some inconsistencies. Thus 5: 16 can be understood as an arrest of Jesus for the purpose of interrogation. In 7: 25 some Jerusalemites express their astonishment that the plan directed against Jesus with a view to killing him has apparently been abandoned. 7: 30, 32 refer to attempts at an arrest which however could not be brought to fulfilment; their collapse is recorded in 7: 45–52. Before which of these instances did the apologia occur? Different layers of tradition have become visible which (as in other passages in the Gospel) are not worked together without seams. Observations of this sort have led me to the conclusion that the Gospel of John is an ancient work which remained incomplete and whose author proceeded with great caution. On this cp. my discussion in *Zeugnis und Gestault*, pp. 7f.

and Pilate, which is concerned with *imperium Romanum* and the kingdom of God: these have their representatives in Pilate and Jesus. But in this passage it is established that for John it is the claim of Jesus to belong to God as Son to Father which constitutes the deepest reason for the opposition of the Jews to him (5: 19; 10: 30–3; 19: 7).

This outline of the story of Jesus and his passion in John is achieved with the help of a tradition which holds the decision by the Sanhedrin to put Jesus to death and Jesus's condemnation to the cross by the Romans further apart in time than is the case in the synoptics.[18] If we must reckon with the possibility that John 11: 47–57 in particular contains traditional elements, then this divergence from the synoptics cannot be explained simply in terms of the theological viewpoint of the fourth evangelist himself. This conclusion is strengthened by the observation that the Johannine tradition is confirmed by Jewish statements. In *b. Sanh.* 43a it is said:

> On the eve of Passover Jesus was hanged and a herald went out 40 days before (and cried): He is to be stoned because he practised magic and beguiled and led Israel astray. Anyone who knows any justification on his behalf should come and testify for him! But there was no defence found for him and so he was hanged on the eve of the Passover.

In an independent form therefore we have here what is contained in John 11: 54, 57. In both cases there is a gap between the decision of the Sanhedrin and its implementation. There is also an agreement between the Talmudic tractate and John 18: 28, 19: 31 as to the timing of the crucifixion,[19] and similarly about the accusation brought against Jesus that he was a beguiler of the people (so John 7: 12). Traces of a tradition of a variant scheme of the trial of Jesus, diverging from the synoptic account, are to be found elsewhere in other passages in non-Christian tradition.[20]

---

[18] The possibility of a considerable interval between the decision to bring about Jesus's death and the final Passover can be discerned in Mark 3: 6. Consequently it is necessary to allow for the possibility that the Markan account of the Passion compresses a sequence of events which in fact stretched over a longer period.

[19] Discussion of the question of the dating of Jesus's death and of the preceding events has recently been renewed, cp. A. Jaubert, 'Jésus et le Calendrier de Qumran', *NTSt* 7 (1960–1), 1–30 and *La date de la Cène* (Paris, 1957), (ET *The Date of the Last Supper* (New York, 1965)); E. Kutsch, 'Chronologie', *RGG* i (3rd edn.), 1813.

[20] Cp. Bammel, *Trial*, pp. 30–2, and also 'Christian Origins in Jewish Tradition', *NTSt* 13 (1966–7), 317–35, esp. 326f; W. Horbury, 'The Trial of Jesus in Jewish Tradition', in Bammel, *Trial*, pp. 103–21. On John 11: 54, cp. Origen, *Contra Celsum* ii. 9: 'when we had convicted him, condemned him and decided that he should be punished, he was caught hiding himself and escaping most disgracefully, and indeed was betrayed by those whom he called his disciples . . .'.

It is therefore not at all certain that John 11:45–57 is 'a Johannine construction ... behind which there is no source', a view drawn by R. Bultmann from J. Finegan,[21] or that it can be understood 'entirely as a remodelling of the Synoptics', to use the formulation of E. Hirsch.[22] Contrary to this view C. H. Dodd sees in it 'a piece of tradition' and regards it as 'improbable in the extreme that the composition of the pericope is the original work of the writer'.[23] From a form-critical angle he sees it as one of 'several scenes in which Jesus does not appear in person', which he regards as typically Johannine;[24] it is fundamentally distinguished, however, from the other scenes of this type by the fact that it is the only one in which the decisive saying is spoken by an enemy of Jesus.[25]

The detailed tradition-historical and redaction-critical analysis of the form and content of the pericope leads to the following insights. John 11:45 is the conclusion of the raising of Lazarus; faith in Jesus had been awakened in many who had witnessed that event. Verse 46 connects this with the next event: some go and inform the Pharisees, who are here, as in 9:13, depicted as the authorities. This information becomes the pretext for convening the Sanhedrin which consists of the chief priests and Pharisees (as at 7:32, 45; 18:3). Because of the signs Jesus performs, this body is plunged into perplexity.[26] The question τί ποιοῦμεν; corresponds to the πολλὰ ποιεῖ σημεῖα. The fact that Jesus's deeds are here described, even by members of the Sanhedrin, as 'signs' rouses the suspicion that the following narrative belonged to the signs source suggested and reconstructed by R. Bultmann, and recognisable also in the conclusion at 20:30.[27] If such a suggestion meets with approval it means that this *Vorlage* also contained a Passion-and-Easter narrative which was closely related to the Lukan tradition.[28] The theme of the scene, the contrast between the 'one' and the 'whole nation', is set up; it is developed as the expression of political anxiety in verse 48 and it reaches its climax in the decisive saying of Caiaphas the

---

[21] J. Finegan, *Die Uberlieferung der Leidens- und Auferstehungsgeschichte Jesu* (Berlin, 1934), pp. 30f; Bultmann, *Johannes*, p. 313 footnote 2, ET p. 409 footnote 8.

[22] Hirsch, *Studien*, p. 93.

[23] C. H. Dodd, 'The prophecy of Caiaphas John XI 47–53' in *Neotestamentica et Patristica, Freundesgabe für O. Cullmann* (Leiden, 1962), p. 135.

[24] In *Neotestamentica et Patristica*, pp. 136f.

[25] 'the general body of oral tradition which, so far as we know it, is shaped by the motive of presenting Jesus himself in significant speech and action'.

[26] On the unusual formulation τί ποιοῦμεν; cp. Bauer, *Johannesevangelium*, ad loc., to whom also Bultmann, *Johannes*, p. 313 footnote 8 (ET p. 410 footnote 5), refers.

[27] The formulations in 11:47f and 20:30f show striking agreement.

[28] On this, see W. Grundmann, *Das Evangelium nach Lukas* (Berlin, 2nd edn. 1961) pp. 17–22; P. Parker, 'Luke and the Fourth Evangelist', *NTS* 9 (1962–3), 317–36. On the connection between 11:47–57 and the passion narrative in John 18 and 19, Bammel concludes similarly: 'the reports in chs. 18 and 19 ... are based on the same source as 11:47ff', *Trial*, p. 29.

high priest, which is said to be prophetic.[29] In verse 49 this is introduced and in verse 50 it is formulated. In verse 51 it is established as prophecy, but in verse 52 it receives comment along the lines of a particularly important Johannine theological statement. If one is to see in 11: 47 the adoption and adaptation of tradition, then verse 52 was certainly not contained in the signs source but is to be traced back to the evangelist. Verse 53 contains the decision of the Sanhedrin, while verse 54 describes evasive action on Jesus's part. Verse 57 reports the decree of the Sanhedrin stating the reponsibility of anyone who knows where Jesus may be staying to pass on the information so that he can be arrested. In other words, an arrest warrant is issued. The two intervening verses 55 and 56 are on the other hand unlikely to be drawn from tradition;[30] they are similar to John 7: 10–13 and in a typically Johannine manner form an introduction to the following narrative.[31] Consequently the elements of tradition which can be traced back to the source comprise verses 47, 48, 49, 50, (51?), 53, 54, 57. It is improbable that they stood next to the raising of Lazarus since it follows from John 11: 2 that, while the Lazarus incident belonged to that signs source, it had a different position from that which the evangelist has editorially given it in his Gospel. Consequently the connecting verses 45 and 46 come from him as well. If one enquires about the context of 11: 47–57 in the signs source, then the cleansing of the Temple emerges as a possibility;[32] according to 2: 23 signs had been performed in Jerusalem by Jesus and 11: 47 could be referring to these. It could also count in favour of this possibility that the synoptic account has given to the Temple cleansing and the events consequent on it the position which the fourth evangelist gives to the raising of Lazarus.

These fragments of tradition give rise to a series of questions. The signs awaken belief in Jesus; the Sanhedrin stands in perplexity over against him. The narrator has in mind an official meeting of the Sanhedrin[33] leading to a

---

[29] Bammel, *Trial*, p. 23: John 11: 48 'contains a comparison between "one man" and the well-being of the whole nation . . .'

[30] Cp. Bammel, *Trial*, p. 35, footnote 121; verse 57 could even be linked directly with verse 54a/b.

[31] Examples of introductions of this sort: 2: 23–5 for 3: 1–21; 7: 10–13 for 5: 2–47 and 7: 15–24; 10: 40–2 for 11: 1–45; cp. also 4: 1–6 for 4: 7–42, and 4: 43–5 for 4: 46–54. They are, therefore, characteristic of Johannine style.

[32] Cp. Bammel, *Trial*, pp. 16–18; the healing of the 38-year-old invalid at the pool of Bethesda (mentioned by Bammel) also belongs to the signs mentioned in 11: 47.

[33] On συνήγαγον, A. Schlatter, *Der Evangelist Matthäus* (Stuttgart, 1929), p. 32: 'That is the established formula for the summoning of the Council or the popular assembly, the parallel word to כילס .' So also Josephus *BJ* 1: 457, *AJ* 5: 332. On συνέδριον cp. also Schlätter, *Matthäus*, p. 170; E. Lohse, *ThWNT* vii, 858–69 (ET *TDNT* vii (1971), 860–71); on John 11: 47–57 the position of Bultmann, as expressed in his commentary on John, has been taken over. Bammel, *Trial*, p. 20: 'The author is thinking of an official meeting of the Sanhedrin'.

decision in this critical situation. If one were to answer 'nothing'[34] to the question about what action of the Sanhedrin is called for by the action of Jesus, then even this policy of inactivity and *laissez-faire* must be rejected: 'If we let him go on in this way, everyone will believe in him and the Romans will come and destroy both our temple and our nation.' The influence of Jesus on the people is thus seen by the members of the Sanhedrin as a danger. The activity of Jesus reinforces the gap between the people and the Sanhedrin. The Sanhedrin members are apprehensive lest the Roman power of occupation and administration should be used to dismiss from office the existing Supreme Council on the grounds of its inability to control the situation, and along with this status to take away the place, that is the Temple, and the people.[35] This fear may originate, historically speaking, in a reminiscence of Herod's treatment of the Council (Josephus, *AJ* 14. 163–84; 15. 6); its formulation is probably determined, however, by the abolition of the Supreme Council during the Jewish war.[36] For in spite of every uncertainty, especially with regard to the high priests, who frequently changed, one thing must be observed: Caiaphas and Pilate held office simultaneously, and simultaneously lost it, the dates of Caiaphas being A.D. 18–36 and those of Pilate being A.D. 26–36. Any intrusion on the Sanhedrin's right of assembly or any threat to its continuation is completely unknown in the period between Herod and the Jewish war.

Perplexity and fear move Caiaphas to his decisive intervention. He is introduced as εἷς δέ (τις)[37] ἐξ αὐτῶν,[38] a formulation which suggests either that the name of an originally anonymous speaker has been inserted by the evangelist into his traditional material, or that the editor of the Gospel is the first to give this person a name. The explanatory reference to John 11: 49 at 18: 14 might support this suggestion. The whole context speaks of the high priest, though in a striking way; for the εἷς δέ τις is not just anybody but the

---

[34] 'τί ποιοῦμεν; is probably a rhetorical question aiming at the answer 'nothing' and grounded in the ὅτι clause. Bauer, *Johannesevangelium*, ad loc.

[35] On τόπος cp. H. Köster, *ThWNT* viii, 204f (ET *TDNT* viii (1972), 204).

[36] Cp. Bammel, *Trial*, p. 25: 'the political presentation of the case of Jesus is typical of the time after 70. . . . Further support is offered there.

[37] The reading of p⁶⁶ is only εἷς δὲ ἐξ αὐτῶν.

[38] On this cp. also Bammel, *Trial*, pp. 38f. On the question of the name, Bammel concludes that it is likely that the office-holder was named and not just introduced by εἷς δέ τις ἐξ αὐτῶν. He refers to F. Blass, A. Debrunner and R. Funk, *A Greek Grammar of the New Testament and other Early Christian Literature* (Cambridge and Chicago, 1961), §301, according to which εἷς δέ τις is an introduction which requires the naming of the person concerned. Bammel draws the conclusion (p. 39): 'The very fact that Caiaphas and not Annas is mentioned here in a passage which has no equivalent in the Synoptics points to the name as being original in the context' (p. 39). However, would that not also apply to a reference to the reigning high priest, without necessitating the mention of his name? For the evangelist it is indeed Caiaphas, but whether the same held for his source is questionable.

high priest himself. May we guess that the original *Vorlage* ran εἷς δέ τις ἐξ αὐτῶν, ἀρχιερεὺς ὢν τοῦ ἐνιαυτοῦ ἐκείνου with Caiaphas being interpolated into the text at a later stage? The basic tradition, in the event of its including a passion narrative, spoke (John 18: 13, 24) only of Annas. Then the evangelist will have constructed the reference to Caiaphas, and he it is who is responsible for the insertion at 11: 49. The relationship between Annas and Caiaphas was conceivably not without tension,[39] perhaps above all a tension between their followers. According to Luke 3: 2 and Acts 4: 6 Annas appears to take public precedence above Caiaphas,[40] and this could also be showing itself in the structure of the Johannine passion narrative. In the same way as Matthew (26: 3, 57) introduced the name of Caiaphas into the synoptic tradition, so also for John it is the latter who is the ultimately authoritative person. So it is Caiaphas who is meant in both John 11: 49, 51 and 18: 13 by ἀρχιερεὺς ὢν τοῦ ἐνιαυτοῦ ἐκείνου.[41] It is true that the high priest in the Temple at Jerusalem was not appointed for a year but counted as fundamentally non-deposable. But it had not been possible to maintain this legal state of affairs since the Syrian domination of 175 B.C. Political authorities had in fact appointed and deposed high priests. The formulation τοῦ ἐνιαυτοῦ ἐκείνου can therefore be understood in terms of cultic practice in Syria/Asia Minor where the leading priests changed annually (in this case the evangelist would be 'wrongly orientated'[42] *vis-à-vis* the Jewish legal situation). Alternatively it may be a reference to a Roman insistence on an annual confirmation of the Jerusalem high priest, which however is not attested elsewhere and can only be deduced from the Johannine construction. The third possible interpretation is the view that the genitive τοῦ ἐνιαυτοῦ ἐκείνου means nothing more than 'in that year when these events occurred'.[43] Whichever view one may prefer it is the

---

[39] On this cp. Bultmann, *Johannes*, p. 497, footnote 4, ET p. 643 footnote 3. Hirsch, *Studien*, pp. 93, 119f, traces the reference to Caiaphas back to the ecclesiastical redactor of the gospel and attributes the reference to Annas to the evangelist. W. Wilkens, *Die Entstehungsgeschichte des vierten Evangelium* (Zollikon, 1958), pp. 79f, leaves the interchange of Annas and Caiaphas in its place undisputed and explains: 'In this way he wants to represent the hearing before the Jewish authority as unimportant. For Caiaphas has indeed a long time earlier passed the definitive sentence (11: 49ff).'

[40] The possibility of an Ἅννας reading at Acts 5: 17 is reckoned with (cp. Bultmann, *Johannes*, p. 497, footnote 4 (ET p. 643 footnote 3)), though admittedly only on the basis of a conjecture by Blass. Wellhausen and Hölscher accepted this version which Hirsch, *Studien*, p. 120, described as 'the correct reading'.

[41] The genitive is lacking in p⁴⁵, e, l, syˢ at verse 51.

[42] Thus Bultmann, *Johannes*, p. 314, footnote 2, ET p. 410 footnote 10.

[43] Thus A. Schlatter, *Der Evangelist Johannes* (Stuttgart, 1930), p. 258): 'Jesus' first activity in Jerusalem and Judaea, chs. 2–4, as also the activity in Galilee which took place before the desert meal which coincided in time with the Passover, is not included by John in this ἐνιαυτός. He includes the period between the apostasy of

high-priestly office which makes the saying authoritative and gives it prophetic weight.

The Fourth Evangelist describes the high priest as a prophet and sees his prophethood as the property of his office (verse 51): 'He did not say this of his own accord, but being high priest (that year) he prophesied.' C. H. Dodd declares that this idea is the reflection of a Jewish belief of the first Christian century.[44] The contemporary Jewish and rabbinic tradition knows about high priests who hear voices and prophesy.[45] While the ancient capacity of the high priest for spontaneous oracles, the so-called Urim and Thummim, had expired after the exile, yet nevertheless in popular estimation the expectation of a prophetic capacity bound up with the office had been tenaciously preserved and constantly nourished.[46] Josephus attributes to John Hyrcanus the roles of high priest, king and prophet (*AJ* 13. 299; *BJ* 1. 68). Especially in Hellenistic Judaism, as Philo above all makes clear, prophecy and high-priesthood were connected together.[47] The Fourth Evangelist uses a tradition in which the prophetic high priest makes the decisive utterance. In this way the account, in which Jesus himself does not figure, gains the form of a narrative in which the authoritative saying is introduced by a word of the Lord.[48] What the high priest says becomes for the Fourth Evangelist the keyword for the whole event bracketed together between 10: 40 and 12: 50. The ideas λογίζεσθαι and προφητεύειν which do not occur anywhere else in John suggest that verses 45 to 51 form the

the Galileans and the Passover of the crucifixion.' But if, as proposed in footnote 16, 5: 2–47 belongs between 7: 13 and 7: 15, there stretches a full year from the pre-harvest time in Samaria (4: 35), through the Galilaean passover (6: 4), the Feast of Tabernacles in Jerusalem (7: 2, 37) and the feast of Temple purification in December (10: 22) to the passover of Jesus's death. Only the early activity of Jesus (1: 19 to 3: 36) falls outside this structure. Wilkens, *Entstehungsgeschichte*, p. 63 note 235, explains: 'The genitive refers rather to the momentous year of Jesus's activity which occurs during Caiaphas' term of office, and is therefore a temporal genitive. . . . In his basic gospel the fourth evangelist describes the activity of Jesus in the course of one year.'

[44] Dodd, in *Neotestamentica*, p. 140: 'We are therefore justified in concluding that the words of Jn. XI51 echo a popular belief of first-century Judaism.' Cp. also p. 139: 'in popular belief prophetic powers were associated with the office of high priest'.

[45] Cp. Schlatter, *Johannes*, pp. 259f; J. Jeremias, *Jerusalem zur Zeit Jesu* 2 (Göttingen, 1958) ii B, 4f, ET *Jerusalem in the Time of Jesus* (London, 1969), pp. 149f. On the high priest, see Jeremias, ibid. pp. 3–17, ET pp. 142–60.

[46] On this, cp. E. Bammel, 'ΑΡΧΙΕΡΕΥΣ ΠΡΟΦΗΤΕΥΩΝ', *ThLZ* 79 (1954), 351–6.

[47] Cp. examples in Dodd, in *Neotestamentica*, p. 139. To this Bultmann refers in *Johannes*, p. 314, footnote 4 (ET p. 411 footnote 2) particularly against Schlatter, *Johannes*.

[48] Cp. Dodd, in *Neotestamentica*, p. 140: 'The words of Caiaphas are accepted as true prophecy, and this is taken so seriously that they occupy the place in a "pronouncement story" which is normally given to a *Herrnwort*.' Neither Caiaphas's words nor the Lord's are derived ἀφ' ἑαυτοῦ; 11: 51; 5: 19; 12: 49; 7: 17.

kernel of the tradition which has come down to the evangelist and has been worked over by him.[49]

The high priest's prophetic statement begins with a sharp criticism of the members of the Sanhedrin, certifying their lack of understanding and their thoughtlessness – 'you know nothing and do not consider' – and making a proposal: 'It is expedient for you[50] that one man should die for the people and the whole people should not come to grief' (11: 50). He and they hold in common the agreed distinction between the individual and the people. It is posed as a question of expediency. The Sadducean position in ethics and politics gave to a man complete freedom in his actions and responsibility for his deeds, and it erected as norms expediency and appropriateness.[51] This position is maintained by the high priest: it is appropriate that an individual should die rather than the whole people perish. His remark takes up a saying which had almost become proverbial and which is attested elsewhere both in non-Jewish and Jewish areas.[52] The question, traceable back to 2 Sam. 20, concerning the rightness of handing over an individual in order to save many others (cp. also Jonah 1) was discussed a great deal in the rabbinate at the time of the Hadrianic persecution.[53] It is questionable whether the saying of Caiaphas implies that the Sanhedrin was engaged in discussing whether Jesus might be handed over to the Romans, since in the first century A.D. there still held good the stern prohibition of handing over a Jew. Bammel therefore concludes 'that the whole subject of extradition is outside the interest of both writer and reader of the passage'.[54] That may be right, especially if one agrees with Bammel that 'the scheme which introduces the idea of care for all (*BJ* 5. 345 refers to this) is to be seen as an independent piece of political wisdom',[55] on the basis of which he can say elsewhere 'that a principle and considerations of this kind were not unknown to members of the Sanhedrin'.[56] If we consider that in the Sanhedrin's decision there is expressed the anxiety of the members about their position, but no proposal is made about handing over to the Romans, then the high priest's declaration gains a decisive significance. What is it aiming at? One thing is absolutely clear and unambiguous: the removal of Jesus. In order to save the people from the fate of perishing (ἀπόληται), a

---

[49] Cp. Dodd, in *Neotestamentica*, p. 141.

[50] Instead of ὑμῖν some manuscripts read ἡμῖν, while in others there is nothing at all.

[51] Cp. A. Schlatter, *Die Theologie des Judentums nach dem Bericht des Josephus* (Gütersloh, 1932), pp. 186, 193, and also *Johannes*, p. 259.

[52] On this, cp. Bammel, *Trial*, p. 26 footnote 81; Bauer, *Johannesevangelium*, on 11: 50; Bultmann, *Johannes*, p. 314, footnote 3, ET p. 411, footnote 1; D. Daube, *Collaboration with Tyranny in Rabbinic Law* (London, 1965); on this, E. Bammel, *ThLZ* 93 (1968), 833–5.

[53] On this, cp. Daube, *Collaboration*.

[54] Bammel, *Trial*, p. 28.

[55] Bammel, *ThLZ* 93 (1968), 834.

[56] Bammel, *Trial*, p. 28.

fate with which they are now threatened, Jesus must die, the one for the whole nation.[57] In this statement the high priest is thinking about the destruction of the people through a Roman intervention in the face of the movement among the people stirred up by Jesus, an intervention which would be spelt out in terms of bloodbath, imprisonment and deportation. As a prophetic utterance, however, this 'perishing' has as background meaning the destruction which God's judgement brings upon mankind (cp. John 3: 16; 10: 27f; 17: 12 etc). In the face of this 'perishing' the death of the one rescues the whole people. That is the prophetic meaning of the high priest's declaration, motivated though it is by mere expediency. In view of the heavy emphasis which the evangelist lays explicitly on its prophetic sense, what is being said is this: without either knowing it or wanting it the high priest unintentionally becomes God's prophet.[58] By virtue of his office he is *jure dignitatis* a prophet. Thus even the actions of God's enemies have to subserve his plan. However great human freedom is and however far it can go, it remains always circumscribed by the will and purpose of God and even at the point of resistance must still submit to them. Bultmann speaks in this context of a 'moment of tragic irony'.[59]

But how then shall the death of the one in the place of and for the sake of (ὑπέρ) the whole people take place?[60] Is Caiaphas thinking of a swift elimination of Jesus by the Jews themselves? This possibility seems to be excluded by their statement before Pilate, when he releases Jesus to them for condemnation: 'It is not lawful for us to put any man to death.' Is the idea that Jesus should be arrested and then subsequently handed over to the Romans? This seems to be indicated, not only by the issue of an arrest warrant as a result of the Sanhedrin session (11: 57), but also by the leading of Jesus before Annas and the subsequent delivery to Pilate (18: 12–28). But on the other hand the Johannine narrative involves Roman military personnel in the arrest (18: 3, 12). That presumes a previous understanding

---

[57] Cp. Dodd, in *Neotestamentica*, p. 138: 'The death of Jesus is regarded as a means by which the Jewish nation may be saved from disaster.' He continues in the same passage: 'It is a λύτρον for Israel. It is the same conception that underlies Mark X 45, only treated in a secular spirit. . . .' On this see the subsequent observations. That one should become a substitute for the whole nation is a secular–political principle of a utilitarian kind; at the same time it is a confession of faith: Mark 10: 45 for a Jewish–Christian form, 1 Tim. 2: 5f for a Hellenistic form.

[58] Cp. Dodd, in *Neotestamentica*, p. 138: 'Whether consciously or unconsciously, the high priest is a prophet *jure dignitatis*: this is an essential element in the passage as it came down to the evangelist.'

[59] Bultmann, *Johannes*, p. 314, footnote 4 (ET p. 411, footnote 2).

[60] On ὑπέρ cp. H. Riesenfeld, *ThWNT* viii, 510–18 (ET *TDNT* viii (1972), 507–16): Riesenfeld looks for the origin of ὑπέρ-statements by reference to Jesus in the Eucharistic words over the cup (pp. 513–15 (ET p. 510f)), within which is expressed the theme of the one and the many.

between the Sanhedrin and the Romans from the beginning, an understanding which has led to their participation in the arrest. Apart from the possibility that different traditions may be overlapping here, it is possible that an interrogation by the Jewish authorities preceding a verdict by Pilate may have belonged within the terms of the negotiated agreement. If this interpretation is right, then by his vote the high priest set in motion a course of action in which the essential elements were these: (1) Preparation for the arrest of Jesus – which, because of the position of the people relative to Jesus, must be implemented with every caution. This point emerges from both synoptic and Johannine versions. (2) Agreement with the Romans as to the arrest and the course of proceedings against him, for which the Jews must hand over the relevant material (cp. 18: 33–5). This procedure could make the fears of the Sanhedrin groundless,[61] for its members would themselves help in putting down the dangerous threat: indeed, they would take the initiative in so doing. Thus far the affair is handled as an internal Jewish matter.[62] But it is only by co-operation with the Romans that it can be settled and finished with (on this there is probably agreement between the evangelist and the traditional report accessible to him). Roman participation, above all, is going to produce a frightening effect on the people who are devoted to Jesus.

III

To the prophetic saying of the high priest the evangelist adds a clarification which is significant for his own theological scheme, in fact 'one of the most characteristic and distinctive ideas of this evangelist'.[63] The evangelist says: '. . . Jesus will die for the nation, and not for the nation only but to gather into one the children of God who are scattered abroad' (11: 51f). Does this

---

61 E. Bammel has put forward the theory that 11: 48b is 'a development from the second century, replacing a different piece of reasoning . . . (its) author knew about the Jewish discussion concerning the question of extradition, and wanted by means of his own embroidery to bring the members of the Sanhedrin close to the position of *delatores* (as certainly v. 48b reads as an *ex eventu* formulation, and that indeed in pro-Roman and not Jewish terminology)', *ThLZ* 93 (1968), 834f. Cp. also Bammel, *Trial*, pp. 27f. One might be attracted to this conclusion if the idea of extradition played any role in verse 48; it seems to us, however, to be primarily an expression of perplexity and anxiety which the high priest sets himself to oppose. That is moreover recognised in Bammel's statement, cited above in the text: 'The whole subject of extradition is outside the interest of both writer and redactor of the passage' (p. 28).

62 Bammel, *ThLZ* 93 (1968), 834: 'to understand the passage entirely in a Jewish context, whether a historical one or one of literary reworking, and therefore to exclude an implicit reference to a Roman trial'; similarly in *Trial*, pp. 26–8: 'The question is treated as being an internal Jewish one.'

63 Dodd, in *Neotestamentica*, p. 134.

take up the tenth petition of the Eighteen Benedictions prayer which, basing itself on the prophetic predictions, runs: 'Sound the great trumpet for our freedom and lift up a banner for the gathering together of our exiles. Blessed are you, O Lord, who gather the dispersed members of your people Israel'? Is it the view of the evangelist that Jesus's death brings about the salvation and assembling of Israel as a renewed people of God to whom may be assigned lordship? C. H. Dodd points out in this connection that the idea of the eschatological gathering of the people of God has deep roots.[64] He alludes to Isa. 11: 12; 53: 5, Ezek. 28: 25, etc., while at the same time affirming that 'the close connection of this with the death of Christ is specifically Johannine'.[65] The statements, to which the interpretation of the prophetic word of the high priest belongs, start with John 10: 16. Jesus who manifests himself as the true shepherd, speaks of his death as the proof of the validity of his position as shepherd.[66] While his flock comprises those whom he leads out of the sheepfold in which they have been previously, now his vision extends further: 'And I have other sheep who are not of this fold; I must bring them also and they will listen to my voice. So there shall be one flock, one shepherd' (10: 16). In this passage it is clear that the bringing together into the one flock by the one shepherd is linked with his death. John 10: 16 is preceded by the statement 'I lay down my life for the sheep' and followed by the statement about the complete voluntariness of this laying down of life (10: 15b and 17f). But it is also clear that the other sheep whom he must bring are not the Jews of the Dispersion: they are not of this fold. The fourth evangelist goes far beyond and indeed remodels the expectation voiced in the Eighteen Benedictions prayer. This is made even clearer in the ensuing passage, John 11: 52. When the request of the Greeks who have come to the feast (probably proselytes,[67] who represent the non-Jews, the nations of the world) is passed on to him, Jesus knows that his

[64] Cp. S–B iv, 212; on the gathering together of the dispersed, iv, 902–10.

[65] Dodd, in *Neotestamentica*, p. 134 footnote 2. An inner connection between the prophecy of the high priest and the evangelist's explanation is something which M. Barker, 'John 11: 50', in E. Bammel, ed., *Trial*, pp. 41–6, would like to propose with the help of the expectation of Messiah ben Joseph. To this Caiaphas alludes, and the evangelist has it in mind. This hope was widespread in Galilee: he must die before the Messiah ben David will come. M. Barker concludes (p. 46): 'The remark of Caiaphas effectively turns against the despised Galileans their own messianic hopes. The Messiah ben Joseph had to die before the Messiah ben David could appear (cf. here Acts 3: 20), and if it was expedient that one man should die for the people, who was Caiaphas to prevent this?' On the question of Messiah ben Joseph, cp. S–B ii, 292–9.

[66] Cp. on this, W. Grundmann, *ThWNT* iii, 550 (ET *TDNT* iii (1965), 548f).

[67] Similarly Bultmann, *Johannes*, p. 323 footnote 6 (ET p. 423, footnote 2). In the text: 'Doubtless these are so-called proselytes; if they are not described as such . . . but rather as Ἕλληνες that is clearly because they are to be understood as representatives of the Greek world.'

hour has come (12:20–3). The hour is his death (cp. 13:1), of which he speaks by means of the metaphor of 'lifting up'.[68] It is the hour of κρίσις for the world of men. The ruler of this world, who determines it, loses his position;[69] into his place there enters the one lifted up from the earth: 'I, when I am lifted up from the earth, will draw all men to myself' (12:31f). Drawing them to himself he gathers them and forges them into 'a unity'.[70] Since Jesus is speaking about his cross whenever he speaks of his exaltation, and since this cross is at one and the same time his own glorification and that of the Father,[71] this drawing-to-himself issues in a following after him in his sufferings, within which at the same time the exaltation occurs (12:24–6).[72] 'The sheep who are not of this fold', that is, Greek non-Jews, are 'those who believe in me through their word' (17:20) and concerning whose unification he prays (17:21–3); these are the ones to whom his disciples are sent out, equipped with the Holy Spirit who brings them to new birth from above, and equipped with the authority to forgive sins (20:21–3); in them he continues his mission and through them his work of drawing men is carried out. If in John 11:52 those whom he wants 'to gather into one' are called the children of God who are scattered abroad, then this term may be understood in a potential sense. According to John 1:12 the authority to become God's sons is the gift of the Logos to those who receive him; to receive him means to believe on his name; to believe on his name is, however, to be born of God. It is made plain in the conversation with Nicodemus that 'being born of God' and therefore 'believing on his name' includes within itself the reception of eternal life. A man receives this

---

[68] Cp. on this, G. Bertram, *ThWNT* viii, 608f (ET *TDNT* viii (1972), 610f); cp. W. Thüsing, *Die Erhöhung und Verherrlichung Jesu im Johannesevangelium* (Münster, 1960), pp. 3–37.

[69] Behind this saying stands the picture of Satan being thrown out of heaven. The presupposition of this is Job 1 and 2 where Satan is the heavenly accuser. This picture is further developed in Rev. 12:7–12, and there are traces also in Luke 10:18, 22:31f and John 12:31. The removal of the accuser, who must give up his place to the advocate, enables this work of assembling and leading to be carried out without any limits being imposed. The activity, dying and rising of Jesus are placed within the context of this eschatological conflict with Satan; in John, this, like all eschatological–apocalyptic affirmations, is referred to the presentness of Jesus in which the future is already concentrated.

[70] Ideas of the ascending redeemer and the journey of the souls to heaven are here making a contribution, cp. Bultmann, *Johannes*, p. 330 (ET p. 431).

[71] The two-sided showing of respect and glorification which applies to the whole career of Jesus are brought to completion in the passion and Easter (7:39; 11:4; 12:23; 13:31f; 17:1, 4, 5, 24). Jesus shows all honour to the Father and glorifies him in that he demonstrates by the laying down of his life his total love for the Father (14:30f). The Father shows all honour to the Son and glorifies him in that he exalts him to himself through death. The glorification and honouring of God's name as Father is his word and his mission.

[72] Cp. on this, Bultmann, *Johannes*, pp. 330f (ET pp. 431f).

from the Spirit into his earthly existence (which is comparable with a mother's womb). This receiving of life takes place through the hearing of the word (6: 63), and its hidden life is released into its perfect form when one dies (3: 1–10, 16; 16: 20–2).[73] Since Jesus gives the authority for divine sonship to those whom the Father has given him (6: 37, 39, 65; 17: 6), those mentioned at 11: 52 are children of God, because they are amongst those whom the Father has given him; this is the authorisation for their becoming children of God. As such potential children of God they are scattered in the world of men but brought to a unity in him and together brought to the Father (17: 20–3). His death releases his work which had been limited to Israel and makes it universal, and this no longer limited work is implemented through his disciples (14: 12). That is the decisive event of his death: the one who for his own people is there on the earth, is now exalted to a possibility of effectiveness which is no longer subject to the previous limitation of being in the flesh. Consequently his death is the event which becomes effective for an historical future and in which the eternal future of the believer is involved (12: 26; 17: 24; 14: 2f).

IV

Does the Johannine interpretation of the high priest's statement, described by him as prophetic, displace an event which originally had a political character? Does it transform a political revolutionary leader, ultimately shattered in confrontation with the Roman occupying power, into 'the saviour of the world' (4: 42)? For one thing is quite clear: it was Pilate who pronounced sentence against Jesus. He condemned him to death by crucifixion and confirmed it in the superscription, 'Jesus of Nazareth, the king of the Jews' (19: 19). Thus Pilate treated Jesus as a Zealot revolutionary. Suspicion of this at least has not been far from the minds of the high priest and of the members of the Sanhedrin. They refer to his influence on the people, which is regarded as growing. This suspicion is strengthened by the fact that according to the Johannine narrative the Romans had already been involved in the arrest of Jesus. The synoptic Gospels underline more emphatically than John the Jewish participation in the event which led to Jesus's crucifixion. But is the Johannine account of Jesus's passion supposed to link up with the fact that in his view Jesus's death releases his work from the limitation to Israel and makes it effective for mankind as a whole? In other words is it part of the movement out of the area of the Jews into that of the cosmos, the whole world? The debate

---

[73] It is possible that the old Christian evaluation of the day of death as a day of birth into eternal life is connected with this statement.

between Jesus and the Jews is concluded with the Sanhedrin's decision to bring about his death; the proceedings before Annas are the bridge leading to the trial and the death. That death is prepared by the Romans and leads to his work for mankind. Jesus's response to Pilate (18: 28 to 19: 21) is determined by the theme which is decisive for this, namely Jesus as the witness to the truth in the face of an *imperium* which is based solely on human might and which leaves open the question of truth.

Now the Johannine account leaves no doubt about Jesus's career's having had political effect. The signs which he does rouse in the minds of the people the idea that he is a messianic prophet and therefore provoke the intention to proclaim him king (6: 14f). According to the evangelist, political expectations and hopes are excited by Jesus, but he turns firmly away from them. His path to kingship does not lead via the battle-field and the gaining of power, but rather through his death on the cross.[74] The disappointment he brings to his Galilaean followers leads, according to the Johannine version, to the great falling away in that area, after which only the Twelve remain (6: 60, 66 to 7: 10). In Jerusalem the people are divided and kept under by the pressure of fear of the priestly authorities, and it is this which forces Jesus to go up to Jerusalem incognito for the Feast of Tabernacles (John 7: 10–13). Admittedly he cannot maintain this incognito and shows himself a free agent over against the pressure of fear (5: 2–47; 7: 15–44). In fact, such is his freedom that this pressure becomes ineffective (7: 45–52) and he brings others into his own freedom (8: 30–6) as is particularly apparent in the case of the man born blind (9: 1–39). The Jews who stand over against him in hostility do not hold back from an attempt at stoning him (8: 59; 10: 31), and finally they make the decision to get rid of him (11: 47–54, 57). But Jesus takes his own people whom he separates from the Jews (10: 1–21), forms from them the people of God's sons (10: 16; 11: 52; 12: 32f) and also gains a powerful influence over the nation (11: 45–7; 12: 9–19;[75] 12: 42f). It is precisely his own liberating freedom, clearly operative once again in his trial (18: 1 to 19: 30), which constitutes the great threat for the high priest and the Sanhedrin. It releases fears which lead to the decision that he must die.[76] The Jews recognise that

---

[74] By the transposition of the day of the anointing and the entry to Jerusalem in John (12: 1–19) this much becomes clear: the one who has been anointed for death enters the royal city for his death in which he is proclaimed as king before the whole world (John 19: 19f) in the languages of the world.

[75] Cp. 12: 19: The Pharisees say to one another, 'You see that you can do nothing; look, the world has gone after him.'

[76] O. Cullmann, *Jesus und die Revolutionären seiner Zeit* (Tübingen, 1970), p. 49, ET *Jesus and the Revolutionaries* (New York, 1970), p. 33: 'According to Jn. 11: 48 the Sanhedrin take the decision to denounce Jesus to the Romans as a political rebel. They do this for fear that the Romans would hold the Jewish authorities responsible

his freedom is based on his relationship to God, and precisely because of this he must die (5: 18; 10: 33; 19: 7). What John is showing is this: Jesus has great support among the people and he finds many followers, but he nevertheless relies not on the people but on the Father (7: 29; 16: 32). So he does not organise the people for revolution as a rebel leader would do. Not every movement among the people is a Zealot undertaking, nor is every person who influences the people a Zealot leader. All this is affirmed by the Johannine account, while at the same time it is not denied that every movement among the people is liable to be misunderstood in a Zealot way.

In the discourse about the shepherd Jesus distinguishes himself from others who make royal claims.[77] In this setting, he speaks of himself as the truly authorised shepherd who dissociates himself from the thieves and the robbers and the hireling.[78] The decisive difference is to be found in the fact that the false shepherds who are branded as thieves and robbers think only of themselves. They use the flock for their own advantage and like the hireling abandon the flock to the wolf who tears them apart and scatters them. The true shepherd is quite different: he lays down his life for the sheep and he gathers together the scattered ones (10: 10–18). By means of the imagery of the shepherd John makes Jesus speak about the essential character of his mission and the identity of his person. The shepherd discourse which stands at the midpoint of the Gospel of John provides the basis for the raising of Lazarus which is followed by the decision to put Jesus to death. It is necessary therefore that attention should be devoted to it finally in the context of examining the questions with which we have been concerned.

if it should so happen that a popular movement in Jesus' favour should assume worrying proportions.' But not every popular movement is political, and there is no statement *expressis verbis* of any denunciation of Jesus as a political rebel. Leading the people astray (John 7: 12) does not happen only in the political sphere. On the question of the Zealots, cp. M. Hengel, *Die Zeloten* (Leiden, 1961); G. Baumbach, 'Zeloten und Sikarier', in *ThLZ* 90 (1965), 727–40, and also 'Die Zeloten–ihre geschichtliche und religionspolitische Bedeutung', *Liturgie und Leben* 41 (1968), 2–25.

[77] Shepherd is a predicate of royalty and divinity; cp. J. Jeremias, *ThWNT* vi, 484–98 (ET *TDNT* vi (1968), 485–502); W. Jost, *Poimen: Das Bild vom Hirten in der biblischen Überlieferung und seine christologische Bedeutung* (Giessen, 1939); I. Seibert, *Hirt, Herde, König* (Berlin, 1969). If one surveys the breadth of association of this image as revealed in I. Seibert's study, then it becomes quite clear that the picture of the shepherd is active in the background of both the metaphors of living water (John 4) and living bread (John 6). Its central position and significance are therefore confirmed; cp. also footnote 82 on p. 315 below.

[78] The expression 'robbers' (λησταί) refers to Zealot leaders (10: 1, 8, 10). Cullmann, *Revolutionären*, p. 53 (ET p. 36), reckons with the possibility that an authentic Jesus-saying lies beneath John 10: 11–13. On the description 'robbers' for Zealots, cp. Hengel, *Die Zeloten*, pp. 25–47.

V

The shepherd discourse is attached without interruption (9: 41/10: 1) to the healing of the man born blind, which reaches its conclusion in 10: 19–21. It consists of a parable which derives its meaning from the healing of the blind man, and its reflective development in 10: 7–18. In the latter passage there appear two of the seven 'I am' sayings of this Gospel, and both are repeated. This in itself indicates their importance. Their theme is taken up once again in the adjacent and final debate between Jesus and the Jews (10: 25–30), this time as the answer to the urgently posed question about his messiahship: 'How long will you keep us in suspense? If you are the Christ, tell us plainly' (10: 24). The explicit question directed at Jesus and his own reply are important for the understanding of the Sanhedrin's decision to put him to death. Jesus responds to the messianic question with a reference to his authority as shepherd which is finally demonstrated in the raising of Lazarus. After this the decision to put him to death follows immediately. This context provides insight into the evangelist's understanding of Jesus.

The connection between the healing of the man born blind and the shepherd discourse is denoted by the fact that the healed man is thrown out of the synagogue community but found and accepted by Jesus. The evaluation by Jesus of the blind man's disability has already been seen to be different from that of the Jews: it is not a divine punishment but the occasion of the revelation of the works of God to him.[79] Jesus had already defined the way of discipleship as a remaining in his word which leads to knowledge of the truth and thus to freedom from sin in a context of belief. The blind man now treads this path. He has to endure the opposition of the Pharisees but in this context he comes to stand by what Jesus had done for him through his revealing word. Thus he recognises him as the one who has come from God (9: 33) and shows his freedom in resistance to Pharisaic pressure. But this causes what his parents had feared would happen to him (9: 20–3): he is thrown out and put under a ban (9: 34). Faced with this threat and pressure, his parents are marked by the bondage of fear, but in contrast with them the man himself is free. He, although banned, is accepted by Jesus.[80] And Jesus interprets the proceedings in terms of his leading out his own and going before them; they follow him, listening to his

---

[79] Since with verbs of teaching and revelation etc. ἐν strengthens the dative, one will have to translate: 'that the works of God may be revealed to him'. Cp. Blass–Debrunner (ET Blass–Debrunner–Funk, *Greek Grammar*), 220, 1.

[80] In John 9: 35–8 there occurs an actualisation of Mark 8: 38: The man born blind has not been ashamed of Jesus and his word but has acknowledged him. He experiences acknowledgement by the Son of man in that he confirms to him: 'You believe on the Son of man.' His belief that Jesus is from God is belief in the Son of man.

voice as he calls them by name. This is what the parable of the true shepherd (10: 1–5) is saying: in this event the κρίμα (9: 39) is effected. The parable which was not understood (10:6) is unfolded by means of a meditation. Jesus is the door to the sheep[81] (10: 7f) and for the sheep (10: 9); he is the truly authorised shepherd; in the laying down of his life this is made visible and also made effective, in that what obtains between him and the Father now obtains between him and his own people. The Father knows him, that is, he has chosen him. He knows the Father, that is, he has entrusted himself to him. He knows his own, that is, he has chosen them after they have been given to him by the Father. They know him, that is, they entrust themselves to him and belong with him to the Father. By means of the relationship with himself into which he calls men, he establishes the relationship with the Father which he himself enjoys and he both seals and extends this relationship through the giving of his life (10: 14–16). The decision of the Jews against Jesus and his own (9: 22, 34) leads to their separation from the synagogue which he himself brings about (10: 7f); thus this passage serves to exhibit the honorific picture of the shepherd.[82]

This theme is taken up again at the Temple feast in Jerusalem on the basis of the question directed by the Jews to Jesus about his messiahship (10: 22–39). Schlatter rightly concludes: 'No statement however rich in content about the mission of Jesus could replace for the Jew what the term "anointed one" meant to him. It was primarily in this term that the prophetic prediction was recalled in the present. The decisive issue therefore hung on this term.'[83] But this term itself was at the same time ambiguous and unmistakable. His answer runs: 'I have told you but you do not believe. . ., because you do not belong to my sheep.' And now once more Jesus speaks about the shepherd and his authority. To the Jews who ask about his messiahship he says: 'My sheep hear my voice and I know

---

[81] If the shepherds before him are thieves and robbers who only consider themselves, then the πρὸ ἐμοῦ shows that he is the true shepherd; it is not to be taken as a matter of time but rather a matter of principle. Whoever comes after him either comes as one sent by him (17: 18; 20: 21) or belongs to the thieves and robbers 'before him'. Thus he alone is the door to the sheep.

[82] Bultmann, *Johannes*, pp. 272–98 (ET pp. 358–91), who brings the shepherd discourse back into another context and also rearranges it internally, expounds the shepherd imagery not in terms of the ancient eastern/Old Testament kingship and divinity context but in terms of gnostic traditions. In these the shepherd has become the revealer (pp. 277–81). Such a view of John's shepherd imagery is attractive. However, if one retains the present position and context, then the features of majesty and divinity obtrude. For it appears at the very moment when, in the light of the exclusion from the synagogue, the authoritative decision has to be made to found a distinctive universal community.

[83] Cp. Schlatter, *Johannes*, p. 241.

them and they follow me, and I give them eternal life and they shall never perish and no one shall snatch them out of my hand' (10: 27f). This saying, which consists of a pair of three line units, shows the personal character of the relationship between Jesus and his own. It is based on hearing his voice. The use of the word 'voice' is striking. The evangelist calls Jesus the Word made flesh (1: 14); the words which he speaks are given him by the Father, for he does not speak for himself (3: 34; 7: 16f; 12: 49f); they are 'spirit and life' (6: 63). Hearing his voice, which is the basis of the link between him and his, shows therefore that his words are not separable from his person, that is, the Word made flesh. They are words which are bound to and cannot be divided from his person. His words serve to establish the relationship with him, and therefore in hearing his word a man hears his voice. His voice calls the individual by name (10: 3) and therefore establishes a personal relationship.[84] Such calling by name is election – I know you, that is, I choose you for myself by calling with my voice so that you follow me. The relationship grounded in this electing call of his voice is realised in following. In this spoken call there is contained the gift of eternal life; those who hear his voice and follow him will never perish whatever may happen to them. They are not lost because they are protected in his hand, and from that hand no destructive earthly power can tear them. For his voice penetrates both the power and the scope of death.

All of this was expressed by the evangelist when he spoke about the voice of the Son of man which calls the dead (John 5: 25–9). The dead are those who, whether alive or deceased, have succumbed to the power of death. But they receive life by listening to his voice. Those who are in the graves, that is, the deceased, will be summoned out by his voice (5: 28f). As an example of this stands the raising of Lazarus,[85] at the end of which it says: 'he cried with a loud voice, "Lazarus, come out." And the dead man came out . . .' (11: 43f). The raising of Lazarus becomes a sign of the shepherd-authority of Jesus; Lazarus is one of his own (11: 3, 5, 35) and he listens to his voice, even though as one who has succumbed to the power of death. In listening to his voice he receives the gift of life. It is precisely this act which brings

---

[84] As regards Mary Magdalene, John 20: 1, 11–18 makes clear that she does not come to faith in the risen one on the basis of the empty tomb, nor because of the angel at the grave, nor as a result of the appearance of the risen one (whom she does not recognise), but rather because of the fact that he calls her by name. She hears his voice, and that qualifies her to be a messenger of the resurrection to his disciples. On this cp. W. Grundmann, 'Zur Rede vom Vater im Johannesevangelium', *ZNW* 52 (1961), 213–30.

[85] This tendency, important to the evangelist, is what causes him to work over the legendary resurrection story. The part of the original conversation between Jesus and Martha which can be discerned in 11: 28, 40 has been replaced by 11: 25f: whoever holds fast to Jesus, the giver of resurrection life, over that person death has no ultimate power. That is the point of the sign of the raising of Lazarus.

about the decision of the Sanhedrin to agree to what the high priest says and to take the decision to put Jesus to death.

One last question must be raised at this point. Where does the name Lazarus come from? Has the Fourth Evangelist taken it from the tradition which quite often he holds in common with Luke (Luke 16: 19–31)? Does he know the story of the rich man and the poor Lazarus? Does he want to show, in the course of his discussion of the insufficiency of a faith based on signs (2: 11, 23–5; 3: 2; 4: 46–53; 6: 2, 14f, 26–35), what the Lukan parabolic narrative is expressing, i.e. whoever like the Jews does not listen to God's voice, whether through Moses and the prophets or through the true shepherd, will not be helped even by the return of one already dead?[86] The Jews impose death on the one who brings resurrection and create mortal danger for the one to whom this resurrection happens (12: 10f). If so, the debate about faith engendered by signs would find in this event its climax and conclusion.[87]

Thus the Fourth Evangelist's account is rounded off. Jesus is the dispenser of that life which no further death can destroy. That is his authority as shepherd, about which Jesus speaks explicitly (10: 29).[88] It is intrinsic to his relationship of unity with the Father who chooses him and to whom he has entrusted himself (10: 14f, 30); it is described as effective in the present – 'the Father in me' – and secure and authorised – 'I in the Father.' For the Jews this is blasphemy and from their side it leads to his death (5: 18; 10: 30–3; 19: 7). So this theologically-based statement is articulated in the account of the Fourth Evangelist: the life-giving of the life-giver brings death to him, but his death is his bestowal of life on mankind. Does the situation attested here correspond to Jesus's own situation? The shepherd discourse and the conversation with Pilate about the kingdom of God distinguish him deeply and fundamentally from the

---

[86] Cp. W. Grundmann, 'Verständnis und Bewegung des Glaubens im Johannes-evangeliums,' *KuD* 6 (1960), 131–54.

[87] In favour of this could be the explicit statement in 11: 47: 'This man does many signs.'

[88] The expression opens up two possible translations which are given by the textual analysis: (1) 'What my (or the) Father has given me is greater than all and no one can tear them out of my Father's hand.' That would then be a reference to the shepherd's authority which the Father has given him. (2) 'The Father, who has given them to me, is greater than everything (or everyone) and no one can tear them out of my Father's hand.' The greatness of the Father, who himself has given his own to Jesus, is the guarantee of their deliverance and protection. Verses 27, 28 and 29f together form three three-membered units. The first concerns how the community is established (verse 27), the second what the community receives from the one who is the shepherd (verse 28), and the third its unity with the Father on which his gift to his community is based. Bultmann opts for the second possibility, *Johannes*, pp. 294f footnote 4 (ET pp. 386f footnote 3), with a reference to a Mandaean text: his possibility is now supported also by the reading in p66.

leaders of the people during his day and time. As the Samaritans called him the saviour of the world, so he stands before Pilate as the witness to the truth for men. And John makes his own affirmation: This is God's eternal Word become flesh, this is the Son who is one with the Father.[89]

[89] The article was translated by Dr D. Catchpole.

The 'triumphal' entry

The tradition of the 'triumphal' entry plays a crucial role in the Markan scheme. The confession of Jesus as messiah in 8: 27–30 had followed a miracle on a blind man (8: 22–6) and had led immediately into a complex of material (8: 31 to 10: 45) structured by three sayings about the suffering Son of man (8: 31–3; 9: 30–2; 10: 32–4) and several ensuing traditions about discipleship. With 10: 46–52 the journey to Jerusalem has reached Jericho where there occurs a further miracle on a blind man. This tradition is clamped to the following tradition of the entry quite unmistakably: in both 'the way' is mentioned (10: 46, 52; 11: 8), in both Jesus is acclaimed in Davidic terms (10: 47f; 11: 10), in both there is a ἱμάτιον reference (10: 50; 11: 7f), in both the theme of salvation is prominent (10: 52; 11: 9), and significantly in both acclamation and following are joined (10: 52; 11: 9). Consequently it appears that the Markan plan is to link 11: 1–10 with 10: 46–52 in much the same way as 8: 27–30 is linked with 8: 22–6. The 'triumphal' entry, therefore, matches the confession and has to do with the disclosure of Jesus's identity and status.

This Markan presentation of the entry into Jerusalem by the one who has already effected a victory is precisely what permits a classification of the story as such. For there is already in existence a family of stories detailing the celebratory entry to a city by a hero figure who has previously achieved his triumph. No doubt the ultimate precedents are to be found in Israelite kingship ritual, cp. 1 Kings 1: 32–40 where acclamation (verse 34) is followed by a ceremonial entry (verse 35) by the king-designate, who rides the royal animal (verse 38) and who precedes a celebrating crowd 'playing on pipes, and rejoicing with great joy' (verse 40). No doubt precedent can genuinely be found in Zech. 9: 9 where an era of universal peace is inaugurated by the arrival of the king in procession, and riding upon an ass, an arrival which is to be greeted with shouts of joy. At all events, a more or less fixed pattern of triumphal entry can be discerned:

(1) Alexander travels from Gaza to Jerusalem (Josephus, *AJ* 11: 325–39) where his previously achieved authority is recognised without conflict. He is ceremonially met outside Jerusalem, greeted, and escorted into the city and then to the Temple where he is involved in cultic activity.

(2) Alexander again is invited to enter Shechem (Josephus, *AJ* 11: 342–5), having been met 'with splendour and a great show of eagerness

on his behalf . . . when he was hardly out of Jerusalem', a proposed visit which would have reached its climax in the Temple (342).

(3) Apollonius is welcomed to Jerusalem (2 Macc. 4: 21f). He is ushered in with a blaze of torches and with shouts, and the welcome is said to be magnificent (μεγαλομερῶς).

(4) Judas Maccabaeus returns home (1 Macc. 4: 19–25; Josephus, AJ 12: 312) after victory over Gorgias, with his associates echoing the language of the psalms as 'they sang hymns and praises to heaven, for he is good and his mercy endures for ever' (4: 24; cp. 4: 33). Similarly

(5) Judas returns from a military campaign (1 Macc. 5: 45–54; Josephus, AJ 12: 348f), passing through Judaea (5: 45) to mount Zion with singing and finally undertaking sacrificial activity. In Josephus's words, 'they came to Judaea, playing harps and singing songs of praise and observing such forms of merrymaking as are customary at celebrations of a victory' (12: 349), while 1 Macc. 4: 55 puts it thus: 'All the people fell on their faces and worshipped and blessed heaven who had prospered them.'

(6) Jonathan Maccabaeus is welcomed in Askalon (1 Macc. 10: 86; cp. 11: 60) without the expected struggle, so the emergence of the men of the city 'to meet him with great pomp (ἐν δόξῃ μεγάλῃ)' clearly implies their acceptance of his authority.

(7) Simon Maccabaeus enters Gaza (1 Macc. 13: 43–8), having already had his status and authority defined (verse 42). Conflict having given way to peace, Simon expels idolatrous inhabitants (verses 47b, 48), cleanses idolatrous houses (verse 47b) and enters the city 'with hymns and praise (ὑμνῶν καὶ εὐλογῶν)'. In a similar vein,

(8) Simon enters Jerusalem (1 Macc. 13: 49–51), peace having again replaced conflict. The pattern of expulsion of inhabitants (verse 50b), cleansing away pollution (verse 50b), and triumphal entry is repeated, though the celebrations are described in unusual detail: 'they entered with praise and palm branches, and with harps and cymbals and stringed instruments and with hymns and songs' (verse 51). The situation in (7) and (8) is summarised later in 1 Macc. 14: 7 as an activation of lordship (ἐκυρίευσεν) which is unopposed, as well as involving a removal of uncleanness.

(9) Antigonus returns from a campaign (BJ 1: 73f; AJ 13: 304–6) with glory, accompanied by soldiers and clothed splendidly, to such an extent that his going to the Temple becomes the occasion for criticism: 'out of keeping with the behaviour of a private person . . . his actions had the indications of one who imagined himself a king' (306).

(10) Marcus Agrippa is welcomed in Jerusalem (Josephus, AJ 16: 12–15), having been met by Herod and brought to the city; the people at

large meet him and welcome him with acclamations prior to his entry and his offering of sacrifice.

(11) Archelaus, having been provisionally appointed king by Herod (Josephus, *AJ* 17: 194–239) and acclaimed as king by his adherents in Jericho, goes to Jerusalem and the Temple in procession. The initial acclamation is combined with an invocation of God as helper (195; cp. *BJ* 1: 570). In the Temple he offers sacrifice and acts in a manner sufficiently regal to provoke later accusations that he had taken power and unduly infringed upon Caesar's authority to bestow the kingship. Specifically he had sat upon a throne and 'had danced and sung as over a fallen enemy' (235), as well as quelling riots in kingly style.

(12) Alexander's 'double' claims kingship (*BJ* 2: 101–10; *AJ* 17: 324–8) and is given a formal welcome by the Jewish population in Rome, of all places. They go to meet him and surround him, shouting good wishes, while he is said to have 'all the trappings of a king' (331).

It thus proves possible to locate the Gospel tradition of Jesus's triumphal entry within a family of stories, all members of which exhibit to a greater or lesser degree the following standard features: (*a*) A victory already achieved and a status already recognised for the central person. (*b*) A formal and ceremonial entry. (*c*) Greetings and/or acclamations together with invocations of God. (*d*) Entry to the city climaxed by entry to Temple, if the city in question has one. (*e*) Cultic activity, either positive (e.g. offering of sacrifice), or negative (e.g. expulsion of objectionable persons and the cleansing away of uncleanness). Mark 11 contains all these major and recurrent features. It also contains minor agreements with occasional features of some of the other stories, for example, the reference to the royal animal (1 Kings 1: 35; Zech. 9: 9), the use of the language of the psalms (see 4 above), the use of the κύριος word group (see 7, 8 above), an earlier decisive event in Jericho (see 11 above). Mark's story thus conforms to a familiar pattern in respect of both its determinative shape and some of its incidental details.

At this point reference ought also to be made to versions of this story other than that in Mark. John's version (12: 12–19), which, in the view of some, may be using an independent non-Markan tradition, works within the same circle of ideas. Once the typical Johannine features of resurrection-inspired recall and reflection are subtracted, as well as the Johannine-redactional link with the Lazarus story, we find ourselves confronted with a story which merely develops details or draws out implications from the synoptic versions: (*a*) The branches used are specified as palm branches (τὰ βαΐα τῶν φοινίκων) – a natural inference in view of texts which see the symbols of kingship as variously crown plus βαΐον (1 Macc. 13: 37) or crown plus φοῖνιξ (2 Macc. 14: 4; cp. Rev. 7: 9);[1] (b) the acclaiming crowd comes out from Jerusalem, rather than explicitly accompanying him into the city – again a natural adaptation, given both John's Jerusalem-centredness and the frequency of the references in other texts to the welcoming delegation (see 1, 2, 3, 6, 10, 12 above and also 1 Macc. 11: 2);[2] (c) Zech. 9: 9 is explicitly cited in 12: 15 as in Matt. 21: 5 which, whether or not John is aware of Matthew, is in each of the two Gospels a natural and indeed necessary inference from the form of the tradition used by Mark. As far as Matthew/Luke are concerned there is no evidence of any non-Markan source. Only at two points might the suspicion arise that MattR and LukeR prove inadequate to explain Matthew/Mark or Luke/Mark variations, that is, the correspondence between αἶνος (Matt. 21: 16) and αἰνεῖν (Luke 19: 37), and the correspondence in the personalising of the shout of acclamation (Matt. 21: 9/Luke 19: 38). These are, however, no indication of alternative Q-type tradition. In the first case, αἶνος in Matt. 21: 16 is part of a quotation from Psalm 8: 2 and is a natural term to use in the overall setting of an entry tradition (cp. 1 Macc. 13: 51: μετὰ αἰνέσεως); LukeR has already introduced αἶνος in 18: 43 diff Mark 10: 52. In the second case, the personalising is an inevitable inference from Mark's version and matches the preoccupation with the status of the leader in other members of the family of such stories; that is, the Matthew/Luke agreement is not an agreement against Mark.

There being no grounds for concentrating on any version of the triumphal entry other than Mark's, we can now discuss briefly the implications of the formal analysis, and then go on to examine how Mark works in a distinctive way within the standard form. First, it is evident that all such stories presuppose an already achieved victory; they do not describe a first move or the opening of a campaign designed to achieve a future victory. On any level, whether Markan or pre-Markan, the absence of any previous social/political conquest places a fatal question-mark against the idea, whether originally suggested by H. S. Reimarus that 'this extraordinary public parade which Jesus not only permitted, but industriously organised, could aim at nothing other than a secular kingdom',[3] or more recently by S. G. F. Brandon that Jesus's actions were

---

[1] On palms as symbols of victory, cp. B. A. Mastin, 'The Date of the Triumphal Entry', NTSt 16 (1969), 79f.

[2] Widespread oriental custom is involved here, cp. Jud. 11: 34; Prov. 7: 15; Tobit 7: 1; Judith 7: 15; Wisd. of Sol. 6: 16; Sira 15: 2; 1 Macc. 9: 39; 1 Thess. 4: 17. Therefore it is doubtful whether the scheme should be confined to 'the joyful reception of Hellenistic sovereigns into a city': R. E. Brown, The Gospel according to John I–XII (New York, 1966), pp. 461f. See also E. Peterson, ἀπάντησις, ThWNT i, 380 (ET TDNT i (1964), 380f).   [3] The Goal of Jesus and his Disciples (Leiden, 1970), p. 92.

'obviously calculated to cause the authorities, both Jewish and Roman, to view him and his movement as subversive'.[4] To the contrary, on the Markan level the presupposed victory is clearly that gained by healings, of which Mark 10: 46–52 is intended as a typical example – an interpretation to which all three other evangelists adhere in their various ways – while on the pre-Markan level (supposing there is one) the story could not do other than receive its interpretative frame of reference from what Jesus is thought to have done previously. Specifically, this implies that, since there is unmistakable kingly messianic colouring in the story, the decision about its historicity will depend not only on its internal viability but also very directly on the extent to which Jesus's pre-entry activity as a whole can justifiably be regarded as messianic. Second, it is apparent that a standard element in the entry stories is movement to the Temple. That being so, our discussion cannot be concluded without coverage of the so-called cleansing of the Temple (Mark 11: 15–19). On the Markan level, the enclosing of this unit within the two parts of the tradition of the cursing of the fig-tree is typical of the evangelist's redactional technique,[5] used on this occasion to make the Temple incident an act of judgement, while on the pre-Markan level (again supposing there is one) the question will arise as to how far there is of necessity the same messianic presupposition as for the earlier material.

The Markan entry story is divisible into two sections, in the first of which the initiative is wholly taken by Jesus (verses 1–7a), while in the second all the actions are taken by Jesus's associates (verses 7b–10). This ordering of events serves to indicate that the actions of others are here silently endorsed by Jesus and seen as the correct inference from his own actions. The claims of others that he is a messianic figure are nothing less than his own claim to such a status. His own actions are entirely concentrated upon the obtaining of the appropriate animal, described by Mark as πῶλος. By that word Mark intends 'an ass'.[6] That this is a very special animal is indicated by three factors. (a) Jesus knows about it and its precise circumstances without being himself *in situ*; (b) he knows, moreover, that it has never previously been used; (c) he names himself the lord of the animal, for that is the appropriate inference from the declaration that ὁ κύριος αὐτοῦ χρείαν ἔχει.[7] The first of these features is presented by a speech whose terms allude

---

[4] *Jesus and the Zealots* (Manchester, 1967), p. 324.

[5] See E. von Dobschütz, 'Zur Erzählerkunst des Markus', ZNW 27 (1928), 193–8.

[6] H.–W. Kuhn, 'Das Reittier in der Einzugsgeschichte des Markusevangeliums', ZNW 50 (1959), 82–91; otherwise, W. Bauer, 'The "Colt" of Palm Sunday', *JBL* 72 (1953), 220–9.

[7] J. D. M. Derrett, 'Law in the New Testament: the Palm Sunday Colt', *NovTest* 13 (1971), 241–58, esp. 245–7.

extensively to the established practice of impressment (ἀγγαρεία). In an extensive study of this section Derrett has drawn attention to the loosing of the animal without formal request (verses 2, 4), the loosing as the act of borrowing and of taking responsibility for the animal because it is tied in the open street (verses 2–4),[8] need as a sufficient justification for impressment (verses 3, 6), the owners' recognition of their obligation to release the animal (verse 6), and the hint of a defined period of time during which the arrangement would last (verse 3). All these details give verisimilitude to the story, but they all belong to a speech by Jesus which is both predictive and a demonstration of his authoritative control – in short, it is christologically determined. The second feature, the newness of the animal, is mentioned in such a way as to register the possibility that the ass might have been used, a possibility amply attested by many and diverse texts (see, for example, 1 Kings 13: 13; Josephus, *AJ* 5: 138 and 6: 301; RH 1: 9; *Martyrdom of Polycarp* 8: 1). Newness, rather than sacred separateness along the lines of Num. 19: 2; Deut. 21: 3; 1 Sam. 6: 7 as sometimes suggested, is confirmed as the intended meaning by Mark 11: 7 where clothing is laid on the animal in place of the usual trappings which went with an ass already in use (see BB 5: 2; Toh. 3: 7). The reference to the animal's not having been previously used recalls not only the similar detail in the burial traditions (Matt. 27: 60; Luke 23: 53; John 19: 41) but also the rabbinic insistence (Sanh. 2: 5) that no one should use the animal on which a king rides. Above all, it matches the word νέος in Zech. 9: 9 (LXX, but not MT).[9] On the Markan level it conforms to a theological pattern which involves Jesus doing what others have not done or cannot do (cp. 1: 27f; 2: 7; 4: 41; 5: 3–5). Again, therefore, a detail of the story is christologically determined. Finally, the third feature represents a confirmation of the christological sensitivity of the other details. Jesus as lord takes charge of the ass which belongs to him. He can be none other than the figure of Zech. 9: 9. A story rightly characterised by O. Michel as 'already full of mysterious links'[10] with Zech. 9: 9 points in a manner subdued but significant to the status of its central actor. He is already the king.

The actions of Jesus's associates (verses 7b–10) demonstrate that they have understood and accepted the implications. Their response to the animal's newness has already been mentioned. Jesus's taking his place upon the ass is followed by two specific acts of homage, the placing of

---

[8] The fact that this detail is integral to the impressment scheme makes precarious a suggested allusion to Gen. 49: 11, cp. J. Blenkinsopp, 'The Oracle of Judah and the Messianic Entry', *JBL* 80 (1961), 55–64.

[9] F. Hahn, *Christologische Hoheitstitel* (3rd edn. Göttingen, 1966), pp. 87f (ET *The Titles of Jesus in Christology* (London, 1969), p. 83).

[10] ὄνος, *TDNT* v (1967), 283–7, esp. 286.

clothing on the road and the cutting of branches. Again christology is involved in both, for the placing of clothing on the ground was a response to the announcement of Jehu's kingship (2 Kings 9: 13) and was followed by a further formal proclamation, 'Jehu is king'. Similarly the use of branches in acclamation ritual is a following of precedent (see 1 Macc. 13:51). All of this prepares for the crescendo in verses 9f. The deliberateness with which the ass is obtained and then used for the short journey to the city is reinforced by the formality of the procession in which Jesus is preceded and followed by the confessing crowd (cp. προάγειν + ἀκολουθεῖν in a processional context: Josephus *BJ* 1: 673; *AJ* 7: 40). The confession itself is constructed on the foundation of Psalm 118: 25f, originally a prayer for salvation and a greeting, a real communication of blessing, to the arriving pilgrims. But now there is more involved than that foundation. A chiastic form puts two ἔρχεσθαι statements between two ὡσαννά calls, and the second ἔρχεσθαι statement gives precise meaning to the first. The coming of the Davidic kingdom is more than a mere spatial movement by a pilgrim.[11] Space has given way to time, geography to eschatology, and all in the interests of christology. The future king is the present Jesus!

As already mentioned, the decision about the historicity of the story depends in part on its internal viability. In this connection the unity of the tradition is almost certain. The precedents for celebratory entry stories are sufficiently often indifferent to the method of transport that one could justifiably ask whether the later part of the story which is closest to the precedents (verses 8–10) genuinely needs the earlier part whose dominant concern is the ass (verses 1–7). Yet the later part is fully integrated with the earlier part by means of the common christology, and the later part must therefore share the vulnerability of the earlier part to historical criticism. The verisimilitude of verses 1–7 by virtue of the unlaboured, almost casual, employment of impressment motifs can be no protection, for a tradition does not have to lack verisimilitude to be unhistorical. Consequently several essential features of the story excite critical doubts: Does not the precise parallelism of this tradition with that of Mark 14: 12–16 suggest a stereotyped form? Does not Jesus's awareness of the existence, the circumstances, and the pre-history of the animal amount, in Bultmann's words, to the 'manifestly legendary'?[12] Does not the thoroughness of the christological impregnation of the story suggest the creative, rather than merely the interpretative, role of scripture? But with that third question we begin to move towards the topic of what might be called the external

---

[11] It may well be that Psalm 118: 25f had already been interpreted messianically: cp. E. Lohse, 'Hosianna', *NovTest* 6 (1963), 113–19.
[12] *The History of the Synoptic Tradition* (Oxford, 1963), p. 261.

relations of this tradition to other messianic traditions with which it may, indeed must, cohere. Here one must again emphasise that a celebratory entry, precisely because it looks backwards to preceding events, cannot survive without another earlier event containing an identical christology. For such a role there is only one candidate, the confession of Peter at Caesarea Philippi (Mark 8: 27–30), whose historicity is therefore vitally necessary for the historicity of Mark 11: 1–10.

Formally, Mark 8: 27–30 is structured antithetically so that a series of incorrect identifications of Jesus by men in general (verses 27b, 28) is set over against an alternative identification of Jesus by the disciple group represented by Peter (verse 29). This alternative identification of Jesus as 'messiah' must, on the Markan level, be viewed as entirely correct for several reasons.[13] Firstly, the identification is the subject of a secrecy command (verse 30), and secrecy commands in Mark, far from implying a rejection of what has previously been stated, in fact presuppose that it is exactly right (cp. 3: 11 reinforced by 1: 11 and 9: 7). Secondly, Mark has already confirmed in 1: 1 the accuracy of the confession of Peter. Thirdly, the form of the tradition itself requires that the inaccurate views stated in verse 28 should not be set antitithetically over against another inaccurate view but rather against an opposite and accurate view, and this formal requirement is reinforced by the sharp contrast between the two groups whose views are here surveyed. Not even the suggestion (in itself insecurely grounded) of a Markan critique of the disciples, nor the argument that 8: 31–3 forces 8: 27–9 to register a critique of a θεῖος ἀνήρ christology,[14] can weaken this conclusion. Given, therefore, the endorsement of Peter's confession at the Markan level, the question arises as to what may have been true at the pre-Markan level, that is, if there was one. At this point we have necessarily in the post-Wrede period to ignore the secrecy injunction in verse 30, but then two options become available. The first is to note the probably secondary and Markan character of verses 31f and to infer that in verse 33 there is preserved an original pre-Markan conclusion to the unit involving verses 27–9,[15] and the second is to consider verses 27–9 without reference to verse 33 at all. These options coalesce, however, in the light of some considerations affecting verse 33 itself. Firstly, even if it were pre-Markan or even historical this would not demonstrate the historicity of

[13] E. Haenchen, 'Die Komposition von Mk 8.27–9.1 und par.', *NovTest* 6 (1963), 81–108, esp. 89f: 'Man trägt in seinen Text etwas Fremdes ein, wenn man das Bekenntnis der Christenheit "Du bist der Christus!" in Munde des Petrus zum Ausdruck einer falschen Christuserwartung erniedrigt.'

[14] T. J. Weeden, *Mark-Traditions in Conflict* (Philadelphia, 1971), pp. 32–4.

[15] Hahn, *Hoheitstitel*, pp. 227f (ET *Titles*, pp. 224f); R. H. Fuller, *The Foundations of New Testament Christology* (London, 1965), p. 109.

verses 27–9, which must stand up to scrutiny in their own right. Secondly, the negativity of verse 33 *vis-à-vis* Peter is certainly fierce and could (if supporting evidence were forthcoming) even be taken as authentic,[16] but it fits easily into the Markan scheme in which the disciples' misunderstanding is inevitable and christologically conditioned, precisely as a pointer to the reader that in Jesus something is happening which is, in the style of apocalyptic, wholly other and wholly beyond man's capacity to understand except through revelation. Thirdly, it stretches credulity to suppose that any community influenced by the confession that Jesus is messiah could possibly transmit a tradition in which Jesus vigorously disputed that confession.

We have, therefore, to assess the possibilities of a pre-Markan existence and of substantial historicity in the case of 8: 27–9 alone. Neither of these possibilities turns out to be particularly well grounded. Firstly, the geographical reference to Caesarea Philippi (verse 27a) cannot carry weight,[17] for geographical references within the gospel tradition at large fluctuate markedly. Secondly, the list of incorrect opinions of Jesus (verse 28) is clearly related to the list in 6: 14–16. In more precise terms 6: 14–16, because it lists none but incorrect opinions – there is no antithetical structure there as in 8: 27–9, since Herod simply selects one of the wrong interpretations – and because it could scarcely exist as a separate unit serving a purpose within Christian tradition, is dependent on and an interpretation of verse 28. Significantly, it serves to highlight the artificiality of verse 28, especially in the case of the suggestion that Jesus is John the Baptist. Four component ideas are severely open to question: first, that one person's activities could only be explained on the basis of his being another person in resurrected form; second, that Herod should anticipate the Christian scheme whereby a general eschatological experience envisaged by apocalyptic should here be brought forward in the case of a specific known individual; third, that the previously executed John in particular should be regarded by him as the person now revived; fourth, that the non-miracle-working John could in any sense provide a strand of continuity through to a miracle-working Jesus. In sum, the list of opinions concerning the identity of Jesus reflects no real historical situation either before or after Easter but is an artificial construction serving christological ends. Thirdly, the raising by the Markan Jesus of the question about his identity is itself at variance with the concerns of the mission of the historical Jesus. It fits uneasily with the theocentric proclamation of the near kingdom, whereas its fits smoothly and easily with the recurrent Markan

---

[16] Hahn, *Hoheitstitel*, p. 227 (ET *Titles*, p. 224).
[17] E. Schweizer, *The Good News according to Mark* (London, 1971), p. 171.

tendency to make various happenings provoke the question of who Jesus is (see, for example, 1: 27; 4: 41; 6: 2; 14: 61; 15: 2) It looks suspiciously like a situation in which a question, instead of generating an affirmation, is in fact generated by it. Fourthly, verse 29 contains a bald, precise and direct christological affirmation in the form οὐ εἶ ... This is exactly in the style of 1: 11 and 3: 11 and closely approximate to 1: 24; 14: 61f; 15: 2, 39.

The evidence seems, therefore, to point towards the conclusion that Mark 8: 27–30 is a Markan construction serving the purposes of Markan theology. If some pre-Markan influence contributed to the production of such a tradition it may be that Peter's having been the first to see the risen one who was in that context affirmed to be χριστός (1 Cor. 15: 3b–5) provided such influence. But in itself 8: 27–30 does not emerge from a pre-Easter context, and it therefore leaves the tradition of the triumphal entry stranded.

At this point a rearguard action in defence of the historicity of Mark 11: 1–10 might be mounted somewhat as follows: If Jesus was crucified as a messianic claimant with the Roman definition of his offence defined by the *titulus* on the cross, then some earlier encouragement of the view that he was messiah must have occurred. The alternative would be a situation in which Pilate would be the creator of christology.[18] Might the historicity of Mark 11: 1–10 be salvaged along these lines?

The Markan narrative of the crucifixion uses several christological terms of which 'the king of the Jews', 'Messiah' and 'the king of Israel' are clearly synonyms (15: 26, 32), all of them being gathered into the term 'son of God' with which the climax is reached (15: 39). The *titulus* itself draws upon the material in 15: 2, 6–15, 16–20 within which ὁ βασιλεὺς τῶν Ἰουδαίων language recurs repeatedly. In the case of 15: 2 we clearly encounter secondary material in context[19] since (*a*) the specific question asked by Pilate receives no preparation in 15: 1 and appears abruptly; (*b*) the generalised accusation πολλά in 15: 3 might more naturally occur before, rather than after, a specific charge; (*c*) the answer of Jesus in 15: 2 is at variance with the presupposition of silence in 15: 4f. Not only is 15: 2 secondary in context but also of doubtful historicity. The terminology used by Pilate aligns Jesus with Jewish kings in general (see Josephus, *BJ* 1: 282; *AJ* 14: 36; 15: 373f, 409; 16: 291, 311, for example) and it is hard to imagine a Roman procurator during a king-less period using such language. The question and answer combination belongs to the context of Christian confession and probably reflects Mark's own technique, in spite of the fact

---

[18] O. Betz, 'Die Frage nach dem messianischen Bewusstsein Jesu', *NovTest* 6 (1963), 20–48, esp. 34.

[19] Bultmann, *History*, p. 272.

that 'king of the Jews' is not strongly attested in Christian texts[20] – though here we should allow for the precedent in Matt. 2: 2, in which context it is immediately defined by more typical ideas (2: 4–6), just as happens to Mark 15: 2 in its own context (15: 27–39).[21] Mark 15: 6–15 presupposes 15: 2 and makes kingship its major theme, but it is also weighed down by the familiar objections to the whole Barabbas tradition and by the clear evidence of an attempt to make Pilate a witness to the innocence of Jesus. Mark 15: 16–20 pursues the same theme in such a way that the claim of Jesus is subjected to ironic parody. Mark 15: 26 itself could be omitted from its context and allow a smooth connection between verses 25 and 27,[22] but support for its historicity is found above all in its greater claim to verisimilitude than that of any of the other 'king of the Jews' texts. The idea of a *titulus* corresponds extremely closely to the practice documented in Cassius Dio, *Roman History* 54.3.7; Suetonius, *Gaius Caligula* 32.2; Suetonius, *Domitian* 10; Eusebius, *H.E.* V 1.434. But one must also observe that, as previously mentioned, verisimilitude does not demonstrate historicity, and, moreover, the precise wording used in 15: 26 has still to be scrutinised in relation to the related material in the surrounding context. In this connection, 15: 26 provides a starting point for a complex of material (15: 27–39) which conforms schematically to the pattern exhibited very clearly in Wisdom 2, 4–5.[23] Like the righteous man, Jesus has made certain claims which form the basis of hostile action (Wisd. 2:13, 16–18, 20; Mark 15: 29, 32; cp. 14: 58, 61f). Like the righteous man, Jesus must be vindicated before death if his opponents are to be convinced (Wisd. 2: 17f; Mark 15: 30, 32). Like the righteous man, Jesus is maltreated, subjected to legal proceedings – and he dies! (Wisd. 4: 16; Mark 15: 37). Like the righteous man, Jesus is recognised by his enemies as 'son of God' (Wisd. 5: 5; Mark 15: 39), an idea which includes the notion of kingship (Wisd. 3: 8; Mark 15: 26, 32). Like the righteous man, therefore, Jesus is vindicated and his claims confirmed, the only difference being that the enemies of the righteous man make their confession in the setting of a disclosure/ revelation of heavenly existence (Wisd. 4: 20 to 5: 8) whereas the representative of the enemies of Jesus does so with particular emphasis at the scene of death (Mark 15: 39). That means that the Markan narrative

---

[20] Historicity is affirmed on the basis of the unusual terminology by P. Winter, *On the Trial of Jesus* (Berlin, 1961), pp. 107–10; E. Lohse, *Die Geschichte des Leidens und Sterbens Jesu Christi* (Gütersloh, 1964), p. 89; Fuller, *Foundations*, p. 135.

[21] Compare the synonymous application to David of the two terms βασιλεὺς Ἰουδαίων and βασιλεὺς τῶν Ἰσραηλιτῶν in Josephus, *AJ* 7: 72, 76.

[22] E. Linnemann, *Studien zur Passionsgeschichte* (Göttingen, 1970), p. 147.

[23] Cp. G. W. E. Nickelsburg, *Resurrection, Immortality and Eternal Life in Intertestamental Judaism* (Cambridge, Mass., 1972), pp. 58–68.

uses a semi-adoptionist scheme but projects back before resurrection that which, strictly speaking, presupposes resurrection. It is to such a scheme that 15: 26 contributes, and it is by virtue of such a scheme, which Mark has imposed with some tension on the crucifixion tradition, that the historicity of the *titulus* has to be doubted.[24] At the hands of Mark the historical fact of the crucifixion of Jesus has been subordinated to the less historical idea of the crucifixion of Jesus the king of the Jews. And that in turn means that the historicity of Mark 11: 1–10 cannot be sustained, either on the basis of the tradition of an earlier event in the pre-Easter sequence (8: 27–30), or on the basis of an appeal to the ground of his ultimate execution (15: 26). That Jesus went to Jerusalem is certain, and to that minimal extent one could affirm historicity. Whether he was greeted like all other pilgrims with the words of Psalm 118:25f,[25] and/or whether an intensity of expectation of the kingdom of God was apparent in his companions,[26] must remain speculative and uncertain.

The review of a series of celebratory entry stories suggested that action in the Temple was a frequently attested component of the common pattern. Therefore the significance of the so-called 'cleansing of the Temple' tradition must be explored. Three preliminary observations must first be made. Firstly, although the celebratory entry scheme includes the element of Temple activity, the record of the latter is not necessarily rendered unhistorical by a conclusion that the entry proper is, as presently described, unhistorical. Arrival in Jerusalem (stated or presupposed) as a prelude to action in the Temple could easily have been expanded christologically to form a fitting introduction. In short, Mark 11: 15–19 has to be examined without prejudice. Secondly, MarkR is responsible for the enclosing of the tradition of Jesus's Temple activity within the tradition of the cursing of the fig-tree and therefore for the bridge-statement in verse 11. Verse 11a clearly overlaps with, and may be an echo of, verse 15a. Verse 11b, if properly attributed to Mark R, is not available to support the suggestion of Brandon that περιβλεψάμενος πάντα hints at '(?) an act of reconnoitring for action on the morrow', action which would directly challenge priestly interests and indirectly attack Roman authority.[27] Thirdly, Mark's version of the tradition can again safely be regarded as the primary one. Matthew/Luke agreements are confined to the affirmative, as against interrogative, introduction to the quotation from Isaiah 56: 7 and the absence of the words πᾶσιν τοῖς ἔθνεσιν. Such agreements cannot sustain any suggestion of an

---

[24] Similarly, Bultmann, *History*, p. 284.

[25] Hahn, *Hoheitstitel*, p. 172 (ET *Titles*, p. 156).

[26] Bultmann, *History*, p. 262.

[27] Thus, Brandon, *Zealots*, pp. 9, 333. Note that περιβλέπειν occurs in the New Testament seven times, of which six are Markan.

independent source. John's version, with its much more elaborate list of the items for sale, its more colourful description of Jesus's intervention, and its significantly different version of Jesus's saying about the house of God, might be independent. On the other hand, the greater detail may be a secondary development, and if the ποιεῖν-saying in Mark 11:17 is secondary in its own context as well as matching the ποιεῖν-saying in John 2:16b, then the Johannine tradition could well presuppose secondary developments in the Markan tradition and therefore emerge as dependent. However, the choice between these two options is not critical since it is unlikely that the ultimate meaning of the traditions is affected. There is no more than minimal risk involved in working from Mark 11:15–19.

Within the section Mark 11:15–19 clearly not all the tradition can be primary. No contribution, except as a transition, is made by verse 19, while verse 18 has to be adjudged MarkR in view of its matching the MarkR passages 1:22; 3:6. In verse 17 an antithesis is set up between οἶκος προσευχῆς and σπήλαιον λῃστῶν. This is done on the basis of the juxtaposition of Isa. 56:7 and Jer. 7:11, the latter probably being attracted to the former by the correspondence between ὁ οἶκός μου . . . κληθήσεται and ὁ οἶκός μου . . . ἐπικέκληται as a result of which the latter phrase is suppressed.[28] Whether verse 17 has 'hit on Jesus' purpose'[29] can only be decided by testing whether the activity which Jesus interrupts so dramatically has changed an οἶκος προσευχῆς into a σπήλαιον λῃστῶν. In other words everything hangs on verses 15f, interpreted in isolation first of all.

It would be tempting to interpret Mark 11:16 in terms of Josephus, *C. Apion* 2:106: 'one further point: no vessel whatever might be carried into the temple, the only objects in which were an altar, a censer and a lampstand, all mentioned in the law'. But Josephus is speaking about the holy place whereas Mark is not. More significantly, the term σκεῦος should not be over-interpreted as a reference to any of the holy vessels, as if Jesus is here interfering with regular cultic activity. The term is frequently used in an entirely secular sense, carrying a range of meanings which includes military equipment, jewellery, baggage, undefined property in general, and containers which may be used for any purpose.[30] Since Mark 11:16 is defined by the preceding statement in verse 15 the natural inference is that

---

[28] Note that πᾶσιν τοῖς ἔθνεσιν (verse 17a), although in Isa. 56:7 and doubtless of considerable interest to Mark (cp. 13:10), has no counterpart in verse 17b. Therefore there is no contrast intended between the use of the Temple by Gentiles and its use by Jews (cp. 1 Macc. 7:37; 3 Macc. 2:10).

[29] F. Hahn, *Das Verständnis der Mission im Neuen Testament* (Neukirchen, 1963), p. 30 (ET *Mission in the New Testament* (London, 1965), p. 38), who nevertheless argued that the double citation was secondary.

[30] C. Maurer, σκεῦος, *TDNT* vii (1971), 358–67, esp. 359.

σκεῦος refers to any container being used by those who bought or sold.[31] A closer parallel than the Josephus text would be Neh. 13: 8, where πάντα τὰ σκεύη οἴκου belonging to Tobiah, clearly standing for his property in general, are thrown out of the temple buildings by Nehemiah. Mark 11: 16 describes an action by Jesus which does not (*pace* Jeremias)[32] presuppose 'the occupation of the temple gates by his followers' but rather coheres with the action described in verse 15. How then may that action be interpreted?

Firstly, the scale of Jesus's intervention must have been small. The notion that Mark has reduced its size and significance lacks all evidential support, and the idea that Jesus and his followers were attempting the seizure of the Temple and treasury with a force 'too strong to be routed and captured'[33] defies all probability. Had this been so, the silence of Josephus, who includes in his accounts many more trivial events than that would have been, is inexplicable. Moreover, the speed and decisiveness of the intervention by the authorities to crush developments which threatened public order had frequently been, and would continue to be, unvaried and unrestrained. The arrest of forty persons by the Temple captain and a considerable support force after the attack on Herod's golden eagle (Josephus, *BJ* 1: 651–3; *AJ* 17: 155–63), the determined suppression of those who mourned for Judas and Matthias in 4 B.C. when they were perceived as a threat to social and political stability (*BJ* 2: 10–13; *AJ* 17: 213–18), the beheading by Gratus of Simon the usurper after his campaign of loot and arson (*BJ* 2: 57–9; *AJ* 17: 173–7), the eliminating of the leadership of the uprising by Athronges (*BJ* 2: 60–5; *AJ* 17: 278–84), the decisive intervention of the Romans to arrest Paul (Acts 21: 30–3), the arrest and execution without trial of Theudas and his collaborators (*AJ* 20: 97–9), the relentless efforts of the authorities to arrest the Egyptian false prophet together with the swift elimination of his followers (*BJ* 2: 261–3; *AJ* 20: 169–72; Acts 21: 38) – all these examples show the standard response of the authorities. In Jesus's case, however, they apparently did not respond.[34] Even when allowance is made for the Markan order as the product of editorial activity, and therefore for the possibility that the arrest occurred rather more immediately after the Temple incident, it remains critical that

---

[31] Cp. N. Q. Hamilton, 'Temple Cleansing and Temple Bank', *JBL* 83 (1964), 365–72, esp. 370. This is probably more true to the link between verse 16 and verse 15 than the suggestion that Jesus was stopping water carriers from taking a short cut through the Temple (J. Jeremias, *New Testament Theology I: The Proclamation of Jesus* (ET London, 1971), p. 145).

[32] Jeremias, *Theology*, p. 228.

[33] Brandon, *Zealots*, pp. 255–7, 330–9. Against this, see E. Trocmé, 'L'expulsion des marchands du temple', *NTSt* 15 (1968), 1–22, esp. 15f.

[34] On the thoroughness of policing arrangements, cp. V. Eppstein, 'The Historicity of the Gospel account of the cleansing of the Temple', *ZNW* 55 (1964), 42–58, esp. 46f.

Jesus was not arrested straightaway or *in situ*, while the disciples were not arrested at all. The action in the Temple must therefore have been trivial in size[35] and, moreover, as Mark himself indicates, an action by Jesus alone.

Secondly, the act of expulsion is definitive. As already noted, an act of expulsion is frequently a component of the celebratory entry scheme. This may throw light on the Markan scheme within which the entry has become subject to christological reflection, but at the pre-Markan stage (if Mark 11: 15f belongs to such a stage) this would be less applicable. Moreover, the expulsions listed earlier are essentially acts of cultic conservatism, designed to re-establish traditional modes of belief and worship, whereas Mark 11: 15 belongs to a setting in which no inroads had previously been made into the traditional practice of Judaism. Indeed, as has frequently been observed, the practice of money-changing and selling doves could easily be justified[36] and was intended to facilitate the traditional practices. One might then have recourse to the idea that a justifiable provision was being used for purposes of unjustifiable exploitation, for example, undue profit-making or financial irregularity. But that idea suffers from two handicaps: (*a*) There is no evidence of such exploitation by the Temple authorities, so it remains only a theoretical possibility; (*b*) Jesus's intervention does not protect the exploited buyers by expelling the exploiting sellers, but instead both buyers and sellers are ejected. The consequence is clear, and the intention therefore evident, in the fact that after Jesus's intervention there is no longer trade as such in the Temple. The fulfilment of an ancient text has in a temporary and preliminary way been achieved: 'There shall no longer be a trader in the house of the Lord on that day' (Zech. 14: 21b).[37]

Thirdly, consideration must be given to the degree of coherence which may exist between verses 15f and verse 17. Had the citation of Isa. 56: 7 alone been employed, and had attention been given to context, the stress would have had to be placed on πᾶσιν τοῖς ἔθνεσιν and the passage would simply have been given a new application as an instrument of polemic. With the assimilated citation attached from Jer. 7: 11, πᾶσιν τοῖς ἔθνεσιν

---

[35] M. Hengel, *Was Jesus a Revolutionist?* (Philadelphia, 1971), p. 16; Schweizer, *Mark*, p. 231. The suggestion of Hamilton, *JBL* 83 (1964), 370f, that 'Jesus by his act suspended the whole economic function of the temple' is probably correct in orientation but too unguarded as far as the scale of the event is concerned.

[36] E. Lohmeyer, 'Die Reinigung des Tempels', *ThBl* 20 (1941), 257–64, esp. 259: 'Diese Konzession brachte wohl ihren Inhabern . . . reiche Gewinne, aber sie diente auch dazu, den vielen Pilgern aus dem Inland oder Ausland ihre Gelübde und Opfer äusserlich zu erleichtern.' Similarly, Eppstein, *ZNW* 55 (1964), 43; Schweizer, *Mark*, p. 233.

[37] C. Roth, 'The Cleansing of the Temple and Zechariah XIV 21', *NovTest* 4 (1960), 174–81; Trocmé, *NTSt* 15 (1968), 18.

moves out of the spotlight, as it were, and is replaced by the antithesis οἶκος προσευχῆς/σπήλαιον λῃστῶν. Yet this polemical antithesis scarcely does justice to the situation described in verses 15f, where the Temple can scarcely be said to have been prevented from being a house of prayer,[38] any more than it can appropriately be labelled a cave of rebels in either Jeremiah's sense of a citadel of hypocritical worship by idolaters or in the later sense of a stronghold of revolutionaries (cp. Josephus, *AJ* 14: 415; 15: 346).[39] The connection between verses 15f and verse 17 is therefore forced and secondary, which means in turn that verse 17 reflects a later anti-Temple tendency in primitive Christianity while the history of the tradition in verses 15f stretches at least as far back as the pre-Markan stage. But does it go even further back to the historical Jesus? This brings us to the next point.

Fourthly, when Mark 11: 15f is understood in terms of Zech. 14: 21 there is an unstrained convergence between it and historical Jesus traditions. For Zech. 14: 21 describes the eschatological order within which God's kingship has been activated and established (verses 5, 9, 16f). In relation to that eschatological rule of God the action of Jesus in the Temple is an anticipatory sign carried out in prophetic fashion. As the prophet of the kingdom of God,[40] Jesus is acting here in line with scripture but pointing forward to that which will be both more comprehensive in scope and more permanent in achievement; in other words he acts here just as in Matthew 11: 5; 13: 16f = Luke 7: 22; 10: 23f.

The conclusion of the study of the 'triumphal' entry and Temple cleansing traditions is now possible. The two have been welded into a single whole under the combined influence of an already existing Jewish pattern and a post-Easter christological conviction. In the Temple incident Jesus is seen as what he was before Easter, the prophet of the near kingdom. In the 'triumphal' entry Jesus is seen as what he later became, after Easter, the Davidic messiah.

---

[38] Eppstein, *ZNW* 55 (1964), 43.

[39] Roth, *NovTest* 4 (1960), 176.

[40] Trocmé, *NTSt* 15 (1968), 18, rightly criticises any attempt at importing messianic ideas into this event.

The two swords (Luke 22: 35–38)

'This record of Jesus' arming of his disciples, or rather his checking on their armament', remarks S. G. F. Brandon,[1] 'has greatly troubled commentators'. The idea that Luke 22: 36–8 really presents Jesus as acting like an officer 'checking' his men's weapons before battle is bizarre; but that the commentators have floundered in a morass of perplexity when faced with this notoriously difficult passage is undoubtedly true. Brandon cites examples of the diverse explanations of exegetes, including myself, who have tried rather desperately to establish the meaning, and indeed to make any sense at all, of this strange pericope. A longer list of interpretations was collected by T. M. Napier, representing the period from Wellhausen to 1938,[2] and they make discouraging reading.

The first question to be considered in any attempt to elucidate Luke 22: 38 ('And they said, "Lord, see, here are two swords." And he said, "It is enough." ') is the relation of this verse, on the one hand to the preceding dialogue, verses 35 to 37, and, on the other, to Luke's version (verses 49 to 51) of the Markan episode of the assault, at or after the arrest of Jesus, on the servant of the high priest (Mark 14: 47; Matt. 26: 51–4; John 18: 10–11). As this verse stands in its context in Luke, it is evidently intended to form part of the dialogue which precedes it (35–7) and which is itself an integral part of the warnings, prophecies, instructions and promises given by Jesus to the disciples at the Last Supper – a section of Luke which, on a small scale, resembles the great Johannine discourses. Yet it does not appear to be logically connected with this material. If it was originally a part of the dialogue which precedes it, it would seem that it must have been intended simply to express the disciples' lack of comprehension and their insensitivity both to the true significance of Jesus's words in that dialogue and to the situation which evoked them. If, as is probably the case, it has been added to that dialogue by Luke himself, it seems that it is a clumsy attempt to establish a connection between the dialogue (verses 35 to 37) and the episode of the attack on the high priest's servant. Our task is to examine the question why Luke, on the assumption that this was the case, composed and inserted verse 38.

Luke has apparently brought together several distinct units of material

---

[1] *Jesus and the Zealots* (Manchester, 1967), p. 340.
[2] 'The Enigma of the Swords', *ExpT* 49 (1939), 467–70.

and related them to one another. These are: the instructions given to the Seventy when they were sent out on their mission (10: 3ff), with the parallel commissioning of the Twelve (9: 3ff); the warning to the disciples that the times have changed and that their original instructions given on those earlier occasions have now to be countermanded (22: 35–7); the saying of the disciples concerning two swords, and Jesus's reply to them (22: 38); the Markan story of the attack upon the servant of the high priest, preceded by the disciples' question, 'Lord, shall we strike with the sword?', and followed by Jesus's healing of the servant's ear (22: 49–51).

At 10: 3–4 Jesus sends out the Seventy, ordering them not to take purse, bag or sandals. This passage is broadly, though not precisely, parallelled in Mark 6: 8–9 and Matt. 10: 9–10, followed also by Luke 9: 3–4, where the orders are given to the Twelve. The source-criticism of this passage is complicated; it is possible that in this material there is an overlap between Mark and Q, and perhaps L as well. However this may be, it is likely that Luke has taken material which, in his source, referred to the sending out of the Twelve, and inserted it in the new context of the commissioning of the Seventy.[3] This passage is taken up at 22: 35: Jesus addresses the apostles and reminds them how they had originally been sent out without purse, bag or sandals. It may be that Luke is himself confused and has forgotten that he had transferred these instructions of Jesus into his new context of the sending of the Seventy; but it is more probable that in Luke's source, which Vincent Taylor may be right in assigning to the L material,[4] the groundwork of verses 35–7 was already associated with the substance of 10: 3–4; both referred to the sending out of the Twelve. The problem of the sources of verses 35 to 38 has been minutely studied by H. Schürmann[5] as well as by Vincent Taylor and others. It appears probable that verses 35 to 37, and conceivably even verse 38 as well, are a Lukan redaction of source-material and were already, in the pre-Lukan stage of the tradition, linked with 10: 3–4 as well as with the preceding 'farewell discourses' of Jesus to the disciples at the Last Supper (22: 21–34).

Jesus reminds his disciples that when he had originally sent them out they went without even the ordinary basic requirements for travel. He asks them whether they had lacked anything, and their answer, 'Nothing', presumably implies that in that successful mission (cp. 10: 17–18) they had been well received; they had found 'sons of peace' to receive their greeting and been given the hire which they deserved as workers (cp. 10: 5–8). But now (22: 36) the situation has changed drastically. In the scheme of

---

[3] See A. Loisy, *Les Evangiles Synoptiques* ii (Ceffonds, 1908), 554–8.
[4] *The Passion Narrative of St Luke*, ed. O. E. Evans (Cambridge, 1972).
[5] *Jesu Abschiedsrede, Lk. 22: 21–38* (Münster, 1953); M. Meinertz, *Neutestamentliche Abhandlungen* xx. 5 (Münster, 1957), 116–39.

successive epochs which Conzelmann discerns in Luke this phrase, ἀλλὰ νῦν, plays a decisive role. It inaugurates a new period, in which the disciples begin once again to be assailed, after a time of immunity during Jesus's ministry, by trials and temptations (πειρασμοί).[6] It is very doubtful whether this saying, or the similar 'epochal' turning-points on which Conzelmann's exegesis of Luke depends, will bear the weight which his theory places on them. Within somewhat narrower limits of interpretation, however, the contrast expressed in Luke's ἀλλὰ νῦν does signify the dramatic change that is going to come in the fortunes of the disciples. Whereas they had been popular preachers and healers, able to count on the support of the public wherever they went, the time is coming when no one will help them. They will have to fend for themselves; they will need purse and bag, and, since every man's hand will be against them to the point of actually threatening their safety, each of them will need to arm himself with a sword, even at the cost of selling his cloak, if necessary, to buy it.

It may be noticed in passing that, as has often been pointed out, in Matthew's version of the Q material at Matt. 5: 40/Luke 6: 29 the cloak (ἱμάτιον) which served the peasant as a kind of sleeping-bag is the most necessary garment of all, which a man would be most reluctant to surrender (cp. Exod. 22: 26–7, LXX). In Luke's version, on the other hand, the order is reversed, as though one would give up one's cloak sooner than one's tunic (χιτών); and this is sometimes taken to indicate that Luke thinks like a Greek city-dweller. In 22: 36, however, the need to buy a sword is so pressing as to demand even the sacrifice of the cloak itself – as though this were the last thing that anyone would want to sell. Perhaps this is yet another indication to add to the evidence adduced by Schürmann that this pericope belongs to pre-Lukan literary tradition.

This passage (verses 35 to 37) falls, then, into an easily-recognised category of the sayings ascribed to Jesus by all the evangelists: that of future, or eschatological, warnings of tribulation, distress and persecution. These naturally tend, as often in the New Testament (Acts 20: 29–31 being one example), to be uttered in the context of a leave-taking. Jesus's warning that his disciples will have to face a hostile world, shunned, boycotted, and in danger of physical assault, is in line with parts of the farewell discourses in the Fourth Gospel, such as John 15: 18–21 and 16: 1–4, with the prophecies of persecution in the eschatological discourses, such as Mark 13: 9–13 and parallels, especially 'You will be hated by all men for my name's sake' (Mark 13: 13, Matt. 24: 9, Luke 21: 17), and the saying

---

[6] H. Conzelmann, *Die Mitte der Zeit* (3rd edn. Tübingen, 1960), pp. 74–6 (ET *The Theology of St Luke* (London, 1960), pp. 80–2), etc.

contained in the Q material at Matt. 10: 34ff/Luke 12: 51ff which warns of coming division and strife within households and families.

The last of these passages is particularly interesting, for whereas in Matthew's version Jesus says, 'I have not come to bring peace (to the earth) but a sword (μάχαιραν)', in Luke's the wording is different: 'Do you think that I came to give peace on earth? No, I tell you, but rather division (διαμερισμόν).' It may well be the case that Luke has deliberately altered the original form of the saying. It is unlikely that he did this through fear that the vivid and striking metaphor of 'a sword' should be interpreted literalistically as implying an intention on the part of Jesus to promote civil war; Luke is not sensitive to such possibilities of misunderstanding.[7] More probably he has altered the wording in order to clarify the meaning of the saying in its application to the actual experience of the early church in times of persecution, and perhaps also because he has reserved the language relating to a sword for the passage we are now considering. In this saying the idea of a 'sword' serves to express, not, as in Matt. 10: 34, the disruption which Christian conversion will bring to the closely-knit family ties that were characteristic of both Jewish and Greco-Roman society,[8] but the total hostility which disciples would encounter; every man's hand would be against them.

This is a warning that the future tribulation, such as was described at 21: 17, is now imminent. It is expressed in the vivid, not to say violent, pictorial imagery characteristic of the eschatological predictions in the Gospels and of the 'farewell' warnings elsewhere in the New Testament, for instance in Luke 17: 31–7; 21: 18–28; Acts 20: 29; 2 Tim. 3: 1–9; 2 Pet. 3: 3ff. Jesus's command that any of his disciples not already in possession of a sword should go to the length of selling his cloak in order to buy one need not be taken literally; indeed, to do so would be perhaps as inappropriate as to press the details of the eschatological warnings given at 17: 31ff and to ask how a man could escape a universal catastrophe by fleeing from his housetop or why the disaster should engulf only one of two most intimate companions and leave the other to survive. The violent language is intended to convey one clear picture: whereas the disciples of Jesus had once been made welcome everywhere, now each must be prepared for a lonely struggle to survive in a bitterly hostile world; no one henceforth will provide him with food or shelter, and he will be in constant danger of attack.

Jeremias[9] argues that as an unfulfilled eschatological prophecy verse 36

---

[7] Cp. Brandon, *Zealots*, p. 316.

[8] Cp. J. Vogt in A. Momigliano (ed.), *The Conflict between Paganism and Christianity in the Fourth Century* (Oxford, 1963), p. 42.

[9] J. Jeremias, παῖς θεοῦ *ThWNT* v, 712.

belongs to very ancient and authentic tradition. This, however, raises far-reaching questions concerning the nature of the eschatological sayings in the synoptic Gospels as a whole. More directly, it leads to the question of the relationship of verses 35 to 36 to the saying in verse 37 and to the rest of Luke's Last Supper discourses. In verse 37 Jesus gives two related explanations of the reason for the drastic change in the situation of his followers. First, he is himself to suffer the fate prophesied in Isa. 53: 12, 'He was reckoned with transgressors.' Jeremias would interpret this to mean that Jesus is to be cast out of the community of Israel as a transgressor (ἄνομος), this being the cause of the coming boycott of his followers. The form in which this prophecy is cited, μετὰ ἀνόμων (אֶת־פּשְׁעִים) ἐλογίσθη, is closer to the Hebrew than to the LXX which has ἐν τοῖς ἀνόμοις. . . . Since Luke commonly follows the LXX, this divergence from that text has persuaded Schürmann and others that the citation is an integral part of the pre-Lukan material of which verses 35 to 36 consist. Although this is very possible, it would be rash to assume that it is necessarily the case. This part of the fourth 'Servant Song' was current in the early church in various forms: 1 Clement, for example, gives it as τοῖς ἀνόμοις without a preposition (16: 13), and it is by no means certain that the insertion of the citation in verse 37 is not the work of Luke himself rather than his source.

The citation is followed by a second explanation of the reason why the disciples must now expect tribulation: τὸ περὶ ἐμοῦ τέλος ἔχει. The meaning of this is ambiguous. Vincent Taylor[10] approves of the interpretation given by Klostermann:[11] 'my life draws to its end'. Eisler,[12] however, maintains that τέλος ἔχει refers not to the end of Jesus's life, but to the fulfilment of his destined role; and in fact the meaning could be, 'the destiny prophesied for me is being fulfilled'. In either case, whether the sense of τέλος is primarily 'end' or 'fulfilment' (and the two possible meanings may be intentionally combined), the question arises whether this sentence is meant, in effect, to repeat and to some extent to clarify Jesus's application of Isa. 53: 12 to himself, or whether it is a second, independent, explanation of the coming tribulation. If the latter seems more probable, then at the pre-Lukan stage of the tradition the saying may have taken the form, 'let him buy a sword. For my life draws to its end (and then you will be left alone to fend for yourselves).' In that case the introduction of the reference to Isa. 53: 12 may have been due to Luke's redaction. According to this view of the matter, Luke may have introduced the citation from

---

[10] *Passion Narrative*, p. 164.

[11] E. Klostermann, *Das Lukasevangelium* (Tübingen, 1929).

[12] R. Eisler, ΙΗΣΟΥΣ ΒΑΣΙΛΕΥΣ ΟΥ ΒΑΣΙΛΕΥΣΑΣ ii (Heidelberg, 1930), 266ff.

Isaiah in order to explain the phrase τὸ περὶ ἐμοῦ τέλος ἔχει which he found in his source, and thereby produced the rather clumsy and ambiguous juxtaposition of δεῖ τελεσθῆναι ἐν ἐμοί and τὸ περὶ ἐμοῦ τέλος ἔχει. Why Luke should have introduced Isaiah's prophecy in this way must be considered later. For the present we must concern ourselves with Luke's placing of verses 35 to 37.

Schürmann believes that the whole pericope, 35 to 38, already belonged, in a pre-Lukan stage of the written tradition, to a farewell discourse at the Last Supper. This may be so, but it is by no means certainly the case. Verses 35 to 37 appear to be a piece of tradition relating to the future lot of Jesus's disciples rather than to the passion story. Schürmann associates it also with those passages in the New Testament which reflect early Christian interest in the mission of the apostles and how they and other ministers in the apostolic church maintained themselves while they were engaged in it; Luke 10: 7; Acts 20: 33; 1 Tim. 5: 17 are examples of these. This is, no doubt, correct, but Schürmann's further assertion is highly questionable: that the maintenance of ministers from the church's common funds or from the common table was a matter closely related to the early Christians' common meals and that the passage we are considering was therefore appropriately located, even at a pre-Lukan stage of the tradition, in the context of the farewell speeches of Jesus at the Supper which was the prototype of Christian common meals. As a prophecy of coming tribulation it could rather, perhaps, have belonged originally to the eschatological material which Luke collected in the discourses in chapters 17 and 21. Luke, however, if not his source, has placed it in the context of the series of warnings and promises which Jesus gives to the disciples at the Last Supper.

Here it forms the last of four units of dialogue which Minear[13] finds 'homogeneous to the content, mood and implications of the Supper'. The themes of these dialogues are Christ's covenantal promises to his disciples (22: 17–19a, 29) and prophetic warnings of their treachery (Judas), denial (Peter), and, in the particular slant which Luke gives to the Isaianic prophecy, lawless conduct: for they are to be the ἄνομοι with whom Jesus is going to be reckoned. All the topics of these dialogues – Judas's treachery in relation to the predetermined fate of the Son of man (22: 21–2), the disciples' quarrel about greatness in its relation to the promise to them as participants in Jesus's πειρασμοί of a table in his kingdom and thrones of judgement over Israel, the prediction of Peter's denial in relation to the promise of his restoration and future leadership, and the saying about buying a sword in its relation to the prophecy of Isa. 53: 12 – have to do,

13. P. S. Minear, 'A Note on Luke 22: 36', *NovTest* 7.2 (1964), 128–34.

according to Luke, with events that are to occur in the immediate future when the hour of Jesus's enemies and the power of darkness are to be manifested in the garden and beyond.

It would seem that Luke has taken from his source Jesus's warning of the future plight of the disciples; he has added to it the citation of Isa. 53: 12, or, if this prophecy was already contained in that pericope as he found it, he has given it a new meaning. If it was already part of this passage in a pre-Lukan stage it must have meant that Jesus was to be cast out of Israel as a lawbreaker. Luke, however, understands it to mean that the disciples have become lawbreakers and Jesus is to be numbered with them. He conveys this meaning, in the first instance, by setting the pericope in the context of this series of promises and warnings which reveal the apostles, Jesus's followers, as lawless and unrighteous men. One is to betray the Lord, one is to deny him, all – even in the setting of the covenant supper and his predicted betrayal by one of their number – quarrel about which of them seems to be great. All of them are ἄνομοι because they, or some of them, are armed, or are going to arm themselves, with swords and resort to the use of the sword in the garden.

Luke has thus imposed a quite new meaning on the old saying about the need to buy a sword. He has done this, first, by either introducing the citation of Isa. 53: 12, or if this was already there by placing it in a new setting and giving it a new application; secondly, by adding the dialogue about the two swords (verse 38); thirdly, by relating the whole pericope both to the preceding warnings and prophecies of treachery and failure on the disciples' part and also to the episode of the assault on the high priest's servant which is to be narrated in verses 49 to 51.

Verse 38 records the disciples' answer to Jesus's warning about his own fate and their coming abandonment to their own devices: 'And they said, "Lord, see, here are two swords." And he said to them, "It is enough" (ἱκανόν ἐστιν).' It is conceivable that this short dialogue may have formed part of the whole pericope, verses 35 to 38, at a pre-Lukan stage of literary tradition. If so, it must have been intended as an inept comment by Jesus's followers on his vivid picture of their coming plight when they would need to equip themselves with purse, bag, and, above all, sword. 'They catch only the surface meaning',[14] and suppose that Jesus is talking literally about swords and actually telling them to go out and buy them on the spot. Such a reaction on their part would, it is true, be in line with the incomprehension and insensitivity which Luke makes them show in their response to his warnings, for instance at 17: 37 and 18: 28, and, in particular, to his prophecies at the Supper about the betrayal and the denial (22: 23ff, 33).

[14] Vincent Taylor, *Jesus and his Sacrifice* (London, 1937), p. 193.

It seems, however, much more probable that verse 38 is Luke's own composition, for the vocabulary and style are strikingly characteristic of Luke. Further, the verse raises notoriously difficult problems if it is taken as an integral part of a pre-Lukan pericope consisting of verses 35 to 38. These include the provenance and purpose of the swords which the disciples happen to be carrying at the Last Supper, the reason why they were carrying neither more nor less than two, and the meaning of Jesus's final words, 'It is enough.' If, however, the verse is recognised to be a Lukan addition to the traditional material contained in verses 35 to 37, inserted, perhaps together with the citation of Isa. 53: 12, in order to bring Jesus's warning about his followers' future need for swords into line with the story of the high priest's servant (verses 49 to 51), it becomes much easier to understand. The preceding prophecies of Jesus concerning Judas's treachery and Peter's denial were shortly afterwards fulfilled in the garden and the high priest's house. Luke understands this traditional prophecy about the need to buy a sword as another similar short-term warning which was also to be fulfilled on that same evening. Hence, by setting it in the context of the disciples' coming treachery and weakness (verses 21 to 34), inserting the citation of Isa. 53: 12 or at least altering its application, and by adding the dialogue in verse 38, Luke has radically changed the significance of Jesus's prophecy and, in so doing, created major difficulties of interpretation. For the prophecy in verse 36 could not be brought into relation with the episode in verses 49 to 51 without violent adjustment and distortion. Nor does verse 38 provide any kind of smooth transition from the prophecy in verse 36 to the story in verses 49 to 51 which Luke takes to be the fulfilment of the former.

The starting-point, it would seem, for the whole of Luke's operation is the incident recorded in Mark 14: 47 which he reproduces at verse 50 and to which, by the additions which he supplies in verses 49 and 51, he gives an interpretation of his own. This event is an armed attack carried out by one of the disciples only (verse 50). Yet the whole body of Jesus's followers (οἱ περὶ αὐτόν) are seen by Luke as being collectively involved in it, as he shows in his addition to the Markan narrative of their question, 'Lord, shall we strike with the sword?' (verse 49). To Luke, it would seem, this violent action, from which Jesus so emphatically dissociates himself, not only by word but by miraculous action (verse 51), identifies the disciples as the ἄνομοι to whom the prophecy of Isa. 53: 12 had pointed. It comes, indeed, as a climax of the offences committed by the disciples, or prophesied of them by Jesus, at the Last Supper: Judas's betrayal, Peter's denial, and the quarrel about greatness which the disciples conceived in terms of those kingdoms of the world which, as Luke made clear by his addition to the story of the Temptations (4: 6), lie under the authority of the devil – the authority of darkness which holds sway in the garden in the 'hour' of Jesus's enemies (22: 53).

In order to explain the assault in the garden in these terms Luke has to force the tradition of Jesus's prophecy about the need for a sword into line with his interpretation of Isa. 53: 12, imposing a new meaning on it, and connecting it with its 'fulfilment' at verses 49 to 51 by means of the dialogue about 'two swords' in verse 38. The latter thus has to be understood in relation, first, to the story of the armed assault as Luke interpreted this, and, secondly, to the warning in verse 36 as Luke reinterpreted this in the light of his application of the prophecy of Isa. 53: 12 to that story.

Mark 14: 47 tells how, after the arrest of Jesus, 'one of the bystanders drew his sword and struck the servant of the high priest and removed his ear'. The way in which this story is presented to the reader is most extraordinary. It has neither prelude nor sequel; indeed, it appears to have no connection with the events that precede and follow it. We are not told who the assailant was. Mark does not say that he was one of Jesus's followers. He is simply one of those anonymous 'bystanders' who appear from time to time in Mark's passion narrative: minor actors in the drama, brought on to the stage unintroduced and casually dismissed without their presence on the scene being explained. Such 'bystanders' appear twice as Peter's interrogators (14: 69, 70), and once at the Cross when they hear Jesus's cry, 'Eloi, Eloi', and say, 'See, he calls Elijah' (15: 35). Lohmeyer[15] thinks that the story is told from the standpoint of those who arrested Jesus, and that one of the disciples, presumably standing about in a state of bewilderment, would appear to them to be a 'bystander'. But this would be a very odd way of describing one of the band of disciples of the man whom the 'crowd' (ὄχλος) had come to hunt down and arrest. The victim of the assault, on the other hand, seems to be someone whom the reader can identify, for he is not simply 'a servant of the high priest' but '*the* servant of the high priest'. We are not told why this man was attacked. It was not in order to hinder the arrest of Jesus, for this had already been effected, and as an attempt at rescue, even as a gesture in an impossible situation, it was a singularly futile effort.

It seems reasonable to infer from Mark's peculiar treatment of the episode that he saw in it a symbolical significance. It would be natural to expect it to have been constructed on the basis of some scriptural type or prophecy, but no passage of the Old Testament seems to have any bearing upon it. The most ingenious attempt to discover a scriptural foundation for the story is perhaps that suggested by Hall.[16] He thinks that

---

[15] E. Lohmeyer, *Das Evangelium des Markus* (Göttingen, 1957), pp. 332ff.

[16] S. G. Hall, 'Swords of Offence', *Studia Evangelica*, i, TU 73 (1959), 499–505.

the incident has been constructed as a fulfilment of Psalm 40 (LXX 39): 7, in a version like that of Aquila: 'ears hast thou dug for me' (ὠτία δὲ ἔσκαψάς μοι),[17] literalistically mistranslating כָּרָה אֹזֶן ('open the ear'), or perhaps confusing this Hebrew verb with כָּרַת ('cut off'). But this seems to be both highly improbable and also irrelevant in Mark's context.

A good case, however, has been made out for the view that the significance of the incident, as understood by Mark, lies in the fact that in the person of his servant a contemptuous insult, directed against his sacred character, was offered to the high priest himself.[18] Mark's curious expression 'the slave of the high priest' is significant. It is repeated by the other three evangelists. The use of the definite article, when the servant is not otherwise identified and the reader has been told nothing about him, suggests that Mark's purpose is to call special attention to his status. He is '*the* servant' of the high priest, his personal agent and representative. An insult offered to such a person when acting as his master's agent is an insult to his master. Daube calls attention to the recognition in Roman law of vicarious insult and damage of this kind: 'iniuria . . . domino per eum (sc. servum) fieri videtur . . . cum quid atrocius commissum fuerit quod aperte in contumeliam domini fieri videtur, veluti si quis alienum servum verberaverit'[19] and also to the biblical examples of such conduct in 2 Sam. 10: 4f and the parable of the wicked husbandmen (Mark 12: 1–5).

Mark has no interest in who struck this blow, nor in what became of him. The whole point of recording the fact that it was struck is that at the very moment when a crowd which had come, as Mark specially emphasises, 'from the chief priests and the scribes and the elders' has laid hands on Jesus, and the moment of the high priest's triumph has arrived, he receives, through his personal representative at the scene of the arrest, an injury of a peculiarly insulting and contemptuous kind, which, moreover, if inflicted on his own person, would disqualify him for his office. As Rostovtzeff points out, the cutting off of an ear is not likely to happen accidentally in the course of a scuffle. It was an intentional act, not done in a bungled attempt to kill but meant to inflict on the high priest, vicariously, an indelible mark of contempt. Rostovtzeff, Lohmeyer and Daube have drawn attention to an Egyptian court case in which 'Hesiod cut off the right ear of Dorion' (*P. Teb.* iii 793), to penalties inflicted under Assyrian and Babylonian law, and to two close parallels to the Markan incident: Antigonus cut off, or slit (the reading varies between ἀποτέμνειν and ἐπιτέμνειν) the ear of Hyrcanus II

[17] See F. Field, *Origenis Hexapla quae supersunt* ii (Oxford, 1875), 151.
[18] See M. Rostovtzeff, Οὖς δεξιὸν ἀποτέμνειν, ZNW 33 (1934), 196–9; D. Daube, 'Three Notes having to do with Johanan ben Zakkai: III, Slitting the High Priest's Ear', *JThSt* n.s. 11 (1960), 59–62; E. Lohmeyer, *Markus*, pp. 332f.
[19] Gaius iii. 222.

to make him unfit for the high priesthood (Josephus, *AJ* 14.13.10); Johanan ben Zakkai did the same to a Sadducee high priest to render him unfit to carry out a cultic service (*Tosephta Parah* iii. 8). Mark, then, is telling us that as soon as his men had laid hands on Jesus the high priest was vicariously marked out, by the symbolical action of an unknown assailant, as disqualified to retain his office. Luke adds to the Markan story the detail that it was the servant's right ear which was cut off.[20] This may merely be due to Luke's fondness for vividly dramatic touches, as when he tells us that it was the right hand of the man in the synagogue which was healed (6: 6, contrast Mark 3: 1/Matt. 12: 10). More probably, however, this detail shows that Luke had taken Mark's point. It was the high priest's right ear which was ceremonially smeared with the blood of the ram of consecration (Lev. 8: 23–4), and at the cleansing of a leper some of the blood of the lamb offered as a trespass offering was smeared on the right ear of the person to be cleansed, as was also some of the oil that he offered (Lev. 14: 14, 17, 25, 28). Luke may thus interpret the incident as a symbol, not only of the disqualification of the high priest, but also of his deconsecration and being rendered unclean.

Luke, however, sees the affair in quite a different light from Mark. The high priest may have been worthy of contempt and rejection; but the armed assault on his representative was lawless aggression. We may compare Luke's treatment of the 'reviling' of the high priest by Paul (Acts 23: 3–5). Both Matthew and Luke believe that the assailant was one of Jesus's companions; but whereas in Matthew and in John it is one man alone who acts and is subsequently rebuked by Jesus (John naming him as Peter), Luke makes all those who were with Jesus responsible for the assault and implies that they tried to involve him in it as well. They ask, 'Lord, shall we strike with the sword?', and, without waiting for an answer, one of them strikes the servant; it is to them all, in the plural, that Jesus addresses his rebuke, ἐᾶτε ἕως τούτου, probably meaning, 'Let my enemies go so far as to do this.'[21] By this rebuke Jesus instantly dissociates himself from his disciples' 'lawlessness', and he then demonstrates his disapproval of their conduct and his own totally different attitude by healing the wounded man. In this way Luke shows that the disciples were rebuked and that Jesus, the

---

[20] John does the same, perhaps following Luke; but since he agrees with Mark against Luke in using ὠτάριον for 'ear' and ἔπαισεν for 'struck', instead of οὖς and ἐπάταξεν, while differing from both Mark and Luke in using ἀπέκοψεν ('cut off') instead of ἀφεῖλεν ('removed'), the precise relation between John and the synoptists here is very hard to determine.

[21] P. S. Minear, however, thinks (*NovTest* 7.2 (1964), 128–34) that these words refer to the fulfilment of Isa. 53: 12: 'You are permitted to go this far, but no farther' (for the prophecy has now been amply fulfilled).

'righteous Servant' was in no way involved in their transgression.[22] Their conduct was such as to mark them out as the ἄνομοι with whom Isaiah had foretold that the righteous Servant, himself free from ἀνομία, would be numbered. Indeed, that prophecy, according to the LXX, went on to say that it was because of their sins that the Servant was 'handed over' to death (παρεδόθη), the word used of the betrayal of Jesus by Luke (22: 48, cp. 22: 4, 6, 21, 22) as also by the other evangelists. It may well have been the appearance of the key-word παρεδόθη which led Luke to apply the Isaianic prophecy to the 'reckoning' of Jesus with the 'lawless' disciples.[23]

If Mark believed that this prophecy referred to Jesus, he saw its fulfilment in the fact that Jesus was arrested as though he were a λῃστής ('brigand' or 'terrorist') and was subsequently crucified together with two λῃσταί (14: 48; 15: 27). At a later period, indeed, this seemed so obvious a fulfilment of the prophecy that a widespread but inferior reading adds after Mark 15: 27: 'And the scripture was fulfilled which says, "And he was numbered with transgressors"', evidently taking this text from Luke 22: 37, and thus quoting it in the form in which it appears there, and not directly from the LXX.

In Luke this interpretation is entirely absent. Jesus is arrested as though he were a λῃστής, it is true, but the two who were crucified with him are not λῃσταί. They are simply 'evildoers' (κακοῦργοι), and Jesus is not in any way 'numbered with' them.[24] To Luke the 'transgressors' are Jesus's disciples whose act of violent lawlessness against the high priest's representative comes after a series of actual and predicted treachery, quarrels to gain such power as the devil alone can give, and denial of Jesus. Luke, therefore, seeing the assault in the garden in this light, applies Isaiah's prophecy to it. He then looks for some previous warning or prophecy of Jesus concerning this transgression, parallel to those which he gave to Judas and Peter. This he finds in his source material in the form of the 'farewell warning' about the coming need to buy a sword.

The two convictions, then, on which Luke's entire construction rests are these: first, that the disciples as a body were guilty of an assault with the sword, an act of violence which Jesus rebuked and the effects of which he

---

[22] In constructing this sequel to Mark's story Luke may have fallen into inconsistency. He tells us that Jesus 'touched the ear and healed him'. But Luke has already reproduced Mark's word ἀφεῖλεν which means that the ear had not merely been damaged but removed. If Luke means that Jesus touched the place of the missing ear and miraculously replaced it, then this was an extraordinary healing, without parallel in Jesus's ministry. It would certainly be an unmistakable demonstration of his attitude.

[23] Possibly another indication that the Hebrew form of Isa. 53: 12 belongs to Luke's source rather than his own writing.

[24] Luke 23: 40, 'You are under the same sentence' has no bearing on this point.

promptly repaired by a miracle; secondly, that the saying about buying a sword, with the interpretation applied to it from Isa. 53: 12, was one of the series of short-term predictions and warnings delivered by Jesus at the Supper and that it was fulfilled on the same evening in that assault. The prophecy did not lend itself easily to this interpretation; Luke was trying to combine and make sense of material that lay before him in Mark and in his L source, and he was not composing freely. How could the disciples actually be expected to get hold of purses and bags, sell cloaks and buy swords late in the evening of the Passover? Were they really meant to stop in the city and try to do these things on their way from the Supper to the garden? How was it that some of them had already obtained swords, as Jesus's words implied that they had? Such questions were inevitably raised as a consequence of Luke's interpretation of verses 35 to 37, but he is not concerned to deal with them. Mark had told him that a sword was used in the garden. Mark was not interested in who used it or where he had brought it from; all that mattered to him was that the high priest's servant's ear was removed. Luke thinks that the disciples were reponsible for the use of the sword in the garden; therefore they must have had at least one sword with them. Further, since they asked, 'Lord, shall *we* strike with the sword?', the man who struck the actual blow could not have been the only disciple with a sword; and Jesus's words, ὁ μὴ ἔχων, seemed to confirm this, for they implied that some of the disciples did have swords.

Luke makes the point clear in verse 38, probably his own composition: 'And they said, "Lord, see, here are two swords." And he said to them, "It is enough." ' Two swords are enough, in Luke's view, to establish the guilt of the disciples as a body, to identify them collectively, and not only one individual among them, with the ἄνομοι of Isa. 53: 12 and bring about the fulfilment of that prophecy, and possibly also to testify to their transgression as 'two witnesses' (cp. Deut. 19: 15). This is probably what Luke intends Jesus to mean by the words ἱκανόν ἐστιν. Luke does not consider the question how the disciples had come into possession of these two swords and, according to his reconstruction of the events, actually to bring them to the Last Supper, any more than Mark troubled to ask why his 'bystander' should have happened to be carrying a sword. If Luke could be questioned about this, he might perhaps reply that the disciples had anticipated Jesus's warning and had brought to the Supper the instruments of their coming 'lawlessness', just as they had brought their rivalries about worldly greatness and Judas had come with his intention to betray the Lord.

The complex and subtle structure which Luke has built on the Markan incident raises problems from which the simpler interpretations offered by Matthew and John are free. In Matthew (26: 50–4) the assault was an attempt to rescue Jesus, who had already been seized; it was rebuked by him with the quasi-proverbial saying, 'all who take the sword die by the sword', and the question, 'Do you suppose that I cannot appeal to my Father, who would at once send to my aid more than twelve legions of angels? But how then could the scriptures be fulfilled which say that this must be?' In John (18: 10–11) Peter tries to prevent the arrest, and Jesus's answer is, 'This is the cup the Father has given me; shall I not drink it?' John, however, takes up Matthew's point in the dialogue between Jesus and Pilate (18: 36): 'My kingdom does not belong to this world. If it did, my followers would be fighting to save me from arrest by the Jews.'

Luke's more intricate composition involves the strange supposition that Jesus believed his disciples to be predetermined to do wrong, compelled to act lawlessly by a prophecy that referred to them and must needs be fulfilled. This, however, would present itself to Luke as only another aspect of the great mystery that was focussed in the paradox that he repeats (22: 22) from Mark: 'The Son of Man is going his *appointed* way; but alas for that man by whom he is betrayed!' Moreover, although the disciples had to become transgressors, this did not mean that they were abandoned without hope to the power of darkness (cp. 22: 53). The warnings that Jesus gave them of their treachery and weakness were relieved by promises: of communion with the Lord in his kingdom, despite their strivings for greatness, of repentance and restoration for Peter, despite the denial. Isaiah, too, showed that although the Servant was 'led to death from their lawlessnesses', they were still 'my (that is, God's) people' (Isa. 53: 8). If Luke knew the Hebrew text (as seems quite possible) of the very prophecy that foretold their lawlessness, he would be aware also that the Servant 'interceded for the transgressors' (53: 12).

If Luke has constructed his story in the light of that prophecy, having to use some very intractable material for this purpose, the many attempts to explain verse 38 as a literal record of an actual dialogue that took place between Jesus and the disciples become irrelevant. Chrysostom, for instance, supposed that the 'swords' were in fact carving knives taken from the table where they had been used for the Passover lamb.[25] Western[26] thought they were fishermen's knives, intended for use when the disciples went back to their fishing in Galilee (John 21: 3), and had nothing to do with weapons, though in a later article the same writer suggested that by ἱκανόν ἐστιν Jesus was either saying that these knives 'are large enough for all the fighting that you will have to do', or asking, 'are they large enough

[25] Cramer, *Catena in Luc.* 22: 50.
[26] W. Western, 'The Enigma of the Swords', *ExpT* 50 (1939), 377, and 52 (1941), 357.

for the fighting which you contemplate?' Helmbold[27] mentions another literalistic explanation: the disciples had found two old swords in Peter's house at Capernaum, left over from past wars, and brought them to defend the party against attack by Herod on their way up to Jerusalem.

Speculations of this kind create immense difficulties of interpretation. Napier[28] imagined that Jesus had discovered that two disciples had provided themselves with swords. He reminded them of his previous instructions to carry no purse or bag; then he said, in effect, 'If, now, you mean to trust to yourselves and think God is no longer sufficient, then if need be sell your cloak and buy a sword.' The disciples missed the point, replied, 'Here are two swords', and Jesus's 'It is enough' is an expression of his sorrow. This explanation altogether fails to take the prophecy of Isa. 53: 12 into account; it is worth noticing, too, that the reading of the 'Western' text, ἀρκεῖ for ἱκανόν ἐστιν, indicates that in antiquity the latter phrase was taken literally. A similar interpretation was proposed by Finlayson:[29] Jesus knew the disciples were arming, but felt it impossible to persuade them to desist; he alluded to the buying of a sword, their attention was distracted, and their unwary reply, 'Here are two swords', revealed the actual situation and prepared the way for Jesus's teaching that 'all who take the sword shall perish by the sword'. This, again, leaves the all-important prophecy out of the explanation, and ignores the fact that Luke did not record the saying of Jesus to which Finlayson believes that the whole passage points.

Eisler,[30] after referring to the discussion of the passage by Schlatter,[31] takes up the question raised by Régnault,[32] how it could have seemed necessary to send a cohort (John 18: 3) to overcome twelve men armed with only two swords. His own answer is that the disciples were carrying two swords each, in the manner of the *sicarii*. This is highly improbable. Had each disciple attended the Supper regularly equipped as an armed *sicarius*, Jesus could scarcely be ignorant of the fact. His comment, 'It is enough', would then seem to express approval; hence his words at Luke 22: 35–7 become unintelligible, as does also the allusion to Isa. 53: 12; and the outcome of it all in the garden would merely show that as *sicarii* the disciples were incredibly feeble and inefficient: twenty-two or perhaps twenty-four swords between them and only one ear to show for all that formidable weaponry!

[27] H. Helmbold, *Vorsynoptische Evangelien* (Stuttgart, 1953), p. 41.
[28] *ExpT* 49 (1938), 467–70.
[29] S. K. Finlayson, 'The Enigma of the Swords', *ExpT* 50 (1939), 563.
[30] Eisler, ΙΗΣΟΥΣ ΒΑΣΙΛΕΥΣ, pp. 266ff.
[31] A. Schlatter, *Die beiden Schwerter*, BFChTh 20 (1916).
[32] H. Régnault, *Le procès de Jésus* (Paris, 1909), p. 92.

Eisler in fact recognises that if the pericope of the two swords is to provide evidence for a theory that the disciples, and perhaps Jesus himself, were militant Zealot revolutionaries, it has to be re-written and transferred to a different context from the night of the betrayal. He acknowledges that Luke's framework for the saying, if it is to be interpreted on these lines, is most implausible; he therefore argues that, as was mentioned above, τὸ περὶ ἐμοῦ τέλος ἔχει (22: 37) bore no reference to the end of Jesus's life, but indicated the fulfilment of his destiny. The pericope belongs, according to Eisler, to a time when Jesus was sending out his followers, some time after their first mission, on a longer journey, equipped and armed. Jesus expected most of them to possess swords already; any who did not must sell even those articles that would be most needed on the journey and buy one.

Others have tried to find evidence in this passage for a Zealot Jesus but without re-working it on Eisler's lines. Brandon,[33] for instance, says that

> the fact (*sic*) that some at least of the disciples of Jesus were accustomed to go about with concealed weapons, after the manner of the Sicarii, is attested by Luke 22: 38. The fact that Jesus had to make sure that the disciples were armed on this occasion (see verses 36, 38) indicates that their weapons were concealed in their garments in Sicarii-fashion.

Brandon, having assumed that verses 35 to 38 mean that Jesus made sure that his disciples were armed before going to the garden, naturally finds Luke's story unconvincing.

> Luke ... endeavours to reduce its (i.e. the arming's) significance by saying that Jesus did so in order to fulfil a prophecy, and that he considered two swords enough for this purpose. The ascription of such an artificial fulfilment of an obscure passage of Isaiah to Jesus on such an occasion does no credit to Jesus and lowers our estimation of the sensibility of Luke. With how many swords the disciples were armed is immaterial; it is scarcely likely that it was only two.[34]

The plain fact seems to be that any attempt to interpret verse 38 literalistically as a source of factual information renders it impossible to make sense of Luke's narrative as a whole. As Brandon suggests, we have to choose between Luke's 'sensibility' on the one hand and a reconstruction along literalistic lines on the other; we cannot have both. Of all the attempts to make sense of Luke 22: 35–8 as a factual record perhaps the best is that of Cyril of Alexandria (*Luc.* 22: 34ff). He understood Jesus to be foretelling the Jewish war. The warning to get a sword and other necessary equipment, though addressed to the apostles, was meant for every Jew. War would come because Christ was to suffer a punishment meant for lawless men and

---

[33] *Zealots*, p. 203.   [34] Ibid. pp. 340–1.

be crucified with λησταί; thus the prophecies of scripture were fulfilled and the doom predicted by the prophets was bound to overtake his slayers. The disciples misunderstood Jesus and thought he was referring to the imminent incursion of Judas. Jesus's reply, 'It is enough', was sarcastic: 'Yes,' he says, 'two swords are sufficient to resist the war that is going to come upon you, a war against which thousands of swords will be of no avail.'

The *titulus*

Death penalties in the provinces used to be registered in the records of the Roman administrator and the execution was, when the circumstances demanded it, reported to Rome either by special message or as an item in the reports on major events which were submitted at regular intervals. These were the acts of official notification.[1] Different from this were the means of informing the general public. The oldest sources, sources not later than the New Testament,[2] mention a *tabula*[3] which was to be carried by the condemned man (or by someone else walking in front of him) on his way to the place of execution, which indicated[4] the αἰτία. The fixing of a tablet[5] with an inscription on the cross is less well testified;[6] possibly because one mention of the *tabula* was considered sufficient by those who described a crucifixion. In any case, the showing of a *tabula* either on the last journey of the delinquent or on the spot where he was publicly put to death was not indispensable, not a constitutive part of the procedure, and therefore not

---

[1] W. Riepl, *Das Nachrichtenwesen des Altertums* (Leipzig, 1913), pp. 271f and especially G. Reincke in *PW* xvi, 1518ff.

[2] Suet. *Calig.* 32; *Domit.* 10.1; Dio 54.8.

[3] Not, of course, identical with the *tabella* on which the sentence was written down and from which it used to be read out by the judge; cp. *Acta Cypr.* iv. pp. cxiif Hartel: 'sententiam vix et aegre dixit verbis huius modi: diu sacrilega mente vixisti ... sanguine tuo sancietur disciplina. et his dictis decretum ex tabella recitavit: Thascium Cyprianum gladio animadverti placet.' The notice in this *tabula* was copied and emended in the record of the administrator.

[4] Significantly it is merely a hint that is given in the formulation of the *titulus* according to the oldest authorities: 'qui causam poenae indicaret/γραμμάτων τὴν αἰτίαν ... δηλούντων'. The report on the Lyonnese martyrs incorporated in Eusebius's church history mentions that one of them was led round the arena πίνακος αὐτὸν προάγοντος ἐν ᾧ ἐγέγραπτο 'Ρωμαιστί 'οὗτός ἐστιν ᾿Ατταλος ὁ Χριστιανός' (5.1.44), implying in this way that the proper juridical reason was not given on the placard and, secondly, that the custom of carrying a πίναξ was not the normal one in this place. Tert. *Apol.* 2.20 presupposes that the *tabella* was the normal accessory, but he harps on the fact that the inscription was not in precise terms.

[5] Not identical with the *inscriptio*, which means the juridical form of the accusation. For the function of the *inscriptio* see L. K. G. Geib, *Geschichte des römischen Criminalprocesses* (Leipzig, 1842), pp. 542ff.

[6] Cp. H. Fulda, *Das Kreuz und die Kreuzigung. Eine antiquarische Untersuchung* (Breslau, 1878), pp. 141f, 204 ('wenn es konstanter Gebrauch ... gewesen ist ...'); O. Zöckler, *Das Kreuz Christi* (Gütersloh, 1875), pp. 429f, 441 (ET (London, 1877), pp. 405f, 417). Chrysostom may presuppose this lack of evidence in that he claims that the robbers' crosses did not have *tituli* and emphasises that the cross of Jesus could already be recognised by the title (84.(85) Homily on John; *PG* 59.461).

laid down in detail. If an execution was meant to serve as a dreadful warning and if, in fact, elements of mockery were not absent from what even lawyers call *Volksfesthinrichtungen*,[7] we cannot expect similar intentions to be foreign to the phrasing of a *titulus*. Even examples of a pedagogical nature[8] are known. And the rhetorical element in the formulation is obvious.[9]

It results from this that evidence of the first or second type, if its authenticity is indisputable, is superior to that of the third or fourth kind. The latter material cannot be taken as giving *eo ipso* the exact and juridically correct reason for the condemnation;[10] it raises additional problems, and carries weight especially in cases where it is supported by other pieces of evidence.

The accounts of the crucifixion of Jesus contain details which belong to all four categories. The most striking piece of information is, however, the mention of the *titulus*. The *titulus*[11] is mentioned in all four Gospels. The term[12] itself is used only by John, whereas Mark and Luke speak of ἐπιγραφὴ τῆς αἰτίας, and Matthew describes it more loosely.

The wording of it is basically the same: ὁ βασιλεύς τῶν Ἰουδαίων. Matthew introduces it by οὗτός ἐστιν ὁ Ἰησοῦς,[13] whereas John renders Ἰησοῦς ὁ Ναζωραῖος. Ev. Petr. 10 reads οὗτός ἐστιν ὁ Βασιλεὺς τοῦ Ἰσραήλ, combining the Matthaean form with the wording of the mocking salutation of Mark 15: 32. The preference for Ἰσραήλ (already so in verse 7) may be conditioned by the negative meaning of Ἰουδαῖοι in the Gospel.[14] The rendering of the *titulus* in the three languages is mentioned

---

[7] Theod. Mommsen, *Römisches Strafrecht* (Leipzig, 1899), pp. 925f.

[8] 'Fumo punitur, qui fumum vendidit' (Lampridius 36). Lampridius 51 narrates that Alexander Severus ordered the crying out of the 'Quod tibi non vis fieri, alteri non feceris' in several cases; cp. A. B. von Walther, *Juristisch-historische Betrachtungen über die Geschichte vom Leyden und Sterben Jesu Christi* (Breslau and Leipzig, 1738; 2nd edn. Breslau, 1777), p. 324. For the functioning of the Golden Rule in the Christian–pagan controversy and especially in the *Historia Augusta* (where the above-mentioned passage is taken from: actually from Alex. Severus 51) cp. J. Straub, *Regeneratio Imperii* (Darmstadt, 1972), pp. 314ff.

[9] Representations by interested parties and equally stubbornness on the side of those who believed they had coined a splendid formulation are not impossible.

[10] R. Eisler, Ἰησοῦς βασιλεύς ii (Heidelberg, 1930), 532, goes too far in assuming that the αἰτία was 'ein amtlicher Auszug aus dem gefallenen Urteil'. For an evaluation of the different forms of notification see Mommsen, *Strafrecht*, pp. 517ff.

[11] J. Gretser, *De cruce Christi* (Ingolstadt, 1600), especially i, 72ff is still indispensable.

[12] The word invaded the Greek language *via* the *Volkssprache* (cp. L. Hahn, *Rom und Romanismus im griech.–röm. Osten* (Leipzig, 1906), pp. 265f). Its usage is therefore not juridically exact, as is also shown by the fact that its meaning is different in juridical language: *titulus* gives the heading of a section in the *Corpus Juris Civilis*.

[13] Followed by *Act. Pil.* x. 13 (rec. B) but without ὁ Ἰησοῦς. For the secondary character of the Matthaean wording cp. A. Dauer, *Die Passionsgeschichte im Johannesevangelium* (München, 1972), pp. 221f.

[14] Cp. the replacement of Ἰουδαῖοι by Ἰουδαία in a number of instances in the old Syriac translation of the Gospel.

only by John, *Act. Pil.* xi and in part of the manuscript tradition of Luke. [15, 16]

The context is not the same. Mark, followed by Matthew, mentions it at the end of the factual description of the execution and before he goes on to describe the reaction of the onlookers. Luke, who places the ἐπιγραφή notice in his account of the remarks which in his representation mock the kingly claim of Jesus, reproduces one mocking interpretation of the *titulus* itself,[17] while leaving it open whether the inscription was meant to convey the same impression. A further clue may be found in the Jewish accusation at the beginning of the trial before Pilate (23: 2).[18] The *titulus* is subordinate to the interest in different reactions. John, who places the notice between the description of the crucifixion and the casting of lots for the seamless garment, adds a judicial detail.

The authority by which the *titulus* was formulated and put up is not mentioned in the synoptic Gospels. John attributes it to Pilate, whereas the *Acts of Pilate* (*Act. Pil.* x. 1; rec. A.) produce the strange description ἐκέλευσεν μετὰ τὴν ἀπόφασιν εἰς τίτλον ἐπιγραφῆναι τὴν αἰτίαν αὐτοῦ . . . καθὼς εἶπαν οἱ Ἰουδαῖοι ὅτι βασιλεύς ἐστιν τῶν Ἰουδαίων,[19] a formulation which emphasises at one and the same time the command by Pilate and a Jewish origin for the formula. Jewish responsibility is claimed by the Gospel of Peter (Ev. Petr. 4: 11); and the same is true for the Sinaitic Syriac.[20]

The passage on the *titulus* was evaluated by Bousset as 'erbauliche Betrachtung der gläubigen Jesusgemeinde', it could not be accepted as historical because its wording constituted a 'Verhöhnung' of the Jews.[21] R.

---

[15] P. F. Regard, 'Le titre de la croix d'après les Evangiles', *RArch* 28 (1928), 96 considers this text form as authentic.

[16] Regard, ibid. 99f, holds that the differences of wording of the *titulus* can be understood this way: Matthew renders the Semitic text, Luke the Greek and John the Latin text, whereas Mark summarises. This last may be true but the interpretation offered for the different texts is speculative.

[17] Cp. 23: 37 εἰ σὺ εἶ ὁ βασιλεὺς τῶν Ἰουδαίων κτλ (but cp. Mani's gospel fr. ii: the soldiers say mockingly: our king Messiah); probably already in view of the *titulus*.

[18] It is there that the singular phrase χριστὸς βασιλεύς is used.

[19] Rec. B X. 5 (P. Vannutelli, *Actorum Pilati textus synoptici* (Rome, 1938), pp. 97f) follows mainly the Johannine account.

[20] Cp. A. Merx, *Das Evangelium Matthaeus* (Berlin, 1902), pp. 414f; cp. pp. 405, 407. Matt. 27: 37 starts in sy[s]: 'and while they were sitting they wrote the trespass and set it over his head'. This looks like an action undertaken on the spur of the moment (like the casting of the lots). The 'they' are in all likelihood the λαός to whom Jesus had been handed over.

[21] *Kyrios Christos* (Göttingen, 1913), p. 56. Cp. J. Weiss and W. Bousset, *Die drei älteren Evangelien* (Göttingen, 1917), pp. 215, 220f. Just the opposite reason for the unhistoricity of the *titulus* is given by E. Haenchen: it is of Christian origin, because it contains the confession which was proclaimed by the Judaeo-Christian

Bultmann added to this the point that the passage is based on Mark 15: 2, a verse which is secondary to 15: 3–5.[22] Bousset's argument does not carry weight, because the *titulus* is not used theologically by Mark, Matthew and John and even Luke bases his evaluation of the trial on 23: 43 rather than on verse 38. Bultmann's observation is substantiated.[23] This does not mean, however, that the βασιλεύς-theme is a secondary intrusion in the Markan text. What is a secondary layer from the literary point of view may, nevertheless, contain information that is historically reliable. Executions used to be public occasions at this time and at many times, and people – unfamiliar with the subleties of the legal position, with charging, fact-finding and condemnation – remembered clearly what had been visible to their own eyes. J. Wellhausen had already set his face against such scepticism[24] and P. Winter's statement: 'if anything that is recorded of his Passion in the four Gospels accords with history it is . . . that the cross . . . bore a summary statement of the cause for which he had been sentenced to the *servile supplicium*'[25] may not be too far from the truth.

The meaning of the *titulus* according to what became the standard opinion of the early church may be illustrated by the interpretation given by Isidore of Sevile, who, pointing to the title of Ps. 57, exclaims: 'spoil not the inscription of the title'.[26] It is the climax of a tendency which tried to supplement Jesus's good confession before Pilate (1 Tim. 6: 13) by the latter's own confession.

communities without any hindrance for a long time. The composition of such an inscription by the Romans would not have constituted a provocation of the Jews (*Der Weg Jesu* (Berlin, 1966), p. 536).

[22] *Geschichte der synoptischen Tradition* (Göttingen, 1931), pp. 293f, 307 (ET p. 272 – the decisive sentence is omitted in the translation – p. 284). E. Linnemann (*Studien zur Passionsgeschichte* (Göttingen, 1970), pp. 134, 154) follows B.-J. Schreiber (*Theologie des Vertrauens* (Hamburg, 1967); *Die Markuspassion* (Hamburg, 1969), p. 52f – he is dependent on R. Thiel, *Drei Markusevangelien* (Berlin, 1938), p. 26 – and especially W. Schenk (*Der Passionsbericht nach Markus* (Berlin, 1974), pp. 37ff) develop the Bultmannian view: two different accounts of the crucifixion were worked together in the actual text of Mark; the *titulus* is part of the second and younger report. Schenk, *Passionsbericht*, p. 40, holds that ἐπιγεγραμμένη was added by the evangelist; that means that the tradition did not necessarily state that the αἰτία was fixed to the cross. J. R. Donahue (*Are You the Christ? The Trial Narrative in the Gospel of Mark* (Missoula, 1973)) does not go into this particular question. H. Braun, *Jesus* (Stuttgart, 1969), p. 50, follows Bultmann, while E. Dinkler, *Signum Crucis* (Tübingen, 1967), p. 306, comes out in favour of the historicity of the *titulus*.

[23] E. Hirsch argues that all the βασιλεύς-references were added by Mark II, they show the attempt to picture Jesus as having been condemned because of his messianic aspiration (*Frühgeschichte des Evangeliums* i (Tübingen, 1940), 163f, 210f). The results of his analysis converge with Bultmann's findings.

[24] *Das Evangelium Marci* (Berlin, 1909), pp. 130f.

[25] *On the Trial of Jesus* (Berlin, 1961), p. 108.

[26] *Contra Judaeos* on Ps. 57; cp. A. L. Williams, *Adversus Judaeos* (Cambridge, 1935), p. 287, n. 3.

Important as it was for centuries, this view has been replaced in this century by the theory that the *titulus* is the chief witness for the trial before Pilate, the precise indication of what was going on on this memorable occasion, and the exact formulation of the *causa poenae*. Βασιλεύς is seen as the confirmation of a claim that had political connotations and was liable to punishment as an attempt at rebellion.[27] The view that Pilate had reason to think of Jesus in these terms while in essence he was mistaken in treating Jesus as a politically dangerous person[28] is a modification of this theory.

The *titulus* does not, however, describe Jesus as a ληστής, a man *novarum rerum cupidus*. Such terms would have been appropriate and even imperative if the *titulus* was meant to define the offence of attempted insurrection committed by the culprit.

The alternative theory that the *titulus* was meant to refer to the crime of *laesa majestas*[29] recommends itself much more strongly. The claim to be a king was according to this view *eo ipso* a challenge to the emperor.[30] This is certainly tenable in the light of the development of the later Roman public law. The Roman rulers of the period of the *Dominium* and certainly of the post-Constantinian period were seen as βασιλεῖς βασιλέων and any claim not vouchsafed by them was bound to be regarded as high treason.[31] The matter was, however, different in the time of the principate. The *princeps* held the *tribunicia potestas* as his main office, he was by no means a king and the *populus Romanus* was still regarded as the very *majestas*. True, the *laesa majestas populi Romani* and that of the *princeps*[32] was already considered as a crime and trials took place in Tiberius's time[33] especially after the fall of Sejanus.[34] This delict, which is equated with ἀσέβεια[35] is, however, hardly

---

[27] Winter, *Trial*, pp. 138ff; S. G. F. Brandon, *Jesus and the Zealots* (Manchester, 1967), p. 328, and, most forcefully, K. Kautsky: 'Hier tritt der ursprüngliche Charakter der Katastrophe wieder deutlich hervor. Hier sind die Römer die erbitterten Feinde Jesu und der Grund ihres Hohns und ihres Hasses liegt in seinem Hochverrat, in seiner Aspiration auf das jüdische Königtum, in demn Streben nach Abschüttelung der römischen Fremdherrschaft' (*Der Ursprung des Christentums* (Stuttgart, 1908), p. 430; for details of ET see p. 19, n. 77).

[28] H. Vincent gives it a further nuance by assuming that Pilate chose to think so for fear of being castigated by the Roman authorities ('Le Lithostrotos Evangelique', *RB* 59 (1952), 526).

[29] E.g. Blinzler, *Der Prozess Jesu* (Regensburg, 1969), p. 311.

[30] Thus H. Windisch: if Jesus professed his messianic character before Pilate, the latter had no choice but to condemn him (*Imperium und Evangelium* (Kiel, 1931), p. 22).

[31] On the other hand a Christian document of this time, like the *Acts of Pilate*, which took this interpretation for granted, had to employ great skill in order to show that the secular authorities acknowledged Jesus's claim to be a king.

[32] Who is, however, not endowed with a special inviolability (Mommsen, *Strafrecht*, p. 582 n. 1).

[33] Tac. *Ann.* IV. 70: VI. 18; Suet. *Tib.* 58. 61.

[34] Cp. *ThLZ* 77 (1952), col. 207f.   [35] Mommsen, *Strafrecht*, p. 540.

applicable, as it presupposed, in the time of the principate at least, direct actions against the *princeps*.[36] The same is even true for *perduellio*.[37] Besides, these laws were binding only for Roman citizens,[38] whereas the trial which took place outside the metropolis and over which the Roman administrator took charge, was conducted according to the principles of *coercitio* (or *Eigenkognition*), thus giving the representative of Rome a far wider choice of action. This does not exclude the possibility that these regulations influenced the frame of mind of a Roman judge in a general way, but it does make it unlikely that quasi-automatic action was called forth by any strange behaviour. Kingly claims outside Rome might be regarded with suspicion in the capital but they did not ipso facto clash with the established order of the day. Besides, the situation in Palestine was so complex, claims of a messianic character were so common[39] and, on the other hand, refuted already by part of the population, that it was a matter of good policy for the Romans to avoid involvement in these issues as far as possible.[40] The interpretation referred to is juridically doubtful and historically unlikely.

The interpretation the passion story itself provides is different. Ὁ χριστὸς ὁ βασιλεὺς Ἰσραήλ – almost a repetition of the *titulus* – is cited mockingly in Mark 15: 32. Χριστός alone is given a mocking interpretation in Luke 23: 39.[41] This certainly gives an indication for the exegesis of the formula of the *titulus*. Luke goes even further by citing the mocking interpretation of the στρατιῶται (verse 37) before actually mentioning the *titulus* itself. This understanding became quite common in the following centuries.[42] We could expect more on the lines of John 19: 21, more of a protest in the early tradition, if the *titulus* had had the intention of defining the actual reason for the condemnation. But the mocking usage of the formula was readily at hand if the *titulus* itself already was meant to give an adverse and ridiculing description of some claim, the nature of which was left in the open.

The Johannine narrative demands special treatment. The reference to

---

[36] Tac. *Ann.* iv. 34: *iniuria*; cp. Mommsen, *Strafrecht*, pp. 541, 583f.

[37] Mommsen, *Strafrecht*, pp. 537f, 540, 546.

[38] Mommsen, *Strafrecht*, p. 543.

[39] Cp. E. Kocsis, 'Der jüdische Messianismus und das politische Problem in der Geschichte Jesu' (Diss. Erlangen, 1959).

[40] The case of the δεσπόσυνοι, who were released even in the time of Domitian (Eus., *H.E.*, 3.20.5), is a telling example.

[41] Luke 23: 39 seems to be a contamination of two versions, one which described the abuse in general terms and which is still documented in D e, and another which gave the wording of the calumny, probably without having introduced it by ἐβλασφήμει.

[42] E.g. in Mani's gospel the Jews call Jesus mockingly 'our Lord Messiah' (E. Hennecke, *Neutestamentliche Apokryphen*, ed. W. Schneemelcher i (Tübingen, 1959), 262).

the inscription is substantially identical with the synoptic account, but for the fact that it contains the supplementary detail that it was rendered in the three languages.[43] The Gospel contains, however, a comparatively long addition which is completely absent from the parallel accounts. This deals with the encounter between the Jewish leaders and Pilate; the former entreat the prefect not to write (any longer)[44] king of the Jews and the latter answers with the epigrammatic phrase: '*quod scripsi scripsi*'.

The addition starts with a remark that many Jews saw the inscription because the place of the crucifixion was near to the town. These onlookers[45] are known from both the Markan/Matthaean and the Lukan account. In the former tradition they are enumerated among those who mock at Jesus (Mark 15:29f; Matt. 27:39ff), whereas the Lukan account remains strangely silent about this feature.[46] While Luke, who calls the onlookers ὄχλος, tends to attribute the mocking action to specific groups, to the ἄρχοντες, the στρατιῶται and the one malefactor, John bypasses any reference to the mocking of the crucified one. The evangelist, who makes

---

[43] Inscriptions in more than one language are well known. In many places it was expedient to promulgate declarations in this form. Their multilingual composition was an accepted practice, although not imperative or even very common. Inscriptions of a more private character were, however, normally produced in one language only. Exceptions, e.g. in funeral inscriptions (examples in Walther, *Betrachtungen*, p. 342), occurred if the person concerned was a figure of great eminence or the society that maintained the cemetery was on the brink of shifting from one language to another. Mockery inscriptions in different languages are certainly uncommon. John, who emphasised the three languages, is likely to have intended to produce something that appeared already to the neutral eye as at least as dignified as the warning inscription of the Temple, which, Josephus maintains, was executed in Greek and Latin (*BJ* 6 §125; the alternative MS. reading ὑμετέροις would refer to an Aramaic wording). The verdict, on the other hand, was to be pronounced in Latin (Mommsen, *Strafrecht*, p. 449, n. 3), as is illustrated by the *Acta Pionii*, where the flow of the narration is interrupted by the remark that the verdict was pronounced in Latin (ch. xx) (the prescription of the Corp. Jur. – cp. Walther, *Betrachtungen*, p. 342 – that the elogium had to be cried out by the herald in Greek and Latin points to a later date). It results from this that the closer the *titulus* is linked with the verdict the less likely becomes the Johannine claim about the three languages. In fact, the inscription is likely to have been written down in the local language (cp. n. 4 on Lyons). The Syriac Schatzhöhle emphasises the point that the inscription was not written in Syriac, and deduces from this that the Syrians are not guilty of the murder of Christ, while the Greek Herod, the Jew Caiaphas and the Roman Pilate are. The inscription is thereby viewed as a condemnation of those by whom it was put up and for whose eyes it was written (53:21ff).

[44] μὴ γράφε do not go on writing; cp. W. Bauer, *Das Johannesevangelium* (Tübingen, 1933), p. 222.

[45] The remark is not a secondary addition (*pace* F. Spitta, *Das Johannesevangelium als Quelle der Geschichte Jesu* (Göttingen, 1910), pp. 379f). Otherwise we would expect to find it after verse 20b. On the contrary, verse 20b is a pedantic interpretation of 20a (ἀνέγνωσαν) which probably came in at the redaction stage.

[46] Verse 35b introduces the mocking of the ἄρχοντες by a καί and presupposes thereby what is lacking in the present text. The καί is omitted by ℵ f13 al.

the soldiers fall to the ground when they realise whom they are about to arrest (18: 6), who deprives the *Ecce homo* scene of any crude feature of mockery[47] and turns it into an occasion for something approaching a confession, must have acted here equally deliberately: while the mocking is not found worth mentioning, those whose mocking action is presupposed are mocked themselves. What we find here is the fragment of a controversy with the Jews. While the first stage is left out, because the mention of the mocking would be at variance with the stylised christology, the answer of Pilate is phrased in such a way that it implies the categorical affirmative that Jesus actually was the messiah of the Jews. The reference to the three languages highlights this from a different side. And the cryptic descriptive appellation Ναζωραῖος[48] is to be taken as a feature similar to that. Such a statement was serviceable in the discussion with the Jews after 70, when they became uncertain whether they still could expect a messiah.[49] This points to verses 20a, 21f having been formulated after the defeat of the Jews. It does not, however, mean that the substance of these verses is not historical.[50] The matter must be left in the balance.

It is this approach of the Fourth Gospel which is taken up in one stream of the Christian tradition and which finds, with respect to the *titulus*, its climax in the claim that Pilate chose the text under the direction of the Holy Spirit: '*et manifestavit propheticum dictum*'.[51]

A Jewish report, in some ways similar to that on the *titulus* is cited in Sanh. 43a.[52] According to this notice a herald marched round for forty days either 'beforehand' or 'in front of him',[53] proclaiming the charges against Jesus and inviting the submission of 'mitigating reasons'. The passage has

---

[47] Mark 15: 19f are not reproduced by John.

[48] E. Stauffer (*Jesus war ganz anders* (Hamburg 1967), p. 191, cp. p. 60), holds that John alone reproduces the correct form of the *titulus*. In this case, however, we would rather expect Ναζαρήνος than Ναζωραῖος. The same argument applies to A. Dauer, according to whom the *titulus* is an 'amtliche Urkunde' in the view of John (*Die Passionsgeschichte*, pp. 176f).

[49] The position taken by Jochanan b. Zakkai is indicative; cp. *NovTest* (1962), 219ff.

[50] Reasons, not altogether convincing, for the historicity of the passage are given by Eisler, 'Iησ. βασ. ii, 530–2.

[51] Tert. *Apol.* 21; for different opinions of the church fathers cp. Fulda, *Kreuz*, pp. 205–7.

[52] 'On the eve of the Passover Jeshu was hanged. For forty days before the execution took place, a herald went forth and cried "He is going forth to be stoned because he practised sorcery and enticed Israel to apostasy. Anyone who can say anything in his favour, let him come forward and plead on his behalf." But since nothing was brought forward in his favour he was hanged on the eve of the Passover. Ulla retorted: Do you suppose that he was one for whom a defence could be made? Was he not an enticer?, concerning whom Scripture says "Neither shalt thou spare, neither shalt thou conceal him." With Jeshu however it was different, for he was connected with the government' (after the Soncino translation).

[53] For the translation problem see *NTSt* 13 (1966/67), 327 n. 4.

been revised several times. The submission of pleas in defence after the conviction is something that exists only in the theory of the Mishnaic code and is contrary to our information about the procedure of the earlier period, which excludes the alteration of the sentence once it has been passed.[54] At this point the principle of Sanh. 6. 1 has exercised an influence on the text.

As for the herald himself, in this case two strands of tradition have been combined. One of these is that a herald preceded the criminal to the place of execution in order to proclaim the reason for the condemnation, the other tells of a proclamation made forty days before the execution took place. The first procedure is the customary one;[55] it will have been carried out in the case of Jesus too. The second, however, will refer to the proscription peculiar to this case.[56] It is in this piece of information that we have the beginning of the tradition about Jesus. It was combined with the information about a detail of the customary procedure for execution and then altered to accord with the principles of the Mishnah. It was in this developed form that the tradition caused the annoyed protest of Rabbi Ullah,[57] which gave rise to a new justification of the procedure supported by reference to special circumstances.[58]

This passage, which goes back to the second century at least, contains two pieces of information of unique value: the indication of the proscription and the detailed formulation about the reason for the condemnation. The form of its proclamation by a herald walking in front of Jesus is even more in keeping with the normal practice[59] than the *titulus*. It seems that this detail had retreated into the background in the Christian reports in favour of the narrative about Simon of Cyrene and, indeed, the warning: 'weep for yourselves and for your children' (Luke 23: 28).

The wording of the Aramaic Toledoth Jeshu[60] is to be seen as a variant version. It is not denied in the text that Jesus misled the people – on the contrary it is emphasised that he directed himself against the Torah (אוריה) – but it is heightened by the statement: 'he rebelled against the great God'.[61] This is meant to be the counter-formulation and mockery of the claim Jesus is said to have made before Caesar, the claim to be a son of

---

[54] Sanh. 44b Bar; j Sanh. 23c; cp. the principle indicated in j Sanh. IV 6 (22b).

[55] Walther, *Betrachtungen*, pp. 323f.

[56] Cp. Festschrift C. F. D Moule (2nd edn. London, 1971), pp. 33f.

[57] He comes out against any ventilating of mitigating circumstances in the case of the enticer and sticks thereby to the older, rigid views, at least in the case of a religious crime.

[58] The rabbis when answering this do not disagree with him in principle. They only give a practical reason ('he was connected with the government') which in their opinion made it desirable to proceed differently in the case of Jeshu (= Jesus).

[59] For the herald's role in the Roman trial cp. Riepl, *Nachrichtenwesen*, p. 333.

[60] L. Ginzberg in Schechter Memorial vol. ii (New York, 1929), 334f.

[61] דימרד באלהא רבא p. 2a l. 24 of the MS publ. by Ginzberg; cp. p. 2b l. 5f.

the great God.[62] The occasion on which this verdict is said to have been pronounced (אברון) by the Jews is different: it is the day when, after certain misfortunes, the corpse of Jesus is paraded through the streets of Tiberias and the Jews thereby make evident their final victory. This shows the development of the tradition and indicates its *Sitz im Leben* in the community of Tiberias, which had become the centre of the Palestinian Jews in Byzantine times.[63]

The written notification of a verdict was another way of informing the public about an execution. Jewish sources insist that in cases of a religious crime 'all Israel' is to be informed.[64] Accordingly Christian sources tell of embassies sent out εἰς πᾶσαν τὴν οἰκουμένην[65] in order to inform about the verdict cast against Jesus. The reason given for the condemnation[66] is in keeping with Jewish law and not directly based on the Gospel reports or the *titulus*. This tradition about Jewish reports is not early. It is, however, in agreement with the procedure laid down by the Mishnah and with factual notices on related subjects going back to the first century.[67] This does not mean that something of this kind happened in the case of Jesus immediately after his death. But it is probable that, at a later stage, when it became apparent that Jesus's following had not dispersed, intelligence went round about the reason for the condemnation of Jesus. It is not inappropriate to take the references as more or less distant reflections of such information. If that is their nature they have to be taken as an explanation from the Jewish side parallel to that offered by the Christians in addition to the mention of the *titulus* incorporated in John 19: 20f.

The existence of direct documentary evidence on the trial of Jesus, available to emperor and senate, is presupposed by Justin[68] and maintained emphatically by Tertullian.[69] The former seems to think of the records of the prefect, whereas the latter claims that a special letter was written to Tiberius. Both these reports[70] (one of them is supposed to be based on a

---

[62] P. 1b l. 21.

[63] The polemical motif is developed even further in the Huldreich version of the Toledoth, according to which a defamatory inscription: 'the children of adultery were hanged at this place and her mother was buried beneath; your mother is covered with shame' was set up on the grave of Mary and her children (J.J. Huldreich, *Sepher Toledoth Jeshua ha-Notzri* (Leiden, 1705), p. 122).

[64] Sanh. 89Bar. – Jehuda even speaks of messengers to be sent to all places (Sanh. 11.4).

[65] Justin, *Dial.c. Tryph.* 108.

[66] μάγος . . . καὶ λαόπλανος (*Dial.* 69), πλάνος (*Dial.* 108).

[67] Especially with Acts 28: 21.

[68] 1 *Apol.* 35 and 38.   [69] *Apologeticum* 5.21.

[70] Outstanding among them is the letter claimed to have been written by Pilate to Claudius. For the theory of a longer span of the life of Jesus and his execution under Claudius see Hippolytus IV, 23.3; cp. W. Bauer, *Das Leben Jesu im Zeitalter der neutestamentlichen Apokryphen* (Tübingen, 1909), pp. 293f.

Jewish account), are produced in the genre of the *Acts of Pilate*. They describe Jesus as accused by the Jews '*Magum esse et contra legem eorum agere*'[71] and testify thereby to the fact that they are a derivation from and correction of non-Christian, most probably Jewish Acts. Their value consists in certain details rather than in the general flow of their account.[72] The letter is merely an imaginative construction.[73]

A unique form of the *titulus* is rendered in the Slavonic Josephus: Jesus the king did not reign but was crucified by the Jews because he prophesied the destruction of the city and the devastation of the Temple.[74] The inscription is said to have been placed on some[75] of the hewn stones with the warning inscription which marked the entrance of the inner court of the Temple. The text itself is a combination of John 18: 19ff[76] and 11:48, 50[77] with the Jewish view expressed in Sanh. 43a (see note 52, p. 360). Historically extremely unlikely, it derives from the Jewish–Christian controversy in late antiquity. It is the Christian counter-formulation to Jewish claims and tries to outmanoeuvre the latter by pretending that this was the official Jewish opinion in the time of Jesus.

The following conclusion arises from this: the evidence about direct and official reports on the trial of Jesus is, although ample, rather to be taken as an attempt to illustrate the event to a later generation than as historically reliable information. Different in nature is the *baraitha* in Sanh. 43a which, besides containing details about the execution of Jesus, gives the reason for the condemnation, the αἰτία in a form that agrees with Jewish law. The wording of the *titulus* as it is reported in the Gospels is in all likelihood authentic.[78] Its juridical relevance is, however, restricted by the influence of considerations and, indeed, emotions of a different nature about its

---

[71] Letter to Claudius (Walther, *Betrachtungen*, pp. 432ff; C. von Tischendorf (*Evangelia Apocrypha* (Leipzig, 1876), p. 413).

[72] Cp. T. Mommsen, 'Die Pilatus-Acten', *ZNW* 3 (1902), 205.

[73] E. Volterra, 'Di una decisione del Senato Romano ricordata da Tertulliano' in *Festschrift C. Ferrini* i (= *Pubblicazioni dell' Universita Cattolica del S. Cuore*, n.s. xvii (Milano, 1947), 471ff), however, advocates the trustworthiness of Tertullian.

[74] Ἰησοῦν βασιλέα οὐ βασιλεύσαντα σταυρωθέντα ὑπὸ (τῶν) Ἰουδαίων διότε ἐπροφήτευσε (τὴν) καθαίρεσιν (τῆς πόλεως) καὶ (τὴν) ἐρήμωσιν (τοῦ) ναοῦ; the text in Eisler, Ἰησ. βασ. ii, 534ff, 542: cp. W. Bienert, *Der älteste nichtchristliche Jesusbericht* (Halle, 1936), pp. 165–7.

[75] Eisler (Ἰησ. βασ ii, 536 and especially 541), thinks of two pillars at the side of a certain gate and of the lintel of the gate itself: the inscription was displayed at each place in a different language.

[76] The three languages, βασιλεύς, Ἰουδαῖοι (removed by Eisler, Ἰησ. βασ. ii, 541), ὅτε . . . εἶπεν (cp. οὐ βασιλεύσας).

[77] ἐπροφήτευσε, τόπος (cp. ναός), ἔθνος (cp. πόλις).

[78] Valid arguments against the Christian origin of its formulation are given by J. Finegan, *Die Überlieferung der Leidens- und Auferstehungsgeschichte Jesu* (Giessen, 1934), p. 78.

formulation. The *titulus* is therefore not to be taken as the 'one solid and stable fact that should be made the starting point of any historical investigation',[79] but rather as a piece of evidence, the importance of which can only be assessed in conjunction with the rest of the material on the trial.

[79] Winter, *Trial*, p. 109; 2nd edn., p. 156. Brandon goes even further by claiming that Jesus was condemned for sedition 'as the titulus shows' (*Zealots*, p. 328).

Romans 13

Chapter 13: 1–7 of Paul's letter to the Romans became perhaps the most influential part of the New Testament on the level of world history. This happened in spite of the fact that the interpretation of the passage has never been found easy and is nowadays more disputed than ever before.

While the interpretations of the patristic period[1] ranged from the identification of the superior powers with evil angels to respect for them as ecclesiastical officials;[2] while, already in pre-Constantinian time[3] an interpretation that lends dignity to the state became dominant, although T. Müntzer turned that into a kind of revolutionary manifesto by maintaining that the governments are instituted to execute the will of God and, conversely, if they fail to do so, those who do the will of God are bound to take the sword into their own hands,[4] nowadays it is asserted that the pericope contains nothing but a 'devastating undermining', the Divine verdict on the Powers that be;[5] and if indeed it were of a positive nature Paul's statement would be in need of radical demythologising.[6]

---

[1] K. H. Schelkle, 'Staat und Kirche in der patristischen Auslegung von Rm 13: 1–7', *ZNW* 44 (1952–3), 223ff.

[2] Didask. 2, 33, 2; 34, 1 (Funk); the Catharens argued similarly; cp. I. v. Döllinger, *Beiträge zur Sectengeschichte des Mittelalters* I (München, 1890), pp. 183f.

[3] Schelkle, *ZNW* 44 (1952–3), 227f.

[4] *Schriften und Briefe*, ed. by G. Franz (Gütersloh, 1968), pp. 242ff. Cp. E. Bloch, *Thomas Müntzer als Theologe der Revolution* (Berlin, 1921; 2nd edn. Frankfurt, 1962), pp. 131ff.

[5] Karl Barth, *Der Römerbrief* (2nd edn. München, 1922), p. 467 (ET Oxford, 1933, p. 483). The author ventilates at length the possibility of revolution and comes out fervently against this attempt 'of willing to do what God does' (p. 474; ET p. 491); these remarks are absent from the first edition (Basel, 1919). Cp. the toning down of this radical point of view in a late statement cited by E. Busch, *Karl Barths Lebenslauf* (München, 1975), p. 478 (ET p. 461). A. A. T. Ehrhardt takes up these views of Barth and attempts to trace the same position *vis à vis* the state which Barth finds in Romans 13 in the Christian documents of the pre-Constantinian period (*Politische Metaphysik von Solon bis Augustin II* (Tübingen, 1959)). For the problem of a more radical position of the young Barth allowing revolution, cp. F. W. Marquard, *Theologie und Sozialismus. Das Beispiel Karl Barths* (München, 1972), pp. 126ff, 135ff; and I. Jacobsen (ed.), *War Barth Sozialist? Ein Streitgespräch um Theologie und Sozialismus bei K. Barth* (Berlin, 1975), especially pp. 34f.

[6] O. Dibelius, *Obrigkeit* (Stuttgart, 1960).

I

Scholars have noticed the unusually isolated character of the passage,[7] and have made the most varied attempts to explain this, ranging as far as interpolation hypothesis (A. Pallis,[8] E. Barnikol[9]). The advice contains elements of a basic understanding of the state, which both in its semi-philosophical terminology and in its point of departure from a theology of creation has no equal in the Corpus Paulinum. That this is not a case of free composition is shown by comparison with 1 Pet. 2: 13ff, a passage which derives not from Romans 13 but from a third tradition which made its imprint on both the New Testament writings.[10] The fact that one finds numerous parallels in hellenistic literature of both pagan and Jewish authorship[11] leads one to seek the roots of this tradition in the Judaism of the diaspora. Indeed M. Dibelius maintained that 'niemand kann überhaupt aus diesem Text entnehmen, dass hier ein christlicher Apostel eine christliche Gemeinde ermahnt'.[12] Even the words διὰ τὴν συνείδησιν need not be seen as a Christianisation of the passage.[13]

[7] E.g. O. Michel, *Der Brief an die Römer* (Göttingen, 1966), pp. 313f. M. Borg, 'A new Context for Romans XIII', *NTSt* 19 (1972–3), 205, on the other hand, tries to link the passage with the main themes of the epistle. While his arguments are not convincing in this respect, he is right in attempting to give the passage itself a historical setting.

[8] *To the Romans* (London, 1920), p. 14 regards verses 1–10 as a clumsy insertion in a continuous context dealing with the correct way of life for Christians. The verses are in accordance with the attitude of the apologists, who, while pointing to dubious machinations, emphasised their own loyalty to Rome. Therefore they are added after A.D. 133. Chr. Eggenberger, 'Die Quellen der politischen Ethik des 1. Klemensbriefes' (Diss. Zürich, 1951), p. 205 reserves judgement on the question of Paulinity of the passage.

[9] 'Der nichtpaulinische Ursprung der absoluten Obrigkeitsbejahung von Römer 13, 1–7' (TU 77 (1961), 65–133). He is followed by J. Kallas, 'Romans XIII, 1–7: an interpolation' (*NTSt* 11 (1964–5), 365ff; W. Schmithals, *Der Römerbrief als historisches Problem* (Gütersloh, 1975); and now J.C. O'Neill, *Paul's Letter to the Romans* (London, 1975), pp. 207f; for criticism cp. K. Aland, *Neutestamentliche Entwürfe* (München, 1979), p. 41.

[10] Cp. D. Daube in E. G. Selwyn, *The first Epistle of St Peter* (London, 1949), p. 488: Romans 13 and 1 Peter 2 used the same source, an 'early Christian code of behaviour within the new community'.

[11] E.g. Jos. *BJ* 2 §140 (cp. M. Dibelius, *Rom und die Christen im ersten Jahrhundert* (SAH, 1941/42), p. 8 (= *Botschaft und Geschichte* (Tübingen, 1956), 182) and, most recently, R. Bergmeier, 'Loyaltät als Gegenstand paulin. Paraklese', *Theokrateia* i (1970), 54ff); Ber. 58a; Aristeas §187ff. Cp. F. Delitzsch, *Paulus des Apostels Brief an die Römer* (Leipzig, 1870), p. 95: '*Der Apostel steht also auf echt jüdischem Boden.*'

[12] *Rom*, p. 10 (= *Botschaft*, ii, 184). Cp. O. Dibelius, *Obrigkeit*, p. 19. For a recent discussion, cp. W. C. van Unnik, 'Lob und Strafe durch die Obrigkeit. Hellenistisches zu Röm 13. 3–4' in *Jesus und Paulus* (Festschrift W. G. Kümmel), eds. E. Ellis and E. Grässer (Göttingen, 1975), p. 41.

[13] A different view, as it seems, is taken by E. Käsemann, 'Römer 13, 1–7 in unserer Generation' (*ZThK* 56 (1959), 374f).

Moreover the attempt to interpret Romans 13 on the basis of the eschatological context,[14] and thus to put a veneer of eschatological Christianity on the passage, and in this way to insert a Christian reservation in the text after all, does not make any proper headway. For the admonitions of Romans 13 are placed side by side without any interconnection, as has been shown by E. Käsemann.[15] And even this context does not allow any substantial limitation of the pronouncement of Romans 13: 1–7.

The state of affairs is all the more peculiar in that on the other hand the passage evinces concrete features of a kind that is otherwise rare in the Epistle to the Romans. Chrysostom expressed the conjecture that Romans 13 is intended to rebut the charge (πολὺς περιεφέρετο λόγος τότε κτλ.) of fostering revolutionary activities (στάσις and καινοτομία, ἀνατροπὴ τῶν κοινῶν νόμων).[16] The conjecture is made of course without any historical backing, but none the less it shows the possibility that first suggested itself to the ancient reader (the same suggestion, but expressed in over-generalising terms, also reappears in K. Bornhäuser[17] and H. Preisker).[18] Indeed the injunction to pay taxes, the emphasis on subordination can have been formulated only with regard to different tendencies on the part of the addressees – whether conjectured or already in evidence (cp. 16: 17).[19] In form too the passage gives evidence of its different setting.

If the stamp of the pericope is thus a Jewish and not a genuine Pauline one (while on the other hand one must assume a concrete reference to Roman conditions) the problem forces itself on us, how such a unique combination could have come into existence.[20] The answer is to be sought in the situation and history of the Roman community. Oriental cults, while permitted with great liberality outside the *urbs*, still came under the critical eye of the city prefect within Rome during the early principate and could

---

[14] Thus M. Dibelius, *Rom*, pp. 9ff. (= *Botschaft* ii, 181ff); W. Schrage, *Die Christen und der Staat* (Gütersloh, 1971), p. 54; and recently Aland, *Entwürfe*, pp. 48, 50.

[15] *ZThK* 56 (1959), 374: the opposite has to be demonstrated in each case. *An die Römer* (Tübingen, 1973), p. 337.

[16] *PG* 60. 615; cp. Schelkle, *ZNW* 44 (1952–3), 227f.

[17] 'Paulus und die obrigkeitlichen Gewalten in Rom' (*Christentum und Wissenschaft* 7 (1931), 201ff).

[18] 'Das historische Problem des Römerbriefes', *Wissenschaftliche Zeitschr. d. Universität Jena*, 1952–3, p. 29.

[19] For this verse cp. the discussion by W. Schmidthals, 'Die Irrlehrer von Rom. 16: 17–20', *ST* 1 (1959), 51ff, who, however, thinks of gnostic opponents within the community. However that may be, even disturbances that were not primarily directed against the state authorities could result in official measures being taken.

[20] Very questionable is the view of H. Schultz (*Jahrbücher für deutsche Theologie* 21 (1876), 128) who thinks that the admonition suits the circumstances of the provincial population better and, for this reason, comes out in favour of the Ephesians as the addressees of Romans 13. The view seems to be shared by E. von Dobschütz, *Die urchristlichen Gemeinden* (Leipzig, 1902), p. 97.

only hope to be tolerated if their loyalty and good behaviour was beyond question.[21] Accordingly the public representatives of Roman Judaism were always loyal to the state, and – unlike many other synagogues of the Diaspora – even subordinate towards the Herodians as their patrons.[22] They gave demonstrative emphasis to this attitude, and even went so far as to make corresponding modifications in their own history, and to create a myth accordingly.[23] On the other hand, it was not easy to maintain such a position. While the Jewish communities in the East possessed a centralised organisation, at Rome they were split into different entities. The Roman law of congregations did not permit the Jews to establish any unity beyond the level of the different synagogues.[24] This meant that different mentalities could find footholds in the respective synagogues, and that it was difficult for those Jews who collaborated willingly with the Roman authorities to quell less desirable tendencies by action within Judaism. This had already become noticeable in the disturbances after the death of Herod. While the establishment of Roman Jewry had supported Herod's policy all the way,[25] large crowds of Jews demonstrated in favour of the false Alexander.[26] Indeed, Roman Jewry was bound to be affected by any kind of development within Judaism to an even higher degree than the communities in Alexandria and Babylonia. It was a matter of pride and, indeed, of missionary strategy for every religious movement to establish a foothold in Rome. We know not only of Christian preachers but also of Simon Magus[27] and of four unnamed Jewish propagandists[28] who made their appearance in

---

[21] E. Schürer, *Die ältesten Christengemeinden im römischen Reiche* (Kiel, 1894), p. 12. Cp. G. Vitucci, *Ricerche sulla praefectura urbi in età imperiale* (Rome, 1956).

[22] For the celebration of Herod's birthday by the Jews of Rome see Persius V, 180; cp. R. Eisler, *Jesous Basileus* i (Heidelberg, 1930), 348 and I. Scheftelowitz, 'Das Fischsymbol im Judentum und Christentum', *ARW* 14 (1911), 20. For the existence of a 'synagogue of the Herodians' cp. H. Vogelstein and P. Rieger, *Geschichte der Juden in Rom* i (Berlin, 1896), app. n. 124.

[23] They emphasised (or invented) their lament on the occasion of Caesar's death (Suetonius, *Julius* 84). For an interpretation of the funeral oration for Caesar, cp. E. Stauffer, *Jerusalem und Rom* (Bern, 1957), pp. 21ff; and W. Kierdorf, *Laudatio Funebris* (Meisenheim, 1980), pp. 150ff.

[24] This has been seen so far only by E. v. Dobschütz, 'Die Entstehung des Römerbriefs', *Deutsch-Evangelisch* iii (1912), 398. Cp. H. Gressmann, 'Jewish Life in Ancient Rome', *Jewish Studies in Memory of I. Abrahams* (New York, 1927), pp. 170ff. G. la Piana, 'Foreign Groups in Rome', *HThR* 20 (1927), 362 was unable to find conclusive evidence for a central governing body, although he was eagerly looking for it. It is probably for this reason that the epistle to the Romans is not addressed to the ἐκκλησία but to the ἅγιοι of that city. It was precisely the lack of a uniform organisation which forced the Roman Christians to become masters in achieving compromise solutions. That they were inclined to press through such solutions, once they had been arrived at, not only in the *urbs* but in the *orbis* as well, was only in keeping with the general atmosphere of the metropolis.

[25] *BJ* 2 §25, 81.

[26] *BJ* 2 §104f; *AJ* 17 §324ff.

[27] Justin, *Ap.* 1. 26; *Act. Verc.* 32.

[28] Jos. *AJ* 18 §65.

the capital. Equally, political movements needed a foothold in Rome in order to get information, to establish influence and to carry out financial transactions. At least two of the synagogues in Rome had strong leanings towards the fatherland and its messianic dreams, as the names chosen by their supporters indicate.[29] Such an environment was open to even more radical agitation. The conflict between the limits drawn from outside and the inner dynamics led of necessity to points of fierce tension in the Jewish community, which as soon as they erupted, were bound to give rise to repressive actions by the Roman officials. The different stern measures taken by the Roman administration between A.D. 18 and A.D. 49 against metropolitan Jewry,[30] the repeated references to 'disturbances',[31] and the equally ominous attempts in Jewish historiography to play down the events,[32] make it quite clear that agitations occurred which could be seen by the uninitiated eye of the Roman police as having involved the whole of Roman Jewry. Maybe the apocalyptic idea that the messianic battle will have to take place in the headquarters of God's enemies played its role in these discussions and actions within Judaism. Maybe an explosive mixture of provocation and shrewd political manoeuvring existed in Rome. In any case, Roman Jewry suffered its most severe blow when the Jews were expelled from the *urbs* in A.D. 49.[33] That this happened under Claudius, who was not at all a committted anti-Semite, is a sign of the hardening of the hand of the Roman administration. Since the beginning of the rule of Nero the Jews had just begun to be able to filter their way in again. Their position was still uncertain.

The Christians, obviously, had shared in the fate of the Jews. The case of Aquila and Priscilla[34] is only additional proof. The situation of those Christians who returned or abandoned an underground existence after A.D. 54 was as unsettled as that of the Jews, if not more so. Not only could they not hope to make use of the shelter and, in case of difficulties, the mediating activities of what soon became the Jewish establishment, not only were the Christians as an apocalyptic movement considered to be very far from a position of enthusiasm for any present order, the Christians in the

---

[29] The synagogue of the Hebrews and the Olive Tree synagogue. This is not seen by J. B. Frey, 'Le Judaisme à Rome aux premiers temps de l'église', *Bb* 12 (1931), 129ff, who denies (147) the existence of messianic expectation in Rome.

[30] Cp. *ZThK* 56 (1959), 295ff.

[31] Suetonius, *Claudius* 25; Dio 60.6.

[32] The actions taken against the Jews are described by Josephus as measures caused by the trespasses of a few Jews who had not even been resident in Rom (*AJ* 18 §84). Philo heaps all the blame on the arch-evildoer Sejanus and stresses that the measures were revoked immediately after the latter's execution (*Leg.* §160f).

[33] A different interpretation is given by E. Schürer, *Geschichte d. jüd. Volkes im Zeitalter Jesu Christi* iii (Leipzig, 1909), 62 (ET ii, 2 (Edinburgh, 1901), p. 23).

[34] Acts 18: 26.

orbis[35] and especially Paul himself had learnt already by bitter experience that Jewish attempts to divert the activities of anti-Jewish officials against the Christians had already started – a tendency which became of crucial importance in the Neronian persecution.

In such a situation it was a matter of vital importance to Paul to dissipate every suspicion. There may have been reason for suspicion against the community and the apostle himself. The man who describes himself as ζηλωτὴς τῶν πατρικῶν παραδόσεων (Gal. 1: 14) must, like Josephus,[36] have at times been tempted to join the ranks of the activist branch of the Pharisaic observance, that is, the Zealots. The man whose reputation was far from good in the Christian communities, who was considered a trouble-maker and someone whose views were vacillating and therefore unreliable had every reason to make clear his political position. If it is true that the letter to the Romans is *inter alia* the apostle's *apologia pro vita sua*, it is likely that chapter 13 is conceived not without awareness of these factors. More important is the problem of the community. The congregation in Corinth – *nota bene* a place much closer to Rome both geographically and in mentality than any other frequented by Paul – had been on the verge of succumbing to the domination of libertines.[37] The situation in Rome was not entirely different, as chapters 14 and 15 of Paul's letter show. There is some evidence for Zealot inclinations in the Christian community at Rome. Romans 16: 17 speaks of those who cause διχοστασίαι and σκάνδαλα; this is expressed in religious language, although it refers rather to resistance against ὑπακοή (verse 19) than to doctrinal aberrations. The coined term ἀνθεστηκότες = insurgents[38] would hardly have been used without some

---

[35] The Christians were in a position different not only from that of the Greeks but from that of the Jews as well. A certain degree of animosity on the side of the Greeks against the Romans was taken for granted. (For the beginnings of this hostility see J. Deininger, *Der politische Widerstand gegen Rom in Griechenland 217–86 v. Chr.* (Berlin, 1971); for the development cp. E. A. Baumann, *Beiträge zur Beurteilung der Römer in der antiken Literatur* (Rostock, 1930)). From the time of Claudius the Romans even tried to satisfy the Greeks. The philhellenic gestures of Nero are the climax of the new policy. The Jews had been supported by the Romans for a long time. From the reign of Claudius, however, the Roman officials shied away from giving the Jewish privileges a generous interpretation and were not disinclined to make such gestures towards the Greek side as did not harm the Jews too much. The Christians were in danger of being ground between two millstones. For the beginnings of Jewish activities against the Christians, cp. the references in 1 Thess. 2: 14f.; 3: 4; Gal. 4: 29.

[36] Josephus describes one Zealot branch as that with cleaner hands (χειρὶ . . . καθαρώτερον *BJ* 2 §258). Eisler's contention (*Jesons Basileus*, ii, 707), that this recognition was given because Josephus himself had belonged to the same or a similar branch of Zealots, has much to recommend it.

[37] Cp. B. Reicke, *Diakonie, Zelos und Festfreude in Verbindung mit der altchristlichen Agapenfeier* (Uppsala, 1951), pp. 233ff. Cp. especially 1 Cor 14: 33.

[38] Jos. *AJ* 18 §100.

reason. The climax[39] of the diatribe, the urge[40] to pay φόρος and τέλος, must equally have been formulated with something in mind that was going on in this milieu. Taxes were a problem for both libertines and activists. It was tempting for the former to make practical use of the privilege of the υἱοί (Matt. 17: 26) and to evade paying taxes. It is well known that the Zealot party was welded together by its resistance against the Roman taxes and that the population gave up or delayed paying taxes in A.D. 66.[41] Such means of evading taxes may have been quite effective in the Empire,[42] whereas in Rome, where a good part of the population was exempt from capitation, any inclination to usurp the privilege of the *civis Romanus* was bound to stir up the hostility of the privileged and to be met by most severe reactions from the side of the state.[43]

The situation, as the 'traveller and Roman citizen', the keen observer from outside might notice, had the facets described above. Certain features in the Pauline presentation can best be explained as allusions to these problems. Even more crucial is another observation, which has been made before:[44] the passage contains elements of argumentation. This is at variance with the normal exhortation in the Pauline letters, even with the call to give honour to the king in 1 Pet. 2: 17. It is equally different from the

[39] It is in keeping with this, that according to *Passio Petri et Pauli* 37 Paul defends himself by citing this verse: I instructed the merchants to pay taxes to the state officials.

[40] The view that the verb in 6a is not imperative but indicative (W. Bauer, *Jedermann sei untertan der Obrigkeit!* (Göttingen, 1930), p. 3; similarly O. Michel, *Der Römerbrief*, p. 319) is at variance with verses 5 and 7.

[41] Jos. *BJ* 11 §404.

[42] Cp. Tert. *Apol.* 42 on heathen who do not pay taxes properly. Akiba permitted certain devices to avoid taxation (BQ 113a).

[43] It was Claudius who had given full jurisdiction to the *procuratores* in matters of taxation, about which people had quarrelled so often *seditione aut armis* (Tax. *Ann.* 12.60; cp. A. Strobel, *ZNW* 55 (1961), 61). This was bound to have its repercussion on the state in the metropolis. The attempt which was made recently (J. Friedrich, W. Pöhlmann and P. Stuhlmacher, 'Zur historischen Situation und Intention von Röm. 13. 1–7', *ZThK* 73 (1976), 131ff) to give Romans 13 its setting in the controversy mentioned by Tacitus (*Ann.* 13: 50f) about the abolition of duties (*vectigal*) which took place in A.D. 58 is interesting but less relevant than is assumed by those who directed attention to it. It is possible to avoid τέλη by various dodges, while it is far more difficult to avoid φόροι. Correspondingly the problem of φόροι is very much in the foreground of Paul's admonition (only φόροι are mentioned in verse 5), whereas τέλη may have come in for the sake of alliteration (τέλος←→τιμή, φόρος←→φόβος). Τέλη were indeed the only problem of the citizens of Rome, who were exempt from φόροι. The incident mentioned by Tacitus is in keeping with this. The battle against τέλη could, however, only be won by collective pressure and not by individual action, while the latter is the situation which Paul supposes his readers find themselves in. Besides, the Roman proletariat is not likely to have permitted newcomers to play a role in its fight.

[44] W. Mangold, *Der Römerbrief und seine geschichtlichen Voraussetzungen* (Marburg, 1884), p. 233.

eulogy of the ruler which we find, with certain differences in detail,[45] both in the Hellenistic and in the Roman world in the forms of the acclamation[46] and of the tractate.[47]

It is tempting to link Romans 13 with the prayer of intercession which is common in the ancient world,[48] which was adapted by the Jews already at an early stage, and reference to which plays a not insignificant role in the self-explanation of the Jews to the outside world.[49] The text of these prayers for the superior powers is only known in outline.[50] The advice to offer such a prayer and the meditation on it already contain elements of reflection on the state, although only expressions of practical wisdom[51] and of apologetic value[52] What we find in Romans 13 is more, is a fuller description of the superior powers than usual, and it attempts a theory of the state as such.

The oldest Jewish formulae dealing with non-Jewish government just speak of the king and his son or his family. This was sufficient. It was however not adequate in the city states of the Mediterranean world with their oligarchic or quasi-democratic constitutions. The Jewish community

---

[45] Cp. I. Opelt, 'Zum Kaiserkult in der griech. Dichtung', *Rhein. Museum* 103 (1960), 43ff.

[46] E.g. the epigram of Action or the Augustus hymn of Philo (*Leg.* §143ff).

[47] E.g. Asclepius's aretalogy on the king (cp. A. F. G. Heinrici, *Die Hermes-Mystik u.d.N.T.* (Leipzig, 1918), pp. 76f).

[48] Oppian, *Halieutika* 2.41; Apuleius, *Metamorph.* XI 17 (prayer in mystery cults).

[49] Cp. the apologetic narration in 1 Macc. 7: 33 and Jos. *AJ* 12 §406.

[50] Ezra 6: 10 (offerings are accompanied by prayers). Baruch 1: 11: περὶ τῆς ζωῆς Ν. βασιλέως καὶ εἰς ζωὴν Β. υἱοῦ αὐτοῦ ἵνα ὦσιν αἱ ἡμέραι αὐτῶν κτλ.; Ros. Sukkah 4. There is little to be said for the theory of H. St J. Thackeray, who thinks that the prayer for the ruler in Baruch 1 came in only after the collapse of the first Jewish revolt, and is inclined to give the whole book a late date (*Septuagint and Jewish Worship* (London, 1921), pp. 89ff). The formula 'king and his sons' is found again in Oppian, *Halieutika* 2.41. L. Biehl, *Das liturgische Gebet für Kaiser und Reich* München, 1937), does not go into these questions.

[51] Jer. 29: 7: it is good for you if the city flourishes; Baruch 1: 11f: καὶ δώσει κύριος ἰσχὺν ἡμῖν; Aboth 3.2: without the state one would devour the other. Cp. M. Rivkes who demands with reference to Sanh. 105a that prayer should be made for the welfare of the kingdom under whose wings we shelter (J. Katz, *Exclusiveness and Tolerance* (London, 1961), p. 165). A more cynical slant is given to this in the Jewish proverb: Don't pray for the death of a king, nobody knows who will succeed him.

[52] Especially Jos. *C. Apion* 2 §196, where Josephus claims that the offerings in the Temple were accompanied by prayers for the κοινὴ σωτηρία (= *salus publica*) which takes preference over private offerings (cp. 2 §77) because man is, it is presupposed, a ζῷον πολιτικόν. This must refer to the prayer for the ruler and is emphasised in answer to the accusation that the Jews are not *sacra colentes* and despise the laws of the state (Juvenal 14.96ff). Cp. Philo, who claims that the Jews are the ones who are φιλοκαίσαρες in their heart (*Leg.* §280), and the defence made by Josephus ('legislator non quasi prophetans Romanorum potentiam non honorandum'; *c. Apion* 2 §75), and the accusations against the Jews cited in Meg. 13b and Jer. Ter. 8. 10 (46b/c).

in Alexandria seems to have pledged its loyalty to the king without mentioning the municipal authorities.[53] We do not know which formula – if any – was used by the long-standing Jewish communities of the Diaspora.[54] The communities in the proud 'free' cities of the Greek world are likely to have mentioned the municipal authorities and more or less disregarded the Roman ones. It was different outside the established Greek commonwealth. The problem became very acute in Rome, a place where the source of authority had been shrouded in mist, where the *princeps* only exercised the *Samtherrschaft*[55] and his official position was that of the *tribunus plebis*, where, on the other hand, every Roman citizen could claim to be a sovereign. It is in keeping with this situation that Rom. 13: 1 and 3 speak of different stages of authority and it is the point of the passage that divine authorisation is bestowed on each of them, without exception: οὐ γὰρ ἔστιν ἐξουσία κτλ.[56]

The claim made in Romans 13 is not new. The book of Daniel emphasises that God will give (δώσει) the power to the king.[57] The Letter of Aristeas states that God stands behind the king.[58] The consequence, however, that the whole pyramidal system of governmental organs is divinely ordained is rarely drawn. Equally τάττειν goes beyond διδόναι; it states a more far-reaching intervention of God. The consideration that the ἄρχοντες cause fear only to the evil and not to the good is equally a stock phrase of political ethics; it is used and paraphrased in Josephus's description of Agrippa's speech to the inhabitants of Jerusalem[59] and likewise by the author of the first Epistle of Peter.[60] The qualification as διάκονος θεοῦ

---

[53] Cp. Aristeas 15f.

[54] If E. Bickermann's theory that the civic prayer for Jerusalem shows marks of Greek influence (*HThR* 55 (1962), 185) is right, it is all the more likely that the synagogue of the diaspora had started to formulate prayers for their respective cities and governments.

[55] T. Mommsen, *Röm. Staatsrecht* ii (4th edn. Tübingen, 1952), 1167ff.

[56] ἐξουσίαι = *potestates*. Only *consul* and *praetor* are in possession of the *imperium* while the rest of the officials have merely a *potestas*. Romans 13: 1–3 seems to emphasise that even the lower ranks of the officials are to be heeded as λειτουργοὶ θεοῦ. The same phrase (τὸν δόντα σοι τὴν βασιλείαν ταύτην ἀρχήν) is found in *Acta Catharinae* V(c) ch. 6. It is hazardous to take this phrase as an argument against an early origin of the text as has been done by E. Klostermann and E. Seeberg in *Schriften der Königsberger Gelehrten Gesellschaft* i (Berlin, 1924), 8off. Cp. the saying of Chanan b. Rabba according to which even the custodian in charge of a well may be taken as ordained by God (Ber. 58a).

[57] Dan. 1: 2; 2: 37ff; 5: 18; cp. E. Stauffer, *Gott und Kaiser im N.T.* (Bonn, 1935), pp. 7ff.

[58] Aristeas 15.

[59] θεραπεύειν γὰρ οὐκ ἐρεθίζειν χρὴ τὰς ἐξουσίας; there is nothing that stops one being whipped sooner than bearing it patiently (φέρειν); forbearance by those who are maltreated (ἀδικούμενοι) leads to a change of mind on the side of those who inflict injustice (ἀδικοῦσιν) (*BJ* 2 §351). Cp. 1 Pet. 2: 15.

[60] 3: 13; the very close parallelism between this passage and the one cited in n. 43 is worthy of note.

which Paul stresses so much, is uncommon. The same is true for λειτουργοὶ[61] θεοῦ[62] – a formula which, although based on Isa. 61: 6, seems to have been coined *ad hoc* with this meaning – and the even more far-reaching statement on the activity: προσκαρτεροῦντες. Taken together this amounts to a fairly extended theology of order[63] which goes far beyond the acclamation or prayer for the king.

It is partly paralleled in the prayer for the ἄρχοντες and ἡγούμενοι which is incorporated in 1 Clem. 61: the reference to different superior powers, the correlation between heavenly and earthly powers, the emphasis on subordination, the description of any resistance as revolt against God are the same, while the rest of the prayer proceeds along different lines. The coincidence is not to be explained by the assumption of direct dependence, as some of the Pauline terms are lacking whereas others are used differently. It has been noted[64] that chapters 6of display Jewish features. It seems reasonable to suppose that a synagogue prayer was adapted and augmented by the Christian community of Rome.

Paul must have known such a text – not necessarily of Roman, but probably of Western origin. It is likely that his formulation in Romans 13 is a carefully designed texture consisting of traditional elements and Pauline additions. The former are to be found in verses 3a, 4b, c (without θεοῦ διάκονος), 5; but other terms as well are likely to have their Jewish pre-history. Pauline, however, is not only the blunt linking of the powers with God, but also the use of the genitive, the emphasis on subordination and the stigmatisation of resistance, and insistence on paying taxes.

Paul does his utmost to combat all political inclinations among the Christians. He not only exhorts his readers in passing to be loyal to the state (as he does later; Phil. 1: 27), but he takes up and gives concrete reference to formulae of basic affirmation of the state, which could be understood by both Jews and Gentiles. The fact too that the proverbial wisdom of Rom. 12: 16 is not taken up suggests political motivation. It is the particular situation of his readers, whether or not the community still consisted primarily of Jewish Christians,[65] that explains the passage most readily.[66]

[61] For the meaning of λειτουργός see F. Oertel, *Die Liturgie* (Leipzig, 1917; 2nd edn. 1965).

[62] Cp. however the statement of Jalqut Shimoni on Ps 132: 9, according to which rulers may act as priests of God.

[63] Cp. O. Eck, *Urgemeinde und Imperium* (Gütersloh, 1940).

[64] W. Mangold, *De ecclesia primaeva pro Caesaribus ac magistratibus Romanis preces fundente* (Bonn, 1881).

[65] For the Jewish character of the Christian community at Rome see Mangold, *Römerbrief, passim*; for a later discussion of the problem cp. W. G. Kümmel, *Einleitung in das Neue Testament* (Heidelberg, 1973), pp. 270f (ET London, 1966, pp. 218ff). Cp. W. Wiefel, 'Die jüdische Gemeinschaft im antiken Rom und die Anfänge des

Romans 13 is written as a warning to the fellow members of the community and even as an *alibi*, a proof of innocence to the officials; it is the beginning of Christian apologetic. Its comprehension is made possible not by emendation but by fitting it into its proper historical context. The passage does indeed contain a theology, and an even more heightened theology of the state can be deduced from it, but it was not the typically Pauline approach that directed its formulation.

II

'When they say, "Peace and security" '[67] (1 Thess. 5:3), a phrase which received fame by its[68] citation in mediaeval mystery plays and at the end of Luther's 95 theses, is the other Pauline reference to the political world. The customary reference to Jer. 6:14 amounts to only a partial parallel;[69] moreover such a reference is unlikely, in that 1 Thessalonians does not give evidence of any explicit Old Testament citations. The half verse must be set in the context of a different tradition.

Ps. Sol. 8:18 relates that Pompey entered Judaea like a father entering the house of his children μετὰ εἰρήνης . . . μετὰ ἀσφαλείας πολλῆς.[70] The psalmist adds that he then poured out the blood of the citizens of Jerusalem like dirty water. The phrase quoted expresses the claim made by the conqueror, and indeed in his own words. For everywhere that Rome makes an appearance, the provision of peace and security is made to justify the loss of autonomy and more than compensate for all the initial terrors. Since the word *pax*, unlike εἰρήνη,[71] has a no more than formally legal content, referring to a transaction rather than a condition (cp. *pactum*), the term demands a supplement to give it substance.[72] This is given by means of an

---

römischen Christentums', *Judaica* 26 (1970), 65ff. ET in K. P. Donfried, *The Romans Debate* (Minneapolis, 1977), pp. 100ff.

[66] This view was put forward in *ThLZ* 85 (1960), col. 837ff. The line of approach was taken up by J. Kosnetter, 'Römer 13: 1–7 eine zeitbedingte Vorsichtsmassnahme oder grundsätzliche Einstellung?' (*AnBibl* 17 (1963), 347ff) and V. Zsifkovits, *Der Staatsgedanke nach Paulus in Römer 13: 1–7* (Wien, 1964).

[67] The Vulgate renders it in such a way that two citations are implied. This is parallel to the tendency of using these terms as formulae of acclamation.

[68] Cp. W. Meyer, 'Der Ludus de Antichristo' in *Gesammelte Aufsätze*, i (Berlin, 1905), 169.

[69] J. B. Lightfoot (*Notes on the Epistles of St Paul* (London, 1895), p. 72) even takes the verse as a 'direct quotation from our Lord's words'.

[70] For the *Pax Romana* concept of Pompey see M. Gelzer, *Pompeius* (München, 1959), p. 94.

[71] It is therefore often – and more adequately – rendered by *felicitas temporum*.

[72] The assumption of a translation from Hebrew, where indeed שלום is often used together with other terms (Rom. 1:7; Gal. 6:16 etc.), can be disregarded in this case.

adjective, complementary noun or significant symbol (*caduceus* or *cornucopia* or the like). It is in such a form that *pax* becomes the programme of the time of the principate. This happens for the first time in the large *aureus* of 28 B.C.,[73] on which the contents of the *Pax* are defined by the addition of a *caduceus*[74] (the same *caduceus* plays an especial role in the history of Thessalonica).[75] The programme is then given concrete expression in the *Ara Pacis Augustae*,[76] the construction of which was begun in 13 B.C. Characterised in this way, *Pax* includes both *urbs* and *orbis*. Within the walls of Rome the term used is *pax et concordia*, since the inhabitants formed the sovereign body, and after the terror of the Civil Wars it is the unanimity among them that is of decisive importance.[77] The corresponding formula for the empire outside Rome is *pax et securitas*. If this is not always in express terms, the reason is that the *Pax Romana* was usually imposed on the peoples by means of warfare. In such a case it was the Roman mercy which first of all showed itself, sparing the stiff-necked instead of wiping them out. On these occasions therefore it is *clementia* that is the object of praise. Where however the subjugation was brought about peacefully (as was initially the case in Judaea), or where the blessings given by Rome had already been familiar for some time, it is not the single event but the mark of complete peace, i.e. *securitas*, that is celebrated.[78] Thus Velleius Paterculus, writing in A.D. 30, makes his description of the present state of affairs culminate in praise of *securitas*.[79] The same eulogy is still found in Aristides.[80] With regard to this it is necessary to take into consideration that a correspondence exists

---

[73] H. Mattingly and E. A. Sydenham, *The Roman Imperial Coinage* I (London, 1923), p. 60; cp. C. Koch, 'Pax' in: *PW* 2nd ser. 18 (1949), col. 2430ff. For the Romans' own interpretation of the *Pax Augusta* cp. H. E. Stier, 'Augustus-Friede und römische Klassik' in *Aufstieg und Niedergang der römischen Welt*, eds. H. Temporini and W. Haase, ii, 2 (Berlin, 1975), 13ff.

[74] *Coins of the Roman Empire in the British Museum*, ed. H. Mattingly, i (London, 1923), p. 112; C. H. V. Sutherland, *Coinage in Roman Imperial Policy* (London, 1951), p. 31.

[75] *A Catalogue of the Greek Coins in the British Museum. Macedonia*, ed. R. S. Poole (London, 1879), p. 117.

[76] S. Weinstock, 'Pax and the Ara Pacis', *JRS* 50 (1960), 44ff; K. Hanell, 'Das Opfer des Augustus an der Ara Pacis', *Skrifter utgivna av Svenska Institutet i Roma*, Acta Instituti Romani Regni Sueciae; quarto series xx (1960), pp. 33ff. For a brilliant interpretation of the concept of Augustus cp. E. Buchner, 'Solarium Augusti und Ara Pacis', *Römische Mitteilungen* 83 (1976), 319ff.

[77] 1 Clem 37: 5, the parable of the body with its praise of συμπνεῖν is a Roman theme *par excellence*.

[78] Apart from *securitas* we find terms like *tranquillitas, stabilitas temporum, quies*, Cp. Tertullian: *rerum quies* (*Apol.* 39).

[79] *Hist. Rom.* ii. 80.

[80] *Orat.* 26; for a searching interpretation of Aristides' speech see J. Palm, *Rom, Römertum und Imperium in der griechischen Literatur der Kaiserzeit* (Lund, 1959), pp. 56ff. Cp. Arist. *Orat. 100* (εἰς ἀσφάλειαν ἐξαρχεῖ), Ps. Arist. *Orat.* εἰς βασ. 37 and already Isocr., *De pace* 17. Cp. W. Gernentz, *Laudes Romae* (Rostock, 1918), p. 142.

between *securitas* and *aeternitas*.[81] If the artistic attributes of *pax* already provide a religious aura, with *aeternitas* a full religious claim, that of political realisation of salvation (*Heilsverwirklichung*) is made.

After the daring attempt of Caligula, who had his three sisters portrayed on a coin as *Concordia, Securitas* and *Fortuna*,[82] the inscription *securitas* was also put on coins from the time of Nero onwards.[83] From this point on the motto became a commonplace on coinage up to Constantius.[84] This could not have happened earlier,[85] because it was only under Nero that the doors of the temple of Janus were shut again for the first time since Augustus.[86] It was possible for propaganda to anticipate something that was not yet permitted to the mintmasters, whose issue had to be a correct proclamation of the present state of affairs.

It may be no chance coincidence that Ps. Sol. 8: 18 is the earliest piece of evidence for this ideology. For Pompey the Great was the first and also the most imposing of the *homines imperiosi* of Roman history. In 1 Thess. 5: 3 too it must be these Latin terms that are taken over, since in Greek, where the term εἰρήνη is understood differently, the inclination to supplement εἰρήνη with a complementary word does not become apparent.[87] Nor is this done in the eulogy of Simon Maccabaeus in 1 Macc. 14[88] which imitates the Greek.

[81] Cp. The references adduced by Fr. Sauter, *Der römische Kaiserkult bei Martial und Statius* (Stuttgart, 1934), pp. 124ff.

[82] Mattingly, *Coins of the Roman Empire* i, p. 152. Claudius issued a programmatic coin which marked the third centenary of the temple of Janus, which bears the inscription *Paci Augustae* and shows *pax* with the wings of *victoria*, the attributes of the *caduceus* (= *felicitas*; cp. *securitas*) and snake (= *salus*) and the *gestus* of *pudor*; *Coins of the Roman Empire* i, Claudius n. 6; cp. Sutherland, *Coinage* p. 127. Cp. the statues of three deities (*Salus Publica, Concordia* and *Pax*), on the *Ara Pacis Augustae* (Dio 54.35.2).

[83] The most complete collection of *securitas* coins is given by J. Bernhart, *Die Münzen der römischen Kaiserzeit* (München, 1942), pp. 124ff. The theme could not be abandoned once *securitas* had appeared on coins. It is due to this that especially in the stormy time of the year of the four emperors *pax* and *securitas* coins are struck; now they represent a programme rather than a factual statement.

[84] *Securitas* and *quies* play a special role in the inscriptions of Constantius; cp. L. Berlinger, 'Beiträge zur inoffiziellen Titulatur der römischer Kaiser' (Diss. Breslau, 1935), p. 54.

[85] A different interpretation is suggested by H. Mattingly, *Roman Coins* (London, 1960), p. 161.

[86] It is typical for both the reality and the aspirations of the time of Claudius that the coin inscription *Paci Augustae* occurs regularly (cp. O. T. Schulz, *Die Rechtstitel und Regierungsprogramme auf röm. Kaizermünzen* (Paderborn, 1925), p. 58): what could not be said of the present time of war against the Britons was projected into the future by reference to the past. Similarly Velleius Paterculus hailed the *revocata pax* of the time of Tiberius (*Hist. Rom.* ii. 89), although the reality was different.

[87] The instances to the contrary, adduced by G. Delling, *Römer 13, 1–7 innerhalb der Briefe des NT* (Berlin, 1962), pp. 40f, do not alter the picture.

[88] Cp. especially verse 8 (μετ' εἰρήνης) and verse 11 (ἐποίησε τὴν εἰρήνην ἐπὶ τῆς γῆς).

It is no less significant that the phrase happened to be incorporated in the Talmud. When Akiba and his fellow-rabbis pay their visit to the capital they find those who live there in a state of security and peace. The welfare of those who do not perform the will of God becomes a tantalising question for those who obey his commandments even in the most trying circumstances. This theodicy problem, which is solved by a new perspective which Akiba becomes aware of,[89] is given depth and illustration by the complaint that the Romans, who do not obey God, live in peace and security.[90]

It is, we remember, a phrase which was coined for the Roman realm outside the city but which is used here to characterise Rome herself and her inhabitants. It should be noted that it is not a phrase that could have been picked up during the stay at Rome that is employed here. Instead, a term is employed that was current in the rabbis' homeland, so much so that it was cited in a theological debate and given point by its incorporation in the description of a visit to the metropolis which took place at the beginning of the second century.

Paul takes up the phrase with polemical intent. Here one must note that he is commenting on an ideology that was in vogue at the time and taking off a generally prevalent self-awareness propagated by the panegyricists and encouraged by the state authorities, not however singling out for attack a formula already made sacrosanct by official proclamation (on a coin). Besides, a distinct confrontation or even hostility against Jewish–Christian eschatology is not noticeable on the other side – it is only imported by the addition of γάϱ or δέ at the beginning of the sentence.[91] Thirdly Paul expresses himself in personal terms (ὅταν λέγωσιν . . . αὐτοῖς).

Thus in this direction the conflict lacks a final sharpness of definition. Moreover Paul is directing himself towards the Thessalonians with these words. Among them, or among some of them, he sees the imminent danger, that the mirage of fulfilled eschatology may cause them to forget the future. None the less he is indirectly making a revaluation of a political ideology that was identical with the imperial government's view of itself, and which the state could expect as a matter of course to be treated with respect. This verse, it would seem, is the one in the Corpus Paulinum where this is done most unambiguously. It is questionable whether Phil. 3: 20 contains an

---

[89] Cp. *Donum Gentilicium*. Festschrift D. Daube (Oxford, 1978), pp. 295ff. For general information cp. G. Stemberger, 'Die Beurteilung Roms in der rabbinischen Literatur' in *Aufstieg und Niedergang der römischen Welt*, II 19, 2 (1979), pp. 338ff.

[90] Makk. 24a: יושבין בטח והשקט .

[91] The additions are well attested – see Tischendorf, *Novum Testamentum Graece* (Leipzig, 1876), ad hoc. – and δέ was even valued as original by B. Weiss. *Textkritik der paulinischen Briefe* (Leipzig, 1896), p. 118.

allusion to emperor worship.[92] In any case it is only implicit in the verse. Here however a critical position is taken expressly.

The wording of the warning – as is shown by verse 3b and the word ὄλεθρος, which is rare in Paul – is governed by apocalyptic motifs. There is, however, no example in apocalyptic literature of so concrete and discriminating a form of polemics.[93] Moreover most significant is the fact that Paul does not remodel the mood he characterises into an apocalyptic sign – or rather into a stage in the evolution of the last things. Thus the impression is reinforced that it is an actual Pauline opinion that is expressed here. This proviso is made by the same Paul who, three chapters earlier, had viewed a political measure of the Roman government in a favourable light.[94] To illuminate such a phenomenon in different ways, on one occasion to set it in the flow of eschatological events, and on another to interpret it purely personally, corresponds fully to the multiformity of apocalyptic impression and thought.

2 Thessalonians 2: 6ff, a passage which is to be taken as Pauline, may serve as an additional piece of evidence for this. The passage cannot be referring to either the Roman state[95] or the mission.[96] For the use of the word νῦν (νῦν . . . οἴδατε is to be rendered: you now come to know[97]) indicates that it is a question of an event that has manifested itself as κατέχον only after Paul's preaching in Thessalonica.[98] Thus it can only be a particular measure taken by the κατέχων, within the narrow limits of a specified period of time. In any case the κατέχων is a person who had the power of momentarily halting the wheel of historical destiny. A closer identification is made possible by verses 3ff. The term ἀποστασία, as was recognised by Bernhard Weiss, refers to what he styles the 'definitive Entscheidung des jüdischen Volkes gegenüber der Heilsbotschaft'.[99] The ἀντικείμενος is an expected figure, who brings to its climax this apostasy, pointedly

---

[92] E. Lohmeyer, *Der Brief an die Philipper* (Göttingen, 1953), pp. 27f. For the more recent discussions of this passage, cp. Aland, *Entwürfe*, pp. 50ff.

[93] In principle it is conceivable that Judaism could have argued along the same lines. In fact, however, Judaism developed its position from the basis of Jewish self-consciousness and was not eager to attack errors or developments within pagan consciousness which, it must be remembered, did not exist as a challenging entity from the Jewish point of view.

[94] Cp. *ZThK* 56 (1959), 294ff.

[95] W. Böld, *Obrigkeit von Gott?* (Hamburg, 1962), pp. 87ff.

[96] O. Cullmann, 'Le caractère eschatologique du devoir missionaire . . .' in *Recherches Théologiques à la memoire de W. Baldensperger* (Paris, 1936), pp. 26ff; *Der Staat im N.T.* (Tübingen, 1956; ET London, 1957); similarly J. Munck, *Paulus und die Heilsgeschichte* (Copenhagen, 1954; ET London, 1959).

[97] E. von Dobschütz, *Die Thessalonicherbriefe* (Göttingen, 1909), p. 279, on the other hand, links it with ἔτι in the same verse.

[98] Rightly so H. Hanse, *ThWNT* ii, 830 (ET ii, 830).

[99] *Lehrbuch der biblischen Theologie des N.T.* (Stuttgart, 1903), pp. 224f.

designated as ἀνομία, and ends in theomachy. The κατέχων inhibits this Jewish persecution of the Christians. It is only indirectly that he delays the end; primarily it is the repulse of the ἀπώλεια that is implied. So one should think of Claudius and his repressive policies against the Jews. The same experience lies also behind 1 Thess. 2: 16. Only here Paul adds that the persecution of the persecutors does not yet proclaim the immediate proximity of the day, but that ἀποστασία must come first. If this ἀποστασία culminates in an individual, one must assume that he too appears in political dress – not indeed preceded by the Roman *fasces* but perhaps in Jewish messianic garb.[100] A further counterpoint of comprehension!

1 Thessalonians 5 and 2 Thessalonians 2 do not speak directly of the state *per se* but rather of manifestations of the political world. They do not contradict each other, but take different approaches in showing the ambivalence of the political powers as revealed to apocalyptic thought, which comprehends world history and salvation history in continual movement – made possible by an extraordinary variability of the apocalyptic scheme itself and of its application to historical events. In each case man interprets the phenomena and signs by his active and passive participation in the events. This means that eschatological reflection lies at the beginning of this perception. Man stands over against the happenings of the political world and does not see himself as entirely subordinate to them. He only criticises, however, so far as his fellow men are led into temptation. There is no time for anything else. The intensified eschatology makes it easy for Paul to regard practical problems as of secondary importance.

The difference from Romans 13 is obvious. On the one side a dynamic–apocalyptic understanding of state and history which embraces the events in continually new and different ways, on the other the static view of the state of a *quod semper ubique*, while, it is to be emphasised, there are no lines of argumentation attributing special distinction and a role in salvation history to the Roman empire.[101] It is impossible to insert the eschatological understanding of 2 Thessalonians 2 – seen with a positive bias – into Romans 13 (as has been done occasionally)[102] and thus even to attribute an eschatological dignity to the state. The Thessalonians

---

[100] Is it the expected ruling of a high priest who claims to give his decision by the authority of God? Or is the ἀντικείμενος a Jewish revolutionary? Is the sitting in the Temple a scene like the one, described by Hegesippus (Eus. *H.E.* 2.23.11ff.), that led to the execution of James the Righteous (similar in appearance but the opposite in contents)?

[101] For references to this appreciation see Palm, *Rom.* pp. 114ff.

[102] Eck, *Urgemeinde*, pp. 66f and Böld, *Obrigkeit*, p. 82.

passages and Romans 13 represent two different types of understanding of the state, which have little in common.

Paul's theology as a whole and in particular his eschatology is largely dictated by apocalyptic. With regard to his view of the state, he undertook, as has been shown, characteristic changes within this framework. Thus the apocalyptic type may be regarded with some certainty as *the* type, in which the Pauline philosophy of the state is moulded.

The development of Pauline theology has not yet been sufficiently investigated. Perhaps the theology of martyrdom in the thought of his middle period may partly explain his sharp attitude towards the political powers, perhaps in the other direction the lessening influence of eschatology may have prepared the ground for Romans.[103] Perhaps such an investigation might throw some more light on the chapter – it will scarcely be possible to uphold the theory of a favourable impression made by the happy *Quinquennium Neronis*. Nor is the solution to wriggle out of the stern meaning of Romans 13 by stating that remarks on the divine ordination of the ruler were quite natural in an environment where so much was linked with the heavenly sphere.[104] We are bound to admit that the passage appears just as much a foreign body when seen from the general viewpoint of Pauline theology as it is evidence for an exceptional case when viewed historically. Therefore, whatever its biblical theological significance may be and however great the momentum it gathered in church history has been, in an account of the Pauline view of the state Romans 13 must be given its place rather in a side aisle than in the nave.[105]

III

The passage is, however, of greatest importance for the characterisation of Paul, the leader of his communities. The distaste for any form of ἀταξία is noticeable from the beginning of the time we can trace his steps (1 Thess. 5: 14). Its combating became a dominant theme the more he encountered the effect of disorder in his foundations. It is in this context that the term προιστάμενοι occurs for the first time. It is significant that the pyramidal structure is meant to be confined to the community.[106] The world is an entity outside (1 Thess. 4: 12), its representatives are ἄδικοι (1 Cor. 6: 1),

---

[103] Thus C. H. Dodd, 'The Mind of Paul I', *New Testament Studies* (Manchester, 1953), p. 118.

[104] Ad. v. Harnack, *ThLZ* 6 (1881), col. 499 (review of Mangold). The observation itself is, of course, true and has been amply substantiated by subsequent research (e.g. Berlinger, *Titulatur*, especially pp. 89f).

[105] Cp. Windisch, *Imperium*, p. 30.

[106] H. v. Campenhausen, 'Zur Auslegung von Römer 13 . . .' in *Festschrift A. Bertholet* (Tübingen, 1950), pp. 109f argues differently.

the Christian task is not to give offence and therefore ἡσυχάζειν (1 Thess. 4: 11). It may be that Paul had been influenced by that rabbinic school of thought that stopped short of considering pagan authorities as divinely ordained[107] and confined itself to a qualified appreciation for practical reasons.[108] But it is typical that, already at the beginning, he is more concerned about the reputation of the communities in the outside world[109] than Jewish missionary literature appears to have been. As soon as he realises that disorder may carry serious consequences for the communities he urges obedience to the government. He enforces this command by giving it an ultimate direction. He achieves this by moving the pyramidal system, which he had recommended as basic to his communities, into the public world. It is this interaction between care for the well-being of the community and circumspection about dangers that may arise from outside that are constitutive factors for Paul's design in Romans 13.

Celsus accuses the Christians of taking no interest in public affairs.[110] What was not entirely true for his time[111] was in all probability valid for the lifetime of Paul. Rendering honour and paying taxes were the only direct contributions for the general welfare which were made by those who lived in the conviction that they possessed a πολίτευμα in heaven. Social status, foreign descent and, indeed, a tense eschatology militated against anything else. It was, however, no less than the government expected of people of this strand of society. In a sense it was even more, if taken together with the apostle's insistence on regular work and his dislike of disorderly, let alone revolutionary, activities. Seneca stresses that the service of a good citizen is never useless: by being heard and seen, by his expression, by his gesture, by his silent stubbornness and by his very walk, he helps.[112] It was in a similar way that Christians were admonished to render their services.[113] Even the

---

[107] That the power is given to Rome from heaven is emphasised by Josephus (*BJ* 5 §307) and admitted in a number of rabbinic statements (Jose b. Kosma in Ab.z.18a (whereas Chanina opposes him) and especially Resh Laquish in Chag. 16a.

[108] Chanina in Aboth 3.2 (men would devour each other without fear but for the government; interesting is Eisler's statement: 'der Stoss seufzer des R. Chanina . . . ist kein vollwertiges Gegenstück (zu Römer 13)', *Jesous Basileus*, ii. 749) and, even more reserved, Gen.r.82 (resistance is equal to suicide).

[109] W. C. v. Unnik, 'Die Rücksicht auf die Reaktion der Nicht-Christen als Motiv in der altchristlichen Paränese' in *BZNW* 26 (1960), 221ff.

[110] Origen, *C. Cels.* viii. 73, 75.

[111] A. Bigelmair, *Die Beteiligung der Christen am öffentlichen Leben in vorconstantinischer Zeit* (München, 1902).

[112] Numquam inutilis est opera civis boni; auditus visusque, voltu, nutu, obstinatione tacita incessuque ipso prodest (*De otio* iv. 6).

[113] Although the pressure exercised on members of the higher strata of society to take over honorary offices caused great difficulties (cp. R. Freudenberger, 'Romanas caerimonias recognoscere' in *Donum Gentilicium. Festschrift D. Daube*) (Oxford, 1978), pp. 238ff.

eschatological view could, as has been shown, result in a positive valuation of certain aspects of governmental activity. The very mutability of the eschatological interpretation of time, for which the Pauline letters give such ample evidence, made it easier for the Christians to adapt themselves to a new situation and to take up new challenges. They resulted in developments which had their own problems, problems the church tried to cope with by a reinterpretation of Romans 13, the essence of which is most lucidly expressed in the text of Bach's cantata:

> Die Obrigkeit ist Gottes Gabe,
> Ja selber Gottes Ebenbild.
> Wer ihre Macht nicht will ermessen
> Der muss auch Gottes gar vergessen:
> Wie würde sonst sein Wort erfüllt?[114]

It needs, there is little doubt, a revaluation in our days. This can be attempted by giving the passage its proper focus, by placing it in a situation which is in some ways, although not entirely, beyond recall, while the apostle's concern and consideration sets an example that it would be unwise to disregard.

[114] Cantata 119 (*Sämtliche von Johann Sebastian Bach vertonte Texte*, ed. W. Neumann (Leipzig, 1974), p. 170).

Biblical criticism criticised: with reference to the Markan report of Jesus's examination before the Sanhedrin

I

In the introduction to the third edition of his *Neutestamentliche Methodenlehre*[1] Heinrich Zimmermann writes that he has not mentioned religio-historical study among the methods of scholarly New Testament interpretation, because he does not know 'which New Testament *pericopae* could be chosen as examples, from the point of view of the history of religions', to demonstrate its use and applicability. His book is accordingly for the most part a full and highly instructive presentation of literary-historical methods, particularly form-criticism and redaction-criticism. The traditions which are shaped in transmission and combined in redaction have nevertheless an historical background. In form- and redaction-criticism this is virtually excluded from examination. These methods are concerned primarily with the moulding of the traditions by congregational *Sitz im Leben* and editorial outlook. Enquiry is directed at the process of literary formation rather than the historical background from which the process begins. Heinz Schürmann justly observes that enquiry into the *Sitz im Leben* of the congregations which proclaimed the Gospel is too limited in scope for him to say that his acceptance of the Gospel is vindicated by it. If, for instance, the Gospel statements on Jesus are to be interpreted only in the light of Easter and Whitsuntide, and cannot be 'traced back to the historical Jesus and into the company of the disciples before Easter', the Christian message would lose 'the *factum historicum*' which is its basis, and could accordingly 'no longer be distinguished from Gnosis'.[2]

Kurt Lüthi, in his review of Adolf Holl's *Jesus in schlechter Gesellschaft*, sums up by saying that New Testament study has foregone 'any direct apprehension of Jesus'. 'The phrase "historical Jesus" ', he says, could only

---

[1] Heinrich Zimmermann, *Neutestamentliche Methodenlehre* (3rd edn. Stuttgart, 1970), p. 7.
[2] Heinz Schürmann, 'Die vorösterlichen Anfänge der Logientradition. Versuch eines formgeschichtlichen Zugangs zum Leben Jesu', in Helmut Ristow and Karl Matthiae (eds.), *Der historische Jesus und der kerygmatische Christus* (Berlin, 1960), pp. 342–70 (370).

signify something 'entirely beyond scientific history.'[3] Lüthi is formulating what could almost be called *communis opinio* of most contemporary exegetes. Here, however, this view is resisted for basic theological reasons as well as from the point of view of exegetical method. I cannot rid myself of the impression that the widespread refusal to elucidate biblical traditions historically stems from the current prevalence of literary-critical methods. By virtue of their very starting-point these methods are more concerned with the factors that form tradition than with historical background. Thus, to begin with, exegetical methods rule out elucidation of the historical *fundamentum in re* for the Christian message; and then this *fundamentum in re* is declared irrelevant, because the student working solely with literary criticism can only attain to the testimony of the witnesses and so to the belief of the church.

Yet the committed faith of the primitive and early Christian witnesses to Jesus left its literary deposit in the Gospels. Can we really be asked to take that faith seriously, and make it our own, without also being interested in its object, the historical Jesus himself? Would not that mean that we should have faith in the faith of the witnesses, although the content of their faith had no longer any relevance for us? Of course the whole biblical message of the Old and New Testaments is determined by the faith of those who have handed it on to us. Of course the biblical writers use various styles of composition, including that of legend, to bring out the meaning of what they transmit for faith. Nevertheless, for anyone who wants to believe today, it is still a decisive question whether behind the different calls to faith there are or are not historical facts. This question may not be weakened or

---

[3] Kurt Lüthi, 'Jesus in schlechter Gesellschaft', *Wort und Wahrheit*, 26 (1971), 463–6 (463). The objection to a faith-motivated interest in the history behind the kerygma is especially forcibly expressed by Georg Strecker, 'Die historische und theologische Problematik der Jesusfrage', *EvTh* 29 (1969), 453–76. Strecker, 468, rightly opposes the claim that the historical Jesus must provide the ground of certainty for faith. For Strecker, ibid., faith's ground of certainty is not attainable outside faith, even in the proclamation of Jesus himself. At 469 he writes: 'The trans-subjective, to which faith refers itself, cannot be understood as an "objective saving fact", as something attainable in general experience, which would also be accessible to the secular historian. Rather, that which gives the believer certainty is not demonstrable; it is inextricably bound up with the event of faith. Certitude of belief only occurs with the accomplishment of faith.' Strecker's position here seems to me to need some modification. Indeed history does not offer the basis for certainty in faith, but it does provide the conditions without which no basis for certainty is possible. The bible in both Old and New Testaments is interpreting historical events, which as events must be accessible to the historian also, so that committed faith can ascribe to them the meaning of saving events. The presupposition for certainty in faith is indeed not demonstrable, but an historical proof that Jesus of Nazareth had never existed could never be removed by any possible ground of certainty for faith. It seems to me that Strecker has made a quantitative problem (how far must the historical *fundamentum in re* extend?) into a qualitative one.

relativised by the observation that the nature of historical fact is a debatable subject. In the present context an historical fact is an historical *factum*, of equal validity however it is transmitted or interpreted, and of equal validity however we relate ourselves to it. In my opinion no historian should lose sight of the question of historical facts in this sense, even when he is aware that any historical fact becomes, the moment it is transmitted, more (or at least other) than historical fact alone. It is the historian's business to evolve methods which bring him as close as may be to historical fact. He should not, however, imitate those many exegetes who rest content with literary criticism alone and declare the historical basis of the biblical message to be unattainable in the first place and in the next place irrelevant. Here a virtue seems to be made out of necessity.

The question of the historical basis of the message is essentially that of continuity between event and report. Only a demonstrable continuity here can be accepted, even from the standpoint of faith, as legitimate development. Thus if, for example, no proto-Israelitic group – however it may be more exactly defined – had the experience of emigrating successfully from Egypt, there would be no grounds for the basic avowal of ancient Israelite faith, that God brought his people out of Egypt. A further implication emerges, in my opinion: the Exodus can only be understood as a saving act of God for Israel, because it was experienced by a definite group of people and because it is open to interpretations other than that of Israelite belief (and so can be seen, for example, as a flight or an expulsion). In other words, the understanding of history as salvation-history presupposes historical events which took place independently of their interpretation as salvation-history and can be understood in a different way. A joke from East-European Jewry may illustrate this.[4] A pious Jew is in a place where it is impossible to eat *kosher*. Driven by the pangs of hunger he goes into a butcher's and asks: 'How much is one portion of ham?' At this instant there is a loud and distinct clap of thunder, for meanwhile a storm has arisen. At the thunder-clap the pious Jew leaves the shop at once and lifts his eyes to heaven with the words 'Mayn't a man so much as ask?!' For no-one else in the whole town does the thunder possess the meaning it has for the Jew in our story. Everyone hears it, but only this one Jew understands it as God's communication to him personally. If it had not thundered so that others too could recognise the thunder, our story would lack *fundamentum in re*, and the Jew's sudden flight from the butcher's would only be the result of his own fancy. If it really did thunder, however, the thunder could be given a corresponding interpretation. If the thunder were

---

[4] [For a version of this joke in Victorian Britain see J. C. MacDonnell, *The Life and Correspondence of William Connor Magee* (2 vols., London 1896), i, 256: ii, 280. *Trans.*]

only a manifestation of the bad conscience of the Jew, his aversion on this account in our story to eating unclean meat would be evinced as simply the product of his fancy.

These considerations compel us to inquire about historical events as they took place, if we wish to understand them as relevant to salvation-history. Yet historical events are virtually untouched in research which is solely directed towards literary criticism. Thus the question of the Last Supper cannot be posed if we only enquire about the *Sitz im Leben* of the community in which the accounts of the meal were formed and handed down. Gerhard Schwarz[5] in his book on Jesus rightly criticised the literary-critical methods which now govern exegesis, and rightly asked for the criteria guiding decisions in (for instance) the important area of christology. 'Do the (christological) statements already presuppose the later christology, or was the later christology only possible because of Jesus' own statements?'[6] Here it seems to me rightly recognised that the criteria for dating a tradition cannot always be found by literary-critical methods. It is indeed in the area of christology that the influence of presuppositions is extraordinarily clear. Sharply expressed, the assumption runs: Jesus was lacking in knowledge about himself, his person and his function, in just the same degree as the church by its Easter faith was instructed concerning him. Everything that brings Jesus, even indirectly, into connection with messianic–christological language is to be understood as church-creation. It is this presupposition – and not any literary-critical necessity – that marks all these passages as church-creation.

Here the Markan account of Jesus's examination before the council will serve to show that this presupposition requires criticism. At the same time it will demonstrate how investigation of religio-historical *milieu* can contribute greatly towards recognition of historical *fundamentum in re*. Indeed we shall be asking what can be, rather than what cannot be, historical.

II

First some literary points must be established. In Mark and Matthew the tradition of Jesus's examination before the council by night, Mark 14: 55–64 (with the mockery following, Mark 14: 65) is inserted into the story of Peter's denial. Immediately annexed to this story is the observation of Mark 15: 1 that 'at once, in the early morning' the members of the Sanhedrin assembled and after deciding accordingly sent Jesus bound to

[5] Gerhard Schwarz, *Was Jesus wirklich sagte* (Wien, 1971).
[6] Schwarz, *Jesus*, pp. 67f.

Pilate. It can therefore be contended that a single sentencing of Jesus by the council has been reported twice, first in the context of the hearing by night and secondly in accordance with the note of time 'at once, in the early morning'. This consideration alone already warrants scepticism from a literary-critical viewpoint as to the historicity of the nocturnal hearing before the Sanhedrin.[7]

This suspicion is strengthened by three further observations.

(1) Mark 14: 55–64 contains christological statements about Jesus. From the presumption that Jesus was first taken to be messiah by witnesses to Christian faith after the resurrection – a presumption that must be critically examined! – it follows necessarily that Jesus and the high priest could not have used christological formulae of this kind. Hence they could only be expressions of the faith of the church, whose members understood Jesus in messianic terms.[8]

(2) In Luke the Sanhedrin do not examine Jesus by night, but only in the morning (Luke 22: 66–71). Some important elements placed by Mark, and Matthew after him, in the nocturnal session are referred by Luke to the morning in a shortened and somewhat altered form. An example is Jesus's reply to the high priest, with its reference, following Ps. 110: 1, to the exaltation of the Son of man to God's right hand. The allusion also made in this reply to Dan. 7: 13 (Mark 14: 62, Matt. 26: 64) is not transmitted by Luke, in accord with his distinctive presuppositions, because it stresses the expectation of the parousia. The formal agreement of the notes of time in Luke 22: 66 and Mark 15: 1 can then be taken as indicating that the earliest tradition of all knew nothing of a hearing by night, and only recorded one in the morning.[9]

(3) Literary resemblances between Mark 14: 55–64 and Mark 15: 2–5 can be taken to show that the first passage (nocturnal hearing before the Sanhedrin) depends on the second (pleading before Pilate). The high priest's two questions to Jesus correspond to Pilate's two questions. Both reports stress Jesus's silence before his judges. Like Pilate (Mark 15: 4), the high priest (Mark 14: 60) asks Jesus: 'Answerest thou nothing?' Now if Jesus was lawfully condemned to crucifixion by Pilate, and if the objections to the report of the nocturnal hearing mentioned under (1) and (2) above are valid, it follows that the report of the proceedings before Pilate was

---

[7] This scepticism was already formulated by Hans Lietzmann, 'Der Prozess Jesu' in *Sitzungsberichte der preussischen Akademie der Wissenschaften*, Phil. -Hist. Kl. xiv (Berlin, 1931), pp. 313–22. It laid the foundation for Paul Winter, *On the Trial of Jesus* (Berlin, 1961).

[8] See for example Ferdinand Hahn, *Christologische Hoheitstitel*, 2nd edn. Göttingen, 1964 (ET *The Titles of Jesus in Christology*, London, 1969.

[9] So for example Winter, *Trial*, p. 25; Hans Werner Bartsch, 'Theologie und Geschichte in der Überlieferung vom Leben Jesu', *EvTh* 32 (1972), 128–43 (139).

already constructed and available when the report of the nocturnal proceedings before the Sanhedrin was drawn up.[10] If we ask whether Jesus's examination before the high priest by night belongs to history, considerations of this kind alone already seem to put us in the wrong and to attribute our question to an illegitimate 'historicizing interpretation'.[11]

Internal analysis of Mark 14: 55–64 also supplies considerations suggesting that Jesus may not have been examined before the Sanhedrin by night. Mark 14: 62 contains a combined scriptural citation linking the concepts of the returning Son of man (Dan. 7: 13) and the exalted Son of David (Ps. 110: 1). It would be concluded almost universally that a combined citation of this kind cannot stem from Jesus himself, but only from the faith of the early church. Likewise, the high priest's question on Jesus's messiahship would be held to imply belief in Jesus as Son of God, that is, the belief of the early church. It is twice reported (Mark 14: 56, 59) that the testimonies of the witnesses against Jesus did not agree. Twice seems once too often, for such a claim needs no repetition.[12] The saying on the destruction of the Temple (Mark 14: 58/Matt. 26: 61) recurs as the gibe of passers-by under the cross (Mark 15: 29/Matt. 27: 39f). In Luke it is missing at both places, but the motif reappears, once again as false witness, in the case against Stephen (Acts 6: 13f). In contrast with Mark and Matthew, who ascribe the saying on the destruction of the Temple to false witnesses against Jesus, John (2: 19–21) gives it as a genuine saying of Jesus at the cleansing of the Temple – a scene which in John stands at the beginning of Jesus's public ministry, but in the other evangelists after the messianic entry into Jerusalem and before the passion. John, for whom the saying is authentic, interprets it allegorically of the three days between the death of Jesus and his resurrection. It is therefore widely concluded that the saying originally circulated in isolation and was first placed in these different contexts as a result of developments in tradition.[13] Nevertheless one must surely also reckon with the possibility that it could have belonged originally to at least one of these contexts!

A further, more fundamental objection to the possible historicity of Mark 14: 55–64 is raised by the view that no one who could be reckoned a witness of the nocturnal hearing will have belonged to the Christian church. Even references to Joseph of Arimathaea and Nicodemus are not relevant here.[14]

[10] G. Braumann, 'Mk 15, 2–5 und Mk 14, 55–64', *ZNW* 52 (1961), 273–8; Joachim Gnilka, 'Die Verhandlung vor dem Synedrion und vor Pilatus nach Mk 14, 53–15, 5', *EKK Vorarbeiten*, Heft 2 (Einsiedeln/Neukirchen, 1970), pp. 5–21 (7, 12); Eta Linnemann, *Studien zur Passionsgeschichte* (Göttingen, 1970).
[11] Gnilka, 'Verhandlung', p. 15.
[12] Linnemann, *Passionsgeschichte*, pp. 109–16.   [13] Gnilka, 'Verhandlung', p. 18.
[14] Eduard Lohse, *Die Geschichte des Leidens und Sterbens Jesu Christi* (Gütersloh, 1964), p. 83.

On the other hand it should be noticed that according to Acts 6: 7, 15: 5 both priests and Pharisees found their way into the primitive church. Among these could have been some with knowledge of what went on during the nocturnal hearing. Likewise we can assume that in the courtyard of the high priest's palace Peter had the amplest opportunity to gain first-hand information on events in the hall of judgement. In arguing now that the Markan account of Jesus's examination before the council is basically historical I proceed from two assumptions: (1) the primitive Christian community had its sources of information on the examination of Jesus by the Sanhedrin; (2) the report in Mark 14: 55–64 is no court record, but only recounts the incidents which were decisive for Christian belief. Ten verses of course could not suffice for a record in due form.

At this point, however, at least a brief debate must be attempted with those who maintain that the Lukan passion-narrative is older and more original than the Markan. So for example it is argued that in Luke the two titles 'messiah' and 'Son of God' are not yet combined in the manner of Mark 14: 61/Matt. 26: 63. In Luke these two titles are divided between the verses 22: 67 and 22: 70. If we can presume that here a stratum emerges older than that in which the two titles are joined, the Lukan account of Jesus's examination before the Sanhedrin will be ascribed to an especially early stage in tradition.[15] As I shall try to show, however, the presumption that Mark 14: 61 presents us with a christological testimony from the early church seems to be false. It is far more likely that we have to do with a true record of what the high priest said! The separation of the two expressions 'messiah' and 'Son of God' accordingly indicates Lukan literary craft rather than especially ancient and original tradition. A number of detailed observations show that Luke has remodelled the tradition that reached him. I mention only the most important. Luke 22: 56–62 deals with Peter's denial. After this 22: 63 notes: 'And the men that held him (Greek αὐτόν) mocked him, beating him.' Luke's text would lead one to believe that this verse concerns Peter, who is spoken of immediately before, if one did not know from Mark 14: 65 that it can only refer to Jesus. Luke here has obscured the meaning of the passage by moving the verse into a different context.[16] In contrast with Mark and Matthew, Luke does not break up the

---

[15] So for example D. R. Catchpole, 'The Problem of the Historicity of the Sanhedrin Trial', in E. Bammel (ed.), *The Trial of Jesus* (London, 1970), pp. 47–65 (65). Among advocates of the priority of the Lukan passion-narrative are: G. Schneider, 'Jesus vor dem Synedrion', *BibLeb* 11 (1970), 1–15; Carsten Colpe, 'Der Begriff "Menschensohn" und die Methode der Erforschung messianischer Prototypen', *Kairos* 13 (1971), 1–17 (13); Jacob Kremer, 'Verurteilt als "König der Juden" – verkündigt als "Herr und Christus" ', *BLit* 45 (1972), 23–32 (29).

[16] Abraham Shalit, review of Winter, *Trial*, in *Kirjath Sepher* 37 (1962), 332–41 (339):

story of Peter's denial by inserting an account of Jesus's examination before the Sanhedrin by night. Mark obviously intended this insertion to emphasise that Jesus's confession of faith happened at the same time as Peter's denial. For literary reasons Luke achieved this emphasis in another way. It is only in Luke 22: 61 that the Lord turns and looks upon Peter as he denies. Mark and Matthew lack this notice because they take literary means to show that confession and denial occurred together, inserting the nocturnal hearing into the story of the denial. Luke did not wish to interrupt this story. His literary scheme therefore compelled him on the one hand to place the mockery before the account of the hearing before the Sanhedrin (not after it as in Mark and Matthew) and on the other hand to locate the whole examination in the early hours of the morning only. Again, the form of Jesus's reply to the high priest's messianic question is obviously secondary in Luke 22: 69 as compared with Mark 14: 62, because here the typical Lukan softening of the early Christian expectation of the parousia is responsible for the Lukan wording. We must then begin with Mark 14: 55–64 if we would investigate the historical *fundamentum in re* of Jesus's examination before the Sanhedrin.

III

The most important unargued ground for the evaluation of Mark 14: 55–64 as unhistorical is the assumption that the christological passages on Jesus are to be understood only as witnesses to the faith of the primitive Christian church.[17] It must therefore first be asked if this assumption is justified. The charge that Jesus drives out devils by Beelzebub the prince of the devils occurs in Mark 3: 22–30/Matt. 12: 22–37/Luke 11: 14–23. According to Luke 11: 20 Jesus answered this charge with the words: 'If I by the finger of God cast out devils, then indeed the kingdom of God has already come to you'. Since this verse is witnessed in Matthew but not Mark it may come from the so-called Sayings Source, which contains old material. The wording in Matt. 12: 28 is of course somewhat less anthropomorphic: 'If I by the spirit of God cast out devils . . .' Here the Lukan text, with its anthropomorphic 'finger of God', appears closer to the original form of the saying. To expel demons and make them powerless is a sign of the end in Jewish apocalyptic thought. The demons are the cause of all failure in man and nature. Their power will therefore be broken at the end.[18]

'There is no vestige of truth in the critical position that Luke had at his disposal a more reliable tradition than Mark.'
[17] Eduard Lohse, *Leidens*, p. 75.
[18] Otto Betz, *Der Paraklet* (Leiden, 1963).

Extraordinary healings were understood by Jesus's contemporaries as acts depriving the demons of their power, and so as miracles. On a critical view of the tradition it can hardly be denied that Jesus performed such healings.[19] Members of the primitive Christian church still performed 'healing miracles' of this kind. (It would be absurd, and out of keeping with the task of evaluating historical sources, to enquire here whether healings of this kind are medically possible.) The rabbinical literature provides one testimony, in my opinion indisputable, from the early second century. Here it is forbidden to allow oneself to be healed in the name of Jesus. The very ancient formulation runs (Tos. Ḥullin ii. 22f):

> The story of Rabbi Eleazar ben Dama, who was bitten by a snake. Jacob of Kephar Sama came to heal him in the name of Jesus ben Pantera [rabbinic mode of reference to Jesus]. But Rabbi Ishmael forbade him and said to him: 'You have no right to do this, ben Dama.' He contradicted him: 'I will give you proof that he may indeed heal me.' But he had no time to do so, for he died. Rabbi Ishmael then said: 'Well is it with you, ben Dama, that you have gone forth [from the world] in peace and have not broken the ordinances of the Wise.'[20]

The attitude which Jesus's opponents adopted to his miracles was similar; they held that the power of evil must be responsible for these healings and that they could only take place by the aid of Beelzebub. Jesus himself, however, saw in them a sign of eschatological power. Thus Jesus's healings already embody the beginnings of later christology.

Even clearer than the reports of the 'healing miracles' of Jesus is the report of Peter's messianic confession in Mark 8: 27–33/Matt. 16: 13–23/ Luke 9: 18–22. According to Mark Jesus asks his disciples whom people take him to be. He receives the most various answers, all of which, however, point to the view that Jesus is the prophet to come in the last days, whom many groups in Judaism awaited.[21] Only Peter explicitly calls Jesus messiah. Jesus's first declaration concerning his suffering follows. It ends with the statement that the Son of man will be put to death, but will rise again after three days. The text immediately continues with the discussion

---

[19] An historical report of this kind seems to me to be provided for instance in Mark 3: 1–6 (Matt. 12: 9–14, Luke 6: 6–11): see K. Schubert, *Der Historische Jesus und der Christus unseres Glaubens* (Wien, 1962), pp. 15–101 (68f).

[20] Tos. Ḥullin ii. 22f (ed. Zuckermandel, 503): parallels in j. Shabb. xiv. 14d foot, b. AZ 27b. See Mordecai Margalioth, *Encyclopedia of Talmudic and Geonic Literature* (Hebrew) (Tel Aviv, 1960), i, 121f.

[21] Deut. 18: 15, 18 (new prophet like Moses); Mal. 3: 23f. (return of Elijah). For expectation of an unidentified eschatological prophet see 1 Macc. 4: 46; 14: 41; Qumran Manual of Discipline (1QSa) ix 11. At 2 Esdras 6: 26 it is said, in connection with the last things: 'Then shall men gaze on those men who once were taken away and who never tasted death since their birth.'

between Jesus and Peter. Peter reproaches Jesus because he has spoken of suffering. Jesus reacts extremely sharply: 'Away from me, Satan! for you think not the thoughts of God, but those of men' (Mark 8: 33). In view of Peter's leading role in the primitive church from the very beginning it is absolutely impossible to regard this verse as a church-formation. A disagreement of the kind described must have been so well known that it could not be blotted out. Further, the subject of disagreement, the concept of messiahship, is historically probable. Jesus somewhat harshly repudiated Peter's triumphalist concept. No doubt is cast on the existence of this disagreement if we assume that Jesus's sayings on his suffering were entirely formulated after the resurrection, because they close with the statement that the Son of man will rise after three days. On the contrary, this state of affairs itself suggests that originally, in place of the prophecy of suffering formulated after the resurrection, a differently-worded disagreement between Jesus and Peter over the concept of messiahship must have occurred. This supposition is fortified by a circumstance which has hitherto been too little noticed. According to the very old formula of belief in 1 Cor. 15: 3, 'Christ died for our sins, according to the Scriptures.' Here for the first time in Jewish religious history the passage on the suffering servant of God in Isa. 52: 13 to 53: 12 is taken messianically.[22] Isa 53: 5 is especially alluded to. The christological reference of the suffering servant of God is so familiar to us as Christians that we do not consider how absurd it must have been for a Jew of the New Testament period to say of the messiah, who should reign over God's kingdom in the last days, that his death was an atoning death. The most obvious explanation is simply that this interpretation goes back to Jesus himself and that Peter objected to it. The first declaration of Jesus's suffering therefore reflects Jesus's reaction to Peter's messianic confession, in the language of the proclamation of the Gospel after the resurrection. Thus the disagreement of Jesus with Peter over the concept of the messiah also belongs to the historical foundations of the Gospels.

Only if we assume that Peter conceived of the messiah in a triumphalist way can we understand why he went in to the court of the high priest's palace. He wanted to be at hand if Jesus was manifested over against his judges as Lord and Christ. The story of the denial reflects the crisis into which Peter entered because his triumphalist interpretation of Jesus's messiahship was not fulfilled.

A further indication that the earthly, historical Jesus was understood to

[22] Georg Fohrer, 'Das Alte Testament und das Thema "Christologie" ', *EvTh* 30 (1970), pp. 281–98 (291); *idem, Geschichte der israelitischen Religion* (Berlin, 1969), pp. 351, 353 (ET *History of Israelite Religion* (London, 1973), pp. 343f).

be messiah by his followers can be found in Mark 10: 35–40/Matt. 20: 20–3. Here James and John, the two sons of Zebedee, ask Jesus if they may sit at his right and left in his kingdom. Pretensions to political power are unmistakably involved. Judas's betrayal might be similarly understood. If his motive was simply to gain money, his suicide after Jesus's death on the cross is incomprehensible; for he must have known the outcome to be expected when he handed Jesus over to enemies with political power. He cannot then have reckoned with the possibility that Jesus would fail before his judges. Judas may have been led to betray Jesus by a motive very like that which drove Peter into the court of the high priest's palace. He wished to force a confrontation in which Jesus could only prove victorious. Judas, the sons of Zebedee and Peter were altogether unprepared to see Jesus as the suffering servant of God. Jesus, then, was taken by his followers to be messiah; and from this standpoint it is not surprising that the examination before the high priest dealt with the messianic question and that Jesus was crucified as 'King of the Jews'.

Luke 12: 8 can also be adduced as evidence for messianic interpretation of the earthly Jesus. 'Everyone who shall confess me before men, him shall the Son of man also confess before the angels of God: but he that denieth me in the presence of men shall be denied in the presence of the angels of God.' The fact that here Jesus is not explicitly identified with the Son of man suggests that we are very close to the original form of the saying. Matthew, aware of this deficiency in assertion, emphasises in his own wording (Matt. 10: 32f) that the Son of man is identical with Jesus: 'Everyone who shall confess me before men, him will I also confess before my Father which is in heaven. . . .' But is is clear even from the indefinite (and so probably earlier) formulation in Luke that the connection between Jesus and the Son of man is so close, that men's relation to the Son of man at the judgement will be decided by their relation to Jesus. Here there is at least a step towards the understanding of Jesus as the Son of man.[23] The unargued assumption that the Gospel statements about Jesus as Christ have no *fundamentum in re* from the time of the earthly, historical Jesus therefore seems to me false. With this established, Mark 14: 55–64 will repay closer examination.

IV

It is striking that Jesus's opponents in the passion narrative – identified as the high priests, the elders and the scribes – are not the same as his

---

[23] On the Son of man see Carsten Colpe, ὁ υἱὸς τοῦ ἀνθρώπου, *ThWNT* viii (1969), 403–81 (ET *TDNT* viii (1972), 400–77) *idem*, 'Der Begriff "Menschensohn" und die Methode der Erforshung messianischer Prototypen', *Kairos* 11 (1969), 241–63; 12 (1970), 81–112; 13 (1971), 1–17.

opponents elsewhere in the Gospels. In the passion, then, according to the Gospels, it is the Establishment of the Jerusalem Temple, that is the Sanhedrin, who lead the opposition to Jesus. Here he was confronted, not as hitherto in Galilee with the adherents of another teaching, but with political power. For that reason this confrontation ended not in theological controversy, but with the cross on Golgotha. The passion-narrative thus depicts the historical situation with fundamental accuracy. If Jesus, as before in Galilee, was to oppose his own self-understanding to the established order, confrontation with political power was unavoidable. It may be that Jesus was wholly aware of this situation and for that reason applied to himself the passage on the suffering servant of God in Isa. 52: 13 to 53: 12. At any rate he was not prepared to play down his message during his stay in Jerusalem. The so-called cleansing of the Temple (Mark 11: 15–19/Matt. 21: 12f/Luke 19: 45–8), which must always be understood with this point in mind,[24] was a provocation of the governing priestly nobility. It was a prophetic sign against malpractices in the Temple, comparable with such Old Testament precedents as are described in Amos 3: 13–15; 7: 10–17 and Jer. 7: 1–15. The wandering preacher of Galilee was, as is to be assumed from the start, no unknown quantity to the priestly aristocrats of Jerusalem. They therefore took his audacious appearance in the Temple as a messianic challenge to their own claim to leadership, and reacted accordingly. This becomes more comprehensible when we recall the ideas typical of that period in the history of Jewish religion. Since the early second century B.C. groups of apocalyptically-minded priests had considered that the Jerusalem Temple was defiled, and governed by unworthy priests. It must be replaced, they believed, by a new heavenly Temple.[25] So we read, for example, in the great apocalyptic survey of history in 1 Enoch 90 (first half of the second century B.C.):

> I stood up to see till [God] folded up that old house. They carried off all the pillars, and all the beams and ornaments of the house were folded up with it. They carried it off and laid it in a place in the south of the land. I saw, till the Lord of the sheep brought a new house, greater and loftier than the first, and set it up in the place of the first which had been folded up. All its

[24] The cleansing of the Temple was certainly not an action of the kind carried out by Zealots, as is often claimed today. For a careful advocacy of this view see S. G. F. Brandon, *Zealots* (Manchester, 1967); *idem*, *The Trial of Jesus of Nazareth* (London, 1968). For criticism see Martin Hengel, *War Jesus Revolutionär?* (Stuttgart, 1970); ET *Was Jesus a Revolutionist?* (Philadelphia, 1971); Günther Baumbach, *Jesus von Nazareth im Lichte der jüdischen Gruppenbildung* (Berlin, 1971); Kurt Schubert, review of Brandon, *Trial*, in *Kairos* 14 (1972), 71–6.

[25] David Flusser, 'The Temple not Made with Hands in the Qumran Doctrine', *IEJ* 9 (1959), 99–104; Kurt Schubert, *Die jüdischen Religionsparteien in neutestamentlicher Zeit* (Stuttgart, 1970), pp. 18–21.

> pillars were new, and its ornaments too were new and larger than those of
> the first, the old one which he had carried off; and the Lord of the sheep
> was within it (1 Enoch 90: 28f).

Jubilees, which belongs to the same milieu and comes from about the
middle of the second century B.C., knows the same idea. In Jub. 1: 27 the
angel of the presence is commanded by God: 'Write for Moses from the
beginning of creation till my sanctuary has been built among them for all
eternity.' The angel of the presence must write out the whole history of the
world from the beginning of creation to the new creation in the last days.
The Essenes of Qumran also knew this expectation of a new Temple at the
end.[26] Because of their opposition to the state of affairs in the Jerusalem
Temple they withdrew to the wilderness of Judaea and regarded their life
there as both a substitute for Temple-worship and a preparation for the
service of the new Temple of the last days.

Nothing is therefore more probable than that the Jerusalem priestly
nobility should have associated Jesus's audacious appearance in the Temple
with ideas of this kind and so secured his arrest and handing-over to Pilate.
Yet they felt themselves imperilled by Jesus's criticism of the Temple in the
sphere which was above all their own. Mark 14: 55–64 is to be understood
from this presumption. Like any investigation, Jesus's examination began
with a general hearing of witnesses. We can gather from the Gospels the
general drift of the evidence for the prosecution. On the Sabbath Jesus
heals sicknesses where there is no danger of death.[27] He has therefore
made a bargain with the Devil (Mark 3: 22, Matt. 12: 24, Luke 11: 15). That
these testimonies were too varied to agree could be conjectured even if it
were not expressly emphasised in Mark 14: 56. A particular charge, noted
outside the tradition as well, concerned the destruction of the Temple.
This was certainly the decisive point for the Jerusalem priestly Establishment.

In this connection we must ask whether or not Jesus spoke of the
destruction of the Temple. In Mark 14: 58/Matt. 26: 61 it is the false
witnesses who claim that he did so, but according to John 2: 19 Jesus did say
something of the kind at the cleansing of the Temple. Mark 13: 1f (Matt.
24: 1f; Luke 21: 5f) must also be taken into consideration: 'And as Jesus
went forth out of the temple, one of his disciples saith unto him, Master,
behold, what manner of stones and what manner of buildings! And Jesus
said unto him, Seest thou these great buildings? there shall not be left here

---

[26] D. Barthélemy and J. T. Milik (eds.), *Qumran Cave 1*, DJD (Oxford, 1955), 134f;
J. M. Allegro (ed.), *Qumran Cave 4*, DJD v (Oxford, 1968), pp. 53f.

[27] Healing of mortal illnesses was permitted on the Sabbath: Schubert, *Religionsparteien*, pp. 34f.

one stone upon another, which shall not be thrown down.' The English exegete and student of comparative religion, S. G. F. Brandon, holds that this saying on the destruction of the Temple is in tension with Mark 14: 57f, where it is described as false witness. He tries to resolve this tension by ascribing Mark 14: 57f to Christian Jews with an affirmative attitude to the Temple, who wanted to avoid Jesus's words of wrath against it. According to Brandon the pre-Markan version of the passion-narrative already impugned the witnesses as false, entirely without historical justification. In Brandon's view, then, we must conclude that Jesus was in fact hostile to the Temple. Brandon infers from Mark 13: 2 that Jesus there intended to allude to actions of his own against the Temple. He sees Jesus accordingly as a sympathiser with the anti-Roman revolutionary movements which also directed themselves against the collaborators with Rome among the Jewish priestly nobility.[28] To foretell the destruction of the Temple does not, however, imply either sympathy with such anti-Roman groups or an active personal share in the destruction. On the contrary, the renowned Pharisaic teacher, Johanan ben Zaccai, who cooperated with the Romans against the rebels in the First Revolt (A.D. 66–70/73),[29] is said to have prophesied to the Temple that it would be destroyed forty years before this came about. 'O Temple, why are you anxious? I know that you will be destroyed' (b. Yoma 39b). Just as Johannan ben Zaccai spoke against the Temple without entertaining any sympathy for the rebels, Jesus prophesied to the Temple that it would be destroyed without wanting to ascribe an active part to himself in the destruction. On the other hand it can easily be understood that the Temple priesthood and their followers should have taken Jesus's words to imply action of his own. The eschatological claim of Jesus, and his criticism of the Temple, could only too easily be misunderstood in this sense.

Why did Jesus have no affinity of any kind with the anti-Roman revolutionary groups? From the numerous arguments for this position[30] I bring forward only one, which seems to me of great weight. The Zealots, from whom the revolt against Rome in A.D. 66 began, received their name because, like the priest Phinehas in Num. 25: 7–13, they were zealous for the Law. This also emerges clearly from Sanh. ix. 6, where the Zealots make away with anyone who has sexual intercourse with a pagan woman. This zeal for the Law is, however, incompatible with Jesus's own attitude to the Law! See for example Mark 7: 15 (Matt. 15: 11): 'There is nothing from without the man, that going into him can defile him: but the things which proceed out of the man are those that defile the man.'

[28] See n. 24 on p. 396 under Brandon.
[29] b. Gittin 56ab; Abhoth de Rabbi Nathan 4; Ekhah Rabbathi I, 244–90 (ed. S. Buber, Hildesheim, 1967, pp. 65–9).
[30] See n. 24 on p. 396, under Hengel, Baumbach and Schubert.

If then Jesus said nothing corresponding verbally to the witness cited in Mark 14: 58, it is clear from the formulation of that verse that statements were before the Temple authorities which linked the widespread expectation of a heavenly Temple at the end with Jesus's appearance in the Temple. David Flusser, the Jerusalem student of the history of religions, is therefore fully justified in saying:

> It is in the highest degree probable that, when Jesus was examined by the High Priest, the first question was whether he had in fact uttered the saying against the Temple. . . . It seems to me to follow from the accounts in the Gospels that the proclamation of the Temple's destruction was for the High Priests the real ground for handing Jesus over to Pilate.[31]

I heartily assent to this thesis of Flusser. It implies, however, that the saying on the Temple has its original *Sitz im Leben* in the account of the examination, although of course it is given as the statement of false witnesses. We must therefore resist the view that 'it was first worked into the scene of the examination before the high priest by the evangelists'.[32]

Jesus's saying on the destruction of the Temple may then be traced back to the interpretation of his attitude to the Temple by others. That an interpretation of this kind should not have been everyone's opinion is more probable than that it should have been advanced unanimously. Thus Mark 14: 59 is entirely right in indicating that 'not even so did their witness agree together'. When even the high priest did not win from Jesus the expression of any viewpoint on these evidences, he could do no other than pose the messianic question in so many words: 'Art thou the Christ, the Son of the Blessed?' The wording of this question is generally attributed to church theology (or perhaps to the Markan redaction) wherein Jesus was already ranked as a Son of God.[33] Such a view seems to me fundamentally false. The expression 'Blessed' is not a usual circumlocution for God among Christians, but it is the current Jewish term: *haqqadosh barukh hu'*, 'the Holy One, Blessed be he'. With his own religious presuppositions the high priest could scarcely have posed the messianic question otherwise than as it is reproduced in Mark 14: 61. There is no trace here of a Christian confession of faith. It is in the highest degree probable that this decisive question of the high priest is verbally reproduced here through the mediacy of an ear-witness, and that we have, so to say, *ipsissima vox* of the high priest! The

---

[31] David Flusser, 'The Trial and Death of Jesus of Nazareth' (Hebrew), *Molad* 2 (1968), 202ff (211), reviewing the book of this title (ET London, 1969) by the Israeli judge Haim Cohn.

[32] Gerhard Schneider, 'Gab es eine vorsynoptische Szene "Jesus vor dem Synedrium"?', *NovTest* 12 (1970), 22–39 (31).

[33] Ferdinand Hahn, *Hoheitstitel*, pp. 126–32, 181 (ET pp. 129–35, 162); Brandon, *Trial*, p. 89; Lohse, *Leidens*, p. 85.

messianic question put to Jesus could not have been worded more Jewishly than is the case in Mark 14: 61! It therefore seems to me, with J. Blinzler,[34] that we should not doubt that this wording indeed goes back to the high priest. It is not a formula of the primitive Christian *kerygma*. Every descendant of David counted from his coronation onwards as an adopted Son of God: see Pss. 2: 7, 110: 1; 2 Sam. 7: 12b, 14. This last verse is already developed in 1 Chron. 17: 11b, 13 with reference to a descendant of David at the end of days. The reference is still clearer in a commentary on 2 Sam. 7: 11–14a from Qumran Cave 4: '*I will be to him a father and he shall be to me a son.* This is the "branch" (*semah*) of David, which comes forth with the "teacher of the Law", who shall be in Zion at the end of days.'[35] The term *branch* according to the Old Testament means the Davidic messiah, Jer. 23: 5; 33: 15; Zech. 3: 8; 6: 12. There can be no doubt that the messiah, the awaited 'Son of David', must also be in the adoptive sense 'Son of God'. The Jewish character of the high priest's question to Jesus is in no way altered by the fact that it could easily be taken by the church in its own Christian sense.

In Mark 14: 62 Jesus's affirmative reply is expanded by a combined citation of Dan. 7: 13 and Ps. 110: 1. Here too we need only find a church-formation if we exclude the possibility that Jesus himself may have linked himself with the expectation of a messianic Son of man. As emerged above in the discussion of Luke 12: 8f, such an assumption would be unjustified. The earthly Jesus has already envisaged himself in such close relationship with the Son of man that it is far more likely that he declared himself Son of man before his judges than that the church created the saying. Thus at the most the reference in Mark 14: 61 to Ps. 110: 1, which obviously assumes exaltation, can possibly be regarded as a product of the church. We are not, however, compelled, in my view, to take it so, for Son-of-man messianology is already combined with the concept of a Davidic messiah in a clearly Jewish context in the pre-Christian period (probably the first century B.C.). In order to assess this state of affairs correctly one must consider that the term messiah is not yet applied to the Davidic messiah in the Old Testament, for which the messiah, the anointed one, is the reigning king of David's line. The term messiah acquired its messianic character when the ideas connected with the Davidic kings were projected into eschatology. In texts from the first century B.C. there are three attestations of the messianic application of the word messiah: Ps. Sol.

---

[34] Josef Blinzler, *Der Prozess Jesu* (4th edn. Regensburg, 1969), pp. 195f. (Cp. ET *The Trial of Jesus* (Cork, 1959), p. 102, representing the 2nd edn.; the 4th edn. is substantially enlarged here). [So, too, Burkitt, in his review of Lietzmann's *Der Prozess Jesu* in *JThSt*, 33 (1932), 64–6 (66).]

[35] Eduard Lohse, *Die Texte aus Qumran, hebräisch und deutsch* (München, 1964), pp. 256f.

17 and 18, the Qumran Manual of Discipline (1QSa), and the Similitudes of Enoch (1 Enoch 37–71) in the passages dealing with the Son of man (1 Enoch 48: 10; 52: 4). Thus the very texts which speak of the transcendent messianic figure of the Son of man apply this term borrowed from Davidic royal ideology to the messiah. The equation of Davidic messiah and Son of man is still clearer when the sayings on the Son of man in 1 Enoch 48: 4 are retroverted into Hebrew. In this process a terminology is brought into use such as is also witnessed in the contemporary messianic texts from Qumran. 1 Enoch 48: 4 runs: 'He shall be a staff to the righteous, whereon they may stay themselves and not fall; he shall be the light of the nations and the hope of the afflicted'. The term 'staff', Hebrew *shebheṭ*, comes from Gen. 49: 10 and Num. 24: 17. It is applied to the Davidic messiah in Test. Judah 24 and the Qumran texts.[36] The phrase 'light of the nations' (Isa. 42: 6; 49: 6) is a combination of Isa. 2: 2 and 9: 1. In Isa. 2: 2 'at the end of the days' all *nations* will come on pilgrimage to the Temple on the hill of Zion, and in Isa. 9: 1 a *light* comes out for men in the land 'of the shadow of death'. If the Son of man according to 1 Enoch 48: 4 is the 'hope of the afflicted', here there is an allusion to Gen. 49: 10, where the ruler from the tribe of Judah is called 'hope of the nations'. Since the 'nations' were named immediately before, the phrase 'hope of the nations' will be reinterpreted in the sense of Trito-Isaiah (Isa. 61: 1; 66: 2) with its eschatological piety of the 'Poor'. This piety of the 'Poor' was also one of the basic elements in the theology of the Qumran Essenes.[37] Thus the 'hope of the nations' became the 'hope of the afflicted'. A pre-Christian Jewish text therefore already combines Son-of-man concepts with Davidic royal ideology in a manner analogous to that of Mark 14: 62. We are then not compelled to ascribe a combination of this kind to primitive Christian christology. Yet this verse also involves a linking of two other concepts, the exaltation and the parousia. These are specifically Christian and do readily suggest an ecclesiastical origin for this element in the combination.

V

These considerations lead to a clear conclusion: there is good ground for seeing in Mark 14: 55–64 ancient, pre-Markan tradition, which has preserved the decisive elements of Jesus's examination before the Sanhedrin in their correct order. Both the imprecisely defined charges in respect of the destruction of the Temple and the assertion that the witnesses

---

[36] Kurt Schubert, 'Die Messiaslehre in den Texten von Chirbet Qumran', *BZ* 1 (1957), 177–97.
[37] Kurt Schubert, *Die Gemeinde vom Totem Meer* (München, 1958), 76–9.

contradicted one another fit the context of the examination well. The climax was the high priest's messianic question, which, as can be made probable, is transmitted in its original form, and the messianic confession of Jesus which followed upon it. This view of the circumstances fits the religio-historical situation of Judaism in the time of Jesus. Study predominantly directed towards literary criticism should not forgo arguments from the history of religions.[38, 39]

[38] Hans Werner Bartsch, *EvTh* 32 (1972) tried to proceed to the historical Jesus from literary criticism. Although he is not concerned 'to objectify certain events in the life of Jesus as facts, in some way to authenticate them by means of source-analysis', he asks 'what in Jesus's deeds and sufferings has proved to be real?' (pp. 130f). Yet, since Bartsch too regards the form-critical method which now governs study as the super-method, without setting it under the corrective of religio-historical study, he renounces any attempt to show that certain events in the life of Jesus are basically factual.

[39] The article was translated by Dr W. Horbury.

The political charge against Jesus (Luke 23: 2)

1. The narrative in Mark

The Third Gospel – by contrast with the older Gospel of Mark which Luke used – specifically states the details of the charge which was brought forward against Jesus before Pilate by the members of the Sanhedrin. Mark 15: 2 indirectly carries the implication that the members of the Great Council must have declared before the Roman judge that Jesus voiced the claim to be 'king'. Only if this is the case can Pilate's question, 'Are you the King of the Jews?', which in the present context has no preparation, be intelligible. Then for the first time it is recorded in 15: 3: 'And the chief priests accused him of many things.' At that Pilate once again directs a question to the accused: 'Have you no answer to make? See how many charges they bring against you' (Mark 15: 4b). Jesus, who had responded to the question about his kingly claim with an unequivocal yes (verse 2c), makes no comment on the specific charges of the chief priests; this causes Pilate some perplexity (verse 5). In the following Barabbas scene the procurator's question shows that in the face of the Jewish crowd he would like to proceed on the basis of the issue of Jesus being 'the king of the Jews' (verse 9). At the same time however it is remarked that the chief priests had handed Jesus over 'out of envy' (verse 10). When the Jews demand the release of Barabbas (verse 11), Pilate asks them: 'What then shall I do with the man whom you call the king of the Jews?' The Jews demand his crucifixion (verses 13, 14b) whereas the Roman regards him as innocent (verse 14a). The title 'king of the Jews' reappears yet again in the scene in which the Roman soldiers scornfully acclaim Jesus (15: 18) and then again in the superscription on the cross (15: 26). Further, in the scoffing words of the chief priests there is another reference to the title, though admittedly in the form adopted by Jewish usage, 'king of Israel' (15: 32). The last mentioned passage is, however, significant from another point of view. It shows, first of all, that the priestly group did not believe in any kingly power of Jesus, understood in the sense of power to step down from the cross. It shows, further, that 'king of Israel' (or 'king of the Jews') is an equivalent paraphrase of 'the messiah'. Mark intends, by setting 'messiah' and 'king of Israel' in apposition, to show that these two titles are identical in content. It is, of course, true that 'king of the Jews' expresses the this-worldly political aspect of the claim.[1] But if Jesus affirmed before the Sanhedrin that he was the messiah (14:61f), then it is clearly on this confession that the charge before Pilate rests, and the latter is intended to place squarely in the foreground a kingly–political claim by the accused (15:2).

For Mark there is virtually no contradiction between the messianic claim and the kingly claim. Before the Sanhedrin some incriminating evidence against Jesus had been sought. The saying about an intended attack on the Temple would have been one such piece of evidence (14:58). But the witnesses did not agree. So the high priest's question was intended to elicit the confession of the accused. Jesus then admitted to being the messiah. This was assessed as blasphemy and a crime worthy of death (14:63f). The messianic, or in other words, the kingly claim of Jesus is thus the only point of the accusation which is brought into the open before Pilate. How this kingly claim was made into a capital crime it is not possible to deduce. No criminal activities of Jesus are recounted, even though the evangelist knows that such must have been brought forward (15:3f). But in that respect he assumes that they were not sufficient to convince the procurator that Jesus had done 'anything evil' (15:14). Viewed as a consecutive factual record of events the Markan report is inadequate, but in theological terms it appears to have a great deal of content. By means of several 'contrast-scenes' the actual kingship of Jesus is disclosed. Even though Jesus is accused as a revolutionary, regarded as a criminal, rejected by the people and scorned by the soldiers, nevertheless everyone is compelled to witness to his identity, even if they do so in complete ignorance and blindness.[2] The historically unimpeachable point of departure in the Markan account is to be seen in the *titulus* on the cross (15:26). From this the charge before Pilate can be inferred.

2. The concrete charges according to Luke

It is necessary to have recognised the weakness of the Markan account as a 'report' if one is to appreciate the way in which Luke does his best to present the course of the Pilate trial in a more coherent manner. At any rate Luke 23:2 presents concrete and precise 'political' charges brought against Jesus. The decisive question is whether these detailed charges have been created by the third evangelist – in line with his conviction about how the history should be reconstructed, or pursuing certain definite theological intentions – or whether he is here following a separate source which is perhaps older than the Markan account.

[1] Cp. F. Hahn, *Christologische Hoheitstitel* (3rd edn. Göttingen, 1966), p. 196 (ET *The Titles of Jesus in Christology* (London, 1969), p. 174).
[2] See Hahn, *Hoheitstitel*, pp. 196f, ET p. 174.

Alongside the section Mark 15: 1–5 stands the passage Luke 23: 1–5:

> Then the whole gathering of them arose, and brought him before Pilate. And they began to accuse him, saying, 'We have established that this man is leading our nation astray; he forbids the payment of tax to Caesar and he is putting it around that he is the Messiah, a king.' But Pilate questioned him, asking: 'Are you the King of the Jews?' But he answered him: 'You say it.' Pilate said to the chief priests and the crowds: 'I find no crime in this man.' But they declared even more insistently: 'He is rousing the people to revolt with his teaching in the whole of Judaea, stretching from Galilee even to here.'

If one wants to separate tradition and redaction in this Lukan section, there are, broadly speaking, two possibilities open. These are represented by two commentaries on the Third gospel. J. Schmid[3] thinks that in this section Luke 'the historian' has remoulded the passage Mark 15: 1–5, which is hardly satisfactory as an historical report, and that he has fashioned it into a narrative which is historically more convincing. In particular he places in the forefront the Jewish accusations which Mark mentions only incidentally and without being specific. Only then does Pilate's question about the claim to kingship follow. The charge brought by the Jews is made concrete, and at the same time unmasked as a slander-ous accusation. Further, it is important to the evangelist that the Roman judge should explicitly affirm the innocence of Jesus (Luke 23: 4; cp. 23: 14, 22).

While Schmid does not accept any parallel Lukan source for the composition of this scene, W. Grundmann[4] is of the opinion that the evangelist has used an extra source alongside the Markan Gospel; he thinks that this forms the thread of the Lukan passion narrative from 22: 14 onwards. Only Luke 23: 3 is taken over from Mark 15: 2. Consequently the special Lukan tradition did not report any real hearing before Pilate but only assumed it from the evidence of 23: 4b.

In a similar way recent investigations of the trial of Jesus part company

---

[3] J. Schmid, *Das Evangelium nach Lukas* (3rd edn. Regensburg, 1955), p. 342. That Luke was here working over material drawn only from Mark had earlier been accepted by R. Bultmann, *Geschichte der synoptischen Tradition* (5th edn. Göttingen, 1961), p. 294 (ET *History of the Synoptic Tradition* (Oxford, 1963), p. 280); J. M. Creed, *The Gospel according to St Luke* (London, 1930), p. 279; J. Finegan, *Die Überlieferung der Leidens- und Auferstehungsgeschichte Jesu* (Giessen, 1934), pp. 27, 38f.

[4] W. Grundmann, *Das Evangelium nach Lukas* (Berlin, 1961), p. 421. Similarly, the view that a special source was available to Luke was accepted by B. H. Streeter, *The Four Gospels* (London, 1924), p. 222, in the context of his proto-Luke theory; A. Schlatter, *Das Evangelium des Lukas* (Stuttgart, 1931), pp. 439f: 'the new narrator'. See also E. Haenchen, *Der Weg Jesu* (Berlin, 1966), p. 518; V. Taylor, *The Passion Narrative of St Luke* (Cambridge, 1972), pp. 84–9; J. Ernst, *Das Evangelium nach Lukas* (Regensburg, 1977), pp. 621f.

from one another over the matter of the Lukan source. J. Blinzler[5] leaves open the question of whether in 23: 2 the evangelist is following a special source or only (on his own initiative) clarifying the Markan narrative. But certainly Luke is taken to reproduce faithfully the historical state of affairs, particularly with respect to the political orientation of the charge. The expression 'king of the Jews' is, in his view, the secularised form of 'messiah' and represents merely a shift on to a profane political level.

The Jewish scholar P. Winter[6] arranges the passion narrative in the Gospel in three strata which are said to exhibit a traditio-historical development in the material. To the oldest (primary) tradition he assigns Luke 23: 2, 3 (alongside Mark 15: 2–5). In any case the exact description of the items of the charge in Luke are not classified as 'editorial accretion'. In another place[7] Winter has traced Luke 23: 1b–3 back to a special tradition (L) available to Luke, but at the same time the attempt is made to show that 23: 4–5 is a later interpolation. Winter's theory plainly coheres with his attempt to demonstrate that the political trial before Pilate is the only historical one. The trial scene before the Sanhedrin (22: 66–71) is similarly understood as an intrusion from the hand of the same interpolator.[8]

Very similar to Winter in his evaluation of the trial of Jesus is S. G. F. Brandon.[9] He does not explicitly take up any position on the source question at Luke 23: 2 and in fact does not engage in any source-critical analysis. But nevertheless he comes to the conclusion that Mark was very probably acquainted with the specific (political) charge against Jesus from the tradition which had become available to him. He has, however, suppressed it in his own account in the interests of political apologetic. Luke, on the other hand, has taken up this point of accusation from the tradition, because in his later situation a more objective record of the trial of Jesus had become possible. In this connection it is clear that Brandon does not want to attribute Luke 23: 2 to the redactional activity of the evangelist. He regards the political points of accusation as historically convincing and indeed justified. This is another case of the evaluation of sources being bound up with a fundamental concern of the author. He is anxious to show the penalty of crucifixion as the consequence of politically revolutionary activity on Jesus's part.

The only study which explicitly concerns itself with the source question

---

[5] J. Blinzler, *Der Prozess Jesu* (2nd edn. Regensburg, 1955), p. 138; similarly in the 3rd edn. (1960), p. 201, and the 4th edn. (1969), p. 278.

[6] P. Winter, *On the Trial of Jesus* (Berlin, 1961), pp. 136f.

[7] P. Winter, 'The Treatment of his Sources by the Third Evangelist in Luke XXI–XXIV' *ST* 8 (1954/55), 138–72, esp. 165f.

[8] Ibid; cp. *Trial*, p. 136.

[9] S. G. F. Brandon, *The Trial of Jesus of Nazareth* (London, 1968), pp. 119f.

in the trial before Pilate has come from H. van der Kwaak.[10] Certainly he does not state explicitly that the divergences between Luke 23: 1–5 and Mark 15: 1–5 go back to the hand of Luke. But he shows in a convincing manner that the differences which are a feature of the third gospel can be explained in terms of the evangelist's purpose and the editorial method.

At the end of this survey we have arrived at the point where the question about possible sources for Luke 23: 2 can be directly posed. In the matter of method the procedure must be first of all to examine whether the verse in question can be explained in terms of the interests and the editorial method of Luke.

3. Luke 23:2. Lukan 'redaction'?

As far as Luke 23: 2 is concerned, one can affirm with Conzelmann:[11] 'If the Lukan Tendenz is recognised, the "proto-Lukan" material disappears.' But the analysis which follows must be concerned not only with the question of whether and to what extent Luke 23: 2 expresses the Lukan purpose in writing (d). Before that it is necessary to ask about Lukan style and vocabulary (b). Further, the evangelist's technique of composition in 23: 1–5 must be scrutinised (c). If it should turn out that 'non-Lukan' or 'anti-Lukan' elements are found, then it will be possible to deduce a source other than Mark. But as long as that is not the case, verse 2 should be held to be the work of the evangelist. That is not, however, to assume that Luke has freely invented the content of the material present in this verse. Schürmann[12] has remarked, on the smaller narrative elements which, like Luke 23: 2, deviate from Mark, that it would be contrary to all our observations of Lukan redactional work in general if we were to regard these minor details as the free artistic creation of Luke. But even someone who, like Schürmann, prefers not to deduce free invention of this sort by the evangelist, will still be able to attribute the verse to Luke's own hand, provided he can demonstrate where the third evangelist has obtained the material setting out the points of accusation (a).

(a) The materials

Contrary to the view of most commentators on 23: 2 the verse does not contain three charges, but only one; this is then particularised in two

---

[10] H. van der Kwaak, *Het Proces van Jezus* (Assen, 1969), pp. 140–4.
[11] H. Conzelmann, *Die Mitte der Zeit* (4th edn. Tübingen, 1962), p. 78, footnote 1, following on from G. D. Kilpatrick, 'A Theme of the Lucan Passion Story and Luke XXIII. 47', *JThSt* 43 (1942), 34–6.
[12] H. Schürmann, *Jesu Abschiedsrede* (Münster, 1957), p. 140, footnote 476.

concrete points.[13] This is shown by the grammatical structure of the second part of verse 2. The twofold καί does not bind together three participles paratactically, but καὶ κωλύοντα and also καὶ λέγοντα are subordinate to the διαστρέφοντα.[14] In addition the two last mentioned participles are brought into a closer relationship with one another since in each case an infinitive follows (διδόναι and εἶναι). Further, Luke 23: 5,14 show that for the evangelist the charge before Pilate can be concentrated and summarised in the accusation of leading the people astray:

23: 2b: this man leads our people astray (διαστρέφοντα)

23: 5:   he stirs up the people (ἀνασείει)

23: 14:   he is one who perverts the people (ἀποστρέφοντα)

The reproach of leading the people astray, or of inciting them, is interpreted by Pilate in exactly the way intended. The Roman procurator is intended to infer that Jesus was wanting to cause the Jewish people to rebel against Rome (23: 14). As to substance the accusation rests on declarations like Luke 19: 48 (cp. Mark 11: 18b); 20: 6 (cp. Mark 11: 32b); 20: 19 (cp. Mark 12: 12a); 20: 26 and 22: 2 (cp. Mark 14: 2). Finally the third evangelist had not only read in Mark that the people listened to Jesus but also that the members of the Sanhedrin for this reason wanted to kill him. It is indeed διὰ φθόνον that they have handed him over to Pilate (Mark 15: 10). As for their charge against Jesus, it is exposed as falsehood. That is the implication of Mark 15: 11, a verse which Luke omits but which tells of how during the Barabbas scene the chief priests had stirred up the crowd (ἀνέσεισαν) so that they would demand the release of the criminal. Even though the reader of the Third Gospel does not have this Markan verse in front of him, Luke's intention is quite clear: it is not in fact Jesus who is the one who leads the people astray, but rather the Jewish leaders who stir them up.[15]

The allegation that Jesus hindered the payment of tribute to the emperor must, after Luke 20: 20–6, appear a total slander. The way in which Luke has in that passage edited his Markan source (Mark 12: 13–17) shows clearly that the evangelist traces this hypocritical question of Jesus's opponents back to their purpose of getting Jesus to incriminate himself with

13 So, as far as I know, only in Grundmann, Lukas, p. 422: 'The leading astray of the people consists of this, that he demanded the withholding of tribute and proclaimed himself the Messiah, i.e. in Pilate's eyes: made himself a king.'

14 See also F. Blass and A. Debrunner, Grammatik des neutestamentlichen Griechisch (9th edn. Göttingen, 1954), §444, 3 (ET A Greek Grammar of the New Testament (Chicago, 1961), §444, 3), with reference to Luke 5: 36; cp. also 5: 37.

15 Cp. on this slant in the account, Luke 23: 18f, 25; Acts 13: 50; 14: 19; 17: 5–8, 13; 18: 12–17; 21: 27f.

an anti-Roman remark 'in order to deliver him up to the authority and jurisdiction of the governor' (20: 20). Since, however, Jesus explicitly permits the imperial tax (verse 25) the opposition are not able to 'catch' him and as a result are reduced to silence (verse 26).

The second specific charge is that Jesus had claimed to be 'the Messiah, a King', i.e. he had assumed for himself a kingship which was political and therefore anti-Roman. This allegation takes up the subject matter of Luke 22: 67–70 (cp. Mark 14: 61f) and anticipates Luke 23: 3 (par. Mark 15: 2).[16] Jesus is 'the Messiah' and at the same time 'the King of the Jews'. That Jesus certainly laid claim to kingship in an unpolitical sense is something which Luke knows and which Pilate also is able to establish (23: 4). So with this last element in the charge the evangelist makes the transition to the procurator's question (Mark 15: 2 = Luke 23: 3). The question about Jesus's claim to kingship, which in Mark occurs without preparation, is made plausible in the Lukan context.

Thus it is apparent that Luke can have deduced the concrete charges of the Sanhedrin authorities from Mark. In this matter he had no need of any new information from any other source. The same applies to 23: 5. Once the scheme of the Third Gospel is known, as well as its dependence on Mark's Gospel, there is no need to postulate as the source of 23: 5 any pre-Lukan summary.[17]

(b) Vocabulary and style

The following analysis of Luke 23: 2 has not merely to enquire statistically about favourite Lukan words but has also to test the pattern of speech for usages characteristic of the evangelist.

(1) ἤρξαντο *with infinitive following* occurs in Matt. once, Mark 8 times, Luke 8 times, Acts once but nowhere otherwise in the New Testament. In front of the infinitive Luke has merely inserted δέ (cp. Luke 4: 21, 20: 9). The statistics already indicate a preference on Mark's part for this usage. Yet it is probable that the third evangelist also writes it on his own initiative each time: Luke 5: 21; 7: 49; 11: 53; 14: 18; 15: 24; 19: 37; 22: 23; 23: 2; Acts 2: 4. Only Luke has in this connection the subject ἅπαν τὸ πλῆθος with the following genitive plural (19: 37) as in our present passage.

---

[16] See also Mark 15: 32: 'the Messiah, the king of Israel'.

[17] Contra Conzelmann, *Die Mitte der Zeit*, p. 79 (ET *The Theology of St Luke* (London, 1961), p. 86, n. 1). Luke, like Mark, stresses the teaching activity of Jesus in Jerusalem (Luke 19: 47; 20: 1, 21; 21: 37; cp. Mark 11: 17; 12: 14, 35; 14: 49). With reference to Galilee, Luke 23: 5 makes the transition to the Herod scene (23: 6–12). Cp. G. Schneider, *Die Passion Jesu nach den drei älteren Evangelien* (München, 1973), pp. 90–3; idem, *Das Evangelium nach Lukas*, Kapitel 11–24 (Gütersloh–Würzburg, 1977), pp. 471–3.

Only in Luke does the infinitive κατηγορεῖν occur after ἤρξα(ν)το (23: 2; Acts 24: 2).

(2) λέγων (-οντες) follows ἤρξα(ν)το with the infinitive in the New Testament in Matt. 16: 22 and 5 times in Luke (Luke 5: 21; 19: 37f, 45f; 23: 2; Acts 24: 2). In that context there stands twice the infinitive κατηγορεῖν (Luke 23: 2; Acts 24: 2). Of these instances it is certain that Luke 5: 21; 19: 37f, 45f stem from Lukan redaction.

(3) κατηγορέω is a favourite Lukan word. In the New Testament it occurs in Matt. twice, Mark 3 times, Luke 4 times, John twice, Acts 9 times, Romans once and Revelation once. The infinitive κατηγορεῖν stands with the object αὐτοῦ only in Luke 6: 7; 23: 2; Acts 24: 2. There is no doubt that Luke 6: 7 goes back to the hand of the evangelist (cp. Mark 3: 2).

Points 1 to 3 show that the statement introducing the details of the accusation has been formulated by Luke. It draws its content from Mark 15: 3.

(4) τοῦτον εὕραμεν takes up the Lukan formulation in Luke 6: 7: the scribes and the Pharisees had wanted for some time to 'find' a point of accusation against Jesus. εὑρίσκω is in itself a favourite Lukan word: 80 of its 176 occurrences in the New Testament are to be found in Luke's work. εὑρίσκω + object + participle, the last expressing an action of the object, occurs (sometimes in a different word-order) in Matthew 5, Mark 6, Luke 11 times, John once, Acts 7 times and Revelation twice. Of the Lukan occurrences only 3 indicate a source (Mark: Luke 19: 30; 22: 45; and Q: Luke 12: 43), whereas in the Matthaean occurrences this applies 4 times (Mark: Matt. 21: 2; 26: 40, 43; and Q: 24: 46). On τοῦτον statistics show Matt. 4 times, Mark 3, Luke 11, John 13 and Acts 20 occurrences whereas in the rest of the New Testament there are only 9.

(5) διαστρέφω. Apart from Matt. 17: 17 = Luke 9: 41 and Phil. 2: 15 (the 'perverse generation'), the only occurrences in the New Testament are Lukan: Luke 23: 2; Acts 13: 8, 10; 20: 30. According to Acts 13: 8 the Jewish magician Elymas was causing the governor Sergius Paulus 'to turn away from the faith'. He was thus 'making crooked the straight paths of the Lord' (13: 10). On the other hand, in the Pilate trial the Jews slanderously accuse Jesus of leading the people astray (Luke 23: 2).

(6) τὸ ἔθνος ἡμῶν is encountered in the New Testament only at Luke 7: 5 and 23: 2. Comparable is τὸ ἔθνος μου in the mouth of Paul (Acts 24: 17; 26: 4; 28: 19). In the Acts passages it is (the 'Lukan') Paul who is speaking, in Luke 7: 5 the Jewish elders say of the Gentile centurion: 'He loves our nation and he built us our synagogue.' In all these passages it is extremely likely that we are dealing with Lukan patterns of speech.

From points 4 to 6 it emerges that in terms of style and word-count – quite apart from actual Lukan interests (cp. no. 6) – the main charge against Jesus has been formulated by the evangelist, and therefore no pre-Lukan source apart from Mark should be proposed.

(7) καί–καί is admittedly not a Lukan speciality, but nevertheless it can be used by the evangelist, even by contrast with his source, as Luke 5: 36b and 22: 33 show. To be set alongside these are the occurrences in special Lukan source-material (1: 15; 2: 46) and in Acts (6 examples).[18]

(8) κωλύω can, on statistical grounds, be reckoned a favourite Lukan word: Matt. 1, Mark 3, Luke 6, Acts 6 occurrences (rest of New Testament 7). Matt. 19: 14 is, like Luke 18: 16, dependent on Mark (10: 14), as is Luke 9: 49, 50. The passages Luke 6: 29; 11: 52; 23: 2 are clearly worked up by the evangelist, which may also be, at least in part, the case at Acts 8: 36; 10: 47; 11: 17; 16: 6; 24: 23; 27: 43.

(9) φόρους διδόναι recalls Luke 20: 22 (in the pericope about paying tribute). There Luke has substituted φόρον δοῦναι for δοῦναι κῆνσον (Mark 12: 14). So the formulation in 23: 2 belongs to the evangelist. Elsewhere in the New Testament φόρος occurs only at Rom. 13: 6f. The recipient is – in line with Mark 12: 14 – in both Lukan passages the 'emperor'. In each case it is only Luke who places the verb at the end of the phrase.

From points 7 to 9 it results once again that this section of the verse is to be attributed to Luke's own hand. The Jewish leaders assert the exact opposite of what Jesus himself had declared.

(10) καὶ λέγοντα ἑαυτὸν . . . εἶναι. The reflexive ἑαυτόν appears in the New Testament as follows: Matt. 5, Mark 5, Luke 12, John 8, Acts 7 times (and 25 instances in the rest of the New Testament). Of the examples in Luke, 3 come from Mark (Luke 9: 23; 11: 18; 23: 35) and 4 from the sayings source (14: 11 twice and 18: 14 twice); in the special material stand 10: 29; 15: 17; 18: 11; 23: 2. Only 9: 25 can be shown to be Lukan redaction of Mark; however, the special material will also have been extensively remodelled by the evangelist (cp. 10: 29). ἑαυτόν and εἶναι follow a verb of speaking elsewhere only at Acts 5: 36; 8: 9. In both these cases we find, as at Luke 23: 2, the present participle of λέγω. This is to be compared with the redactional usage in Luke 10: 29 (θέλων δικαιῶσαι ἑαυτόν), similarly Acts 16: 27; 19: 31; 25: 4. Statistics for the infinitive εἶναι indicate a Lukan preponderance (Matt. 6, Mark 8, Luke 23, John 3, Acts 20, other New Testament occurrences 65).

(11) χριστὸν βασιλέα. The direct linking of the messianic title with βασιλεύς is attested elsewhere in the New Testament only at Mark 15: 32. The combination appears in Luke not as a reminiscence of this Markan text, but by virtue of a combination of the messianic confession of Mark

---

[18] Schürmann, *Abschiedsrede*, p. 32. Cp. Blass–Debrunner, *Grammatik*, §444, 3.

14: 61f with Pilate's question about Jesus's kingship, Mark 15: 2. Equally, John 19: 12 ('everyone who makes himself a king sets himself against Caesar') is no indication of some special Luke–John tradition available at this point; for the fourth gospel also depends here on Pilate's question, 'Are you the king of the Jews?' (18: 33, cp. 19: 3), drawn from the Mark tradition. What Luke wants to say by means of the βασιλέα placed in apposition to 'messiah' is plain from Acts 17: 7. In the synagogue at Thessalonica Paul preached Jesus as the messiah (verse 3). Jews and god-fearing Hellenists responded in faith (verse 4). At this the rest of the Jews, moved with envy, stirred up a riot, in order to haul Paul and Silas up before the politarchs. The legal action concerned comprehensive incitement to disorder and rebellion against the imperial regulations. The offence against the imperial δόγματα was regarded as an expression of the confession, 'another is king, Jesus' (verse 7). Here Ἰησοῦν is in apposition (just as βασιλέα is at Luke 23: 2).

(12) λέγων βασιλέα εἶναι finds, both in terms of form and content, its parallel in Acts 17: 7: βασιλέα λέγοντες εἶναι. In both places the kingship of Jesus is regarded (by the Jews) as directed against the regulations of Caesar, while Luke for his part understands the kingship in a non-political sense (Luke 1: 33; 22: 29f; 23: 42). Furthermore we meet here once more the Lukan theme of the Jews, who accuse Jesus of stirring up a riot, being themselves in fact the ones who stir up a riot.

Points 7 to 12 demonstrate once again that Luke is assembling material which he knows about from Mark. He has given it his own linguistic and stylistic character.

A corresponding conclusion can also be reached in respect of 23: 1, 4, 5. But we must at this point do without a detailed spelling out of the case for this view. It does not turn out to be possible to demonstrate on stylistic grounds the existence, and availability to Luke, of a non-Markan (literary) source.

(c) Method of composition in Luke 23: 1–5

The editorial composition of Luke 23: 1–5 can be convincingly interpreted as a Lukan working over of the Markan source in order to achieve the presentation of a coherent and comprehensible account. From the procurator's question, Mark 15: 2, Luke concludes that the Sanhedrin authorities must previously have accused Jesus of being a messianic pretender and in that situation produced many allegations against him. By reconstructing such allegations out of the Markan material, the evangelist is able at the same time to fashion the Pilate scene into a regular proceeding in which first of all the *delatores* appear and then the accused is granted opportunity for self-defence.[19] Finally this setting of the scene also gives the evangelist opportunity to cause Pilate to attest before the Jews the innocence of Jesus. Although the Jews have listened to this from Pilate, they nevertheless persist with their claim that Jesus is an (anti-Roman) inciter of the people (verse 5). The mention of Galilee then provides the catchword for the scene 'Jesus before Herod' (cp. 23:6f).

If it is permissible to understand the scene 23: 1–5 in this way as a Lukan construction, conversely it follows that a pre-Lukan context 23: 1–2, 4–5[20] is unlikely. A unity of this sort must certainly be disputed since verse 1, like verse 2, clearly assumes the Markan source, which is all the more true, of course, at verse 3. The charge concerning tribute to Caesar stands formally in relation to Luke 20: 20–6, a pericope which is plainly dependent on Mark. But if 23: 2 assumes at this point the Lukan redaction of Markan material, then this verse cannot be pre-Lukan. The declaration of Pilate in opposition to the accusers (verse 4) cannot follow unless and until Pilate has (by means of the question to Jesus in verse 3) convinced himself of Jesus's innocence.[21]

(d) The purpose of the account

An important purpose of Luke's two-volume work is to produce political apologetic *vis-à-vis* the Roman state.[22] This is plain also from the charges against Paul and the demolition of these in Acts (17: 7; 24: 2–5, 10–21; 25: 7f; 26: 2–23).

After the arrest of Jesus and the hearing before the Sanhedrin the Jewish leaders bring charges against Jesus before the Roman governor, the allegations which they produce being known to be false. The points of accusation are so planned that they are bound to rouse the interest of the Roman Pilate (23: 2): Jesus is said to have wished to stir up the Jewish people, in that he demanded the withholding of tribute to Caesar and played the role of a messianic claimant. This state of affairs would necessarily be of interest to Pilate in his official capacity. Yet the allegations

---

[19] See A. N. Sherwin White, *Roman Society and Roman Law in the New Testament* (Oxford, 1963), pp. 24–6; cp. van der Kwaak, *Het Proces*, pp. 140f.

[20] Suggested by Streeter, Schlatter and Grundmann (see above, footnote 4 on p. 405).

[21] This does not mean that Pilate understood Jesus's reply as a negative (thus Grundmann, *Lukas*, p. 422). Rather the evangelist assumes that Pilate realises the unpolitical (Lukan) interpretation of kingship (cp. Conzelmann, *Mitte*, pp. 78f (ET *Luke*, pp. 85f).

[22] Cp. on this, Conzelmann, *Mitte*, pp. 128–35 (ET pp. 138–44); G. Schneider, *Verleugnung, Verspottung und Verhör Jesu nach Lukas 22, 54–71* (München, 1969), pp. 193–6; cp. the more differentiated statement of the same author in his recent article 'Der Zweck des lukanischen Doppelwerks', *BZ* 21 (1977), 45–66, esp. 59–61.

are demonstrably wide of the mark. Jesus had affirmed the payment of the imperial tax (20: 20–6); his messiahship is not kingship in a political sense as the Jews understand it and as they want to make the governor believe (cp. 19: 11; 22: 24–30; 23: 35, 37, 39). In fact it consists of serving (22: 27). Therefore it is a gross calumny when the Jews accuse Jesus of political rebellion. In reality it is they themselves who not only approve of uproar (23: 18f, 25) but even arouse it (Acts 13: 50; 14: 19; 17: 5–8, 13; 18: 12–17; 21: 27). Pilate is able to convince himself that Jesus is guiltless (Luke 23: 4, 14f, 22), and he is anxious to let him go free (23: 16, 20, 22).

4. Conclusion

Luke 23: 2 relies, according to the foregoing analysis, on the material in Mark which Luke has edited in order to reconstruct a specifically detailed charge from the Jewish side before Pilate. That the evangelist has thereby grasped in its essentials the historically true position can be indirectly confirmed from the Jewish tradition about Jesus, a tradition which sees in Jesus one who led the people astray.[23, 24]

---

[23] Cp. *b. Sanh.* 43a (*baraita*): Jesus practised magic and 'enticed Israel to apostasy and rebellion'. Blinzler, *Prozess*, p. 42, wants to explain the claim that Jesus was a beguiler and instigator of rebellion in terms of the Jewish situation of the second century when Christianity had come to be regarded as 'heretical'.

[24] This article has been translated by D. R. Catchpole.

The trial before Pilate

'The most interesting isolated problem which historical jurisprudence can present' – such is a characterisation given to the trial of Jesus.[1] The Roman part of it is no exception to this.

The nature of the trial before Pilate is indicated in the introductory terms used by Mark: δήσαντες . . . παρέδωκαν (15: 1). The binding of Jesus is not mentioned in the Second Evangelist's introduction to the Sanhedrin trial, as indeed the fettering of a person who is still only under accusation is unusual.[2] The term implies that Jesus's judicial position was different from that after the arrest, in other words that the deliberation of 15: 1a, which sums up the nocturnal events, did not refer to these as a preliminary interrogation[3] but constituted an act that had its procedural consequences.[4] The position is different in John, where Jesus is bound immediately after his arrest (18: 12) and kept fettered during the night (18: 24). The difference is conditioned by the fact that here Jesus is, when taken captive, a ζητούμενος, whose fate had already been decided upon – pending the emergence of mitigating circumstances.[5] Mark and John agree in describing Jesus's situation at the beginning of the trial before Pilate as that of a culprit. Matthew follows Mark, whereas Luke omits this detail.[6]

Παραδίδωμι is a word that is used in a more general and even half-metaphorical way quite often in Christian language.[7] This secondary

---

[1] A. T. Innes, *The Trial of Jesus Christ. A legal Monograph* (Edinburgh, 1899), p. 2.

[2] For the position according to Roman law, where the personal status of the accused man is affected only in so far as he is not permitted to apply for one of the civic offices and where only imprisonment is mentioned as a means of *coercitio* see T. Mommsen, *Römisches Strafrecht* (Leipzig, 1899), pp. 391ff.

[3] Thus P. Winter, *On the Trial of Jesus* (Berlin, 1961), p. 27.

[4] Not noticed by E. Hirsch, *Frühgeschichte des Evangeliums* (2nd edn. Tübingen, 1951), pp. 164f.

[5] Cp. *Festschrift C. F. D. Moule* (2nd edn. London, 1971), pp. 33–5.

[6] His formulation could be taken to mean that no condemnation had taken place (Winter, *Trial*, pp. 28ff). Rather, the opposite is the case. No appeal for an admission of guilt is possible without a charge; equally no statement like that of 22: 71. Further, verse 71 presupposes that enquiries had been made before and that their result is considered to be confirmed by Jesus's own attitude *vis-à-vis* his judges. That means, the Lukan scene only becomes comprehensible if we presuppose the existence of an account which is not recorded in the actual text. Luke 22: 1f does not meet this demand; on the contrary, the wording is less formal than in Mark, let alone in Matthew. So it must be a scene like the one described in John 11: 45ff.

[7] E.g. Papyrus Egerton A. 1. 29. The same may be true for Mark 1: 14; John 3: 36 e sy[hmg] (referring to the Baptist) and especially Mark 9: 31 (παραδίδοται is *passivum*

usage which is based on reflection on the passion story is, however, not likely at a place where both the *traditor* and those to whose keeping the culprit is handed over are juridical persons – whatever overtones may be present.[8] The same word is used in John 18: 31, 35, at the beginning of the Jews' dealings with Pilate and of the interrogation of Jesus. In both cases it is in a reference at the beginning of a dispute and not in a factual description that the term occurs.[9] This is true to the Johannine style of presentation which disregards an even flow of narration. Substantially, however, the two traditions agree.

The point is confirmed and even stressed by John 18: 35: τὸ ἔθνος . . . καὶ ὁ ἀρχιερεὺς[10] παρέδωκαν. The two nouns refer to the two representatives in Judaism. כהן and חבר – the latter is not a γερουσία but the whole community, the *Volksgemeinde*[11] – are named in the inscriptions on the coins of the Hasmonaean period.[12] The formula has an

---

Divinum; nothing can be deduced from it for the details of the trial of Jesus). Technically it means the transference from one authority to the other (John 18: 35) or from one stage of the proceedings to the next (*AJ* 20 §200: Ananus with his Sanhedrin παρέδωκε James to be stoned). The word receives the subsidiary meaning of treachery if the handing over is performed to an outside power (the term παράδοσις is used in *BJ* 7 §415 for the handing over of the Zealots by the Jewish authorities of Alexandria to the Romans: they had been fugitives – §413 – and were therefore not under the jurisdiction of the Jewish γερουσία; the fact that they had already committed murders in Alexandria is given as an additional reason). This notion is expressed by ἐκδιδόναι even more strongly *AJ* 14 §15; Eusebius *H.E.* 1.5.1. Cp. D. Daube, *Collaboration with Tyranny in Rabbinic Law* (Oxford, 1965), pp. 7f; D. Schirmer, 'Rechtsgeschichtliche Untersuchungen zum Johannes-Evangelium' (Diss. Erlangen, 1964), pp. 133ff, 179ff.

[8] This is especially the case in the references to Judas, ὁ παραδιδοὺς αὐτόν (John 18: 5; cp. 18: 2; 6: 64, 71; 12: 4; 13: 2, 11, 21).

[9] A. Dauer, *Die Passionsgeschichte im Johannesevangelium* (München, 1972), p. 122 holds that the first passage is the elaboration of a source, in which the handing over was mentioned in the form of a narration. This is doubtful and even more so the attribution of the dialogue to the theology of the evangelist.

[10] א* (C. von Tischendorf, *Bibliorum Codex Sinaiticus Petropolitanus* (Leipzig, 1863), p. 59*); L *b* (which in the opinion of A. Jülicher, *Itala* iv (Berlin, 1963), 196 represents the text of the Itala for this verse). *ff²* (*principis sacerdotum*) may be dependent on a similar, although less precise text (*servus principis* etc?). *e*, representing the *afra*, has the same reading. G. D. Kilpatrick (*Festschrift M. Black* (Edinburgh, 1969), pp. 203ff) observed a tendency to replace ἀρχιερεῖς by -ρεύς, because the wider usage of the word had become obsolete. It is, however, difficult to see that this tendency should have invaded a chapter in which two high priests had already been mentioned by name. Apart from this the passage in question is different because it is of a piece with the preceding.

[11] E. Schürer, *Geschichte des jüdischen Volkes im Zeitalter Jesu Christi* i (Leipzig, 1901), 269 (ET – based on the 1890 edition – i. 1.284). Josephus employs a different terminology. When referring to the Sanhedrin he describes it in its different components and uses therefore with preference the plural formulation, which includes the members of the high-priestly families.

[12] A. Reifenberg, *Jewish Coins* (Jerusalem, 1947), pp. 40–2.

official ring and, used in this context, means that the recognised authority of Judaea had taken a decision in consequence of which Jesus was standing before Pilate.

Accordingly no accusation is raised in these strands of the tradition and not even the reason for the condemnation is reproduced in a satisfactorily formulated form in the section on the trial before Pilate. Jesus is taken as a κακὸν ποιῶν (John 18: 30), just as the two other persons who will be crucified with him are briefly styled as κακοῦργοι (Luke 23: 33). No witnesses are called nor even is the condemnation rendered in unmistakable words. The verdict is presupposed;[13] it is the basis of the following scenes. No indication is given that Pilate deals with the question *ab ovo*. What is asked and stated by him, is done with reference to what had been found before by the Sanhedrin.

True, the question: σὺ εἶ ὁ βασιλεὺς τῶν Ἰουδαίων has been taken to mean that a new accusation is being dealt with, that a political trial is about to start after the religious trial[14] or as the only trial proper.[15] Such an economy seems probable and has therefore become the classical approach in *Prozessforschung*. A complete separation is, however, not possible: the scene before Pilate starts with the taking up of the findings which had been made before. Even if the Gospel reports on the Sanhedrin trial were unreliable, some form of investigation leading up to βασιλεύς κτλ. must have initiated the proceedings and preceded the reports on the Roman part of them. The knowledge Pilate has about the material (John 18: 33b) makes it likely that he had been instructed in a form not dissimilar to the direction of his own examination.

It is, of course, possible to avoid this conclusion by assuming that it was the Sanhedrin itself that raised a new and different accusation in front of Pilate.[16] Possible as it is, this theory presupposes an action on the side of the Jewish authorities which is far less in accord with Jewish law than any other course attributed to them: it involves the denunciation of someone who is not liable to punishment according to Jewish law and who is, at the same time, not charged by the Romans. It demands ἔκδοσις rather than παράδοσις – without external pressure to do so. Paul, following an iron

---

[13] J. Wellhausen, *Das Evangelium Johannis* (Berlin, 1908), p. 83 sees two lines in the Johannine account: one according to which the Jews act as accusers, another in which they just demand execution and 'verbieten ihm (Pilate), in die *merita causae* einzugehen'.

[14] E.g. J. Blinzler, *Der Prozess Jesu* (Regensburg, 1969), pp. 278ff.

[15] Winter, *Trial, passim*; H. H. Cohn, *The Trial and Death of Jesus* (New York, 1971), pp. 142ff.

[16] E.g. E. Stauffer, *Jesus war ganz anders* (Hamburg, 1967), p. 188. The view that a different accusation was put foward in front of Pilate is taken already in *Const. Apost.* v. 14.

rule of Jewish behaviour, admonishes the members of his community not to frequent heathen lawcourts in matters of dispute (*lites*), although they were in the unhappy situation of being unable to benefit any longer from the services of the local Jewish court.[17] The same is all the more true for capital cases and indeed those Jews who were able to execute judgement themselves. Such a procedure was not employed *vis-à-vis* the followers of Jesus, the early Christians.[18] The case in Josephus, where ἐκδοῦναι is used, indicates how Jewish authorities were likely to react: Florus commands (ἐκέλευσεν) the Jewish authorities to ἐκδοῦναι those who had offended him, but his request is resisted.[19] It shows that the horror with which מסר is used in talmudic times[20] lays open a feeling that is deeply rooted and was present in the Jewish mentality at an earlier time. The theory is not absolutely impossible,[21] but very unlikely.

If, then, there was a connection between the Sanhedrin investigation and the one carried out by Pilate, the link must be found in the question with which the Roman prefect, according to the reports of all the four Gospels, starts his interrogation, the question of Jesus's kingship. The part in the Jewish statement that caught his interest and fitted the framework of his understanding is phrased by him in these words. It does not mean that the Jews had described Jesus as king–pretender nor that, in doing so, they made themselves guilty of great deceit consciously committed.[22] The political relevance was not necessarily stressed by the Jews – βασιλεύς has primarily a religious meaning in Jewish language. It may rather have been brought out by the Christian narrators who wanted to make Pilate reject an insinuation with these particular overtones.

Neither the truth of the accusation nor the nature of the claim is investigated. This points to a religious charge which the prefect was unable

---

[17] 1 Cor. 6: 1ff.   [18] Cp. the case of James.

[19] The term is used in *BJ* 2 §30a.   [20] Daube, *Collaboration*, p. 19.

[21] Symptomatic and at the same time enigmatic is the case of Jesus b. Ananias, who after having started to utter cries against Jerusalem and the Temple while standing in the latter, is arrested, chastised by τινες τῶν ἐπισήμων δημοτῶν and, because he continued, was brought (ἀνάγειν) by the ἄρχοντες before the Roman ἔπαρχος. The governor flayed him to the bones, but let him go, whereupon he continued with his lament for several years (*BJ* 6 §300–9). It is to be assumed that the Jewish authorities, who obviously had failed to get hold of him while he was still in the precinct of the Temple, tried and punished him first, then handed him over to the Romans in order to achieve a severer punishment, i.e. execution. Having been set free by the Roman judge he can continue because the Jewish authorities, having handed him over to the Romans, cannot touch him again. The story shows that capital punishment was not any longer in Jewish hands at that time. For an interpretation of this Jesus's prophecy of doom cp. A. Schalit, 'Die Erhebung Vespasians . . .' in *Aufstieg und Niedergang der alten Welt* ii. 2 (Berlin, 1975), 276, 322–7.

[22] Thus Blinzler, *Prozess*, p. 279.

to re-examine rather than to a political accusation which would have called for further enquiry in order to find out more about accomplices etc. Instead, the culprit's confession is invoked and, subsequently, a series of attempts is launched by Pilate to make Jesus give an innocent interpretation to this charge. That means Pilate looks for mitigating circumstances, whereas the matter itself is seen by him as a *fait accompli* according to the Mark/John report. This allows conclusions with regard to the judicial nature of the proceedings.

Mark, Luke and John agree in claiming that the decision was not taken as a matter of routine but only after several interludes. The number of scenes varies and their description too, but the basic feature is the same.

Additional elements occur in the course of these proceedings on the side both of the prefect and of the Jews. This is elaborated especially in the Fourth Gospel, whereas Mark, who summarises the proceedings, gives only hints. First, Pilate tries to rid himself of the matter, the nature of which is not explained to him. The Jewish demand, that he should fall in line with their findings without any ado, is well in keeping with the tendency to turn the legal situation to one's maximal advantage, known from Josephus's interpretation of Caesar's edicts and other sources. The suggestion made by Pilate in John 18: 31a, λάβετε αὐτὸν ὑμεῖς, καὶ κατὰ τὸν νόμον ὑμῶν κρίνατε αὐτόν,[23] is the obvious answer, which forces the Jews to give a reason[24] and to demand execution explicitly.[25] The second additional

---

[23] The Syriac text allows two different translations: judge him according to your law; and judge him as it (is) law.

[24] It seems that elements belonging originally to 18: 30f were transposed by the evangelist to 19:6b, 7. The two elements of John 19: 6 (σταύρωσον/λάβετε κτλ.) are taken at face value and given a very articulate interpretation by A. Schlatter: the Jews insist on depriving Jesus of his honour completely and they know that this is only achieved if he is executed at the hands of the Romans (*Der Evangelist Johannes* (Stuttgart, 1930), p. 344). This point is taken up by W. Grundmann: Jesus was handed over to the Romans for execution in order to separate him completely from Judaism; stoning would have been an honour for him, for this mode of execution would have meant the recognition of Jesus as belonging to them (*Jesus der Galiläer* (Weimar, 1940), p. 162). The view could find support in R. Otto's interpretation of Mark 14: 22, a verse which points to Jesus's expectation of being 'broken' like bread, i.e. stoned to death (*Reich Gottes und Menschensohn* (München, 1934), pp. 251, 253f; ET (London, 1938), pp. 296, 300f). The theory presupposes not only full Jewish jurisdiction even in capital cases (cp. John 19: 6a) but the successful attempt to lure Pilate into carrying out an action which the Jews themselves could have taken. The possibility of complex Jewish schemes has been ventilated once and again (cp. J. D. M. Derrett, *Law in the New Testament* (London, 1970), pp. 389ff), but this one has little foothold in the sources, quite apart from the fact that – cp. note 199, p. 442 – the Jews were not afraid of implementing 'separation', even by carrying out executions by way of crucifixion. W. Koch (*Der Prozess Jesu* (Köln, 1966), p. 169) appears to be influenced by the Schlatter–Grundmann theory. *Act. Pil.* 4.3f narrates that the Jews would have been able to stone Jesus, but they wanted him to be

feature is the giving of a choice between Barabbas and Jesus. The suggestion is only meaningful if the two persons were understood to represent different aims and standpoints[26] and thereby gave a chance to confuse the ranks of the Jews and to outmanoeuvre those who wanted to have their own way. Additional moves on the side of the Jews are accusations (Mark 15: 3)[27] and attempts to exercise pressure on the prefect (John 19: 12).[28] Both these features, interesting as they are for the literary development of the narrative as well as the historical situation they attempt to mirror, are not relevant for the description of the legal situation.

There occurs, however, one element in the narrative which is to become of 'crucial' importance: the silence of Jesus, a gesture which already puzzled the earliest opponents of Christianity so much.[29] Mark, followed by Matthew and Luke, reports the ambiguous[30] σὺ λέγεις in reply to Pilate's question about his kingship, and emphasises that after this Jesus said οὐκέτι οὐδέν (15: 5).[31] Luke gives the motif its setting in his account of the Herodian trial (23.9). John has both features (18: 37; 19: 9), although they are flanked by lengthy pronouncements which definitely are stamped in the Johannine mould.

The matter is different with the verses which introduce the Johannine σὺ λέγεις. A theological ingredient is present only in 18: 36a, c. Apart from this two topics are dealt with which are closely linked with the *materia* itself. Verse 36b touches upon a problem that had played a certain role in the Johannine account of the arrest[32] and the Sanhedrin proceedings (18: 20):[33] the involvement of the disciples in the activities of their master. While

crucified and it is for this reason that they hand him over to Pilate; this text seems to coincide with the view discussed above.

[25] For the latest attempt to trace a pre-Johannine tradition in the verses see Dauer, *Passionsgeschicte*, pp. 145f.

[26] Mark emphasises the political activity of the counterpart of Jesus, carried out in the (!) στάσις and thereby makes clear the difference. John, who only touches upon the subject in passing, reduces the political significance of Barabbas.

[27] J. Wellhausen: 'Schade, dass der Inhalt der Anklage nicht angegeben wird' (*Das Evangelium Marci* (Berlin, 1909), p. 128).

[28] For an interpretation see *ThLZ* 77 (1952), col. 205ff.

[29] Celsus (Origen, *C. Cels.* ii. 35); Porphyry fr. 63 (*Porphyrius 'Gegen die Christen'. 15 Bücher Zeugnisse, Fragmente und Referate*, ed. A. von Harnack, SBA 66 Phil. -hist. K., pp. 4f).

[30] Even more so with the Johannine addition: ὅτι βασιλεύς εἰμι.

[31] It is for this reason that the silence motif appears at a later stage of the Johannine tradition. For the historical evaluation see C. H. Dodd, *Historical Tradition in the Fourth Gospel* (Cambridge, 1963), p. 104.

[32] 18: 8b; it belongs to the basic layer of the story because the urging question of Jesus is inconsistent with the power of the divine name displayed in the redactional material.

[33] It is there rather the problem of secret, possibly heretical teaching that is at stake than revolutionary activity (thus Winter, *Trial*, p. 49). Cp. the parallel in

Jesus's negative reply there had led to his first buffeting,[34] it is here again that, by emphasising an otherworldliness for his kingdom of such a kind as to prohibit his disciples from raising arms for it, he explicitly protects those disciples against recriminatory actions[35] which undoubtedly would have followed any admission of political ambitions.[36] The other statement of Jesus is an enquiry as to who caused Pilate to presume his kingship: ἀφ' ἑαυτοῦ . . . ἢ ἄλλοι. The question seems to be irrelevant, because only the accusation matters in the circumstances. It even seems inappropriate, evasive[37] and out of place: 'so spricht kein Angeklagter sondern der Herr'.[38] In fact, the matter is different. An assumption and charge, conceived and formulated by Pilate independently, would not only have meant something amounting to a new trial but would have given Jesus the opportunity to speak his mind freely. A charge communicated through the Jews would, on the other hand, have forced him to raise a counter-accusation against those who are named by Pilate in his answer. Such a procedure might have brought Jesus into collision with the rule that required a Jew who was unfortunate enough to stand in the dock of a Gentile court to say nothing that might imperil his fellow-countrymen. In asking this question and complying with the Jewish code of behaviour[39] Jesus proves to be a loyal

Aristobulus 48f: Moses received the teaching in two forms, esoteric and exoteric instruction.

[34] It is the judicial buffeting parallel to that of Mark 14: 65 (and possibly Luke 23: 6ff), different from the scene of mockery in 19: 2ff (with its parallels in Mark 15: 16ff and Luke 22: 63ff).

[35] A parallel may be found in *Asc. Is.* 5.13, where Isaiah discharges his fellows and sends them to Tyre and Sidon, saying 'The cup was prepared only for me.' The verse is already a Christian addition, as the mention of the 'cup' and of 'Tyre and Sidon' indicates, and it may be influenced by the account of the trial of Jesus. For the historical problem whether the disciples became involved in the proceedings against Jesus, cp. Mark 14: 70, a passage which may possibly imply a hunt after the followers of Jesus, and Ev. Petr. v. 26, which actually states that the disciples had to go into hiding because they were accused of having intended to burn down the Temple. The circumstantial evidence speaks against the claim of the Gospel of Peter.

[36] Vespasian ordered an ἀναζήτησις of all the scions of the Davidic family, causing a persecution thereby (Hegesippus acc. to Eusebius *H.E.* iii 12; cp. E. Meyer, *Ursprung und Anfänge des Christentums* i (Stuttgart, 1921), 72, n. 2). J. Klausner, *The Messianic Idea in Israel* (London, 1955) rightly states that such an utterance as that of John 18: 36 would have been impossible for a Jewish messiah.

[37] R. von Mayr, 'Der Prozess Jesu', *Archiv für Kriminal-Anthropologie und Kriminalistik* 20 (1905), 276.

[38] Dauer, *Passionsgeschichte*, p. 253. In fact, bold utterances are known from both the reports on Jewish martyrdoms (2 and 4 Macc.) as well as those on the pagan martyrs of Alexandria (*Acta Alexandrinorum. De Mortibus Alexandriae nobilium fragmenta papyraica Graeca*, ed. H. A. Musurillo (Leipzig, 1961)).

[39] Two points result from this. Firstly, not to frequent heathen courts at all in questions of litigation (cp. 1 Cor. 6: 1ff); secondly, not to give witness against a fellow-countryman, brother etc. Both elements are present in the Messiah Sutra

Jew.[40] He does so in most trying circumstances: not even the accusers are exposed by him.

True, the silence[41] of Jesus is often explained by reference to Isa. 53: 7: οὐκ ἀνοίγει τὸ στόμα . . . ἄφωνος οὕτως οὐκ ἀνοίγει τὸ στόμα αὐτοῦ.[42] The parallel cannot, however, mean that the remark is unhistorical.[43] Too many features of the story point in the same direction. Equally it should not be taken as an admission of guilt; neither the Roman legal system[44] nor the reaction of Pilate, as it is recorded in the Gospels,[45] allows this interpretation. The silence is the conclusion drawn and posture adopted by the one who had already invoked divine justice against the Sanhedrin[46] and who is now not any longer willing to defend himself. The petition for the enemies, which Luke records as having been uttered on the mount of Calvary[47] and to which is appended the legal phrase: 'they do not know

which is based on a Syriac document: 'bring not your complaint before the magistrate . . . if you know the details of the matter you need not give any information thereof' (verse 13of; cp. P. Y. Saeki, *The Nestorian Documents and Relics in China* (2nd edn. Tokyo, 1951), p. 138).

[40] One is tempted to think of Jonah, who, according to Jewish tradition was so eager to 'insist on the honour of the son (= Israel)' that he tried to flee and even to attempt suicide in order to escape carrying out an action which was detrimental to his nation, Mekilta Pis'cha 1 (Lauterbach I. 9). The 'sign of Jonah' may be interpreted against this background rather than as a sign of penitence.

[41] The silence in front of the court is not unique. Certain traditions, in contrast to the standard tradition represented by Xenophon, Plato etc., attribute silence or an almost resilient gesture to Socrates (Philostrat. *Vit. Apoll.* 8.2; Maximus of Tyre, *Diss.* 3), and make Apollonius adopt the same position in his trial while pointing to the great example (*Vit. Apoll.* 8.2; cp. 8.7 – the statement is in fact the beginning of a long speech). There is, however, no reason to suppose that this model, if it had been established already by Jesus's time, played a role either in Jesus's own mind or in the evangelist's report – the link between Socrates and Jesus which J. G. Klopstock establishes in his famous rendering of Portia's dream (*Der Messias* vii. 399ff) is entirely due to the great poet's ingenious vision. Cp. H. Gomperz, 'Sokrates Haltung vor seinen Richtern', *Wiener Studien* 54 (1936), 32. The silence of Jesus b. Ananias (Jos. *BJ* 6 §302) is different: he remains silent when he is maltreated; it is not a silence in the courtroom.

[42] W. Zimmerli and J. Jeremias, *The Servant of God* (London, 1957), p. 99. For the correction of an attempt at criticism of Jeremias's view cp. J. Jeremias, *JThSt* n.s. 11 (1960), 140ff.

[43] Zimmerli and Jeremias, *Servant*, note 458 remark that the fact that no scriptural reference is given points in favour of the historicity of the silence. Cp. Dodd, *Tradition*, 103f and Dauer, *Passionsgeschichte*, 128 (taken from a pre-Johannine report).

[44] Sallust, *Catilina* 52: 'magistratus de confesso sumat supplicium'; cp. Blinzler, *Prozess*, p. 282.

[45] It is an almost Johannine phrase which is used in Mark 15: 5.

[46] This is the meaning of Mark 14: 62: God will give judgement different from that pronounced by his earthly representative and he himself will have to see the Son of man on the clouds; cp. TU 88 (1964), 24.

[47] 23: 34. Cp. Ignatius's prayer for the persecutors (*Phil.* 12: 3). For the interpretation cp. J. Jeremias, *Neutestamentliche Theologie* i (Gütersloh, 1971), 283 (ET (London,

what they do',[48] only gives expression to what had been practised by Jesus before.[49]

The Lukan report differs from this in many ways. The Jews are described as those who start with accusations (ἤρξαντο . . . κατηγορεῖν) about which details are given (23: 2; cp. 23: 5). This could be taken as pointing to a new trial rather than to a supplement to the preceding one. The Herodian trial could function as a subsidiary piece of evidence for this view: what made it possible for Pilate to undertake a *remissio*[50] was the circumstance of an open or relatively open question not tied too closely by the strings of previous transactions.

The fact that Jesus was a Galilaean stimulated Pilate, it is said, to enter upon this course of action (23: 7). Γαλιλαία is, however, a stock phrase in the Lukan formulae characterising Jesus's activity[51] and, owing to this, inserted into the formula of accusation. Its occurrence in 23:5 is therefore to be taken as Luke's way of accounting for Herod's involvement in Jesus's trial and his way of understanding the episode, whereas the scene itself has its climax and clue in 23: 12. The 'friendship' which must have been brought about by Pilate's giving away of something – something that was noticeable to the outsider – cannot have been caused by his considering Herod Antipas as the *forum domicilii*. The jurisdiction of the tetrarch in his realm was never in doubt. What the Herodians were aiming at was influence in Jerusalem, was a kind of προστασία τοῦ ἔθνους,[52] was the ἐπιμέλεια τοῦ ἱεροῦ[53] – the former was claimed in a dramatic gesture shortly after the trial of Jesus;[54] the latter was formally acquired in A.D. 44.[55]

1971), pp. 298f), and K. Bornhäuser, *Das Wirken des Christus durch Taten und Worte* (Gütersloh, 1921), pp. 224ff.

[48] For the interpretation see D. Daube, 'For they know not what they do', TU 79 (1961), 58ff.

[49] We have to think especially of the enemies of Jesus in Mark 10: 45. It is this address which is in keeping with the context.

[50] Cp. E. Bickermann, 'Utilitas Crucis', *RHR* 112 (1935), 206.

[51] Acts 10: 37; 13: 31; cp. Luke 4: 31. Jesus's movement from there to Judaea as the centre of his activity likewise (Luke 4: 44 ('Iουδαία seems to be the original reading); 6: 17; 7: 17; Acts 10: 37). Cp. U. Wilckens, *Die Missionsreden der Apostelgeschichte* (Neukirchen, 1961).

[52] *AJ* 20 §251; the term is here used in relation to the high priests, but the leadership fell into the hands of the Herodians when they were given the right to appoint and depose high priests (*AJ* 20 §15f).

[53] *AJ* 20 §222; cp. 20 §15.

[54] Philo, *Legatio*, 300.

[55] Josephus speaks of Herod of Chalkis in *AJ* 20 §15. But the right was in all likelihood already exercised by Agrippa I. One may wonder whether the incident mentioned in Luke 13: 1, where Pilate mixed the blood of some Galilaean pilgrims with that of their sacrificial animals was the first occasion for Antipas to try to establish some sort of sovereignty in the Temple area – unsuccessfully and therefore resulting in animosity. The Gospel of Peter, where Antipas presides over a *consilium* of judges of

In sending Jesus (who was supposed to have offended against the Temple) to Herod Antipas Pilate asked for his judgement (or advice) in this matter and thereby meets one of the demands of the Herodians or gives at least the appearance of doing so. Such an event could be taken as a demonstrative gesture and be given the characterisation found in Luke 23: 12,[56] at the end of a passage which otherwise had undergone a certain deterioration. The scene gives rather the impression of being another attempt to refer the case to the Jewish side – this time to an authority not necessarily in agreement with the Sanhedrin[57] – than a *delegatio* as part of a new trial.

Of overriding importance is the point of disagreement with Mark/John, the accusation of the high priests. The form of the Alexandrian[58] texts, which consists of three[59] elements, starts with an accusation based on Deut. 13 – that is to say, it summarises (hence εὕραμεν) the accusation before the Jewish court and the findings of the Sanhedrin, which were presupposed only and not spelled out in the preceding section of Luke's narration.[60] It adds two points which, one would think, had been sufficiently dealt with long before: Jesus had admitted none of these accusations.[61] What, however, made their repetition necessary was to give evidence for what was the Roman representatives' opinion in this matter. The ἀνάκρισις – only the main point, βασιλεύς, is mentioned, under which the tax question seems to be subsumed – results in nothing that is incriminatory:[62] οὐδὲν

which Pilate is only a member, presupposes a judicial situation of this kind. The exemption of the Temple courtyard from Roman jurisdiction – more marked after A.D. 44 than before – is well known from contemporary sources. The representative of the Herodian house acted as justice of the peace within this area (and as a guarantor *vis-à-vis* the Romans). The account of the Gospel of Peter retrojects this situation into the time of the trial of Jesus.

[56] The cumbersome expression φίλοι μετ' ἀλλήλων, periphrastic construction πρὸς αὐτούς and the wording ἐν ἔχθρᾳ suggest a Semitic background. The pericope itself, on the other hand, is different in style. Lukan are ἅπαν τὸ πλῆθος, ἐρωτάω, εἶπεν πρός; ἄξιος and χαίρειν, listed by F. Rehkopf (*Die lukanische Sonderquelle* (Tübingen, 1959), pp. 92ff) as pre-Lukan, are in fact not un-Lukan, as the usage in Acts shows.

[57] Thus Bickermann, *RHR* 112 (1935), 205ff.

[58] The Western text, on the other hand, turns it by its additions and the omission of Καίσαρι (which is likely for Marcion and which makes it, according to W. Bauer, *Das Leben Jesu* (Tübingen, 1909), p. 197 refer to the Temple tax) to a code of Christian behaviour which is very much in line with what we know of the ethical standards in the Marcionite church.

[59] Different G. Schneider, p. 407f in this volume. If the καί were epexegetical, we would equally expect a καί in front of διδάσκων in verse 5.

[60] Cp. p. 417.

[61] It is important to note that Luke 20: 20ff is – contrary to Mark – introduced by reference to the political and juridical dimension of the question. The ἐσίγησαν added by Luke to the Markan report makes it quite clear that Jesus won victory in this dispute.

[62] σὺ λέγεις (23: 3) has like 22: 70 a negative meaning for Luke.

εὑϱίσκω αἴτιον (23: 4). This statement forces the high priests to fall back to . the first point of accusation. After the Herod scene, which must be seen as being concerned with this point at issue, even the first accusation (and with it the others as well) is denied: 23: 14f, 20, 22. Pilate repeats his opinion three times before all sections of Jewish society[63] and Luke underlines the finality of this (23: 22 τϱίτον). He even goes so far as to eliminate the ridiculing βασιλεὺς τῶν Ἰουδαίων of Mark's Barabbas scene (15: 9) in his own report.

The innocence of Jesus could have been stated without the outlining of the points of accusation in detail. As they are mentioned prominently it must have been done with a particular purpose. Jesus's own fate, the fact that he was killed although innocent, cannot have been the reason. Can the situation of Christianity at a time nearer to Luke's own have given rise to the detailed mentioning of these points?[64] Romans 13: 5f is phrased in such a way that it presupposes an inclination to make use of the privilege of the heirs of the kingdom, a certain resistance against the paying of taxes[65] either in the Christian community or in such circles as could be associated with it. To defeat such suggestions and, even more, to convince the Romans that such ideas, which were likely to be put into their heads by the Jews, did not exist among them, was of vital importance for nascent Christianity – not only in Rome.[66] Ἑαυτὸν Χϱιστὸν βασιλέα εἶναι is the only formulation of this kind in Luke, indicating in this way that something specific, the Davidic pretension, is implied. Such a notion, in normal circumstances not necessarily of consequence, became dangerous in the years of the revolt and after it when the Romans chased those persons, who by virtue of their descent might become focal points for subversive activities.[67]

---

[63] The λαός of verse 13 is still present in verse 23. This may be a difference compared with the preceding scene where the πλῆθος or ὄχλος are the followers of the Sanhedrin.

[64] Cp. Matt. 17: 25. The word κῆνσος indicates that the problem of the Temple tax is linked with that of the tribute. It is only for the latter that verse 25c is formulated from the believer = υἱός. Cp. also W. Horbury, above, p. 265.

[65] φόϱος is used as in Luke 23: 2; not κῆνσος as in Mark 12: 14.

[66] For the Roman situation see p. 370f – Luke's rephrasing of the centurion's confession: ὄντως . . . δίκαιος (23: 47) – at first glance surprising because it avoids the christological confession which Mark had produced – becomes meaningful in the assumed context. It was of vital importance to bring out clearly the innocence of Jesus at the end of the account of the passion.

[67] BJ 6 §114f. The removal of John, the γνωστὸς τῷ ἀϱχιεϱεῖ (John 18: 15), to Patmos may have been part of the same operation. The relegatio was a comparatively mild punishment, mainly accorded to honestiores. It is Luke too who rewrites the Gethsemane pericope and produces a different version of the arrest. Is it possible to go so far as to assume that inclination to resistance is in his opinion a form of the πειϱασμός, the danger of which is stressed so much in his account (22: 40, 46)?

It results from this that the accusation of the πρεσβυτέριον τοῦ λαοῦ is a Lukan heading, under which umbrella are put together the findings of the Sanhedrin with other points which were sensitive spots in the evangelist's own time. From this it may be deduced that the impression that Luke follows a different scheme for the trial before Pilate[68] is based only on editorial material and is not, even on this level, carried through systematically.[69] The Barabbas episode agrees with the Markan/Johannine scheme and the Herodian 'trial', whether historical or unhistorical,[70] is, taken by itself, capable of being interpreted as a fact-finding mission with the possible intention of counteracting the Sanhedrin's claims. The final decision of Pilate is rendered in a way almost identical with that of Mark. The source analysis of the Roman part of the Lukan trial leads to a result different from that of the Sanhedrin trial: whereas the latter is based on a source independent from and, perhaps, superior[71] to Mark, it is in the trial before Pilate that the main thread, interwoven with a few features of different provenance, is Markan.

The 'strange episode concerning Barabbas'[72] is only a subsidiary feature in the Fourth Gospel. It had invaded the pre-Lukan tradition at an early stage[73] and it is, although firmly embedded in the Markan text as we possess

[68] *Pace* Bickermann. The charges are Lukan, but the evangelist has chosen to describe the way in which Pilate deals with them from the basis of Mark (Luke 23: 3). This would point against the existence of a continuous pre-Lukan narrative on the Roman trial. Verses 1f are to be viewed together with verse 5 (cp. the similar καί plus participle formulation). Probably it was originally one entity. Luke moved what is now verse 5b/c in order to have a foothold for the Antipas story and replaced it by verse 2c.

[69] 23: 14 refers only to the first 'accusation'.

[70] It has certainly not evolved from an interpretation of Ps. 2: 1 (thus M. Dibelius, 'Herodes und Pilatus' in *Botschaft und Geschichte* i (Tübingen, 1953), 278ff). In this case we would expect the βασιλεύς-trial to have been given a far greater prominence, an importance not dissimilar to that given in Ev. Petr.

[71] D. Catchpole, *The Trial of Jesus* (Leiden, 1971), pp. 153ff. The question arises as to what was the end of the pre-Lukan report cited by the evangelist in ch. 22. Some mention of the Roman trial is to be presupposed. It cannot be ruled out that the evangelist who cut off the beginning did the same with the final section at the end of the source. But there is one point in his account which is to be explained neither by his own tendency nor by the influence of Mark: the role of the crowd. Whereas the crowd does not come in in Mark before 15: 8 and has to be agitated by the high priests against Jesus, it is here the case – contrary to what is usual in the main body and again in the crucifixion story (verse 35) of the Gospel – that the crowds are present right from the beginning (verse 4) and take an active part. Might it be that this feature stems from pre-Lukan tradition? Remembering the deviating traits in the Barabbas scene of that Gospel, it appears likely that the source went on with verse 18 and concluded with verse 24. A short mention of the crucifixion itself may have been the concluding remark of the source.

[72] S. G. F. Brandon, *Jesus and the Zealots* (Manchester, 1967), p. 258.

[73] Luke 23: 16 is identical with 23: 22d. The evangelist established a bridge by inserting λαός in 23: 13, a passage where the crowds have nothing to do; on the

it now, an insertion in the summarising *Ur*-account. This does not mean, however, that it is just a 'legendary embellishment'.[74] The state of affairs points to two streams of tradition at an initial stage, comparable with the two traditions of Stephen's death[75] one of which explained the action of the crowd by reference to the choice given to it (owing to this the σταύρωσον is moved into the scene), whereas the other replaced the crowd by a smaller segment of the population.[76]

The *privilegium Paschale* makes sense as a Jewish custom (thus John 18: 39): one prisoner is released in remembrance of Israel's salvation from Egypt. In a similar way the Jews felt compelled to buy out, and were busy buying out, fellow-countrymen who had fallen captive especially at this time.[77] The release is likely to have been a royal prerogative *vis-à-vis* the Sanhedrin.[78] The Roman prefects whose office was in the succession of the Hasmonaean kings carried on with this. If such a custom existed in Jerusalem at that time, it is most likely that the demand was normally put forward by the people (as is the case in Luke 23: 18). If, in answer to this, a choice was given by the authorities – this is certainly a possibility[79] – it had to be a choice between persons who were 'in the same condemnation'. That means, Jesus was in all likelihood in the situation of a condemned person[80] –

---

other hand, he may have omitted the beginning of the Barabbas scene. The state of affairs shows that Luke selected pieces of different provenance for his account.

[74] Thus R. Bultmann, *Geschichte der synoptischen Tradition* (Göttingen, 1957), p. 293 (ET (Oxford, 1963) p. 272); M. Grant, *Jesus* (London, 1977), p. 165. Even F. Hahn ('Der Prozess Jesu nach dem Johannesevangelium', *Evangelisch-Katholischer Kommentar. Vorarbeiten*, Heft 2 (Neukirchen, 1970), pp. 13ff) considers the tradition as '*vorjohanneisch*'.

[75] Cp. Acts 6: 11ff with 7: 57f and cp. F. Spitta, *Die Apostelgeschichte* (Halle, 1891), pp. 96ff and K. Bornhäuser, *Studien zur Apostelgeschichte* (Gütersloh, 1934), pp. 71ff.

[76] John 19: 6. This is a standing feature in the Fourth Gospel. The last statements on the multitude are found in 10: 41 and 12: 19.

[77] Pes. viii. 6 refers to this, not – *pace* Blinzler, *Prozess*, pp. 371ff – to the Passover amnesty.

[78] And therefore not listed by Josephus as a privilege accorded to the Jews by the Romans (a different view in Brandon, *Zealots*, p. 259). The parallels adduced from the Graeco-Roman world (see Blinzler, *Prozess*, pp. 303ff) are relevant only so far as they may help to explain the Roman attitude of carrying on with the practice. The role of grace in Jewish penal law demands a special investigation.

[79] It would point to a somewhat circumscribing practice in the apprehension of the *privilegium* – a development not difficult to understand.

[80] It was, *nota bene*, a verdict by the Sanhedrin. Bickermann, *RHR* 112 (1935), p. 239 tries to escape this conclusion by assuming that an introductory remark to the scene, reporting the condemnation to death of Jesus by Pilate, was suppressed by Mark. The same would have to be supposed to have happened with the beginning of the Lukan account – a most unlikely coincidence. R. W. Husband, *The Prosecution of Jesus* (Princeton, 1916), pp. 268ff; *idem*, 'The Pardoning of Prisoners by Pilate', *AJT* 21 (1917), 110ff, on the other hand, argues unconvincingly that Barabbas was not yet convicted. The arguments assembled by Cohn, *Trial*, pp. 163ff carry weight, if any, only under the unproven supposition that Jesus was not yet *rite* condemned.

in the same way as Barabbas was awaiting execution. It is not less likely that the choice given to the people was a real one: Jesus had been tried for a crime different from that of the ληστής[81] Barabbas. The outcome could not be seen as decided beforehand,[82] as the peoole had not been involved so far. And indeed, men like Josephus take great pains to give a picture in which the attitude of the main population is distinguished from the activities of the fanatics. So far the story is not untrustworthy[83] and points strongly away from any revolutionary behaviour on the part of Jesus himself. What is due to the evangelist's redaction is the direct link between the choice of Barabbas and the σταύρωσον of the people, whereas the latter is likely to have happened at a later stage of the proceedings (cp. John 19:6).

No verdict pronounced by Pilate is cited in either the synoptic Gospels or the Gospel of John. What is mentioned, however, is his intention and, indeed, his command to scourge Jesus. Luke, who reports the intention (23:16), fails to mention the execution of the punishment. John speaks about it at some length (19:1), whereas Mark and Matthew briefly mention the act in their summary of the events. Luke's report suggests a scourging before the Barabbas scene and John, on the other hand, places it afterwards, whereas the first two evangelists give no clear indication as to when it happened.[84] It is not an ancillary punishment to the execution,[85] and must therefore be either an act of cruelty to please the public or a punishment for some minor offence. John, who links it closely with the mocking, has moved in the first direction, whereas Luke, who ventilates the question of guilt in the same sentence, points to the other alternative. It is more likely that a measure that was considered as an order of punishment could look like an act of brutality than that the opposite happened. If we have to take the punitive character of the measure seriously, it is necessary to trace the reason. Jesus's silence must have been taken as contempt of court by Pilate and caused the reaction of the enraged prefect.[86]

The final verdict is supposed to be alluded to in John 19:13: ἐκάθισεν ἐπὶ βήματος. This phrase is valued as the only clear witness for a Roman

---

[81] Winter, *Trial*, pp. 96ff tries unsuccessfully to dispute the linking of Barabbas with insurrectionist activities.

[82] Jesus must have been a man of a type different from that of Barabbas; the story makes sense only under this supposition. This points against O. Cullmann's interpretation: the same crime and the same verdict (*Der Staat im N.T.* (2nd edn. Tübingen, 1961), p. 34; ET London 1957, pp. 47f).

[83] Was the nomination of Barabbas as eligible for amnesty a scheme of Pilate in order to test the loyalty of the Jews? In any case, the extension of the amnesty to a case which was only punishable according to Roman law might be taken as a success of the Jews.

[84] Mark seems to put the punitive measures together.

[85] See p. 44of.

[86] Cp. John 18:22.

condemnation,[87] and it is seen as the beginning of the proceedings *e superiori* which are concluded by the verdict pronounced from the same βῆμα.[88] In the Johannine scene it is, however, the mocking remark: ἴδε ὁ βασιλεὺς ὑμῶν that follows, a remark that is raised to another level by the evangelist as is indicated by the mentioning of the hour. The situation is parallel to verse 5 where he says: ἰδοὺ ὁ ἄνθρωπος. The progression to βασιλεύς in verse 14 – and its emphasis in verse 15 – has meaning only if something had been done with the person concerned in the meantime. Scourging and mocking are actions that preceded verse 5. A new act is, however, supplied if ἐκάθισεν is taken as a transitive form;[89] it describes a final climax of the mocking scene, the culprit is placed on the judgement seat and, in keeping with this, spoken of as βασιλεύς. Interpreted this way the pericope – whether its position in the sequence of events is correct or not[90] – does not provide the required information about the state of the trial itself.[91]

The word that comes nearest to a juridical description is used by Luke: ἐπέκρινεν (23: 34). It does not describe the giving of sentence,[92] but rather a decision, rightly or wrongly[93] taken within a larger procedural context. The other evangelists avoid even such a description and allude to the end of the scene before Pilate in the shortest possible wording.

Which is the procedural form that satisfies these data? The evaluation of the facts has retreated into the background almost completely, and the question whether a punishment, and if so which one, is advisable, dominates the scene. This not only demands that the fact-finding, summing-up and verdict of another authority should have preceded, but equally that the decision of the former should have been of such a kind that it could not be overruled in substance. It appears that the case was not such as to be dealt with by the *coercitio* of the prefect or even by ordinary Roman provincial trial. Neither the one trial[94] nor a new trial[95] seems to be the

---

[87] J. Blinzler, 'Der Entscheid des Pilatus – Exekutionsbefehl oder Todesurteil?', *MThZ* 5 (1954), 175; *Prozess*, pp. 346ff.

[88] Blinzler, *Prozess*, pp. 341f.

[89] As the parallel in Ev. Petr. v. 7 suggests. Cp. A. v. Harnack, *Bruchstücke des Evangeliums und der Apokalypse des Petrus* (Leipzig, 1893), pp. 63f; and P. Corssen, "Εκάθισεν ἐπὶ βήματος', *ZNW* 15 (1914), 339f. So too in Ev. Barnabae (ed. L. and L. Ragg (Oxford, 1907), p. 479); the passage refers there to Judas in the guise of Jesus. But cp. J. A. T. Robinson below, n. 52 on p. 469.

[90] Cp. Winter, *Trial*, pp. 101f, 106.

[91] Mommsen already made it likely that no *Vollverfahren* took place. Thus there was no need for Pilate to mount the βῆμα (*Römisches Strafrecht* (Leipzig, 1899), pp. 240f). Differently Blinzler, *Prozess*, p. 356.

[92] Thus A. Plummer, *St Luke* (Edinburgh, 1913), p. 527.

[93] Thus 2 Macc. 4: 47, where the word is used.

[94] Winter, *Trial*, *passim*.

[95] G. Aicher, *Der Prozess Jesu* (Bonn, 1929); E. Stauffer, *Jesus. Gestalt und Geschichte* (Bern, 1957; ET London, 1960).

Roman trial but a procedure based and dependent on the Sanhedrin trial. The possibilities to be taken into consideration in this case are a handing over without any scrutiny and comment or a short examination and decision guided by the principles of Roman administration. The former view may find support in the simple παρέδωκεν by which the end of the Roman part of the narrative is described in all four Gospels[96] and the nearly complete absence of details of a strictly judicial procedure. On the other hand it must be mentioned that whatever may be said about Christian enlargements of the story,[97] certain dealings took place which would find their natural conclusion in a formal decision taken by the prefect. True, such a decision is nowhere reproduced in the passion accounts, but it is presupposed in Acts 13: 29,[98] and the later tradition which attributes to Pilate a formal κρίμα[99] could hardly have arisen without any trace in its nascent form.[100] The ἐπίκρισις, found in the description of Luke, is therefore to be taken as the term which comes nearest to the essence of the judicial action in the Gospel account of the Roman 'trial'. 'Επίκρισις is a decision based on such investigation as was necessary for the consideration of imperial interests. On the other hand, it was a scrutiny 'mit gebundener Marschroute'[101] that was carried out: the case itself was not re-examined, only the political consequences of whatever actions had been decided on.

One element has been disregarded so far, the role played by the people. The evangelists unanimously emphasise that their intervention was decisive. The *Volksgericht* had been in action in Rome until the time of Augustus and was valued as an expression of liberty.[102] Such an institution, well known from the Jewish past[103] and still in force in the autonomous communities of the Empire,[104] could not be met with disapproval *a limine* by

---

[96] Cp. p. 416f.

[97] Cp. Bultmann, *Synoptische Tradition*, pp. 297ff (ET p. 275ff).

[98] The handing over takes place although no *causa* was found; this implies that a *causa* was supplied by Pilate. D, on the other hand, supplies a reference to a κρίμα given by the Sanhedrin.

[99] E.g. *Act. Pil.* ix; cp. E. von Dobschütz, 'Der Prozess Jesu nach den Acta Pilati', *ZNW* 3 (1902), 89ff.

[100] Certain details which gave support to the impression of a Roman judgement came in later: the three languages (cp. p. 354f), the centurion and the interpretation of John 19: 13 as referring to a formal action of Pilate.

[101] R. von Mayr, *Archiv für Kriminal-Anthropologic und Kriminalistik* 20 (1905), 305. L. Wenger (*Die Quellen des römischen Rechts* (Graz, 1953), p. 287) inserts this statement into his acount of the events although it is substantially at variance with his own view of the separate trials.

[102] Mommsen, *Strafrecht*, p. 171.

[103] Lynch law, still commonly practised in this period (cp. Acts 7: 58) was only acceptable to the legal mind as a way of executing the people's justice.

[104] J. Colin, *Les villes libres de l'Orient gréco-romain et l'envoi au supplice par acclamations populaires*, Coll. Latomus 82 (Brussels, 1965). Colin's theory was endorsed – with a

the Romans. Indeed, the Barabbas scene shows that those assembled before the βῆμα[105] were viewed as the representatives of the people qualified to make a choice. The voices of the people, although not regarded as sufficient to decide the outcome of a trial, were valued not just as *vanae voces populi* but viewed with regard by the Romans when it came to the question of the political feasibility of a verdict, and in fact the importance of the multitude in wider political issues became of decisive importance exactly at the time of Pilate. There is a straight line from Mark 15: 15 (βουλόμενος τῷ ὄχλῳ τὸ ἱκανὸν ποιῆσαι) to the report of Eusebius on Attalus's execution: τῷ ὄχλῳ χαριζόμενος ὁ ἡγεμών.[106] The impression the Gospel reports[107] convey, that it was this intervention that tipped the scales in Jesus's disfavour and made the prefect arrive at the decision he issued, is historically not at all unlikely. Examination of this factor in the events confirms the view that political considerations had their part in the Roman side of the proceedings. The care for the preservation of peace[108] is certainly no sufficient reason for the condemnation of Jesus (not even under the *vinculum* of *coercitio*) but it is a satisfactory argument if Jesus was already *rite* condemned.[109]

Does this hypothesis find support in the information we receive outside the trial proper about the execution of Jesus or does such evidence demand a different solution? The summarising accounts in Acts and in the synoptic Gospels, which go back in substance to a period prior to the literary activity of the Christians[110] have to be taken into consideration. The accounts of the events preceding and following the trial come in as subsidiary evidence.

The third prediction of the passion (Mark 10: 32ff) contains a more detailed description than the preceding ones (8: 31ff; 9: 30ff) and mentions the ἔθνη to whom Jesus is to be handed over. Mark constructs the following part of the sentence in parataxis and thereby leaves it open whether the Gentiles or – more likely – the high priests perform the subsequent actions

certain proviso – by F. Bovon, *Les derniers jours de Jésus* (Neuenburg, 1974), p. 68; cp. p. 43.

[105] Colin, *Villes*, pp. 13ff makes a good case for the variant ἀναβοήσας.

[106] Eusebius, *H.E.* v. 1.50; cp. Colin, *Villes*, pp. 126ff.

[107] Matthew alone adds the ominous τὸ αἷμα αὐτοῦ κτλ. (27: 25). It is a form of oath (*Schwurformel*), the meaning of which is: his blood be on us, if we do wrong with the man whom you are about to hand over (ὑμεῖς ὄψεσθε). For a new interpretation, according to which the phrase 'his blood on our heads' testified to the innocence of the person concerned, cp. G. Baum, *Die Juden und das Evangelium* (Einsiedeln, 1963), pp. 105f.

[108] Thus, in defence of Pilate, J. F. Stephen, *Liberty, Equality, Fraternity* (London 1873; new edn. Cambridge, 1967), p. 87; cp. Innes, *Trial*, pp. 101ff.

[109] The theory suggested here finds its closest ally in the reconstruction of the events given by S. Liberty, *The Political Relations of Christ's Ministry* (Oxford, 1916).

[110] C. H. Dodd, *The Apostolic preaching and its developments* (London, 1936). E. Stauffer, *Die Theologie des N.T.* (Stuttgart, 1941), pp. 329ff; ET (London, 1955), p. 339.

of humiliation and the execution,[111] whereas both Matthew and Luke refer to misdeeds of these ἔθνη. The plural formulation is, however, not handed down unanimously: sy[s] reads τῷ λαῷ[112] in Matt. 20: 19, Mark 10: 33, and l omits the object altogether. Obviously different traditions[113] have come together[114] and the attempt to integrate them has not been wholly successful.[115] It is surprising that no more definite reference to the Romans is given in this formula, that none of the opprobrious terms for them is used, and no mention is made of the judicial activity of Pilate. This state of affairs is explained more easily by an ἔθνη-formulation into which other notions crept than from the opposite starting point. The corresponding formula in Luke 24: 20 which lacks any reference to the Romans[116] and treats the passion entirely within a Jewish horizon,[117] confirms this view.

The formulae in Acts do not seem to coincide with this. The χεῖρες ἀνόμων (2: 23) must allude to non-Jewish involvement,[118] as the notion of the nefariousness of the executioner is completely absent from the Jewish mind. Acts 13: 28 too takes this line and even names Pilate as the one whom the Jews asked (ἠτήσαντο). It is, however, striking that the activity attributed to the Roman prefect does not go beyond the granting of a request – a remark that seems to refer to the popular demand at the Barabbas scene[119] – and that in the probably superior[120] part of the textual tradition, even the resulting event[121] is described in such a way that it indicates a Jewish rather than a Roman action.[122] Pilate appears on the

---

[111] Equally n in its rendering of Matt. 20: 19.

[112] Burkitt adds the plural in his translation.

[113] If not we would expect the Syriac text form to be the same in all three Gospels.

[114] See Merx, *Matthaeus*, p. 288; *Die Evangelien des Markus und Lukas* (Berlin, 1905), p. 361.

[115] The Lukan formulation is interesting: μαστιγώσαντες ἀποκτενοῦσιν – at variance (even terminologically) with the Lukan trial report but (rather) in agreement with the Roman procedure of crucifixion.

[116] *Pace* Blinzler, *Münchener Theol. Zeitschrift* 5 (1954), 173f. *Prozess*, pp. 341–428.

[117] παρέδωκαν has here the wider meaning drawn attention to in n. 7, p. 415f. So it agrees with the following verb: both terms describe different sides of the same action.

[118] Otherwise H. Conzelmann, *Die Mitte der Zeit* (Tübingen, 1954), p. 84 (ET London 1961, pp. 90f), although so only for the level of Luke's redaction.

[119] αἰτεῖσθαι is used in the description of the choice (Mark 15: 8; Matt. 27: 20; Luke 23: 23) and equally as a stock phrase in the parallel formula of Acts 3: 14, where it clearly refers to this incident. It is to be kept in mind that the κατοικοῦντες ἐν Ἰερουσαλήμ are seen as the principal actors.

[120] Cp. J. H. Ropes in F. J. F. Jackson and K. Lake, *Beginnings of Christianity* iii (London, 1926), 262f.

[121] *Ut interficeretur.*

[122] The Egyptian reading ἀναιρεθῆναι was, together with Acts 5: 30; 10: 39, taken as evidence by I. M. Wise that Jesus was actually hanged and not crucified (*The Origin of Christianity* (Cincinnati, 1868), p. 29).

stage[123] just as a foil for the Jews whose deeds are qualified by terms stronger than those used in the Gospels; they are called προδόται (7: 52) and almost stigmatised as ἐκδόται.[124] The very fact that the Romans are passed over in silence in the rest of the formulae (3: 15; 4: 10; 5: 30; 10: 39) underlines this concentration. Their sketch of events turns out to be consistent with the passion prediction formulae, while the difference in terminology shows them to be independent sources.[125]

The *Testimonium Flavianum* presents a different picture: an ἔνδειξις is performed by the πρῶτοι ἄνδρες,[126] a fact that causes Pilate to ἐπιτιμᾶν Jesus to the cross.[127] It is a denunciation or, as Rufinus puts it,[128] *accusatio* that had been discharged by the Jews. The phrase has been taken to exclude a Jewish trial.[129] But this is not necessarily the case[130] as not even the formal verdict pronounced by Pilate is reported. Still, the text as it

[123] The Egyptian text only implies Pilate's choice between Barabbas and Jesus, whereas the Western text has Jesus handed over to him and attributes a role to the prefect that stretches even beyond Jesus's death, more in keeping with the Gospel reports than the alternative text. E.J. Epp's evaluation of the passage is hereby to be corrected (*The theological Tendency of Codex Bezae Cantabrigiensis in Acts* (Cambridge, 1966), p. 58).

[124] 2: 23 is to be constructed this way: delivered over through the hands of lawless men you nailed etc. In the Western text λαβόντες has a very different meaning, for the illumination of which see Epp, *Theological Tendency*, pp. 60f. T. Zahn, *Apostelgeschichte* (Leipzig, 1919), p. 112 comes out in favour of the Western text, which he interprets differently.

[125] Dibelius put forward the hypothesis that the first literary products of the Christian communities were concerned with the description of Jesus's passion, that the Gospels as we have them are passion narratives extended backwards. This is correct and yet not correct. Certainly the description of the Lord's suffering was a subject of meditation and source of influence for every one of his followers, the more so as soon as oppression and persecution began and Jesus's example gave strength to his disciples. That means that Gethsemane, mocking, crucifixion and death will have been narrated early on. Is this the case, however, also for the legal procedures? The piety of the individual would have been less affected by this subject. As far as Christian apologetics are concerned, they can only have had a chance of success in the Palestinian area if (a) they asserted the ascension and coming again of the one condemned, and (b) they were in the position to make some answer to the accusations of witchcraft, seduction of the people and blasphemy against the Temple, i.e. it was necessary for the description of Jesus's life to play a certain role from the beginning. The Roman part of the trial, however, apart from the Barabbas scene, was left out as irrelevant. The result of this is that the account of the two trials derives from a later stage in Christian development, a stage when enlightenment concerning the Roman side was of vital importance for the Christians. The account of the trial in the Gospel of Mark is therefore already a formation which goes back to the community outside Palestine.

[126] Eusebius, *Theophany* renders ἄρχοντες instead.

[127] *AJ* 18 §64.

[128] Jerome adds the paraphrase: 'invidia nostrorum principum' (*ex libr. vir. de Jos.* c. 13).

[129] Th. Reinach, 'Josèphe sur Jésus', *REJ* 35 (1897), 16f.

[130] Cp. the argument of Blinzler, *Prozess*, pp. 46f.

stands attributes a greater measure of activity to the Romans. It coincides in this respect with Tacitus's reference to Jesus.[131] Both statements seem to reflect the state of jurisdiction which had evolved at the turn of the century.[132]

The examination of the material from the different sources reveals a surprising degree of consonance about the nature of the Roman proceedings. To transfer this to the juridical level is not easy, as our knowledge of the provincial trial is very scanty indeed.[133] Still, certain points can be fixed. As the Jewish code of law had been applied in the examination and condemnation of Jesus and no independent enquiry had been carried out by Pilate, it is likely that the delict (*Tatbestand*), as it had been expressed by the Jewish court, was accepted by the Roman judge. This could be linked with the idea of a Roman trial in such a way as to assume that Pilate went into the matter so far as to find out whether the case was a punishable delict according to Roman law as well or not.[134] A *Delibationsverfahren*[135] (interrogatory proceedings) of this description is, however, not noticeable in the sources. The elements of an investigation carried out in accordance with principles which differed from those of the Sanhedrin are absent.[136] The βασιλεύς-theme is not given a new, a political interpretation. If it had been, an investigation into the activities of the disciples would have been unavoidable. It therefore seems likely that not only the case itself but the punishment according to Jewish law was accepted as a presupposition by the Roman prefect, that what is called the *Subsumptionsfrage* was taken as having been settled by the Sanhedrin.[137] What was left to Pilate was to decide whether the punishment applicable

---

[131] *Ann.* xv. 44.

[132] In a similar vein Tacitus gives Pilate the title *procurator* which had become common in the historiographer's own time; for the question see H. Volkmann, 'Die Pilatusinschrift von Caesarea Maritima', *Gymnasium* 75 (1968), 130–2; D. M. Pippidi, 'Discutii in Jurul lui Pontiu Pilat', *Studii Clasice* 12 (1970), 182ff; R. Szramkiewicz, *Les Gouverneurs de province à l'époque augustéenne* (Paris, 1971); E. Stauffer, *Die Pilatusinschrift von Caesarea* (Erlangen, 1966). It was already in 1905 that O. Hirschfeld had assumed that the title of Pilate had been ὑπάρχων/*praefectus* rather than ἐπίτροπος/procurator or ἡγεμών/*praeses* (*Die kaiserlichen Verwaltungsbeamten* (2nd edn. Berlin, 1905), p. 385). His thesis was confirmed by the first inscription where Pilate was mentioned, the inscription of Caesarea.

[133] Mommsen, *Strafrecht*, p. 356: 'Die Ueberlieferung ist hinsichtlich der genaueren Feststellung ihrer (der statthalterlichen) Kompetenzgrenzen, insbesondere der denselben beigelegten Strafgewalt sogut wie stumm.'

[134] von Mayr, 'Ursprung', 299.

[135] The term is used by von Mayr. He is misled by the statements of Origen (*ad Africanum* 14; *In Rm.* vi. 7) which he distorts and considers relevant already for the time of the trial of Jesus (pp. 285f, 299).

[136] E.g. no questioning of witnesses; different von Mayr, 'Ursprung', 301.

[137] E. Schürer, *Geschichte des jüd. Volkes im Zeitalter Jesu Christi* i (Leipzig, 1901) 481 (ET (Edinburgh, 1892), i. 2. 73f).

according to Jewish law was politically expedient from the point of view of Roman administration. Distributing the weight in this way allows for the reconciliation of what is otherwise irreconcilable:[138] Pilate's decision and his repeated doubts about Jesus's guilt. It allows for the emphatic statement of his own – judicial – innocence,[139] while he was morally all the more guilty. Such a reconstruction is in keeping with the general evidence for the period. The judicial system was left intact by the Romans as far as possible,[140] at least in the time of the early principate. Moreover, it was certainly the local law that was applied ordinarily, apart from conditions in which extraordinary measures had to be taken *per coercitionem*. Thus it is concluded by no less an authority than Theodor Mommsen that Jesus was apprehended according to the old criminal code of the time of the kings.[141] A convenient way to check the activity of the local courts and to reverse the worst decisions taken by them was the introduction of a regulation that required Roman permission for the execution of death penalties.[142] It seems that Judaea had just arrived at this stage of development in the time of Pilate.[143] It is this impression of the practice of the Roman provincial administration that favours the view that, if there was a verdict by the Sanhedrin, it was only supplemented and put into force by a Roman *exsequatur*.[144]

[138] A condemnation for an offence committed against the *lex Julia* is irreconcilable with the emphasis in Pilate's impression of Jesus's innocence. However much the Roman representative was obliged to examine possible sources of unrest, he was not at all compelled to condemn someone whom he considered not guilty.

[139] Mommsen stated that the confirmation of a verdict by a Roman representative could not easily have been given without a re-examination of the preceding trial (*Strafrecht*, p. 241; similarly von Mayr, 'Ursprung' 285). It is the almost complete absence of revisionary features that makes him culpable from a historian's point of view. Mommsen once added the qualification to his description of the judicial situation: 'dass er (the Roman representative) dieses Recht (confirmation) nicht ausübte, ohne sich über die Schuldfrage selbständig orientiert zu haben, versteht sich von selbst' ('Die Pilatusakten', *ZNW* 3 (1902), 199; cp. *Strafrecht*, p. 241; similarly von Mayr, 'Ursprung', p. 285) and expressed hereby what was desirable from the Roman point of view and became the practice in the course of time. The almost complete absence of this element is the characteristic feature of the Roman part of the trial of Jesus. Pilate 'beschloss unrömisch' – this statement of Klopstock (*Der Messias*, vii, 765) receives meaning in this context.

[140] For the Roman intention to grant πάτρια ἔθη, which included the judicial system, cp. Jos. *AJ* 14 §194; 16 §35.

[141] 'das alte königliche (= jüdische) Strafrecht, nach welchem Jesus gerichtet worden ist' (*Strafrecht*, p. 120 n. 1).

[142] This inaugurated a development that resulted in the reservation of capital cases for the Roman courts.

[143] See *Studies in Jewish Legal History* (London, 1974), pp. 35ff. Cp. also C. H. Dodd, 'The Historical Problem of the Trial of Jesus' in *More N.T. Studies* (Manchester, 1968), p. 92.

[144] Similarly F. Dörr, *Der Prozess Jesu in rechtsgeschichtlicher Beleuchtung* (Berlin, 1920).

The word used for Pilate's action is the same that had been used before for the transition from the Sanhedrin to the Roman proceedings: παρέδωκεν. We would therefore expect an act similar in nature and appearance. Indeed, that is emphasised by the addition of αὐτοῖς, which we find in the whole manuscript tradition of John 19: 16, in a considerable part of the manuscripts of Matt. 27: 26[145] and in a substantial minority of witnesses to Mark 15: 15.[146] The state in the Markan tradition can be explained as an intrusion from Matthew, whereas the evidence of the Matthaean manuscripts points rather in favour of the authenticity of αὐτοῖς than otherwise.[147] In any case, the meaning of the sentence in both Mark and Matthew demands that those to whom Jesus is delivered are the same as those on whose behalf Barabbas is released. The same is true for Luke who paraphrases: τῷ θελήματι αὐτῶν. The following verses in Luke and John do not disagree with this,[148] whereas in Mark and Matthew the mocking follows, which is performed by στρατιῶται in the πραιτώριον and therefore supposed to point to Roman custody.

Attempts have been made to smooth out the divergency by giving παρέδωκεν a metaphorical interpretation[149] or by devaluing the Johannine statement as due to a 'jüngerer Interpolator'.[150] The matter is, however, more difficult, as this tradition occurs already in the first reference to the trial in early Christian literature, in 1 Thess. 2: 14f: τῶν Ἰουδαίων τῶν . . . τὸν κύριον ἀποκτεινάντων Ἰησοῦν.[151] The same is maintained in the Ascension of Isaiah,[152] the Gospel of Peter,[153] by Justin[154] and Aristides,[155] in the Kerygma Petrou,[156] the Syriac Didaskalia,[157] the Apostolic Constitutions,[158] in the Epistle of Barnabas,[159] in Melito of Sardis,[160] in

---

[145] ℵ 1 DLNΘ f1 892.1010 al lat sys arm (erased in ℵ*AB).

[146] FW sys ph h georg 54.282.c.

[147] Merx, Matthaeus, pp. 407f.

[148] 'Wie jetzt der Vers 16. . . steht und lautet, wird Jesus den Juden zur Hinrichtung übergeben' (Wellhausen, Johannes, p. 86).

[149] Blinzler, Prozess, p. 340.

[150] E. Schwartz, 'Aporien im vierten Evangelium', Nachr. v.d. Kgl. Ges. d. Wiss. Göttingen (1907), p. 356. F. Spitta emends αὐτοῖς in the same verse out of existence (Das Johannes-Evangelium (Göttingen, 1910), p. 378).

[151] For an interpretation cp. ZThK 56 (1959), 259ff.

[152] They delivered him to the king and crucified him (xi. 19).

[153] v. 5: καὶ παρέδωκεν αὐτὸν τῷ λαῷ. The first editor had omitted these words. Without knowing this Harnack already expressed his doubts whether verses 5f refer to soldiers or not (Bruchstücke, p. vi).

[154] Apol. 1. 35.38; Dial. 97, 104; cp. 16f, 32, 72, 85, 133.

[155] ὑπὸ τῶν Ἰουδαίων προσηλώθη (Apology, Armenian and Syriac version, ch. 2).

[156] Cp. E. Preuschen, Antilegomena (Giessen, 1905), p. 91.

[157] Ch. 13.21.

[158] The Greek text claims that the Jews acted likewise as κατήγοροι καὶ μάρτυρες καὶ κριταὶ καὶ τῆς ἀποφάσεως ἐξουσιασταί (5.14.12) and adds that the execution was

Tertullian,[161] in part of the *Acta Pilati* literature,[162] in the Slavonic Josephus,[163] and in many other places.[164, 165] A generalising interpretation is, at least in a number of cases,[166] impossible. The relevance of these statements is strengthened by their conformity with the claims made in Jewish sources.[167] The alternative view is of course widely held,[168] but usually expressed with certain qualifications.[169]

The apparent divergency raises a difficult problem. The remission of the culprit to the local court after the confirmation of the sentence by the Roman governor seems to be the obvious thing to do. 'L'exécution du condamné devrait revenir, logiquement, aux Juifs' – as E. Bickermann puts it.[170] Examples from the same period support this view. The jurisdiction of Herod the Great over his sons was checked by Augustus. The execution, however, was left to him after a court in the Roman colony of Berytus[171] had investigated the case on the emperor's instruction. Attention has been drawn to this fact in recent discussion.[172] Two somewhat dissimilar cases are not less telling. When a Roman soldier had performed an action that could be taken as an offence against the Temple privilege, his tribune, Celer

carried out by δήμιοι (5.14.14). The part played by Pilate in his ἀνανδρία is linked with this in a way which is not absolutely clear.

[159] *Barn.* 5: 2.12; 6: 6f; 7: 5.9.

[160] *Homily* §92 (The Chester Beatty Biblical Papyri VIII (London, 1941) fol. 20 v.).

[161] *Apol.* 21; *Adv. Judaeos* 10.

[162] Bauer, *Leben Jesu*, p. 202.

[163] W. Bienert, *Die älteste nichtchristliche Jesusbericht. Josephus über Jesus* (Halle, 1936), p. 129. Cp. the claim made by the Jew of Celsus (ii.4): ἐκολάζομεν.

[164] Cp. Bauer, *Leben Jesu*, pp. 199ff.

[165] Another piece of evidence may be found in the parable of the vineyard. The story, which soon was taken as symbolising the fate of Jesus, runs in Mark ἀπέκτειναν αὐτὸν καὶ ἐξέβαλον (12:8), whereas both Matthew and Luke transpose ἐξέβαλον/ἐκβαλόντες . . . ἀπέκτειναν (the Western MSS. in Matthew follow Mark). The former reading may point to a Jewish execution. The latter may be taken to refer to an ἔκδοσις and a subsequent execution, the organs of which are not clearly indicated. It is, however, questionable whether such a far-reaching interpretation of the *minutiae* is admissible.

[166] Bauer, *Leben Jesu*, p. 202.   [167] Cp. p. 360ff.

[168] The Messiah Sutra describes the Trial as conducted entirely in a Roman court; but, it is true, on the instigation of the Jewish scribes and after unsuccessful attempts on their side to get rid of Jesus in other ways (v. 182ff; Saeki, *Nestorian Documents*, pp. 143ff). The Samaritan chronicle, which makes detailed mention of Jesus, does not produce a formal Sanhedrin trial (eds. J. Macdonald and A. J. B. Higgins, *NTSt* 18 (1971/72), 62, verses 63ff, although the יצלב ('let him be crucified') suggests a Jewish execution.

[169] Exceptions: *Const. Apost.* 7.23.2 and *Syriac Didaskalia* 5.19.5 (here together with Herod).

[170] 'Utilitas crucis', *RHR* 112 (1935), 222.

[171] Cp. *ZDPV* 84 (1968), 73ff.

[172] Bickermann, 'Utilitas', 222; P. J. Verdam, 'Sanhedrin and Gabatha', *Free University Quarterly* 7 (1961), 13ff.

by name, was handed over to the Jews for execution by special order of the emperor:[173] παραδοθῆναι Ἰουδαίοις πρὸς αἰτίαν ἐκέλευσεν καὶ περισυρέντα τὴν πόλιν οὕτω τὴν κεφαλὴν ἀποκοπῆναι. A Roman soldier who had torn a holy scroll was led – obviously a compromise solution – to execution διὰ μέσων of his Jewish accusers.[174] The cases show that in certain circumstances the Romans were not unwilling to expose a Roman soldier to the hostility of the Jewish crowd or even to hand over a Roman officer to Jewish punishment and execution. The execution was not considered a sovereign act (*Hoheitsakt*) which had to be reserved to the Romans at all costs. Mommsen was aware of the general situation and felt compelled to give special reasons for a Roman execution of Jesus: the cruelty and untrustworthiness of the local personnel and the Jewish inclination to lynch law. He thought that Roman intervention could not be considered as strange especially in the situation of the Jewish commonwealth.[175] His arguments show a certain degree of uneasiness about giving the execution of Jesus its proper place within the larger horizon of what appears to have been the case in the Roman provinces. This may be sufficient reason for a re-examination of the data in the case of Jesus.

It is here that the first impression seems to point in quite a different direction. A centurion is mentioned as having taken up his position near to the cross; soldiers are present. These features and, most importantly, the cross as a means of execution seem to point to a Roman participation, an involvement of the overlord to a degree which it is difficult to reconcile with the results reached from the scrutiny of the trial. It is in all probability due to these telling details[176] that scholars felt stimulated to engage in, so to speak, a revision of the trial working backwards from its sequel, and to look for features in the accounts of the trial which could be brought into line with this. The results of these attempts to prove a greater

---

[173] *BJ* 2 §246; *AJ* 20 §136. Σύρειν/περισύρειν is used in these passages. The same term is used in *BJ* 7 §154: Simon b. Giora was in Rome and executed subsequently. The word seems to indicate the Roman mode of execution, where the display of the culprit before the execution is the public event in the majority of cases, whereas the execution itself is the public occasion in the realm of Jewish law. The term is used in Ev. Petr. v. 6 and Justin, *Apol.* 1. 35 for the description of the execution of Jesus performed by Jews (the story mentioned by Ephraem (eds. Aucher and Mösinger (Venice, 1828), p. 165) seems to be a distant reflex of this case). Σύρειν occurs in Acts 14: 19, in the description of the applications of lynch law against Paul. Similar words are used in the Toledoth-Jeshu tradition. Another parallel may possibly be found in the account of the passion of Jesus which is given in the Martyrdom of Eustathius; cp. J. N. Birdsall, 'The Martyrdom of St Eustathius of Mzketha' and the Diatessaron: An Investigation', *NTSt* 18 (1971/72), 454.

[174] *BJ* 2 §231: διὰ μέσων τῶν αἰτιωμένων ἀπαχθῆναι.

[175] *ZNW* 3 (1902), 199f.

[176] Cp. p. 356.

measure of Roman participation were unsatisfactory. Another way to link the picture of the execution directly with the findings about the trial would be to assume that the Sanhedrin, responsible for the execution, borrowed Pilate's officers and soldiers to perform the execution, since the Romans had in any case two others to execute.[177] This theory could be given support by certain statements in apocryphal literature.[178] Before adopting this view it might, however, be advisable to scrutinise the given data about the execution more closely while keeping in mind that these details, vivid as they are, do not necessarily represent the oldest stratum of tradition in integrity but are particularly likely to have been exposed to embellishment, and that therefore the evidence drawn from individual features has to be supplemented as far as possible.

The event that sets the pace is the arrest. It cannot therefore be ignored. The only verse from which Roman participation can be deduced is John 18: 3. It mentions a σπεῖρα that is said to have been 'taken' by Judas[179] and a χιλίαρχος; it seems to point to a Roman unit consisting of at least 600 servicemen and commanded by a χιλίαρχος, which was preceded and followed by some Jewish auxiliaries.[180] Σπεῖρα and χιλίαρχος are, however, terms which are used for Jewish as well as Roman units or ranks.[181] In the latter case σπεῖρα may even be used for a detachment consisting of more (2 Macc. 8: 23) or less (Judith 14: 11) than 1,000 men, while the term χιλίαρχος is employed with the precise meaning indicated by the word, or it may point in a more loose sense to leaders in Israel. A detachment of the magnitude of a Roman σπεῖρα was hardly appropriate for the task to be performed at Gethsemane. The taking of a prisoner into non-Roman custody would be unlikely if the arrest was carried out by a Roman officer.[182] The terms of the Roman army were, however, taken up by their satellites. At the same time they were used more vaguely, giving expression to the vain pretension of their bearers. So, the view may be taken (although with a certain *caveat*) that the σπεῖρα was the Temple-guard of Jerusalem, while the χιλίαρχος (John 18: 12) was the deputy of the στρατηγὸς τοῦ ἱεροῦ (or even identical with that person; Luke 22: 52). Likewise the δοῦλος ἀρχιερέως is to be seen as a person of such calibre

---

[177] This idea was suggested by an anonymous specialist who read the manuscript for Cambridge University Press.

[178] The Jews had requested (ἠτήσαντο) a *custodia* from Pilate according to *Act. Pil.* XIII. 1 (rec. A).

[179] A. Merx (*Das Evangelium des Johannes* (Berlin, 1911), p. 427) rightly asks: 'wie kann Judas eine Kohorte nehmen?'.

[180] For the latter cp. J. Pickl, *Messiaskönig Jesus in der Auffassung seiner Zeitgenossen* (2nd edn. München, 1935), pp. 88f.

[181] Catchpole, *Trial*, p. 149 with reference especially to *AJ* 17 §215.

[182] H. H. Cohn's argument to the contrary (*Trial*, pp. 71ff) is very forced.

that offending him could be taken as dishonouring the high priest himself.[183]

The use of such a detachment would be in keeping with the Temple charge which had been raised against Jesus. The carrying out of the arrest in daylight was impossible because of the support Jesus and his followers drew from the crowds. Jesus himself gives vigorous expression to this theme of the night arrest (Luke 22:53), and his answer is only meaningful if addressed to Jewish persons. Apart from this, the interpretation the scene receives in John 18:36 points against Roman participation in the arrest.

Jesus is mocked by the στρατιῶται – Matthew rightly adds τοῦ ἡγεμόνος. There is little doubt that it was the Roman force that made fun of him.[184] Is its mention, however, original in the context? The text runs smoothly from verse 15 to verse 20b. The suggestion may be ventured that originally there was only the remark καὶ ὅτε ἐνέπαιξαν αὐτῷ ἐξάγουσιν κτλ. and that this was supplemented later in order to assimilate it to John 19:2f. There, it had its proper location, in the context of a disciplinary procedure (μαστιγόω). In Luke we find it in 23:36: Jesus is hanging on the cross and the soldiers are described as προσερχόμενοι (from the two other crosses?) – might this be the original location for the scene?

Scourging is part of the crucifixion in Roman Law. It is the secondary punishment (Nebenstrafe), administered concurrently with crucifixion. This is the reason why exegetes tend to link Mark 15:15 (φραγελλώσας)[185] with the main punishment (Hauptstrafe), the crucifixion,[186] and use this in turn as a pointer for a Roman execution. This interpretation contradicts the meaning of the sentence and does not lead to the envisaged result, as the scourging ought to take place when the delinquent is already fixed to the

---

[183] For an interpretation of the action see D. Daube, 'Three Notes Having To Do with Johanan ben Zakkai', JThSt n.s. 11 (1960), 594. By the violation of his immaculate physical appearance a person could be impeded from executing his priestly functions: AJ 14 §366: ἀποτέμνει αὐτοῦ (Hyrcanus II) τὰ ὦτα . . . εἰς . . . λελωβῆσθαι; Prologus Monarchianorum: amputasse sibi . . . pollicem dicitur, ut sacerdotio reprobus haberetur (Mark). So the δοῦλος was in all likelihood a priest who had special duties with regard to serving the high priest. The parallel from Livy 29.9 (Pleminius has his nose and ears cut off by soldiers) adduced by J. Lengle, (Römisches Strafrecht bei Cicero und den Historikern (Leipzig, 1935), pp. 8f) is less stringent. A different view on the composition of the arrest party is taken by J. A. T Robinson in this volume, p. 470f. See also G. W. H. Lampe, above pp. 344–5.

[184] A different view is taken by A. Merx, Das Evangelium Matthaeus (Berlin, 1902), pp. 406ff.

[185] Omitted by B, the scribe of which very often tries to avoid difficulties. G. Strecker, 'The Passion – and Resurrection Predictions in Mark's Gospel', Interpretation 22 (1968), 434f views the mocking as a Markan composition; there is little to be said for this theory.

[186] O. Zöckler, Das Kreuz Christi (Gütersloh, 1875, pp. 433f; ET London, 1877, p. 410); Bauer, Leben Jesu, p. 207.

cross,[187] whereas Mark, after 15:15, goes on to narrate Jesus's way to Calvary.[188]

The scourging therefore has to be taken separately. And, indeed, scourging can take place independently, as a special form of punishment.[189] That such a punitive measure was the intention of Pilate is evidenced by Luke 23:16. Luke does not mention a scourging in verse 2, the passage parallel to Mark 15:15. Mark, whose report on the scene before Pilate is very short, seems to have summarised the incident in verse 15.[190]

Putting to death by way of crucifixion is, of course, taken as the main pointer to an execution performed under Roman supervision. Crucifixion is considered as a way of execution that is characteristic of the empire. It is this presupposition that directed the minds of scholars: 'daraus ist mit Sicherheit zu schliessen, dass er nicht von der jüdischen Obrigkeit, sondern von den Römern zu Tode gebracht worden ist'.[191] From a Jewish point of view, however, the matter was different: it was the beheading that appeared as the execution *more Romanorum* (כדרך שהמלכות עושה).[192] Surprisingly, even this mode of execution was adopted by the Jewish courts as one of the possible ways of implementing the death penalty.[193] Crucifixion, on the other hand, was a mode of execution that was not at all unknown in Hasmonaean Judaea.[194] A new piece of evidence has recently emerged from Qumran. The Temple scroll[195] gives the ruling that a man who informed against his people (רכיל) and delivered up (משלים)[196] his people to a foreign nation and did evil to his people, is to be hung on a tree 'and he shall die';[197] likewise the man who committed a crime punishable by

---

[187] Mommsen, *Strafrecht*, p. 920; cp. Livy 1. 26.

[188] *Act. Pil.* ix. 5 describes the action in such a fashion that it is more in agreement with the Roman practice of execution. Is the same also true for Pet. 2:24 where the text could be taken to imply a scourging to death on the cross?

[189] Such a punishment is envisaged in *Dig.* 48.2.6: 'levia crimina audire et discutere de plano proconsulem oportet et vel liberare eos, quibus obiciuntur, vel fustibus castigare vel flagellis servos verberare' (Ulpian). Equally Leg. 13.6: '... castigandum dimittere'. Cp. the case of Ananos – in some ways not dissimilar to that of Jesus – who is scourged by the prefect (*BJ* 6 §304) but dismissed subsequently. Is *BJ* 2 §306 (μάστιξιν προαιχισάμενος ἀνεσταύρωσεν) an indication for two separate acts?

[190] Dobschütz, *ZNW* 3 (1902), 104 equals this with the 'verberatum crucifigi' of Livy 33.36, 'das über die zeitliche Folge beider Akte nichts aussagt'.

[191] W. Brandt, *Die evangelische Geschichte* (Leipzig, 1893), p. 147.

[192] Sanh. vii. 3; cp. Keth. 30a.   [193] Sanh. vii. 1.

[194] Cp. *Festschrift C. F. D. Moule* (2nd edn. 1971), p. 162ff.

[195] The text is reproduced and commented upon by Y. Yadin, 'Pesher Nahum (4QpNahum) Reconsidered', *IEJ* 21 (1971), 1ff. Cp. M. Wilcox ' "Upon the Tree" Dt 21:22f. in the New Testament', *JBL* 96 (1977), 85ff.

[196] The meaning is identical with that of מוסר ; cp. note 20.

[197] A parallel to this procedure (as opposed to what became the Mishnaic rule) is to be found in Targ. Jer. 1 to Num. 25:4; cp. M. Hengel, *Nachfolge und Charisma* (Berlin,

death and who has run away into the midst of the gentiles and has cursed his people.[198] The specifications show that the regulation is not just a sectarian rule[199] but a code that enjoyed wider recognition.[200] The related document of 4QNah 6ff indicates a tendency to apply this mode of execution, which, according to the most likely restoration of the text, is a time-honoured procedure,[201] especially to those who are 'seekers after smooth things', that means to those who favour an objectionable Torah interpretation or have contact with outlandish ideas[202] or institutions. Conversely, the administration of this death penalty does not seem to be impossible in the case of Jesus;[203] its actual choice could even give an indication of the kind of accusation raised against him.[204]

Mark does not give details about those who crucified Jesus.[205] Mark 15:23 mentions that Jesus is offered myrrh – it is a Jewish custom to give a person who is about to be executed an intoxicating drink.[206] This detail, therefore, rather points to a Jewish execution than to a Roman one.

1968), pp. 64f. It is probably the same practice that is alluded to in the parable of Meir cited in Sanh. 46b.   [198] 1. 9f.

[199] *Pace* Yadin. This is all the more true if Yadin should be right with his interpretation that the pesher aimed at defending Alexander Jannaeus's crucifixion of 800 Jews. 'Sectarians' had no reason for establishing such a rule for their particular group. Running away from them was likely to take place in the direction of the main body of Judaism. The rule, if not taken over from pre-Qumran Judaism, must have been formulated with the intention of being implemented in the whole land of Israel.

[200] Winter's claims (*Trial*, pp. 90ff) appear to be outdated.

[201] For a discussion of the proposal of Yadin and the reasons for his own agreement with it, cp. J. A. Fitzmyer, 'Crucifixion in Ancient Palestine, Qumran Literature and the N.T.', *CBQ* 40 (1978), 499ff. For further discussion, cp. J. M. Ford, ' "Crucify him, crucify him" and the Temple Scroll', *ExpT* 87 (1975/76), 275ff.

[202] The 80 witches who were hanged/crucified by Simon b. Shetach (Sanh. VI. 4) could be enumerated under this heading.

[203] It *may* even give a hint of the reason why Jesus was crucified. The first crime listed in the Temple scroll ('informed against his people' etc.) cannot have been relevant. It may however be different with the second ('committed a crime punishable by death, fled into the midst of the Gentiles' etc.). John 11:47ff describes the occasion of such a verdict (albeit from a Christian point of view) and carries on with a cryptic reference to the withdrawal of Jesus to a territory that was not under the jurisdiction of the Sanhedrin, and that his status was therefore that of a ζητούμενος (11:56). This would do justice to the first two qualifications in this paragraph, whereas the third ('cursed his people') may be taken to be implied by the contempt of court, which is expressed by the withdrawal.

[204] If it was not the general formulation (וְעוֹשֶׂה רָעָה) that was adduced against Jesus, it is likely that his withdrawal was taken as an offence against the Sanhedrin.

[205] An indication might possibly be given by verse 28 (ἄνομοι), a verse which, however, is omitted in the best mss. In Luke 23:36 στρατιῶται are mentioned, who present ὄξος. But they are described as προσερχόμενοι. This does not really point to their acting as executioners of Jesus. Cohn, *Trial*, p. 204, raises the question whether the men of the escort on the way to Calvary were identical with the executioners in attendance at the place of crucifixion.

[206] Cp. S–B i, 1037.

Another indication might be found in the presence of the two other persons who are crucified. They are only mentioned subsequently in Mark – not in the description of the road to Calvary, whereas Luke adds them in this earlier section. Already the Markan report is stylised; the intention is to bring out the innocence of the one, to whose right and left very different persons were crucified. It is therefore not a foregone conclusion that they were the only ones to suffer crucifixion that day.[207] They are described as λῃσταί, as political insurgents, like Barabbas (Mark 15: 7), probably taken captive together with him after the στάσις. Barabbas had been held in Roman custody, in all probability the λῃσταί too. Their execution was entirely a Roman matter.[208] A Roman officer must have been in command of the procedure. The Jews had no title to the persons while still alive, or to the bodies. On the other hand it is only natural that the Jews were concerned about their fate and interested in carrying out the prescriptions of the Torah about the burial of the bodies, and in doing so before the beginning of Sabbath. The remark in John 19: 31ff may therefore be historical. It may be that it is this feature that caused the confusion we find in John, where we get the impression that the στρατιῶται who cast lots for Jesus's garment are under Pilate's orders.

The Jews' concern for Jesus's body had to go so far as to demand a burial and to ensure that it would take place before Sabbath. The Gospel accounts, whatever they say in detail, emphasise that it was a disgraceful burial Jesus was in danger of encountering.[209] The story of Joseph of

---

[207] Rather the opposite is likely. Executions tended to be postponed for the rare occasions when the prefect was present in Jerusalem, occasions which coincided with the Jewish feasts. A considerable number of delinquents must have awaited death. The term popular execution (*Volksfesthinrichtung*) receives a special meaning in this context.

[208] Schürer, *Geschichte*, i, pp. 470f (ET i.2, p. 61) mentions that the civic executioners were replaced by military ones in the time of the principate; this may account for changes in the tradition underlying the Gospel reports. P. Winter (in W. Koch, *Zum Prozess Jesu* (Köln, 1967), p. 44) assumes that pagan soldiers of the *auxilia* from Sebaste or Caesarea were in charge of the execution and rules out definitely the possibility that other persons were involved. For the *auxilia* and their role cp. G. L. Cheesman, *The Auxilia of the Roman Imperial Army* (Oxford, 1914). Later forms of the tradition deviate from this. While a stray Jewish source – cp. p. 204f – takes the malefactors as followers of Jesus and lets them be executed by the Romans together with Jesus, it is the appendix of the *Marienklage* which indicates that the two persons had been killed by the Jews (xi. 38; cp. ii. 55; vii. 36, ed. M.A. v.d. Oudenrijn (Freiburg, 1959)); equally *Const. Apost.* 15.14.

[209] Several devices were worked out in order to counter such an impression. The story of the anointing at Bethany implies that, whatever happened to the corpse of Jesus, due honour had already been given to the body in advance (for an interpretation of the story see D. Daube, *NT and Rabbinic Judaism* (London, 1956), p. 301). The scene would receive additional importance, if the B. Weiss theory could be maintained, according to which the Q document concluded its report on Jesus with a version of the anointing story; for criticism see *Festschrift G. Stählin*, eds. O. Böcher and K.

Arimathaea asking for Jesus's body presupposes that special measures had to be taken to spare his body such maltreatment. Thus his case was different from that of the two ληϲταί who, from a Jewish point of view, were not criminals tried by an indigenous court.[210] Special burial places for criminals found guilty by Jewish courts are known from Sanh. vi. 7. The Christian antipolemics are therefore more in keeping with a Jewish execution and a subsequent burial of disgrace either attempted or carried out than with a different mode of execution. The petitioning for the body to the Roman authority after the carrying out of the execution[211] is to be considered slightly irregular. More in accordance with the supposed state of affairs would be the narrative of the Gospel of Peter according to which Joseph of Arimathaea's request to Pilate was made before the execution was enacted.[212] The Gospel reports about a subsequent petition either reflect the influence of a different view about the legal situation or are due to a certain degree of confusion.

The centurion, whose statement is cited in Mark 15: 39, was in all probability the person who had been in command of the execution of the ληϲταί. Whether he had been in direct control of the crucifixion of Jesus,[213] or had just been asked to keep an eye on Jesus as well, or even had no function with regard to Jesus, is not stated in the sources. The passage, although in some ways the climax of the Markan passion account, does not contain information of such precision that it could be used as a basis for the reconstruction of the events.

Haacker (Wuppertal, 1970), pp. 40f. Mark 15: 42ff, on the other hand, claims that Jesus did receive an honourable burial and John 19: 40 adds that even the anointing of the body could be carried out before the beginning of Sabbath. While it is implied in these passages that the followers of Jesus succeeded in doing what they did against the wishes of the Jews, we hear in the Gospel of Peter that Herod himself had intended to give Jesus an honourable burial. This latter claim is obviously a compromise solution which aims at out-manoeuvring completely such traditions which claimed that the enemies of Jesus actually succeeded in giving Jesus a burial of disgrace.

[210] In Ebel Rabbati 11. 8 it is stated that nothing is to be denied to those who were condemned by the government. In the case of Jesus on the other hand some Jews, it is said (Luke 23: 35), felt at liberty to deride him.

[211] To take the ἔχετε of Matt. 27: 65 as indicative formulation and to interpret it as a refusal (similar to John 19: 22), would be in consequence of this. A Jewish *custodia* at the grave is assumed in the version of the Toledoth reproduced by Agobard (cp. H. L. Strack, *Jesus, die Häretiker und die Christen nach den ältesten jüdischen Angaben* (Leipzig, 1910) p. 15*).

[212] Ev. Petr. 2: 3ff. The verse is also preserved in the second text of the Gospel which was published recently by R. A. Coles (*The Oxyrhynchus Papyri XLI* (London, 1972), p. 15 (fr. line 12f)).

[213] That is the Matthaean interpretation of the Markan report. W. Schenk, *Der Passionsbericht nach Markus* (Gütersloh, 1974), pp. 22f, assumes that the centurion had been introduced in the underlying tradition as standing *vis-à-vis* the Temple.

A scrutiny yields the result that the main traits of the pieces of evidence point rather to a Jewish execution than to a Roman one. The view advanced here was taken as obvious in the Jewish world and held by Jewish scholars up to the middle of the nineteenth century and even later.[214] Among Christian scholars it was established by G. Möbius,[215] taken up here and there and renewed with great vigour by A. Merx.[216]

It must, however, be added that the sources are by no means uniform and they are heavily overlaid with legendary colouring. It is not at all certain that critical investigation has succeeded in removing those tinges of colour which were added later and in uncovering the oldest stratum of the tradition, let alone in tracing the facts themselves. What is said is said with a caveat. It is possible to arrive at a different solution, while it is, however, hardly admissible to make such a view the starting-point for a reinterpretation of the examination before Pilate.

On the other hand, the course of events suggested here agrees with and renders support, albeit slight, to the interpretation of the trial before Pilate given above. This view too had been taken for granted by Jewish scholars for a long time. J. Salvador held that the Sanhedrin only needed the countersignature of the Roman authority.[217] H. Grätz described Pilate's action as 'die Bestätigung des Todesurteils oder vielmehr die Erlaubnis zur Hinrichtung'.[218] The characterisation of the Roman side as endorsement of the verdict of the Sanhedrin or, even less, as the permission for execution, is an approach that has been favoured among legal historians since the days of J. Steller.[219]

Significant is the almost complete absence of political motifs in the trial before Pilate. Neither is there any investigation into a *laesa majestas* accusation, nor is Jesus styled a revolutionary.[220] True, such motifs come in in the Lukan account, but only in order to be refuted, to be rejected, in a passion story which otherwise does not disagree with the report of the

---

[214] S. Krauss, *Das Leben Jesu nach jüd. Quellen* (Berlin, 1902); Catchpole, *Trial*, W. Horbury in *Festschrift C. F. D Moule*, pp. 103ff.

[215] *Dissertatio de crucis supplicio* (in *Thesaurus theologico-philologicus sive sylloge dissertationum ad N.T. loca* (Amsterdam, 1702), pp. 234ff).   [216] *Matthaeus*, p. 402ff.

[217] *Histoire des Institutions de Moise et du peuple Hébreu* ii (Paris, 1828), 28ff; cp. Catchpole, *Trial*, pp. 16ff.

[218] *Geschichte der Juden* iii (4th edn. Leipzig, 1888), 306. The statement (p. 307), that Pilate dealt with him according to Roman law 'as the scourging shows', is not entirely in agreement with this. His treatment evinces the tendency to move away from a position firmly held in the earlier editions of his work (he had maintained in the 2nd edn. that Jesus was stoned in accordance with the Deuteronomic law (iii (2nd edn. Leipzig, 1863), p. 245).

[219] *Defensum Pilatum exponit J. Steller* (Dresden, 1674).

[220] The Gospels would hardly have called those who were crucified on the same day λῃσταί, if there had been any inclination in the tradition to give Jesus a similar appellation. Any connection with the insurrectionists is denied with irony in Mark 14: 43/Matt. 26: 55.

Second Gospel and which thereby indicates that, in the opinion of Luke, the Markan narration was of an unpolitical nature.

What may be taken to be political elements come in in part of the apocryphal tradition. It so happens that the fragment of the Gospel of Peter which was found in Egypt starts with the climax of the proceedings against Jesus. The point at issue, which must have been mentioned in an earlier part, can still be traced. As the disciples have to go into hiding because they are under suspicion of having attempted to burn the Temple,[221] it is to be assumed that a similar accusation had been raised against Jesus as well. This cannot have been in a preceding Sanhedrin trial – the trial, the end of which is preserved in the fragment, is the one and only trial.[222] The first judge is Herod who stands for his family, for the ambition to gain, and indeed the achievement of gaining, control over the Temple.[223] In this capacity he is the foremost judge of Jesus who must have been accused of having offended against the Temple – a point of accusation from which Pilate dissociates himself.

The accusation referring to the Temple saying is mentioned briefly in the Acts of Pilate.[224] The reason is the same as in the Gospel of Peter: the proceedings before the Roman judge are the only action mounted against Jesus.[225] The Temple *logion* used as a point of accusation before Herod's or Pilate's court was bound to receive an additional political flavour. But it is significant that the motif is to be found only in these sources and that even here it does not go so far as to change the narrative completely.[226]

One last question has to be tackled: the position of Pilate in Christian tradition. The evidence – it is claimed[227] – seems to point in favour of a gradual exculpation of Pilate and a corresponding incrimination of the Jews. The one tendency seems to call for the other. This again could be taken as an indication that the original tradition was completely different from what is now found in the New Testament reports. It is this considera-

---

[221] Ev. Petr. v. 26.

[222] Herod gives order that Jesus should be apprehended. That means he had been left unfettered so far. This leaves no room for a Sanhedrin trial and verdict.

[223] Cp. 423f.

[224] *Act. Pil.* IV (in the wording of Matthew).

[225] The compiler of the Apostolic Constitutions who produces two court scenes blunders in giving the accusation 'enemy to the Romans, adversary of Caesar' its setting in the Jewish one (v. 14).

[226] It was Roman policy to give protection to indigenous cults wherever possible. An accusation of sacrilege committed against the Temple would, if established, have had the most serious consequences for the accused. It would have settled the matter without more ado. It must be concluded therefore that the point was not raised in the trial before Pilate; probably because it had been impossible beforehand to find conclusive evidence to support such an accusation.

[227] Winter, *Trial*, pp. 51ff; Brandon, 'Pontius Pilate in History and Legend', *History Today* 18 (1968), 523ff.

tion that is taken to invalidate the relevance of features discussed above.

The oldest datable reference to the trial, 1 Thess. 2: 15, does not mention Pilate. Only one of the summaries of Acts gives his name, as that of a man who performs a subsidiary activity (Acts 13: 28). But Pilate figures prominently already in Acts 4: 27, in 1 Tim. 6: 13 to the exclusion of anyone else. The Apostles' Creed follows the same pattern. The Gospel reports highlight the part played by Pilate up to the disposal of the body.[228] The corresponding figure of the centurion forms the climax of Mark's account.[229] The trial before Pilate is, at least in post-Markan tradition, fuller and certainly more colourfully presented than the Sanhedrin trial.

The development is not, however, exclusively in the direction of the supposed tendency. True, there are indications – for example, the wife of Pilate (Matt. 27: 19)[230] and the washing of hands[231] – which could be taken as pointing this way. But are they meant to exonerate Pilate? Do they not, in fact, involve him in a greater measure of guilt? The verse is part of the Barabbas scene, which comes nearer than anything else in the passion story to the presumed tendency – but this is part of the early stratum of tradition and, as is evidenced by John,[232] is abbreviated in its later development. If exculpation can be found, it is rather the tendency to exculpate Antipas than Pilate.[233] The presumed tendency did not even later become dominant. The Syriac Didaskalia (5.14.3) and the early Christian literature composed in Latin[234] are not at all well-disposed towards

---

[228] The detail Mark 15: 44 seems to be stray tradition like that found in Matt. 27: 19.

[229] The centurion's statement could be taken as the final admission of those who were responsible for the death of Jesus.

[230] For an interpretation of the tradition cp. E. Fascher, *Das Weib des Pilatus* (Halle, 1951). For the stressing of the responsibility of the Jews in Matthew's account, cp. D. P. Senior, *The Passion Narrative according to St. Matthew* (Leuwen, 1975), p. 338. For an examination of the formula reproduced in Matt. 27: 25, cp. H. v. Reventlow, 'Sein Blut komme über sein Haupt', *Vetus Testamentum* (1960), 311ff.

[231] The emergence of such a tradition is only intelligible on the supposition of an interacting of two judicial systems. Matthew, who reproduces it (27: 24), takes it only as a pointer to Jesus's own innocence. The gesture is turned against the Jews in Ev. Petr., the gospel which makes Pilate leave the judicial council.

[232] 'The statement, which is often made, that the Johannine account is influenced by the motive of incriminating the Jews cannot be substantiated, when it is compared with the other gospels' (Dodd, *Tradition*, p. 107).

[233] The mediaeval excerpt said to derive from the gospel of the Nazarenes which was discovered by B. Bischoff (cp. Hennecke–Schneemelcher i. 100 Nr. 34), attributes the death of Jesus solely to the machinations of some Jews who bribe (Roman) soldiers to scourge and crucify Jesus.

[234] Cp. A. Ehrhardt, 'Pontius Pilatus in der frühchristlichen Mythologie', *EvTh* 9 (1949/50), 443. That means, we encounter this unfavourable portrait of Pilate in an environment where such an exculpation should have been most necessary, whereas in fact we meet the tradition about the dominance of the Jewish proceedings in the East, in a climate, where political considerations and attempts to influence the Roman government are less likely to have played a role.

Pilate.[235] It was not until the post-Constantinian era, a period when the principle of heredity in rulership was stressed, strict observance of the rules on the part of civil servants was enforced to the exclusion of any independent action, and the idea of *Roma aeterna* was given official sanction, that the Emperors felt responsible for the reputation of their forebear Tiberius and his servant Pilate,[236] and it was left to the Germanic king Chlodwig to wonder what he himself would have done if he had lived at the time of the Gospel events.

In the times of the early principate it was easier to cope with undesirable measures taken by Roman provincial governors. Everyone knew of good and bad administrators, and the political bell-wethers knew of those who had fallen into disgrace. It was therefore the task of the shrewd propagandist to associate certain measures with such a person, if he wanted to bring about a reaction or even to stir up the public conscience. Masterminds in this respect were the Jewish historiographers. Thus Philo, after having dealt in a book now lost with the anti-Jewish activities of Sejanus, that example of a disobedient servant and would-be impostor, heaps all the blame for the Alexandrian disturbances on Flaccus, who came to a cruel end.[237] Josephus selects three incidents in the time of Pilate in order to show the Roman *superbia* in the first half of the Roman rule.[238] He was able to do so because Pilate was deposed and probably forced to commit suicide.[239] Such a procedure, which, for domestic consumption, could easily be linked with the topic of the *mors persecutorum*, was readily at hand for a Christian apologist. The Christian community was not unaware of the delicate position of Pilate as a protégé of Sejanus, as the reference John 19: 15 indicates.[240] That such an association proved to be a mark of Cain was experienced by no less a figure than Herod Antipas, who in A.D. 37 was deposed under the pretext that he had plotted with Sejanus – a reason which was still found adequate by Josephus two generations later.[241] This is an approach that was not far from the mind of Christian apologists

---

[235] A. Ehrhardt, 'Pontius Pilate', 442f. Cp. G. A. Müller, *Pontius Pilatus* (Stuttgart, 1888), pp. 52f. The fundamental work on the tradition is still W. Creizenach, *Pilatus-Legenden* (Halle, 1874).

[236] The *Acts of Pilate* (cp. ch. xii: περιτεμνόμενος τῇ καρδίᾳ) and especially the appendix reproduced by C. von Tischendorf (*Evangelia Apocrypha* (Leipzig, 1876), pp. 449ff) received the impact of this situation. It is similar with Augustine, who claims that Pilate became only guilty in a small measure (*Sermo*, 44.3.7; cp. B. Blumenkranz, *Die Judenpredigt Augustins* (Basel, 1945), pp. 192f).

[237] For an analysis of Philo's design cp. Schürer, *Geschichte*, iii, 677 (ET iii 2, 439f).

[238] *AJ* 18 §55ff, 85ff. The same technique is employed by Josephus when he deals with the Jews in Egypt during the Ptolemaic period: all the blame is heaped on Cleopatra, the person whose memory was stigmatised by Augustus (*c. Ap.* 2.60).

[239] Eusebius, *H.E.* ii. 7.

[240] For an interpretation cp. *ThLZ* 77 (1952), 205ff.   [241] *AJ* 18 §250.

who claimed that only certain emperors acted against Christianity.[242] In this case it was expedient to call them ill-advised, whereas a criticism of a governor could be expressed more openly.

True, it is an unsympathetic picture of Pilate the Gospels give. This is especially true for the Fourth Gospel, which characterises him as yielding to pressure to such a degree that he acts contrary to what he knows is his duty. But surprisingly no attempt is made to explain the trial before Pilate in this way. The guilt of association – association with Sejanus – could easily have opened the way for a picture of the trial of Jesus that would have appealed to the enlightened elements of Roman society and might even have resulted in a re-opening of the trial. In fact this was not even done in Christian times.[243] Pilate is made witness of the resurrection in certain apocryphal sources,[244] but he is never said to have pointed to the sacrificial meaning of Christ's stripes.

An anti-Jewish bias certainly existed in the early church. But was this already the case in New Testament times? The very fact that Nicodemus and Joseph of Arimathaea and indeed Gamaliel are singled out as respectable persons; that Mark boasts of the following Jesus had among the scribes of the Pharisees[245] and points to the scribe who is not far from the kingdom at the end of the description of Jesus's ministry;[246] that John knows of certain Pharisees who were favourably disposed towards Jesus,[247] while Ἰουδαῖος as an opprobrious term seems to be used only for the leading men in Jewry;[248] that the oldest Christian chronicle refers to a multitude of priests who turned to the faith,[249] do not support the thesis. Even Caiaphas is described as a man with prophetic gifts (John 11: 51) – how easy it would have been to blacken his portrait, to picture the high priest as an antitype to a whitewashed prefect.

[242] For the frank Christian criticism of Nero and Domitian cp. R. Klein, *Tertullian und das römische Reich* (Heidelberg, 1968), pp. 58ff. Tertullian boldly claimed that to be condemned by Nero was to be condemned in good company.

[243] Instead he is made to repent his decision (especially in the letter to Claudius); that means, a theological motif directs the imagination.

[244] Pilate's letter to Claudius (Tischendorf, *Apocrypha*, pp. 413ff); the same motif is inserted by Agobard into his summary of the Jewish Toledoth Jeshu (cp. Strack, *Jesus*, p. 15*).

[245] Mark 2: 15f. The ℵ B reading seems to represent the original text.

[246] He stands for a whole branch in Judaism. The Nicodemus scene in the fourth gospel is probably a developed form of the same story. For the tendency to give names to the nameless cp. B. Metzger, *Festschrift J. Quasten* (Münster, 1970), pp. 79ff.

[247] E.g. 9: 16. Cp. *Miracles* (ed. C. F. D. Moule), p. 197 and J. Bowker, 'The Origin and Purpose of St John's Gospel', *NTSt* (1964/65), 400f.

[248] W. Lütgert, 'Die Juden im Johannesevangelium', *Festschrift G. Heinrici* (Leipzig, 1914), pp. 147ff.

[249] Acts 6: 7; for an analysis of the source reproduced at this place cp. J. Jeremias, 'Untersuchungen zum Quellenproblem der Apostelgeschichte', *ZNW* 36 (1937), 205ff.

Caiaphas is a prophet because he is endowed with the Old Testament gifts. And it is this heritage that causes the bitterness on the side of the Christians. The Jews are seen as those who, in pestering Pilate, a sceptic, a man of this world, have forfeited the promise given to them. The passion predictions, which are dotted with references to Isa. 53, are meant to drive home this point. This type of presentation was familiar in the world of the Bible. It results from this that these references are made in the context of a struggle 'within', and not in order to denounce the Jews to the Roman authorities.

In fact, the tendency of the Gospels is very different in kind. This tendency is indicated by the change from Mark 8:31 (ὑπὸ τῶν πρεσβυτέρων καὶ τῶν ἀρχιερέων καὶ τῶν γραμματέων) to 9:31 (εἰς χεῖρας ἀνθρώπων). It is the world[250] that becomes involved in the proceedings. The same is intended, although less clearly achieved, by the phrase τοῖς ἔθνεσιν, a phrase which is probably based on עמים or רבים and is therefore a circumscribing interpretation.[251] It is in keeping with this that Acts 4:25–7 places ἔθνη and λαοὶ Ἰσραήλ side by side, as those who brought about the death of Jesus. Later tradition seizes upon the executioners at the cross, gives them names and makes them representatives of the principal nations. So it happened with Pilate who in this context, with an emphasis differing from that of the Creed,[252] is directly[253] charged with the crucifixion:

---

[250] The same tendency to include the heathen world as equally culpable is to be found in the D ff² form of Mark 13:9f. Luke 24:7 describes Jesus as having been delivered εἰς χεῖρας ἀνθρώπων in the D it form. This text form is not likely to be original, as was observed by A. Merx (*Die Evangelien des Markus und Lukas* (Berlin, 1905), pp. 518f). It is, however, indicative of the generalising tendency.

[251] One of the reasons for the prominence given to the Gentiles is found in Ps. 22, which served as a proof-text for the passion of Jesus. The list of the enemies of the psalmist is introduced by dogs' (verse 17). As the equation of dogs with Gentiles was standard already in the time of Early Christendom (Matt. 7:6; Mark 7:28; Rev. 22:15; cp. Phil. 3:2), it was inviting to elaborate on the part heathen powers had played in the proceedings against Jesus.

[252] The early Christian confessions do not go further than claiming that Jesus was crucified sub/ἐπί Pontius Pilate (the exception being *Const. Apost.* 7.23.2: ὑπό is a paraphrastic formulation). For the meaning of the mentioning of Pilate – the name is occasionally omitted – cp. T. H. Bindley, 'Pontius Pilate in the Creed', *JThSt* 6 (1905), 112f: it was brought about by chronological, not primarily by theological interests (therefore the addition καὶ Ἡρώδου in *Const. Apost.* 6.30.8). The presumed chronology was challenged recently by E. Powell, *Wrestling with the Angel* (London, 1977), pp. 118ff.

[253] It is at this point that the traditions on Judas and Pilate become assimilated; cp. F. Ohly, *Der Verfluchte und der Erwählte. Vom Leben mit der Schuld* (Opladen, 1976), pp. 22f.

. . . Pontius ille Pilatus
Teutonicae gentis,
Crucifixor cunctipotentis.[254]

Everyone became guilty – therefore ἄνθρωποι ἁμαρτωλοί (Luke 24: 7) –
so that everyone might have a share in the fruits of Christ's death.

Historical, genealogical association is one way of expressing the meaning
of the cross. The direct equation and blunt confession is another form. It is
found in Paul Gerhard's lines:

ich, ich und meine Sünden. . .
die haben dir erreget
das Elend, das dich schläget.[255]

[254] Chytraeus (cited by Walther, *Bericht*, p. 112); for the tradition on a German place of
origin of Pilate cp. Müller, *Pontius Pilatus*, pp. 50f and especially K. Hauck, 'Pontius
Pilatus in Forchheim' in *Medium Aevum Vivum. Festschrift W. Bulst* (Frankfurt, 1960,
pp. 104ff).

[255] In the hymn: 'O Welt, sieh hier dein Leben'. For the latest examination of the
literature on the trial cp. W. G. Kümmel, 'Jesusforschung seit 1965. Der Prozess
und der Kreuzestod Jesu', *ThR* n.s. 45 (1980), 295ff and A. Strobel, *Die Stunde der
Wahrheit* (Tübingen, 1980).

JOHN A. T. ROBINSON

'His witness is true': A test of the Johannine claim

In any study of the Jesus of history the place of the Fourth Gospel and the use to be made of its evidence is problematic. And nowhere is this issue more acute than in the events leading up to his conviction and death. For John has an extensive and detailed narrative of these events which differs at a number of vital points – not least in its chronology – and yet where the degree of overlap with the other accounts is greater than anywhere else. C. H. Dodd has observed how extensive and detailed this parallelism is[1] – so much so that one of two conclusions is inevitable. Either John's account evinces literary dependence on that of the synoptists or it embodies an independent tradition with serious claims to take us back to the facts and interpretation that created and controlled the common Christian preaching. With now the growing weight of contemporary scholarship, I cannot find the former a credible explanation, and Dodd's own examination of the passion narrative, from which he begins his massive exposition,[2] is a sufficient statement of the case.[3] But if John's is an independent voice, how are we to assess how he stands to the truth of the

---

[1] *Historical Tradition in the Fourth Gospel* (Cambridge, 1963), pp. 29f.

[2] Ibid, pp. 21–136.

[3] Cp. the conclusion of R. E. Brown, *The Gospel according to John* (New York, 1966–70), ii, 791: 'The Johannine Passion Narrative is based on an independent tradition that has similarities to the Synoptic sources. Where the various pre-Gospel sources agree, we are in the presence of a tradition that had wide acceptance at a very early stage in the history of the Christian Church and, therefore, a tradition that is very important in questions of historicity.' He goes on: 'The acceptance of the thesis of an independent, early tradition underlying John should make us cautious about assuming too quickly that the doctrine, apologetics, and drama *created* the raw material basic to the scenes involved. In our opinion, John's genius here as elsewhere consisted in re-interpreting rather than in inventing.' F. Hahn, 'Der Prozess Jesu nach dem Johannesvangelium–Eine redaktionsgeschichtliche Untersuchung', *EKK*, ii (Zürich, 1970), 23–96, and A. Dauer, *Die Passionsgeschichte im Johannesevangelium* (München, 1972), both support the fundamental independence of the Johannine tradition but give more weight to redactional motifs. I do not myself share the presupposition, common to Dodd and the form- and redaction-critics, that this evangelist stood in an external relationship to his tradition and that one can separate out pre-Johannine material; cp. my *Redating the New Testament* (London, 1976), chapter 9. But that does not affect the value of their contributions, as Dodd himself, *Historical Tradition*, p. 17, recognised that it would not undermine his case if the opposite presupposition were made.

453

454   J. A. T. ROBINSON

matter? For the claim of the Johannine community is that 'his witness is
true' (John 21: 24), which in turn is based on the personal testimony of
19: 35: 'This is vouched for by an eyewitness, whose evidence is to be
trusted. He knows that he speaks the truth, so that you too may believe.'
While it is the truth of faith that he is primarily concerned with, this is
not to be dissociated from the truth of fact. For to him the faith is the truth
of the history, what *really* happened, from the inside.

How may we test his claim? It can only be *a posteriori*, by asking whether,
in the light of all the evidence, his account yields a credible picture of
the total situation, explaining not only what *he* gives us but what others
independently tell us. This does not involve saying that John states the
whole truth or nothing but the truth. But he does claim that in the essential
relation of the Word to the flesh he is giving us the truth. The purpose of this
chapter is to test that claim with specific reference to the theme of this book,
the relationship of the spiritual to the political in the life, teaching and
death of Jesus.

We may begin by noting two tributes in recent writing on this subject to
the testimony of John. In the course of his balanced discussion of the
political question in *Jesus and the Revolutionaries*, Oscar Cullmann writes:

> According to John 18: 36 Jesus replies to the political question of Pilate
> (the only one which interested him), 'Are you the King of the Jews?' with
> the decisive answer, *which I could have used as the motto for this presentation*: 'My
> kingdom is not of this world.'[4]

In other words, Cullmann believes that John has got it right – that his
interpretation provides the correct clue to the essential understanding of
the matter.

Equally, Alan Richardson punctuates his treatment of the Gospel
evidence in his book *The Political Christ* with reluctant tributes to the
testimony of John. For he is one of those who start with a very low
expectation at this point. Indeed, in his own earlier commentary[5] he
committed himself to the position that not only is John historically
worthless as an independent source but that he had no concern for
historical or chronological accuracy. Yet time and again in Richardson's
later book we have such concessions as:

> Here again John (19: 13) brings out the truth of history, even if he
> composed the trial speeches himself.[6]
>
> Does John in 6: 15 in his characteristically allusive way hint that this [viz.,

---

[4] *Jesus und die Revolutionären seiner Zeit* (Tübingen, 1970), p. 61 (ET London, 1973), p.
42. Italics mine.
[5] *The Gospel according to St John* (London, 1959).
[6] *The Political Christ* (London, 1973), p. 28.

being taken for the leader of a nationalist movement] was a serious danger to Jesus during his ministry?[7]

John with his usual penetrating eye for the real issue brings out the truth of the matter when he makes the Jews (the Jews!) protest to Pilate, 'Everyone who makes himself a king is an enemy of Caesar' (19: 12).[8]

John repeatedly shows that he is very well informed about Jewish affairs in the period before the Jewish War.[9]

At this stage we merely note these as impressions that, whether for reasons of theological insight or historical information (or both), the Johannine picture is not as far removed from reality as it has been customary to assume. But we can only convert impressions into something more substantial by working through the evidence in greater detail. This we may do by fastening upon the incidents, in the order John records them, that bring into focus the relationship between the spiritual and the political, between the kingship of Christ and the kingdoms of this world.

The first, that of the cleansing of the Temple as recorded in John 2: 13–22, is chiefly significant for what is does not say. It constitutes the first and most dramatic challenge to the synoptic picture. Not only in its placing, at the very beginning rather than at the very end of Jesus's ministry, but in its significance, it stands in striking contrast to the Markan tradition. Few have thought that John is nearer to the truth in this regard. Dodd himself believed that the synoptists were here to be preferred.[10]

In John the cleansing of the Temple has nothing to do with the challenge that culminated in the arrest of Jesus. According to Mark (11: 18) it served as the trigger for the final determination of the chief priests and scribes to do away with Jesus. It is interesting that there is no sign of this link in Matthew, and in Luke (19: 47) it is the *teaching* of Jesus in the Temple that decides them to act. Indeed, in all four Gospels it is his teaching that is given as the real ground of their fear and opposition (Mark 11: 18; 12: 12 and pars.; 14: 64 and pars.; Luke 19: 47; 20: 1; John 18: 19–21; 19: 7). It looks as though we have here a purely Markan piece of editorial interpretation. For if the cleansing of the Temple had really provided the occasion of the arrest, it is remarkable that it should receive no mention at all in the subsequent proceedings. It was the threat to *destroy* the Temple that was brought up against Jesus (Mark 14: 57f = Matt. 26: 60f; cp. Mark 15: 29 = Matt. 27: 39f; Luke refers to it only, indirectly, in Acts 6: 14), and this in the synoptists is not associated with the cleansing of the Temple. If the cleansing had occurred in the highly-charged context in which the synoptists place it, it could not but have assumed, whatever its motivation,

[7] Ibid, p. 28.   [8] Ibid, p. 38.   [9] Ibid, p. 41.
[10] *Historical Tradition*, pp. 162, 211.

a political significance. Indeed the dilemma is, Why was Jesus not apprehended on the spot? S. G. F. Brandon, who sees it as a political coup not merely in consequence but in intention, is acutely aware of this, and he can explain it only by the totally unsupported hypothesis that Jesus *must* have been accompanied by an armed force powerful enough to have prevented his arrest.[11] It is at least worth asking whether the Johannine version may not be correct in saying that it was political neither in intention nor in consequence, and was not followed by arrest or prosecution because it occurred in a totally different context.

For John the cleansing of the Temple has nothing to do with the political scene. It is an act of religious zeal for the purity of the holy place, a prophetic protest by Jesus against turning his Father's house into a market (cp. Zech. 14: 21; 1 Macc. 2: 24–6; 2 Macc. 10: 1–8; Mark 11: 16), that is, against trying to serve God and money (cp. Matt. 6: 24 = Luke 16: 13). It is explained by a different scripture (Ps. 69: 9) from those adduced in the synoptists (Isa. 56: 7; Jer. 7: 11), and this scripture is introduced not as Jesus's motive at the time (as in Mark 11: 17 and pars.) but as the disciples' subsequent reflection that such zeal for God would be the death of him (John 2: 17; cp. 12: 16). To the evangelist himself the incident would appear to be a sign of the spiritual truth that in order to give life the temple of Jesus's own body must be consumed (καταφάγεται) and die (cp. 2: 17, 21; 6: 51–8; 12: 24; and 2: 18–21 with 6: 30–5). Despite assertions to the contrary, it is not presented as an act of *force majeure*. The 'whip of cords' (2: 15) was, it seems, 'something like (ὡς – supported now by p⁶⁶ ᵃⁿᵈ ⁷⁵) a whip' made up on the spot (ποιήσας) from the rushes (σχοινίων) used for the animals' bedding[12] and (if the phrase τά τε πρόβατα καὶ τοὺς βόας is taken in apposition to πάντας[13]) confined in its application to the sheep and oxen. But, whatever precisely happened, the act is presented as one of religious enthusiasm, not to say spiritual fanaticism, with no perceptible politcal overtones. In this it differs from the purging of the Temple described in Josephus (*AJ* xvii. 149–63) by two men with good Maccabaean names, Judas and Matthias, of the image of the golden eagle set over the great gate by Herod, which was clearly political in motivation and immediately provoked military reprisals.

Jesus's words in John, 'Destroy this temple and in three days I will raise

---

[11] *The Fall of Jerusalem and the Christian Church* (London, 1951, 2nd edn. 1957), pp. 103f; *Jesus and the Zealots* (Manchester, 1967), pp. 332–4; *The Trial of Jesus of Nazareth* (London, 1968), pp. 83f.

[12] So Brown, *John*, i, 115.

[13] So RV; E. Hoskyns and F. N. Davey, *The Fourth Gospel* i (London, 1940), 203; and Dodd, *Historical Tradition*, p. 157, who compares Matt. 22: 10 and defends the use of the masculine πάντας where nouns of different genders are comprehended under a collective term.

it again' are not, as in the 'false witness' reported by the synoptists, a threat that *he* would destroy the Temple (those who will do this are the Romans, 11: 48), but a statement that *if* this Temple is demolished,[14] Jesus will raise up another, 'in a trice'. The nearest parallel is the saying connected with the cursing of the fig-tree, which is closely associated in the synoptists with the cleansing of the Temple: 'If you say to this mountain, "Be removed and thrown into the sea", it will happen' (Matt. 21: 21), where 'this mountain' (cp. 'this temple' in John 2: 19) probably has the overtones of the holy mount of Zion, as in Isa. 25: 6f, etc. In other words, the debate in John 2: 13–22, as in 4: 20f (where 'this mountain' for the Samaritan woman means Gerizim), concerns the offering of worship in spirit and in truth in contrast with its materialistic corruption. The saying 2: 19 is not throwing down a political gauntlet but challenging to purity of faith (cp. again Mark 11: 22f). There follows (John 2: 20) the same crude misunderstanding between Jesus and 'the Jews' as there is later between Jesus and Nicodemus. For Jesus is not talking of rebuilding Herod's Temple, any more than spiritual rebirth has to do with entering the womb a second time (3: 4): 'the temple he was speaking of was his body' (2: 21). The political dimension is at this point far removed. Later it will be very relevant, but not now.

R. E. Brown, while siding with the majority of commentators in preferring the synoptic dating of the cleansing,[15] agrees that the saying about the Temple's destruction could scarcely have left such a dim and divisive memory at the trial (cp. Mark 14: 59) had it only been uttered shortly beforehand. He therefore allows that this points to an earlier context for the saying. But I have long been convinced[16] that John's setting of the entire complex makes much better sense – quite apart from removing the very real difficulty to which Brandon's hypothesis of a *force majeure* represents such a desperate solution.

It has often been observed that the synoptists' placing of the cleansing was forced upon them. It is one of the few incidents outside the passion narrative which they had no option but to locate in Jerusalem, and their outline included only one visit to Jerusalem. John, on the other hand, could have put it at the beginning, middle or end of the ministry. That he puts it at the beginning is, I believe, due to the fact that it belongs, as J. Armitage

---

[14] For the imperative for the conditional, cp. Dodd, *The Interpretation of the Fourth Gospel* (Cambridge, 1953), p. 302, who argues that the Johannine form of the saying is more primitive than the Markan.

[15] One of the exceptions, ironically, is V. Taylor, *The Gospel according to St Mark* (London, 1952, 2nd edn. 1966), pp. 461f, who prefers John to Mark. Similarly J. Blinzler, *Johannes und die Synoptiker* (Stuttgart, 1965), p. 84f.

[16] Cp. my 'Elijah, John and Jesus', in *Twelve New Testament Studies* (London, 1962), especially pp. 40f. I reproduce some sentences from that article here.

Robinson observed a long time ago in his book, *The Historical Character of St John's Gospel*,[17] to that period in Jesus's ministry when the understanding of his role was dominated by the figure of 'the coming one' designated for him by John the Baptist. As M. Goguel put it,[18] 'When Jesus preached and baptized in Peraea, it was as a disciple of John the Baptist that he did it.' When therefore he first went up to Jerusalem it was deliberately to set in motion the opening act of the programme of Malachi that had inspired John's preaching, the promise of the messenger of the Lord coming suddenly to his Temple like a refiner's fire to 'purify the sons of Levi and refine them like gold and silver, till they present right offerings to the Lord' (Mal. 3: 1–3, 8f).[19]

That there was a connection between this action of Jesus and the mission of John is borne out by the association of the two in the Synoptic account. Jesus, challenged for the authority by which he purges the Temple, refers his questioners to the baptism of John (Mark 11: 27–33 and pars.). In the position which it occupies in the synoptists it appears to be a trick question parried by a clever riposte. The Baptist has been off the stage for a long time and the source of his activity seems to have nothing to do with the case. As H. E. Edwards put it, 'Is it likely that if John the Baptist had disappeared from public view *two years before* this incident it would still have been dangerous for any member of the Jerusalem aristocracy to disavow belief in him?'[20] But if the Johannine placing is correct, the connection is at once apparent. Jesus's right to act can be accepted only if the source of the Baptist's mission is acknowledged. For the authority behind the one is the authority behind the other: if John's activity was 'from God', then so was Jesus's. It was a complete answer. Were the Markan question in John or the Johannine placing in Mark, I suggest that no one would doubt that the cleansing of the Temple occurred during the period when the people were still 'all wondering about John, whether perhaps he was the Messiah' (Luke 3: 15).

Moreover the dating of the incident in the Fourth Gospel fits with the external evidence in so far as we can reconstruct it. In John 2: 20 the Jews say, 'It has taken forty-six years to build this temple.' Now Josephus tells us in *AJ* xv. 380 that the reconstruction of the Temple by Herod began in the

---

[17] London, 1908, 2nd edn. 1929, pp. 27–31.

[18] *Jean-Baptiste* (Paris, 1928), pp. 250f.

[19] For the connection between the cleansing of the Temple and the religious ideal of zeal for the purity of Israel that inspired both the Baptist and Qumran, cp. E. Stauffer, 'Historische Elemente im vierten Evangelium', in E. H. Amberg and U. Kühn (eds.), *Bekenntnis zur Kirche: Festgabe für E. Sommerlath* (Berlin, 1960), pp. 31–51 (especially p. 48). He accepts the Johannine placing of the story in the 'Baptist' period of Jesus's ministry (pp. 38, 41, 49f).

[20] *The Disciple who Wrote these Things* (London, 1953), p. 191.

eighteenth year of his reign – that is, in the year 20–19 B.C.[21] The forty-sixth year would then be A.D. 27–28 on inclusive counting. It is impossible to arrive at certainty for the absolute dating of Jesus's ministry but on balance it seems most probable that Jesus was baptised towards the end of 27 and crucified in 30.[22] The Passover referred to in John 2 would then be that of 28, with the final Passover, at which the synoptists place the cleansing, in 30. The forty-six years would therefore fit the earlier occasion with remarkable precision, but not the latter. Now, according to the Mishnah (*Shekalim* 1.3), the tables of the money-changers for converting into the Temple currency the annual half-shekel tax enjoined by Exod. 30: 13 were set up in the Temple from the 25th day of Adar, that is, three weeks before Passover.[23] This comports with the statement in John 2: 13 that Passover was 'near' when Jesus went up to Jerusalem, which is then followed in 2: 23, after the cleansing, by the time-reference 'at the Passover, during the feast'. R. Schnackenburg, who rejects the Johannine placing, nevertheless concedes that this looks like 'a precise detail which seems to support the date given by the evangelist for the cleansing of the temple, the beginning of the public ministry of Jesus'.[24] The only way to set aside the otherwise irrelevant and apparently motiveless reference to forty-six years (a number for which no convincing symbolic reason has been found)[25] is to insist, with C. K. Barrett,[26] that the aorist must mean that John was

---

[21] Cp. J. Finegan, *Handbook of Biblical Chronology* (Princeton, 1964), pp. 276–80. Josephus has another statement in *BJ* i. 401, putting it in Herod's fifteenth year, but it is generally agreed that this is less reliable. In any case this would make the date earlier still and even less compatible with the synoptic placing of the cleansing.

[22] Cp. the judicious article by G. B. Caird, 'The Chronology of the NT', *Interpreter's Dictionary of the Bible* i (New York, 1962), 601–3.

[23] That the cleansing of the Temple occurred at Passover-time is the one common factor in the divergent datings, and the burden of proof must lie heavily on those who would wish to put it at any other season. F. C. Burkitt, 'W and Θ: Studies in the Western Text of Mark', *JThSt* 17 (1916), 139–50, argued for the feast of the Dedication, and T. W. Manson, 'The Cleansing of the Temple', *BJRL* 33 (1951), 276–80, for Tabernacles. But the specific provision for the money-changers' tables to be set up prior to Passover makes this very arbitrary. Manson's attempt to get round this by saying 'there would probably always be some tables in the Temple precincts' is unconvincing. And unless, with him, we gratuitously excise Mark 11: 13b ('for it was not the season of figs') in the interests of a naturalistic easing of the offence of the story, the closely-attached cursing of the fig-tree precisely fits the Passover season – one of leaves without fruit – in a way that Tabernacles (autumn) or the Dedication (winter) does not.

[24] *Das Johannesevangelium* i (Freiburg, 1965), p. 366 (ET *The Gospel according to St John* i (London, 1968), p. 352).

[25] Augustine, for instance, *In Joh.* 10, noting that in Greek letters 'Adam' had the numerical value of 46, applied it to Jesus's own age (cp. John 8: 57, 'not yet fifty years old'). But this bears no relation to the quite explicit statements of the text.

[26] *The Gospel according to St John* (London, 1955), p. 167.

mistaken, supposing that the construction of the Temple had by then stopped, whereas we know that it went on till 63 (Josephus, *AJ* xx. 219). But Brown[27] cites what he calls the 'perfect parallel' from Ezra 5: 16 (LXX): 'From that time until now [the Temple] has been in building (ᾠκοδομήθη) and is not yet finished'. It is surely easier to believe that the evangelist knew what he was talking about and got the date right.

Though it is peripheral to our purpose here, I would venture the suggestion that other material associated with the Jerusalem ministry and placed, unavoidably, by the synoptists in the final visit, may also properly belong to the period when Jesus is still acting out the Baptist's programme. We have seen how the cursing of the fig-tree, symbolising the doom of Israel (cp. Hos. 9: 10, 16f), which is intertwined by Mark with the cleansing of the Temple, supplies the closest parallel to the saying in John, 'Destroy this temple. . . .' The cursing might almost be designed as an act of prophetic symbolism to spell out the Baptist's warning: 'Bring forth fruit worthy of repentance. . . . Every tree that fails to produce good fruit is cut down and thrown on the fire' (Matt. 3: 8–10 = Luke 3: 8f). The *parable* of the fig-tree in Luke 13: 6–9, instead of being, as is often supposed, a variant tradition of the same incident, could then be Jesus's reflection upon his own action two years previously (counting inclusively in the Jewish manner) and thus bear out its early dating.

> A man had a fig-tree growing in his vineyard; and he came looking for fruit on it, but found none. So he said to the vine-dresser, 'Look here! For the last three years (or, this is now the third year) I have come looking for fruit on this fig-tree without finding any. Cut it down. Why should it go on using up the soil?' But he replied, 'Leave it, sir, this one year while I dig round it and manure it. And if it bears next season, well and good; if not, you shall have it down.'

If then the cursing, like the cleansing, belongs to Jesus's early Judaean ministry, this could explain why the withering attack on the Jewish leaders which follows in Matthew contains two further echoes of the Baptist – the accusation of not believing him when even tax-gatherers and prostitutes did (21: 32) and the adoption by Jesus of his description of them as a 'viper's brood' (23: 33; cp. 3: 7). Perhaps therefore what seems to us so harsh was a deliberate part of that ministry of the mightier one to winnow and to burn

---

[27] *John*, i, 116. It had already been cited by J. H. Bernard, *St. John* (Edinburgh, 1928), ad loc.; C. H. Turner, 'Chronology of the New Testament', in *Hastings Dictionary of the Bible* i (Edinburgh, 1898), 405; and earlier by J. B. Lightfoot, whom little escaped, in an unpublished section of his lectures at Cambridge in 1873 (see the reference in my *Redating the NT*, p. 277). John 2: 20, he said, 'speaks volumes for the authenticity of the gospel'. Cp. also his *Biblical Essays* (London, 1893), pp. 30f.

(Matt. 3: 11f = Luke 3: 16f) which at that time Jesus was content to accept from John.[28]

After John's arrest (Mark 1: 14) Jesus is presented as coming into Galilee with an understanding of his mission very different from that of this Elijah figure drawn from Mal. 3 and 4. Luke (4: 16–19) makes Jesus introduce it in terms of Isa. 61, and according to the Q tradition Jesus justifies his activity to John's emissaries by referring them to Isa. 35 and 61 (Matt. 11: 2–6 = Luke 7: 18–23). The rôle is no longer that of the mighty one sent to purge and to judge but of the gracious one anointed to seek and to save and to heal. Between the Jordan and Galilee the synoptists set the story of a spiritual crisis which is depicted in Q as three successive temptations that Jesus faces and rejects. Doubtless this is a schematised account of temptations born of real-life situations over a longer period (cp. Luke 22: 28), though the news of John's arrest (Matt. 4: 12) could well have forced reappraisal of the rôle that his preaching had sanctioned. For was the confrontation and violence to which it led really the way of the kingdom? The path of precipitate action in the Temple (Matt. 4: 5–7; Luke 4: 9–12) began to look less compelling. Rejection of it could perhaps have stemmed from the incident described in John 2: 13–22.[29] For on reflection the evangelist sees it as suicidal, the action of a religious enthusiast whose zeal is self-consuming. In itself it was a spiritual rather than a political act, motivated by purity of passion for his Father's house rather than the quest for popular support or temporal power. But the Q narrative sees it as linked with two other highly political temptations, whose origin in life could well be associated with the next incident in John to be considered. It is interesting that Matthew relates the incident to the news, this time, of the Baptist's *death* and to another withdrawal to the wilderness (ἔρημον τόπον) which that provoked (14: 13).

If it is John who enables us to understand the religious *rather than* the

---

[28] For further such connections, lying behind John 3: 5 and Luke 9: 52–56, cp. again my *Twelve New Testament Studies*, pp. 41f.

[29] R. E. Brown, 'Incidents that are Units in the Synoptic Gospels but dispersed in St John', *CBQ* 23 (1961), 152–5, while agreeing with what I go on to say below about the other two temptations, parallels this one with the urging of Jesus's brothers in 7: 1–4 to him to go up to Jerusalem and show himself to the world. This cannot be excluded, but the correspondences are not great. In an earlier attempt at the same exercise (which Brown does not mention) H. Preisker, 'Zum Charakter des Johannesevangeliums', in F. W. Schmidt, R. Winkler and W. Meyer (eds.), *Luther, Kant, Schleiermacher in ihrer Bedeutung für den Protestantismus: Festschrift für G. Wobbermin* (Berlin, 1939), pp. 379–93, parallels Luke 4: 2–4 (improbably) with John 4: 31–34; Luke 4: 5–8 with John 6: 14f; and Luke 4: 9–12 with John 7: 4–6. He argues that the temptations are lifted out of the 'mythical settings' given to them by the synoptists and later supplied with historical ones by John. But again, if the 'mythical' settings had occurred in John and the 'historical' in the synoptists, no one would have dreamt of making such a judgement of priority.

political significance of the Temple cleansing (and there is in fact nothing in the synoptic accounts themselves as opposed to their context to suggest otherwise), it is John in 6: 1–15 who enables us to appreciate the political *as well as* the religious meaning of the desert feeding.[30] This meaning could not be deduced from the Markan narrative, yet when introduced makes startling sense of it. The clue lies in the Johannine conclusion, 'Perceiving that they were about to come and take him by force to make him king, Jesus withdrew again to the hills by himself' (6: 15). There is indeed good manuscript support here for the reading 'fled' (φεύγει)[31] – which is scarcely likely to have been invented. Jesus's hand is forced and he finds himself compelled to rapid evasive action. Suddenly the political and paramilitary overtones of this messianic meal become evident. From Mark we could, if we were looking for it, sense the manic excitement of the crowds and their lost and dangerous condition of lacking and looking for a leader (Mark 6: 33f; for the political background of 'sheep without a shepherd', cp. Num. 27: 17; 1 Kings 22: 17; Ezek. 34: 5). Then there is the significance, again if we were looking for it, of the fact that they were all men (ἄνδρες). John (6: 10) agrees with Mark (6: 44) and Luke (9: 14) in so describing the five thousand. Matthew appears to miss the point in order to heighten the miraculous by adding 'besides women and children' (14: 21; and also in 15: 38).[32] For the context of this desert assembly is evidently the same as that described in Acts 21: 38: 'Then you are not the Egyptian who started a revolt some time ago and led a force of four thousand terrorists (ἄνδρας τῶν σικαρίων) out into the wilds?' The wilderness was the natural place from which false prophets and messianic pretenders might be expected (Matt. 24: 24–6) and Josephus testifies later (*AJ* xx. 97–9, 167–72, 188) to several such abortive risings by individuals promising signs and giving themselves out to be a 'prophet' (John 6: 14; cp. Mark 13: 6; Acts 5: 36f).[33] Of the same Egyptian that Acts mentions Josephus writes:

> A charlatan, who had gained for himself the reputation of a prophet, this man appeared in the country, collected a following of about thirty thousand dupes, and led them by a circuitous route from the desert to the

---

[30] On this, cp. Dodd, *Historical Tradition*, pp. 212–17; *idem*, *The Founder of Christianity* (London, 1971), pp. 131–9; T. W. Manson, *The Servant Messiah* (Cambridge, 1953), pp. 69–71; H. W. Montefiore, 'Revolt in the Desert?', *NTSt* 8 (1962), 135–41; and earlier, as so often, Lightfoot, *Biblical Essays*, pp. 151–3.

[31] Including ℵ*, the old Latin, Tertullian and Augustine. It is adopted by Brown.

[32] Unless χωρίς could here mean 'without any admixture of women and children', as Dodd suggested to Montefiore (*NTSt* 8 (1962), 137). But he did not repeat this in his own discussion of the passage.

[33] Cp. P. W. Barnett, 'The Jewish Sign Prophets – A.D. 40–70 – Their Intentions and Origin', *NTSt* 27 (1981), 679–97.

mount called the mount of Olives. From there he proposed to force an entrance into Jerusalem and, after overpowering the Roman garrison, to set himself up as tyrant of the people, employing those who poured in with him as his bodyguard.[34]

Such, no doubt, was the kind of programme that many of the crowd were expecting from Jesus in the wilderness. If, as John says, they proposed to make him 'king', it could for them have meant no more than when Josephus uses the same word to describe how, 'as the several companies of the seditious lighted upon anyone to head them, he was immediately created a king (βασιλεύς)' (AJ xvii. 285).[35] Yet a bid for national power was a serious possibility, for with 'the country . . . a prey to disorder . . . the opportunity induced numbers of persons to aspire to sovereignty (βασιλείαν)' (BJ ii. 55). Indeed of John 6: 15 William Sanday wrote: 'There is no stronger proof both of the genuineness and of the authenticity of the Fourth Gospel than the way in which it reflects the current Messianic idea.'[36]

This clue explains also the sudden and otherwise unaccountable ending to the story in Mark (6: 45): 'As soon as it was over he made (ἠνάγκασεν, forced) his disciples embark and cross to Bethsaida ahead of him, while he himself sent the people away.' Evidently Jesus could not trust his associates not to share the surge of the crowd and constitute themselves his bodyguard. Then, we read, 'after taking leave of them (ἀποταξάμενος αὐτοῖς), he went away εἰς τὸ ὄρος by himself alone' (6: 15). Here perhaps we may have the setting in life for the temptations to a populist programme which the synoptists represent him as rejecting in principle from the beginning (Matt. 4: 1–4, 8–10; Luke 4: 1–8) but which could well have taken their particular form from the loaves and the mountain (cp. Matt. 4: 8, εἰς ὄρος) of this desert crisis. If so, they will belong not so much to the first transition in Jesus's self-understanding, from the prophet of doom to the charismatic liberator, but to the second critical turning in his ministry – though, as we have said, if Matthew is right, this too may have been triggered off by reflection upon the fate of John (with Matt. 14: 13 cp. also 11: 12–14 and 17: 9–13). This time it was the shift arising from the dangerous misunderstanding to which the title of Messiah, or anointed one, lay exposed. For it was open to be interpreted not only in religious but in political terms, as the equivalence of 'Christ' and 'king' in popular usage makes clear (Mark 15: 32; Luke 23: 2, 35, 37; cp. Acts 17: 7, 'They . . . assert

---

[34] BJ ii. 261f. Tr. H. St J. Thackeray (Loeb Classical Library).

[35] I have followed here the translation of A. N. Sherwin-White, *Roman Society and Roman Law in the New Testament* (Oxford, 1963), p. 25. R. Marcus in the Loeb edition takes προϊστάμενος to mean 'made himself king', which seems less likely in the context.

[36] *The Authorship and Historical Character of the Fourth Gospel* (London, 1872), p. 124.

there is a rival king, Jesus'). When therefore, as John 6: 15 records, this equation became explicit, Jesus was compelled to a corrective, beginning with the Twelve. For the reply elicited from Peter in Mark 8: 29, 'You are the Christ', is followed not, as in Matthew's addition (16: 17–19), by acclamation, but by rebuke, the verb ἐπιτιμάω recurring three times in 8: 30, 32, 33. Thenceforward Jesus must insist with uncompromising abruptness on spelling out his mission in terms rather of a Son of man vindicated only out of suffering and death, for which the models were this time to be found in Dan. 7 and Isa. 53. (For the same contrast between Christ on the lips of others and the Son of man on Jesus's own, cp. Matt. 26: 63f; Luke 22: 67–9.) This testing of the terms on which he could count on the disciples' loyalty is presented by the synoptists without occasion or motive as the climax of the Galilaean ministry (Mark 8: 27–30 and pars.). But in John it is explained by the desert crisis. It is this last which was the real turning point, of which the testing of the disciples' faith (6: 66–9) and the need for withdrawal (7: 1) were the consequences. Thereafter care to avoid a premature dénouement, which this crisis so nearly provoked, becomes decisive (7: 2–9).

Yet John makes it clear that the real truth of what it is to be the messiah or king of Israel (both of which titles he uses more than any of the synoptists) is not to be denied or repudiated of Jesus. Indeed they are introduced in the opening chapter (1: 41, 49) as essential ingredients of what it means to confess him as the Son of God (1: 49). But after chapter 6 the debate about how, and in what sense, Jesus can be the messiah becomes more subtle and more ironic (7: 25–52). Then in chapter 10 the argument focusses upon the category of the shepherd, which, as Walter Grundmann has rightly stressed,[37] is intimately associated with that of divine kingship. In Ezek. 34, a chapter which underlies the whole of John 10 (and cp. again Ezek. 34: 5 with Mark 6: 34 – the sheep without a shepherd), the shepherd is linked with the hope of a Davidic messiah: 'Therefore I will save my flock, and they shall be ravaged no more . . . I will set over them one shepherd to take care of them, my servant David; he shall care for them and become their shepherd. I, the Lord, will become their God, and my servant David shall be a prince among them' (34: 22–4). It is understandable therefore that the claim by Jesus to be the true shepherd of Israel provokes the question, 'How long must you keep us in suspense? If you are the Messiah say so plainly' (10: 24). It is the same question that in Luke (22: 67) is later thrown at Jesus by the Sanhedrin. And the answer, though superficially different, is in fact the same: 'If I tell you', he says in Luke, 'you will not believe.' 'I have told you', he says in John, 'but you do not believe' (10: 25;

[37] Pp. 295–318 above.

cp. 8: 25, 'Who are you?' . . . 'What I have told you all along' (NEB margin)). For in John the messianic secret is not that Jesus says nothing, but that he says everything openly to the world (18: 20) – yet only his own sheep can hear and believe (10: 26f).

Throughout this tenth chapter Jesus is at pains to distinguish himself as the good from the worthless shepherds of Israel,[38] echoing in 10: 12 the words of the prophet Zechariah: 'Alas for the worthless shepherd who abandons the sheep' (Zech. 11: 17). In particular he dissociates himself from the pretenders claiming to enter and control the sheep-fold of Israel. The contrast is not with those who have gone before him, as the πρὸ ἐμοῦ of 10: 8 has inevitably suggested. But this is very doubtfully part of the true text.[39] The contrast is with those who come without authorisation and 'climb in some other way' (10: 1). Jesus does not come 'of his own accord', but with the authority of him who sent him (7: 28f; 8: 42f): they come in their own name, saying ἐγώ εἰμι, and claiming to be the Christ (Mark 13: 6 and pars.; 13: 21–3 and pars.; Luke 17: 23). The purposes for which the two come are diametrically opposed: for Jesus it is to give life, for them it is to take life (10: 10). And whereas he voluntarily and of his own accord lays down his life for the sheep (10: 11, 15, 17f), they by their resort to violence have their lives taken from them (10: 18). So far from being the nationalists they claim, true Israelites (cp. 1: 47), they are ἀλλότριοι (10: 5), foreigners to God's people (cp. Matt. 17: 25f). They are burglars and bandits (10: 1, 8), λῃσταί, the word that is to be used subsequently for the political insurrectionary Barabbas, who is contrasted with the true 'king of the Jews', Jesus (18: 40). It is the term too that Josephus uses for the Zealots, and he gives vivid examples of these terrorists and their methods (*AJ* xvii. 269–85, xx. 160–72; *BJ* ii. 55–65, 264f, 433–40; iv. 503–13). One in particular (*AJ* xvii. 278–84; *BJ* ii. 60–5) offers an ironic commentary on John 10. After speaking of 'the great madness that settled upon the nation because they had no king of their own to restrain the populace by his moral example (ἀρετῇ), Josephus goes on to tell of an unknown shepherd Athronges, who 'had the temerity to aspire to the kingship, thinking that if he obtained it he would enjoy freedom to act more outrageously; as for meeting death, he did not attach much importance to the loss of his life' (very different from voluntarily laying it down). He 'donned the diadem' and took the title of 'king', and with his marauding bands slaughtered Romans and compatriots alike, killing, as Josephus puts it, 'sometimes in

---

[38] For the setting in life of this parable in the concluding challenge to the Jewish leadership, see further 'The Parable of the Shepherd' (John 10: 1–5)' in my *Twelve New Testament Studies* pp. 67–75.

[39] It is omitted *inter alia* by p₄₅ ᵛⁱᵈ, ₇₅,, ℵ*, R, *al*, lat, syˢ·ᴾ, sa – a powerful combination. It is bracketed in the United Bible Society's text.

hope of gain and at other times from the habit of killing'. The contrast with the 'good' shepherd, especially as it is drawn out in John 10: 10, could scarcely be more striking.

It is the determination to present Jesus as the true messiah or king of Israel and yet to make clear that he repudiated the overtones of political violence with which it was *bound* to be associated that dominates the tragic irony of the Johannine passion story. Before moving to this, however, we should note the build-up to the arrest and trial of Jesus which John is careful to record. In Mark there is an early reference to a plot of Jewish factions to make away with Jesus (3: 6), but then no plans or procedures are mentioned until the very end (11: 18; 12: 12; 14: 1f), when things are rushed through in hugger-mugger fashion (14: 55–64; 15: 1–15). In John there are a series of abortive attempts at arrest or violence to Jesus's person (7: 30, 32, 44; 8: 20, 59; 10: 31, 39), leading to a formal meeting and resolution of the Sanhedrin when a warrant is issued for his arrest and he is publicly declared a wanted man (11: 46–57). Bammel[40] has subjected this passage to close analysis and concluded that its parallels with Jewish usage and tradition afford good confidence that it represents reliable historical material. He summarises its main points as follows:

> (a) a picture of the prosecution of Jesus which makes the legal proceedings begin a considerable time before the crucifixion;
> (b) the fact that the legal processes are started and carried out solely by the Jews;
> (c) the part played by Caiaphas and the arguments presented by him;
> (d) the withdrawal of Jesus.

He goes on: 'Each of these elements looks strange, but together they give a picture which is thoroughly consistent, and is paralleled in more than one detail by traditions which do not merely reproduce the Fourth Gospel.'[41] Indeed the meeting and resolution of the Sanhedrin and the part played by Caiaphas seem to be reflected independently in Matt. 26: 3f. There however this tradition is combined with Markan material which sets it a bare two days before Passover and with a dating of the crucifixion which contradicts the clear determination that 'it must not be during the festival ... or there may be rioting among the people' (Matt. 26: 2, 5). The Johannine chronology is altogether more intelligible.[42]

---

[40] '*Ex illa itaque die consilium fecerunt*' in E. Bammel (ed.), *The Trial of Jesus* (London, 1970), especially pp. 29–35. Cp. Brown, *John*, i, 441f; ii, 799; Dodd, *Historical Tradition*, pp. 27f.   [41] *Trial*, p. 35.

[42] It would take us wide of our purpose to enter in detail into the whole question of the dating of the crucifixion, but it is one where (in contrast with the cleansing of the Temple) there is substantial critical support for the Johannine chronology.

In John Jesus goes into hiding after the warrant for his arrest until six days before Passover (11:54; 12:1). Then 'the next day the great body of pilgrims who had come to the festival, hearing that Jesus was on the way to Jerusalem, took palm branches and went out to meet him' (12:12f). In all the records of the triumphal entry[43] there is the same tense mixture of the spiritual and the political. The distinctive emphasis of John is to present Jesus's action as the conscious *corrective* of a planned political ovation. In the synoptists it is Jesus himself who stage-manages his entry on a donkey (Mark 11:1–7 and pars.) and the crowd which spontaneously cuts brushwood from the fields (Mark 11:8) or branches from the trees (Matt. 21:8). In John it is the crowd which takes the initiative, coming out from Jerusalem to greet him with a reception calculated to evoke the spirit of Maccabaean nationalism (12:13).[44] It is Jesus who counters this by an apparently spontaneous action: 'But (δέ) Jesus found a donkey and mounted it' (12:14). The 'but' is omitted in the NEB. J. N. Sanders[45] however is surely right in interpreting it as 'a prompt repudiation of the crowd's acclamations'. The purpose of the act of prophetic symbolism is clear. It is to say 'King of Israel' (12:13), yes: but not that sort of king (12:15).[46] There is no suggestion in John, as in Luke (19:37), that the disciples had any part in the demonstration, or even in finding and preparing the donkey (Mark 11:1–7 and pars.). They are merely recorded as not understanding. For, as the evangelist stresses, the true significance of what happened could only be understood later in the light of the distinctive and paradoxical manner in which Jesus was in fact to enter upon his glory (12:16). Like all the history in the Fourth Gospel it is written 'from the end' and its telling has been moulded by that 'calling to mind' which must wait upon the gift of the Spirit (14:26). Yet what is 'remembered' is not only

---

[43] Cp. E. D. Freed, 'The Entry into Jerusalem in the Gospel of John', *JBL* 80 (1961), 329–38 (for dependence upon the synoptists), and D. M. Smith, Jr, 'John 12:12ff and the Question of John's Use of the Synoptics', *JBL* 82 (1963), 58–64 (against dependence).

[44] Cp. W R. Farmer, 'The Palm Branches in John 12.13', *JThSt* n.s. 3 (1952), 62–3; and R. H. Lightfoot, *St John's Gospel* (Oxford, 1956), p. 238. Cp. in particular 1 Macc. 13:51 (the only other occurrence of βαΐς in the biblical writings) and 2 Macc. 10:7 (φοίνικας). The fact, if it were a fact (which it is not), that palms did not grow in Jerusalem (e.g. R. Bultmann, *Das Evangelium des Johannes* (Göttingen, 1941), p. 319 (ET *The Gospel of John* (Oxford, 1971), p. 418); to the contrary, H. St J. Hart, 'The Crown of Thorns in John 19.2–5', *JThSt* n.s. 3 (1952), 72), would not necessarily indicate that John did not know his topography but that they had been brought in earlier (for liturgical purposes; cp. Neh. 8:15) and were used with premeditated purpose; cp. Brown, *John*, i, 456f.

[45] J. N. Sanders and B. A. Mastin, *The Gospel according to St John* (London, 1968), p. 288.

[46] The point of the quotations from Zech. 9:9 and (as he argues) Zeph. 3:16 is well brought out by Brown, *John*, i, 462f.

'that this had been written about him' but 'that this had happened to him': not merely interpretation but event. Sanders's comment at this point is again apposite:

> So far from being 'hardly possible as history' (Barrett, p. 347), his [John's] account may well reveal a better understanding than the other evangelists' of Jesus's dilemma, as 'Son of David' by right, and conscious of a mission to save Israel, yet refusing to adopt the only policy that the majority of his people would understand or accept.[47]

For John the entry into Jerusalem, with its tragic-comic 'God bless the king of Israel!', presents the reader in advance with the clue by which the trial of Jesus is to be interpreted: its proceedings turn more insistently than in any other gospel upon the question, 'Are you the king of the Jews?' (18: 33).[48]

Indeed the whole of the latter part of John's Gospel is presented as a kind of cosmic political trial, of which it is the function of the last discourses to supply the heavenly dimension or spiritual interpretation. This was brought out in a most original but neglected article by Théo Preiss, 'Justification in Johannine Thought', originally submitted to the *Festschrift* for Barth's sixtieth birthday in 1946 and translated in the posthumous collection of his essays, *Life in Christ*.[49] As far as I know, it has received no mention in any subsequent commentary on John.[50] Preiss drew attention to the markedly juridical emphasis in John's Gospel (and Epistles), in such categories as legal agent, witness, judge, judgement, accuse, convict, advocate.[51] The whole action is viewed as a 'gigantic juridical contest' between Jesus as the authorised *persona* of God and 'the Prince of this world', culminating in a great reversal of judgement, when it will be seen that it is the latter who is condemned and Jesus who has won the case by his exaltation to the Father. This will become apparent only in the light of the work of the Paraclete; for he, as both defending and prosecuting counsel, will call the victorious lives of Christians to witness in the court of heaven to clinch the great demonstration of how matters really lie.

Meanwhile in the earthly events, for those who have the eyes to see it, 'the

---

[47] *John*, pp. 288f.

[48] In John's passion narrative there are 12 occurrences of βασιλεύς (plus 3 of βασιλεία), compared with 4 in Matthew, 6 in Mark and 4 in Luke. This is the more notable in view of only 2 occurrences in John of ἡ βασιλεία τοῦ θεοῦ.

[49] ET (London, 1954), pp. 9–31.

[50] It is one of the merits of Hahn's article, 'Der Prozess Jesu nach dem Johannesevangelium', *EKK* ii, 95, that he commends it, albeit briefly. Surprisingly, it does not even receive mention in A. E. Harvey's *Jesus on Trial. A Study in the Fourth Gospel* (London, 1976), which came out too late to be taken into account here, but which expands the same thesis in a most suggestive manner.

[51] Key passages for these terms are John 5: 22–47; 7: 45–52; 8: 13–18, 28, 45f; 12: 31–3, 44–50; 14: 30f; 15: 22–7; 16: 7–11, 33; 18: 29 to 19: 16.

judgement of this world' (12: 31) is about to be played out with all its ambiguities and double meanings. It is the world that supposes it is doing the judging. Pilate, as the unwitting representative of the higher power, not merely of Caesar but of God, exercises the royal ἐξουσία granted to him (19: 11). He takes his seat on the tribunal as judge (19: 13). Yet the ἐκάθισεν could be deliberately ironical, carrying the overtones also of the transitive sense of 'setting' upon the judgement-throne the Man to whom the right to pass judgement has been committed (cp. 5: 27). The transitive sense cannot be the primary one,[52] though echoes of this way of thinking in the early church are to be found in the Gospel of Peter 3: 7, 'They put upon him a purple robe and set him on the judgement-seat and said "Judge righteously, O King of Israel!" ', and in Justin, *Apol.* i. 35.6, 'They tormented him, and set him on the judgement-seat, and said, "Judge us".' In both these cases it is the Jews who do this; but in John it would be part of the irony of Pilate's action. For, in contrast with the synoptists, John has Pilate himself bring out the prisoner in his purple cloak and mock radiate crown[53] and publicly present him to the Jews as their king (19: 14). And the political implications of the scene are drawn out to the full: 'If you let this man go, you are no friend to Caesar;[54] any man who claims to be a king is defying Caesar' (19: 12); ' "Crucify your king?" said Pilate. "We have no king but Caesar", the Jews replied' (19: 15).

Of course the story is written up to bring out the theological dimensions of the drama that is being enacted. But once again John appears to be giving the truth, as he sees it, *of* the history, rather than creating *ex nihilo*. As Brown says,[55]

> The Synoptic Gospels never adequately explain why Pilate yielded to the importunings of the crowd and the priests. . . . John's picture of Pilate worried about what might be said at Rome has a very good chance of being historical. According to Philo, *Ad Gaium* xxxviii. 301f, Pilate was naturally

---

[52] Despite Harnack, Loisy, Macgregor, and most recently I. de la Potterie, 'Jésus, roi et juge d'après Jn. 19: 13: ἐκάθισεν ἐπὶ βήματος', *Bb* 41 (1960), 217–47. For a full survey, cp. Dauer, *Passionsgeschichte*, pp. 269–74, who comes down against. As Bultmann observes, *John*, p. 664, 'an αὐτόν would be indispensible'. Dodd, *Historical Tradition*, p. 119, and Hahn, *EKK* ii, 48–50, are also decisive for the intransitive. (For striking parallels for the procurator taking his seat on the βῆμα cp. Josephus, *BJ* ii, 172, 301.) Yet other commentators are surprisingly open to a secondary meaning: e.g. Barrett, R. H. Lightfoot, Brown, and Lindars, ad loc.

[53] Cp. Hart, *JThSt* n.s. 3 (1952), 66–75. Even if his theory is not substantiated the irony remains.

[54] For 'Caesar's friend' as a title of honour, cp. E. Bammel, 'Φίλος τοῦ καίσαρος', *ThLZ* 77 (1952), 205–10; E. Stauffer, *Jesus. Gestalt und Geschichte* (Bern, 1957), pp. 110f, ET *Jesus and his Story* (London, 1960), pp. 109f; Sherwin-White, *Roman Society*, p. 47.

[55] *John*, ii, 890f.

inflexible and stubbornly resisted when the Jews clamored against him until they mentioned that the Emperor Tiberius would not approve his violating their customs. 'It was this final point that particularly struck home, for he feared that if they actually sent an embassy, they would also expose the rest of his conduct as governor'. . . . A shrewd ecclesiastical politician like Caiaphas would have been quite aware of the prefect's vulnerability and prompt to probe it.[56]

Yet in all this the non-political and non-violent nature of Jesus's kingship is made explicit in John 18: 36f:

> 'My kingdom does not belong to this world. If it did, my followers would be fighting to save me from arrest by the Jews. My kingly authority comes from elsewhere.' 'You are a king, then?' said Pilate. Jesus answered, '"King" is your word. My task is to bear witness to the truth. For this was I born; for this I came into the world, and all who are not deaf to truth listen to my voice.'[57]

Taking up, as the passage does, the previous injunctions at the arrest, 'Let these others go' (18: 8) and 'Sheathe your sword' (18: 11), there could not be a clearer disavowal of power-politics. Yet, equally, the manner in which the religious charge against Jesus, which for the Jews is the real gravamen in all the Gospels (Mark 14: 63f and pars.; John 19: 7), was capable of being twisted into the political is nowhere more fatefully evident than in John. He stresses that the two aspects were inseparable. In this Gospel the arrest of Jesus is already the work of Roman soldiers, as well as of the constables of the Jewish court (18: 3, 12).[58] This Roman involvement has been much questioned, and even denied.[59] But if one's first reaction is to

---

[56] It was precisely this sort of denunciation to Rome by his subjects that led to Pilate eventually losing his post in 36–37 (Josephus, *AJ* xviii. 88f).

[57] Cp. the echo in the last words of the test of messiahship in 10: 27: 'My own sheep listen to my voice.'

[58] The ὑπηρέται, a word which John always uses in its technical sense, were not 'temple police' (NEB) but constables of the court of the Sanhedrin acting in its judicial capacity. Cp. Matt. 5: 25; Mark 14: 65; John 18: 22; Acts 5: 21f; and note the irony of John 18: 36: '*my* ὑπηρέται'.

[59] E.g. by Blinzler, *Der Prozess Jesu* (4th edn. Regensburg, 1969), pp. 90–9; ET of 2nd edn. 1959: *The Trial of Jesus* Westminster, Maryland, 1959), pp. 63–70; and Bammel, p. 439 above. It seems to me most improbable that John did not intend to use σπεῖρα and χιλίαρχος, like the rest of the New Testament writers, as the equivalents of the Roman *cohors* and *tribunus*. (So in revised ET of E. Schürer, *History of the Jewish People in the Age of Jesus* i (Edinburgh, 1973), p. 372, n. 86.) Of course the LXX does not do so because it is not talking about the Romans; but its parallels certainly do not bear out the desired meaning of σπεῖρα as a small detachment (e.g. 2. Macc. 12: 20!). Such resort becomes plausible only if Roman participation is utterly improbable – but see below. M. Goguel, *La Vie de Jésus* (Paris, 1932), p. 315 (ET *The Life of Jesus* (London, 1933) pp. 468f), and P. Winter, *On the Trial of Jesus* (Berlin, 1961), pp. 44–9, make the point that Roman

find it strange and historically improbable, it may on reflection again bear out, and indeed explain, the synoptic account. All the synoptists concur – and it is the only point in the story at which Luke agrees verbatim with Matthew and Mark – that Jesus asked the question of his captors, 'Do you take me for a bandit, that you have come out with swords and cudgels to arrest me?' (Mark 14: 48 and pars.) Now if we stop to ask who would arrest a ληστής, and how, the answer is obvious. It was certainly not the Jews who apprehended Barabbas (John 18: 40) or the two ληισταί crucified with Jesus (Matt. 27: 38; Mark 15: 27). It was the Romans; and they would take the proper military precaution of doing it in force. What is distinctive about the arrest of Jesus is that the Jewish authorities took the initiative and collaborated. They did so because the informer was in their pay and was answering the call of the Sanhedrin, which John alone reports, 'that anyone who knew where he was should give information, so that they might arrest him' (11: 57). The words of Jesus to Pilate in 18: 36 ('my followers would be fighting to save me from arrest by *the Jews*')[60] presuppose again that it was the Jews, not the Romans, who were out to seize him (cp. 19: 11). Their reasons for wanting him were religious (11: 47f), though doubtless the Jewish establishment was able easily enough to obtain Roman assistance by representing him, then as later, as a danger to the peace. But in the first instance he was a wanted man on the Jewish list, for whom a summons was out from a properly convened Jewish court. So it is to this court that he was handed over – by the Romans.

So far from this being irregular or improbable there are close parallels in the story of Acts 21 to 23.[61] There too 'the officer' (χιλίαρχος) commanding 'the cohort' (τῆς σπείρης)[62] took a force of soldiers to keep the peace (21: 31f), and he too supposes he has gone out against a ληστής: 'Then you are not the Egyptian that started a revolt some time ago and led a force of four thousand terrorists out into the wilds? (21: 38). We are not told how

participation in the arrest goes against John's tendency (as they see it) to place responsibility for the death of Jesus on the Jews while exonerating Pilate, and cannot therefore be regarded as his invention. H.-W. Bartsch, 'Wer verurteilte Jesus zum Tode?', *Nov Test* 7 (1964/65), does not think Winter establishes this. But I would regard Roman participation as in any case entirely natural under the circumstances, and in no way 'astonishing' (C. K. Barrett, *The Gospel of John and Judaism* (London, 1975), p. 71; though he is wrong in saying that in John 'the Romans *rather than* the Jews arrest Jesus' (italics mine)).

[60] I owe this point to Hahn, *EKK* ii, 40.

[61] On the legal aspects of this, cp. Sherwin-White, *Roman Society*, pp. 48–70.

[62] As has often been observed (e.g., Lightfoot, *Biblical Essays*, pp. 160f), John's similar use of '*the* cohort' in 18: 3, 12 may reflect knowledge of the fact (cp. Josephus, *BJ* ii. 224; v. 244) that prior to the Jewish war a Roman cohort was regularly quartered in the Turris Antonia and always mounted guard to prevent disorders at the feasts. After 70 a radical change took place in the garrisoning of Palestine; cp. Schürer, *History*, i, 366f.

many troops he took – obviously not the whole cohort of six hundred men (later he detached two hundred to convoy Paul to Caesarea (23: 23)). As Bernard comments on John 18: 3:[63]

> It is not . . . to be supposed that John means that the whole strength of the regiment (cf. Mark 15: 16) was turned out to aid in the arrest of Jesus; the words λαβὼν τὴν σπεῖραν indicate no more than that Judas had got the help of 'the cohort', i.e. a detachment, with whom the commanding officer of the garrison came (verse 12), in view of possible developments.

Moreover, there is no difficulty about the fact that the Romans deliver the prisoner bound to the Jewish authorities. For in Acts, even though Paul is a declared Roman citizen (22: 25–9) and is in Roman protective custody, he is on a charge before the Jewish high court (22: 30; 23: 28f), and it remains within the power of the Sanhedrin to apply to the commandant to bring him before them (23: 15). Subsequently Lysias reports: 'I found that the accusation had to do with the controversial matters in their own law, but there was no charge against him meriting death or imprisonment' (23: 29).[64] That would have been the end of it as far as the Romans were concerned, were it not that, thanks to information received (μηνυθείσης, the same technical term as in John 11: 57), a plot against Paul's life had been uncovered (23: 30).

With Jesus too, since the threat of civil violence turned out to be equally unfounded, that would have been the end of it for the Romans – *had not the Jews been able to represent their religious charge of blasphemy as at the same time the political one of high treason.* And this is really the nub of the whole affair. The strength of the Johannine account is that it gives, I believe, a better explanation of the relationship of the two than any other.

All the Gospels agree that Jesus went to his death on a political charge and yet that the participants in the drama, the Jewish leaders, Pilate, and Jesus himself, all knew in their hearts that this was a false charge. The real accusation lay elsewhere, yet it was the political one that could, and must, be made to stick. As Dodd succinctly sums up the situation,

---

[63] *John*, p. 584.
[64] This had not prevented the commandant, like the magistrates at Philippi (16: 22), ordering a preliminary flogging (22: 24f), and it is interesting that it comes at the same stage and is described by the same term (μαστίζειν) as in John's account of the trial of Jesus (19: 1). Yet it is regularly asserted (e.g. by B. A. Mastin in Sanders and Mastin, *John*, pp. 399f; and B. Lindars, *The Gospel of John* (London, 1972), pp. 363f) that John has deliberately or ignorantly turned upside down the Markan–Matthaean order, where, quite properly, the (severer) *flagellatio* occurs after the sentence (Matt. 27: 26; Mark 15: 15) as a regular part of the preliminaries to crucifixion (cp. Josephus, *BJ* ii. 306; v. 449; Livy xxxiii. 36; Sherwin-White, *Roman Law*, pp. 27f). Luke (23: 16, 22) also mentions the threat of a preliminary beating in the same place as John, but we are not told whether it was carried out.

The priests had a double aim in view: Jesus must be removed by death; he must also be discredited. The death sentence therefore must be legally and formally pronounced by the governor. The surest way to secure such a sentence would be to cite the Defendant on a charge of political disaffection. But such a charge would by no means discredit him in the eyes of the Jewish public; quite the contrary. It was for the Sanhedrin to show that he was guilty of an offence against religion.[65]

The one charge that met both requirements was that of claiming to be the Christ, which could be interpreted from the religious point of view as the blasphemous one of making himself Son of God (John 10: 33–6;[66] cp. 5: 18; 19: 7) and from the political point of view as the seditious one of pretending to the throne. And the Gospels agree on the fatal way in which these three terms, Christ, Son of God and King, could slide, or be made to slide, into one another (Matt. 26: 63; 27: 42f; Mark 14: 61; 15: 32; Luke 22: 67–70; 23: 2, 35, 37; John 1: 41, 49; 18: 33; 19: 7).

The first requirement of any satisfactory account of the trial is that it should be able to show how the political charge, though recognised to be disingenuous, could still have seemed plausible. The strength of an interpretation like Brandon's is that Jesus's position must have been *patient* of the construction put upon it in Luke 23: 2, 'We found this man subverting our nation, opposing the payment of taxes to Caesar and claiming to be Messiah, a king.' The weakness of such an interpretation is that it does not do justice to the knowledge that this construction was fundamentally a lie. This is nowhere made clearer than in John. Not only is the reader appraised unequivocally of the inner truth, but the disingenuousness of the Jewish leadership over their real charge against Jesus is subtly conveyed. They begin their dealings with Pilate by trying to get away without being specific at all: 'Pilate went out to them and asked, "What charge do you bring against this man?" "If he were not a criminal", they replied, "we should not have brought him before you".' (18: 29f) When that fails, as it must, they go for the capital charge of treason (18: 33 to 19: 6). When Pilate finds no case on that one, they fall back on the real offence (for the Jews) of his blasphemous claim to be Son of God (19: 7) – though taking the trouble to dress up their charge in the pagan terms of being a son of God (υἱὸν θεοῦ)[67]

[65] *Founder*, p. 156. For the interrelation of the religious and political charges, cp. also Brown, *John*, ii, pp. 798–802.

[66] Cp. the βλασφημία here with that in Mark 14: 64 = Matt. 26: 65. It appears to attach to the theological implications of 'Son of God' rather than of 'Christ' (cp. Luke 22: 66–71).

[67] Dodd, *Historical Tradition*, pp. 113f, rightly draws attention to the absence of articles here – though I would hold that they should be omitted, with strong manuscript support, in 10: 36, where, for different (and this time Jewish) reasons, the logic of the argument equally requires it (cp. my *The Human Face of God* (London, 1972), p.

or a θεῖος ἄνθρωπος and thus play on the Roman prefect's fear of the supernatural (19: 8f, cp. Matt. 27: 19).[68] Finally, with that getting them nowhere, they return to the political tack and out-manoeuvre Pilate with the utterly cynical claim of being more loyal to Caesar than he (19: 12–16).

Of the three charges in the Lukan indictment – that Jesus was a disturber of the peace, a rebel against Rome, and a claimant to the throne of Israel – it is the last which stands out, and upon which alone Pilate seizes (Luke 23: 3; though cp. 23: 14). The trial turns on his supposed claim to kingship (Mark 15: 2 and pars.; John 18: 33): it is not simply that he is one more insurrectionary like Barabbas (Mark 15: 7; Luke 23: 19; John 18: 40) or the two others crucified with him (Matt. 27: 38; Mark 15: 27). The Gospels are unanimous that he was condemned to execution as messianic pretender to the throne of Israel, 'the king of the Jews' (Mark 15: 26 and pars.; John 19: 19). They all agree too that he did not express it in this way himself, but threw the question back when it was put to him with 'The words are yours' (Mark 15: 2 and pars.; John 18.37). Pilate's refusal therefore, according to John (19: 21f), to alter the *titulus* at the request of the Jews to 'He said, I am king of the Jews' was entirely correct. It was not he who said it but they – as Mark also makes Pilate insist: 'the man *you call* the king of the Jews' (15: 12). Yet, for John, in the deepest and truest sense he *was* 'the king of the Jews'. So Pilate is made to testify to it. As Dodd put it earlier,[69] with a true sense of the juridical context in which the whole drama is being played, 'He is thus, as it were, subpoenaed as an unwilling witness to Christ's authority, as Son of Man, to judge the world (as Caiaphas was subpoenaed to testify that He died to gather the scattered children of God (11: 50–2)).'

No one is arguing that the Johannine account of the trial or of anything else is to be assessed primarily by the canons of factual accuracy. That indeed is to judge things 'as the eyes see' (7: 24), 'by worldly standards' (8: 15), rather than with true discernment, and inevitably to misunderstand and misrepresent. John is concerned primarily with theological verity rather than with historical verisimilitude.[70] Yet, once again, it is the truth of

189). The absence of articles in 1: 14 and 5: 27 shows that John's usage in this regard is far from accidental (cp. also Mark 15: 39 = Matt. 27: 54).

[68] Cp. Dodd, *Historical Tradition*, p. 114: 'The whole episode therefore is entirely in character, and to all appearances it owes nothing to theological motives. Thus in the one place where the course of the narrative directly invites theological exploitation, it remains on a strictly matter-of-fact level. This is surely a very remarkable feature in a work so dominated by theological interests.'

[69] *Interpretation*, p. 436.

[70] For the elaboration of this, cp. my 'The Use of the Fourth Gospel for Christology Today' in B. Lindars and S. S. Smalley (eds.), *Christ and Spirit in the New Testament: Studies in Honour of C. F. D. Moule* (Cambridge, 1973), pp. 61–78.

the history that he claims to present, not of a fictitious tale. So we may end with Dodd's concluding assessment of the Johannine trial scene:

> Here we have for the first time an account which, though it leaves some gaps, is coherent and consistent, with a high degree of verisimilitude. . . . It is pervaded with a lively sense for the situation as it was in the last half-century before the extinction of Jewish local autonomy. It is aware of the delicate relations between the native and the imperial authorities. It reflects a time when the dream of an independent Judaea under its own king had not yet sunk to the level of a chimera, and when the messianic ideal was not a theologumenon but impinged on practical politics, and the bare mention of a 'king of the Jews' stirred violent emotions; a time, moreover, when the constant preoccupation of the priestly holders of power under Rome was to damp down any first symptoms of such emotions. These conditions were present in Judaea before A.D. 70, and not later, and not elsewhere. This, I submit, is the true *Sitz im Leben* of the essential elements in the Johannine trial narrative.[71]

The case we have been arguing does not depend on claiming that John alone gives us the truth, or that his account is distinctively different. Indeed the argument has at most points been that it is he who enables us to make full sense of the synoptists, even when he diverges from them. Yet it is not primarily in additional information, however valuable and illuminating, that his contribution lies, but in the interpretation that he allows us to see in, rather than imposes upon, the common story. In particular he draws out the fascinating and fateful ambiguities, religious and political, inherent in the categories in which the person and work of Christ were compassed. I believe therefore that Cullmann was correct in saying that his reconstruction in *Jesus and the Revolutionaries*, based as it is on material supplied by the synoptists, receives its most succinct and profound expression in John. Whether John has got it right (if he has) from theological insight or from

---

[71] *Historical Tradition*, p. 120. Cp. C. H. Turner, *Studies in Early Church History* (Oxford, 1912), p. 191: 'I should feel minded to urge every student who wants to understand the meaning of the Roman empire in history to master two brief passages in the Bible, the story of the opening of relations by Judas Maccabaeus with Rome in 1 Macc. 8, and the fourth evangelist's account of the trial before Pilate.' Sherwin-White, *Roman Society*, p. 47, concludes: 'After the survey of the legal and administrative background it is apparent that there is no historical improbability in the Johannine variations of this sort from the synoptic version.' He strongly defends (pp. 32–43) the historicity of John 18:31, 'we are not allowed to put any man to death', which is crucial also to the credibility of the synoptic accounts. So too Dauer, *Passsionsgeschichte*, pp. 143–5.

Since completing this study I have seen an unpublished paper, 'The Trial of Jesus', by Fergus G. B. Millar, editor of the *Journal of Roman Studies*, from which he kindly allows me to quote. In it he says, 'I wish to suggest that the most convincing account we have of the events leading up to the Crucifixion is that of John. . . . It is John who allows us to see what really happened.'

inside historical knowledge, or both, depends upon judgements about his tradition that involve far wider considerations. But that 'his witness is true' on the fundamental issue of the relationship of the spiritual to the political is a claim which must be judged to have stood the test.

Index of authors

477

Index of references